Churchill 1874–1922

CHURCHILL

1874–1922

BY
HIS GODSON

EARL OF BIRKENHEAD

Edited and
with a Foreword
by
Sir John Colville

HARRAP
London

First published in Great Britain 1989
by HARRAP BOOKS LTD
19-23 Ludgate Hill, London EC4M 7PD

ISBN 0 245–54779–7

Designed by Jim Weaver

Printed in Great Britain by
Mackays of Chatham Limited

Contents

Part 3   The First World War

Part 4 The End of the Coalition

Epilogue

Acknowledgements

The copyright in all Sir Winston Churchill's writings vests in C & T Publications for the purposes of this biography, and grateful thanks are extended to them for permission to quote. As to other works, Lord Bonham Carter has kindly given permission to make copious quotation from *Winston Churchill as I Knew Him*, by his mother, Lady Violet Bonham Carter. Acknowledgement is also made to Weidenfeld and Nicolson Ltd, for passages from *Churchill: A Study in Failure* by Robert Rhodes James, and to Century Hutchinson for passages from *Herbert Henry Asquith* by J. A. Spender.

Introduction

This book is the first half of what was conceived as a full Life of Sir Winston Churchill by Frederick, second Earl of Birkenhead. He was Churchill's godson and son of his greatest friend, F.E. Smith, later first Earl. Frederick Birkenhead had completed what is here published, before his death in 1975, taking the story up to 1922 when Churchill's political career seemed to be finished – for the second time.

Robin, third Earl of Birkenhead, then took on the task but he too died after continuing the narrative to 1940.

Following Robin Birkenhead's death Sir John Colville, Churchill's long-time Principal Secretary and confidant, agreed to write the last phase. He had only just completed the Foreword when he too, in October 1987, died suddenly.

There is no one left sufficiently close to Churchill who could be asked to substitute. Accordingly, it has been decided to publish Frederick Birkenhead's account alone. Robin Birkenhead's contribution,since perforce he did not have his father's unique insights, is published privately as a separate volume.

The last chapter in this book – an intimate account of Churchill's life at Chartwell (his country home now owned by the National Trust) during the 'Wilderness Years' 1924–39 – is jointly written by both Birkenheads, Frederick and Robin.

Foreword

Even before Sir Winston Churchill died in January 1965 thought was given, by Sir Winston himself as well as by others, to the choice of his official biographer. His son Randolph much wished to be chosen, thus emulating Sir Winston's own much praised life of his father, Lord Randolph Churchill. Sir Winston, who for many years had only occasionally been on good terms with his son, was at first dubious; but he was finally moved by Randolph's passionate desire for the appointment and encouraged by his diligence in writing the life of the seventeenth Earl of Derby. He therefore agreed to Randolph's request.

So Randolph, ably supported by his friend Michael Wolf, collected a band of bright young historians, moved the massive archives to his house at Stour in the heart of the Constable country and, with the creation of a beautiful garden as his sole diversion, set about the task. He wrote fluently and well. He planned to write his father's life in five volumes, one to be published annually, together with companion volumes containing the documents. The finance for the operation was provided by a company called C. & T., consisting of Messrs Heinemann, the American publishers Houghton Mifflin and the *Daily Telegraph* (which had already once bought the copyright of the papers to finance Winston Churchill's *History of the Second World War*, and then generously returned it to Sir Winston). The copyright was thus acquired by C. & T. with provisions to cover payment of the biographer and his staff, and the element of profit to be divided between Randolph and his three sisters.

In the spring of 1968, after the two first volumes of the biography had been published, and their long companion volumes carefully collated by the team of 'bright young men', Randolph died with the work only completed up to the outbreak of the First World War. After many meetings between the owners of C. & T. and the trustees of the Chartwell papers (Sir Leslie Rowan and myself) it was agreed to invite a bright survivor of Randolph's 'bright young men', Martin Gilbert, to complete the official biography. It was also agreed that Frederick, second Earl of Birkenhead, should be invited to write a single-volume life of Churchill which could be expected to reach a wider public than the more detailed multi-volume Official Life. Only Lord Birkenhead, apart from the Official Biographer, was to have access to the Chartwell papers.

Lord Birkenhead had no need to hurry, for his book was not to appear till after the fifth and last volume of the Official Life was completed; but he soon became mortally ill. Nevertheless, he struggled bravely on and by the time he died, in 1975, he had brought the story up to the years immediately following the First World War, together with the main part of a chapter describing Churchill's contented life at Chartwell in the 1920s and 30s. He was well qualified for the task. Not only was he Churchill's godson (one of his only four godchildren), but he was the son of his greatest friend, F. E. Smith, first Earl of Birkenhead and Lord Chancellor, who had died in 1930. He had been Captain of Randolph's house at Eton, and had often met and listened to his godfather. Moreover he had written several highly acclaimed biographies, including those of his father ('F. E.'), of Walter Monckton, of Lord Halifax and of Professor F. A. Lindemann, one of Churchill's most intimate advisers before and during the Second World War and also a close friend of the Smith family. Thus both personally and by research he was especially well acquainted with Churchill's life and times.

On Freddie Birkenhead's death, with the book far from completion, his son Robin – who had to his credit an excellent life of Wilberforce – took over the task; but he too died tragically young in 1985, having brought the story up to the end of 1940. I had lent him my war diaries (since published), as I did to Martin Gilbert, and he had asked me to read through his manuscript in due course, to make suggestions and to point out errors. I had done this for Martin Gilbert.

Robin, unlike his father, did not know Winston Churchill, and when the Second World War ended he had only just celebrated his ninth birthday. Thus his contribution (which is in any case a first draft) depends largely on already published works, including Martin Gilbert's Official Life, and there are few personal touches. I have taken it on myself to amend his contribution and, in places, to elaborate it, as I should have done had he lived to send me the manuscript, bearing in mind that all I have is a first draft which the author had had no time to correct. I have retained by far the greatest part of the draft which, despite gaps which he would undoubtedly have filled, seems to me a true and competent account of Churchill's life from the fall of Lloyd

George's Coalition Government in 1922 to the end of that year, 1940, which enshrined England's and Churchill's finest hour.

I have been asked to finish the story. To do so in detail would only amount to repeating much of what Martin Gilbert has meticulously researched and written, as well as my own diaries which have been published in *The Fringes of Power*. However, during the last twenty-five years of Winston Churchill's life I was as closely associated with him as anybody but his own immediate family – indeed, more so than most of them apart from his wife, Clementine, his daughter Mary and, latterly, his son-in-law, Christopher Soames and, in his last years, his faithful and devoted secretary, Anthony Montague Browne. Therefore I have endeavoured to round off what two Lords Birkenhead have written with an epilogue attempting, as Lady Violet Bonham Carter did for an earlier period, to describe Winston Churchill as I knew him. It was a Winston Churchill markedly different from the ambitious, selfish and often ruthless young man described by Freddy Birkenhead.

It may, and almost certainly will, be said that already too many lives of Winston Churchill, and essays about him by distinguished men, have been published. They vary in both quality and accuracy, but only Lady Violet's brilliant work and Mary Soames' life of her mother seem to me to capture his vivid personality; nor can any of them attempt to vie with Randolph Churchill's and Martin Gilbert's studious and exhaustively researched volumes. However, both Birkenheads have quoted liberally from Robert Rhodes-James' excellent biography, from Lloyd George's voluminous memoirs, from Harold Nicolson's lives of Curzon and King George V and from Winston Churchill's own writing. Much that has been written about Churchill, or fantasized on the television screen, is ignorant and fallacious; but in their choice of quotations the two Birkenheads were wisely selective and they have succeeded in presenting a true portrait of a great statesman whose achievements and failures have never ceased to fascinate.

Sir John Colville
1987

Part 1

Young Churchill

Chapter 1

The First Twenty-Five Years

The child was born on the full tide of England's power and glory. In 1874 Queen Victoria had occupied the throne for thirty-seven years, and presided over an Empire on which the sun never set. European wars were now merely evil or glorious memories – things of the past – and were to remain so for nearly forty years. England was still the commercial power-house of the world, and the Pax Britannica preserved a blessed and general tranquillity. The British Navy guarded the trade routes and, supreme above all others, defended her against all conceivable foreign dangers. Everything seemed so fixed and ordered in its place that the thought of change would have seemed like some monstrous reversal of nature. The rich, and those who for long – with no thought of incongruity – were referred to as 'the lower classes' might almost have been members of different species.

Income tax, two years before, had been a few pence in the pound, endured with much groaning and forecasts of doom, but in 1874 Gladstone proposed its total abolition. Beer, undiluted and of formidable strength, was a penny a pint, and fifty fresh eggs could be bought for a shilling. The countryside was almost completely unspoiled, and the rash of jerry-building which was to defile so much of it was a nightmare that lay in the distant future.

It was indeed a period of immense national prosperity. There was a rising birth-rate, an average wage rate, and at least temporarily, a falling rate of pauperism and unemployment. Four years before British agriculture had reached its highest point of achievement. 'The Repeal of the Corn Laws in 1846 had steadied prices, but gave no check to agricultural prosperity for another generation to come because America was not yet ready to flood England with her farm products.' And, as A. J. P. Taylor observed, there was social as well as international peace:

3

The revolutionary disturbances earlier in the century had died away. In 1872 Karl Marx consigned the First International to an early death in New York. Trades Unions had been legalised and had become respectable. Trade Union leaders had taken on a middle-class appearance, their stomachs encircled with heavy gold watch-chains. Many of them were staid Liberal MPs. Strikes were almost forgotten.[1]

But there was, of course, a dark side to this glittering scene. This was a world for the great and the rich with their cool-gardened country houses, but one of singular misery for the poor. There was a 10-hour Act in the factories, but most had no conception of the meaning of leisure, never taking a holiday and slaving for inhuman hours in a six-day working week to earn a near-starvation wage. The towns were Gehennas of smoke, filth and pollution, and the old died in droves from infections of the throat and lungs. In the winter came the stifling pea-soup fogs, like that described with genius by Dickens at the beginning of *Bleak House*, bringing more death and disease in their train.

In the great world Palmerston, 'the last candle of the 18th century', had been dead for nine years. John Stuart Mill had departed the year before, and Livingstone had perished in Africa; and now, in the year of Winston Churchill's birth, Gladstone and Disraeli bestrode the mid-Victorian scene like colossi – Gladstone's first and greatest Ministry ending in that year – and Lord Randolph Churchill, showing few signs as yet of political genius, entered Parliament for the first time as Member for Woodstock.

In public life the spoken word was at this period the most potent and indispensable factor. Statesmen studied and refined this weapon with the same care that a samurai warrior gave to his sword. To excel at a great meeting was to bestow an emotional experience upon those who flocked to it, for men would come for miles to listen to a master of the art, as they might throng to the singing of a great operatic tenor. Its supreme exponents had carefully nourished their gift, some so mastering the art of elocution that they could sink their voices to a whisper, and yet be heard at the back of great halls. Nor did such men rely on preparation or contrivance. They spoke as a bird flies – thinking on their feet, soaring on 'the unpinioned wing', and, to an entranced audience, approaching the climax like the resolution of some great piece of music. Winston Churchill was to realize a politician's vital need of this acquirement, but although his speeches were to achieve immortality he could hardly be called a natural orator.

Such were a few of the characteristics of the age in which the child

1. A. J. P. Taylor, *Sunday Express*, 2 January 1972.

was born. To contemporaries it seemed to be an age of unshakeable English predominance, an age of marmoreal permanence. The fact that Winston Churchill was born a member of the aristocratic upper classes and remained – through changing scenes and transformed social conditions – in essence a man of his own time was to condition his life and thinking.

The birth took place at Blenheim Palace on 30 November 1874, and the child Winston was the first son of Lord Randolph Churchill, the second surviving son of John, seventh Duke of Marlborough, and Frances, daughter of the third Marquess of Londonderry. Lord Randolph's wife was Jennie, second daughter of Mr and Mrs Jerome of New York City.

The birth was two months premature, probably owing to the lovely and impetuous Jennie having a fall when out walking with the guns through the bracken and oak trees of the Great Park, and to a rough ride home in the pony carriage. There was therefore much agitation at the Palace, where nothing was ready for the confinement which had been planned to take place at the Churchills' rented house in Charles Street. Mr Hope, a leading London obstetrician, was unable to reach Blenheim in time as there were no trains running on Sunday, and Dr Frederic Taylor of Woodstock, the sleepy little town outside the gates of Blenheim, was called upon to deliver the child. There was, of course, no baby linen, and this had to be borrowed from the wife of a solicitor in Woodstock who was shortly expecting a child.

Jennie was taken with her pains suddenly at 6 p.m. on Sunday, and was hurried into a dingy set of rooms on the ground floor in the passage to the right which leads from the Great Hall to the Long Library. This dark refuge was known as Dean Jones' Rooms, mean and bare, with an iron bedstead, and overlooking a small inner court. The rooms, in such melancholy contrast to the magnificence of most of the house, had been occupied by a Dean, who had been private chaplain to the great Duke, and whose florid countenance looks down from the murals of the Great Dining Saloon, painted by Laguerre. It is not a face suggestive of the spiritual vocation, and it seems strange that this fleshy priest should have haunted the ugly rooms that bear his name, but many who had slept there had been terrified by his ghostly visitations. Winston's birth there at least exorcized this phantom, and he has never been seen since, the rooms being afterwards occupied without complaint by a gentle and gifted organist from Birmingham, Mr Perkins, who came to Blenheim to play the Willis organ in the Long Library. Perhaps the Dean recognized the advent of a more powerful presence.

There was something appropriate in the boy's precipitate appearance in the world, which reminds us of certain other actions of his early life, for it was pushing, dangerous and inconsiderate. Appropriate also that Winston was born in this superb baroque palace set in the lush green Oxfordshire countryside.

Although he would have been the last to reflect upon the matter, or to attach importance to it, he could not avoid his birth. Blenheim was to be his second home from childhood onward, so that its atmosphere became part of him, causing him to accept its magnificence as a mode of life perfectly natural to him, and the great men whom he met there as his friends and equals. He moved with perfect ease in the greatest houses of the day, and although for most of his life he was short of money, and in every sense an adventurer, he was always a member of the magic circle, and managed all his life to live like a patrician.

* * *

Winston was to become familiar with every aspect of Blenheim. The excitement would begin when the carriage left the torpid streets of Woodstock and passed under the first Blenheim archway; and then on over the Vanbrugh bridge – one of the worst bones of contention between architect and Duchess. It carried one over part of the immense lake which was made by Capability Brown in the 1760s, and remained the central feature of the superb Blenheim gardens. He became familiar with the interior of the Palace, with the hidden spiral staircases, so provocative and so dangerous to children, the Great Hall with its hooded leather chairs for the powdered footmen, the Saloon with its gold plate, and Dean Jones glaring eternally from its walls, the 'icy emptiness of Hawksmoor's Long Library', with its white bearskin rugs and Willis organ: but above all, the unforgettable Blenheim smell, compounded from heaven knows what ingredients, which when one entered the house fell upon the nostrils like a benediction.

And as soon as the boy's intelligence developed, and with it his sense of historical grandeur, this surely was the place to nourish it. The tapestries in the State Rooms depicting the battle of Blenheim, the puffs of artillery-fire, and the Duke on his rearing horse, would have been enough to send his pulses hurrying with strong emotions, and it was natural that in time this fertilizing agent would lead him to devote a massive biography to his ancestor which some regarded as a majestic labour of love, and others as a shameless piece of special pleading.

When in due course, while writing of his father Lord Randolph, he described Blenheim it is easy to see that it was the historical glory of the place that left the deepest impression on his mind, effacing gentler and more subtle memories. The passage, which should be quoted as an example of his early prose style, shows an undoubted love of language, but also a lack of suppleness and real insight. It was as though he had set the scene with rather stylized and mechanical eloquence, instead of with deeply experienced emotion and feeling. It also suggests that he had already an undue fondness for the instruments of percussion even in describing a scene of architectural genius or of pastoral beauty. He was never to escape fully from their bewitching fascination:

> The cumulative labours of Vanbrugh and 'Capability' Brown have succeeded at Blenheim in setting an Italian palace in an English park without apparent incongruity. The combination of these different ideas, each singly attractive, produces a remarkable effect. The palace is severe in its symmetry and completeness . . . The approaches are formal; the wings are balanced; four equal towers maintain its corners; and the fantastic ornaments of one side are elaborately matched on the other. Natural simplicity and even confusion are, on the contrary, the characteristic of the park and gardens. Instead of that arrangement of gravel paths, of geometrical flower beds, and of yews disciplined with grotesque exactness which the character of the house would seem to suggest, there spreads a rich and varied landscape. Green lawns and shining water, banks of laurel and fern, groves of oaks and cedar, fountains and islands, are conjoined in artful disarray to offer on every side a promise of rest and shade.
>
> The whole region is as rich in history as in charm; for the antiquity of Woodstock is not measured by a thousand years, and Blenheim is heir to all the memories of Woodstock. There kings – Saxon, Norman, and Plantagenet – have held their courts. Ethelred the Unready, Alfred the Great, Queen Eleanor, the Black Prince loom in vague majesty out of the past.
>
> Woodstock was notable before the Norman conquest. It was already a borough when the Doomsday Book was being compiled. The park was walled to keep in the foreign wild beasts of Henry I. Fair Rosamond's Well still bubbles by the lake. From the gatehouse of the old manor the imprisoned Princess Elizabeth watched the years of Mary's persecution. In the tumults of the Civil Wars Woodstock was held for King Charles by an intrepid officer through a long and bitter siege and ravaged by the victorious Roundheads at its close. And beyond the most distant of these events, in the dim backward of time, the Roman generals administering the districts east and west of Akerman Street had built their winter villas in this pleasant, temperate retreat; so that Woodstock and its neighbourhood were venerable and famous long before John Churchill, in the early years of the eighteenth century, superimposed upon it the glory of his victories over the French.[2]

* * *

All this was rich nourishment for a young romantic, but whatever

2. Winston S. Churchill, *Lord Randolph Churchill*, p. 1–2.

the past of Woodstock, it was inevitable that in Winston's mind his illustrious ancestor, John, the first Duke, should tower above it, dwarfing all else, elevated as is the slim monument erected to him in front of the palace. We should therefore note briefly the origins of his family, although those dim and forgotten figures have long since been relegated to history's capacious dustbin.

The youngest son of Wandril, Lord of Courcelles, came to England from France with William the Conqueror. His descendant John, Lord of Currichill, or Chirechile, 'since called Churchill in Somersetshire', had a son called Sir Bartholomew de Churchill, 'a man of note in the time of King Steven', who defended the castle of Bristow against the Empress Maud and was slaine afterward in that warr.' In the time of King Edward I, the lordship of Churchill was seized by the Crown and given to some favourite. The family was apparently not without vicissitudes, for we come eventually to Roger, who was reputed to be a blacksmith. But this worthy's great-grandson John restored the position, and solidly improved the fortunes of this branch of the Churchill family, which rallied strongly from its social decline. He was a lawyer who married into the Winstone family and arranged for his son Winston, father of the great Duke, to marry into the still more distinguished Drake family, people with a far purer lineage than the Churchills. In the Civil War the Drakes were Parliamentarians and the Churchills Royalists, a true salvation for the Churchills at a time of flux. Since Winston was the father of John, first Duke of Marlborough, and the Duke of Berwick and Alba was the son (by James, Duke of York – later James II) of Winston's daughter Arabella, he could make the proud boast of being the progenitor of the two greatest captains of the age. Indeed, this, and the writing of a history of the Kings of England during the Commonwealth called *Divi Britannici*, were his claims to fame.

The Churchills were later to be linked with another eminent family, the Spencers, who, originally descended from shepherds, by 1504 owned estates at Wormleighton in Warwickshire, and subsequently at Althorp in Northamptonshire. John Spencer was knighted by Henry VIII, and in 1603 the Spencer of the day was made a baron. The third Lord Spencer was created Earl of Sunderland in 1643 by Charles I. He married Lady Dorothy Sidney, the 'Sacharissa' of Waller's poems, at Penshurst in 1639, and died with his friend Falkland by cannon-fire at the battle of Newbury. Dorothy administered Althorp during her son's minority of nineteen years. This son, the fourth Lord Spencer and second Earl of Sunderland, had been brought up by his mother as a staunch Protestant, joining William Penn in a demonstration against the wearing of surplices in Tom Quad, Christ Church, in defiance of the wishes of Charles II.

During the Protectorate, Sunderland travelled over Europe, becoming at an early age ambassador in Madrid and afterwards in Paris. It was he who first acquired the magnificent collection of pictures which was supplemented by succeeding generations of his family at Althorp. The fact that he held high office under kings of such different opinions as Charles II, James II and William III suggests, to put it kindly, a certain flexibility.

In 1699 the link with the Churchill family was formed, when his son Charles, the third Earl of Sunderland, while still Lord Spencer, married Lady Anne Churchill, second daughter of the Duke of Marlborough. This Spencer was an ultra-Whig with republican opinions which were not at all to Marlborough's taste, but because the Duke's only son did not survive him, the fourth Earl of Sunderland inherited Blenheim and the Marlborough dukedom from his aunt, the eldest daughter of the Duke of Marlborough, Henrietta, Countess of Godolphin and, by Special Remainder, Duchess of Marlborough. It was by this marriage with the Spencers that the Marlborough blood, title and estates have descended to posterity.

On becoming Duke, Charles Sunderland, by a family arrangement, handed over Althorp to his younger brother Jack, whose son was created Earl Spencer in 1765. It was a misfortune for the Marlborough branch of the family that the old Duchess Sarah, grandmother of Charles and Jack, was prejudiced against them on account of their gross extravagance. But if she had to choose between the two she preferred Jack, and bequeathed to him most of the family property which was not entailed and confined to Blenheim. It is for this reason that the greatest family pictures and Marlborough silver were to be found at Althorp and not at Blenheim. Not content with this, Sarah alienated other possessions from the Marlborough branch to another daughter who was married to the Duke of Montagu, whose heiress married the third Duke of Buccleuch. Proof of this unfortunate prejudice of Sarah, the sword of Ramillies and Marlborough's campaign maps today repose at Boughton in Northamptonshire. Spencer now became the family name of the Dukes of Marlborough, until 1817, when the fifth Duke of Marlborough changed it by licence to Spencer-Churchill.

We may round off this brief family history by noting that Lord Randolph Churchill's elder brother George, a brilliant but wayward character who became eighth Duke, married first Bertha, daughter of the first Duke of Abercorn, whom he treated with studied cruelty, and secondly, Lilian Hammersley of New York ('Duchess Lily'). Lord Randolph had three brothers who did not survive childhood, and six sisters. In those days of unquestioned privilege and social grandeur, their marriages were almost invariably to men of great possessions. Of the sisters, Cornelia married Ivor Guest, first Lord Wimborne, Rosamund the second Lord de Ramsay, Fanny the second Lord Tweedmouth, Anne the seventh Duke of Roxburghe, Georgiana the fourth Earl Howe. Of the six girls Sarah alone was allowed to content herself with a commoner, Lt. Colonel G. C. Wilson, and remained happy in spite or because of this fact.

Lord Randolph's elder brother George had one son by his marriage to Bertha – Charles, the ninth Duke of Marlborough, Winston's cousin 'Sunny' to whom he became deeply attached, and who was to remain a lifetime friend. On the whole the Dukes of Marlborough since the immortal John had been a dull lot, apart from the fifth Duke who was profligate, immoral and eccentric. However, the fourth Duke had employed Capability Brown to landscape the Blenheim gardens and commissioned Reynolds and Romney to paint members of the family. This had indeed been a period of glory, and when George III visited Blenheim in 1786 he is said to have murmured in awe: 'We have nothing to equal this.'

Winston's cousin Sunny, in search of an injection of dollars to revive the waning financial health of Blenheim, made a marriage of convenience with the lovely, but reluctant, American heiress Consuelo Vanderbilt. Then again the glories of the Palace revived. The footmen wore powdered hair. They powdered every day, washing the hair with soap, combing it out, setting the hair in waves, and then applying the violet powder which was mixed with flour, causing the hair to set hard, like cement. No footman was ever engaged at Blenheim unless he was six feet tall or more. They wore maroon plush breeches, maroon coats, waistcoats with silver braid, flesh-coloured silk stockings and silver-buckled shoes.

The inside staff at Blenheim during this renaissance was forty when there was no entertainment, and the outside staff forty to fifty, but when the Palace was thrown open these numbers greatly increased. The Duke also kept a hunting department at his home farm at Bladon with a staff of twelve. He kept twenty grey thoroughbred hunters, famous throughout the land, and twenty exquisite bay carriage horses. The chief electrician presided over a staff of four, and there were carpenters and decorators whose duty it was to collect flowers from the garden and arrange them in every room in the palace. The two Lodge Keepers, one at Blenheim, one at Woodstock, were over six feet tall. They were dressed in black coats with silver buttons, buff breeches, gaiters and a cockaded top hat, and each carried a long staff. There was also a dairyman and a dairymaid, a nightwatchman and an Airedale police-dog, and a professional cricketer to instruct the Duke. Two wine specialists from

London unpacked the wine, and stocked the two vast cellars. Twenty gamekeepers presided over the shooting, in Irish green velvet coats with brass buttons, and black billycock hats, each bearing a long staff.

The Duke also owned a hunting lodge, Sysonby, at Melton Mowbray, which he would visit from time to time with the modest retinue of the Groom of the Chambers, two footmen, three housemaids, three in the kitchen, an odd man, the stud groom, second horsemen and stable helpers. This army was conveyed both ways in a special train. The ninth Duke of Marlborough held sway like a Renaissance prince, and this was the Blenheim which Winston, as a mature man, was to know, its fantastic ambience familiar to him through repeated contact, and accepted by him as a normal mode of life.

* * *

Lord Randolph Churchill was twenty-five at the time of Winston's birth. Although his father, the seventh Duke, had had a respectable political career, having been a member of Derby's third Cabinet and Disraeli's first, it was primarily a tribute to his position. The political genius of the family was only to flower in true glory in his son Randolph, though he by the time of Winston's birth, had not yet shown any signs of unusual promise. He was the Conservative member for the family seat of Woodstock, but had as yet made little mark in the House and had indeed shown an almost clownish political ineptitude during his early electioneering.

Winston's mother, Lady Randolph, was twenty at the time of his birth. She was the daughter of Leonard Jerome, a financier and entrepreneur who had settled in New York in 1855. He joined the Stock Exchange, becoming partner in a brokerage business with William R. Travers, and made and lost several fortunes in a dazzling career. He was at one time principal proprietor of the *New York Times*, became consul in Trieste, and was widely known for his passion for horses and racing (he owned the stout-hearted Kentucky), for ocean-going yachts, and the opera, where his interest in the singers was said not to be confined to their voices. He was to be remembered as one of the founders of the American Jockey Club, and as builder of the race-track near New York which bore his name – Jerome Park. He was clearly a man of charm and *panache* – a public figure adored by the crowds when at the top of the wave, dignified and courageous when in temporary eclipse. On Sundays he would drive his four-in-hand up Fifth Avenue, waving to his friends in the passing church parades, and as a contemporary wrote:

Jerome sat on the box and handled the reins. With a huge bouquet of flowers attached to his buttonhole, with white gloves, cracking his whip ... the four horses would rush up Fifth Avenue, on towards the Park, while the populace said, one to the other: 'That is Jerome.'[3]

He built a mansion in Madison Square with stables three stories high, and above the stables a private theatre where such artists as Patti were invited to rehearse, but there were moments of seclusion and defeat when his wings were clipped. From these he each time rallied, and re-established himself. Jerome and his wife, Clara Hall, had four daughters of whom three survived – Clara, Jennie, Camille who died at the age of seven, and Leonie. Of these, Clara was to marry Moreton Frewen, a sort of genius *manqué* who suggested to some a thwarted Elizabethan. He was a learned but unsound student of economics and bimetallism and the father of Clare Sheridan the sculptor; Leonie married John Leslie of County Monaghan, father of the author Sir Shane Leslie, while Jennie (socially ambitious, as were all the sisters), made what seemed a better match with Randolph.

* * *

This injection of vigorous American blood was no bad thing for an old aristocratic English family, and the 'Jerome constitution' was held by many to be the explanation of Winston's extraordinary stamina once he had passed through the stresses of boyhood. Well might Lord Randolph have been bowled over by Jennie's outstanding loveliness, for she had the dark beauty of a creole, some indeed seeing in her something of the stealthy grace of a wild animal. Lord D'Abernon remarked on his first sight of her at Viceregal Lodge in Dublin when her father-in-law, the seventh Duke, was Viceroy:

> I have the clearest recollection of seeing her for the first time ... The Viceroy was on the dais at the farther end of the room surrounded by a brilliant staff, but eyes were not turned on him or on his consort, but on a dark, lithe figure, standing somewhat apart and appearing to be of another texture to those standing around her, radiant, translucent, intense. A diamond star in her hair, her favourite ornament – its lustre dimmed by the flashing glory of her eyes. More of the panther than of the woman in her look, but with a cultivated intelligence unknown to the jungle.

A perceptive description this, and perhaps that suggestion of animal grace in Jennie could be attributed to an admixture of Iroquois blood in her mother's family. She and Randolph had met at Cowes in August 1873, where Leonard Jerome had taken a small house, Rosetta, for his

3. Anita Leslie, *Jennie*, p. 9.

wife and daughters. (It stands to-day exactly as it was in 1873.) Suffering one of his temporary reverses on Wall Street, he could not join them. Here, in an atmosphere conducive to romance, with the riding lights of yachts reflected in the water, Randolph and Jennie met at a dance given by the officers of the cruiser *Ariadne*, guardship in Cowes Roads for the Prince of Wales. Randolph was at once infatuated by Jennie's beauty, and arranged for an introduction to her, the morose gloom with which he had embarked on the evening dissipated in an instant. Jennie appeared to respond to his advances with equal alacrity, but it is possible that there was a certain element of calculation in her attitude. There was at least no ambiguity in the position of Randolph's father, to whom any relationship was clearly repellent.

> It is not likely [he wrote on 31 August] that at present you can look at anything but from your own point of view, but persons from the outside cannot but be struck with the unwisdom of your proceedings, and the uncontrolled state of your feelings, which completely paralyses your judgement; never was there such an illustration of the adage '*Love is blind*' for you seem blind to all consequences in order that you may pursue your passion; blind to the relative consequences as regards your family & blind to trouble you are heaping on Mamma and me by the anxieties this act of yours has produced . . .

Nor was what Randolph had been able to tell the Duke, and what he had already heard about Mr Jerome, likely to reassure a man who, as we have seen, expected his children to marry into English families with resounding titles:

> . . .I can't say that what you have told me is reassuring. I shall know more before long but from what you have told me and what I have heard this Mr J. seems to be a sporting, and I should think vulgar kind of man. I hear he drives about 6 and 8 horses in N.Y. (one may take this as a kind of indication of what the man is.) I hear he and his two brothers are stockbrokers, one of them bears a *bad* character in commercial judgement in *this* country, but which of them it is, I do not know, but it is evident that he is of the class of speculators; he has been bankrupt once; and may be so again . . . I am deeply sorry that your feelings are so much engaged; and only for your own sake wish most heartily that you had checked the current before it became so overpowering.[4]

The Duke wished to postpone the marriage for a year, but Randolph, who already displayed great obstinacy and determination, persuaded his father to antedate it to after the approaching election, in which he was elected member for Woodstock. The Duke next took issue at the

4. Blenheim papers.

marriage settlement. Mr Jerome was naturally shocked by the British practice of making the bride completely dependent upon her husband, and wished to settle £2,000 a year on Jennie to secure her position should things go wrong. The Duke fought this eminently reasonable proposal tooth and claw, holding that it was unheard of that Miss Jerome should 'be made quite independent of Lord Randolph Churchill in a pecuniary point of view', which in such a case, the Duke held, was 'without precedent'. In the end a compromise was reached in which Mr Jerome was forced to yield most of his safeguards. We can well sympathize with his rueful words to the Duke:

> It is quite wrong to suppose that I entertain any distrust of Randolph. On the contrary I firmly believe there is no young man in the world safer, still I can but think your English custom of making the wife so utterly dependent on the husband most unwise.[5]

Randolph had never had the slightest intention of allowing his father's prudential warnings to influence his choice, and the pair were married at the British Embassy in Paris on 15 April 1874.

* * *

The first two years of Winston's life were spent at the rented house in Charles Street, and at Blenheim. During this time there occurred an event which transformed his childhood, the engagement of Mrs Everest as his nanny at the beginning of 1875. Lord Randolph was nervous, much occupied with affairs, and in the end desperately ill, and had little time for his children except to load them with reproaches. He appeared in any case to be almost entirely deficient in paternal feelings. Jennie was equally remote. The young and ambitious American woman, aided by her glowing beauty and vivacity and the advantage of her marriage, was making a strenuous and wholly successful onslaught on London Society – in those days a jealously guarded enclave. In Winston's childhood his mother's selfishness and ambition, endorsed by the customs of the day, left him completely deprived of maternal love, although it should be remembered that when his career was beginning mother and son came together, in a partnership free from scruples, for its advancement. But we shall see Jennie emerging as a far more formidable character than appears in the social climber of this early period. Always a better wife than mother, she was to remain loyal to Lord Randolph in his ghastly decline, and throughout his most painful moments of humiliation.

Winston would inherit this admirable constancy. The less he proved himself an old-fashioned Churchill, the more he revealed his Jerome

5. Ibid.

inheritance. Politics, oratory, style, were derived from his father. From Jennie came determination, undeviating ambition, an iron constitution, and a clear vision of the future. Selfish and frivolous as she was at this time, her virtues should be clearly recognized. She was utterly fearless, superb in disaster, and prepared to face any enemy. She had also great musical powers, which Winston did not inherit, almost sufficient to make her a concert pianist, and when this wild American girl, whom the Duchess of Marlborough had imagined to be so common and vulgar, sat down to the piano at Blenheim and played with exquisite skill the old lady was entranced at an accomplishment notably lacking in her own daughters.

Winston felt no resentment at his parents' indifference, regarding it as the common lot of children. Indeed, there is something pathetic in the unrewarded love he lavished upon his father and mother, writing of the latter:

'She shone for me like the evening star. I loved her dearly, but at a distance ... My mother always seemed to me a fairy princess: a radiant being possessed of limitless riches and power.' Into the gap left by his mother's obsession with pleasure stepped Mrs Everest, the perfect substitute: 'My nurse was my confidante. Mrs Everest it was who looked after me and tended all my wants. It was to her I poured out my many troubles, both now and in my schooldays.' Winston's debt to this splendid woman is beyond assessment. Though often insensitive in human relations, he was deeply conscious of this one, and left a tender picture of her in the reminiscences of his youth – of her stories of her last charge, 'little Ella, the daughter of a clergyman in Cumberland', her love of Kent, which she always called 'the garden of England', her dread of 'sitting in wet feet', her detestation of 'Roman practices'.

In 1895 he hurried from his military duties at Aldershot to her death-bed and later wrote: 'When I think of the fate of poor old women, so many of whom have no one to look after them and nothing to live on at the end of their lives, I am glad to have had a hand in all that structure of pensions and insurance which no other country can rival and which is especially a help to them.' Who can doubt that when he wrote these words it was not the anonymous destitute and deserving millions but Mrs Everest who was in his heart and mind?

But if it was his old nurse who held the key to Winston's heart – while his mother's glittering image shone for him in remote glory – when his intelligence matured, it was the worship of his father which dominated and indeed obsessed his early life. The business of fostering this image (which was entirely of his own invention) was to be complicated by the fact that his father never admitted him into the slightest intimacy, treated him with icy indifference, and as his own health declined, grossly underrated his son's ability and despised his character. But no rebuffs, however brutal, could prevail against Winston's hero-worship for this cold but brilliant man:

> He seemed to own the key to everything or almost everything worth having. But if ever I began to show the slightest sign of comradeship, he was immediately offended; and when once I suggested that I might help his private secretary to write some of his letters, he froze me into stone.

In spite of this:

> I conceived an intense admiration and affection for him; and after his early death for his memory. I read industriously almost every word he had ever spoken and learned by heart large portions of his speeches. I took my politics almost unquestioningly from him.

And so the worship of the son was proof against the glacial indifference of the father. No hardening by experience was to disturb the myth, and in Lady Asquith's words: 'Until the end he worshipped at the altar of his unknown father.'[6]

* * *

But all this was in the future, and we must return to Christmas 1874, which Randolph and Jennie spent at Blenheim, when Winston was baptized there by the Duke's chaplain, and passing over a few years to January 1877, when a gross indiscretion by Lord Randolph made necessary a period of rustication in Ireland, his father, the Duke, having been persuaded by Disraeli to accept the position of Viceroy in order to get Lord Randolph out of England.

There is no need to relate in detail this ridiculous business, which can be found set out at length in Randolph Churchill's *Life* of his father, Winston. It is only necessary to say here that it concerned a love affair between Lord Randolph's elder brother Blandford and Lady Aylesford, who with her husband had been members of the Prince of Wales's circle. Lord Randolph, springing with typical impetuosity to his brother's help in an effort to prevent Aylesford from divorcing his wife, so mismanaged matters that he practically accused the Prince of having an affair with the lady himself, and most incautiously threatened to produce letters to support this charge.

He was unwise enough to remark in the presence of others: 'I had the Crown of England in my pocket.' The Prince greatly resented this probing among the extensive débris of his erotic life. It should be remembered that this was an age of gross snobbery, and of servile

6. Violet Bonham Carter, *Winston Churchill As I Knew Him*, p.27.

genuflexions before the heir to the throne. Even Winston, describing the episode in his biography of Lord Randolph, could not refrain from a deferential kowtow, referring to 'the deep displeasure of a great personage'. The act of *lèse-majesté* was therefore the more outrageous, and it did not stop there. Lord Randolph chose to interpret a letter from the angry Prince – who was mercifully absent in India at the time – as either a demand for an apology or a challenge to a duel.

This latter possibility was so appalling that it led to a *démarche* from the Prime Minister and the Lord Chancellor, ordering Lord Randolph to apologize. He did so, some months later, signing a letter drafted by the Lord Chancellor, but adding a surly postscript of his own which deprived his surrender of any grace, and made it impossible for the Prince to accept it. On his return from India he made it clear that he would not in future be prepared to meet the Randolph Churchills, or to visit any house where they were received.

Lord Randolph, contemptuous and morose, may have cared little for this demotion, but it was a severe blow, temporary but devastating, to Jennie's solid progress; for although the Prince had other equally delectable ladies in tow, he was becoming a captive at her chariot wheels, and her ostracism was a guarantee that the rest of Society would abjectly follow the Prince's lead. That the Prince should suddenly be forced to defect, through her husband's folly, was a disaster so complete that only an aspiring hostess of the Edwardian era could fully measure it.

Disraeli, as so often, found a solution. The Duke of Marlborough must drag himself away from his career in England and his life at Blenheim, and go to Ireland as Viceroy, taking his erring son with him as unpaid private secretary, and thus removing him from the glare of Royal censure. 'It will,' he said, 'put an end to it all.' But if the Aylesford scandal was a thunderbolt from heaven for Jennie, its effect upon Lord Randolph was to mature and harden him. To Winston, writing of him afterwards, it seemed that

> a nature originally genial and gay contracted a stern and bitter quality, a harsh contempt for what is called 'Society', and an abiding antagonism to rank and authority. If this misfortune produced in Lord Randolph characteristics which afterwards hindered or injured his public work, it was also his spur. Without it he might have wasted a dozen years in the frivolous and expensive pursuits of the silly world of fashion; without it he would probably never have developed popular sympathies or the courage to champion democratic causes.[7]

The family set off for Dublin in January 1877, and this Irish interlude

7. Winston S. Churchill, *Lord Randolph Churchill*, p. 60.

was the time which gave Winston his first memories of the world. He could recall vividly, as a middle-aged man, its sounds, smells and places – 'Little Lodge' where they lived, and the fine Irish rain falling on grey buildings. He remembered his grandfather, the old Duke, unveiling a statue of Lord Gough – scarlet soldiers on horseback, and a black faceless crowd behind them – and the theatre being burned down just before he was to go there for a pantomime, and the manager burned with it, all that was left of him his keys; and of how nervous Everest was of the Fenians, and how he fell off his donkey when she thought a procession of them was approaching, and suffered concussion of the brain. Looking back across the years, he listened again to the rain pattering on the shrubberies round the house, to him huge and mysterious as forests, and remembered how he hid there from the governess who sought him for lessons; remembered too a long white building with green shutters, and what to the eye of childhood seemed a vast lawn as wide as Trafalgar Square, where in the fresh purity of early morning the sleek blackbirds with their yellow bills hopped and pecked on the dew-soaked grass.

There were memories of his mother too, but now in different guise to his later ones – not the goddess with the diamond star in her hair, but in a riding habit 'fitting like a skin and often beautifully spotted with mud'.

It was during this period in Dublin that Winston's brother Jack was born, in February 1880. No two brothers could have presented a greater contrast, although their mutual love was lasting and complete. For Jack had none of Winston's daemon, being a charming but unremarkable man who married the entrancing Lady Gwendeline Bertie, and became a stockbroker of modest attainments.

* * *

The Irish interlude was, as Winston wrote, the period when Lord Randolph's precocious and abnormal powers were forged in the fires of resentment. In his hunting and wanderings over the Irish countryside he also gained a deep insight into the miserable lives of the Irish poor when he was secretary of the Famine Fund Campaign organized by the Duchess. His general knowledge of Ireland, acquired at first hand, stood him in good stead when the time came to oppose Gladstone's Home Rule Bill. Meanwhile his temper became morose and his mood resentful and exacting, as he brooded over the insults and injuries, as he saw them, that Society had heaped upon his wife and himself in the Aylesford fracas, and as his character hardened, it acquired a steely force in which it had before been lacking:

'This, however,' said his friend Rosebery, 'was the turning-point of his life. The *saeva indignatio*, excited in him by this social conflict, turned to politics. That was the vent for his suppressed wrath.[8]

8. Lord Rosebery, *Lord Randolph* (1906) p. 37–8.

Lord Randolph and Jennie, taking Winston and Jack with them, returned to England in February 1880 to prepare for the General Election which took place in April. Lord Randolph held Woodstock with 512 votes, a reduced majority reduced by 60, but the Government of Disraeli – now Lord Beaconsfield – was routed, a defeat which ended the Duke of Marlborough's term as Viceroy of Ireland. Mr Gladstone and the Liberals, after victory, had a majority of 46 over the Tories and the Irish combined. The Conservatives were in pathetic disarray, their Front Opposition Bench, in Winston's words, 'cumbered with the ancient and dreary wreckage of the late Administration', their leader and inspirer Beaconsfield's stimulating presence removed from the House of Commons. And yet, as Winston wrote later in his Life of Lord Randolph, an extraordinary reversal of fortune was at hand in which his father was to play a major part:

> Who could have foreseen that these dejected Conservatives in scarcely five years, with the growing assent of an immense electorate, would advance to the enjoyment of twenty years of power? It needed a penetrating eye to discover the method, and a bold heart first to stem and finally to turn the tide. . . . Who without the audacity of genius would have dared to force the Conservative party to base the foundations of their authority with confidence upon the very masses they dreaded and to teach those masses to venerate and guard the institutions they had formerly despised? . . .

The Randolph Churchills moved into a house at 29 St James's Place. Their general ostracism by London Society over the Aylesford business gradually abated, and the Queen was said to have agreed to forgive the *enfant terrible*. Three years were to pass before the outraged Prince allowed a reconciliation to be arranged, and it was Lord Beaconsfield's opinion that the quickest way back to his favour would be some drastic success in Parliament. They were to stay in St James's Place for two years, when after a visit by Lord Randolph to America the family moved to 2 Connaught Place.

The various solvents of Mr Gladstone's Government were soon at work. The process of undermining it had begun with the episode of Charles Bradlaugh refusing to take the oath in the House, which led to the formation of the most successful splinter group in Parliamentary history, the Fourth Party.[9] This made for the dimming of the prestige both of the Liberal Government and of the Conservative Opposition under Sir Stafford Northcote, and for the emergence of Lord Randolph Churchill as a tactician of genius, and a debater of daring panache.

Such was the background of Winston's life – a father totally immersed

9. Consisting of four Conservative MPs led by Lord Randolph, and including Lord Salisbury's nephew, Arthur Balfour.

in politics, a frivolous mother, and an adored and adoring nurse. He was now to undergo a new and grim experience.

* * *

This began in 1882, shortly before his eighth birthday, and it was to prove a *via dolorosa*. Victorian preparatory schools were frequently places of Dickensian horror, but this one on the surface seemed comfortable and well run, the food being better than many of the boys enjoyed at home. It was St George's at Ascot, a place of pitch-pine boarding and gothic windows, and stained glass in the WC, and outside shrivelled pine-trees and dirty heather. The Headmaster was the Rev. H. W. Sneyd-Kynnersley, who was inordinately proud of his aristocratic connections, his coat of arms, and his red Dundreary whiskers which 'waved on either side of his flaccid cheeks like a bat's wings', and which he was in the habit of fondling during lessons. Winston was miserable at the thought of being left alone in this alien place:

'After all, I was only seven, and I had been so happy in my nursery with all my toys. I had such wonderful toys: a real steam engine, a magic lantern, and a collection of soldiers already nearly a thousand strong. Now it was to be all lessons.'

It would not have been so bad if the lessons had been presented to him in a comprehensible way, or if he had seen any practical advantage in them. As it was, he resisted them and authority with unbroken spirit, and his attitude towards the governing system at St George's might be taken as the first exercise of his formidable will-power. However harsh the punishments, the less willing was he to alter his behaviour. It was a characteristic that persisted through childhood, youth and early manhood, and indeed through his whole life. But the failure to understand what they were trying to teach him was his greatest affliction, and his direct and acquisitive mind was baffled by meaningless instruction.

It was not that there was anything wrong with his understanding: he simply had no mental structure of elementary knowledge on which to build, so that lessons which assumed that he had were baffling and profoundly discouraging. Failure to understand them, moreover, was rewarded by beating by the Headmaster of such ferocity that the taint in his character appears obvious to us today:

'No Eton boy,' said Winston, 'and certainly no Harrow boy of my day ever received such a cruel flogging as this Headmaster was accustomed to inflict on the little boys who were in his care and power. They exceeded anything that would be tolerated in any of the Reformatories under the Home Office.'[10]

In Winston's case there were no doubt ample causes of the Headmaster's displeasure. He was hopelessly unsuited for school life – brash, rebellious, and so unamenable to discipline that even in its harshest form it left no impression on his unyielding nature, and not a dent in his extraordinary will-power. It was like some wiry grass springing back instantly after it had been trampled on. But while one thinks of this Headmaster with a certain repulsion, one should also reflect that in Winston's case he had much to bear. The small, red-haired boy was lazy, slovenly, unpunctual, rebellious and slow to learn, and his transgressions had passed into folk-lore by the time a new boy, the renowned Maurice Baring, arrived at St George's after Winston's departure.

> Dreadful legends were told about Winston Churchill, who had been taken away from the school. His naughtiness appeared to have surpassed everything. He had been flogged for taking sugar from the pantry, and, so far from being penitent, he had taken the Headmaster's sacred straw hat from where it hung over the door and kicked it to pieces. His sojourn at this school had been one long feud with authority.[11]

Winston was, of course, frequently beaten. His sufferings at this school might have been softened by parental sympathy, but he received little or none. Lord Randolph – totally immersed in politics, cold and enigmatic with his son – never wrote, and his mother, occupied with her social life, was equally indifferent. Even for the period, their selfishness was abnormal, and Jennie's was to continue for some years to come. Winston's pathetic appeals to his mother and father to visit him – appeals to echo *ad nauseam* from Harrow and Sandhurst – were ignored, and he was left 'to count the days and hours to the end of every term, when I should return home from this hateful servitude, and range my soldiers in line of battle on the nursery floor'.[12]

*   *   *

Even Lord and Lady Randolph realized at last that all was not well with their son, and he was removed from St George's at the

---

10. Winston S. Churchill, *My Early Life*, p. 20.
11. Maurice Baring, *The Puppet Show of Memory*, p. 93.
12. Winston S. Churchill, op. cit., p. 21.

end of the summer term of 1884. Winston's last year at this school was a time of great political activity for Lord Randolph. He made the immortal 'chips' speech at Blackpool in which he ridiculed Gladstone's habit of felling giant trees, and inviting the press to inspect the débris, probably the most withering political attack of his career. Then, his seat at Woodstock having been abolished in consequence of a new Reform Bill, he announced that he would fight the Central Division of Birmingham, challenging the great Joseph Chamberlain and John Bright in their own radical stronghold, a bold venture which stirred Tory working-men to their depths, and made Lord Randolph their adored hero.

He was also engaged in a successful fight for the control of the important Union of Conservative Associations, and Winston later believed that this success was the true foundation of his political fortune. It was also due to his efforts that the Primrose League[13] received official recognition. His fierce opposition to the party leadership was relaxed, and it is possible that he had come to some accommodation with Lord Salisbury as to the terms on which he would be prepared to join a future Conservative Government.

Winston left St George's, and was sent in the middle of the following term to a very different type of school. It was conducted by two gentle elderly sisters in an elegant Regency house in Hove within sight and sound of the sea. It was no doubt thought that the invigorating Brighton air would benefit Winston's health, and another reason for the choice was the presence in Brighton of the Randolph Churchill family doctor, the renowned Robson Roose, who practised there as well as in London, and whose presence, as we shall see, almost certainly saved Winston's life in the first of his many brushes with death.

In the winter of 1884–5 Lord Randolph made a four-month visit to India, perhaps to recover from a recent illness, but more probably because he had reason to believe that if Lord Salisbury formed a Government after the next General Election he intended to make Randolph his Secretary of State for India. The new school was in every way a delightful change for Winston. Gone were the harsh discipline, the terrible floggings, the censorious masters. He was allowed to ride three times a week, and was now addicted to a fat family dog called Chloe about whose health he constantly inquired in letters becoming ever more buoyant.

13. The Primrose League was founded by Lord Randolph and his friends in commemoration of Lord Beaconsfield.

* * *

Lord Randolph's first office came in June 1885 when Gladstone's Government was defeated on a minor amendment to the Budget, and at once resigned. Lord Randolph had already told Lord Salisbury with extraordinary effrontery that he would not join any Government in which Sir Stafford Northcote was Leader of the House of Commons. This gesture of almost insolent defiance, coupled with a haughty refusal to see Salisbury before his departure for Balmoral, surprisingly won him the day, and he became Secretary of State for India in a 'Caretaker Government' which took office until a General Election could be held. It need only be said that his tenure of this office was brief but successful, and during it the annexation of Burma to the Crown was accomplished. The Election took place in November, and it was then that Lord Randolph stood against Bright in Birmingham.

He lost this election, but entered Parliament via South Paddington, where an admirer stood down for him. Gladstone was victorious but by a margin which made the Government dependent on the Irish vote. So long as the Salisbury–Parnell alliance held the result was a dead heat. Salisbury for the moment continued in office, but resigned in January 1886. Gladstone formed his third Cabinet in February, making clear that he would try to introduce a measure of Irish Home Rule. The proposal, involving a separate Government for Ireland, caused a massive split in the Liberal Party, such leaders as Hartington and Joseph Chamberlain, leaving Gladstone, transferring their talents to the Conservatives under the title of Liberal Unionists.

Lord Randolph had long determined to meet any Gladstone proposal for Home Rule by fervent support for Protestant Ulster, for which there was then no question of partition, and which, contrary to religion and descent, would be brought under a Dublin Parliament. Travelling to Belfast, he made a stirring speech of defiance in the Ulster Hall and coined the memorable phrase: 'Ulster will fight, and Ulster will be right.'

* * *

We shall be struck by the number of Winston's terrifying escapes from death as a child. He was small for his age and somewhat puny in physique, and the moments of peril were usually due to some reckless physical action, taken to prove his virility. But the first and closest call was due to natural causes, and came in March 1886 when he collapsed with pneumonia at school. He was attended with wonderful devotion by Robson Roose, whose frequent reports to Lord Randolph clearly show the extreme danger of Winston's condition, and the loving care with **which he was tended.**

To Lord Randolph. Sunday 14 March 1015 p.m.

Memo W Churchill. Temp 104–3; right lung generally involved – left lung of course feeling its extra work, but as yet free from disease! Respiration more frequent. Pulse increased!

N.B. This report may appear grave, yet it merely indicates the approach of the crisis which, please God, will result in an improved condition should the left lung remain free.

I am in the next room and shall watch the patient during the night – for I am anxious.[14]

To Lord Randolph 15 March 6 a.m.

The high temperature indicating exhaustion I used stimulants, by the mouth and the rectum, with the result that at 2.15 a.m. the temp had fallen to 101, and now to 100, thank God. I shall give up my London work and stay by the boy today.[15]

To Lord Randolph Churchill 15 March 1 p.m.

We are still fighting the battle for your boy. His temp is 103 now, but he is taking his nourishment better and there is no increase in lung mischief. As long as I can fight the temp and keep it under 105 I shall not feel anxious, and by Wednesday the fever ought to have subsided and the crisis be past. Nourishment, stimulants and close watching will save your boy. I am sanguine of this . . . Pardon this shaky writing. I am a little tired.[16]

To Lord Randolph Churchill.

Your boy, in my opinion, on his perilous path is holding his own well, right well! The temp is 103.5 at which I am satisfied, as I had anticipated 104. There can *now* be no cause for anxiety for some hours (12 at least) so *please* have a good night as we are armed at all points.[17]

Then there was a sudden alarming return of the fever.

To Lord Randolph Churchill 16 March 1886.

We have had a very anxious night but we have managed to hold our own. The temp is now 101, the left lung still uninvolved; the pulse shows still good power and the delirium I hope may soon cease and natural sleep occur, when one might hope that he would awake free from the disease – on the other hand we have to realize that we may have another 24 hours of this critical condition. I have given you a statement of fact; your boy is making a wonderful fight, and I do feel please God he will recover.[18]

14. Chartwell papers.
15. Ibid.
16. Ibid.
17. Ibid.
18. Ibid.

On 17 March Robson Roose, was able to write to Lord Randolph with intense and obvious relief:

> I have a very good report to make. Winston has had 6 *hours quiet sleep*. Delirium has now ceased. Temp 99, respiration 28. He sends you and Her Ladyship his love.[19]

On 17 March the doctor wrote to Lady Randolph urging the need for constant vigilance:

> Forgive my troubling you with these lines to impress upon you the absolute necessity of quiet and sleep for Winston and that Mrs Everest should not be allowed in the sick room today – even the excitement of pleasure at seeing her might do harm! and I am so fearful of relapse knowing that we are not quite out of the wood yet.

But no relapse took place, and, as his uncle Moreton Frewen expressed it to Jennie, Winston had been given back to her 'from the very threshold of the unknown'. The convalescence, after so grave an illness, was long, but at the end of it his irrepressible character at once asserted itself, and he wrote to his mother with all the old bounce and assurance, saying that he had completely recovered his own strength, and bragging about how he had beaten Robson Roose's son in an examination.

'I am in good health,' he concluded. 'It is superfluous to add that I am happy.'

* * *

Meanwhile the Liberal Government, which had been labouring heavily, was brought down in June 1886 on the Home Rule issue. Gladstone resigned, and a General Election in July gave the Tories and Liberal Unionists a majority of 188 over all other parties. Lord Randolph had been in large part the architect of this triumph, and the Prime Minister, Salisbury, was uneasily aware that his promotion to high office was now inevitable: 'He feared Lord Randolph Churchill must be Chancellor of the Exchequer and Leader [of the House of Commons], which I do not like,' recorded the Queen on 25 July. 'He is so mad and odd, and has also bad health.'

This bleak conclusion was to be amply justified, in spite of Lord Randolph's excellent beginning as Leader of the House of Commons,

19. Ibid.

where he showed a tact and patience by no means expected in one so volatile and unpredictable. But his strange character was soon at work in the Cabinet, dividing colleagues and eroding his own influence and reputation. The Prime Minister was never misled by his brilliant parliamentary ascendancy, and had no illusions about him: 'His character,' he said, 'is quite untamed. Both in impulsiveness and variability and in a tendency which can be described by the scholastic word *vulgaris* he presents the characteristics of extreme youth.'[20] We can now see that in Lord Salisbury Lord Randolph met a more powerful will than he even imagined.

Meanwhile Winston was following his father's career with naive but avid wonder, for although he was only eleven his interest in politics, particularly Lord Randolph's, was already astir. He remained happy and content in this school by the sea with the two gentle old ladies, writing the usual schoolboy letters, asking if he might learn the 'cello, begging his mother to come and see him in the *Mikado*, play the piano at the school concert and present the prizes; and begging, as usual, in vain. Lord Randolph also visited Brighton without bothering to call on his adoring son, who wrote plaintively:

'You never came to see me on Sunday when you were in Brighton.'[21]

But perhaps Lord Randolph was too preoccupied in November with his own troubles to spare time for his son, for his own self-inflicted ruin was at hand, and 1886 was to see his meteoric career brought to final ruin. On 20 December he wrote to the Prime Minister from Windsor, saying that as the Secretary of State for War refused to decrease his estimates for the coming year, he could 'not continue to be responsible for the finances'. He was implored by Lord George Hamilton, who was also staying at Windsor, not to send this suicidal letter, but insisted on doing so, failing even to inform Jennie of this grave step. Her first knowledge of the event came from the morning paper. Lord Randolph had utterly and wantonly destroyed himself. As his distraught secretary cried out to Jennie at that shattered breakfast table, 'He has thrown himself from the top of the ladder, and will never reach it again.'

The pretext for Lord Randolph's resignation – War Office economy – concealed other and more profound differences.

> In which direction was the Conservative Party to go, and who was to lead it? Over a wide series of subjects Lord Randolph had stumbled into serious conflict with the Prime Minister, to the point where the latter would be pressed no more ... Such was Lord Randolph's prestige that the

20. Salisbury to Fitzjames Stephen, 30 December 1886.
21. Chartwell papers.

Government tottered, but it did not fall. Lord Randolph found himself out of office, without a following, and utterly isolated.

We shall see him again in the background of this story – a doomed and baleful figure – his body deceitfully normal and responsive, his brain disintegrating with the stealthy onset of *locomotor ataxia*.

His resignation had been a profound relief to Lord Salisbury, whose position had indeed been briefly menaced, but who when asked if he would bring Lord Randolph back answered: 'Have you ever heard of a man having a carbuncle on his neck wanting it to return?'

* * *

Winston remained at the Hove school for another four terms, and Lord Randolph consulted his brother-in-law Edward Marjoribanks about a suitable public school for him.[22] Marjoribanks, whose son Dudley was down for Harrow, wrote to the Head Master, the Rev. J. E. C. Welldon, who replied that he would be happy to accept Winston, who would be placed temporarily in a small house, and afterwards in the Head Master's own. In December 1887 Winston and Jack were deserted again when their parents went to Russia, leaving them with Mrs Everest, who became seriously ill with diphtheria. They were then sent to the Duchess Fanny at Blenheim, and on 23 January 1888 Winston returned to school. The Duchess greeted his departure with a certain relief:

'Winston is going back to school today,' she told Lord Randolph. '*Entre nous* I do not feel very sorry for he is certainly a handful . . . I am sure Harrow will do wonders for him for I fancy he was too clever and too much the Boss at that Brighton school . . . Jack is a good little boy and not a bit of trouble.'[23]

The time had come for Winston to take the Entrance Examination to Harrow, about which he was full of bluster and misplaced confidence. The examination was far more difficult than he had envisaged in his bragging letter to Lady Randolph, and he made a sorry hash of it. . . . However, wrote Winston forty years on, 'It was from these slender evidences of scholarship that Mr Welldon drew the conclusion that I was worthy to pass into Harrow. It is very much to his credit. It showed that he was a man capable of looking beneath the surface of things: a man not dependent upon paper manifestations. I have always had the greatest regard for him.'[24]

22. Edward Marjoribanks was the eldest son of the first Baron Tweedmouth. He married the third daughter of the seventh Duke of Marlborough, Lady Fanny Spencer Churchill.

23. Blenheim papers.

24. Winston S. Churchill, *My Early Life*, p. 23–4.

It is curious in a boy thought so brash and fearless that, although he may have jested about it in after-life, Winston worked himself into an appalling state of nerves over this examination, only just scraped through it, and was horribly sick in the train on the way back to Brighton.[25] But his buoyant spirits were not for long lowered by this ignoble showing, and he was soon babbling in letters to his mother about the beauties of Harrow; of how much he liked Welldon and his sisters, and how urgently he required money. *'My funds are in rather a low condition, and the Exchequer would bear replenishing.'*

Winston entered Harrow on 17 April 1888, where he was taken into Mr H. O. D. Davidson's 'Small House', in which he remained until April 1889 when Welldon received him into his own. He was placed in the Third Division of the Fourth Form, the bottom form in the school, under his English master Mr Robert Somervell. There were only two boys lower than himself, and these were soon removed by illness, leaving Winston the bottom boy in the school. This unpretentious position was a source of some embarrassment to him when the roll was called, and the boys filed past the master in order of school seniority:

> Lord Randolph Churchill had only just resigned his position as Leader of the House of Commons and Chancellor of the Exchequer, and he still towered in the forefront of politics. In consequence large numbers of visitors . . . used to wait on the school steps in order to see me march by; and I frequently heard the irreverent comment: 'Why, he's last of all.'[26]

However, the two terms spent in his form were not wasted, and Winston was to remember for the rest of his life with gratitude the influence of his English master, Somervell, under whose guidance: 'I got into my bones the structure of the ordinary British sentence – which is a noble thing.' After two terms he had done sufficiently well to move to a higher Division.

* * *

But apart from English, the familiar pattern of failure at once began to reassert itself at Harrow. Winston, of course, blamed every lapse of understanding upon the senseless curriculum, the methods of teaching, the dreary incomprehensible subjects. All the old, maddening faults which had fired Sneyd-Kynnersley's savage temper persisted now. The masters clearly recognized his abilities and originality, but were so exasperated by his slovenly methods that H. O. D. Davidson was driven to the unusual course of sending a cry of

25. Blenheim papers.
26. Winston S. Churchill, op. cit., p. 24.

despair to Lady Randolph which almost amounted to an ultimatum.

'His forgetfulness, carelessness, unpunctuality and irregularity in every way have really been so serious that I write to ask you, when he is at home to speak very gravely to him on the subject.'[27]

Davidson and Somervell had seriously considered stopping Winston's '*exeat*', and threatened that if he did not mend his ways he would have to be most severely punished. We may imagine how these words of doom were received by Lord Randolph in his state of morose depression. But these strictures made no more lasting impression on Winston than those that had gone before.

It was thought incongruous that such a misfit should win the Declamation Prize open to the whole school – the recitation of 1,200 lines of the *Lays of Ancient Rome*. His own explanation would have been that the poems appealed to him, unlike the classics or mathematics, and that he had an excellent memory. 'The Exchequer would bear replenishing' – how often were such remorseless reminders to Lady Randolph on his lips at this inauspicious time! They became, indeed, a positive bombardment, and further diminished Lord Randolph's sagging opinion of his son's character. Nor did Winston understand that his parents' financial position had been greatly restricted by their own gross extravagance, and they were neither generous nor understanding in supplying his needs. Lord Randolph's own weakness in this direction in no way tempered his reproaches. He convinced himself that his son was an incorrigible spendthrift, and as Winston approached Sandhurst, he expressed his opinion in letters which by then flew like showers of poisoned arrows.

At Harrow Winston always had to write and ask for journey money and other legitimate expenses, and when at his wit's end, too frightened to make further demands on his parents, would ask Everest for it. Sometimes she lent it to him, and sometimes entered it in her book, earning tart reprimands from Lady Randolph. But after Winston had been at Harrow for two years, a close friend of his parents, Lady Wilton,[28] entered his life, and his pecuniary troubles were somewhat eased. She decided for some reason to befriend the boy, writing to him regularly over the signature 'Your deputy mother', and enclosing gifts of money from her house The Hatch, near Windsor, or of mandarine oranges from her villa in the South of France.

Lord and Lady Randolph, immersed in their own affairs, and by no

27. Chartwell papers.
28. Lady Wilton was the daughter of William Russell, and married the fourth Earl of Wilton, a rich landowner, in 1885.

means exhilarated by their eldest son's progress, continued to neglect him. Winston repeatedly sent letters to them imploring them to come to Harrow, but almost invariably in vain. He hated the prospect of being one of the few boys without visitors on Speech Day:

'I wish you would try and get someone to come down here on Speech Day. I suppose grand mamma Duchess could not come. Try and get Auntie Clara to come if no inconvenience to her. Do get someone as I shall be awfully "out of it" if no one comes.' But by joining the Rifle Corps as soon as was possible, he found an enduring interest throughout his Harrow days, which did something to offset his parents' lack of interest. It would be wrong to suppose that all Winston's work was slovenly. He ended his first term third in the form, and in addition to his prize for declamation won a 'copy', or award, for his work in history. Winston himself was to be largely responsible for creating this impression of failure in youth. From the pinnacles of fame he would enjoy exaggerating his early stupidity and failure, as his friend to be, F. E. Smith, exaggerated the poverty of his childhood to enhance the brilliance of his later career. Welldon always believed in Winston, and his other masters also sensed something unusual, something latent, in the boy, and this was the reason for their continued interest in him in spite of everything.

He did not see much of his parents, even in the holidays. Winston and Jack were usually sent to the seaside with Mrs Everest, and it was in the summer of 1888 that they went to Ventnor near which Everest's brother-in-law was a senior warder at Parkhurst Prison. They spent Christmas in 1888 with their parents at 2 Connaught Place, when Winston and Jack both became ill, Winston being quite unpleasantly afflicted with a serious infection of the throat. This did not prevent Lord and Lady Randolph from leaving the two children, who were taken by Mrs Everest on a short visit to Ventnor.

*   *   *

Winston got his 'remove'[29] when he returned to school towards the end of January 1889, and another 'copy' for history, but he had not shaken off his illness and spent some time in the sanatorium. Welldon promised to take him into his own House the following term, informing Lord Randolph: 'He has some great gifts and is, I think, making progress in his work.' The Head Master had evidently decided to give the indifferent parents a discreet flick of the whip, for he continued:

29. He moved one division higher to the second (instead of the third) division of the Fourth Form.

> It has occurred to me that as you are naturally occupied through the week it would perhaps not be disagreeable to Lady Randolph and yourself to come here from Saturday to Monday sometime when Winston is in the House and the weather is warm enough to make life enjoyable ... You would have at least the opportunity of seeing what Winston's school life is like.

Winston added his own entreaties, but Lord Randolph did not come. Indeed, eighteen months were to elapse between Winston's arrival at Harrow and his father's first visit.

He failed to attend Speech Day in the summer term of 1889, atoning slightly for this lapse by giving Winston £7 2s 6d to buy a bicycle, from which he immediately fell, concussing himself. Recovered, he wrote to his mother: 'You have never been to see me. Do try to get Papa to come. He has never been.' But this oft-repeated prayer was not answered until Lord Randolph's first visit in November 1891.

After pondering the difficult question of Winston's future Lord Randolph decided that he should go into the Army. There was humiliation for the boy even in this choice:

> This orientation was entirely due to my collection of soldiers ... They were all of one size, all British, and organized as an infantry division with a cavalry brigade. My brother Jack commanded the hostile army. But by a Treaty for the Limitation of Armaments he was only allowed to have coloured troops, and they were not allowed to have artillery.[30]

Lord Randolph finally made a visit of inspection, looking at the toy soldiers arranged in formation of attack 'with a captivating smile'. At the end of it he asked Winston if he would like to go into the Army, to which he at once agreed. For years the besotted boy thought that his father had discerned in him the seeds of military genius, and it was only later that he learned that Lord Randolph had come to the conclusion that he was too stupid to go to the Bar.

So in September 1889 Winston joined the Army Class. This meant extra lessons in the evening and on half-holidays, and to some extent a diversion from ordinary work (which is no doubt the reason why he never rose above the Lower School in his four and a half years at Harrow). As Winston was not strong in mathematics, it was decided by his Army Class tutors that he should try for Sandhurst rather than Woolwich. His general education was severely curtailed by these arrangements, and huge gaps left in his knowledge.

In his own words: 'Henceforward all my education was directed to

30. Winston S. Churchill, op. cit., p. 27.
31. Ibid.

passing into Sandhurst, and afterwards to the technical details of the profession of arms. Anything else I had to pick up for myself.'[31]

In the spring term of 1890 Winston obtained his remove into the First Division of the Fourth Form. In the summer he was due to sit for the Preliminary Examination for Sandhurst, but Welldon decided that he was not yet ready for it. His reports were appalling, and provoked a letter from Lady Randolph that for a moment shook even Winston:

> Dearest Winston you make me very unhappy – I had built up such hopes about you and felt so proud of you – and now all is gone ... My only consolation is that your conduct is good, & that you are an affectionate son, but your work is an insult to your intelligence ... I will say no more now, but Winston you are old enough to see how serious this is to you – and how the next year or two and the use you make of them will affect your whole life – stop and think it out for yourself before it is too late.[32]

His father, of course, was even more displeased. He had strongly resented Winston's long delay in thanking him for a present of £5, and the offhand letter in which he had eventually done so. He now threatened to send him away with a tutor in the holidays. But Winston took the Preliminary Examination for Sandhurst in November 1890, and passed in all subjects, causing Welldon, no doubt, to expel a deep sigh of relief.

* * *

But the year 1890, full of dolour as it had been for him, disclosed a new interest to Winston, for in the summer of that year his father rented a small property, Banstead near Newmarket. Lord Randolph's old interest in racing had revived since his resignation, and his filly L'Abbesse de Jouarre – known to the racing public as 'Abscess on the Jaw' – carried his colours of pink, chocolate sleeves and cap (afterwards adopted by Winston) to victory in the Oaks, the Manchester Cup and other races, winning £10,000 in stake-money in her racing career.

Shane Leslie, Winston's cousin and son of Jennie's sister Leonie, vividly recalled those old days at Banstead when Winston first closely entered his life as the black sheep of the family. They were first cousins, and there were seven others of Jerome stock who were invited to Banstead. 'Winston,' said Shane, 'had few admirers among adults except for his aunt Leonie, and his beloved old nurse Mrs Everest.'

Winston was about six years older than his cousins, and showed every sign of a dominating character. The children's chief occupation at Banstead was digging out a moated hut in the garden called 'The Den', with help from the gardeners' boys. It was, of course, designed

32. Chartwell papers.

by Winston. The Den was two-chambered, carpeted with straw, and surrounded by real water in the wet season. Then a drawbridge could be let down over the puddles that formed in the moat, and the fort was defended by an immense catapult which fired unripe green apples. In all these battles and combinations Winston was the unquestioned leader. Receiving their orders in the damp straw, the cousins were told by him that they were awaiting attack from 'the enemies of their country'. In Winston's army there were only two strictly enforced rules – first, that he was always General; secondly, that there was no promotion.

There was no question of his supremacy being challenged. At church one Sunday a formidable butcher's boy was pointed out to Shane, whom Winston had met in single combat after a challenge. His superiority was further attested by the sights which he alone was allowed to witness at an Aquarium, the strong man and Miss Zazel being shot from a gun. From only one spectacle was he debarred, Mrs Everest refusing to allow him a glimpse of Barnum's 'Boneless Wonder', although the thought of this prohibited horror lingered pleasantly for years in his mind.[33]

Shane Leslie remembered that Winston in the days of The Den was 'most objectionable', but his unpopularity was felt mainly by adults, Shane and the other cousins loving and following him.

> His Marlborough aunt and his Roxburghe aunt brought up at Blenheim were his enemies. Boys in those days were supposed to be polite to their elders, but Winston simply did not care what he said. He was utterly different from his brother Jack who was also present at the making of The Den. Jack was polite, without character, but Winston was the exciting one.[34]

In 1891 Lord Randolph left on a long visit to South Africa. His health was now rapidly declining, as also were his fortunes, and he hoped to make some money for his wife and family. But it was accepted by them that he would never recover his health or make a successful return to politics. Jennie did not accompany him, but plunged instead even more avidly in social gaiety, now surrounded by competing admirers of whom the most successful was Count Charles Kinsky, a fascinating diplomat and sportsman who rode his own horse Zoedone to victory in the Grand National in 1883. At length Lord Randolph reappeared at Banstead, a stricken and alarming figure made even more disturbing by the growth of an unkempt beard. But to the children he was a grizzled and bearded hunter returned from Africa. Shane associated him only with the skins of lions and horns of hartebeest. He offered Lord Randolph the fruits

33. The image was to be used by Churchill with devastating effect years later in an attack on Ramsay MacDonald.
34. Sir Shane Leslie, Bart. to author.

of his own hunting in the local bush – a filthy and empty old bird's nest gathered in winter. Lord Randolph stared madly at him and turned away without a word, but later, when reminded by Leonie that he was Shane's godfather, gave him his first half-sovereign. Bearded and silent, Lord Randolph was a cause of trembling in all who passed, so that when he was in it the house was heavy with gloom.

Yet desperate as was Lord Randolph's plight, he had the most devoted succour. Jennie was now bracing her powerful and fearless character to the support of her dying husband through the foulest weather and to the end of the journey. Their relations had deteriorated, but in this respect she knew her duty. She was supported by a faithful servant, the butler Walden. This devoted man valeted Lord Randolph and Winston, whose clothes were often ragged until he reached the dignity of uniform. He was equal to every social occasion in their service, even to climbing trees when accompanying Lord Randolph lion-hunting in Africa, or holding him back from falling overboard during his last nightmare world journey. He was entrusted with Lord Randolph's travelling wardrobe, including a lead-lined coffin in which to bring him home if he died in the tropics. As far as Winston was concerned, Lord Randolph treated him as though he had no belief in him and no hope. Mrs Everest remained the most important part of the boy's life, and twice, so Leonie said, saved him from death. At Harrow, when she went there to see him and some of the boys laughed at him for being visited by his nurse, he kissed her goodbye in front of them – a brave and touching gesture.

*　　*　　*

Welldon and Winston's Army Class tutor Moriarty wanted him to spend four weeks of the summer holidays in 1891 in France, but he made such a violent protest that the idea was shelved and he was given a tutor instead. But there was no avoiding it, and in the end he was packed off to Versailles in the Christmas holidays, much to his annoyance, and after a long fight.

Lord Randolph had returned from South Africa while Winston was still away. Winston asked his father to get him an extra week so that he could see something of him, but Lord Randolph vetoed the idea on the grounds that Winston must work for the next Sandhurst Examination in June. His mother was at this moment engaged in 'trying to get Papa to sacrifice that terrible beard', but so far with no success. In March Winston became Fencing Champion of the School, and was given £2 by Lord Randolph for a gift for his instructor. He immediately spent this on a clock, and asked his father for more. Lord Randolph was again **enraged by his extravagance, writing furiously to say that Winston had** already got through £10 and that if he succeeded in entering the Army 'six months of it will see you in the bankruptcy court'.

But there was no doubt about the boy's skill at fencing, and in April he won the Public Schools Championship at Aldershot. Again he had begged his father to watch him perform, but was coldly informed that Lord Randolph proposed to go racing at Sandown on that date.[35] 1892 was not a good year for the Churchill family. Winston failed in the next, or 'Further', Sandhurst Examination, although his marks, particularly in history, were respectable. And in the summer of that year his parents, owing to the gross extravagance for which they had so frequently reproached their son, were themselves in a lamentable financial position. They were forced to give up 2 Connaught Place and, to save money, to move to 50 Grosvenor Square with Duchess Fanny. In October Banstead too was sacrificed, but anxiety over this matter merely increased Lord Randolph's irritability at Winston's expenditure.

Winston, who had been joined at Harrow by his brother Jack in September, again failed the Sandhurst Examination in November. He was pleased, however, that his mathematical marks had greatly improved since the first attempt, as it was a subject by which he had hitherto been completely baffled:

> We were arrived in an Alice-in-Wonderland world at the portals of which stood 'A Quadratic Equation'. This with a strange grimace pointed the way to the Theory of Indices, which again handed on the intruder to the full rigours of the Binomial Theorem. Further dim chambers lighted by sullen, sulphurous fires were reputed to contain a dragon called the 'Differential Calculus' . . .I have never met any of these creatures since. With my third and successful examination they passed away like the phantasmagoria of a fevered dream.[36]

We have seen that Winston worshipped physical courage to an inordinate degree. On the eve of leaving Harrow he was still of a small and unimpressive physique − 5 feet 6 ½ inches, with a chest measurement of only 31 inches − very small by Sandhurst standards. That chest was hairless, and his hands were white and delicate as a woman's. Anthony Storr was undoubtedly right in saying:

> The physical courage which he consistently and sometimes rashly showed was not based upon any natural superiority of physique, but rather upon his determination to be tough in spite of lack of height and muscle. His search for physical danger in early youth and his reckless self-exposure in France, even though his behaviour put others in danger, bears witness to

35. Chartwell papers.
36. Winston Churchill, op. cit., p. 34.

the fact that his courage was not something he himself took for granted, but rather something which he had to prove to himself.[37]

This tendency then, began in youth, but never left him. Several of his less happy appointments as Prime Minister were due rather to a man's courage than his ability, and he would sometimes ask a much-wounded hero to bare his scars.[38]

It was this desire for physical courage which led to his second providential escape from death. At his aunt Lady Wimborne's estate Canford, near Bournemouth, he fell thirty feet while trying to jump from a bridge to the top of a fir-tree growing in a chine beneath. (He had been playing a game of tag with his brother Jack and a cousin.) A kidney was ruptured: he was unconscious for three days, and in bed for two months. It is clear that his intense desire to display physical courage prompted him to make the leap, and his survival was almost a miracle.

He was sometimes taken in 1893 during his long convalescence to witness as an absorbed spectator Mr Gladstone's last great battle. Although not perceptive in personal matters, he began to notice an ominous flagging in Lord Randolph's contributions to date. He longed for the time he could go to his father's aid, thinking of how strong a prop Austen Chamberlain was of his own father, and how Herbert Gladstone had helped the Grand Old Man to fell oak-trees, and was his constant and trusted companion.

In this year, in Lord Randolph's house, Winston met many of the Parliamentary leaders – Balfour, Joseph Chamberlain, Rosebery, Asquith and Morley. A sort of groping fascination for their craft began to possess him:

'It seemed a very good world in which these men lived; a world where high rules reigned and every trifle in public conduct counted: a duelling ground where although the business might be ruthless, and the weapons loaded with ball, there was ceremonious personal courtesy and mutual respect.'

Winston had now left Harrow and been sent to a crammer, for his last and desperate assault on Sandhurst.

* * *

He took the examination in August 1893, and was at last successful, passing not well enough for an infantry cadetship, but well enough to be offered the easier entry into the cavalry. He had in fact scraped

37. Anthony Storr, *Churchill Revised*.
38. Sir Louis Spears to author.

in, although his marks in English history were superior to any other candidate taking the subject, and proving once again that his ability was unquestioned when his interest was engaged.

Winston heard of his success when he and Jack were setting off for a walking holiday in Switzerland. His mercurial spirits shot up at the news; all previous failings and backslidings were wiped from his mind, and he could hardly wait to tell his adored father, whose praise, he felt, he had at last fully earned. Winston had always yearned for the panache of the cavalry, with its chargers with jingling bits, and its peacock uniforms, but it was more expensive than the infantry, and Lord Randolph was angry beyond all reason because he had arranged with the Duke of Cambridge[39] for Winston to get a commission in the 60th Rifles.

But Winston was intoxicated by his modest achievement – about the only positive one of his scholastic career – and in this mood he wrote to his father from Lucerne a letter which enraged Lord Randolph by its complacency. He was taking the cure at Kissingen, and from there sent Winston an odious letter which must be quoted in full as an illustration of how far this brilliant mind had been poisoned by sickness, so as to plant in him a deep irrational resentment of his eldest son, verging on hatred, and a desire to humiliate and wound. The boy after all, however narrowly, had passed the examination. It is a letter that can only be excused by the condition of the writer:

> My dear Winston. I am rather surprised by your tone of exultation over your inclusion in the Sandhurst list. There are two ways of winning an examination, one creditable and the other the reverse. You have unfortunately chosen the latter method, and appear to be much pleased with your success.
>
> The first extremely discreditable feature of your performance was missing the infantry, for in that failure is demonstrated beyond refutation your slovenly happy-go-lucky harum scarum style of work for which you have always been distinguished at your various schools. Never have I received a really good report of your conduct in your work from any master or tutor you had from time to time to deal with. Always behind-hand, never advancing in your class, incessant complaints of total lack of application, and this character which was constant in your reports has shown the natural results clearly in your last army examination.
>
> With all the advantages you had, with the abilities which you foolishly think yourself to possess and which some of your relations claim for you, with all the efforts that have been made to make your life easy and agreeable & your work neither oppressive or distasteful, this is the grand

39. Grandson of George III and Commander-in-Chief of the British Army.

result that you come up among the 2nd rate & 3rd rate class who are only good for commissions in a cavalry regiment.

The second discreditable fact in the result of your examination is that you have not perceptibly increased as far as my memory serves me the marks you made in the examination, & perhaps even you have decreased them, inspite of there being less competition in the last than in the former examination. You frequently told me you were sure to obtain 7000 marks. Alas! your estimate of your capacity was, measured arithmetically, some 700 marks deficient. You say in your letter there were many candidates who succeeded whom you knew; I must remind you that you had very few below you, some seven or eight. You may find some consolation in the fact that you have failed to get into the '60th Rifles' one of the finest regiments in the army. There is also another satisfaction for you that by accomplishing the prodigious effort of getting into the Cavalry, you imposed on me an extra charge of some £200 a year. Not that I shall allow you to remain in the Cavalry. As soon as possible I shall arrange your exchange into an infantry regiment of the line.

Now it is a good thing to put this business vy plainly before you. Do not think that I am going to take the trouble of writing to you long letters after every folly & failure you commit & undergo. I shall not write again on these matters & you need not trouble to write any answer to this part of my letter, because I no longer attach the slightest weight to anything you may say about your own acquirements & exploits. Make this position indelibly impressed on your mind, that if your conduct and action at Sandhurst is similar to what it has been in the other establishments in which it was sought vainly to impart to you some education, then that my responsibility for you is over.

I shall leave you to depend on yourself giving you merely such assistance as may be necessary to permit of a respectable life. Because I am certain that if you cannot prevent yourself from leading the idle useless unprofitable life you had led during your schooldays & later months, you will become a mere social wastrel, one of the hundreds of the public school failures, and you will degenerate into a shabby unhappy & futile existence. If that is so you will have to bear all the blame for such misfortunes yourself. Your own conscience will enable you to recall and enumerate all the efforts that have been made to give you the best of chances which you were entitled to by your position to & how you have practically neglected them all . . .[40]

But it must be remembered that this was the tragic twilight of Lord Randolph's life, which would be over in less than eighteen months. Winston had for the moment become an obsession in his afflicted mind, and he wrote to his mother the Duchess Fanny still agitating this murky pool, and apparently under the extraordinary illusion that Winston had

40. Chartwell papers.

been at both Eton and Harrow: 'I have told you often and you would never believe that he has little claim to cleverness, to knowledge or any capacity for settled work. Nothing has been spared on him ... The whole result of this has been either at Harrow or at Eton to prove his total worthlessness as a scholar or a conscientious worker. He need not expect much from me ...'

* * *

The savage assault by an idolized father, so full of contempt and resentment, was a shock, violent if evanescent, for Winston. 'He was a good deal depressed,' said his tutor who had escorted him to Switzerland and now told him that his arrival at Sandhurst would be a new clean page in his life, an opportunity for a fresh start such as occurred only once or twice in a lifetime. Winston was, then, shocked and disappointed after his father's attack, but he was not deeply pierced by the charges, for he could have found a thousand self-justifications, and his contrition was brief. But he was cautious enough to keep to himself his third narrow escape from death, which took place in the lake at Lausanne, and appears to have been due to the carelessness in Winston which his father so greatly deplored.

He and another boy took out a boat from which they dived into the lake a mile from shore, and a suddenly rising wind caused the boat to drift away from them. Swimming after it, they began to tire and Winston at last realized the extreme danger: 'Up to this point no idea of danger had crossed my mind. The sun played upon the sparkling blue waters. The wonderful panorama of mountains and valleys, the gay hotels and villas still smiled. But I now saw Death as near as I believe I have ever seen him. He was swimming in the water at our side whispering from time to time in the rising wind.' Winston managed to approach the boat, but each time a gust drove it further away: 'But by a supreme effort I caught hold of its side in the nick of time ... and rowed back for my companion who although tired had not ... realized the dull yellow glare of mortal terror that had so suddenly played around us.'[41]

Lord Randolph, as Rosebery wrote in his elegant memoir, was now 'dying publicly by inches', as the paralysis turned its screws within him. But as is common in this merciless disease, he was unaware of his own condition. The body continued to fulfil its functions; the brain sank in the grip of a baleful decay. Winston, when he wrote his father's Life, was to describe this bleak decline with warmth, and a delicacy that must have been difficult to achieve: 'The victim becomes less and less

41. Winston S. Churchill, op. cit. pp. 5–46.

able to realize his condition. In the midst of failure he is cheered by an artificial consciousness of victory. While the days are swiftly ebbing he builds large plans for the future; and a rosy glow of sunset conceals the approach of night.'[42] Enemies had already walked out of the House of Commons during his speeches, rather than listen to his thick and muddled sentences; and friend had absented themselves from a spectacle that was now too painful to contemplate – the slow quenching of a once brilliant light. And now, when Lord Randolph returned to England in the autumn, he carried out, to the despair of his family, a nation-wide programme of speeches: 'But the crowds who were drawn by the glamour of his name departed sorrowful and shuddering at the spectacle of a dying man, and those who loved him were consumed with embarrassment and grief.'[43]

When Winston returned to London he found another communication from the Military Secretary telling him that he had, after all, been given an infantry cadetship. Before leaving for Sandhurst, Winston wrote to his father asking him for a quarterly allowance, reinforcing this plea by writing to his mother: 'Please try to persuade him. It would be much better and cheaper than the present arrangements which are:

> 'Spend as much as I can get
> Get as much as I can.'

Lord Randolph refused to consider this suggestion, and Winston was given a monthly allowance of £10 for small necessities, a niggardly and absurd concession which was to lead to incessant financial troubles.

He entered the Royal Military College on 1 September 1893. A new life opened before him, spartan, backbreaking, and governed by an iron discipline. Yet he was strangely content, for it was a new point of departure. He was at last put to work he could understand, which did not affront his intelligence or baffle his understanding, work which, as he clearly realized, was a direct preparation for his military career.

There were long field days, days of fresh air and aromatic smells in the bracken of Chobham Common, and the pine-woods of Camberley. Tactics, Fortification, and Topography were eagerly absorbed, and Drill, Gymnastics and Riding toughened his inadequate physique. He found himself digging trenches, constructing breastworks, revetting parapets with sandbags, putting up *chevaux de frise*, cutting railway lines with slabs of guncotton, and learning how to blow up masonry bridges. He practised making contoured maps of the rolling countryside. At the end of each day, in a bare monk-like cubicle, he fell into the sleep of complete physical exhaustion. After a short time at Sandhurst he wrote to his

42. Winston S. Churchill, *Lord Randolph Churchill*.
43. Ibid.

mother, 'I am cursed with so feeble a body that I can hardly support the fatigues of the day; but I suppose I shall get stronger during my stay here.'

He enjoyed the life because he experienced a sense of real progress, and looked back with pain on 'my grey schooldays'. The Army did not accept excuses for scamped work, and the remorseless discipline was an admirable corrective for a slovenly and feckless mode of life, although it left no lasting effect on Winston's rebellious and incorrigible nature. Nothing, in fact, could do so. Above all other work at Sandhurst he loved riding. In later years Winston was to be regarded as the perfect example of the unathletic man who despised games; but no one in his youth could have pursued horsemanship and, later, polo with a greater passion.

The discipline, even though its effects were evanescent, wrought an astonishing change in the puny and rather disordered boy who had left Harrow. Even Lord Randolph was betrayed into unusual warmth in a letter to his mother, the Duchess Fanny, in October:

> I took Winston to Tring on Saturday . . . He has much smartened up. He holds himself quite upright and has got steadier. The people at Tring took a great deal of notice of him but [he] was very quiet and nice-mannered. Sandhurst has done wonders for him.'[44]

This friendly gesture of Lord Randolph meant much to Winston. He began to feel that he was at last on the threshold of the intimacy and friendship for which he yearned when his father took him to important political parties at Lord Rothschild's house at Tring, or to stay with his racing friends, or to see the acrobats and jugglers who so amused Lord Randolph. Winston's hero-worship for his queer parent was at its height:

> In fact to me he seemed to own the key to everything or almost everything worth having. But if ever I began to show the slightest idea of comradeship, he was immediately offended; and when I suggested that I might help his private secretary to write some of his letters, he froze me into stone.

In fact Lord Randolph's sickness was now far advanced, although Winston did not realize this. His clouded mind was no doubt mollified by the fact that Winston was, after all, to go into the infantry – thus, as he repeated *ad nauseam*, saving him £200 a year – but the old irrational antagonism remained.

44. Chartwell papers.

* * *

When Winston complained of his puny physique at Sandhurst, he was not exaggerating or indulging in self-pity. He suffered a good deal from eyeache and much from toothache. He was also a victim of boils, suffering a bad one on his cheek which had to be lanced. He was told by the breezy surgeon that boys of his age were subject to such disorders, and that they were a sign of good health. In his second term he suffered from agonizing boils on his buttocks, and for some time was unable to ride.

Winston's examination results at the end of his first term were creditable. He spent Christmas at Blenheim with his cousin Sunny, and Sunny's mother Bertha, Marchioness of Blandford, first wife of the erratic seventh Duke. Back in London after Christmas, Winston spent the rest of the holidays at Knightsbridge Barracks Riding School to steal a march on the other cadets, who did not ride as part of their training during their first term, although they were allowed to ride for pleasure. As a result of this advantage he was put at the head of the ride, a success acknowledged by his father in an unusually friendly letter.

But in April 1894 the fragile *détente* between the two was shattered by the unfortunate affair of the gold watch, and Winston was back again in his father's bleak disfavour. By a mixture of ill-luck and carelessness Winston had dropped a gold watch given to him by Lord Randolph into a deep place of the Welsh Stream. He dived in, but could not stay in the icy water for more than ten minutes. The next day he had the pool dredged but without success. Eventually, after borrowing twenty-three men from the Infantry Detachment, getting the fire engine, and pumping the pool dry, the watch was retrieved, but in a bad state. Winston sent it at once to Dent, the watchmaker, but unfortunately his father went in there a few days later about his own watch, and the fat was in the fire.

'I have written a letter to Winston he won't forget,' he told Lady Randolph, and in the course of it he said:

> Jack has had the watch I gave him longer than you have had yours; the only expense I have paid on his watch was 10/6 for cleaning before he went back to Harrow. But in all qualities of steadiness, taking care of his things & never doing stupid things Jack is vastly your superior. Your vy much worried parent Randolph S. Churchill.

Lady Randolph allied herself with her husband, writing one of her pained letters to Winston:

'Oh, Winny what a harum scarum fellow you are! You really must give up being so childish . . . I shall scold you well when we meet.'[45]

---

45. Chartwell papers.

At this time Colonel J. P. Brabazon,[46] an officer of great distinction and panache, was commanding the 4th Hussars at Aldershot. A man who had served with outstanding gallantry in the Second Afghan War and the savage fighting round Suakim in 1884, he was strongly reminiscent of a Ouida hero. He inquired on one occasion of the stationmaster at Aldershot: 'When is the London twain?' 'It has gone, Colonel.' 'Gone! Bwing another.' Brabazon was an old friend of the Randolph Churchills, and Winston decided to enlist his help in inducing Lord Randolph to change his mind over the cavalry commission. His persistence in this direction after the gold watch fiasco is a clear indication of the ruthless force of that one-track mind already at work, impervious to failure or opposition, which was to remain the outstanding characteristic of Winston Churchill throughout his life.

Winston, in his last term at Sandhurst, became involved in a lively episode arising out of a campaign, in the interests of public decency, to separate the bars of the Empire Theatre from the adjoining promenade, where accommodating ladies of the town paraded their charms, particularly on Saturday evenings. Partitions were erected for this purpose, and Winston, at the head of a mob of two or three hundred, stormed the partitions, Winston making a passionate speech on the shattered barricades. This was his first political speech.

* * *

There were soon to be no more waspish letters from Lord Randolph, whose life was now approaching its lamentable end. In June 1894 Lord Randolph decided to go on a world tour with his wife. In view of his desperate condition they were to be accompanied by a Dr Keith, and the ever-loyal valet Walden. Winston arranged to have regular reports from Dr Roose on his father's progress, but afterwards noted sadly: 'I never saw him again except as a swiftly fading shadow.'

The tour was a fiasco – a period of sustained agony for Lady Randolph. Lord Randolph was now disintegrating physically before her eyes, and in addition to this terribly visible decline, his behaviour in public was quite unpredictable and often shocking in character. From Government House, Singapore she wrote to her sister Clara: 'He was very bad for two days, and it was dreadful being with strangers.' But he refused to return home, as Lady Randolph and Dr Keith wished. He had, in some bygone existence, annexed Burma, and was determined to

46. For an excellent account of this office see Winston S. Churchill, *My Early Life*, pp. 76 et seq.

see it, even if he had to do so alone. It was while in Rangoon that Lady Randolph's misery was deepened by a letter from her devoted admirer Count Kinsky who, tired at last of waiting for her, had become engaged to be married. This, in the midst of gloom, was a grievous blow: 'I hate it,' she wrote to Clara. 'I shall return without a friend in the world and too old to make any more now.' But these sufferings in no way weakened her purpose, and brought out to the full this woman's innate strength of character, iron will and serene courage, all long concealed by social manoeuvres and ambitions. At whatever cost, her full loyalty was given to her husband. But Lord Randolph, although dying by inches, had remained strangely happy in a disconcerting condition of euphoria, and the changing and exotic Eastern scenes kept morbid reflections at bay. This unnatural vivacity held out until he reached Burma, but when it failed: 'The change was sudden and complete. The journey was curtailed [in Madras], and in the last days of 1894 he reached England as weak and helpless in mind and body as a little child.'[47]

In the meantime Winston and Jack again went to Switzerland with a tutor for their summer holidays. Before leaving he stayed with his grandmother, Duchess Fanny, in Grosvenor Square, writing to Lady Randolph later from Brussels: 'The Duchess was getting very "difficile" when we left, & it was perhaps as well that we came off here.' Duchess Fanny also sent Jennie her own comments on the pair: 'Jack is really excellent and steady, Winston appears to be pleasant. I lectured him freely before he left and he certainly takes reproof well tho' perhaps it does not make much impression.'[48] One has the familiar impression of homilies politely endured and immediately forgotten – and the impressions always left by the two boys – Jack a little insipid and ductile, Winston brash and untameable.

Winston had now set his heart on winning the Sandhurst Riding Prize in the hope that such a success might yet persuade his father to allow him to join the cavalry. Meeting the Duke of Cambridge by chance at Sandown, he found that the Duke had entirely forgotten his promise to ease Winston into the 60th, which seemed to offer a means of escape from the infantry to his ever-sanguine mind. Winston narrowly missed the prize, achieving a most creditable second place with 190 marks out of 200 – clear proof of the excellence of his horsemanship. The final Sandhurst Examinations followed, in which Winston again acquitted himself with credit, passing out 20th in a class of 130. The results were not known until January 1895, when Lord Randolph lay dying in his mother's house in Grosvenor Square, but he was able, according to

47. Winston S. Churchill, *Lord Randolph Churchill*, p. 819.
48. Chartwell papers.

Winston, to ask in a lucid moment how his son had passed.

After attacks of acute mania and delusions, Lord Randolph, as if exhausted by the frenzy of his distemper, died quietly on 24 January 1895. 'For a month,' as Winston wrote afterwards in his biography, 'at his mother's house, he lingered pitifully until very early in the morning of January 24 the numbing fingers of paralysis laid that weary brain to rest.'[49] He was buried in the churchyard at Bladon near Blenheim, after the funeral service in Westminster Abbey.

At the time of his father's death Winston was sleeping at another house in Grosvenor Square, and had crossed in haste to the one where his father lay dying. Winston's cousin, Shane Leslie, also preserved a vivid memory of that scene – of his mother's sudden appearance in his room in the small hours, and being dressed by her in mourning. They too hurried to Grosvenor Square where Lord Randolph's body lay. But his enduring memory was not of the dead man, but of Winston, who, business-like and completely in charge of events, was slitting open and arranging telegrams from all parts of the Empire. 'He was the Head of the family,' reflected Shane: 'he had taken possession.'[50]

* * *

'It remained for me only,' Winston was to write many years later, 'to pursue his aims and vindicate his memory.' Lord Randolph's death marked the end of Winston's boyhood, and the beginning of his full maturity as a man. His grandfathers on both sides were both dead, and his Jerome grandmother was soon to follow them. Everest too was soon to go, and the days of the old Duchess were numbered. Soon Winston, Jennie and Jack would face the world alone. He had already begun the subjugation of his mother:

> I was now in the main the master of my fortunes. My mother was always at hand to help and advise; but I was now in my 21st year and she never sought to exercise parental control. Indeed she soon became an ardent ally, furthering my plans and guarding my interests . . . We worked together on even terms, more like brother and sister than mother and son.[51]

It was true that Lady Randolph no longer tried to exercise parental control. We shall see her constantly attempting to do so when Winston was in India, and only ceasing when she realized the utter futility of her efforts. Winston was now prepared to accept full responsibility

49. Winston S. Churchill, *Lord Randolph Churchill*.
50. The late Sir Shane Leslie, Bart. to author.
51. Winston S. Churchill, *My Early Life*, p. 71.

for his family group. He had only the smallest inheritance. But his loveless childhood had conferred one priceless boon upon him – an armoured self-assurance. Was he not to write forty years later in his *Life of Marlborough* with an eye clearly on his own case:

> It is said that famous men are usually the produce of an unhappy childhood. The stern compression of circumstances, the twinges of adversity, the spur of slights and taunts in early years, are needed to evoke that ruthless fixity of purpose and tenacious mother wit without which great actions are seldom accomplished.

And, of the Mahdi:

> Solitary trees, if they grow at all, grow strong; and a boy deprived of a father's care often develops, if he escapes the perils of youth, an independence and vigour of thought which may restore in after life the heavy loss of early days.[52]

In the meantime, after leaving Sandhurst, he viewed the world not with apprehension, but with wonder and delight. 'It opened,' he said, 'like Aladdin's cave.'

Indeed, one of the aspects of Winston that most impresses us is that never from this time did he have a dull or idle moment.

> I could count almost on my fingers the days when I have had nothing to do. An endless moving picture in which one was an actor . . . When I look back on them I cannot but return my sincere thanks to the high gods for the gift of existence. All the days were good and each day better than the other. Ups and downs, risks and journeys, but always the sense of motion, and the illusion of hope.[53]

* * *

Lady Randolph, at Winston's suggestion, arranged with the Duke of Cambridge for Winston's transfer to the 4th Hussars. Lord Randolph on his world tour had written to Winston to put all thought of the cavalry out of his mind, but Winston, no doubt wishing to justify his flouting of this order, claimed to have heard his dying father in one of his last coherent mutterings ask: 'Have you got your horses?', a remark which (if indeed it was ever made) might well have been uttered in delirium. But it was entirely characteristic of

52. Randolph Churchill, *Winston S. Churchill*, Vol. I., Youth, p. 241.
53. Winston S. Churchill, *My Early Life*, p. 69.

Winston to be able so readily to convince himself of anything on which he desired reassurance. He reported to the 4th Hussars on 18 February 1895 at Aldershot, receiving his commission on 20 February.

He began with the arduous training of a recruit officer, which included a backbreaking course in the riding school 'which exceeded in severity anything I had previously experienced in military equitation', and made him fear a recurrence of an old hernia as the horses were broader than the 'Sandhurst screws' to which he was accustomed. Again and again he bit the tan of the riding-school, and rose, bruised and shaken, replacing his little gold-braided pork-pie cap while the troopers grinned with delight at seeing an officer share their sufferings. Even before finishing this course the young officers were often allowed to ride with their troops at exercise and to take part in the cavalry drill. The panache of the manoeuvres excited Winston, and was never obliterated from his memory, a perfect stimulant to the romanticism of his character:

> There is a thrill and charm of its own in the glittering jungle of a cavalry squadron manoeuvring at the trot, and this deepens into joyous excitement when the same evolutions are performed at a gallop. The stir of the horses, the clank of their equipment, the thrill of motion, the tossing plumes, the sense of incorporation in a living machine, the suave dignity of the uniform – all combine to make cavalry drill a fine thing in itself.[54]

He began riding in steeplechases, and, as soon as he could borrow enough money, to play polo. Having promised his mother that he would not take part in races, he rode in the 4th Hussars Subalterns' Challenge Cup and he wrote about it to his brother Jack:

> It was very exciting, and there is no doubt about it being dangerous. I had never jumped a regulation fence before and they are pretty big things as you know. Everybody in the Regiment was very pleased at my riding, more especially as I came in third. They thought it very sporting. I thought so too. It has done me a lot of good here and I think I may say I am popular with everybody.[55]

It was an illusion under which he frequently suffered.

54. Ibid. p. 73.
55. Chartwell papers.

* * *

We can see that Winston's character had already changed since his father's death. It was he who was with his adored old nurse to comfort her when she died in 1895; he who was present at her funeral, and who paid for the headstone erected on the grave. He had, as Shane Leslie noticed, accepted responsibility for his family, and was determined to function as its head. He had discovered that his mother and father had spent nearly all their money, and his own meagre resources were soon to help shore up Lady Randolph's chronic extravagance. Winston was often tormented by financial anxiety, and had difficulty in equipping himself to join the 4th Hussars. The cost of joining, including one charger, he estimated at £653. 11. 0., Duchess Lily having already given him another horse worth £200.

There is nothing more striking in his private life that in spite of the poverty which persisted until his last years, he always succeeded living *en grand seigneur* and indulging every extravagant wish. Now Cox, the Bankers, obligingly lent him money to buy polo ponies, and before long he had ordered a satin jacket and cap in the chocolate and pink of his father's racing colours. Winston had for long been captivated by Lord Randolph's political career, and after his death his own interest in politics quickened. It is clear that although he was dazzled by the excitement of his new military life, and loved the Army, a cold process of calculation was at work, and he already had no intention of remaining in it indefinitely. He wrote to his mother in August 1895:

> It is a fine game to play – the game of politics – and it is well worth waiting for a good hand – before really plunging.
>
> At any rate – four years of healthy and pleasant existence – combined with both responsibility & discipline – can do no harm to me – but rather good. The more I see of soldiering – the more I like it – but the more I feel convinced that it is not my *métier*. Well, we shall see – my dearest Mamma.

It should be noted at this point that Winston had already a strong foretaste of the future – that his destiny lay in politics rather than in arms, and that his whole life would be spent in their pursuit. He had already, in his close study of Lord Randolph's career, mixed a rich compost in which his own would germinate and flourish. His other occupations and skills, writing and painting, were always to be mere appendages to his political life. His later calm and resilience in the face of disaster was at least in part due to the fact that his life from the start had been a battle, with a useless father and a selfish and frivolous mother, a battle in which there had been many a grim defeat until he became hardened to the condition. He had no financial resources, and little education. He was driven from the first by a voracious and gnawing ambition, too obvious and naive to be offensive. The extreme egocentricity (which repelled some) was already marked, but it was also from the beginning the secret of his success. He was egocentric in that he never allowed anything to divert him from his purpose. He was as much a self-made man as Nuffield or Henry Ford, for, apart from birth, he started life with no advantage.

But some time must pass before the decisive step into politics could be taken. The two instruments with which he would cut himself clear from a life of mediocrity were the sword and the pen, but neither was yet developed. Meanwhile his position must be established; his name must become known: and a measure of financial stability must be achieved. One perceives that he had hardly entered the Army before beginning to regard it as a mere stepping-stone to better things.

* * *

First, Winston decided, he must educate himself, but the crowded days at Aldershot left little time or energy for reading. From a surfeit of riding and drilling and military routine he sank into a sort of mental torpor: 'From this "Slough of Despond" I try to raise myself by reading & re-reading Papa's speeches – many of which I almost know by heart – but I really cannot find the energy to read any other serious work.'[56]

In the autumn of 1895 the 4th Hussars moved to Hampton Court and Hounslow. In those spacious days the military year consisted of a seven months' summer training season, and a five months' winter season of leave. Winston had spent all his money on polo ponies, and could not afford to hunt, for the family finances were as usual in the doldrums. So for the winter leave he and a fellow-subaltern, Reginald Barnes, decided to go to Havana where a guerrilla war between Spanish overlords and Cuban rebels was in progress. His sole object in doing so was the hope of coming 'under fire', like a *débutante* prepared to run considerable risks in order to win a kiss.

It is strange, after two World Wars, to reflect that this was the consuming desire of every ambitious young officer in the Army in those piping days of peace. The world seemed lapped in tranquillity, and a man who desired excitement must seek it out wherever he saw it, and ruthlessly pursue it. Winston, using with equal impudence effrontery and influence and cajolery, was as gifted in the art of self-propulsion as any young officer in the armed forces, and to ambition, in his case, was

56. Chartwell papers.

added the lure of excitement.

> From early youth I had brooded about soldiers and war, and often I had
> imagined in dreams and day dreams the sensations attendant upon being,
> for the first time, under fire. It seemed to my youthful mind that it must be
> a thrilling and immense experience to hear the whistle of bullets all around
> and to play at hazard from moment to moment with death and wounds.[57]

Employing now for the first time the method he was to employ *ad
nauseam* in the future, Winston exerted influence in high quarters.
He used this means without the slightest shame or embarrassment,
and with the utmost persistence, and it is probable that without it his
swift emergence might never have taken place. He appealed now to his
father's old friend and colleague in the Fourth Party, Sir Henry Wolff –
then British Ambassador in Madrid – to procure for him the necessary
permits from the Spanish authorities.

Having duly received these, which promised a warm welcome by
the Spanish Captain-General, Winston sailed from Liverpool in the
Etruria at the beginning of November 1895 for New York. Here he
stayed with a remarkable friend of the Jeromes, the lawyer Bourke
Cockran, whose rare gifts and glowing eloquence made an indelible
impression on Winston. Bourke Cockran had opposed Cleveland for
the Democratic nomination in 1892, causing much controversy, and
the next year was to campaign for the Republican nominee McKinley.
He lived in a superb apartment on Fifth Avenue, and brought Winston
immediately under his thrall. Reading Winston's words, we can see that
he was no ordinary man:

'I have never seen his like, or in some respects his equal. He
looked uncommonly like the portraits of Charles James Fox ...
His conversation, in point, in pith, in rotundity, in antithesis and
in comprehension exceeded anything I have ever heard.' Another
indication of this man's perception was that he was the first person to
recognize that Winston had a natural bent for politics, and a particular
understanding of their nature, and the letters between them in which
Bourke Cockran emphasized this fact are astonishing in their foresight.

After a week in New York Winston and Barnes sailed for Havana,
arriving there on 20 November. Winston was already in a state of
exaltation at the prospects ahead, and captivated by the enchanting
tropical beauty of this island – 'The Pearl of the Antilles' as her
Spanish overlords called her. 'The minds of this generation' he was to
write forty years later, 'exhausted, brutalized, mutilated and bored by

---

57. Winston S. Churchill, op. cit., p. 85.

war may not understand the delicious yet tremendous sensations with which a young British officer bred in the long peace approached for the first time the actual theatre of operations.' When the coast of Cuba, blue and shadowy, began to define itself on the horizon he felt as if he was sailing with Long John Silver and was gazing for the first time at the mysterious shores of Treasure Island: 'Here was a place where anything might happen . . . Here I might leave my bones.'[58] He was intoxicated by the beauty of the place, the city and harbour, the gentle slopes and rolling savannahs, the groves of Spanish cedar, mahogany, pine, date palm and black olive. So rich was the soil that even wooden fence-posts sprouted like garden plants. The climate was temperate yet ardent.

Winston had arranged to send despatches from the front to the *Daily Graphic*, for which he was paid £5 a letter. This was his first essay in a system he later perfected – to combine experience in the field with the establishment of his name as a writer and the earning of ever-increasing rewards. Thus he aimed to make his name known and in the end be sufficiently independent to leave the Army.

Winston and Barnes were affably received by the Captain-General, Marshal Martinez Campos, and advised by his ADC that if they wished to see fighting they should join the mobile column then being mounted by General Valdez, intercepting it for this purpose. With much difficulty and some danger they reached Sancti Spiritus, the town where the mobile column was expected. It was a desolate little place more than twenty miles from Havana, and smallpox and yellow fever were raging there. They spent the night in a filthy tavern, and awaited General Valdez's arrival.

When he came, with a strong force of 3,000 infantry and two squadrons of cavalry, they presented themselves, and were again well received and told that the column would leave the plague-ridden town before first light. Next morning, shortly before dawn had revealed the festering squalor of the place, the column began its march to the village of Igaura. On 29 November General Valdez heard that a large force of guerrillas was encamped to the east of the village, and on 30 November he marched to attack them.

There was a low mist as they moved off in the early morning, and suddenly the rear of the column was involved in heavy firing: 'As no bullets seemed to come near me I was easily reassured. I felt like the optimist who did not mind what happened, so long as it did not happen to him.' It was Winston's twenty-first birthday, and it was perhaps fitting that he then first 'heard shots

58. Winston S. Churchill, op. cit., p. 86.

fired in anger', and heard bullets smacking into flesh or whistle
through the air. Later a horse was struck near him, and as he
looked at the dying animal he realized that the bullet had passed
within a foot of his head:

'So at any rate I had been "under fire" – that was something.
Nevertheless I began to take a more thoughtful view of our enterprise
than I had hitherto done.' From that moment the column was
continually in contact with the insurgents for three days. On 1
December he described in his despatch how he had been bathing
with Spanish officers in a river when a volley of shots passed
over their heads. They pulled on their clothes and organized a
hasty defence, driving back the enemy. That night bullets were
fired into the hut where Barnes and Winston were sleeping, and
wounded an orderly outside it.

Next day Valdez fought a major action which became known
as the Battle of La Reforma, during which Winston remained at
the General's side in what, owing to Valdez's contempt for death,
proved to be the most dangerous and exposed position on the field.
Winston later described the battle to his mother in a letter from his
Havana hotel:

'The General, a very brave man – in a white and gold uniform
on a grey horse – drew a great deal of fire on to us, and I think
I heard enough bullets whistle and hum past to satisfy me for some
time to come.'[59]

Winston and Barnes stayed with Valdez throughout the battle,
and were recommended by him for the Rioja Cruz, or Red Cross,
a Spanish decoration for officers, which Winston later received but
was not allowed to wear.

Looking across the years at this Cuban adventure, it was the
evidence of the senses rather than the details of battles that remained.
He saw the long column crawling snake-like through the dripping
woods where the immortelles flamed against the deep, deep green.
Sometimes the Spanish officers from mere *joie de vivre* would slash
with machetes at the melons hanging above their heads, and send the
juice flying. And he would see the halts for rest, the off-saddling of
the horses, and catch again a fragrant whiff of bacon in the pan, and
the smell of wood fires and horse sweat, and listen to pony squealing
to pony across the forest track before he climbed into a hammock for
the long, invigorating siesta.

*   *   *

59. Chartwell papers.

Childhood and Adolescence

Churchill's father, Lord Randolph Churchill, second son of the seventh Duke of Marlborough. Shooting star of the Tory party. 'He had no belief in Winston and no hope.' (*Press Association*)

Winston Churchill's beautiful American mother – Lady Randolph Churchill (née Jennie Jerome), the second daughter of Leonard Jerome, financier and entrepreneur, and his wife Clara. (*John Hillelson Agency*)

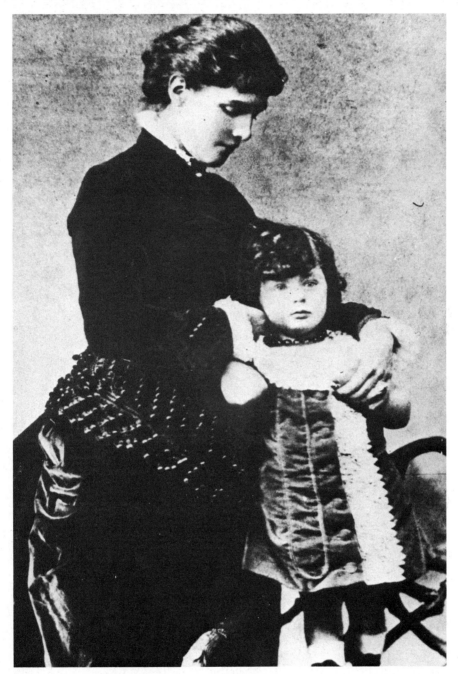

Winston Churchill at the age of two with his mother in 1876. *(Popperfoto)*

The six-year-old Winston poses in a sailor suit. 1880. (*Camera Press*)

Winston pictured with his aunt, Lady Leslie. *(Popperfoto)*

Lady Randolph Churchill with her sons Winston (*right*) and John in 1885. *(Popperfoto)*

Churchill (*left and inset*) as a cadet at the Royal Military College, Sandhurst, which he entered on 1 September 1893. He wrote to his mother: 'I am cursed with so feeble a body that I can hardly support the fatigues of the day; but I suppose I shall get stronger during my stay here.' (*Mary Evans Picture Library/Popperfoto (inset).*)

Winston found it difficult, after this excitement, to come to a definite conclusion about the rights and wrongs of the Cuban affair. His natural inclination was to sympathize with the weaker party trying to dislodge an oppressive overlord, but experience of the insurgents in the field had convinced him that they were cowardly, cruel and incompetent: 'Their army, consisting to a large extent of coloured men, is an undisciplined rabble,' he wrote in 1896, and he thought it most improbable that such people could provide a better régime for the Cuban people than could the Spanish colonists. On the contrary, he believed that bad as the colonial rule was, a Cuban government would be infinitely worse. Winston was also not unmindful of the fact that after the kindness he had received it would appear churlish and unmannerly to his Spanish hosts if he did not support their cause. But he saw no prospect of them winning the war: his real belief was in American intervention in Cuba, and when this came in 1898, and the United States went to war with Spain, he wrote in favour of American annexation of the island.

For the first (but not the last) time in his life voices were raised in abuse of Winston's participation in a foreign imbroglio, particular resentment being expressed at his acceptance of the Spanish medal. Even Winston realized dimly that his behaviour was lacking in common sense:

> To travel thousands of miles with money one could ill afford, and get up at four o'clock in the morning in the hope of getting into a scrape in the company of perfect strangers, is certainly hardly a rational proceeding ... What is it then that we want? It is that lure of youth – adventure, and adventure for adventure's sake.[60]

Winston opposed to the criticism and hostility an indifference which was to harden into a horny carapace as his adventures unfolded.

* * *

The 4th Hussars were to sail to India in the autumn of 1896. Generous leave was given to officers, and facilities for arranging their affairs before leaving. It was a delightful period for Winston, 'almost the only idle spell I ever had'. He was able to live at home with his mother, going to Hounslow Barracks two or three times a week. He now had five polo ponies, and played the game at Hurlingham and Ranelagh. He abandoned himself to the pleasures of the London season. In this period of deep tranquillity no exterior threat menaced the unbroken peace and prosperity, and men's eyes were now turning to the Diamond Jubilee in the coming year. Society itself, in which Winston was as of right welcomed, was then a potent force with its own rules hard as iron,

60. Winston S. Churchill, op. cit., p. 89.

its ramparts almost impossible for outsiders to scale. There is a strong nostalgia and regret for the past in Winston's recollections, long after, of this powerful closed circle:

> In those days English society still existed in its old form. It was a brilliant and powerful body, with standards of conduct and methods of enforcing them now altogether forgotten. In a very large degree everyone knew everyone else and who they were. The few hundred great families who had governed England for so many generations and had seen her rise to the pinnacle of her glory, were interrelated to an enormous extent by marriage. Everywhere one met friends and kinsfolk. The leading figures in Society were in many cases the leading statesmen in Parliament, and also the leading sportsmen on the Turf. Lord Salisbury was accustomed scrupulously to avoid calling a Cabinet when there was racing at Newmarket, and the House of Commons made a practice of adjourning for the Derby. In those days the glittering parties at Lansdowne House, Devonshire House or Stafford House comprised all the elements which made a gay and splendid social circle in close relation to the business in Parliament, the hierarchies of the Army and Navy, and the policy of the State.

* * *

Winston filled every moment of his time before embarkation. Many exalted persons were curious to know how Lord Randolph's son was turning out, and Winston missed no opportunity of meeting them. This was partly because he enjoyed the sort of parties they gave, and partly because he realized cold-bloodedly that a collection of influential friends might be of decisive help to him in the future. He particularly enjoyed his frequent invitations to Lord Rothschild's house at Tring, and to Duchess Lily's house, Deepdene near Dorking, where she lived with her new husband Lord William Beresford, who had won the VC in the Matabele War, and whose panache was much to Winston's taste.

It would be too harsh to suggest that Winston was now seeking the friendship of the great entirely for the use he could make of them to further his own ends, for he was also now passionately interested in politics and was deeply intrigued to meet the men at the top, and study their conversation. But the other object was never far from his mind, and it is beyond doubt that he made a formidable list of contacts and friendships of which he was to make constant and remorseless use to further his career – Asquith, Balfour, Chamberlain, Wolseley (the Duke of Cambridge's successor as Commander-in-Chief of the British Army), were but a few of those whose usefulness he now coolly assessed.

It was at Deepdene in 1896 that he met Sir Bindon Blood, a leading commander on the Indian frontier, and lost no time in adding him to the list. He was another flamboyant figure who boasted proudly that he was a direct descendant of the Colonel Blood who had stolen the Crown Jewels in the seventeenth century. But for Winston he had a more contemporary usefulness.

'He had come home fresh from the successful storming of the Malakand Pass in the autumn of 1895. If future trouble broke out on the Indian frontier he was sure to have a high command. He thus held the key to future delights. I made good friends with him.'[61] He did more: he extracted from the General a promise that if he ever commanded another expedition on the Indian frontier he would take Winston with him.

Winston knew nothing of storied India, her culture, history and ancient civilization, and was not concerned to learn. It is astonishing that an imagination so romantic and ardent should not have been fired by a glamour so tremendous. He referred to the sub-continent as 'the tedious land of India', and made desperate efforts to wriggle out of his commitment – trying to become correspondent to the *News Chronicle* in disordered Crete; to join Kitchener's coming expedition up the Nile; to join the 9th Lancers' expedition to Durban, to go anywhere in fact that offered some action and was sufficiently remote from the 'tedious land of India'. It is easy to understand what an intolerable nuisance he was, and the reasons for his unpopularity are not far to seek.

But it was all in vain. He had not yet perfected his technique of wire-pulling. He became angry and abusive to his mother for not helping him more effectively:

> When I consider that I am letting the golden opportunity go by I feel that I am guilty of an indolent folly that I shall regret all my life. A few months in South Africa would earn me the S.A. medal & in all probability the company's Star. Thence hot foot to Egypt – to return with two more decorations in a year or two – and beat my sword into an iron despatch box. Both are within the bounds of possibility and here I am out of both. I cannot believe that with all the influential friends and all the men who would do something for me for my father's sake – that I could not be allowed to go – were those influences properly exerted.
>
> It is useless to preach the gospel of patience to me. Others as young are making the running now and what chance have I of ever catching up? I put it down here – definitely on paper – that you really ought to leave no stone unturned to help me at such a period. Years may pass before such chances ever come again. It is a little thing for you to ask, and a smaller thing for those in authority to grant – but it means so much to me . . . You can't realize how furiously intolerable this life is to me when so much is going on a month away from here . . . [62]

61. Ibid. p. 101.
62. Chartwell papers, 4 August 1896.

One can vividly sense the corrosive egoism and biting frustration when everything seemed at stake and the penalties of delay to be written before him in huge characters. Perhaps Lady Randolph was becoming weary of these nagging importunities, for she appears to have sent no answer, and the 4th Hussars sailed from Southampton on 11 September 1896.

By the time of embarkation Colonel Brabazon the flamboyant had, to Winston's deep regret, been forced to hand over the command of the 4th Hussars to a Colonel Alexander – who appeared a poor substitute since, through no fault of his own, he had seen no action of any kind in thirty years' service. Reginald Barnes, Winston's companion in Cuba, was adjutant, and Hugo Baring, another officer, was among his closest friends.

Winston, as we have seen, felt nothing but a dull, surly indifference to this new experience, and always a bad sailor, was irked by the long, steaming-hot journey, unstirred even by its novelty, although he passed the time pleasantly enough, playing picquet with Baring and chess with another friend, Kincaid Smith. He also took part in a moot or mock trial of a breach-of-promise case, and for two reasons was profoundly relieved by the result. He found himself able to speak for twenty minutes without learning his speech by heart, and was by no means disconcerted by his strange natural impediment of being unable to pronounce sibilants, from which he had always suffered.

The fact that he could speak so long without notes or preparation must also have delighted him, for he had no natural power of extemporary speech, and for the rest of his life relied on a full written manuscript, from which he produced results worthy of the greatest actor. But in all his long experience he was never to master the true art of speech; never to learn to think upon his feet, or, like his friend F. E. Smith, 'to soar upon the unpinioned wing'. Sometimes, he would brace himself to speak impromptu and in his later years he often did so well; but his brilliant readiness in ordinary conversation deserted him in the House of Commons, except at Question Time, if he rose to his feet unprepared, and he was frequently plagued by nervousness and lack of confidence. His speech at the moot therefore was a triumph not repeated for several years, and there was elation in his letter to Lady Randolph describing the trial:

> . . .I was counsel for the defence. To my relief I showed myself able to speak without notes or preparation for twenty minutes and as I succeeded in keeping the audience in constant laughter – my harangue was a success. My impediment did not seem to interfere with my articulation at all and of all who spoke I was the best heard.[63]

63. Chartwell papers.

This defect in speech was so marked as to have deterred a man less dogged and persevering, and less hell-bent on success in political life. His attempt to pronounce the letter 'S' emerged in a strange lisping hiss, and he was sufficiently disturbed by it to consult a throat specialist who found no organic defect, and gave Winston exercises in speech, telling him that the impediment could be conquered by perseverance. This was a quality in which he was certainly not wanting, and before leaving for India he could be heard pacing the garden paths of country houses, resolutely declaiming with many hisses: 'The Spanish ships I cannot see for they are not in sight.'[64]

* * *

Winston's boredom at the prospect of India was dispelled for a moment by his first glimpse of the city of Bombay, which seemed half drowned in the sea, lying flat against the promontory of the Malabar Hills. Its palms and palaces spread out in a wide crescent before his eyes. He felt a sudden intense eagerness to land, and his reckless behaviour in doing so led to another serious incident which had a lasting effect upon him. While he was being rowed from the ship to the quay of the Sassoon Dock in a small boat he felt distinctly queasy, and in his eagerness to reach terra firma he grasped a ring on the quayside at a moment when the boat fell steeply in the trough of a wave, 'giving my right shoulder a sharp and peculiar wrench'. His shoulder was not actually dislocated, but he had received an injury which lasted for life, often crippling him for polo, and for years suddenly reappearing and causing dislocation at unpredictable moments — taking a book from the library shelf, or even sleeping with his arm under the pillow.

From Bombay the 4th Hussars travelled by train to their station, Bangalore in the Deccan, breaking their journey in a rest camp in Poona, where Winston was invited to dinner by the Governor, Lord Sandhurst. At his table, encouraged by copious draughts of champagne, Winston showed the side of his character that most irritated his elders, and from his own account of the evening seems for once to have been dimly aware himself that he had given grounds for annoyance:

> I have forgotten the particular points of British and Indian affairs upon which he sought my counsel. All I can remember is that I responded generously. There were indeed moments when he seemed willing to impart his views; but I thought it would be ungracious to put

64. Randolph S. Churchill, *Winston S. Churchill*, Vol.I., p.293.

him to so much trouble; and he very readily subsided. He kindly sent his aide-de-camp with us to make sure we found our way back to camp.[65]

The city of Bangalore stands in the centre of the Mysore tableland, and the cantonments stretched away towards the north-east, the troops being housed in large, cool colonnaded barracks shaded by endless double avenues of trees. Winston soon found that although by day the sun struck with ferocious power, the nights were cool and fresh, and the climate at that elevation unusually healthy. He was entranced by the profusion of flowers, which here rioted in a glory impossible in a cold climate:

> The roses of Europe in innumerable large pots attain the highest perfection of fragrance and colour. Flowers, flowering shrubs and creepers bloom in glorious profusion. Snipe (and snakes) abound in the marshes; brilliant butterflies dance in the sunshine.[66]

We have already noted that whatever his financial difficulties, Winston managed throughout life to live *en grand seigneur*, and it is impossible to imagine him in any other condition. Now, as a needy subaltern in India, he began as he intended to continue. He, Reginald Barnes and Hugo Baring, pooling their resources, found a 'palace of white and pink' with a heavy tiled roof and deep verandahs supported by white columns round which was coiled a mass of bougainvillaea. The house stood in a compound or garden of about two acres in which, to Winston's delight, were already 150 standard roses. There was stabling in the compound for thirty horses and ponies.

The young men's needs were served by a staff of almost laughable proportions. There were three butlers to manage the household, wait at table and supervise the stables; six dressing boys or valets, and a syce (groom) to each horse and polo pony. Besides these, there were also at their disposal two gardeners, three water-carriers, four dhobies or washermen, and one nightwatchman.

This sort of ménage clearly could not be maintained on pay of 14/s. a day supplemented by an allowance from his mother of £500 a year paid quarterly, with £3 a month allowed for the upkeep of two horses, although such an income with the prevailing value of money would have been ample for any normal subaltern. But Winston flatly refused to forgo the luxuries which now beckoned him. He raised the wind by borrowing whatever was necessary at exorbitant rates of interest from all too accommodating native money-lenders. Every officer was warned

65. Winston S. Churchill, op. cit., p. 113.
66. Ibid. p. 114.

against these sinister usurers, but Winston contemptuously ignored the warning. He neither understood nor cared about money. He merely required that it was present in sufficient quantities to supply his needs.

> I always found them most agreeable; very fat, very urbane, quite honest and mercilessly rapacious. All you had to do was to sign little bits of paper, and produce a polo pony as if by magic. The smiling financier rose to his feet, covered his face with his hands, replaced his slippers, and trotted off contentedly till that day three months.[67]

A well-tended Indian garden is an earthly paradise, and it provided him with a new and absorbing interest. 'We now have 50 different kinds of roses,' he told his mother in January 1897, 'La France, Gloire de Dijon, Maréchal Niel and the rest of them – and all the rest we planted on arrival have come up into bright coloured flowers. I take the greatest interest in their growth.'[68] And in February, the enthusiasm still strong upon him, he told her that: 'I have 250 rose trees and 70 different sorts so that every morning I can cut about 3 great basins full of the most beautiful flowers which nature produces.' He asked her to send him English seeds – wallflowers, stocks and such like, which were unknown in the district, but which he felt sure would flourish in the rich dark soil.

The heavenly garden provided another delight. Winston had always loved butterflies, and his own passion for bright colours had long been satisfied by their gaily pied and iridescent wings. He had hunted a few common varieties in the old childhood days at Banstead, and he wrote of the butterflies he later saw in Uganda:

> Never were seen such flying fairies. They flaunted their splendid liveries and inconceivable varieties of colour and pattern in our faces at every step. Swallow-tails, fritillaries, admirals, tortoiseshells, peacocks, orange tips... flitted in sunshine from flower to flower, glinted in the shadow of great trees, or clustered on the path to suck the moisture from any swampy patch . . . so intoxicated by feasting that I could pick them up quite gently in my fingers . . .[69]

Here at Bangalore, fluttering over the tropical creepers were also to be seen in rich profusion the jewels of the butterfly kingdom – purple emperors, white admirals, swallow-tails, and a hundred other exotic specimens, many of which he could not at first identify. He began to make a collection, sending to England for collecting boxes,

67. Ibid.
68. Chartwell papers.
69. Winston S. Churchill, *My African Journey*.

setting-boards and killing-bottles. But while awaiting these he began his collection, which, as he told his brother Jack, came to an untimely end:

> My butterfly collection, which included upwards of 65 different sorts, has been destroyed by the malevolence of a rat which crawled into the cabinet and devoured all the specimens. I have, however, caught the brute and had him killed by Winston the terrier, and have begun again perseveringly.[70]

In this way he settled down pleasantly enough to his new life, which also, of course, included many military duties. His day began in a manner that seems a trifle decadent: he was shaved while still half asleep by one of his Indian servants.

'Just before dawn every morning one was awakened by a dusky figure with a clammy hand adroitly lifting one's chin and applying a gleaming razor to a lathered and defenceless throat.' By six o'clock the regiment was on parade and drilled and manoeuvred for an hour and a half. Then a return, hot and sweaty, to the almost sensual luxury of cooling baths at the white-and-pink house, and breakfast in the mess. Stables and Orderly Room followed from nine to half-past ten. It was then necessary to seek refuge in the house again before the sun reached its ferocious zenith. The distances in the cantonments were too great for walking, and the officers cantered on hacks from one point to another:

> But the noon-day sun asserted his tyrannical authority, and long before eleven o'clock all white men were in shelter. We nipped across to luncheon at half past one in blistering heat and then returned to sleep till five o'clock. the station begins to live again. It is the hour of polo.

Winston played every evening in as many chukkas as he could arrange, and his passion for the game is beyond question. This should be emphasized, for in later life he was to play no games of any kind, and indeed seemed to regard them with contempt. The author recalls a discussion between Winston and his friend F. E. Smith,[71] who was still an ardent games player, about a young man Smith believed to show promise. He said not only was the young man likely to take a First Class at Oxford, but was also almost certain to be given his Rugby 'Blue'.

'What does it matter,' asked Winston with withering scorn, 'whether he gets his Rugby Blue or his Rugby Green, or his Rugby dung-colour?'

70. Chartwell papers.
71. Afterwards Earl of Birkenhead.

But at this time of his life in India he was as anxious to succeed at polo as any conventional public schoolboy avid for success at football.

* * *

Chapter 2

India to the Boer War

He had not been many weeks in India before he went to Secunderabad in the dominions of the Nizam of Hyderabad to play polo, and there met the girl he regarded as the first great love of his life, and to whom he surrendered at least part of his heart (evidently keeping a good deal in reserve). Her name was Pamela Plowden, a girl of dazzling beauty, and daughter of the British Resident in the state. Winston rode through the city of Hyderabad with her on an elephant, explaining to Lady Randolph: 'You dare not walk or the natives spit at Europeans – which provokes retaliation leading to riots.' He dined with her parents, and was enchanted by the stately and civilized atmosphere, remarking that a dinner with ladies present 'is delightful in this country after nearly three months of messes and barbarism'.

He might well be impressed, for the Residents of Hyderabad lived like Renaissance princes. The residency was really a palace. It was conceived on a vast scale, and built with the expiring elegance of the early nineteenth century. A tranquil refuge from the clatter of the city, it stood in an exquisite compound shaded by banyans, peepuls, tamarinds and mahogany trees, and full of ferns and canna lilies. As we follow Winston's relationship with Pamela Plowden we become aware of a strange absence of passion on his part, and we have an uneasy feeling that she meant a great deal less to him than his own career, that he was never in love, and halted on the threshold of those bitter-sweet regions.

Winston was oafish and rude in Anglo-Indian circles, the mediocrity of which he stressed in letters to his mother which grew ever more peevish and discontented. He refused to pay or return calls, and showed the cruelty of youth to a society which was certainly not stimulating, but which was friendly and well-meaning, and deserved better treatment: 'I saw a lot of horrid Anglo-Indian women at the races,' he told his mother in October 1896: 'nasty vulgar creatures all looking as though they thought themselves great beauties', and

62

a month later he wailed: 'This is an abominable country to live in.'[1]

It is to Winston's discredit that he showed no interest in the storied past of India, in her history, religions or architecture. In November 1896 we find him complaining to his mother:

> If I could only get hold of the right people my stay here might be of value. Had I come to India as an M.P. – however young and foolish, I could have had access to all who know and can convey. As a soldier – my intelligent interests are supposed to stop short at Polo, racing and Orderly Officer. I vegetate – even reading is an effort . . .[2]

But he was not deploring his ignorance of India. Such knowledge, given the slightest interest or curiosity, could have been acquired by sending for books on Indian subjects. But he had no such interest. He was fretting himself into discontent because the political career which dominated his mind seemed to be stuck in the doldrums, and his natural vivacity now masked a hideous boredom.

But he was shrewd enough to realize that he was inadequately educated, and that this would weigh heavily against his grandiose plans for the future, and intelligent enough to be conscious of an aching desire for knowledge. In his usual dogged, almost canine manner he began his quest. He started with certain strong advantages – a wide vocabulary and a love for the manipulation of words – 'for the feeling of words fitting and falling into their places like pennies in the slot', and a marvellous ear which enabled him to place words in the most harmonious juxtaposition. But owing to his lack of education he found himself again and again using words whose meaning he did not fully understand, and although he admired these words, he stopped using them for fear of being ridiculous. He began to feel an inferiority complex about the young men he had met from the Universities, who were systematically instructed by learned men, and who could put forward trap questions and baffling arguments formidable as the gladiator with his entangling net. But it was consoling to reflect that they paraded their erudition like a stockbroker's diamond, and were, after all, only at their books while he and his friends were commanding men and defending the Empire.

These reflections did not remove his doubts. Above all he longed for a wise instructor who would shine a lantern into the darkness of his ignorance, and would submit himself to cross-examination on the subjects that passed uncomprehended before Winston's mind. Winston

---

1. Chartwell papers.
2. Ibid.

had, for example, heard a thing called Ethics mentioned. What exactly were Ethics? He would, he said, have paid a man well for an hour and a half's lecture on the subject in all its aspects. And what was the 'Socratic method' that he had once heard someone mention? But there was no one at Bangalore to enlighten him.

But there was still history. The pageantry of history had always beguiled him, although his knowledge of it was by no means comprehensive, and his prejudices were unusually blatant. Messages now reached Lady Randolph demanding what Winston thought to be the standard works on this subject. He began at the end of 1896 with the eight volumes of Dean Milman's edition of Gibbon's *Decline and Fall of the Roman Empire*, and, while his friends were sleeping in 'the glistening middle hours of the Indian day', he devoured this great work, scribbling his opinions industriously in the margins of the page, and becoming a strong partisan of the author 'against the disparagement of his pompous-pious editor'.

From Gibbon he passed to Macaulay's *History of England*, immediately captivated by the extraordinary virtuosity of that historian's style, and deceived by his devastating self-confidence. Enchanted by the hard gem-cutting sentences and the lava flow of narrative, he accepted the message as gospel, although distinctly shaken by Macauley's violent indictment of Winston's own great forebear the Duke of Marlborough. He discovered afterwards with relief how far, in the absence of a tutor, he had been misled by Macaulay's genius:

'There was no one at hand to tell me that this historian with his captivating style ... was the prince of literary rogues, who always preferred the tale to the truth, and smirched or glorified great men and garbled documents as they affected his drama.'[3] It is ironical to note that when Winston came to write his own account of his great ancestor he did so with a partiality and a special pleading worthy of Macaulay himself.

A one-man university without dons, Winston, confronting an ocean of ignorance, took further steps to fill in some of the vast gaps in his knowledge – Plato's *Republic*, Aristotle's *Politics*, Schopenhauer on *Pessimism*, Malthus on *Population*, Darwin's *Origin of Species* – all were doggedly consumed until the temperate weather of November degenerated into the baking inferno of May. What is so impressive about it was the avidity with which he laboured and the passion with which he sought enlightenment:

3. Winston S. Churchill, *My Early Life*, p. 121.

It was a curious education. First because I approached it with an empty, hungry mind, and with fairly strong jaws; and what I got I bit; secondly because I had no one to tell me: 'You should read the answer to that by so and so; the two together will give you the gist of the argument.' 'There is a much better book on that subject,' and so forth. I now began . . . to envy those young cubs at the University who had fine scholars to tell them what was what; professors who had devoted their lives to mastering and focussing ideas in every branch of learning; who were eager to distribute the treasures they had gathered before they were overtaken by the night.[4]

But his envy for these pampered youths was softened by a pity that closely verged on contempt. They were, after all, in a backwater, many of them (unlike him) 'leading frivolous lives in the midst of precious fleeting opportunity.'

* * *

No one could have accused Winston of this particular fault. He had not swerved by an inch from his original purpose: he now regarded India as a sort of provincial gaol in the workings of which he took not the slightest interest. He was trying desperately not to waste time, going through an elaborate process of self-education, and seeking to inform himself on history and politics to equip himself for the life to come. Apart from this his sole desire was to leave the Army as quickly as he could, but before doing so to see as much action as possible whenever a skirmish or a frontier war gave promise of it. We shall see him pushing his way into these with astonishing effrontery.

He watched with envy and resentment friends who were stealing a march on him and forging ahead. The thought of Kitchener's expedition up the Nile still glowed before his eyes and beckoned like an *ignis fatuus*. Lord Fincastle had won three medals in Egypt and Captain de Moleyns the DSO in South Africa, and their success brought bitter reflections on his own stagnation. He felt overcome by *accidie*, longing to see active service, to win fame and fortune describing it, and then leave the Army and enter politics, now more than ever conscious that it was at Westminster only that the great game was played. We notice particularly at this time the utterly ruthless manner in which he was prepared to exploit others for his own ends. His mother, with her powerful contacts, was now his agent and ally, on whose influence he blindly relied.

The time had not quite come when he became the dominant and she the recessive partner, though it was fast approaching. There still lingered enough of the old relationship for her to send Winston sharp

4. Ibid, p. 122.

and frequent letters of well-deserved reprimand, but their relations were swiftly changing. At the moment she was the only person to whom he could write, his sole link with the great world. He had already written to her about his *idée fixe*. '*Please do your best*,' he wrote urgently: 'I should not have forgiven myself if an expedition started next year and felt it was my own fault I was not there.' And from Calcutta during Christmas he added: 'I revolve Egypt continuously in my mind. Two years in Egypt my dearest Mamma – with a campaign thrown in – would I think qualify me to be allowed to beat my sword into a paper cutter and my sabretache into an election address.'[5]

It was her influence which, after much pestering, induced a reluctant Kitchener in December 1896 to put Winston's name on the list for special service with the Egyptian army, although there were no vacancies at that moment in the cavalry. Winston's drooping spirits revived like a watered rose, but, determined not to spend a dull period waiting in Bangalore, he told his mother in the New Year of 1897 that he proposed to come home on leave. This was more than she was prepared to tolerate, and she wrote to him with unusual sharpness, and a large degree of justification:

> 26 February 1897 . . . It is absolutely out of the question, not only on account of money, but for the sake of yr reputation. They will say & with some reason that you can't stick at anything. You have only been out 6 months & it is on the cards that you may be called to Egypt. There is plenty for you to do in India. I confess I am quite disheartened about you. You seem to have no real purpose in life & wont realize at the age of 22 that for a man life means work, and hard work if you mean to succeed. Many men at yr age have to work for a living & support their mother. It is useless my saying more – we have been over this ground before – it is not a pleasant one.[6]

Useless indeed – for he was no longer even faintly impressed by such charges – if indeed he ever had been. His reply, jaunty and self-centred, was not softened by a word of apology, explanation or contrition, and his intention to go on leave was completely unchanged: 'I set great store on going to Egypt if they go this year,' he calmly told his mother. 'I long for excitement of some sort and the prospect of joining an English expedition attracts me immensely. I do hope you will not relax your efforts.[7]

5. Chartwell papers.
6. Ibid.
7. Ibid.

Lady Randolph must have been wounded and angered by this dusty answer, but it is clear from her own letter that she still had no conception of the strength and obstinacy of her son's character, while to accuse him of a lack of purpose in life shows an almost grotesque want of perception. In this little exchange, therefore, Jennie revealed her ignorance of Winston's inflexible will-power, and he in turn served notice that he was no longer affected by maternal censure or appeals *ad misericordiam*.

* * *

His early months in India had been marred by a series of unpleasant injuries – first in an overturned carriage as the result of a practical joke;[8] when he cut his knee so deeply that he could not play polo for ten days; then in the rifle butts he was struck by a ricochet, sustaining a wound an inch and a half deep near his left thumb, and having to submit to twenty minutes' agonizing probing before the splinter could be extracted. Later, in February 1897, he was so badly blistered on manoeuvres by the terrible Indian sun that he was driven again to the Medical Officer: 'The inflammation caused by the burns on my chin has inflamed all the glands of my throat & the blister is a horrible sight. I however keep dressings continually on and so manage to go about my business – though in a bandaged condition.'[9]

In February he was able to boast to his mother that he was acting for a time in the key position of Brigade Major as well as Adjutant, and that 'soldiering prospects are very prosperous . . . Responsibility is an exhilarating drink.'

But Winston showed far less sense of it in his financial transactions. He had, with his increased allowance for a cavalry officer and Lady Randolph's £500, an income of £800 a year, which with the value of money in those days and the cheapness of living in India compared to England, should have been more than sufficient for his needs. But something grand and lordly in his blood – some *Grand Seigneur* residue of that Blenheim–Marlborough background – ensured that, then as afterwards, he demanded high living as his natural lot, and was satisfied by nothing but the best in life.

He had already received a sharp reprimand from his mother on the subject of his overdrawing at Cox's Bank and general extravagance, but his lofty indifference to these squalid details led to one of his cheques

8. After a wild dinner one of Winston's friends had fastened the reins to the horse's collar instead of his bit.
9. Chartwell papers.

being dishonoured, a most humiliating and disturbing experience at any time, and particularly heinous at this – no fit conduct indeed for an 'officer and gentleman'.

Lady Randolph was, of course, devastated by the news, but her reproaches on this occasion were tempered by the recognition that her son's reckless follies and financial incompetence were only equalled by her own. Pain, therefore, rather than anger marked her reply:

> My darling boy, you can't think how all this worries me. I have so many money troubles of my own I feel I cannot take on any others . . . Darling I lay awake last night thinking about you and how much I wanted to help you – if only I had some money I wld do so. I am so proud of you and of all yr great and endearing qualities. I feel sure that if you live you will make a name for yourself but I know to do it you have to be made of stern stuff – and not mind sacrifice and self-denial . . .[10]

Winston gave a somewhat casual explanation of the shaming episode of the bounced cheque, saying that he had given it to the recipient post-dated, but as he was still overdrawn when it matured, he had asked the man to wait a little longer before presenting it. He had refused to do so. There is reason to think that even Winston, at least briefly, was shaken by this affair. This time too he felt that he owed it to his mother to express contrition. What he was not prepared to do was to admit that his own extravagance alone had landed him in this mess; or to reduce the standard of living which had saddled him with the crippling debts which hung like an albatross round his neck:

> All this worries my awfully. Indeed I don't know what will happen in the near future. I must raise a certain sum of money on a Life insurance or some other security & pay off these pressing liabilities lest I obtain a most unenviable reputation . . . Of course spending your capital means loss of income – already alas so small, but not to do it is to be almost dishonest in my case.[11]

*   *   *

When the hot weather of 1897 approached he sailed from Bombay early in May for the leave on which, against the strong wishes of his mother and the advice of his own friends, he was so obstinately determined: 'Having so newly arrived, hardly anybody wanted to go,' he observed naively: 'I thought it was a pity that such good things should go a-begging, and I therefore volunteered to fill the

10. Chartwell papers.
11. Ibid.

gap.' He was punished by a ghastly voyage – sweltering heat and fearful sea-sickness from which he did not emerge until the ship was two-thirds across the Indian Ocean.

From a new shipboard friend, Colonel Ian Hamilton – to whom he became devoted, and who was to play an important part in his life – he heard that Greece and Turkey were at war over Crete, and he had decided, if his mother could arrange it through her influential friends in the usual way, to go as war correspondent and special observer to the operation. He promised to take no part in the fighting, 'but would merely see the fun and tell the tale'. But by the time the ship reached Brindisi the war was over, and he consoled himself by visiting Rome instead:

> I read again the sentences in which Gibbon has described the emotions with which in his later years for the first time he approached the Eternal City, and though I had none of his credentials of learning, it was not without reverence that I followed in his footsteps.[12]

Winston had been moved by his exploration of Rome mainly on Gibbon's account, for he was not then, nor ever became, an ardent sightseer. He described this visit as a 'well-conceived prelude to the gaieties of the London season', and a striking aspect of his early life is the quick alternations of scenes of violence in remote countries and the leisured ease of London Society. The lush green and lovely surroundings of Goodwood and the grisly crags of the Indian Frontier – there could hardly be greater contrasts. Yet it was at Goodwood, when staying with the Duchess Lily and Lord William Beresford, that he heard of the revolt of the Pathan tribesmen in these grim northern fastnesses, and soon read in the papers that a Field Force of three Brigades had been formed under the command of Sir Bindon Blood.

Going to the top as usual, Winston immediately wired to the General, reminding him of his promise of the previous year, made to him at Deepdene in the old Hounslow days, that if he ever commanded another expedition on the frontier he would allow Winston to join him. With extraordinary impulsiveness and without waiting for a reply, he packed his bags in wild haste, and left for India by the quickest and most expensive route, expecting a message from Blood at every port, and suffering accumulating agonies when none appeared.

Sir Bindon, he had once said, by virtue of his position, 'held the key to future delights'. Surely he would not fail Winston now? But not until he had been back in Bangalore for several days did he hear

12. Winston S. Churchill, op. cit., p. 133.

from the General, who had no vacancy but advised Winston to come up as press-correspondent:

'When you are here I shall put you on the strength at the first opportunity. I have hardly managed to get any of my pals on my staff – though I have asked for several. However if you were here I think I could, and certainly would if I could, do a little jobbery on your account.'[13]

Thus reassured, Winston obtained an extra month's leave from his obliging Regiment, and prepared to leave for the North. Mindful of the other side of his two-pronged strategy, he sent a peremptory request to his mother to find a paper for him to represent. She was successful with the *Daily Telegraph*, and Winston also arranged to send 300 words a day to the *Pioneer* of Allahabad, the paper on which Kipling had served as a cub reporter. Lady Randolph had done her best but only succeeded in getting £5 a column from the *Daily Telegraph*, half the price asked by Winston. He did not particularly mind this, but was incensed because she had, on the advice of Lord Minto, arranged that his articles should be unsigned.

This anonymity, he angrily informed his mother, would completely disrupt his grand strategy:

> I had written them with the design . . . of bringing my name before the electorate. I had hoped that some political advantage might have accrued . . . However I left the decision in your hands and you have decided – not for the first time upon a negative course . . . I will only add that if I am to avoid doing 'unusual things' it is difficult to see what chance I have of being more than an average person.[14]

Winston was justified on this occasion in protesting about his mother's weak and foolish decision.

*   *   *

At the Bangalore station the clerk pushed an ordinary ticket through the pigeon-hole. Winston asked the man how far it was to his destination – Nowshera, the railhead of the Malakand Field Force. The Indian clerk consulted a time-table and replied impassively that it was 2,028 miles. A five-days' journey therefore lay before him in the worst of the Indian heat, and he looked forward to it with apprehension.

But he soon found that the Indian railways had given much thought and care to hot-weather travel. He had plenty of books, ice and tobacco, and the carriage was a sort of oasis in a scorching desert.

13. Chartwell papers.
14. Ibid.

Those large leather-lined Indian railway carriages, deeply shuttered and blinded from the blistering sun and kept fairly cool by a circular wheel of wet straw which one turned from time to time, were all adapted to the local conditions. I spent five days in a dark padded moving cell.

He read by lamplight or by a cautiously admitted shaft of the dreaded glare from outside.[15] On the sixth morning after leaving Bangalore he stood on the platform of Nowshera, and from there made his way forty miles across the plains in appalling heat before the tonga – a small cart drawn by relays of galloping ponies – began to climb the steep ascent to the Malakand Pass. Winston was yellow with dust when he presented himself at the Staff Office, only to find that the General was away on a punitive expedition against the unruly Bunerwal tribe, one of the most formidable of the Frontier.

While waiting for Sir Bindon to return Winston acquired, with some pride, an entirely new faculty. He learned to enjoy whisky.

. . . I liked wine, both red and white, and especially champagne; and on very special occasions I could even drink a small glass of brandy. But this smoky-tasting whisky I had never been able to face.

He now found himself for five days in heat abnormal even for India, with nothing to drink except tepid water with lime juice or tepid water with whisky:

Faced with these alternatives I grasped the 'larger hope'. I was sustained in these affairs by my high morale. Wishing to fit myself for active-service conditions I overcame the ordinary weaknesses of the flesh. By the end of these five days I had completely overcome my repugnance to the taste of whisky. Nor was this a momentary acquirement. On the contrary the ground I gained in those days I have firmly entrenched, and held throughout my whole life. Once I got the knack of it, the very repulsion from the flavour developed an attraction of its own; and to this day, although I have always practised true temperance, I have never shrunk when occasion warranted it from the main basic standing refreshment of the white officer in the East.[16]

During this period of waiting he learned that a new method of photography had been discovered which would in time enable doctors to photograph bones in the human body, and ascertain the nature of

15. Winston S. Churchill, op. cit., pp 133–4.
16. Ibid., pp. 136–7.

fractures. A song was sung about it by the soldiers with a haunting and lively refrain:

The inside of everything you see
A terrible thing, an 'orrible thing is the new photographee.

Winston found that for the rest of his life he had only to hear or hum this song to summon the past as vividly as by Proust's madeleine to float before his senses – to catch a whiff of the cow-dung fires of those northern valleys, or the clean smell of horse sweat as they plodded up steep hills; to see again that landscape of lunar bleakness, the grisly untamed mountains where no birds sang, the troops winding through rugged defiles – and taste anew the fierce excitement and glorious hope of youth.

*   *   *

The activities of the Malakand Field Force were continually interrupted by political officers attached to the Army who patched up local truces, often preventing military operations and making themselves extremely unpopular with subalterns like Winston avid for glory. At first, in fact, he found little excitement, but his moment came when he was invited by Sir Bindon, 'if he wanted to see some tough fighting', to join Brigadier P. D. Jeffreys's Brigade which was to go on a punitive expedition into the Mahmund Valley. It was intended in this operation to punish the Mahmunds for an attack on the British camp, and during it Winston was to experience some of the horrors of war.

Between Afghanistan and the Indus stretches one of the most formidable mountain systems in the world, and this frontier had been for centuries a scene of unending vigilance, and a local problem of enormous complexity. It was through the passes that pierce these mighty ranges like narrow sword-cuts that the invaders from Central Asia had poured to the rich plains of India. In their deep and tortuous ravines were found those bodies of fanatical tribesmen who could scarcely wring a livelihood from their stony soil, and were therefore always avid for loot, for the capture of a caravan, or for a bloody raid on the settled districts beneath them. Malakand is at the north end of this frontier.

It was forbidding territory, and the Pathan tribesmen most formidable enemies with hideous methods of revenge and punishment, and the habit of mutilating horribly all enemy soldiers who fell into their hands, dead or alive. Winston in later life was to be accused, like Napoleon, of a love of war, and certainly his zest for it in youth survived the terrible scenes he witnessed in the Malakand Valley and later at the battle of Omdurman.

The most savage fighting so far in his life took place on 16 September 1897. He had set out with the Brigade at dawn on a grey pony, riding with the Bengal Lancers, and reached the head of the valley before a brisk skirmish began, lasting for an hour, with tribesmen gathered on a conical hill. The British force was then divided into three punitive groups. One of these, to which Winston attached himself, was to make its way up a long spur to the left of the mountain towards a village whose roofs could be seen shimmering in the heat among the boulders and waving Indian corn of the mountain-side.

Winston handed his pony to a soldier, and began to plod up the hillside with the infantry. The heat was grilling, and he was somewhat disconcerted that he could see no sign of the Brigade which had marched out 1,200 strong, and now seemed to have been swallowed up by the valley. His own party – 5 officers and 85 Sikhs – appeared small, indeed dangerously inadequate. The village they had come to castigate was abandoned, and Winston, with an officer and eight Sikhs, lay down and rested while the others poked about in the mud-houses of the deserted village.

He was abruptly roused when the mountain-side suddenly sprang to life. He saw the flash of swords in the sun from behind rocks, and bright flags waving. Blue-and-white figures 2,000 feet above him began dropping from crag to crag like monkeys swinging down liana ways, and the howls, infinitely menacing, with which the Pathans entered battle could be heard.

Winston and his eight Sikhs began firing with their Martini rifles at the figures on the hill. He had borrowed a rifle from one of the men, telling the Sikh to pass him the ammunition. In the midst of this excitement the Battalion Adjutant suddenly appeared behind them and ordered him to retire. Winston and his Sikhs rose to obey when a volley from the hillside cut through the group like a swathe, laying five of them low, the men falling with a sound like fireirons dropped rattling into a grate. Winston at first thought they had lain down again, and so in a sense they had – two killed and three wounded. One man was shot through the breast and spouting blood: another lay on his back kicking in agony.

Winston knew that it was a point of honour on the frontier never to leave wounded men behind in a retreat: 'Death by inches and hideous mutilation are the invariable measure meted out to all who fall in battle into the hands of the Pathan tribesmen.' They began dragging down the hill, humping and crashing them against the rocks like shattered golliwogs, disregarding their groans of anguish. There was no rearguard of any kind behind them, for Winston had waited till the bitter end before retiring, and apparently no supporting party in front, for they had mistaken the knoll on which it was supposed to be waiting. At one point Winston, glancing to his left, saw that the Adjutant had been shot. Half a dozen Pathans emerged from the houses and made for him, and the men carrying the Adjutant dropped him and fled at their approach. The leading tribesman rushed upon the prostrate officer and began slashing and hacking him with his sword.

Winston was filled with a berserk rage and a wild urge to kill.

'I forgot everything else at this moment except a desire to kill this man. I bore my long cavalry sword well sharpened . . . I resolved on personal combat *à l'arme blanche.*' He was only twenty yards away from the Pathan. With other tribesmen joining the man, Winston gave up the idea of cold steel, and fired desperately with his revolver, driving the Pathans away. Under heavy fire he at last reached the right knoll which was being held by Sikhs. They made furious gestures at him to hurry, and in a moment he was among them.

But the dangers were not yet over, and there was still nearly a mile of the spur to traverse before the plain was reached. They staggered on down, cursing and sweating, slipping and falling, now little better than a mob but with a fair number of their wounded, although one officer and twelve men were left, wounded or dead, to the horrors in store for them. When they reached the plain the tribesmen, now frenzied with excitement, had gathered in a wide half-moon around the flanks of the survivors, but some disciplined and well-directed firing at last forced them to withdraw up the hillside. During this rather desperate day's work Winston had repeatedly exposed himself to danger, and was among the last to retreat. In his published despatches he was modest about his own part in the affair, but three days after the action wrote to his mother:

> When the retirement began I remained till the last and here I was perhaps very near the end. If you read between the lines of my letter [despatch] you will see that this retirement was an awful rout in which the wounded were left to be cut up horribly by these wild beasts. I was close to both officers when they were hit almost simultaneously and fired my revolver at a man at 30 yards who tried to cut up poor Hughes' body. A subaltern . . . and I carried a wounded Sepoy for some distance . . . My pants are still stained with the man's blood. We also remained till the enemy came within 40 yards firing our revolvers. They actually threw stones at us. It was a horrible business. For there was no help for the men that went down. I felt excitement and very little fear.

Referring to physical courage, Winston continued:

> But at any rate whatever I do afterwards, no one can say anything against me on this score. I rode on my grey pony all along the skirmish line where everyone else was lying down in cover. Foolish perhaps but I play for high stakes and given an audience there is no act too daring or

too noble. Without the gallery things are different.[17]

In this, as in another action a fortnight later, Winston showed himself to be without fear, and in October 1897 Sir Bindon Blood wrote warmly to Colonel Brabazon about his young friend:

> He [Winston] is now pro tem. an officer of native infantry of the 31st P.I. [Punjab Infantry]. I have put him in as he was the only spare officer within reach, and he is working away equal to the ordinary subalterns. He has been mentioned in despatches already, and if he gets the chance will have the V.C. or a D.S.O.[18]

But Winston declared that he would feel amply rewarded by the mention in despatches when he heard from his mother of Blood's intentions:

> I am more ambitious for a reputation for personal courage than anything else in the world. A young man should worship a young man's ideals ...'

And to his brother Jack he wrote:

> I had no military command and only rode about trying to attract attention – when things looked a little dangerous. Perhaps my good grey pony caught the Speaker's eye. I hope it is true. Being in many ways a coward – particularly at school – there is no ambition I cherish so keenly as to gain a reputation for personal courage.[19]

* * *

Winston was seen to be in a state of suppressed excitement when he returned to Bangalore, and glowing with a radiant self-satisfaction too naive to be offensive. But his mother did not like the bombastic tone that crept into his letters. 'Be modest,' she urged him. 'All your feats of valour are sure to come out, and people will know. Let it be from others, and not from yourself ... Let them *drag* things out of you.'

On his return to Bangalore he sat down and wrote *The Story of the Malakand Field Force*. He was indignant, as we have seen, that his despatches had been made anonymous, over the signature 'By a young officer', and this book was designed to boost his name and forward the Grand Design. He worked at high pressure, writing for five hours a day, and was able to send the MS home on 31 December

17. Chartwell papers.
18. Ibid.
19. Ibid.

1897. Lady Randolph was as usual saddled with all the arrangements. She sent the book to the literary agent A. P. Watt, and it was published by Longman in April 1898.

Winston rushed the book through because he knew that Lord Fincastle was about to publish a work on the same subject, and he was determined to be the first. There was no time for the proofs to be sent to India for revision, and Winston made the mistake of entrusting this task to his uncle Moreton Frewen, who made a sorry hash of it. Far from correcting drafting errors, he inserted a great many more, and changed words and indeed whole sentences. The punctuation was particularly lamentable.

Winston was wild with rage and mortification when the advance copy arrived, and he saw the full extent of the butchery, which at first quite ruined the pleasure he would have felt at the favourable reception given to the book. But the critics did not seem to notice anything wrong, and when he had read the first bundle of reviews he was deeply gratified by the compliments paid him. 'The reader must remember,' he wrote in *My Early Life*, 'I had never been praised before.' He recalled that the only comments that had been made on his work at school had been 'Slovenly', 'Bad', 'Very bad', etc.

> Now here was the great world with its leading literary newspapers and vigilant erudite critics, writing whole columns of praise! ... I was thrilled. I knew that if this would pass muster there was lots more where it came from, and I felt a new way of making a living and of asserting myself opening splendidly out before me. I saw that even this little book had earned me in a few months two years' pay as a subaltern.[20]

* * *

A disturbing item of news, however, awaited him in Bangalore, typical of the financial anxiety which dogged this family, but in which his mother rather than himself was now the delinquent party. Hopelessly extravagant and incompetent in money matters, she found herself under the necessity of raising £17,000 by a new loan, the security for which was to be life-insurance policies on her own and Winston's lives. She had arranged – without bothering, or daring, to tell him – that Winston should guarantee the premiums on these policies to the tune of approximately £700 a year.

Now the dominant partner in this strange alliance, Winston addressed to his mother a letter of reproach comically reminiscent of those he was accustomed to receiving from her, but far more tolerant:

20. Winston S. Churchill, op. cit., p. 166.

28 January 1898 ... Speaking quite frankly on the subject – there is no doubt that we are both you & I equally thoughtless – spendthrift and extravagant. We both know what is good – and we both like to have it. Arrangements for paying are left to the future ... We shall vy soon come to the end of our tether – unless a considerable change comes over our fortunes & dispositions ... I hope you will not mind my writing in a candid manner. I sympathize with all your extravagances – even more than you do with mine – it seems just as suicidal to me when you spend £200 on a ball dress as it does to you when I purchase a new polo pony for £100. And yet I feel that you ought to have the dress & I the polo pony. The pinch of the whole matter is we are damned poor.[21]

They were – for the sort of lives they insisted on leading. Winston, after stipulating that Jack should share his liabilities in this matter, agreed to his mother's request, but wrote to her again two days later with deepening resentment:

... In three years from my father's death you have spent a quarter of our entire fortune in the world. I have also been extravagant: but my extravagances are a very small matter beside yours ... If this letter does not please you – you must balance your annoyance against my reluctance to be £700 a year poorer & then I think you will admit that my side of the account is the heavier.

I hope you will write me a special answer to this letter ... I write in full love and amity and you will do very wrong to be angry at the unpleasant things it is necessary to express. ... [22]

It is as though he was gently but inexorably asserting his own superior will-power, and proclaiming his dominance in the partnership for once and all. His way of life did not alter. He continued to work on his book *Savrola*, his sole and self-revealing attempt at the novelist's craft, which he had laid aside while writing *The Malakand Field Force*, and in February 1898 travelled to Meerut, 1,400 baking miles to the north, to play in the inter-regimental polo tournament, where the 4th Hussars were beaten in the second round by the eventual winners, the Durham Light Infantry. But his mind was less upon the game than upon the war that was in progress in the northern frontier in Tirah where the Afridis had revolted, the war in which he was as always eager to participate.

Winston decided to go 600 miles north from Meerut to Peshawar, the railhead of the Tirah Expedition, rather than return with the

21. Chartwell papers.
22. Ibid.

others to Bangalore. In doing so he ran a grave risk. He had already had an inordinate amount of leave, and if he now made this journey, and failed to be accepted by the Expedition, it would mean overstaying his leave by at least forty-eight hours, and exposing himself to extreme humiliation and severe punishment. In taking such a risk Winston seems not only reckless, but to have been almost the sport of impulse; but the lure of further adventure, and perhaps a second book describing it, routed discretion.

At Peshawar he sought his friend Ian Hamilton, now commanding the 3rd Brigade of the Tirah Expeditionary Force, and from him he learned that the commanding officer, General Sir William Lockhart, had an ADC who wielded a remarkable influence, which some thought was quite disproportionate to his rank and position. His name was Captain Aylmer Haldane.

The formidable Haldane did not receive Winston effusively, but promised to put his name before the General. Winston waited in sharp anxiety as Haldane entered the General's office. When he returned he told Winston, to his intense surprise, that Lockhart had decided to appoint him an extra orderly officer on his personal staff. Once again a reckless gamble had succeeded, and there was no longer the slightest danger from his Colonel:

'The Adjutant General published my appointment in the Gazette. Horses and servants were despatched by the Regiment from far-off Bangalore, and I became the close personal attendant of the Captain of the Host.'[23] For some weeks, none the less, he was treated distantly and coldly as a self-invited newcomer. Contrary to every instinct, he was forced to remain silent at meals, speaking only when addressed. It is easy to see in imagination that red-haired bumptious figure, crushed by this appalling and unnatural restriction.

But he greatly strengthened his position when he gave sensible advice on the advisability of the Chief of Staff of the Expedition entering into a newspaper controversy about the conduct of operations with a journalist who had written damaging criticism of the campaign. Winston persuaded the Chief of Staff that it was beneath his dignity to reply. After this he was taken into the confidence of the Staff, and generally treated like an adult. But this was not to prove one of Winston's lucky excursions. The operations which he awaited so eagerly began to languish, and the fighting gradually petered out on the Afghan border. In spite of this Winston rode over nearly the whole frontier, writing to his mother the meaning words: 'I know all the Generals who are likely

23. Winston S. Churchill, op. cit., p. 170.

to have commands in the next few years.' [18 March 1898.]

He was now entitled to three months' leave, and having sent a letter to Lord Charles Beresford[24] in defence of the campaign, which was published in *The Times* of 3 May, he sailed from Bombay to England on 18 June 1898 to pull further strings in London. It was a moment of setback and of failure:

'Thus the beaver builds his dam, and thus when his fishing is about to begin, comes the flood and sweeps his work and luck and fish away together. So he has to begin again.'[25]

The whole philosophy of his early life is contained in this simple analogy, and we shall see how the unswerving will, the abnormal persistence, were rewarded by luck equally fantastic in the pursuit of what now seemed to be a gleaming *ignis fatuus* – glory in Egypt.

* * *

For Winston dimly realized that among the many people who had been antagonized by his forward thrust was the Sirdar of the Egyptian Army, Sir Herbert Kitchener. He began to realize the full extent of his unpopularity in certain quarters. People began to ask how he got all these campaigns, how he could be a newspaper correspondent and a serving officer at the same time, why the Generals were so weak with him, and above all, by what right he criticized his superior officers.

Lady Randolph, intriguing away on his behalf, found that it had suddenly become heavy going: even Lord Roberts, an old friend of Winston's father and under considerable obligation to him, refused to help Winston to get to the front, and Winston's powerful friend Lady St Helier[26] failed completely with the Adjutant General, Sir Evelyn Wood. The way seemed firmly barred. But at this black moment Winston had one of those extraordinary strokes of luck that make one think that some protective Providence was certainly watching over him. The Prime Minister, Lord Salisbury, having read and admired Winston's book on the Malakand Campaign, invited Winston to visit him at 10 Downing Street: 'The Great Man, Master of the British world . . . received me at the appointed hour and I entered for the first time that spacious room overlooking the Horse Guards Parade in which I was afterwards . . . to see much grave business done in Peace and War.' The interview was friendly, and ended with a formal remark by Lord Salisbury that if he could ever be of help to Winston the latter must call upon him. Thus

24. Admiral and Member of Parliament, and brother of Churchill's friend Lord William.
25. Winston S. Churchill, op. cit., p. 172.
26. Formerly Lady Jeune, and a woman of great influence in the political and military field.

encouraged, Winston, with incredible effrontery, wrote in due course to Lord Salisbury about his consuming desire to go to Egypt, and suggesting that the Prime Minister should telegraph to Lord Cromer, the political master of Egypt, saying that on personal grounds he wanted Winston to go, and that Cromer should inform Kitchener of this fact. Having succeeded in this bold manoeuvre, he then instructed Lady St Helier to tell Sir Evelyn Wood that the Prime Minister had now intervened on Winston's behalf, and that the Adjutant General should therefore redouble his own efforts.

Two days later Winston was informed by the War Office that he had been attached as a supernumerary lieutenant to the 21st Lancers for the Sudan Campaign. His intrigues in high places had brilliantly succeeded, and the wishes of the mighty Kitchener had been ignored by the War Office.

*   *   *

All he now needed was leave from the Indian Army authorities to take part in the Sudan Campaign. But he departed without waiting to hear whether this leave from his regiment had been granted. This was, of course, yet another insolent flaunting of military discipline, but this longed-for excursion was too vital for Winston for him to take any chances. He had already arranged to write despatches for the *Morning Post* for £15 a column.

He was too busy to write many letters home, and we can best follow his part in this campaign as a series of pictures and glimpses flashing out from many a golden phrase in his despatches, and in the book he later wrote – *The River War*. First to Cairo with its domes and minarets and feathery palm-trees against the sunset, its brief twilights, its disdainful camels, and the dark coming suddenly like a handclap; and all over the city a smell never to be forgotten, a clogging mixture compounded of urine, ordure and vegetable decay, the smell of Cairo. When he reported at the Abbasiye Barracks there was the bustle and excitement of an army preparing for war, and his own frantic haste and terror of missing the battle. Then followed the movement of the Regiment 1,400 miles into the heart of the continent – partly by train, and then by stern-wheeled steamers to Assouan. At Luxor on 5 August he was suddenly struck by the transformation of the scene from the London he had known such a short time before – the dinners and balls – and here the khaki everywhere, the lumbering barges full of horses, the muddy river, and beyond it the palm-trees and the sails of dahabiahs and feluccas.

Winston remained in buoyant spirits at the thought of the approaching adventure, and was entranced by the journey through a strange and ever-changing countryside. There was a freshness and a carefree atmosphere about their progress which made it altogether delightful. The early mornings were cool and stimulating; the journey full of incident. Sometimes they would have to land, and lead their horses round a cataract. Everyone was excited and gay and full of expectation; and Winston found his own pulses hurrying with strong emotions. One disturbing speculation haunted him – how the flouted Sirdar Kitchener had taken the news that his specific orders about Winston had been overridden by the War Office, and whether he was even now contemplating some odious revenge – ordering him to be sent back to the base, or to come on with the remounts after the battle. Winston flinched at every stop when the insignia of a staff officer became visible, and only when they had reached Wadi Halfa did he begin to feel safe. A fortnight after leaving Cairo they arrived at Atbara, the camp and railway base of the army, 'where the waters of the Atbara flow into the mighty Nile'.

And from there followed a nine-days' march up-river towards the Dervish capital Omdurman. After passing the Shabluka Cataract they became jumpy, expecting to see an enemy behind every thorn-bush. The heat was intense, even for this continent, and seemed focused upon them as through a burning glass. Their water bags were drained long before the afternoon had passed, and it was delicious in the evening when the ferocious sun had sunk 'to drink, and drink and drink again from the swift abundant Nile'. They could only cover eight to ten miles a day in the blistering heat on the final march, and as it continued without incident they came to believe that the Dervishes would not fight.

But suddenly on 1 September the enemy was sighted, looking like a long brown smear on the distant horizon. And then there came a meeting not without drama between Kitchener and Winston in the field, when Winston was sent to describe the disposition of the enemy to the Sirdar after studying it from the top of the black hill of Surgham – a meeting marked by Winston's slight uneasiness and Kitchener's monumental calm. Then came Winston's return to the zariba, and the orders to stand to arms at 2 p.m. Behind the palisade he attached himself in his casual way to Sir Reginald Wingate, Director of Intelligence, and other senior officers, and with them enjoyed a picnic luncheon of extraordinary gaiety, spread on biscuit boxes, which reminded him of some *fête champêtre* before the Derby. They ate bully beef, and a young naval officer called David Beatty later threw over a bottle of champagne from his gunboat on the Nile. There was to be no fighting that day, but on that following the enemy was brought to battle. The battle of Omdurman opened with appalling carnage in the ill-equipped Dervish army, after which the 21st Lancers were sent on a reconnaissance to discover what enemy forces still stood between Kitchener and the city, and, if possible, drive them away.

The four squadrons left the zariba, trotting in a southerly direction, and ascending the Surgham Hill once more saw the whole plain of Omdurman spread out beneath them, and the domes and minarets of the vast mud city. Trotting over the hard sand, they came suddenly under fire, and before they realized what was happening the reconnaissance had become a charge. Winston had foreseen and longed for such a moment, the apotheosis of his military life. Because of his dislocated shoulder he discarded his sword for a Mauser pistol. He sheathed the sword with some difficulty at the gallop, and drew the pistol. He was the right-hand troop leader but one. He was now in a world of swirling dust and savage blood-curdling shouts and screams. They charged a nullah full of Dervish spearmen in crescent formation: 'They all fell,' he wrote soon after the battle, 'knocked A.O.T. [arse over tip].'[27] One of his troopers also fell, and was immediately hacked to pieces. Winston pulled up to a trot and rode round firing his Mauser into contorted Dervish faces, killing: '3 for certain − 2 doubtful − one very doubtful.'

Then the Emirs reformed their ranks and an intense Dervish fire started. Winston, for a moment isolated, managed to rejoin his troop having emptied his pistol, but 'without a hair of my horse or a stitch of my clothing being touched'.[28] But for a fleeting moment, and for the first time in action, he had known fear − chilling and repellent: 'I felt myself absolutely alone. I thought these riflemen would hit me, and the rest devour me like wolves.' Now the Lancers moved off at a trot towards the flank of the enemy, and the Dervishes were forced to retreat, having inflicted on the Regiment in a few minutes losses of 5 officers and 65 men killed and wounded, and 120 horses − nearly a quarter of its strength.[29] Such were Winston's personal experiences on this occasion.

It is interesting to note that most of his romantic attitude survived this experience, as it had that other grim affray on the Indian frontier, in spite of the fact that at Omdurman the full horrors of war were again clearly brought before him. Describing the aftermath of the battle, he wrote:

27. Chartwell papers.
28. Ibid.
29. Winston S. Churchill, op. cit.

But now from the direction of the enemy there came a succession of grisly apparitions; horses spouting blood, struggling on three legs, ... men bleeding from terrible wounds, fish-hook spears stuck right through them, arms and faces cut to pieces, bowels protruding, men gasping, crying, collapsing, expiring.

Yet forty years later when describing the battle he would write, 'This kind of war was full of fascinating thrills', and that 'Death was a sporting element in a splendid game',[30] and of the charge in which he took part: 'The British fought with sword and lance as in the days of old.'[31] But in fairness we should remember his more immediate reflections contained in a letter to Lady Randolph written two days after the battle. One friend, Grenfell, had been killed; another, Dick Molyneux, wounded; and there were other such personal losses:

These things – and at the time they were reported as worse – made me anxious and worried during the night and I speculated on the shoddiness of war. You cannot gild it. The raw comes through. The metaphors are mixed but expressive.[32]

But at whatever cost, he had fulfilled his ambition, and he had pursued his aim with extraordinary canine persistence, not accepting the refusal even of the all-powerful Kitchener, impatiently brushing his hostility aside, and afterwards sharply rebuking him in print for desecrating the Mahdi's tomb. In spite of what he had seen and his words to his mother – in spite of the losses and horrors of battle – war continued to hold for Winston a powerful and glittering lure. It required the mechanized butchery of the Great War to dispel this illusion, and even that not completely.

* * *

Winston soon discovered what bad odour he was in with the authorities, and on 16 September wrote to his friend Ian Hamilton:

...I am in great disfavour with the authorities here. Kitchener was furious with Sir E. Wood for sending me out and expressed himself freely. My remarks on the treatment of the wounded – again disgraceful – were repeated to him and generally things have been a little unpleasant. He is a great general but he has yet to be accused of being a great gentleman.[33]

30. Winston S. Churchill, op. cit..
31. Ibid.
32. Chartwell papers.
33. Ibid.

And later, in the New Year, he wrote to his mother on the same subject:

> I shall merely say that the victory of Omdurman was disgraced by the inhuman slaughter of the wounded and that Kitchener was responsible for this.[34]

The battle over, the glory remained to be harvested. He would, of course, write a book about the Egyptian campaign. It was to be called *The River War*, and he began it at once on the ship that was taking him back to England, working on it deep into the stifling nights, affecting a bizarre combination of the sharp antithesis of Macaulay and the rolling sentences of Gibbon:– 'and I stuck in a bit of my own from time to time'. He was pleased with his progress, and was able to assure his mother later: 'The chapter describing the fall of Khartoum Gordon's death etc is I think quite the most lofty passage I have ever written'.[35] He felt that he had now really begun to grasp the business of putting a book together, although the reader will notice that he had yet to master the art of punctuation.

He was now convinced that he must leave the Army, relying on his pen (which had already proved far more remunerative than his commission) to support him. He therefore made his plans for the year 1899 – to return to India and win the Inter-Regimental Polo Cup, always a constant ambition; to send in his papers, and relieve his mother of paying an allowance; to finish the new book, and to keep his eyes open for a chance of entering Parliament. He was in the main to carry out this programme, keeping himself unaided for twenty years until in 1919 he inherited a valuable property from a long-dead great-grandmother.[36]

While in England he made three political speeches – at Rotherhithe, Dover and Southsea. These were successful, although at Dover his inability to think on his feet caused him to lose his train of thought, with an agonizing silence until he recovered it. He met the ablest young Conservative MPs, such intellectuals as Lord Hugh Cecil, Lord Percy and Lord Balcarres. Once again he was baffled by these men's power of dialectic. Their minds sharpened upon the University grindstone, they would put forward preposterous arguments which they defended with wayward logic and brilliant agility. Winston, when clearly in the right, was mortified that he could not dispute with them. He was so intellectually outgunned that he was made to appear clumsy and ridiculous, and

34. Ibid.
35. Ibid.
36. Frances Anne, Marchioness of Londonderry.

Churchill, aged 22, with the 4th Hussars in India, 1896. He later wrote that his main interest there was polo. *(Popperfoto)*

Boer and First World War

Churchill as a prisoner during the Boer War, when Foreign Correspondent for *The Morning Post*. He represented the paper for £250 a month. He was captured on 15 November 1899 and later wrote: 'I hated every moment of my captivity more than I have hated any other period of my whole life.' *(Popperfoto)*

Pictured in South Africa after he had escaped from Pretoria prison camp.
(*Topham Picture Library*)

An often-reproduced but interesting poster of Churchill with a price on his head.
(*Popperfoto*)

Churchill as an officer of the 11th Hussars, watching Army manoeuvres. 1910.
(Popperfoto)

Churchill watches the march-past of the 47th Division after they had liberated Lille in October 1918. His brother, Major John Churchill, is on the left. Behind him is his life-long Civil Service secretary, Eddie Marsh. *(Popperfoto)*

it was no consolation to be told that he was only being teased. Although he consoled himself by the reflection that these powers were a mere trick picked up in Oxford and Cambridge, he was so shaken by his exposure that he seriously thought of going to Oxford to forge similar weapons. But the need for Greek barred his way: 'I could not contemplate toiling at Greek irregular verbs after commanding British regular troops.'[37]

He was now more than ever consumed with the desire to be famous, and it was in this mood that he wrote to Pamela Plowden in November 1898, shortly before returning to India. It is a curious letter, and although he speaks of his love he does so in an offhand and almost jaunty manner, with no hint of passion, and it is obvious that he had not the slightest intention of committing himself. Ambition ruled the heart. 'This is a pushing age,' he tells his mother, adding rather superfluously: 'we must push with the best.'

He left for India in December 1898, again working on *The River War* on shipboard. He became friendly on this voyage with an outstanding newspaper correspondent, G. W. Stevens of the *Daily Mail*, who was a fellow-passenger. Stevens was at once amazed at Winston's originality, ambition and force of character. They discussed *The River War*, and Stevens, himself an accomplished writer, was able by tactful hints to tone down the baroque splendours of Winston's prose style, and convince him that restraint could also be effective. His ambitions were now crowding his mind to the exclusion of almost every other thought, and there is something touching and pathetic in his words to Lady Randolph in January 1899: 'What an awful thing it will be if I don't come off. It will break my heart for I have nothing else but ambition to cling to.'[38]

* * *

The Inter-Regimental polo tournament was to be held at Meerut, cradle of the Indian Mutiny. But first there was a fortnight's practice in the state of Jodhpur where they were guests of the renowned Sir Pertab Singh, who was the Regent of the state, a legendary figure whose twin deities were polo and war.

There were practice games where Sir Pertab pointed out their faults – frightening games, for the ground was quickly obscured by a thick cloud of red dust raised by the ponies' hooves, a miasma from which turbanned figures emerged at full gallop, and the ball whistled unseen past Winston's head. On their last night in Jodhpur disaster overtook Winston, who, slipping on some stone stairs, again dislocated his shoulder and sprained both ankles. Bitterly

37. Winston S. Churchill, op. cit., p. 215.
38. Chartwell Papers.

disappointed, he told the captain of the team that he must be left out, and the reserve player used in his place.

But after much discussion it was decided to play Winston, and he took the field with his right upper arm strapped to his side to keep his shoulder in place. It was his role as No. 1 'to engage in a ceaseless duel with the opposing back, who, turning and twisting his pony, always endevoured to put his opponent off-side'. It was thought that if Winston could thus occupy the opposing back and ride him out of the game he would not have to strike the ball too often, and so would spare his shoulder, and yet still serve his team usefully.

In spite of this severe handicap the 4th Hussars reached the Final of the tournament, where they met the 4th Dragoon Guards. Winston stuck to the opposing back like a terrier with a rat, and in the midst of a confused *mêlée* near the enemy goal he found the ball beside him, and was able to tap it feebly between the posts. This goal brought the score to two–all, and shortly after this the ball came towards him travelling fast, and he was again able to deflect through the goal. After a desperately close last period in which the 4th Hussars grimly held on to their lead, and Winston several times thought: 'Would God that night or Blücher would come', the bell sounded, and the Regiment had fulfilled a cherished ambition – to win the Inter-Regimental Tournament – a consummation for which they had been working for the last three years.

In March 1899, his polo glory won, Winston finally left India, and sent in his resignation from the Army on the way home. Kitchener's ADC Major Watson, on whom he relied for much important briefing for *The River War*, was forbidden by his chief to provide any help or information, so Winston stopped for a week in Cairo on his way home to collect material there, and to pick the brains of Lord Cromer, who for two and a half hours expounded to him the past history of the Sudan, and caused him to revise his first hero-worshipping impressions of General Gordon. He reached England at the end of April 1899, and his military life appeared to be over.

Chapter 3

The Boer War

I n June 1899, three months after leaving the Army, Winston decided
to press on with the career which had never been long absent from
his mind even in battle. He was invited to contest a by-election at
Oldham, a large working-class constituency in Lancashire. His fellow
Conservative aspirant was James Mawdsley, General Secretary of the
Amalgamated Association of Cotton Spinners; this honest son of toil
and Winston, the grandson of a duke, made a drolly incongruous
couple. It was as a Tory democrat ardent for the improvement of
the people that Winston put himself forward, and in order to curry
favour with the Chapel element – strong in the constituency – he held
forth with profound cynicism in his election address against 'lawlessness
in the Church', and inveighed ponderously against the ritualism being
introduced into it in some quarters.

As Winston had not the slightest interest in such matters, and only
had recourse to prayer at moments of extreme physical danger, there
was opportunism as well as naivety in his attitude. Lord Salisbury's
Government was saddled with the Clerical Tithes Bill, which had
been introduced by Arthur Balfour and was designed to help the
poor clergy of the Church of England. It was a measure greatly disliked
by Nonconformists everywhere, and in particular by the Methodists in
Oldham. Indeed, as the campaign progressed it seemed probable that
this unfortunate millstone would most adversely affect it, and Winston,
observing uneasily his supporters' hatred of the Bill, became deeply
anxious. A raw and inexperienced politician, he now made a serious
error. He decided to throw the Bill overboard, and undertook that it
would not have his support if he was returned to Parliament.

'As I was ignorant of the needs which had inspired it,' he wrote
later, 'and detached from the passions which it aroused, the temptation

to discard it was very great. I yielded to the temptation.'[1] It was an act both stupid and faintly disreputable which he was afterwards to recognize and regret. Winston was defeated at the poll, the swing to the Radicals being about 2 per cent, and this action caused the first blight on his reputation, like an early autumn frost. 'I thought he was a young man of promise,' observed Arthur Balfour coldly, 'but it appears that he is a young man of promises.' Winston's contrition was genuine but evanescent, and he admitted that he had made a serious *faux pas*: 'It is not the slightest use,' he said, 'defending Governments or parties unless you defend the very worst thing about which they are attacked.'

But he had got the taste of the political battle he had longed for, and its atmosphere – the entry into a teeming smoky hall to cheers and boos and a din as tumultuous as their clattering cotton machines, an uproar so long imagined which powerfully stirred his senses:

> It has been a strange experience and I shall never forget the succession of great halls packed with excited people until there was not room for one single person more – speech after speech, meeting after meeting – three even four in one night – intermittent flashes of Heat & Light & enthusiasm – with cold air and the rattle of a carriage in between: a great experience.[2]

Apart from politics, Winston was busy with the proofs of *The River War*. Free now from the restraints of military discipline, he strongly attacked Kitchener for desecrating the Mahdi's tomb and carrying off his head in a kerosene tin. As he was putting the finishing touches to this task, the South African War began, and, although he could not foresee it, this war, and the events which flowed from it were to make him a national figure.

*   *   *

The South African war, abhorrent to many English Radicals, was linked with the discovery of gold on the Witwatersrand in 1886, which attracted a horde of British speculators and pioneers whose arrival seemed a knell of doom to the Dutch (known as Boers) who had settled in South Africa two hundred years before, and later established two republics, the Transvaal and the Orange Free State. The Boer President Paul Kruger therefore used every effort to restrain the hungry visitors – who were known as Uitlanders – from acquiring the vote or settling permanently in the area, while some British leaders,

1. Winston S. Churchill, op. cit.
2. Winston Churchill to Pamela Plowden. Lytton papers.

particularly Milner and Chamberlain, were thought to be anxious to increase British power in the Transvaal, to build a railway from Cairo to the Cape, and bring the question to an issue. Milner was instructed to meet the Boer leaders at Bloemfontein, and press the Uitlanders' claims. The negotiations having broken down, further discussions also failed, producing an ultimatum from Kruger which in turn led to the outbreak of war in October 1899.

Winston, who had foreseen the approaching war, was as usual anxious to be at the front. He had arranged with his friend Oliver Borthwick of the *Morning Post* to represent that paper for £250 a month, a most favourable contract. As usual, he remembered his comforts, and his list of stores contained many bottles of whisky, claret and port. He sailed on the *Dunottar Castle* on 11 October. On board also was Sir Redvers Buller, the Commander-in-Chief of the British Army, with his staff. Always indifferent to exalted rank, Winston dismissed him as bovine and unimpressive, although civil enough in the few words they exchanged. It was a rough passage at first as the ship seethed through the night past Ushant, and Winston told Lady Randolph of his misery, but after Madeira it was calm and pleasant and hotter every day as they steamed due south, although he was tormented by the absence of news.

His quickly ripening friendship with one of the other journalists on board, J. B. Atkins of the *Manchester Guardian*, helped him to pass the time agreeably. Atkins at once recognized an arresting quality in his colleague, 'plunging along the deck "with neck outthrust", as Browning fancied Napoleon.' He listened to Winston's talk with sharpening admiration, noticing how he delighted in manipulating words and phrases in a manner which was at once arabesque and sensual:

> It was obvious that he was in love with words. He would hesitate sometimes before he chose one or would change one for the better . . . But when the prospects of a career like that of his father, Lord Randolph, excited him, then such a gleam shot from him that he was almost transfigured. I had not before encountered this sort of ambition, unabashed, frankly egotistical, communicating its excitement and extorting sympathy. He had acquired no reverence for his seniors as such, and talked to them as though they were of his own age or younger.[3]

On 29 October a homeward-bound vessel passed close to the ship and a blackboard was held up from it to say that there had been three battles and that the Boers had been defeated. This news,

3. J. B. Atkins, *Incidents and Reflections*, p. 122.

which seemed to suggest that the war would be over before they reached Cape Town, cast gloom over the whole ship's company. On 31 October the *Dunottar Castle* sighted that 'fairest cape in the world', but Buller and his staff decided to continue their slow and unhurried progress to Durban on the ship.

Winston and Atkins elected to disembark and to join their fortunes in an attempt to reach Durban before the Commander-in-Chief by a four-day journey by steamer and rail. 'We would go,' said Atkins, 'to the sound of the guns near Ladysmith,' where they believed that the heaviest fighting would take place. They caught a little mail steamer in which they had an excruciating passage, when Winston vomited his heart out, and on the Natal railway they found that the line had been cut some way short of their goal. They pitched their tent therefore in the railway yard of the small town of Estcourt where the news had reached them, and there, drinking wine from Winston's abundant stores and strolling in the sunshine, they waited on events.

Two familiar figures from the past suddenly re-entered Winston's life in this dim and improbable place. He saw first the squat, powerful figure of Leo Amery who, in some bygone existence, he had pushed into Ducker at Harrow, and then, when hanging about the street trying to pick up crumbs of information for his paper, suddenly saw that man of destiny in his life, Aylmer Haldane, inscrutable and sardonic, emerging from his office.

Haldane had been given temporary command of the Dublin Fusiliers. He now invited Winston to accompany him on an armoured train along ten miles of railway in the direction of Colenso to assist the cavalry in their reconnaissances. Winston for some strange reason was, according to Haldane, 'not at all keen' to go. Had he only known, this lumbering joke of a train, derided by the troops, thinly armoured and vulnerable to any cutting of the line, was to take him along a rail which led to fame and glory, and to enable him once again to display courage and resource in action.

* * *

The best and fullest account of this famous episode is that sent by Winston to the *Morning Post*, and afterwards embodied in *My Early Life*. There is also in existence Captain Haldane's report on the affair written in prison in Pretoria, and later sent to his Chief of Staff. Winston's account has remained unchallenged, and it would be superfluous here to describe the exploit in detail. Although Winston had not wished to go on this expedition, he told Atkins, who had refused to accompany him, 'But I have a feeling, a sort of intuition, that if I go something will come of it. It is illogical, I know.[4] Never was pure instinct more fully justified by events.

The armoured train travelled, slow, clanking and pathetically vulnerable, about fifteen miles along the line to Chieveley, when Haldane was told that the Boers were in the town, and that he was to retreat to Frere. As he did so the enemy suddenly opened up with artillery, one shell hitting the leading truck. The train was on a down-gradient at high speed, but three-quarters of a mile from Frere several leading trucks were derailed by a stone placed on the line by the enemy lying in ambush. Winston at once offered his services to Haldane in an attempt to get the train moving again, and: 'Knowing how thoroughly I could rely on him, I gladly accepted them and undertook to keep down the enemy's fire while he endeavoured to clear the line.'[5]

Haldane failed in this last intention. Under intense fire from rifles, Creusot and Maxim shells, Winston called for volunteers, and was heard to say: 'Keep cool, men.' He set to work to free the engine, and with what Haldane describes as 'indomitable perseverance', he continued his task. Seeming to bear a charmed life, he used the engine as a ram in an attempt to pull and push the two trucks clear of the line, moving continuously up and down the track or standing in the open for more than an hour, with bullets constantly smacking the trucks or screaming away in ricochet. The engine driver was wounded and badly frightened, and protested violently about the non-union conditions, but Winston, by a blend of threats and cajolery, brought him back to his duty: 'No man is hit twice on the same day,' he told the man, promising that he would be decorated. 'Buck up a bit,' he added, 'I will stick to you,' and throwing off his Mauser pistol and field glasses, helped the driver to pick up twenty wounded men and put them on the tender of the engine.

At last, after frenzied efforts, Winston and his party succeeded in freeing the engine: all the wounded were now in the cab, and Haldane gave orders that it should retreat out of range to Frere. 'The cab . . . was now crammed with wounded,' he said, 'who would have been scalded had a shell struck the boiler,' and the front of the engine was in flames. He withdrew his men from the now useless trucks, and made a sortie for a group of buildings 800 yards away from which he had hoped to offer further resistance, shouting, 'Now mind – no surrender!' Winston jumped out of the engine cab and ran back to join Haldane, but by that time the soldiers had waved white flags without authority, and the whole party were rounded up like cattle.

But Winston wriggled and twisted like a hare before the enemy

4. J. B. Atkins, op. cit., p. 128.
5. Captain Haldane's despatch to Chief of Staff, Natal Field Force.

caught him. Suddenly seeing two figures in plain clothes on the line, and realizing that they were Boers, he ran back in the direction of the engine with the men firing their rifles at him. Still unhit, he crawled up the bank of the railway cutting and tried to reach the Blue Krantz river where there was cover, but was cut off by a horseman galloping towards him, rifle in hand. Winston was unarmed, having left his pistol during the train fracas, and it was only then that he surrendered. It was 15 November 1899. Winston was soon to convince himself that his Boer captor was General Botha. It was a dramatic story, a *dénouement* of the sort he loved, but it was almost certainly mistaken, although Botha may well have played some part in his capture.

* * *

Winston's part in this episode was a justly renowned example of heroism generously acknowledged in the despatch written by Haldane from his prison cell in Pretoria, although his own heart was heavy with captivity:

> I would point out that while engaged on the work of saving the engine, for which he was mainly responsible, he was frequently exposed to the whole fire of the enemy. I cannot speak too highly of his gallant conduct.[6]

But perhaps the most convincing tribute came from a private soldier in the Durham Light Infantry, who was at Winston's side throughout the battle, writing to his sister:

> Thanks to young Churchill . . . who was with us as correspondent for some paper, we managed to get the engine clear after about an hour. Churchill is a splendid fellow. He walked about in it all as coolly as if nothing was going on, & called for volunteers to give him a hand to get the truck out of the road. His presence and way of going on was as much good as 50 men would have been. After the engine got clear he came about 1/2 mile on it and then coolly set off & walked back to help the others.'[7]

There are two examples chosen from several accounts of Winston's courage and leadership. Equally remarkable had been his intelligence when addressing his mind under murderous fire to the technical difficulty of freeing the engine. This was a problem quite outside his experience: he was not by nature a practical man; yet he had shown, under extreme pressure, almost the resource of an engineer or a mechanic in coping with this novel and unexpected demand. All the

6. Randolph S. Churchill, *Winston Churchill*, Vol. I, p. 472–4.
7. Captain Aylmer Haldane's despatch to the Chief of Staff, Natal Field Force.

officers in Estcourt, when the news reached them, were convinced that Winston and the engine-driver would be given the Victoria Cross.

And yet how characteristic it was of this single-minded, inflexible youth that immediately after capture, with the din of this desperate affair still ringing in his ears, his first thoughts should have been, not of his own achievement, but of the effect it would have on his political career. As he and Haldane trudged wearily under guard over the sodden veldt Winston remarked that in the train battle he had been constantly in the limelight, and that the event could not fail to help in opening the door for him to enter the House of Commons.[8]

But there can be no doubt that Winston also thought that he deserved a decoration for his part in this affair, for he wrote, when a Member of Parliament, to Joseph Chamberlain in 1901, saying that some railwaymen and Durham Light Infantrymen had sent testimonials of his action to the authorities, and that the officer in charge had also commended him, but that the despatch had not been thought important enough to publish. He asked Chamberlain to see that the papers sent by the soldiers and railwaymen and the officer's despatch were forwarded to the War Office with the object of gaining him a decoration:

> As it is I suspect that the authorities think the whole thing merely a piece of journalistic humbug, which it was not. Of course in common with all other Members of Parliament, I care nothing for the glittering baubles of honours for *my own* sake, but I have like others – as you know – to 'think of my constituents', and perhaps I ought also to consider the feelings of my possible wife.[9]

* * *

On arrival in the Boer capital Pretoria, officer prisoners were confined in the State Model School, and other ranks in a camp on a nearby racecourse. From the outset Winston pined in confinement like a wild animal in a cage. 'Certainly,' he said, 'I hated every minute of my captivity more than I have hated any other period of my whole life.' The mere fact of restraint was abhorrent to him – the grey, dreary prison, the agony of being excluded from great events, cooped up with uncongenial men, one of a flock of sheep ready to follow the bell-wether down any path. At first he sought release by claiming, as a journalist, to be a non-combatant, but his role on the armoured car made this claim impudently absurd. It was rejected by the Boer authorities after a long correspondence, and he immediately

8. Chartwell papers.
9. Aylmer Haldane, *A Soldier's Saga*, p. 147.

turned his mind to escape. The State Model School at this time held 60 officers, and the buildings were placed in a quadrangle surrounded on two sides by a high wire fence, and on the others by an iron grille. He soon found that Haldane was working out a plan of escape with a Sergeant Brockie of the Imperial Light Horse, who had passed himself off as an officer, and was fluent in Afrikaans and Taal, a debased form of Dutch which was the local language.

Winston at once tried to attach himself to this party, but found Haldane strangely reluctant. He argued that Winston was such a prominent figure that his absence would be immediately noticed and would jeopardize the escape. He also thought (although he did not say so), that Winston was far too excitable and voluble to be safe; that he had already drawn unwelcome attention to himself by loud arguments about who was responsible for the war,[10] and by stalking up and down the yard in Napoleonic parody. He believed also that Winston, who never joined in camp games, took too little exercise to be fit enough for escape, and knew that he would be hampered by his weak shoulder. But when Winston wanted something sufficiently he was inexorable in argument and persuasion, and not over-scrupulous in method. He did not hesitate to remind Haldane that he could have escaped on the armoured train; of all that Haldane owed him for his conduct on that occasion, and of how grateful he had professed himself. He drove Haldane into reluctant agreement in which Brockie, who did not trust Winston, was sullenly forced to join.

The plan was to escape from the 'round house', a circular latrine in the backyard of the prison chosen because the electric light did not shine directly upon it. They would wait until the sentry outside had turned his back – or turned aside, as he often did, to talk to another guard. An abortive attempt was made on 11 December, but the sentry did not budge, and they returned to their quarters. Haldane and Winston again went to the latrine on the following night. The day had been an anxious one for Haldane, who was disturbed by Winston's over-excited state, and by the fact that he was again indulging in his Napoleonic stalking in the yard, head sunk in his shoulders, hands clasped behind his back, every line of his body seeming to proclaim the coming adventure.

Inside the latrine they waited in extreme tension, every nerve screwed to the topmost peg, for a chance to get over the wall, but again the sentry did not move. Again they left, passing Brockie – who accused them of being scared before entering the latrine himself to make his attempt. But he too was no luckier with the sentry, and was also forced to return. Winston then said to Haldane, 'I am going over again, don't follow

10. Joseph Chamberlain papers, Birmingham University, 4.5.01.

immediately,' and this time he saw the sentry turn aside to light his pipe.

It was the moment he had been awaiting, and without delay he jumped on to the ledge of the wall and dropped silently into the garden below, where he crouched in some grass bushes waiting for the others to join him. His position was dangerous in the extreme, as he had little cover, and people were constantly passing to and fro. He waited according to his own account, for one and a half hours for the others to join him.

After the first quarter of an hour Winston had managed to attract the attention of an officer using the latrine for a natural purpose, and whisper to him a message for Haldane that he had succeeded in getting out, and that Haldane should now join him as soon as possible. Haldane then tried to do so, but was sent back at the point of the sentry's rifle, and realized that there was no further chance of escape that night. After a long (and for Winston agonizing) wait, Haldane returned to the latrine and established contact with him by tapping. He whispered that he and Brockie had been stopped, but, according to Winston, agreed that it was impossible for the latter to climb back over the high wall, and that he must go alone. He wished him good luck.[11]

* * *

There was clearly a misunderstanding here, for Haldane wrote that he was 'bitterly disappointed' to find that Winston had gone, and added: 'I resist the temptation of stating what Brockie said on the subject.[12] Haldane was to return to this grievance in his *Diaries*, published in 1924. But Winston was for the rest of his life passionately convinced that he had acted throughout in a completely honourable manner. It will be necessary to return to this question in due course.

Meanwhile Winston was faced with the appalling problem of covering 300 miles of wild and hostile country to the frontier with Portuguese territory, without map or compass, speaking no relevant language, and with every man's hand against him. He had £75 in his pocket. 'But I felt I would have a run for my money and see how far I could get.' All he knew was that there was a train to Delagoa Bay in Portuguese East Africa each night. He felt that it offered his only, if desperate, chance. Having waited in the garden for an hour and a half, he walked out of the gate into the road, passing in a heart-stopping moment another sentry who stood in the roadway at a distance of two or three yards. The scene was illuminated not only by the camp electricity but also by a brilliant and baleful moonlight. He dared not look behind him, and restrained an

11. Aylmer Haldane, op. cit., p. 153.
12. Ibid, p. 156.

overwhelming impulse to break into a run. Humming a tune to himself, he walked through the streets of Pretoria to the outskirts of the city. The streets were full of burghers, but he was in a civilian suit, and they paid no attention to him. Haldane had observed his intense excitement at the moment of escape: he was still highly stimulated but not frightened, for he now regarded recapture as certain.

His prospects indeed appeared hopeless. There was a long and dangerous journey ahead. His escape would be discovered at dawn: the hue and cry would then start, and he would be hunted like an animal.[13] All the exits seemed barred. He knew that the country was patrolled, the trains searched, and the line guarded. He had only four slabs of chocolate and, ignorant of the language, could not without extreme hazard buy food. He decided to abandon the plan he had formed with Haldane of walking the whole way, and decided that he must find the railway. Without a compass he turned to the stars. 'Orion shone brightly. Scarcely a year before he had guided me when lost in the desert to the banks of the Nile. He had given me water. Now he should lead me to freedom.'[14]

After walking south for half an hour he struck a railway line. Ignorant of whether or not it led to Delagoa Bay, he saw no choice but to follow it. It was a warm and velvety evening with a million stars. 'The night was delicious. A cool breeze fanned my face, and a wild feeling of exhilaration took hold of me.' He walked briskly along the line, making detours round Boer picket forces, until after two hours he reached a station, and beyond it crawled into a ditch to await a train. He argued that it would stop at the station, and then move on slowly enough to make boarding it possible. At last he heard the sound of an approaching goods train which stopped at the station with much clanking of couplings and a hiss of steam. As it started again Winston waited until the engine had passed, hurled himself upon a truck, and after an agonizing struggle managed to remain crouching on the couplings between two wagons. Then he crawled up into one of them, and burrowed into the sacks of coal inside.

The incredible fortune that had so far preserved him continued, until once again one finds nothing fanciful in the thought that some divine providence shielded this man. He dropped off the train just before dawn, quenched a raging thirst at a stream, and after walking for a few hours, sheltered from the blistering heat in a grove of trees. The only living thing near him seemed a portent of doom – a huge vulture which

13. Winston Churchill himself is the only evidence for the next part of the escape. See 'London to Ladysmith', *Strand Magazine*, December 1923, and *My Early Life*.
14. Winston S. Churchill, op. cit., p. 286.

seemed to be waiting with sinister expectancy, and from time to time made ominous gurgling noises.

He waited until nightfall, then returned to the line in the hope of boarding another train. But after six leaden hours this hope died, and, all exhilaration and euphoria now spent, and replaced by something approaching despair, he began to plod wearily along the line, forced to make wider and wider detours to avoid detection, crawling on his belly, falling into swamps, in immediate danger from the bright moonlight illuminating every detail on the veldt. Now he tasted to the full the terrors of loneliness – on the run at night in a hostile country with every man's hand against him. His will-power began to sag, but he was spurred on by the unendurable prospect of a long imprisonment.

At last he saw lights in the far distance which, he imagined, were Kaffir fires. Vaguely registering in his exhausted mind that the Kaffirs hated the Boers, and might therefore help him, he trudged on towards them. After hours of slow, numbing progress, he recognized from the winding gear that he was approaching a coal-mine. He knew that there were English living in the mining areas of Witbank and Middelburg. Now near the end of his tether, he took a desperate risk, and knocked on the door of a house. It was opened by a tall man with a moustache who received his bedraggled caller with hostility: 'I saw before me,' wrote the stranger later, 'a man below medium height and dripping water from the waist. His hair was red, his eyes blue, and his face inclined to be freckled.'

The man covered Winston with a revolver, and listened with stony scepticism to his story that he was a burgher who had fallen off a train and lost his way in the dark. The householder, who thought that Winston was a Boer spy, still kept him covered as he sat slumped in a chair, and told him sternly to speak the truth. With a feeling of final defeat and exposure he muttered, 'I am Winston Churchill.'

* * *

His host put aside his revolver and said unexpectedly, 'Thank God you have come here. It is the only house for twenty miles where you would not have been handed over.' He proved to be John Howard, manager of the Transvaal and Delagoa Bay Collieries at Witbank. Living with him was another official, a Mr Dewsnap, who by some strange freak of chance came from Oldham. He gave Winston a crushing handshake and whispered, 'They'll all vote for you next time.' As Howard could not trust his servants, Winston was hidden in the deepest recesses of the mine, where he became aware of swarms of white rats with pink eyes. Unlike most men, they caused him no repugnance, and he even grew fond of these sinister companions, writing later, 'They seemed rather nice little beasts.'

Winston remained under Howard's care for three days until the hue and cry began to die away, for the Boers made an intensive search of the area. He was then allowed a brief walk in the moonlight, and was moved from the mine and the rats to the back room of the manager's office. Howard – now as deeply involved in the escape as Winston himself – arranged for him to be put on a train to Delagoa Bay hiding under bales of wool belonging to a Dutch friend of Howard well disposed to the English. The mine was connected with the railway by a branch line, and the wool bales would be loaded at the mine's siding. A hiding-place would be made for Winston in the heart of the bales.

He found that agreeing to this suggestion was the most harrowing decision of his entire escape. Fortune until this moment had lavished her favours upon him, and liberty was now so close that the mere thought of failure at this stage was to Winston insupportable. He had to brace himself strongly to express agreement.

At 2 a.m. on 19 December Winston was taken out to the yard and concealed among the bales. He was given a pistol, two roast chickens, cold meat and cold tea. He had memorized the names of the stations, and through a chink in the wooden truck could see their names as the train lumbered east across the Transvaal. There were long and frightening halts while the train lingered at sidings. A particularly terrifying delay took place at the dreaded frontier town Komati Poort, only a few hundred yards from the border, where a search was probable. Through his chink he could see people moving about, and hear shouting and whistling. He tunnelled deep into the centre of the bales, covered himself with a sack, and lay waiting with a thumping heart. At last the train started again, and at the next station, peering through the chink, he saw Portuguese soldiers and read the name Resana Garcia. As the train left this place Winston was so transported with joy and relief that he thrust his head through the tarpaulin cover of the truck, crowing and shouting like a maniac, and even firing his pistol into the air as a *feu de joie*.

It had been an even closer call than Winston knew. Charles Burnham, the Witbank storekeeper who was privy to the plan, and had accompanied the train, had moments of acute anxiety. He had prevented Winston's truck being shunted into a siding at Middleburg by tipping and standing drinks to a porter; had bribed the guard and a shunter with a bottle of whisky to prevent the same disaster at Waterval-Onder. At Komati Poort this invaluable ally had arranged with his friend, the chief detective at the station, that although the rest of the train was searched the wool was to continue on its journey without interruption.

In the late afternoon the train reached Lourenço Marques: here Winston slipped out of his truck and mingled with the crowd. He made his way to the British Consulate, where he heard of the Black Week through which the British Army had passed during the nine days of his escape – disasters at Magersfontein, Colenso and Stormberg – more shattering than any since the Crimean War. The Consul was anxious for Winston to leave the town, which was full of Boer sympathizers, and he sailed for Durban in the weekly steamer that evening.

On arrival there he realized, with a sense of intoxication, that like Byron he had woken up famous. 'I was a popular hero,' he said, 'and was received as though I had won a great victory.' The town was in a state of wild carnival, and the harbour a forest of welcoming flags. After the grim and humiliating reverses of Black Week, Winston's escape was a tonic, a thrilling adventure that lifted men's hearts with new hope. The people went wild with joy, and he was nearly torn to pieces as he was carried on the shoulders of the crowd to the steps of the Town Hall where, after a spurious display of reluctance, he was induced to make a speech. The headlines of the world press trumpeted the news of his escape: telegrams poured in from every quarter. He was not only a national but a world figure.

He left by train that afternoon for Pietermaritzburg, and thence to Sir Redvers Buller's headquarters at Chieveley. Buller wrote to Lady Londonderry in a manner subtly revealing of his own limitations: 'He really is a fine fellow, and I must say I admire him greatly. I wish he was leading regular troops instead of writing for a rotten paper.'[15]

* * *

Haldane and Brockie also escaped in due course, but their adventures passed almost unnoticed. Haldane's friends indeed maintained that he never forgave Winston for escaping alone, when they had agreed to leave as a party of three or not at all. Winston on the other hand remained for the rest of his life acutely sensitive to suggestions that he had in any way behaved dishonourably during the escape; that he had taken an unfair advantage over his companions, or broken his parole.

The last charge, of breaking his parole, is patently absurd, for there was no parole system in operation in the camp, all prisoners being held under guard together. As to the rest, Winston wrote with convincing sincerity:

> My conscience is absolutely clear on the whole episode; I acted with perfect comradeship and honour the whole way through . . . After our attempt on the 11th we were all fully resolved that we must at all costs get over the night of the 12th. There was no more agreement or bargain

15. Chartwell papers.

or stipulation, as to who should go first, or how we should go than there is among a dozen people in the hunting field who are waiting to take their turn at an awkward gap. When I had got over I waited for an hour and a half at imminent risk of recapture, for the others to come, and the fact that they were not able to come seemed to me and seemed to them to deprive me of all reasonable chance of escape. In these circumstances it is monstrous that any misunderstanding, however honest, for which I am not in the slightest degree responsible, should be allowed to serve as a basis for the abominable charges and slanders of which I have been repeatedly the object.[16]

Haldane, as we have seen, greatly admired Winston's courage and ability, but in this matter he undoubtedly felt a sense of grievance, although he did not fully express it at the time, and only disclosed its true nature in his *Diaries* written in 1924. Since this work was not published, it is necessary to quote the relevant passages from it to gain a fair impression of the nature of Haldane's complaint.

When he approached me on this subject [joining the escape], I did not hide from him how greatly, in my opinion, his presence with us would add to the risk of capture ... The absence of Churchill, who was regarded by the Boers as a valuable hostage, was certain to be noticed within twelve hours, a limit of time which would not allow a sufficient interval to elapse in order to give us a chance of reaching the Portuguese frontier ...

I feared that my talkative friend would by his presence compromise the prospects of success. However, Churchill had done gallant work at the time of the armoured train mishap ... and I was loth to seem ungenerous as would be the case if I went off without him ...But I made it clear to him that I was the leader in the plan of escape and that he would be expected to conform to orders ... It never crossed my mind that he did not clearly grasp what his share was to be ... That he and I were to go *together* was a clear and definitely explained arrangement.

Of the night of 12 December, when Brockie accused Haldane and Winston of being afraid, Haldane wrote:

Churchill said to me: 'I am going over again, don't follow me immediately,' thus proving once more that he understood that we were to go in company. Not grasping what he had in his mind I waited ... Meanwhile Churchill had disappeared into the latrine,

16. Winston S. Churchill, Memorandum of 1912 on his escape. Chartwell papers.

and as neither Brockie nor I for a moment imagined that he would attempt to go while I was not with him, we went into the dining room, intending after a hurried meal to try again ... I must admit that I was surprised and disgusted to find myself left in the lurch, for Churchill had walked off with my carefully thought-out plan or what he knew of it, and had simply taken the bread out of my mouth. Brockie, I need hardly say, was furious ... It requires no effort of memory at this distance of time to recall his sneering reference to 'your trusted friend – a nice kind of gentleman!' ... Nor was he alone in his abuse of the escaped war-correspondent, for many, indeed most, of our fellow-prisoners, some of whom had pressed me to let them share in the enterprise and who now began to realize the far greater difficulties of evasion in the future, joined in the chorus of vituperation that arose and continued for some days ... Had Churchill only possessed the moral courage to admit that in the excitement of the moment, he saw a chance of escape and could not resist the temptation to take advantage of it, not realizing that it would compromise the escape of his companions, all would have been well ...

I can honestly say that I feel nothing but regret that a man of such splendid ability and brilliant parts, whom I once regarded as my friend, but whom, since the events recorded, I have never felt I could really trust, should have allowed himself to commit an action followed by prevarication, which I firmly believe in his innermost soul he has bitterly regretted ever since.'[17]

These extracts convey fairly and fully the burden of Haldane's grievance. The matter had clearly festered in his mind through the years, but his charges can scarcely be justified. It is possible that Winston did not fully grasp the inflexibility of Haldane's resolve that the escape must be made as a group of three or not at all. Even so, when he went back to the latrine on 12 December he told Haldane that he was going to make another attempt, and asked him not to follow too quickly. In the belief that Haldane would join him, he waited in the garden – at great personal risk – for more than an hour. Haldane had later tried to follow him, but was seen by the sentry and sent back at the point of the rifle. At the worst, this must have been a misunderstanding on Haldane's part. When Winston said to him, 'I am going over again', Haldane said that he did not grasp what Winston had in mind. Why not? It was surely obvious that he was announcing a second attempt to escape, and telling Haldane not to follow too quickly, in order to lessen the risk of detection. What else could Haldane have imagined Winston meant by the words: 'I am going over again; don't follow immediately'?

17. Aylmer Haldane's Diary. Haldane papers. Copy in Chartwell papers.

No doubt Winston was, as Haldane said, in a state of high excitement, but once he had broken out, and waited so long in vain in the garden, it was clearly ridiculous to expect him to crawl humbly back, even if it had been possible for him to scale the twelve-foot wall, which, with his injured shoulder, was a task completely beyond his power. Winston remained convinced that he had acted in every respect as a man of honour, and his belief was well founded. He was later to justify this conviction in four successful libel actions. In one of these, against *Blackwood's Magazine*, Haldane refused to testify on his behalf.

*   *   *

On 6 January Sir Redvers Buller arranged a lieutenancy for Winston in the South African Light Horse – 'The Cockyolly birds', as he called them in reference to their plumed hats – while allowing him to remain a war correspondent. This is at first sight puzzling, because it was his duplication of those roles at Omdurman which had caused it to be ruled that the two functions could not again be combined. Probably the arrangement was made possible by the fact that the commission was unpaid.[18] Winston was also able to arrange a commission for his brother Jack in the same Regiment, although deeply distressed that he was quickly wounded and put out of action.

He remained in South Africa for a further six months, but although he had stirring adventures, it was somehow an anticlimax after the drama of his escape. But he found the life one of glowing physical pleasure – soft little whistles an hour before dawn, stamping from the horse lines, breakfast in the dark and the smell of sizzling bacon, the loaded wagons and the saddling up; the long marches across open savannahs where a bugle-call could be heard for miles; the endless veldt, the stubborn kopjes, and here and there a wrecked bridge and the débris of war: and then the off-saddling and the horses turned out to graze.

He passed ungrazed through the shambles of Spion Kop – 'the strangest and most terrible scenes I have ever witnessed'[19] – while Jack lay wounded beside him; rode with the advance forces into starving and long-beleaguered Ladysmith, a moment of extreme exhilaration, and in June, after the capitulation of Pretoria, entered the town with his cousin Sunny Marlborough, and, with the memory of his own captivity vivid in his mind, threw open the prisoner-of-war camp to its almost hysterical inmates.

18. Chartwell papers.
19. Ibid.

After the relief of Ladysmith, Winston wrote to Joseph Chamberlain saying that he hoped that the nation would not complain of this entanglement: '. . . for it makes a fine page in English history'. He told Chamberlain that he expected a further long and hard campaign before the end:

> I earnestly hope that the resolve of the country will not weaken, but I fear that they will regard a new series of misfortunes, such as may easily come to us, as an anticlimax. However, we all have entire confidence in Lord Roberts. If he cannot carry this war to a prosperous issue, no one else in the British Empire will succeed. I hear that he has had occasion to put Lord Kitchener in his place several times and there is no doubt here as to who commands the army and whose brain directs its movements.'[20]

It was now time to go, his laurels unwithered. Lord Roberts had arrived as Commander in Chief, with Kitchener as his Chief of Staff. The war appeared to be over. The Conservative Government had decided that the moment was ripe to hold a General Election, and Winston knew that he must return to try his fortune at Oldham. He sailed for home on 4 July 1900 in the *Dunottar Castle*, the ship in which he had met the taciturn Buller in what now seemed some bygone age. As usual he 'carried his office with him', finishing *Ian Hamilton's March*, which appeared in October. *Savrola* had been published in February 1900.

His mother was not at Southampton to meet him when his ship docked on 20 July. She was busy with preparations for her marriage to Captain George Cornwallis-West – surely one of the most sanguine unions ever solemnized. The bridegroom was twenty years younger than Lady Randolph – indeed, almost exactly the same age as Winston – and the most handsome man in London. He had few thoughts in his head beyond creating havoc in the animal and feathered worlds, to an extent remarkable even in his day and age. His letters to Lady Randolph (singularly devoid of passion) were diligent and humourless chronicles of well-shot woodcock, partridge, snipe, and cunningly lured salmon and trout, and so absorbed was he in the technique of destruction that he found little time to mention anything else.

He was charming but absurd, and his union with this brilliant, forceful woman seemed to augur ill for the future. This doomed young man was impoverished after paying Lady Randolph's debts – pressing as always – and the marriage lasted for only thirteen uneasy years before he sought solace in the arms of Mrs Patrick Campbell. The strangely assorted couple were now to make a journey round the world,

20. Chamberlain papers. [Birmingham University] 7.4.1900.

and her house in Great Cumberland Place was let. Sunny Marlborough, therefore, with his usual generosity offered to Winston the unexpired part of the lease of his rooms at 105 Mount Street, and he was to remain there in comfort and happiness until 1906.

Chapter 4

The Young Tribune

We have seen how Winston, while still in Africa, sent a despatch to the *Morning Post* drawing attention to the need for more irregular corps of cavalry to emulate the Boers at their own game and inquiring: 'Are the gentlemen of England all fox-hunting?' This incautious phrase gave a chilling advance notice of the attitude to be expected from him, and a foretaste of the profound odium in which he would soon be held.

By the time Pretoria had fallen (5 June 1900) most people in England thought, erroneously, that the war was over, and it was at this point that it seemed to Winston that the Government made a serious mistake. There was to be no negotiation with the Boer Republics: they were to surrender, or be blotted out. It was an error of the most expensive kind, for there were still in the country thousands of brave and desperate men prepared to fight guerrilla actions for years, and leaders of the highest calibre to command them – Botha, Smuts, De Wet, Hertzog, and others who had already proved themselves born leaders in the field.

The nature of the struggle also changed for the worse. The wandering partisan soldiers no longer wore uniforms, and mingled with the civil population, who even when they had taken the oath of neutrality sheltered the guerrillas in their farms, from which they emerged to attack isolated British detachments. To prevent this the British military authorities were forced to depopulate whole districts and confine their populations in concentration camps. The railways were continually being cut, and it was impossible to keep the camps fully supplied. Sometimes owing to these circumstances, sometimes due to incompetence, disease broke out in them and resulted in the death of several thousand women and children. The farms of oath-breaking owners were burned, but the result was not to subdue the Boers but only to make them more desperate. Winston watched this process of both

105

sides inflicting 'frightful reciprocal injuries' with profound misgiving, but in the meantime the 'Khaki Election' was held in September, and he returned to England to pursue his dream.

* * *

It was a different and more rapturous Oldham than the place where he had failed before that now received him with a Roman triumph. The town was in fiesta. It was like that intoxicating moment at Durban again – flags and banners stiff and rattling in the grey streets – and shouts of welcome that were nectar in his mouth. Only then did he fully grasp the fame his escape had won him. And at a great meeting in the Theatre Royal he told the full story. When he mentioned the name of Dewsnap, the Oldham engineer who had wound him down the mine, the audience shouted, 'His wife's in the gallery', and wild jubilation followed.

Winston fought the election mainly on the issue of the Boer War, arguing that it was just and necessary, that the Liberals had been wrong to oppose it, and that it must be fought to a finish. His opponents, Mr Emmott and Mr Runciman, supported the country in the war, but alleged gross incompetence in its prosecution. His fellow Conservative candidate was a quiet and unassuming man called Crisp. Joseph Chamberlain himself came to speak for Winston – a significant event, as it was the only speech delivered by him in the whole campaign outside his own 'Midland District' kingdom. They drove to a great meeting together in an open carriage to the boos and groans of an immense hostile crowd:

> I watched my honoured guest with close attention. He loved the roar of the multitude, and with my father could always say: 'I have never feared the English democracy.' The blood mantled in his cheek, and his eye as it caught mine twinkled with pure enjoyment.[1]

'The Oldham election was fought at concert-pitch and spotlit from start to finish', and there were ominous signs that Winston had already made many enemies. Dirty accusations reflecting on his honour were freely made and passionately refuted. It was said that he had been driven from the Army in disgrace; that he had gone to war as a correspondent because he was too cowardly to do so as a soldier; and that had he not resigned he would have been cashiered. No one hit harder than this young man, and few were more insensitive to the feelings of others, but no one was more deeply wounded or mortified by slanders than he, or recoiled from them with more outraged resentment. The election became

1. Winston S. Churchill, op. cit., p. 373.

more violent and personal as its climax approached. The tone was set by Chamberlain with the slogan: 'Every seat lost to the Government is a seat gained to the Boers', and most Conservatives loped without protest in the wake of his caravan. Liberals, even those who had supported the war, or lost sons in it, found themselves stigmatized as 'Pro-Boers', and an unlovely chauvinism poisoned the atmosphere.

When the votes were counted it was seen that the Liberals and Labour were the stronger party in the constituency: the poll was held by Mr Emmott, while Winston ousted Runciman from second place, being elected by the small margin of 230 votes, a number of Liberals who voted for Runciman having given him their second vote from good will for a brilliant young man, or admiration of his war record:

> I walked with my friends through the tumult to the Conservative Club. There I found already awaiting me the glowing congratulations of Lord Salisbury. The old Prime Minister must have been listening at the telephone, or very near it, for the result. Then from every part of the country flowed in a stream of joyous and laudatory messages. Henceforward I became a 'star turn' at the election.[2] I was sought for from every part of the country.[3]

He spoke in Manchester for Arthur Balfour, and the great audience rose and shouted at his entry, and after this:

> I never addressed any but the greatest meetings ... For three weeks I had what seemed to me a triumphal progress through the country. The party managers selected the critical seats, and quite a lot of victories followed in my train. I was twenty-six. Was it wonderful that I should have thought I had arrived? But luckily life is not so easy as all that: otherwise we should get to the end too quickly.[4]

This was the consummation. All the dreams of India, as he read Gibbon in his sweltering tent, all the strivings at desperate moments of action, had been preparations for this moment of achievement. Cheers and boos, multitudes hostile or adoring, carriage drives between meetings – those were his confused memories of his triumph. Boos there had been in plenty, for from the first Winston used violent and provocative language towards the party he was soon to join, and uttered words difficult to forgive and forget:

2. At that time polling was spread over six weeks. Churchill's result was one of the first.
3. Winston S. Churchill, op. cit., p. 374.
4. Ibid, p. 375.

The Liberal Party, he said, was 'hiding from the public view like a toad in a hole, but when it stands forth in all its hideousness the Tories will have to hew the filthy object limb from limb'.

This sort of language was, of course, designed solely to draw attention to himself, and the personal and political animosities it aroused were to haunt him mercilessly for years, and to obliterate him temporarily in 1915 – a fact difficult to fathom now, for the abuse seems so boyish and naive today as to be completely devoid of offence.

* * *

After this success, and before taking his seat, Winston took stock of his financial position and decided that he must increase his working capital. He therefore embarked on lecture tours in Great Britain, Canada and the United States. And how characteristic was his choice of chairman of the British venture! '*De l'audace*,' said Danton, '*toujours de l'audace*,' and Winston too, as always, was content only with the highest: the Commander-in-Chief of the Army, Lord Wolseley, for London; Lord Rosebery for Edinburgh; Joseph Chamberlain for Birmingham; in each town a chairman of national renown.

His tour of the United Kingdom was the most lucrative of the three ventures, netting £3,782 15*s.* 5*d.*; that in America the most exhausting. But it was memorable for the chairing of his meeting in New York by Mark Twain. The creator of Huckleberry Finn introduced Winston in a speech which might be regarded as a model of the chairman's art:

> I think that England sinned when she got herself into a war with South Africa which she could have avoided, just as we have sinned by getting into a similar war in the Philippines. Mr Churchill by his father is an Englishman, by his mother he is an American; we are kin. And now that we are also kin in sin there is nothing more to be desired. The harmony is perfect – like Mr Churchill himself, whom I now have the honour to present to you.[5]

During the last lectures of his tour, in Winnipeg, he heard of the death of Queen Victoria. Then as later, he cherished a romantic view of the monarchy which held for him a compelling mystique. He was now intensely curious to know how the new King would measure up to his responsibilities. Winston had always in his published work referred to the Prince of Wales with an awe and reverence he considered suitable to the heir to the Throne. In a letter from Winnipeg to his mother, in January 1901, he struck a somewhat different note:

5. Chartwell papers.

... So the Queen is dead. The news reached us at Winnipeg and this city far away among the snows — fourteen hundred miles from any British town of importance — began to hang its head and hoist half-masted flags. A great and solemn event: but I am curious to know about the King. Will it entirely revolutionise his way of life? Will he sell his horses and scatter his Jews or will Reuben Sassoon be enshrined among the crown jewels and other regalia? Will he become desperately serious? Will he continue to be friendly to you? Will the Keppel be appointed 1st Lady of the Bedchamber? ... I am most interested and feel rather vulgar about this matter. King Edward VII — gadzooks what a long way that seems to take one back! I am glad he has got his innings at last, and most interested to watch how he plays it ...[6]

At the end of the lecture tours he found that with his book earnings he was now worth £10,000. This entirely self-made man glowed with justifiable pride, which is clearly revealed in his letter to Lady Randolph after he had made his reckoning: 'I am very proud of the fact that there is not one person in a million who at my age could have earned £10,000 without any capital in less than two years.'[7]

* * *

He took his seat with a sense of exhilaration on 14 February 1901. He was in the place he had long been determined to occupy: the oyster was at last opened. There were some, then and afterwards, who through dislike or envy maintained that his struggle to succeed had been overstressed — that he had a great advantage in being Lord Randolph's son, and in his high station in life. But we have seen with how few material assets he set out; how adamant had been his purpose, and how single-minded his advance. It was almost as though he had gone forward blinkered against distractions from his goal. He had not been content to dream: he had turned dreams into reality. We cannot doubt that his path was a far thornier one than that ridden by his father, and for Winston there was no pocket borough like Woodstock to lubricate his entry into Parliament.

After his success and sudden fame, followed by rhetorical triumphs at the election, it was not unnatural that he should feel that he was firmly established. Had he been given to introspection he would have realized that he had already incurred a great deal of unpopularity, and had his character been more malleable he might have made some effort to reduce

6. Chartwell papers.
7. Ibid.

it. Fashioned as he was, he could only take pride in the fact that he was so blatantly an adventurer and an opportunist. As such, and with only his own enterprise, courage and ability to rely upon to make his fortune, it had been sometimes necessary to cut corners with a sharpness that did not endear him universally.

> ... And it may be noted that the young Churchill made no attempt to conceal his ambition. He possessed Lord Randolph's lack of interest, amounting almost to carelessness and which some attributed to patrician arrogance, about his reputation among the majority of mankind. Nor, as time passed, did he make any attempt to dispel the suspicion and dislike with which he was regarded by the majority of the House of Commons.[8]

'To the insatiable curiosity and enthusiasm of the child,' wrote the Liberal publicist A. G. Gardiner, 'he joins the frankness of a child. He has no reserves and no shams. You are welcome to anything he has, and may pry into any corner you like. He has that scorn of concealment that belongs to a caste which never doubts itself.'[9]

Everyone round him, therefore, was aware of that insatiable ambition gathering itself under him like some powerful and uncontrollable horse, for he saw no reason to conceal it. Indeed, so exclusive a passion was it that other instincts seemed to wither in its glare. But he was saved by his warmth from the worst effects of this consuming fever, and by a delightful *gaminerie* which reminded some of his father. But in spite of his brilliant talents there had always lingered about Lord Randolph something faintly disreputable, indefinably raffish, which was entirely absent in the son. His complete lack of duplicity disarmed some who might have been repelled by his ambition, and the perceptive noticed in extenuation of it how he always 'thought with his heart'. In the words of Asquith's daughter, his friend and confidante Violet Asquith, later Bonham Carter (that 'wonderful person', as he called her):

> No doubt there were moments when his emotions vitiated his judgment, but far more often his heart acted as his mind's pathfinder and guide. His emotional response to situations and events was nearly always a true one. The right way to his mind was through his heart and his imagination. I have spent hours with him in fruitless argument, battering in vain on a closed door. If by some lucky phrase, some form of words, some vivid image, I could find the way to his imagination

8. Robert Rhodes James, *Churchill. A Study in Failure*, p. 14.
9. A. G. Gardiner, *Prophets, Priests and Kings*, p. 108.

or emotions, all barriers would fall. His intellect was often inaccessible. His heart was an open city.[10]

It is to this brilliant woman, so politically aware, so psychologically perceptive, that we owe the most revealing glimpses of Winston at the beginning of his political career, although she did not meet him until 1906. Where others saw naked opportunism and shameless ambition, she was immediately aware that from the door of this furnace emerged, strong and inescapable, the glare of genius. And she had no difficulty in accepting the last words of his opening sentence to her: 'We are all worms. But I do believe that I am a glow-worm.'

She was staggered by the extraordinary gaps in his knowledge. When she quoted him, in order to prove that words had a magic and music apart from their meaning, Keats' immortal lines:

> Charmed magic casements opening on the foam
> Of perilous seas, in faery lands forlorn—

His eyes blazed with excitement. 'Say that again,' he said. 'Say it again – it is marvellous!'

'But,' I objected, 'you know those lines. You know the Ode to the Nightingale.' He had apparently never read it, and never heard of it before.

His comic ignorance was again evident when she quoted to him from the poet William Blake. He listened to this new revelation avidly and with rapture, remarking, 'I never knew that the old Admiral had found time to write such good poetry.'

No clearer examples could be found of his loss in being denied a general education by the demands of the Army Class. At Bangalore, groping for knowledge on his own, vast areas of enlightenment had escaped him completely, but Violet Asquith knew at once that she had encountered something new and extraordinary: 'I was transfixed, transported into a new element; I knew only that I had seen a "great light". I recognized it as the light of genius.'

Everything under the sun was new to him: his approach to life was full of ardour and enraptured surprise, 'seen and appraised as on the first day of creation'. Even the eternal verities appeared to him an exciting personal discovery. The whole world of thought was virgin soil. He had no small talk, and did not attempt to make any, and no knowledge of the thoughts and feelings of other people. He had in any case not the slightest interest in them and remained as 'impervious to atmosphere as a diver in his bell'.[11] Hence his petrified silence at dinner parties when next to some strange woman, agonized by

10. Violet Bonham Carter, *Winston Churchill As I Knew Him*, p. 34.
11. Ibid.

her failure to establish contact. When he was not talking he would often sit there hunched and remote, drooped like an old man, and he appeared to be, and indeed was, in a different world. His concentration on himself was already obsessive, and when it was not engrossing his mind he was sitting in silence merely to recharge his batteries. But he could be stirred in an instant from this daunting seclusion by the mention of some matter of interest into a monologue matchless and dominating.

When others saw only uncouthness and bad manners, Violet understood that it was instead a profound immersion in his own problems. She was therefore able to discern, as few others did, that beneath the egotism and diamond-hard ambition was a touching simplicity, a naivety even, which had its own appeal, and gaps in his armour against which he was defenceless; and that: 'although armed to the teeth for life, he was at the same time highly vulnerable. He would need protection from, and interpretation to, a humdrum world which did not easily apprehend or understand his genius.'[12] This was a true judgment, but it was shared by few people at the time.

Another who felt an equal affection for Winston was the late Lord Rosebery, son of the fifth Earl, the Liberal Prime Minister, who first met Winston in 1898. Their first encounter was at Guisachan, the home of Winston's uncle Lord Tweedmouth. He was then sixteen, and Winston about twenty-three. Memories lingered in Rosebery's mind of discarding tail-coats and assuming velvet jackets for the smoking-room. Vivid also in his recollection was the night when there was a stampede after dinner to the door of the dining-room, in an effort not to be the last out, because the evening before Haldane[13] had been in that position, and had been buttonholed by Winston, and subjected to a half-hour monologue on the political situation.

Rosebery believed that Winston had been devoted to Violet Asquith before Clementine Hozier, the girl he was to marry, entered his life. Indeed, Rosebery claimed that Winston once remarked to him, 'I behaved badly to Violet because I was practically engaged to her.' But he maintained that on the whole Winston as a young man was so obsessed by his political career that he had shown little interest in women, or indeed in anything else.

But he recalled an evening when he and Winston took two Gaiety girls out on an occasion which ended with each going home with his partner. Rosebery happened to meet Winston's girl the next day and on asking her what had happened learned that

12. Violet Bonham Carter, op. cit., p. 34.
13. Lord Haldane, Secretary of State for War, 1905–12.

Winston had merely talked inexorably into the small hours on the subject of himself.[14]

Winston was still an unimpressive figure, red-haired and somewhat puny, and the iron stamina which later carried him through so much had not yet matured and hardened. But the perceptive noticed that his hands were exquisite – small, delicate and artistic, and that he was not a little proud of them. His health was still suspect. There was an evening when he was to speak for Rosebery (then Lord Dalmeny) in his constituency, but was so unwell that he had to be given oxygen before his speech. The doctor on this occasion warned him that he must not smoke more than two cigars that night, and he responded by buying the two largest in the shop. Rosebery looked back on their youth together with deep affection. Winston, he thought, was the staunchest of friends – no fair-weather friend, but one through Hell and high water, although he was capable of ruthlessness in his own interest.[15]

But what he mainly remembered was that Winston was entirely different from all other people of his age. There was no one in the least like him, for in his twenties he seemed already a natural statesman. His lisp at this time was at its worst, and Rosebery remembered him speaking in Dalkeith when it was painful and embarrassing to listen to him. But he gradually mastered this impediment, and even turned it to his own advantage with the same courage and resolution he had shown so often in battle. He had already in embryo most of the qualities he was to display so abundantly in the Second World War, and it was notable, as Earl Alexander of Tunis observed to the author, that these qualities all had their opposites – 'He was sentimental, yet ruthless, kind, yet cruel. He was inclined to be a bully.'[16]

Those who regarded him with interest noticed how feverish and exclusive was his concentration on the business of the moment, and how completely it was forgotten when exhausted. In A. G. Gardiner's words:

> It may be the attraction of war or peace, of social reform or of a social order – whatever it is he will plunge into it with all the schoolboy intensity of his nature. His loves may be many, but they will always have the passion of a first love. Whatever shrine he worships at, he will be the most fervid in his prayers.[17]

14. Sixth Earl of Rosebery to author.
15. Ibid.
16. Earl Alexander of Tunis to author.
17. A.G. Gardiner, *Pillars of Society*, p. 51.

He always seemed to be acting a part – the panther-like Napoleonic striding back and forth which had so struck Haldane in the prison camp, the histrionic gestures:

> He is always unconsciously playing a part – an heroic part. And he is himself his most astonished spectator. He sees himself moving through the smoke of battle – triumphant, terrible, his brow clothed with thunder, his legions looking at him for victory, and not looking in vain. He thinks of Napoleon; he thinks of his great ancestor. Thus did they bear themselves; thus in this rugged and awful crisis will he bear himself. It is not insincerity: it is that in that fervid and picturesque imagination there are always great deeds afoot with himself cast by destiny in the Agamemnon role. Hence that portentous gravity that sits on his youthful shoulders so oddly, those impressive postures and tremendous silences, the body flung wearily in the chair, the head resting gloomily in the hand, the abstracted look, the knitted brow.[18]

These mannerisms indicate that Winston had already acquired the essential attributes of a man of destiny – that he was shielded in his own mind from self-mistrust, and that his strong sense of humour would never include a derogatory picture of himself. It is also worth recalling that this early estimate was realized in full when he was called upon to rally the nation in its hour of greatest need.

Another fault which repelled many was his unusual egocentricity. And here it should be remembered that if his mind had not been so stonily and almost inhumanly focused on his own advancement, he would never have emerged from the mediocrity into which his father's contempt had consigned him. And here too Violet Asquith supplies the charitable explanation that it was mainly due to his self-absorption, to his exclusive preoccupation with his own problems.

Placed next at table to the enchanting Lady Horner, he was so morose and silent that this most polite and charming of women exclaimed in anger, 'I don't like people who make me feel as though I wasn't there.' Diana Lister, afterwards Lady Westmoreland, was so outraged by Winston's surly abstinence from conversation that she rose from the table, and finished her meal at the sideboard. But so remote was Winston from normal social obligations that he did not even notice her absence from his side until the end of the meal, when he inquired vaguely, 'What happened to that jolly little trout?' When chided after this he was sincerely contrite, explaining that a vital issue was occupying his mind to the exclusion of everything else. He had in fact 'a power of concentration amounting almost to an obsession'. But

18. op. cit. p. 57–8.

he was hopelessly insensitive to the human element in existence, and was to remain so through Life. He had not the faintest idea of what was passing in the minds of other people. Most men feel an interest, and many show great subtlety in understanding the springs of action of their fellow-men, in grasping the reasons for their behaviour, the strength and weaknesses which govern it, and most intelligent men are, like De La Rochefoucauld, fascinated by gaining a psychological insight into the secret impulses of their fellows, and believe that 'Gnothe seauton' – 'Know thyself' – is one of the most fundamental precepts of human wisdom. But although Winston was pre-eminently *human* himself, he had an almost inhuman indifference to these matters. He had, as Lord Moran was to write after his death, 'no antennae' with which to establish close contact with the minds of others. Nor had he the slightest desire to do so. This curious hiatus in his mental equipment was sometimes a grave political handicap, and the cause of many errors of judgment.

He allowed himself at this time few distractions, and we can safely say that he did not require or miss them. But he enjoyed dining or staying at the great houses, in all of which he was a welcome guest through birth or old friendships – Londonderry House, Blenheim Palace – his second home – Stafford House; weekends at Taplow, home of the ill-starred Grenfell family, its lovely gardens sharply descending to the quietly flowing green river beneath; or the Duke of Sutherland's Dunrobin, that enchanted castle in the mists of a northern sea.

He remained loyal to polo, his first and only passionate love in the world of sport, enjoyed hunting and an occasional day's shooting. But his heart was not fully in any of these pursuits, for he still set up an elaborate office in his bedroom in any country house in which he was staying, and was capable of leaving a grand shoot after the first drive if a political idea suddenly occurred to him which required immediate thought and study.[19] He had in fact no engrossing pastimes, and the obsessive habit of concentration on his own problems held him in an iron grasp.

He had already begun to predict gloomily that, like his father's, his life would be brief, allowing him little time for great achievements, reminding us of Cecil Rhodes: 'So much to do. So little time,' a foreboding far from justified by events. Winston persisted with this prediction of early death for years to come, at last drawing from Lady Randolph the tart rejoinder: 'Well, you'd better hurry up about it. You're nearly forty.'[20]

19. The Earl of Rosebery to author.
20. Margaret, Countess of Birkenhead, to author.

*   *   *

Winston was now face to face with his real life, and he was only to remain on the back benches for five years. He grew up in a period when England had transformed herself from a largely pastoral nation into the greatest industrial power in the world, and the mightiest in Europe. She had not been menaced by a European Power since the overthrow of Napoleon. Her homeland and Imperial trade routes were protected by a navy so large and powerful as to give an assurance of complete and perfect security. The mere thought of forceful change in this inviolate realm would have seemed beyond the bounds of rational thought.

Members of Parliament when Winston entered it were unpaid, and were called upon for a considerable outlay in their constituencies, so that only prosperous men in both parties were likely to seek admittance. He was not among these; and hence came his determination to increase his working capital so that he could support Parliamentary life for five or six years without undue anxiety.

Although London was extolled as the richest city in the world, its opulence masked an appalling squalor beneath, and this poverty was accepted as a fact of life, a matter for private charity rather than Government intervention.

We shall see later how when Winston was at the Board of Trade, he became more fully aware of the harsh inequalities of the age, and the degradation of the poor. He never registered such questions owing to his self-absorption and insensitiveness unless they were directly and forcibly brought to his attention. But when this young aristocrat suddenly grasped the plight of these unfortunates, his conversion to their cause was almost comical in its swiftness.

*   *   *

There were were certain signs of erosion in the fabric of the great monument of prosperity and peace, but they were too small for anyone to realize what they portended. Keir Hardie, a Scottish miner, had entered the House of Commons in 1892, cloth-capped, the first working-class Member, and backed by union funds. Eight years later he formed a new party which was the nucleus of the future Labour Party. The trade unions were beginning to flex their muscles, and the Fabian Society maintained a shrill intellectual obbligato.

The Liberal Party, still deeply divided over the issue of the war in South Africa, was at least united in its opposition to the Government's demand for unconditional surrender. Their wish was that the Boers should be assured that their co-operation would be sought, and that with the conclusion of peace they would receive their full share in the rights of self-government. To this demand the Conservative Prime Minister, Lord Salisbury, had returned a dusty answer, implying that in the circumstances it might be necessary to shelve self-government for generations.

The Election had not transfused much new blood into the Conservative Party: 'The stable remains the same', said the Liberal leader, Sir Henry Campbell-Bannerman, but as Violet Asquith commented, 'The Cecil stable still provided most of the best horses.' Lord Salisbury, the man who had broken Lord Randolph Churchill, was Prime Minister; his nephew Arthur Balfour was Leader of the House of Commons. Another nephew, Gerald Balfour, and a cousin, Lord Balfour of Burleigh, were Cabinet Ministers. The Prime Minister's eldest son, Lord Cranborne, was Under Secretary of State for Foreign Affairs. Younger sons, Lord Hugh and Lord Robert Cecil, were among the backbenchers.

* * *

Winston was at this moment lacking in a definite political objective or a coherent political philosophy. He therefore turned to his father's speeches and to his hallowed (if slightly tarnished) memory, for inspiration and guidance. He continued to lean heavily on both, and it is significant that apart from the advancement of his own political career his main occupation until 1905 was the biography of Lord Randolph, the research for which may have played some part in his swift disenchantment with the Tory Party.

> Certainly the contemplation of the events of the 1880s was not likely to heighten Winston's estimation of the Conservative Party in general and certain individuals in particular . . . It was Churchill's opinion before he embarked on the book that the party had treated his father badly; he emerged with the conviction that it had treated him scurvily . . .[21]

The research for this book brought Winston under the influence of Sir Francis Mowat, Head of the Civil Service, and an ardent admirer of Lord Randolph, whom he had served at the Treasury when Randolph was Chancellor. Winston realized at once that Mowat's financial views were an exact reflection of those of his father, and for the next years he was to follow them blindly, seeming indeed to regard Sir Francis as a sort of *alter ego* of Lord Randolph:

> He represented the complete triumphant Victorian view of economics and finance; strict parsimony; exact accounting; free imports whatever the rest of the world might do; suave steady government; no wars; no flag waving; just paying off debts and reducing taxation and keeping out

21. Robert Rhodes James, op. cit., p. 16.

of scrapes . . . *laissez-faire* and *laissez-aller*. Let the Government reduce itself and its demands upon the public to a minimum; let the nation live of its own; let social and industrial organisation take whatever course it pleased, subject to the law of the land and the Ten Commandments. Let the money fructify in the pockets of the people.[22]

* * *

With these and other thoughts occupying his mind, some half digested and dimly understood, Winston began to consider the best tactical moment for his maiden speech. He realized that it would be an ordeal more unnerving even than the ordinary initiation, for not only had his fame preceded him but the memory of Lord Randolph's career was still fresh in the minds of all – that golden soaring of the rocket in sudden glory into dark night; the sad descent of the stick. Winston had also made many enemies, and must have anticipated that some who awaited his *début* would do so in a feline hope of failure.

He consulted many about the moment when he should take the plunge – 'the supreme ordeal', as his ardent imagination now regarded it. He approached it 'with awe as well as eagerness', and the mere thought of failure was a greater deterrent than any he had faced in battle. Some advised caution and delay, and a pause until he had more surely gauged the capricious ear of the House. Others, when the question of the Boer War approached for debate in February 1901, told him that this was his chance and his subject, and that he must not fail to grasp the nettle. He believed that this was the true advice.

We have seen that the war was still dragging on, a humiliation and embarrassment to the British Government, and had deteriorated from an ordinary conflict into odious guerrilla strife; into the burning of farms, and the establishment of concentration camps. However necessary this was, the process was abhorrent to the radical element in the Liberal Party, who had denounced the war from the outset. Winston was divided in his opinions, as was the House of Commons. He believed in the justice of the war, but believed too, even then, that at the end there must be magnanimity. He spoke after dinner on 18 February in the Debate on the Address to a packed House waiting – some, no doubt, with hostility – to appraise him.

One can picture [wrote one of his biographers[23]] the scene of 1901; the hansom cabs and carriages clattering across the pavements of New

22. Winston S. Churchill, *Thoughts and Adventures*.
23. Virginia Cowles, op. cit., p. 79.

Palace Yard and pulling up in front of the entrance to Westminster Hall; the lobbies lit by flickering gas jets; the Strangers' Dining Room filled with men and women in evening dress; the Chamber itself with Members elegantly attired in striped trousers and frock coats, some of them half reclining on the benches with their silk hats tipped over their foreheads; the wives and daughters in voluminous, rustling skirts, taking their seats in the gallery and gazing earnestly at the crowded floor.

It was an audience representing a society wielding a power intellectual and material, and an influence – greater, perhaps, than any that has been known since – a truly intimidating audience, one indeed 'to excite the fears and the emulations of an orator'. It was a scene scarcely less daunting than Clemenceau's Paris as Winston was later to describe it – 'a terrible society, grimly polished, loaded with explosives; trellised with live electric wires.'

* * *

But the issue of the South African War, in which he had fought, and which he understood so well, seemed to offer the best hope. He had learned that a young Welsh firebrand called Lloyd George, who was passionately pro-Boer, would be called at about 9 o'clock, and that he could if he wished speak after him. Lloyd George had put down an amendment framed in moderate terms, but it was uncertain until the last moment whether he would move it. Winston had of course devoted even more than his usual intense labour to this speech. As he was unable to say anything, except a sentence or two in reply to an interruption, which had not been written down and memorized, it was necessary to foresee any possible crises and emergencies, and to have answers to them ready to hand. 'I need not recount,' he wrote of this crucial maiden speech, 'the pains I had taken to prepare, nor the efforts I had made to hide the work of preparation.'

The necessity of anticipating every unexpected question and insidious danger lurking in his path enormously increased the strain of the ordeal. In spite of his command of the language – already superb, but as yet too tropical and luxuriant – that fatal blockage still prevented him from 'thinking on his feet', and abolished spontaneity. Lloyd George immediately announced that he did not intend to move his amendment, and embarked on a violent and intemperate speech. Winston had prepared in succession sentence after sentence to latch on to Lloyd George's speech after he had finished, but 'each of these poor couplings became in turn obsolete. A sense of alarm and even despair crept across me. I repressed it with an inward gasp.'

Beside him on the bench sat a brilliant, if wayward, Conservative

parliamentarian, Thomas Gibson Bowles, who observed the expression
of gathering panic on Winston's mobile features as he groped for an
opening. At this most opportune moment he whispered to the petrified
young man, 'You might say: "Instead of making his violent speech
without moving his moderate amendment, he had better have moved
his moderate amendment without making his violent speech." ' Winston
grabbed at this life-giving sentence like a drowning man clutching at a
plank placed in his way by some divine chance:

'Manna in the wilderness was not more welcome! It fell only just
in time ... I was up before I knew it, and reciting Tommy Bowles's
rescuing sentence. It won a general cheer. Courage returned.'[24]

Winston spoke from the corner seat above the gangway behind the
Government front bench, the seat from which Lord Randolph made
his fatal speech of resignation. After the inspired beginning, it was
a fine performance pleasing in succession both sides of the House
acutely divided upon the issue. He was cheered by his own side
when he attacked Lloyd George with the words: 'I do not believe
that the Boers would attach particular importance to the utterances
of the honourable member. No people in the world have received so
much verbal sympathy and so little practical support as the Boers.'
But when he continued, a moment later, 'The Boers who are fighting
in the field – and if I were a Boer, I hope I should be fighting in
the field—' there was a warm response not only from the Liberal
Opposition but also from the Irish Nationalists: and he was aware
of a stir on the Treasury Bench below him, like a sudden catspaw
of wind ruffling a still lake, when Joseph Chamberlain shifted in
his seat and muttered to George Wyndham, 'That's the way to
throw away seats.'[25]

Winston then strongly denied the charges of treachery by one
side and barbarity by the other, arguing as an eyewitness and a
combatant that this war compared with most others had been waged
with unusual chivalry and humanity on both sides. He appealed
for delay in establishing the new Transvaal constitution after the
war until the British settlers had returned, and argued that a civil
rather than a military Government should be set up immediately:
'The Boer farmer is a curious combination of the squire and the
peasant, and under the rough coat of the farmer there are often
to be found the instincts of the squire.' He had been ashamed to
see such men 'ordered about peremptorily by young subalterns as
if they were private soldiers'. He hoped that the Colonial Secretary
would

24. Winston S. Churchill, *My Early Life*, p. 361.
25. Ibid.

leave nothing undone to bring home to these brave and unhappy men who are fighting in the field that whenever they are prepared to recognize that their small independence must be merged into the larger liberties of the British Empire there will be a full guarantee for the security of their property and religion, an assurance of equal rights, a promise of representative institutions, and last but not least of all, what the British army would most readily accord to a brave and enduring foe – all the honours of war.

This chivalrous attitude towards an enemy in the process of defeat and disintegration struck a warm and responsive chord among the Liberals, and his closing sentence profoundly moved the whole House, and appealed strongly to that vein of sentiment and respect for filial loyalty which exists in every House of Commons.

'I cannot sit down,' he concluded, the ghost of Lord Randolph standing at his shoulder, 'without saying how very grateful I am for the kindness and patience with which the House has heard me, and which has been extended to me, I well know, not on my own account, but because of a certain splendid memory which many honourable members still preserve.'

It was a masterly ending, genuinely pious as well as astutely contrived. Winston received congratulations from both sides of the House, far warmer than convention demanded. He was also praised the following day in the same debate by one future Liberal Prime Minister, Herbert Asquith, and, in a letter, by another, Henry Campbell-Bannerman. The Parliamentary reporters were also laudatory in the extreme, although there were predictable reservations in the Radical press. The ordeal was over, and Winston was taken to the Smoking Room and plied with 'the usual restoratives', accompanied by congratulations. Later he was introduced at the Bar of the House to Lloyd George, who after praising Winston's effort remarked, 'Judging from your sentiments, you are standing against the Light.' Winston answered lightly, 'You take a singularly detached view of the British Empire.' 'Thus,' he said, 'began an association which has persisted through many vicissitudes.'[26] His relief after this speech was profound, and in retrospect he said of it, 'It was a terrible, thrilling yet delicious experience.'[27]

* * *

After the maiden speech there was much speculation as to the

26. Winston S. Churchill, op. cit., p. 362.
27. Randolph S. Churchill, op. cit. Vol II, p. 12.

direction Winston's political career would now take. It seemed improbable that his temperament would allow him to become a good party man voting with docility at the command of the whips. On the other hand, his ambition for office was obvious, and an attitude too rebellious and defiant of his own leaders would clearly not advance it. One fact soon became apparent – that he did not intend, like many members, to recline for months on the laurels of his maiden speech until they became withered, before intervening again in debate.

A young man in a hurry, he spoke twice again in the following week on South African subjects, and made his next important contribution on 12 March 1901 in the case of General Colville, an officer who had been appointed Commander-in-Chief at Gibraltar after service in South Africa. Certain alleged episodes of military misconduct in the war were unearthed and used against him nearly a year later, and he was dismissed from his command by the Government. This seemed to the Opposition shabby behaviour, too closely resembling the digging-out of a fox, and they demanded a debate. This took the form of an all-party amendment demanding an inquiry into the Colville case, and began badly for the Government, which was criticized from all quarters for this belated act of retribution.

Winston was again on familiar ground, and spoke brilliantly in defence of the Government in what was generally supposed to be a debating speech, but was as usual the result of hours of preparation, and of anticipation of the points that might be raised. He defended the Government by using arguments that appealed equally to the Opposition, referring to the tendency he had noticed among military officers –partly from good nature and partly from a dislike of public scrutiny – to suppress unpleasant facts, to sweep them under the carpet, and to allow incompetent officers to linger on in commands, 'in the hope that at the end of the war they may be shunted into private life without a scandal'. Loud Opposition cheers had scarcely subsided when he suddenly rounded on them:

> On whom does the responsibility for the continuance of the system rest? When Lord Roberts went out to South Africa he struck out a new and true line. The truth, the whole truth, was to be told to the country frankly and fairly. The House will remember the publication of the Spion Kop despatches and the reception that the publication met with from honourable and right honourable gentlemen opposite. That settled the policy of candour in military matters for some time to come at any

rate. That is why the despatches contained no incriminating matter in regard to General Colville.

He ended his speech with the unanswerable point that selection was the only hope for increased efficiency in the Army, the only way of preventing the senior ranks from being clogged with incapable men:

> The principle of selection is challenged, and would be destroyed if a Commission were appointed in this case . . . I exhort the right honourable gentleman [the Secretary of State for War] not only for the sake of the army, but also in the interest of the House, not to budge an inch from the position he has taken up.

The amendment was soundly defeated, and there was little doubt that Winston's speech had contributed substantially to the result. He claimed, and with justice: 'I really seemed to be finding my footing in the House.'[28]

'Nothing could be more remarkable,' wrote the leading Liberal political journalist H. W. Massingham after this speech, 'than the way in which this youth has slipped into the Parliamentary manner . . . He did it to perfection. Mr Balfour showed his gratitude by vehement and repeated cheering.'[29] It might be added that to make the languid, epicene Balfour cheer 'vehemently and repeatedly' was in itself a miracle to cherish. Fully conscious of his success, Winston wrote to his mother:

> . . . There is no doubt that the speech turned votes and shifted opinion at the time when the current was running very strongly against the Government. George Wyndham and all my friends think that as a Parliamentary coup it is far bigger than I have ever done.[30]

* * *

Those who remained curious about the direction his career would take received a resounding answer when he passed (on 13 May 1901, two months later) from ingenious defence of the Government to formidable attack upon it for excessive military expenditure in peace-time. This was at first sight a curious theme for one who was later in life to urge massive rearmament on a listless Government, and to become one of the greatest war leaders in English history. But we should remember

28. Winston S. Churchill, op. cit., p. 312.
29. *Daily News*, 13 March 1901.
30. Chartwell papers.

that he had written of Lord Randolph's death, 'There remained for me only to pursue his aims and vindicate his memory'; remember too that this was a subject which engaged Winston's emotions more deeply than any other, for it was upon this issue – military expenditure in relation to social reform – that Lord Randolph had made his fatal gesture, and had fallen, not only from office, but from public life.

Winston took six weeks to prepare this speech, and 'learned it so thoroughly off by heart that it hardly mattered where I began or how I turned it'. It was designed to restate Lord Randolph's thinking in the form of a general attack not only on the Government's policy, but upon the mood and tendencies of his own Conservative Party, to urge peace, economy and the reduction of armaments. The immediate cause of this intervention was the announcement, a few days before the Colville debate, by the Secretary of State for War, Mr St John Brodrick, of an expensive and far-reaching scheme for the enlargement and expansion of the Army on continental lines, which provided Winston with the opportunity of making the finest speech of his early Parliamentary life, loudly cheered by the Liberal Opposition, but far less enthusiastically received on his own side of the House.

He began by contrasting the soaring costs of the Army with his father's efforts to restrict military expenditure, the note of filial piety beginning by now to jar a trifle in the ears of Conservative members:

> If I might be allowed to revive a half-forgotten episode . . . I would recall that once upon a time a Conservative and Unionist Administration came into power . . . and when the time came round to consider the Estimates the usual struggle took place between the great spending departments, and the Treasury . . . The controversy was bitter, the struggle uncertain, but in the end the Government triumphed, and the Chancellor of the Exchequer went down for ever, and with him, it now seems, there fell also the cause of retrenchment and economy, so that the very memory thereof seems to have perished, and the words themselves have a curiously old-fashioned ring about them.

He then quoted from Lord Randolph's letter to Lord Salisbury, adding: 'Wise words stand the test of time, and I am very glad the House has allowed me, after an interval of fifteen years, to lift again the tattered flag I found lying on a stricken field.'

On that bygone occasion Lord Randolph had refused to consent to Estimates of £31,000,000. Parliament was now being invited to approve more than £59,000,000. Winston continued with increasing vigour and indignation, every question falling like a hammer-blow:

What has happened in the meantime to explain this astounding increase? Has the wealth of the country doubled? Have the armies of Europe doubled? Is the commercial competition of foreign nations so much reduced? Are we become the undisputed master of the markets of the world? Is there no poverty at home? Has the English Channel dried up, and are we no longer an island? Is the revenue so easily raised that we do not know how to spend it? Are the Treasury buildings pulled down and all our finances fled? . . .

Speaking of the need for someone to protest against the daily increases in the defence burden, he added, playing again the gambit of family loyalty:

'If such a one is to stand forward in such a cause, then, I say it humbly, but with I hope becoming pride, no one has a better right than I have, for this is a cause I have inherited, and a cause for which the late Lord Randolph Churchill made the greatest sacrifice of any Minister of modern times.' Turning to Brodrick's scheme, he was unmerciful in analysis. Three Army Corps were to be reserved under it for foreign emergencies: 'Why,' he asked, 'three corps?' One was quite enough to fight savages, and three not enough even to begin to fight Europeans.

He answered, in a striking passage, Members and Ministers who spoke glibly and with composure about a European war:

> . . . we must not expect to meet the great civilised power in this easy fashion . . . I will not expatiate, but there has been a great change which the House should not omit to notice. In former days, when wars arose from individual cases, from the policy of a Minister or the passion of a King, when they were fought by small regular armies of professional soldiers, and when their course was retarded by the difficulties of communication and supply, and often suspended by the winter season, it was possible to limit the liability of the combatants. But now, when mighty populations are impelled on each other, each individual severally embittered and inflamed – when the resources of science and civilisation sweep away everything that might mitigate their fury, a European war can only end in the ruin of the vanquished and the scarcely less fatal dislocation and exhaustion of the conquerors . . . The wars of peoples will be more terrible than those of kings.

He spoke in bitter language of the great expenditure demanded by the Secretary of State, which would not even make the country safe:

> . . . if we went to war with any great Power his three army corps would scarcely serve as a vanguard. If we are hated they will not make us loved . . . If we are in danger, they will not make us safe. They are

enough to irritate; they are not enough to overawe. They cannot make us invulnerable, but they may very likely make us venturesome.

He concluded by saying that the weapon upon which the country must rely was the economic command of markets and the Navy's command of the seas:

> . . . we shall make a fatal bargain if we allow the moral force which this country has so long exerted to become diminished, or perhaps destroyed for the sake of the costly, trumpery, dangerous military playthings on which the Secretary of State for War has set his heart.[31]

This speech had held the House entranced for an hour by its force and by the speaker's command of language and masterly grasp of his material. It was a brilliant success – with the Opposition, and the press which served it, Massingham bestowing on it one of his warmest eulogies: '. . . In its elevation of purpose, its broad conception of national policy, and in the noble and delicate movement of its closing sentences, I recall nothing like it since Gladstone died . . . In the years to come the author should be Prime Minister – I hope Liberal Prime Minister – of England.'[32]

This prediction was not calculated to boost Winston's sagging position in the Conservative Party, to which his speech had also administered a serious blow, for it marked a definite divergence of thought and sympathy from his own side. In A. J. P. Taylor's words:

> He entered Parliament during the Boer War, with the special distinction of having escaped from Boer captivity. He was something of a war hero. Yet, far from breathing fire, he urged that the defeated Boers be treated with generosity – much to the annoyance of the Conservatives who had elected him. Next, though a former officer in the Army, he went on to criticise the Army Estimates and declared that the Royal Navy was Britain's sure defence. This was the attitude of an isolationist, even of a Little Englander, not of an imperialist, and he swung still further away from imperialism when he championed Free Trade against Joseph Chamberlain's campaign for Tariff Reform.[33]

He had in fact taken a long stride towards the most fateful decision of his early political life – that of changing his Party.

31. Hansard, 13 May 1901.
32. *Daily News*, 14 May 1901.
33. A. J. P. Taylor, op. cit., p. 18.

Chapter 5

Crossing the Floor

Winston had already, writing to his mother in March, made disparaging references to the disorder of the Conservative Party, the dissatisfaction in the ranks, and the 'shocking lack of cohesion' to be found there:

'The Government is not very strong ... The whole Treasury bench appears to me to be sleepy and exhausted and played out ...'[1] To dissipate this gloom and inject some life into the proceedings Winston and a few friends formed a small group of rebellious Tory members, which included Ian Malcolm, Lillie Langtry's son-in-law; Lord Percy, son of the Duke of Northumberland; Arthur Stanley, the Earl of Derby's younger son; and Salisbury's son, Lord Hugh Cecil.

It was for Winston yet another genuflexion before Lord Randolph's shrine, for we cannot doubt that the 'Fourth Party' was in his mind. This was to be sure a somewhat pallid reflection of that great splinter group, but it succeeded in causing a certain amount of annoyance to Ministers. The parliamentary manners of this body were later frequently appalling, and they became known as the Hughligans, or Hooligans. It was also significant that the Hooligans spent far more of their time with members of the Liberal Party than with their Conservative colleagues.

During these early years Winston concentrated his efforts on two main objectives – Army reform and economy – the first because he understood the subject, and the second because he had inherited it from his father. That it was a pious obligation is further suggested by the fact that the instinct of economy was so conspicuously absent from his own life. But it should not, as Violet Asquith

1. Chartwell papers.

emphasized, be thought that he slavishly aped Lord Randolph's views. He simply accepted them unquestioningly as a rubric of faith. So far he had shown no interest in social problems, and not the slightest awareness of the social upheaval towards which the country was slowly but surely progressing. His interest was in ideas: of people he knew nothing.

'I like the working man,' he was fond of saying, but he had not the slightest idea what he was like or how his mind worked. 'The People' were to him a political abstraction, which his inability to probe the minds of others made it impossible for him to fathom in human terms. He was the grandson of a Duke; and, brought up at Blenheim, accepted class distinction as a matter of course:

> He knew nothing of England beyond the society of political London and the great aristocratic houses. The life of ordinary Englishmen was beyond his ken, until he studied it from outside as the head of some government department. He apprehended social problems with extreme benevolence, but along with an air of gracious giving. He wished to remove poverty and injustice, not to achieve any fundamental change, and claimed rightly to be at heart a conservative even in his most radical days.[2]

Soon, for example, at the Board of Trade he was to discover (with almost comical indignation) the condition of poverty, and to throw himself into alleviating it with all the fervour of a freshly discovered cause, as he had once thrown himself into the pursuit of glory. It had to be brought before his eyes before he became aware of it. But once this had happened his reaction was to be immediate and warm, as Charles Masterman, one of the ablest of the young Liberal idealists, clearly perceived:

> Winston swept me off to his cousin's house, and I lay on his bed while he dressed and marched about the room, gesticulating and impetuous, pouring out all his hopes and plans and ambitions. He is full of the poor whom he has just discovered. He thinks he is called by Providence to do something for them. 'Why have I always been kept safe within a hair's breadth except to do something like this?'[3]

But Masterman, like Taylor, perceived the limitations of his commitment: 'He desired in England a state of things where a benign upper

2. A.J.P. Taylor, op. cit., p.16.
3. Lucy Masterman, *C.F.G. Masterman*, pp.97-8.

class dispensed benefits to an industrious, *bien pensant*, and grateful working class.'

* * *

Meanwhile he continued to urge the need for economy, and later was even to oppose the building of eight new dreadnoughts. This was a strange posture for a future First Lord who was to bring the Fleet fully prepared into war, but was again due to Lord Randolph's memory; to what *The Times* called his 'hereditary tradition of hostility to the Service Estimates'. At the beginning of 1902 he found himself increasingly out of tune with his Conservative colleagues, writing to the former Liberal Prime Minister, Lord Rosebery: 'I cannot make speeches in the country with any satisfaction now. I cannot work up the least enthusiasm on the Government's behalf: and yet popular audiences seem to gape for party clap-trap.'[4] But late in the year he discovered a certain interest in Balfour's Education Bill which transferred the administration of primary and secondary schools from the School Boards to the Local Authority, and brought Church Schools under the same control. It was a measure also close to Lord Hugh Cecil's heart, and he made one of the greatest speeches of his life on the Second Reading.

It was Winston's growing friendship with Lord Hugh, and his intense admiration of his superior mind, that had led him to espouse a most improbable cause – resistance to a Bill for allowing a man to marry his deceased wife's sister. To Winston's uncomplicated and secular reasoning such a relationship appeared 'a very excusable and often reasonable arrangement', but his protests were swept angrily aside by Lord Hugh in a torrent of theological argument:

> He was scandalized at my ignorance of Ecclesiastical Law ... The object of the Christian Church, he explained, was to enlarge the bounds of family affection to the widest possible extent without admitting within those bounds the possibility of sex disturbance ... Dethrone the principle of prohibited degrees, and in hundreds – nay in thousands – of households, the position of these devoted women, hitherto unquestioned, would become a target for comment and calumny. He stressed our duty to preserve the structure of humane, enlightened, Christian society. Once the downward steps were taken, once one's moral and intellectual feet slipped upon the slope of plausible indulgence, there would be found no halting-place short of a general Paganism and Hedonism, possibly agreeable from time to time in this world of fleeting trials and choices, but fatal hereafter through measureless ages, if not indeed through eternity itself.[5]

4. Chartwell papers.
5. Winston S. Churchill, *Thoughts and Adventures*, pp.35-6.

One can imagine Winston gaping as though paralysed by a snake, while this tirade engulfed him, but his friendship with its author caused him, none the less, to join with him in obstructing the passage of the Deceased Wife's Sister Bill. Lord Hugh, in spite of his exalted notions, eventually gained his point by the most dubious and amoral means – by crawling so slowly through the lobby that the clock struck four before the division ended, and this Private Member's Bill (which required the vote to be taken before the clock struck) was killed. Its supporters were enraged, and received Lord Hugh with howls of fury when he re-entered the Chamber, accusing him of 'not playing the game'. But he was one of those intellectual zealots who believed that the end justified the means, and was quite unmoved by the abuse: 'What was all this talk of "not playing cricket" when the transcendental character of the marriage tie was at stake? . . . We were not playing a game; we were discharging a solemn and indeed awful duty.'

In this manner, bemused but loyal Winston discharged his 'awful duty' in the sacred name of friendship. It proved to be a sterile gesture, for later 'in the growing tolerance of the age I was ultimately induced to acquiesce in the legalizing of a man's marriage with his deceased wife's sister'.

This act of devotion brings the question of Winston's friendships to our attention. Those held in close regard were seen by him as an élite, demanding an unconditional loyalty, a magic circle to be forgiven all backslidings, and to be held immune from all criticism. This strict code by no means applied to his many ordinary acquaintances, but only to those who found their way into the small inner circle. The nature of this privilege was best described by one of those who was especially close to him in pre-war days – Violet Asquith:

> His friendship was a stronghold against which the gates of Hell could not prevail. There was an absolute quality in his loyalty, known only to those safe within its walls. Their battle was his own. He would concede no inch of ground, no smallest point against them. In a friend he would defend the indefensible, explain away the inexplicable, even forgive the unforgivable.
>
> The inner citadel of the heart held first and foremost his relations – in the widest sense. His strong family feeling embraced not only his mother and his brother Jack, but cousins, uncles, aunts –the whole Guest tribe and 'Sunny' Duke of Marlborough. (He confided to me that one of his reasons for preferring the post of Colonial Under Secretary to that of Financial Secretary to the Treasury was that Sunny had once held it.)[6]

6. Violet Bonham Carter, op. cit., p. 146.

There occurred another event, in April 1902, which widened the gap between Winston and his Party, and which he would have done well to ponder deeply. There had been a contentious debate on the case of a Mr Cartwright, who was being held in South Africa under the authority of martial law, and prevented from visiting England after serving a year's sentence for uttering a seditious libel on Kitchener during the war. The Liberals saw in this restriction a gross infringement of personal liberty, and Winston led a Tory back-bench revolt and voted with the Liberals.

Mr Joseph Chamberlain was the guest of the Hooligans at dinner that night. 'I am dining in very bad company,' he said to his mutinous hosts. Winston and the others justified their conduct on the ground of the arrogant and arbitrary behaviour of the Government, but Chamberlain answered tartly, 'What is the use of supporting your own Government only when it is right? It is just when it is in this sort of pickle that you ought to have come to our aid.'

He paused at the door before leaving and, turning, remarked with a peculiar emphasis:

'You young gentlemen have entertained me royally, and in return I will give you a priceless secret. Tariffs! There are the politics of the future, and of the near future. Study them closely and make yourselves masters of them, and you will not regret your hospitality to me.' This was a portentous warning.

* * *

Lord Salisbury resigned in July 1902, and was succeeded as Prime Minster by his nephew and heir-apparent, Arthur Balfour. This 'autumn rose', in Lytton Strachey's lovely phrase about an earlier statesman, was intellectually superior to almost all other members of the House of Commons, a man who seemed indeed the quintessence of civilization – scholar, philosopher and mathematician; a man of letters, and an adornment of the 'Souls', that social clique devoted to the Higher Thought. Sometimes his commanding intellect seemed to be dissolved in languor, and in such a mood he would rise in the House and dreamily improvise on some abstract theme like a musician on a violin. It was said of Balfour that he gave to politics the first mind of his generation, and men learned to appraise the deceptive gentleness of his manner, the perfect courtesy, and to dread the reproofs, sudden and annihilating as the stroke of a tiger's claws, which he would suddenly and unexpectedly administer.

Winston had attacked this formidable man freely, but it is most unlikely that it was on account of this that Balfour (although he chose another Hooligan, Lord Percy, and replaced Hicks-Beach as Chancellor of the Exchequer by C. J. Ritchie), did not offer Winston any Ministerial office. He was above such pettiness, and in any case did not make any major reconstruction of his Government. But it would be naive to assume that this neglect did not strongly influence Winston in the decision he was soon to take. His political ambition was still as intense as ever: he was hungry for greatness, and he must have felt that in his own Party his progress was blocked. The immediate effect of the Prime Minister's neglect of his obvious claims was to drive him farther to the Left, and into closer relations with the Liberal leaders, of whom Morley and the former Prime Minister Rosebery exerted the strongest influence upon him.

Winston was now sufficiently dissatisfied to hanker for a new alignment of the parties, and it was in this restless mood that he wrote to Rosebery on 10 October:

> I enclose you a letter from the man on my committee on whom I chiefly depend. It is a striking letter. If by an 'evolutionary process' we could create a wing of the Tory party wh could either infuse vigour into the parent body or join a central coalition, *my plan* would become most important as an incident in or possibly as the herald of the movement. But the risk & peril of it would be vy great, & it would carry consequences to me wh I cannot foresee; & only the conviction that you are upholding the flag for which my father fought so long & so disastrously would nerve me to the plunge. The Government of the Middle – the party wh shall be free at once from the sordid selfishness & callousness of Toryism on the one hand & the blind appetites of the Radical masses on the other – may be an ideal wh we perhaps shall never attain, wh could in any case only be possessed for a time, but which is nevertheless worth working for: I for my part see no reason to despair of that 'good state'.
>
> But I should like to bring you & Beach together. There lies the chance of a central coalition. 'Tory-Liberal' is a much better name than 'Tory Democrat' or 'Liberal Imperialist'; & certainly neither paradoxical nor unprecedented. The one real difficulty I have to encounter is the suspicion that I am moved by mere restless ambition: & if some definite issue – such as Tariff – were to arise – that difficulty would disappear.[7]

But Lord Rosebery was guarded. He warned Winston that he must not compromise his future by premature action. 'Some day, perhaps not long hence, the psychological moment may come for a new departure, but it is not yet.'[8]

But there was no question that Winston, in spite of great distrust, had already by aggressive tactics established a definite position in the political world by the autumn of 1902, although his party leaders

7. Rosebery papers.
8. Chartwell papers.

were not yet disturbed about their position in the country. L. S. Amery, who had been with him in South Africa and whom he had earlier pushed into 'Ducker' at Harrow, wrote: 'The young Whig *fronde* in the Tory Party, of which Winston Churchill was the leading spirit, could spend its energies on worrying the Secretary of State for War in Parliament without seriously disquieting the party leaders.[9]

But there was already a stirring in the dovecots. That 'definite issue' – Tariffs – had already arisen, and although it did not lead to a 'government of the Middle', it caused Winston before long to abandon the Conservative Party and cross the floor of the House. In his Budget in April 1902, Sir Michael Hicks-Beach had before his replacement reintroduced a registered duty of three-pence a hundredweight on imported corn and grain, and a duty of fivepence a hundredweight on imported flour and meal. He argued that it was necessary to enlarge the basis of taxation because of the growing demands on the Exchequer, particularly by the Service departments; that the registration duty, which had survived Peel's repeal of the Corn Laws, had not been abolished until 1868, and that this must have been a mistake. But he denied that the tax heralded a protectionist policy.

* * *

Winston was shaken by this departure, and expressed misgivings in the House, but voted for the Budget, possibly, as his son has suggested, because 'he knew that his father's old friend Hicks-Beach was at heart a staunch free-trader, and also that he was under the safe Treasury patronage of two eminent civil servants, Sir Francis Mowat and Sir Edward Hamilton, both notable and articulate free-traders.[10]

As far as was humanly possible, Balfour sought to diminish tensions, and to sail in the fairest weather he could find, and under the most tranquil skies. It was indeed in comparatively cloudless days that Joseph Chamberlain produced his seismic shock. On 15 May, in a speech in Birmingham shortly before the Whitsuntide Recess, he informed an astonished nation that the Empire was in peril of dissolution, and that a supreme crisis could only be met by hooping the barrel firmly with a system of Imperial Preference. This would, of course, involve the taxing of food, the adoption of Tariffs, and the abandonment of Free Trade. Although this revolutionary policy had been expounded to

9. L.S. Amery, *My Political Life*, Vol. 1, p.222.
10. Randolph Churchill, op.cit., Vol.II, p.50.

the Prime Minister, it had not been authorized by the Cabinet. Balfour did not declare for or against the proposal, and Government and Party were sharply divided.

Few speeches in English history have had greater or more enduring repercussions. It united the Liberal Party, and brought disunity to the Conservatives; it led to a drastic shifting of the political balance of power from Right to Left. On Winston Churchill its effect was decisive. It provided him 'with what he needed most, a cause and a theme. It was not as a crusader or a missionary that he had entered politics, but rather as a fish takes to water or a bird to the air, because they were his natural element.'[11] He was also, one might add, a young man in a hurry with a monomania about achieving greatness. He was already out of harmony with the Conservative Party, and when the Protection issue was raised he was disposed to view all their actions in the most critical light.

But it would be wrong to conclude, as some have, that his espousal of Free Trade was a gesture dictated entirely by naked ambition and the pursuit of power, and that his belief in it could have been neutralized by a ministerial appointment. There is in fact no reason to doubt the truth of his own words: 'I am sure that in those days I acted in accordance with my deepest feeling and with all that recklessness in so doing which belongs to youth and is indeed the glory of youth and its most formidable quality.'[12]

For Winston, sitting at the feet of Mowat and others, had swallowed the Free Trade doctrine in one voracious gulp, and in doing so was embracing a cause fervently believed in by the majority of the British people. This belief (or legend) was simply that Britain's industrial and commercial pre-eminence had been the direct result of Free Trade and its concomitant cheap food. Any deviation from this hallowed policy would mean the loss of her world markets, and land her people again in the starvation and horror of the 'Hungry Forties'. This was the dogma unquestioningly accepted by men and women in all walks of life, and which also carried with it the rider that Free Trade ensured peaceful relations with all the world, whereas Protection led inevitably to wars. Winston was not only certain of the truth of this proposition, but was also convinced that his father would have embraced the same cause. The arguments against Free Trade were cogent and powerful, but far less easy to grasp or to enunciate than the simple declaration of faith in its favour. We are fairly safe in assuming that Winston did not probe them with undue diligence.

11. Violet Bonham Carter, op.cit., p.99.
12. Winston S. Churchill, *Thoughts and Adventures*, pp. 5-6.

* * *

His zest for this battle was hardened by the memory of Chamberlain's contemptuous treatment of Lord Randolph when he refused to admit him as a Parliamentary candidate in Birmingham; for still at any recollected slight on his idol, Winston's face would become transformed by fierce and sudden anger. On 25 May he set out his views to Balfour. After telling the Prime Minister that he was utterly opposed to anything which would alter 'the Free Trade character of this country', he concluded:

> I feel perhaps that I may have sometimes been the cause of embarrassment to the Government. It is difficult to write about such things because of obvious rejoinders, but I should like to tell you that an attempt on your part to preserve the Free Trade policy & character of the Tory Party would command my absolute loyalty. I would even swallow six army corps – if it would make any difference & sink all minor differences. But if on the other hand you have made up your mind & there is no going back, I must reconsider my position in politics.[13]

This letter is significant. At twenty-seven he is already addressing the aloof Prime Minister as an equal, almost laying down conditions for his own conformist behaviour. And, by offering to abandon one cherished principle – the army corps – he proves how strong and genuine was his belief in Free Trade, and that he was already prepared to sacrifice a strongly held belief in order to achieve a greater end.

If he was not yet finally committed to the Liberals, he was already prepared to work with them, and during the summer of 1903 was a leading instigator of the Free Food League, which was established in July in opposition to Tariff Reform, and in which sixty Conservative Free Traders in the House of Commons joined. His path to the League was not always smooth, and he received a daunting snub from Archibald Salvidge, the Liverpool brewer and powerful Tory Party manager whom he had invited to meet other Unionist Free Traders at a dinner party at the House of Commons. It was hoped that Salvidge would announce the fidelity of the industrial North to Free Trade, but when he discovered its purpose he chose to regard the dinner as a disloyal gesture to Chamberlain, and abruptly left the table.

Although Winston was now opposed root and branch to Chamberlain's policy, he could not repress his admiration for the man's daring and resolution, and was also – perhaps uneasily – conscious of many favours received at his hand: '. . . although I disagree with him so utterly, yet he has been very kind to me'.

13. Chartwell papers.

Chamberlain had indeed been kind to Winston, and his generosity
continued in spite of the young man's violent attitude:

> In any case [Chamberlain assured him] and whatever happens, if you
> fight your battle fairly and squarely, you may rely on my interest and
> good-will. P.S. Is it really necessary to be quite so personal in your
> speeches? You can attack a policy without imputing all sorts of crimes
> to its author. Mr Gladstone was a good model in this aspect, & in all the
> Home Rule controversy he almost entirely avoided personal attack.[14]

Now that Winston was poised on the brink there were not wanting
powerful influences to urge him to take the plunge. His formidable
aunt Cornelia, Lady Wimborne, begged him to do so without delay:

> You know, I am sure, how deeply interested I am in your career.
> I feel the present moment is such a critical one for your fortunes
> ... Of one thing I think there is no doubt & that is that Balfour &
> Chamberlain are one, and that there is no future for Free Traders in the
> Conservative party. Why tarry!

*   *   *

Meanwhile it was public knowledge that the Government was a house
of discord. The position of the enigmatic Prime Minister alone remained
in doubt, and he continued to cloak his thoughts in a mysterious silence.
Both sides had high hopes of him and competed like rival Jesuits to bring
about his conversion to their own way of thought, Winston referring to
him in the House of Commons as 'a great Free Trader out of school
hours'. But Balfour obstinately refused to resolve their doubts, or to
break his baffling silence on the burning issue of Tariffs, and imposed a
gag upon discussion of the subject in Parliament until a Board of Trade
inquiry had reported on it.

This extraordinary decision gave Winston an excellent opportunity
for goading the Prime Minister, and he wrote derisively to *The Times*:

> The great question of the day may be argued in the Palace and the
> coal hole. Every Chamber of Commerce may debate it. Every public body
> may pass a resolution. It is on the agenda of the Eton Debating Society. It
> is in order in the Parliament of Peckham. There is one place in the British
> Empire where it is 'taboo'. The House of Commons, most interested, most
> concerned, most responsible, is to be gagged and smothered by a cynical
> and ingenious abuse of its own procedure.[15]

14. Ibid.
15. *The Times*, 16 July 1903.

But although the Prime Minister may have failed to make his own decision, he could not prevent others from doing so, and the cracks in the Conservative Party were splitting open into chasms. On 9 September Chamberlain wrote to Balfour resigning from the Government, and notifying him of his intention to conduct a campaign for Tariff Reform in the country. But the Prime Minister, at a Cabinet Meeting six days later, did not see fit to inform his colleagues of Chamberlain's resignation, merely remarking that he was in favour of some undisclosed fiscal reform. But, at the same time, he disembarrassed himself of the Free Trade Ministers in his Government, forcing the resignations of Mr Ritchie, Lord George Hamilton, Lord Balfour of Burleigh, and the Duke of Devonshire, and filling two of the vacant offices with a pair of convinced Protectionists – Austen Chamberlain and Alfred Lyttelton.

In Winston's words:

> He was careful to shed Free Trade and Protectionist blood as far as possible in equal quantities. Like Henry VIII he decapitated Papists and burned Hot Gospellers the same day for their respective divergences from his central, personal and artificial compromise.[16]

Although Balfour, so intelligent, so *rusé*, seemed yet to be unaware of, or indifferent to, the growing hostility of public opinion, and the approaching disruption of his own party, both were abundantly clear to the 29-year-old Winston. The latter after only three years in Parliament wrote to the Duke of Devonshire and acutely remarked: 'We are on the eve of a gigantic political landslide. I don't think Balfour and those about him realise at all how far the degeneration of the forces of Unionism has proceeded, and how tremendous the countercurrent is going to be.[17] These were prescient words.

* * *

Clear signs of a sharp impatience began to appear in Winston's constituency. His Chairman at Oldham, Mr Travis Clegg, himself a Free Trader, warned him that unless he agreed blindly to follow Balfour (now believed to be in favour of Protection), he would be repudiated by the constituency party. But Winston had already gone too far to be disturbed by any threats from this quarter. An unsent letter he wrote on 24 October to Lord Hugh Cecil described his attitude without the slightest ambiguity:

> I am an English Liberal. I hate the Tory Party, their men, their

16. Winston S. Churchill, *The World Crisis 1911-1914*, p. 28-9.
17. Holland, *Life of the Duke of Devonshire*, Vol.2, p.320.

> words & their methods. I feel no sort of sympathy with them ...
> It is my intention that before Parliament meets, my separation from
> the Tory Party and the Government shall be complete and irrevocable,
> and during the next session I propose to act consistently with the Liberal
> Party. This will no doubt necessitate a re-election which I shall not hesitate
> to face with all its chances.[18]

On 8 January 1904 his local constituency party formally repudiated
him for his failure to support Balfour, and passed a resolution saying that
he had forfeited their confidence as Unionist member. He treated this
gesture with disdain, explaining that it was Balfour who had changed the
fundamental policy of a Party which had been Free Trade for fifty years,
and that no charge of broken pledges could be fairly made against him.

Perhaps the last straw was the public humiliation inflicted on him
by Balfour on 29 March during the debate on the Easter adjournment.
Winston was now more detested by his own party than any other man
in the House of Commons. This hatred was venomous in its intensity.
He was a traitor to his party and his class; ugly emotions which were a
bitter forecast of the general abhorrence in which he was soon to be held
by Tories, some of which remained with him, clinging and inseparable,
for decades to come. Now, when the Government was tottering, and
the fortunes of the party were at a low ebb, Winston's attacks on the
failing Administration in its hour of weakness and need further enraged
Conservatives; but he persisted doggedly in sight of the kill.

On this occasion the party rank and file led by the Prime Minister,
who had decided to show the claw rather than the velvet glove, refused
to hear him. Balfour declined even to listen to his opening sentences,
and walked out of the Chamber, followed by the other Ministers. Then
seventy or eighty Tory members followed their leader in a body, like
sheep following the bell-wether, leaving Winston with an audience of
less than a dozen of his own side, most of them Free Traders. This was
not a spontaneous demonstration but a coldly organized insult reflecting
the hatred in which he was now held. He volunteered to resign his seat
at Oldham, but the Association did not accept the offer. They probably
realized that there must be a General Election within eighteen months,
and did not want to have two elections in so short a time.

* * *

On 22 April 1904 Winston suffered another public disaster, breaking
down in the middle of a speech on the Trades Disputes Bill, a speech

18. Chartwell papers.

which was described as 'Radicalism of the reddest type',[19] before it came to its humiliating end. This failure was a direct penalty of his peculiar method of oratory. He had been speaking with his usual apparent confidence, with vivid imagery and daring asides, to make retaliatory forages at the expense of the Government and Joseph Chamberlain:

'It lies with the Government', he was saying, with normal vigour and emphatic gestures, 'to satisfy the working classes that there is no justification –' but at this point he suddenly dried up. He had absolutely lost the thread of his argument, and in a horrible moment realized that his mind was a complete blank, and that the next words refused to come. He tried desperately to reassemble his speech, and began again: 'It lies with them to satisfy the electors . . . It lies with them . . . What?' he barked at a member trying to supply the key word and failing to do so. He picked up the scraps of paper from the bench: others picked them off the floor. The linking words were not there. Once more the stranded orator tried again, muttering desperately: 'It lies with them to satisfy the electors . . .' but the log-jam was complete, and he sat down, murmuring thanks to the House for its courtesy.

Wild and foolish rumours at once began to circulate about his health, and it was recalled that Lord Randolph, during his last illness and in premature senility, had broken down with the same humiliating results. Was Winston's incandescent flame to be pathetically quenched in the same way? But there was nothing wrong with his health. We have already seen that he was incapable, or believed himself to be so, of 'thinking on his feet', although he was one of the most brilliant monologists of his age. When seated in an armchair or at a table, and stirred in conversation, his thoughts followed in sequence, disposing themselves in superb imagery, and flashing out in golden unpremeditated phrases without a pause for reflection, a natural and organic process. But some profound mistrust of his power of speech, some psychological blockage, inhibited him from speaking in the same way on his feet in public.

Hence his speeches had the Sheridanesque quality of concocted impromptu, where everything was contrived rather than natural. His speeches were in fact prodigious feats of memory, but 'memory is mechanical, and its breakdown, like that of a machine, is absolute'. This incident should have revealed to anyone who did not already understand it the secret of his public eloquence – the grinding hours writing and memorizing long speeches, burning the midnight oil for weeks on end. A lesser man might well have found his confidence irretrievably sapped by this unnerving fiasco, but Winston was a man of the toughest – indeed, insensitive – fibre, and brushed it aside. Speech was the cutting tool of

19. *The Daily Mail*, April 1904.

his trade, and he could have no more lost confidence here than have abandoned politics altogether.

Nor did he change but rather intensified the old cumbrous methods of preparation. More detailed and fuller notes, more elaborate engines and fulcrums against breakdown, and even more laborious memorizing followed the collapse of memory. He would rise to speak in future holding what resembled the manuscript of a book, but such was his histrionic skill that he seldom needed to glance at it, and an impression of easy spontaneity was maintained. We may regard his recovery from this disaster as yet another proof of the iron determination of his character.

He was speaking in the following month, on 16 May, with all the old ardour. This was his last speech, as it transpired, from the Conservative benches, on the Second Reading of the Finance Bill, and it castigated the Government for financial extravagance; to reinforce his argument, it revealed a cynical change in his attitude towards the Boer War, which he now referred to as 'that immense public disaster'. As he bitterly attacked Chamberlain and his 'New Imperialism', Members melted away until there was scarcely a Protectionist left in the House.

* * *

On 31 May Winston crossed the floor at last in an atmosphere strangely devoid of drama. As though guided by a ghostly hand, he made his way to his father's old place, the corner seat below the Opposition gangway, from which in bygone days Lord Randolph had sprayed his jets of ridicule on Gladstone and Stafford Northcote, and sat down beside David Lloyd George. This formal transfer of allegiance completed the hatred and contempt in which he was already held by the Conservative Party. The taint of the renegade had now become a disgusting stench.

Said Joseph Chamberlain's honourable son Austen: 'His conversion to Radicalism coincided with his personal interests.' Leo Maxse, editor of the *National Review*, remarked: 'He is half alien and wholly undesirable.' Bonar Law, a Prime Minister to be, described him briefly and succinctly as a 'turncoat'.[20]

This intense resentment was to be deepened by the fact that from the fall of the Balfour Government in 1905 until May 1915, Liberal Governments were continually in office, and Winston Churchill was in office with them. It was therefore thought by Conservatives that by 'ratting' to the Liberals shortly before the Conservative disaster at the polls in 1906 he had shown a cynical and unscrupulous pursuit of power at the expense of principle. To repeat Rhodes James's penetrating comment:

20. Robert Rhodes James, op.cit., p.21.

The personal and political animosities that he had aroused during his brief and spectacular advance in 1900-1905 were to stalk him relentlessly, were to temporarily destroy him in 1915, and were never to be wholly eradicated. In politics, both individuals and parties have long memories. Churchill, within five years of active politics, had arrived – but at a price.[21]

And yet although he had changed his party once, and would do so again, he was not a true party man. Again in Rhodes James's words:

Churchill stood apart from Party in the sense that he had no permanent commitment to any. Few men could indulge in the exchange of party acerbities with greater vigour, yet he always regarded Party as essential in the sense that the horse is essential to the rider.

For this reason we shall see that when the Second World War came, and he was urged by some to be 'above Party', he decided with great shrewdness to provide himself with a firm base by becoming Head of the Party. To be 'above party', he clearly realized, is to be powerless.[22]

* * *

Winston found himself in mixed company in the Liberal Party. There were men of his own background there – Edward Grey, Rosebery and Crewe – and in spite of the divergence of their views, he was devoted to Morley, with whom he frequently dined. There were also the Radicals led by Lloyd George, and including a strange menagerie of pacifists, teetotallers, nonconformists, and cranks. But although he was held in suspicion by many of these, he ignored them, and was warmly received by Lloyd George, Asquith and Morley, who were in no doubt of the value to their party of this new, if turbulent, recruit. He now realized that his days at Oldham were numbered, and cast round for another constituency. He was approached by the Liberals in the North-West Division of Manchester, which although a Tory stronghold was the cradle of doctrinaire Free Trade, and in April 1904 accepted their invitation to contest the seat at the next election.

In Manchester he was to make many Jewish friends to whom he endeared himself by his robust opposition to the Aliens Bill of 1904, which the Government was forced to abandon. He also met a man whose genius and abnormal dedication to the task in hand closely resembled his own – a young Jewish doctor called Chaim Weizmann, who planted in him an enduring sympathy with Zionism, and whose

21. Ibid, p.23.
22. Rt. Hon. Harold Macmillan to author.

slogan 'The difficult we do at once; the impossible takes longer', was perfectly in time with his own impatient spirit.

He spoke in Wales on the same platform for the first time with David Lloyd George, whose influence upon him was at once powerful. The young girl Winston was to marry in 1908 formed the impression that in these early Liberal years 'he was completely under Lloyd George's thumb – wholly absorbed and fascinated by him'.[23] Reform and the amelioration of the plight of the humble was the bond which united them. But although the first impact of this fascinating creature was overwhelming, there was a most significant difference between them. As A.J.P. Taylor wrote: 'The differences between Churchill's Radicalism and the deeper Radicalism of Lloyd George was already showing. Churchill was merely lessening the edge of economic harshness. Lloyd George aimed at a Welfare State which would transform society.'[24] In other words, Winston's radicalism was essentially conservative. It was based on generosity. Born and bred as he was, it was inevitable that this generosity should be devoted to improving the lot of the poor and under-privileged, without any questioning of the social order in which he had been brought up and saw no reason to doubt, while in his early years Lloyd George's passionate desire was to tear up the whole rotten system, as he saw it, root and branch, and lay down paths for the workers which led 'through fields of waving corn'.

Lloyd George welcomed Winston to the reformist fold, but with certain reservations. In August 1904 he said that

> He was very glad to see the young men on the other side forsaking their evil ways and turning towards the Light ... The marvel to him was not that they were with them now but that they had not been with them for three years. He knew that they were perfectly sick of the Tory Government and all its ways, but one could not expect people to rush all at once from their party ties. They had expected the Tory Government to repent; having given room for repentance and finding that there was no hope of them they had come over to the other side ... What had driven them? The extravagant expenditure and reactionary legislation, culminating eventually, as the natural outcome of all this, in the policy of Mr Chamberlain to tax food and restore the Protectionist régime.[25]

* * *

In the prolonged death throes of the Conservative Government Winston did not waste his powder on minor victims. Now speaking from Liberal

23. Lady Spencer-Churchill to author.
24. A.J.P. Taylor, op.cit., p.19.
25. Lloyd George papers.

platforms, he directed his fire against two former friends and partners – Balfour and Chamberlain. It will be apparent by now that there was little if any subtlety in Winston's character, and even less cruelty, but his attack on Balfour in Manchester at this period was so feline and penetrating that it can only have been accidental.

> I am not surprised, he said, that Mr Balfour has declared that he does not intend to dissolve Parliament. Abdications have taken place in the history of the world . . . but you will see that they have usually been made by masculine not by feminine monarchs. Kings have abdicated but never Queens, and it is one of the attractive qualities that his nature displays a certain femininity. No doubt it is that element in his nature which prompts him to cling to office on any terms as long as it is possible to do so.[26]

These words revealed with deadly, if unintentional, clarity something of which many have been vaguely aware – the epicene quality in Balfour's complicated and baffling character.

Later, and after another damaging speech by Winston calling on him to resign after a Government defeat, Balfour was to take his revenge. Winston had attacked him in a sensitive spot, and he retaliated in kind by sneering at Winston's inability to speak without laborious preparation.

> It is not on the whole desirable to come down to this House with invective that is both prepared and violent. The House will tolerate . . . almost anything within the rule of order which evidently springs from a genuine indignation aroused by the collision of debate, but to come down with these prepared phrases is not usually successful . . . If there is preparation there should be more finish, and if there is so much violence there should certainly be more veracity of feeling.[27]

But if this thrust was supposed to penetrate the joints in Winston's armour it failed, since he remarked gleefully to a friend after the debate: 'He caught me in my weak place – the preparation.' But, he told her, he had thought Balfour's speech excellent. In fact, although he greatly disliked being opposed or contradicted in private, he was able to regard the blows delivered in debate with an artist's detachment. 'Blood might flow but there was no poison in the wounds that he inflicted or received.'

He had already dismissed Chamberlain contemptuously at the National Liberal Club in the words 'The country thought Mr Chamberlain was . . . a prophet with a message. They have found him a politician groping for a platform.' He then renewed the assault on Balfour in Glasgow in November 1904, and continued in 1905 to be a leading

26. *The Times*, 28 January 1905.
27. Hansard, 24 July 1905.

protagonist of Free Trade in speeches which exacerbated the loathing in which he was now held by the Conservative Party.

By February the Government was seen to be dying fast, but still refused to give up the ghost. Winston administered another vicious kick to its ailing body when Balfour failed to appear in the House during a Private Member's motion of censure on his 'policy of fiscal retaliation'. Never one to mince words, he said: 'To keep in office for a few more weeks and months there is no principle which the Government is not prepared to abandon, no friend or colleague that they are not afraid to betray, and no quantity of dirt and filth that they are not prepared to eat.'

In February too Winston made a most significant departure. He revealed himself as a Home Ruler. This gesture was of particular importance because it disclosed a fundamental rejection of one of his father's strongest convictions. Lord Randolph had shown a bitter hostility to Irish Home Rule. By this unfilial rejection Winston gave notice that he was accepting one after another the articles of Liberal faith, that he was no longer guided by a vanished hand, but was at last following his own or at least a Liberal star.

On 4 December Balfour realized that the game was lost, resigning at last, and Sir Henry Campbell-Bannerman formed a Liberal administration.

* * *

Winston's hour had now come. So long superciliously ignored by Balfour, he was now offered the Financial Secretaryship to the Treasury under the new Chancellor of the Exchequer, Herbert Asquith. At this point he showed both effrontery and shrewdness, persuading Campbell-Bannerman instead to appoint him Under-Secretary of State for the Colonies. The main reason for this request – a bold one indeed for a young man being offered office for the first time – was that the Secretary of State, Lord Elgin, sat in the House of Lords, so that Winston would have sole charge of Colonial business in the House of Commons, and frequent opportunities for displaying his skill. It may also have been that the governing of the colonies appealed more to the instinct of grandeur in his character than did the intricacies of the Treasury, and he may have felt a doubt (entirely justified) of his grasp of even the elements of finance. He chose as his Private Secretary Edward Marsh, a civil servant in the Colonial Office, and a close friend of his aunt Leonie Leslie. 'Eddie' Marsh – who had a fastidious interest in literature, and was afterwards to become a patron of young writers such as Rupert Brooke, and Editor of *Georgian Poetry* – served Winston in every office he held for the next thirty years and was his devoted friend.

Parliament was dissolved in January 1906: the campaigning for the General Election had already begun. This was an important month in Winston's life: his massive and pious biography of Lord Randolph, begun in 1902, was published on 2 January, and on the 3rd he went north to contest his seat. In North-West Manchester William Joynson-Hicks, a solicitor (afterwards famous as 'Jix') was the Conservative candidate, and the campaign was fought chiefly on the issue of Free Trade, although Winston also pledged himself to religious equality, reduction of spending on armaments, and reform of the administration of Ireland.

The tone of his campaign was set by the aggressive announcement:

> I am glad that the Government elected in 1900 is about to be dissolved. Few Parliaments in our modern experience have been less worthy of respect. A majority elected under the spell of patriotic emotion, upon a national issue, in the stress of an anxious war, has been perverted to crude and paltry purposes of party. Seven more years of dodge and dole and dawdle! Seven years of tinker, tax and trifle! Seven years of shuffle, shout and sham! *Do not be taken in again.*

In the wake of this alliterative blast he entered the familiar election atmosphere – the carriages rattling from meeting to meeting, the drab streets glistening in the rain which fell constantly on the steaming horses, the shouting, the fierce loyalties and hatreds, the relaxed and happy suppers after the last meeting, the post-mortems over wine and cigars at the Midland Hotel.

> Like any contest in which Winston Churchill played a part, it was dominated by his personality. The crowds struggling to get into his meetings were so great that he was often obliged to address dense throngs outside the hall and hundreds jammed upon the stairs inside before he could reach the platform. On one occasion the sheer weight of the audience in an overfilled hall threatened to bring down the floor. There were cries of 'The floor is giving way,' and a panic was feared. 'Let us do justice,' said Winston coolly, 'even though the floor fall,' and proceeded with his speech – while the floor mercifully held. Mr Balfour, who was defending his seat in a neighbouring division on Manchester, was neglected by the crowds. The press, the public and the limelight were all focused on the fight in the North West. Winston had stolen the picture from the ex-Prime Minister.[28]

At no time in living memory had there been an election of such frenzied tumult or charged with such electrical excitement. There was a sense in the air of some great impending change. Winston's

28. Violet Bonham Carter, op.cit., pp.127-8.

meetings were systematically interrupted; the disdainful Balfour was the incongruous object of blatant and violent rowdyism, and Joynson-Hicks had his carriage stoned. Winston clearly recalled this election afterwards, for it was deeply stamped on his mind for many different reasons:

> My individual fight was part of a vehement national revolt against the Conservative Government. Nothing like it had been seen in the memory of mortal man, and nothing like it was seen until 1931 . . . No one, however, could possibly suppose that the final results would be so sweeping. Even the most ardent Liberal would never have believed it. When we rose up in the morning all the nine seats were held by Conservatives. When we went to bed that night all had been won by Liberals. Arthur Balfour was out, and with him all his friends.
>
> Some of us belonging to the victorious party had a supper at the Midland Hotel. There was a gallant little man, a Mr Charles Hands, on the staff of the *Daily Mail*, who had been a correspondent in the South African War and whom I had known there . . . He wrote extremely well, but of course on the Conservative side. I invited him to supper. 'What did you think of that?' 'It is,' he said, 'a grand slam in doubled no trumps.'

* * *

And so indeed it proved, for the results of Manchester were reflected in every part of the country. Bastion after bastion, supposedly impregnable, fell to the Liberals until it was clear that a landslide was in progress. The Conservative Party had long outstayed its welcome, and had become an object of deadly tedium to the people.But it was not only against the public weariness of a moribund Government that the Conservatives were fighting. They had also to contend with the most formidable cluster of slogans – some of them fraudulent – that have ever led a political party to triumph at the polls.

Four main issues – the 'Chinese slavery' fiction, or the charge that Chinese indentured labour had been used in conditions of slavery in South Africa; the catch-phrase of 'dear food'; the teetotallers' hatred of the licensed trade; and the unpopular Unionist Education Act – all these and other bitter draughts for the Tories were drawn from the same somewhat contaminated well.

Winston's own majority over Joynson-Hicks was 1,241, but in the country the Liberal victory was so overwhelming that even the most sanguine prophets of the party were staggered. 'They had prayed for rain,' it was said, 'and been given the deluge.' When Parliament met the figures were 513 Government supporters, of whom 377 were Liberals, and on the opposition benches 157 Tories. This last forlorn group, huddled like the cowed survivors of a disaster at sea, only reached up to the first gangway.

In the new House of Commons the Government benches would soon be seen to bristle with exultant Liberals, so long excluded from power and place. It was not a situation in which chivalry was likely to be extended to the vanquished. Armoured in their immense majority, the victors were to permit themselves every form of arrogance and ill manners. They regarded the crushed remnant on the Opposition benches with neither pity nor generosity, but merely with contempt, and the vast Liberal phalanx was unrestrained in triumph. There were many strange faces and even stranger characters in it, with a fair admixture of cranks and fanatics. Such men, thought the Tories, have never before been seen at Westminster.

The merciless newcomers seemed to accentuate the upheaval that had taken place. Winston Churchill, in fact, was to find himself in strange company. It was a fascinating question what his relations with these people – many wholly alien to him – would be, and what he would think of them.

Part 2

In Office

Chapter 6

Under-Secretary of State
for the Colonies

12 December 1905-12 December 1908

Winston's attitude to this great phalanx of almost faceless men soon became evident – he simply ignored them. He betrayed not the slightest interest in them personally, and it was impossible to conceive any communication between himself and them in any medium other than politics. They may well have been dazzled by his political performances, and regarded the exotic creature with the wonder with which one watches a peacock spreading its tail, but he and they spoke different languages, and inhabited different worlds, and within his total lack of interest in the processes in other minds, there could be no other communication between them.

Now, serving under a Secretary of State who was in the House of Lords,[1] an opportunity was disclosed for a much fuller indulgence than ever before of his leaping ambition. An outstanding authority on this period, Ronald Hyam, described the 'short and lively partnership of Elgin and Churchill' as constituting 'the watershed between the nineteenth-century empire and the twentieth-century commonwealth'.[2] Their most important achievement was the establishment of self-governing constitutions in the Transvaal and the Orange River Colony.

In his new Department Winston exercised far more than the influence of an ordinary Under-Secretary. At times he would irritate and embarrass the Secretary of State, but always, with his dim awareness of human relationships, would convince himself that they were working in perfect harmony. The Secretary of State was no man of straw but a canny Scot, able in administration although inarticulate in debate, and in no way prepared to countenance Winston's flights of fancy. Winston

1. Ninth Earl of Elgin.
2. R. Hyam, *Elgin and Churchill at the Colonial Office*, p.545.

was aware of Elgin's endowments, but thought him slow and painfully lacking in imagination, regarding him with a sort of patient respect or, in Edward Marsh's words, as 'a rugged old thane of antique virtue'. Most of the friction between them was due to Churchill's ambition. It was his object to become a full Cabinet Minister at the earliest moment, and in the pursuit of this aim his ruthless and selfish side often asserted itself at Elgin's expense. He maintained separate and direct contact with men in high office, and (sometimes no doubt without realizing it) depreciated Elgin, his own reputation growing to the detriment of his superior. Three weeks before Asquith actually became Prime Minister, Winston was shamelessly asking for the reversion of the Colonial Office, claiming that during the past two years 'practically all the constructive action and all the parliamentary exposition has been mine'.[3]

Another tendency which disconcerted Elgin was Winston's habit of writing minutes of devastating frankness, which showed his complete indifference ot the need for concealing from the office his many disagreements with his chief. This habit Elgin regarded as not only personally disloyal to him but destructive of the proper conduct of departmental business.[4] Elgin observed with growing irritation Winston's apparent inability to distinguish between major and minor issues. Owing to his compulsion always to be doing something, every day was a day of crisis. He would minute at equal length and with the same copious eloquence on the dethronement of an African chief and the establishment of a new constitution. He noticed strange and irrelevant details. In reading the estimate for the Seychelles he observed that the income from unique postage stamps there was the same as the annual expenditure on education and religion. He exaggerated the importance of everything he touched. Every approaching problem, large or small, loomed immediately for him portentous with crisis and doom.

Nor was his ravenous appetite to be contained within the confines of his own department, and he was as free with his advice to other departments as he was to his own. The explanation, of course, was that fantastic reservoir of energy, those teeming ideas – good, bad and ridiculous – straining for release, like flood-waters piling to burst a dam. He was utterly incapable of relaxation, like a racing engine that cannot idle, and his power of concentration amounted almost to obsession. But, as we shall see in this short review of his period of office, his contribution and activity were for a junior Minister prodigious, and have probably

3. R. Hyam, op.cit., p.489.
4. Ibid., p. 490.

never been equalled by any other Under-Secretary before or since.

* * *

Chinese labour was the first colonial problem with which the Liberal Government had to deal. In 1904, on Milner's advice, the Secretary of State, Lyttelton, had allowed the introduction of indentured Chinese labour to work in the mines on the Rand. The tender humanitarian Liberal instincts were outraged by this decision, and 'Chinese Slavery' was one of their most cherished battle-cries in the General Election of 1906 which resulted in so huge a Liberal majority. To Conservatives this form of attack was nauseating – indeed, the most malodorous red herring of all those thrown in their teeth during the campaign. They repudiated the charge with fury, and regarded the Liberal slobbering over the Chinese without examining the facts as tinged with characteristic cynicism and with a hypocrisy which they found hard to stomach. An ordinance sanctioning this experiment had been passed by the Transvaal Council, and in June 1904 the labourers had begun to arrive. Milner justified the measure by the labour shortage in the mines, on the profits of which his reconstruction programme depended, and he had become convinced that it could not be met from South African sources alone. Milner, a great proconsul and a hero of the Imperialist movement, had a contempt for parliamentary democracy, was intent only on his work of administration, and certainly did not concern himself unduly with the political repercussions of his policy at home. This is not the place to examine the ethics of Chinese labour, apart from noting that 'slavery' was a gross and unscrupulous misnomer; that the Chinese labourers earned wages fifteen times as high as they could command in their native land; and that Milner's economic objective was unquestionably achieved. We should, however, clearly understand that there were other facts that made the ordinance ill-advised. It alienated organized labour in Britain at a time when its support was most needed by the Conservatives. The policy asked for trouble from the working class for two reasons; it excluded a field of potential emigration, and it implied a commodity view of labour which was likely to be anathema to articulate trade unionists.[5] The precedent of dealing with labour shortage by importing foreigners might, after all, be extended to Britain to the severe disadvantage of the unions when in a favourable bargaining position. The policy also greatly disturbed the 'Nonconformist Conscience', and it was asked with horror what would happen when hordes of young men were placed in compounds without their wives or women.

5. Robert Blake, *The Conservative Party from Peel to Churchill*, p.173.

The answer was all too clear – in the jargon of the day 'nameless practices'; and although today we are readier to give them a name, even then everyone knew what was meant.[6]

The Colonial Office did not like the measure, but Alfred Lyttelton, who was clay in Milner's hands, had justified it by claiming that it was a temporary expedient which could be amended or withdrawn. He urged continual vigilance to ensure that Chinese wages were never less than African wages, and care in the administration of the regulations. These, however, were open to harsh and frequent misinterpretation, and many irregularities occurred on the side of both Chinese labourers and white employers.

It was impossible in practice for the Liberal Government to end this system at a stroke, however much they affected to abhor it, without inflicting a heavy blow on the mining industry. Winston Churchill, on whom now descended the outraged moral feelings of Government supporters in the House of Commons, disliked the Chinese ordinance, although he realized that the term 'slavery' was a ridiculous exaggeration. As he was now in a responsible official position, his public remarks on the subject were set in a most uncharacteristic minor key, and marked by an unwonted caution. In his election address he had made the following reference to Chinese labour:

> My opinions on the subject of Chinese labour are unchanged, except that having had access to official information I hold them more strongly than ever. A Liberal Government, while it is forced to bear any part of the responsibility, is bound to do its utmost to restrict such a system, and to put down its abuses.[7]

The phrase 'while it is forced to bear any part of the responsibility' indicated the desire of the home Government to establish self-government in the Transvaal with all possible speed, thereby disembarrassing itself of the odious duty of implementing the Chinese Labour Ordinance, over which it had little effective control, and ridding itself for good of this unfragrant detritus of its predecessor. Chinese labour had had some bearing on the outcome of the election, and it was necessary to honour the election pledges. Campbell-Bannerman had indeed, in a moment of exuberance in 1905, committed himself to stopping immediately the recruitment and embarkation of coolies. Unfortunately, shortly before this robust declaration, and contrary to Lyttelton's suggestion to suspend recruitment for six months, some 14,000 further licences for the importation of coolies had been issued.

6. Ibid.
7. Randolph Churchill, op.cit., Vol.II, p.117.

Cabinet colleagues therefore persuaded the Prime Minister to confine his pledges to no further recruitment.[8]

Although Lord Elgin thought the gloomier predictions of the effect of the withdrawal of Chinese labour exaggerated, his Scottish realism convinced him that it was out of the question to repatriate the Chinese all at once. That would involve a reversal of policy without consulting the colony, and would be bitterly resented in South Africa; it would be disastrous to the mining industry; imply a breach of faith with the labourers, and involve the Government in enormous claims for compensation. The mine-owners would also protest that they had been the victims of a betrayal, for the Conservative Government had led them to believe that they would be safe until a Transvaal elected Assembly decided the matter.[9] It was finally decided that the November licences should remain valid, but that nothing should be done to add to the number under contract until Transvaal opinion had been properly declared. The Government decided to amend the regulations by giving the coolies access to ordinary courts of law, by assisting the repatriation of those who could prove a genuine desire to return home, by more careful administration, and by abandoning penalties which were in practice inoperative. Winston summed up the position thus:

> In short it amounts to this – that the Chinese will have to go, but that reasonable time – even perhaps six years – will be given for their gradual and I trust comparatively painless extinction.[10]

In defending their policy in Parliament spokesmen for the Government were at pains to repudiate the charge of 'slavery' which they had flaunted with such reckless mendacity in their electoral propaganda. Winston's particular disclaimer, in which he travestied the language he loved, became famous and will survive as a dubious monument to his flamboyance:

> A labour contract into which men enter voluntarily for a limited and for a brief period, under which they are paid wages which they consider adequate, under which they are not bought or sold, and from which they can obtain relief ... may not be a desirable contract, may not be a healthy or proper contract, but it cannot in the opinion of His Majesty's Government be classified as slavery in the extreme acceptance of the word without some risk of terminological inexactitude.

8. Randolph S. Churchill, op.cit., p.118.
9. Hyam, op.cit., p.65.
10. WSC. Ref. CO 291/96.

This and the Government's other contortions in the search for compromise did not appease Radical opinion at home, nor was it likely to meet with enthusiasm in the Chamber of Mines. The Chinese labour problem continued to bedevil Churchill. On 27 November 1907 an extra shipload of 1,000 coolies was embarked, the result of an administrative blunder made in June 1905. On arrival in Durban on 6 January, the coolies were found to number 2,129. All but 259 had licences. Repatriation of the 259 would have cost the Transvaal Government £12,000. It was decided to turn a blind eye on the discrepancy in the hope that the 259 would pass unnoticed.

* * *

Winston's next House of Commons speech as Under-Secretary was a complete, humiliating, notorious disaster. It had been revealed that Milner had authorized the corporal punishment of Chinese labourers without the safeguards of the law, and that he had not objected to illegal flogging. The occasion of Winston's debacle was a motion moved by a Liberal back-bencher, William Byles, concerning the conduct of Milner. Winston replied by proposing an amendment which declared that the House 'while recording its condemnation of the flogging of Chinese coolies in breach of the law, desires, in the interests of peace and conciliation in South Africa, to refrain from passing censure on individuals'. His original attitude was that 'Britain was too great a country, that the Liberal Party's success at the Election had been too overwhelming, and that the situation in South Africa was too critical to warrant the Government "engaging in the task of making martyrs".'[11] This generalization was by no means to the taste of the Radical elements in the party, eager for blood, but Winston persuaded the Government to allow him to put down his amendment.

He was the chief Government spokesman in the debate on the censure motion which took place after dinner in a House already rendered restive and ill-tempered by acrimonious proceedings in the afternoon. Churchill's speech was lamentable, but he was once again the victim of his own peculiar method of preparation. As always, everything had been long assembled and polished, and the mood of the House anticipated, and there could be no retreat even when he realized, as he did, that he was striding into a fiasco. He plodded grimly on, claiming that he did not wish to revile or harry Milner, but using none the less contemptuous phrases which he delivered in a harsh and grating voice which appeared to carry an unpleasant sneer that enraged the Opposition. In rasping tones he compared Milner with Parnell, adding

11. Randolph Churchill, Vol.II, p.176-7.

that the difference between them was that Parnell was innocent whereas Milner was not. The fault was one of manner, not of feeling; and Winston himself had engaged in the task of making martyrs.

Hyam described the speech as 'pompous and patronising'; Robert Rhodes James wrote:

> Read today, it is a good speech; it certainly seemed so when rehearsed to his new secretary, Edward Marsh; but it was fatally ill-tuned to the temper of the House.[12] Lord Winterton, who had listened to this unhappy effort and was a personal friend, had no doubt 'that this first ministerial speech of Mr Churchill's was a complete failure. His many enemies in the Conservative Party exultantly claimed that he was finished.'[13]

The disastrous performance was indeed long remembered against Churchill by his enemies among the Conservatives, and not less vindictively by Milner's friends. Among these was a young man of genius, Rudyard Kipling, who had long idolized Milner as fulfilling his ideal of 'the strong man working alone', and who read Winston Churchill's speech with incredulity and disgust. Kipling's memory was long and tenacious, and his character one that did not forgive or forget. Certainly he never forgot this speech of Churchill's which he regarded as the ultimate betrayal, the supreme Judas kiss.

As for Winston, he recognized his failure, but, as we have noticed before, failure inflicted no morbid or neurotic scars upon him. As for the renewed Conservative detestation, he had long reconciled himself to this condition and was stonily indifferent to it. He knew by experience that any failure, however humiliating, would be quickly obliterated by the next success. This he rightly believed would be his lot. His next speech was brilliant, and within two years he was in the Cabinet.

* * *

Letters Patent establishing the so-called Lyttelton Constitution for the Transvaal had been issued on 31 March 1905. Letters Patent obviate the necessity of a Bill being passed through Parliament. This Constitution was in fact the product of Milner's brain. The Treaty of Vereeniging declared that 'as soon as circumstances permit, representative institutions, leading up to full self-government, will be introduced.' There was conflict between the parties on that question, but the cardinal question was clearly when that moment should arrive.

The political parties formed in the Transvaal in 1904 were Het Volk by the Boers, and the Progressive Association and the Responsible

12. Robert Rhodes James, op.cit., pp.30-1.
13. Winterton, *Orders of The Day*, p.19.

Government Association by the British. The Lyttelton Constitution which never came into effect, found favour with none of these parties. The Progressive Association at first thought it acceptable, but when by November they saw hopes of winning the election they announced that if the British Government was not in sympathy with their views they would agitate for full responsible government.

The voters' roll had been compiled on the 1898 list of burghers, which was by then completely out of date. Another oversight in the Letters Patent was that the soldiers of the British garrison had not been disqualified from voting. Lyttelton had not wished to amend the solemn instrument, and hoped that a declaration of the Government's intention would suffice. Het Volk and the Responsible Government Association made five recommendations to the High Commissioner, who himself put forward an amendment which would increase the number of constituencies and seats.

* * *

Such was the position when the Liberals took office in December 1905. The unpopularity of the proposed Constitution and the flaws in the Letters Patent made it possible and seemly for the new Government to review the impasse without exposing themselves to the charge of reversing their predecessors' Imperial policy.

A Cabinet Committee under the Lord Chancellor, Lord Loreburn, of which among others Elgin, Morley and Asquith were members, was established in December to review the whole question. Winston was not a member, but this did not prevent him taking an active part in it. After much worried deliberation it was decided to scrap the Lyttelton Constitution, and to opt boldly for immediately responsible government. This generous decision was not registered without misgiving on the part of certain Ministers, although Lord Elgin from the first expressed a cautious approval. Winston, his mind full of the victor's duty of magnanimity to the vanquished, firmly made up his mind that this was the just and honourable course, and afterwards indulged in no doubt or vacillation, although fully aware of the dangers involved.

In January 1906 Jan Smuts, representing the Het Volk party, visited London to confer with Ministers, among whom was Winston. Sometimes Churchill's attention – utterly indifferent as he usually was to the personalities of others – could be captured in an instant and held for a lifetime by a single man, and that man likely to be one of genius. It happened with Chaim Weizmann. Now he felt this sudden electrical contact established with Jan Smuts, who so little time before had been his enemy, but who was to become an intimate and venerated friend whose sage counsels he was to seek for the rest of his life.

Elgin, after meeting Smuts, was less effusive. Slow to kindle, he found the Boer leader 'very pleasant and plausible; but so far as I can judge, he did not leave behind him any undue impression'.[14]

Smuts was at pains to foster the impression that it was he who had persuaded Liberal Ministers to accept responsible government. But in fact they were in no need of blandishments or promptings from without. They did not require conversion, for they had already made up their minds, although the decision was not formally taken until the Cabinet Meeting of 8 February when the Lyttelton Constitution was finally abandoned. Smuts was anxious to persuade the Government to give up the principle of 'one vote one value' in the delineation of constituencies, but in this he did not succeed.

* * *

The Government appointed a Committee to visit South Africa and inquire into disputed questions on which Ministers were lacking information. Winston fully grasped the need for such a committee of inquiry, but he was profoundly disturbed by the fact that

> a 6 months' delay in settling the fundamentals of the Constitution will, through economic pressure and political uncertainty, drive away British voters from the Transvaal, and alienate from the Mother Country the affections of the rest . . .[15]

These anxieties were confirmed by a letter from Lord Selborne[16] on 2 March:

> . . . I am in deep anxiety as regards the effect of the period of suspense . . . What will happen in the interval heaven only knows. The capitalists will suffer, but I do not care for them. But the population which I do care for and cherish, miners, artisans and trading and labouring classes, will suffer quite terribly. Already the Banks are calling in over-drawn accounts and are everywhere pressing for money that is lent. Everywhere work is being shut down; building operations are being stopped, and artisans and clerks are every day being turned off. This is not a funny picture; it is one of very real danger and distress. The reason is that capital is frightened; the future is unsettled . . .[17]

14. Hyam, op.cit., p.125.
15. Ibid., p. 140.
16. Second Earl of Selborne, High Commissioner in South Africa and Governor of the Transvaal and Orange River Colony.
17. Chartwell papers.

The Committee arrived in South Africa on 24 April and presented their report in July.

> As a result of its inquiries, the committee favoured manhood suffrage (as the Cabinet had suggested), the retention of the voters basis and the old magisterial districts (which would save time and make a concession to Boer sentiment), a residential qualification of six months and single-member constituencies, a point on which the Boers gave the most strenuous resistance. Het Volk accepted 'one vote one value' in exchange for manhood suffrage and other arrangements which would reduce the over-mighty subjects of the Rand compared with the country districts.[18]

In all these matters Winston made a strong personal contribution to Liberal thinking, out of all proportion to his subordinate office. That summer was a period of incessant work preparing the Constitution in which he played a major part throughout. So rapid was the progress that on 31 July he was able to give the House of Commons a clear outline of the Government's proposals. This time there was to be no hectoring, no clumsy solecisms. It was in the accents of a statesman that he reached his noble peroration:

> We are prepared to make this settlement in the name of the Liberal Party. That is sufficient authority for us; but there is a higher authority which we would earnestly desire to obtain. I make no appeal, but I address myself particularly to the right honourable gentlemen who sit opposite, who are long versed in public affairs, and not able to escape all their lives from the heavy South African responsibility. They are the accepted guides of a Party which, though in a minority in this House, nevertheless embodies nearly half the nation. I will ask them seriously whether they will not pause before they commit themselves to violent or rash denunciation of this great arrangement. I will ask them further whether they will not consider whether they cannot join with us to invest the grant of a free Constitution with something of a national sanction. With all our majority we can only make it a gift of a Party; they can make it the gift of England.

But in spite of this melting invitation, and perhaps partly because of its detested sources, the Government's proposals encountered bitter attacks by the Unionist Party.

* * *

When the House rose for the summer recess Winston went abroad with relief and a sense of having been at grips with great issues. First he went to stay with his friend Baron de Forest at Deauville, where he

18. Hyam, op.cit., p.141-2.

was briefly enchanted by the gaiety of the little town, the sea and the surrounding coast and washed-out skies that Boudin loved to paint. But as usual he was incapable of relaxation, and saw these things only as a vague background to the recollection of recent political events which were still teeming in his head like a dream that will not fade.

From de Forest's magnificent steam yacht, on which most men would have found repose, he addressed on 15 August a 35-page handwritten document to the King, setting forth 'some considerations wh could not well be stated in a public or formal manner'. This remarkable effusion[19] illuminates at once Winston's fundamental grasp of the situation in South Africa, his phenomenal industry, his abnormal obsession with the issue of the moment, his sometimes dangerous instinct to put all to the hazard, and his strong belief in the consequences of a gift freely and generously bestowed.

The King appeared to be less convinced, answering through his Private Secretary that he was by no means certain of the wisdom of granting immediate responsible government to the Transvaal:

> The King quite understands that the granting of self Government was unavoidable, but in solving the many difficult problems in S Africa, it might be dangerous to assume that the Transvaal is simply a colony desirous of self Govt., like any other of His Majesty's Dominions, and the King knows you will agree with him in thinking that it would be deplorable to run the risk of having another war in South Africa or of losing the Colony where we have spent so much blood and money . . . The King can well understand that the onus of all these discussions in Parliament was thrown upon your shoulders and no doubt severe criticisms were made from both extremes, but His Majesty is glad to see that 'you are becoming a *reliable* minister and above all a serious politician.'[20]

Winston, of course, nourished a romantic veneration for any occupant of the throne, irrespective of merit, but it is perhaps surprising that he found this reply, as he told his brother Jack, a 'gracious' one. In reply to another question of the King as to the effect of the Constitution on immigration, he replied with another immense screed, almost as long as the first.[21]

He spent a fortnight at Ernest Cassel's villa, and here (when not writing on the political situation) he spent the days climbing the mountains of the Valais with his host, and the evenings playing bridge.

19. Royal Archives, 15.8.06.
20. Ibid.
21. Ibid., 20.8.06.

Apart from an occasional day's hunting or polo, Winston had taken no physical exercise since his Army days, and found himself seriously distressed on the slopes, writing to his mother:

> Cassel & I climbed the Eggishorn yesterday. A very long pull & I should never have got home without the aid of a mule. *Le vieillard* tramped it all out like a bird. Rather discreditable to me, I think.

As to bridge, it was said by some that Winston was the worst player in London, and that only his friend F. E. Smith could be remotely compared with him. He was aware of this fact, telling his mother: 'I cannot say how I hate losing money at Bridge. It is a wretched game when you are a bad player & hold the worst of cards.'[22]

After Switzerland, to Breslau for the German manoeuvres, and here again the King was watching his movements with a certain anxiety, caused by well-justified suspicions of his detested nephew, that *enfant terrible* the German Kaiser. He used Campbell-Bannerman to convey a warning to Winston: 'A day or two ago the K[ing] told me you were going to the manoeuvres, and asked me to warn you against being too communicative and frank with his nephew. I have no doubt you will, as the penny-a-liners say, "Exercise a wise discretion".' After the manoeuvres he went to Vienna and Venice, and thence to Eichorn to shoot partridges.

On 29 September he wrote to Lady Randolph from Siena:

> ... As I told you I do not desire any change this year, & I am quite contented where I am. There are enormous advantages in lying quiet & doing nothing at intervals. Youth so often loses by being over-eager & what is the use of being in a hurry when one has twenty years in hand. Next year will be the Colonial Conference which will be full of interest & I have the OR [Orange River] Constitution & Nigerian Railway still to pilot through the House of Commons . . .[23]

By October Winston was back at his desk at the Colonial Office, and we may conjecture that it was with relief that, after his long holiday, he found himself once more at the centre of affairs. On 6 December the new Transvaal Constitution was promulgated by Letters Patent, and the first General Election was held on 20 February 1907. A British majority of possibly 9 and certainly 5 was forecast and Winston wrote to the King that 'a clear Boer majority is outside the bounds of possibility'. He should have refrained from prophecy. The result of the

22. WSC to Lady Randolph. Chartwell papers.
23. Ibid.

election was a majority of 5 in the Legislative Assembly for the Het Volk party, and Winston's putative captor in the Boer War, General Botha, became Prime Minister. The Orange River Colony was granted a similar Constitution by Letters Patent on 5 June 1907, and an election was held in November, at which Oranjie Unie won 30 out of the 38 seats.

Ultimate federation of the South African Colonies had long been the agreed aim of both Parties, and the Constitutions were framed with that object in mind. A conviction was formed, that federation was the solution. The economic advantages were overriding, and it was believed that federation would ensure a strong, stable, independent South Africa. One of its main attractions to its begetters was that it would be an impartial solution, and therefore more likely to ensure civilized treatment of the Africans. The case for Federation was strengthened by the troubles in Natal, where the weakness of the small white community led to narrow-mindedness and parochialism, and led Campbell-Bannerman to write to Elgin in 1907: 'Those Natal people of yours are tiresome to the last degree. I hope federation will soon squelch them.' The 'native question', 'that ever swelling sea of dark humanity', as Winston called it, was also a matter of serious concern. In South Africa there was one white man to five Africans. 'The growth of this great population,' he wrote, 'is indeed a dark cloud spreading over the future of South Africa',[24] while Elgin gloomily predicted 'that the time must come when there will be danger of a collision between the white and coloured races, unless the relations between them are fair and suitable.'[25] The British framers of the Transvaal and Orange River Colony Constitutions did not forget the Africans, but there was little they could do in a practical sense, because of Article 8 of the Treaty of Vereeniging which said: 'The question of granting the franchise to natives will not be decided until after the introduction of self-government.' It was believed that South African opinion on the native question was improving and would continue to improve. It was, however, clear that the South African authorities had no idea what the Africans were doing, or what their real aims and aspirations might be.

It was generally hoped that federation would help to provide the answer to this daunting question. But while Ministers would offer every encouragement, they would do nothing to compel it. Federation must now be the work of South Africans themselves.

Lord Selborne argued the case for union in a memorandum of July 1907, and once in power the three Afrikaner parties [Cape, Transvaal, and Orange Free State] adopted it with enthusiasm and with the support

24. WSC to Sir Walter Hely-Hutchinson, 19 May 1906.
25. CO 291/97.

of their oppositions. White public opinion in South Africa moved steadily towards the new conception – partly, perhaps, out of a vaguely idealistic belief that the time had come to bury the hatchet and make a new start on the basis of white equality, but more importantly because an African rebellion in Natal in 1906 led many to believe union essential for white security – some also saw in union the best safeguard against any further British interference in South Africa. There were also strong economic reasons for union: the four colonies were interdependent, and yet without political union their material interests were so divergent that any customs union seemed almost certain to collapse.

Accordingly a national convention, consisting of 30 members appointed by the four colonial parliaments, and 3 non-voting members from Rhodesia, met from October 1908 till February 1909 under the chairmanship of the Chief Justice of the Cape. A Federal Constitution was drafted and unanimously approved by the convention, and it was carried with few dissentients in the parliaments of the Cape Colony, the Transvaal, and the Orange River Colony, and by a 3 to 1 majority in a referendum in Natal. It was enacted by the British Parliament in September 1909, substantially as it had been submitted to the British Government. The South Africa Act came into force on 31 May 1910, and the four colonies became the Union of South Africa, an event which seemed to most at the time a clean and desirable end to the business.

* * *

A major event of the spring of 1907 was the Colonial Office Conference, which had not met since 1902 when the Colonial Premiers had assembled in London for the Coronation of Edward VII. Liberal Ministers regarded the approaching Conference (which demanded a great deal of preparation) without much enthusiasm. There was a long debate on membership of the Conference, chiefly in regard to the Australian state premiers who wished to be invited. Winston was in favour of inviting them all, if they wished to come. Elgin, who thought that an overloaded Conference would break down, was strongly against the innovation. A long battle of words between them followed, fought by Winston with the extraordinary tenacity and passion with which he invested every issue that was currently occupying his mind, however minor; but he was forced to bow to Elgin's decision.

The Conference met on fifteen days in April and May. Winston was not a member of it, but had no intention of effacing himself from its proceedings, and, having asked permission to speak, held forth at length. This Conference was one of considerable significance, and its effects were ably summed up by Hyman in the following words:

In retrospect, the conference of 1907 marks an important stage in the evolution of the commonwealth. As Professor Hancock has observed: 'In spirit it was far closer to the Commonwealth Club of 1926 than to the Colonial circus of 1887.[26] It is now authoritatively regarded as probably the most important of all the conferences held before the outbreak of the First World War. All these conferences were in varying degrees affected by the difference of opinion between the advocates and the opponents of federalism, between those who wished to formalise the ties of empire, and those who did not; between those who believed that imperial unity was possible only by maintaining the vague ties of friendship and those who believed that they must organise themselves with formal machinery in order to survive. Although the conflict was not finally settled in 1907, it is clear that the anti-federalists won an important victory. The conflict between the two conceptions of imperial organisation was tacitly decided. Negative decisions are never very exciting, but they can be very significant. Much more than half the work of government consists in securing the quiet lapse of unwelcome proposals, which is what the Liberals achieved in 1907, with decisive help from the Canadians. Imperial unity as an ultimate goal was silently rejected. In the view of their opponents, the Liberals had opted for autonomy and disintegration, rather than centralisation and integration. If Elgin was described as 'unimaginative' it was largely because he did not share the 'imaginative' – but impracticable – visions of the federalists.[27]

* * *

The Conference was accompanied by much exhausting social activity, public and private, including the bestowal of the Freedom of the City of London upon the Premiers. One can imagine how bored Winston was by these unavoidable ceremonies. In the midst of them a rumour, wilder than most, was circulated that he was engaged to Botha's daughter, Helen. This was duly discredited and refuted. On 1 May he had been sworn of the Privy Council, no doubt in recognition of his work on the Transvaal and Orange River Constitutions and in preparation for the Conference.

Before his old enemy, General Botha, left London he wrote to Winston in language that carried an agreeable flavour of reconciliation:

> Before I leave it is my pleasant duty to write and thank you most heartily for the way in which you have received and helped me in the discussion of the burning questions of the Transvaal. It has been indeed a pleasure to have been here and to have strengthened our acquaintance.

26. Professor Hancock, *Smuts*, i, 134.
27. Hyam, op.cit., p.321.

I know how glad my Government will be when I tell them of what
assistance you have been to them, and what a thorough grip you have
of all matters relating to the Transvaal.

I am well aware of the fact that you and the other members of the
Government have as it were staked your reputation on the Transvaal, and
I can assure you that my colleagues and I and that important section of the
public who support us will see to it that your reputation is not imperilled
and that the splendid confidence reposed by you in us will prove a source
of strength, nay more a great victory to you.

May I also wish you every success and say that I soon hope to
see you at the top of the ladder?[28]

* * *

Churchill's superiors had been regarding his work at the Colonial Office and his performances in the House of Commons with
an admiring eye, and on 9 September 1907 the Prime Minister,
Campbell-Bannerman, wrote a letter which both encouraged and
gratified him:

Now that we have had a little breathing time, I feel impelled, on
looking back over the Session, to send you a special line of congratulation
and recognition of the part you have had in our success. There cannot
be two opinions on one point, viz. that the most conspicuous event
in the year is the creation of a self-governing state in the Transvaal
and in the Orange Colony. It is not only the greatest achievement of
this Government (which is a comparatively small matter) but it is the
finest & noblest of the British power in modern times. And you have
so identified yourself with this courageous & righteous policy, and so
greatly contributed to its successful enforcement that a large part of the
credit must always be attributed to you.

I cannot thank you too greatly for the help you have given in
this and in other matters, and the constant readiness and effectiveness
with which you have upheld true principles of government amid
the débris and wreckage left by the blunders and crimes of recent
years.

Take a good holiday and mind your health in this pilgrimage you
are undertaking. Don't overdo it.

Your sincere friend and grateful colleague . . .

Strong wine this for a young head, but Winston's self-confidence had
been cemented so hard by his success in office that it is unlikely that
he was unduly exhilarated by it. He was now impatiently awaiting the
moment when he should become a full Cabinet Minister.

28. Chartwell papers.

He went to the Continent for a few weeks (visiting the French manoeuvres in September) before undertaking 'this pilgrimage' to East Africa.

We have seen that Winston had few intimate personal friends outside his family. The subjectivity of his own character and his complete indifference to that of others normally prohibited such intimacy. 'Winston was different as a politician and a private person,' said Sir Desmond Morton to the author. 'He was prepared to let down a fellow-politician when it suited his book, but never a private friend. The others were just "politicals" playing the same game as himself. Private friends were admitted to the same category as his family.' Once in the magic circle they were sacrosanct, and, whatever enormities they might commit, Winston would have perjured himself in their defence.

His companion at the French manoeuvres, F. E. Smith, was perhaps the closest and dearest of these friends. They had been introduced at the Bar of the House of Commons, while waiting for a division, when the Parliament of 1906 had run some months of its course. F. E. Smith was angry with Winston for leaving the Conservative Party and 'breaking a continuity', and did not wish to meet him. 'But from that hour,' Winston wrote, 'our friendship was perfect. It was never disturbed by the fiercest party fighting. It was never marred by the slightest personal difference or misunderstanding. It grew stronger as nearly a quarter of a century slipped by, and it lasted till his untimely death.'

The star of that brilliant parvenu F. E. Smith had 'shot suddenly into the political skies, like a meteor in reverse, from earth to heaven, from obscurity into fame.' No reputation had ever before been so instantaneously established by a maiden speech. The House had been swept by gales of laughter; the Conservative back-benchers roared in ecstasy, and their leaders rolled about on the Front Bench in convulsions of amusement and delight. F. E. Smith not only made himself famous on that memorable night; he struck the first and only effective blow at that swollen Liberal majority, which never seemed quite the same again; driven the colossus into the open and shown that it had feet of clay.

Although one of this formidable pair had come from a palace and the other from a modest middle-class home in Birkenhead, there was an obvious bond between them. They were both, in the truest sense, adventurers, had made their own way in the world by their own unaided effort. Winston was at once attracted by F.E.'s character: 'He had all the canine virtues in a remarkable degree – courage, fidelity, love of the chase.' He was also to an unusual extent humbled by the force and discipline of this man's mind and his superb power of speech. For when F. E. spoke it was like the flight of a strong bird. He would speak for an hour, without a note, without hesitation, in language which might have been the result of days of preparation, but which flowed by the light of genius into his head. Winston greatly admired this supreme gift, which he would never possess, but he was a trifle awed by his new friend's other attainments, for F. E. was one of the most merciless vituperators of the day, with a tongue like a skinning knife, and Winston was a little afraid of him: 'Even I,' he wrote, 'who knew him so well, refrained from pushing ding-dong talk too far when others were present lest friendship should be endangered.'

That gleaming weapon of oratory – how dearly Winston would have loved to command it. Although he did not understand F.E.'s legal genius, he realized how complete his rhetorical equipment was – 'The bludgeon for the platform; the rapier for a personal dispute; the entangling net and unexpected trident for the Courts of Law; and a jug of clear spring water for an anxious perplexed conclave.' But it was the miracle of his friend's impromptu speaking and power to think on his feet that so deeply impressed him, and he wrote of his later mastery of the Upper House: 'To hear him wind up a debate from the Woolsack, speaking for an hour at a time without a note, with hardly an alteration of tone, dealing with point after point, weaving them all into an ordered texture or argument, darting aside now here now there upon some retaliatory foray, but returning always surely and easily to his main theme, and reaching his conclusion without the slightest appearance of effort; all this constituted an impressive and enviable gift.'

F. E. Smith felt none of the irritation, even repulsion, which many Conservatives experienced in Churchill's presence. The alleged arrogance of manner left him cold, and he was immediately drawn to the man beyond it:

> To those who know him well it is very remarkable how complete is the public misconception of the man. He is looked upon as reserved, insolent, and even domineering. For these illusions his own demeanour is (unintentionally) much to blame. He has no small talk; and says everything which comes into his mind. Sometimes caustic and disagreeable things come into it, though in private life this very seldom happens. He walks through the Lobbies ... with an air appropriate to Napoleon Bonaparte on the morning of the crisis of 18th Brumaire. He does not mean to be either reserved or rude; but he contrives to give the impression to those who know him little that he does not desire to know them more.

But F. E. brushed all this aside as irrelevant:

> Only his friends understand him well. And they know that there is no man in public life in England with a heart so warm, with a simplicity

so complete, with a loyalty so unswerving and so dependable. He has, indeed, in the intimacy of personal friendship a quality which is almost feminine in its caressing charm. And he has never in all his life failed a friend, however embarrassing the obligations, which he felt it necessary to honour, proved at the moment when he honoured them.[29]

Embarking at Syracuse towards the end of September, Winston visited Cyprus, and arrived in Malta early in October, where he was joined by Edward Marsh and Colonel Gordon Wilson, his aunt Sarah's husband, who were to be his travelling companions.

The journey developed into an official progress. Winston behaved like a Viceroy of India graciously touring his dominions. He bombarded the Colonial Office with long memoranda upon every country he visited, which were far from being to the taste of the civil servants, or of Lord Elgin himself. On a certain Saturday in December no less than eight of these immense rigmaroles descended upon the table of one of the ablest officials, Sir Francis Hopwood,[30] where they were received with a marked lack of enthusiasm. But from Winston's own lordly point of view the journey was a complete success, marred only by the death at Khartoum, from choleraic diarrhoea, of his faithful servant Scrivings. It would not have been in character if Winston had given the slightest consideration to the inconvenience which his activities might be causing to Lord Elgin and his officials, or to the problems which his memoranda would leave for Elgin's successor. It was quite sufficient to that abnormally self-centred mind that it had become absorbed by these new places and was forced to express itself upon the scene immediately before his eyes with total indifference to the effect on others. But he also became fascinated by the animal life in these strange places in the intervals between inspections – stalked lions, speared wart-hogs and looked with wonder on crocodiles, hippopotami, and a white rhinoceros. And in Uganda he renewed an old and consuming passion, the study of butterflies.

He defrayed the expenses of the journey by writing five articles for the *Strand Magazine*, which were afterwards published as a book, *My African Journey*. He received £750 for the articles and a further £500 for the book rights. He also wrote accounts of his travels in vivid letters to Lady Randolph and Jack. He arrived home on 17 January 1908, after a five months' absence. His house, No. 12 Bolton Street, had been let, and was not yet available to him. He therefore stayed at Lord Ridley's house in Carlton House Terrace.

*   *   *

29. First Lord of Birkenhead, *Contemporary Personalities*, pp. 114-15.
30. Permanent Secretary to the Colonial Office.

During Winston's absence in East Africa it had become obvious to his colleagues that Campbell-Bannerman's life had begun to fade quietly away, and that his resignation could not be long postponed. It was also clear that Asquith would be his successor. The King was convinced that the old Prime Minister's day was over, and discussed with Asquith the reshuffling of the Cabinet he might desire to make on Campbell-Bannerman's resignation.

Asquith recorded that the King 'had heard gossip that Winston was anxious to get into the Cabinet, keeping his present office of Under-Secretary. He was opposed to this, and said that Queen Victoria had vetoed a similar proposal by Lord Rosebery in favour of Sir Edward Grey . . .' Asquith had replied that Winston had every claim to Cabinet rank. There can be little doubt that Winston accepted Violet Asquith's love and intense admiration for him in order to advance his claims in that quarter. He had never seen anything wrong in exploiting high authority, and there could be few higher than the adoring daughter of the coming Prime Minister, who was a close confidante of her father. She was a priceless asset which he was not likely to overlook, although it must be remembered that she was as ambitious for his future as Winston himself. And when later Asquith came to form his Government, we know from her own evidence that she wrote to her father and 'adjured him to make the most of Winston'. Asquith admired his daughter and respected her political judgment. His reply was propitious: 'You need have no fear on W's account. He will be well looked after & provided for in your absence.'[31] It was obvious that his days at the Colonial Office were now numbered. Looking back on his time there, we should remember that Elgin had not chosen Winston as his Under-Secretary, and that it was Churchill who had forced his way into the office for reasons not difficult to plumb and to the inconvenience of others: 'I had some difficulty in securing my wish as it involved considerable alteration in other minor offices,' he had written airily to Lord Hugh Cecil.[32]

What did the incongruous pair in reality make of each other? When Elgin's time came to leave the Colonial Office he wrote to his successor, Lord Crewe:[33]

> . . . When I accepted Churchill as my Under Secy I knew I had no easy task. I resolved to give him access to all business – but to keep control (& my temper). I think I may say I succeeded. Certainly we have had no quarrel during the 2½ years, on the contrary he has again and

31. Bonham-Carter, op.cit., p.153.
32. Chartwell papers.
33. Robert, Marquis of Crewe K.G., successively Viceroy of Ireland, Lord President, S. of S. for the Colonies and S. of S. for India, Leader of the House of Lords.

again thanked me for what he had learned and for our pleasant personal relations. I have taken a keen interest in his ability and in many ways attractive personality. But all the same I know it has affected my position *outside* the *Office* – and the strain has often been severe. On 'questions' alone hours have been spent (Hopwood who has of late relieved me of much of this work could if he chose tell you many tales). I admit that most of this is personal and perhaps ancient history and I should not have mentioned it had it not been for the Tour of last autumn. That originally was intended to be a purely sporting and private expedition – & I really don't know how it drifted into so essentially an official progress; but if you consult more serious documents than the *Strand Magazine* you will find the character it assumed. And therefore it has left behind it matters with which you will have to deal, for the course is strewn with memoranda – Malta, Cyprus, Somaliland, East Africa, the Nile &c. I do not discuss any of them. I believe most of them hopelessly to be unpracticable at least as they stand . . .[34]

In spite of these signs of natural exasperation, Elgin had written to Winston in December 1906, when there had been rumours of Churchill's promotion, from his home, Broomhall in Scotland:

. . . I have been dreading every post to find the rumours true and that I was to lose your help. You might think it unkind if I said I 'hoped' not to hear – but however it may turn out I shall always look back on your cooperation during this year of toil & strife with peculiar satisfaction – and with real gratitude to you not only for the courage and ability with which you have fought our cause – but for the invariable consideration you have shown for me & my opinions.[35]

One cannot doubt the sincerity of this letter, for Elgin was not a man capable of insincere official generalizations, and Winston was touched by it and moved into replying with equal warmth:

. . . It is very kind of you to write such generous things about our association. No one could ever have had a more trustful & indulgent chief than I have been most lucky to find on first joining a Government: I have learned a vy great deal in the conduct of official business from your instruction and example which I should all my life have remained completely ignorant of, if I had gone elsewhere. Believe me, I value vy highly the words of approval you have bestowed.

Perhaps we may see this couple in the form of two horses of different ages and temperament harness to a carriage which each

34. Crewe papers.
35. Chartwell papers.

intends to pull according to its own wishes. One is young, headstrong and high-mettled, and might well drag the carriage to disaster, unless restrained by the other, which is old, wise and obstinate. Winston had undoubtedly made a strong impression in this first office, but in doing so he had been driven into revealing his bad as well as his good qualities, his weaknesses as well as his strength.

Chapter 7

Marriage and the Cabinet

In 1908 two outstanding events occurred in Winston Churchill's life. In April he entered the Cabinet and in September he was married. Early in that year Campbell-Bannerman was dying, a sad ghost of a man. Asquith, as his successor designate, presided over the Cabinet and led the House of Commons, but during March government languished and came almost to a standstill, urgent decisions having constantly to be deferred owing to the Prime Minister's continuing absence. The King, enjoying himself in the Biarritz sunshine, would have preferred the change to have taken place after his return, but at the beginning of April Campbell-Bannerman's doctors at last persuaded the dying man that he must resign immediately.

During these painful and uncertain weeks Asquith, who, prodded by his daughter, recognized that Winston had earned promotion, gave much thought to his future and considered three posts for him – the Colonial Office, the Admiralty and the Local Government Board. There is no doubt that Churchill would have welcomed promotion in the Colonial Office, with whose workings he was so familiar; he was also strongly attracted by the Admiralty – 'in its amenities and attractions far the most pleasant and glittering position in the Ministry'. Here, however, there was a personal and genuine obstacle in his path, as the First Lord of the Admiralty at this time was his uncle by marriage, Lord Tweedmouth, and his intense family loyalty prevented Winston from pressing this claim. He was most reluctant to accept the Local Government Board which Asquith urged upon him, remarking to his secretary Edward Marsh that he had no intention of being 'shut up in a soup kitchen with Mrs Sidney Webb'. Although he had for some time been conscious of a growing interest in social questions, he did not feel himself sufficiently experienced in domestic politics to carry through the necessary measures of social reform.

We are probably right in conjecturing that Winston wrote to Asquith with unusual diffidence because he was anxious to avoid a tedious office, for ignorance of a subject had never deterred him from grappling with it if he wished to do so:

> Dimly across the gulfs of ignorance I see the outline of a policy wh I call the Minimum Standard. It is national rather than departmental. I am doubtful of my power to give it expression. If I did, I expect before long I should find myself in collision with some of my best friends – like for instance John Morley, who at the end of a lifetime of study & thought has come to the conclusion that nothing can be done.

He went on to develop the theme of his own ignorance and unworthiness, and then appealed to Asquith:

> In all this, as in the Bills I have mentioned, the Local Government Board must inevitably be the fountain. I do not underrate the great honour you have done me in seeming to wish me to encounter such awful labours & responsibilities. I hope your arrangements may permit some other disposition of offices. I am sure you will find people much better qualified than I for service in this arena.[1]

But Winston added, 'No condition personal to myself shall prevent me from serving you where you wish . . .'

* * *

Asquith became Prime Minister on 8 April, and that day wrote to Churchill from Biarritz where he had gone to wait upon the King:

> My dear Winston,
>   With the King's approval, I have the great pleasure of offering you the post of President of the Board of Trade in the new Administration.
>   It is my intention to seek the consent of Parliament to placing this office on the same level as regards salary & status, while retaining its present title, with the Secretaryships of State . . .
>   I shall hail with much gratification your accession to the Cabinet, both in public & personal ground . . .

This Cabinet post was, of course, a milestone in Winston's political career. With considerable shrewdness he decided to renounce the extra salary resulting from the Presidency of the Board of Trade being raised in status to a Secretaryship of State, and when the debate took place on the second reading of the Board of Trade Bill by which the salary of the President was raised to £3,000 per annum he was thankful that his

---

1. Chartwell papers. WSC to HHA, 14 March 1908.

decision had been accepted. Writing on 27 April 1909, he recorded:

> The debate last night was poisonous. I was vy glad that I had adopted a course wh left me unassailable personally. The jealousy of the 'private member' for the 'front bench' was clamant. The division however was satisfactory, & now the bill will go up to a committee and have only two more stages in the House of Commons ... I think it is all right but a sinister element may be introduced by the Budget into the feeling of the House ...[2]

At this time appointment to the Cabinet required re-election. As a rule the Opposition did not contest the seat involved, but in this case the festering Conservative hatred of the renegade Churchill and the longing to avenge the disaster of 1906 caused them to fight, and Winston's old opponent Joynson-Hicks defeated him by 429 votes. There is a danger of forgetting how vindictive and persistent this hatred was. The mistrust had an element of permanency, and it was only to be shaken off in 1940. Although the reasons for it can be understood, one cannot but deplore its malevolence. Even at this distance we can still clearly wind it in the ecstasy of the Tory press of the day at his defeat, exultant as at some crucial triumph in war. This howl of fulfilment is characteristic of many others:

> Churchill out – language fails us just when it is most needed. We have all been yearning for this to happen, with a yearning beyond utterance. Figures – oh yes there are figures, but who cares for figures today? Winston Churchill is out, OUT, OUT![3]

By now hardened to such loathing, Winston could regard this as a purely passing rebuff. The safe seat of Dundee was made available to him, the sitting Member having been created a peer on Asquith's succession. In this working-class constituency the main threat came from a strong Labour candidate likely to attract a large number of former Liberal votes. Another slight hazard was a fourth candidate obscurely masquerading as a 'Christian Socialist prohibitionist'. But Winston, glittering in his most effulgent Radical plumage, triumphed with a majority of 2,709 over his closest contender, the Conservative candidate. In Dundee he found a resting place for fifteen years.

After Winston's defeat in Manchester his kindly friend John Morley diagnosed his failure there as relying on 'mere computation of other people's opinions, without anxiety about his own'. Not for the first time Violet Asquith showed far more perception about his true nature:

2. Ibid. WSC to Clementine Churchill.
3. *Sheffield Telegraph*, 25 April 1908.

So far from concentrating on 'a mere computation of other people's opinions without anxiety about his own', his error – if he erred – was in the opposite direction. He was so wholly possessed by his own opinions that he often failed to take that of others into account, even as a practical factor in a situation. He never had his ear to the ground. Nor would he have felt much interest in its message even if he heard it. It was his own message which concerned him and which he was determined to transmit. He possessed neither the sensitive antennae nor the servile inflexibility of the demagogue.[4]

In other words, we may repeat that he had not the slightest idea of the thoughts that were passing in the minds of other people, nor the slightest interest in what they might be. This must be clearly recognized as the greatest of Winston Churchill's natural shortcomings.

*   *   *

At a dance given by Lady Crewe in 1905, Winston had been captivated by the beauty of a girl he had never seen before, and at once asked his mother to introduce him to her. She was Clementine, daughter of Sir Henry Hozier and his estranged wife, Lady Blanche Hozier, who was a friend of Lady Randolph. She was a girl of dazzling beauty whose classical features might have been chiselled by Praxiteles. Sir Alan Lascelles, who first met her when she was sixteen years old, never forgot this first vision and how when she entered the room her appearance 'was quite electrifying – the loveliest creature you ever saw, like someone making an entry on the stage, yet without any artifice or self-consciousness'.[5] He was suddenly reminded of Burke's lines on Marie Antoinette as he watched her entering the room:

It is now sixteen or seventeen years since I saw the Queen of France, then the dauphiness, at Versailles; and surely never lighted on this orb, which she hardly seemed to touch, a more delightful vision. I saw her just above the horizon, decorating and cheering the elevated sphere she just began to move in – glittering like the morning-star – full of life, and splendour and joy.

Winston, having asked his mother to introduce him to Clementine, did not seem to know what to do next. At his most gauche and uncouth, he did not ask her to dance, to sit down, or to join him at supper. He merely stared at her in silence. He made, in fact, a deplorable impression, and so oppressive did his presence become that after an

4. Bonham Carter, op.cit., p.157.
5. Sir Alan Lascelles to author.

awkward period she arranged to be rescued from him by a friend. She did not see him again until 1908.

Clementine – or Clemmie, as she was always called by her friends – lived during these years at Abingdon Villas with her mother, Blanche Hozier. They were chronically short of money, and Clementine, who was fluent in French, gave French lessons for 2/6d. an hour. At some time in 1908 her aunt, Lady St Helier, invited her to a dinner party to which she was reluctant to go, as she was not only tired, but had no clean gloves (which were *de rigueur* at the time). Winston was also bidden, and was no more eager to attend than she. Edward Marsh found him at 12 Bolton Street shortly before dinner, and threatening not to go. Marsh told him that it would be unpardonably rude if he failed to appear, and Winston set off late and in a vile temper.

Clementine in consequence found herself with an empty place on one side at dinner until Winston arrived half-way through the meal and slumped into the place beside her. With no preliminary greetings he asked her abruptly: 'Have you read my book?', referring to his biography of Lord Randolph. When she was forced to reply in the negative he said: 'I will send it round tomorrow morning in a hansom.' After dinner Clementine found herself cornered by the First Lord of the Admiralty, Lord Tweedmouth, but Winston with some adroitness told the First Lord that there was an admirable picture of Nelson in the passage, and when he left to look for it at once appropriated his chair next to Clementine. They both stayed so late that they were in fact the last to leave, and in the end Winston said, 'I will take Miss Hozier home.' But it was strange and disappointing to her that in spite of his promise he never sent the book.

After that evening she encountered Winston at several dances in London, but he made no move towards her and showed no signs of proposing. To her it seems that the reasons for Winston's four-year delay and extraordinary courtship with its sporadic ardour were that at the time he admired a number of other young women, while she herself was much absent in the country, often at seaside lodging-houses. But it is also safe to conjecture that that devouring addiction, politics, also distracted his mind from even so ardent an affair of the heart. In spite of Winston's sluggish approach, though, events moved quickly after Lady St Helier's dinner in 1908. His brother Jack's marriage to Lady Gwendeline Bertie, in Clementine's opinion, precipitated Winston's decision. Lady Randolph did her best to smooth the lovers' path. She invited Lady Blanche and Clementine to spend a weekend at Salisbury Hall. Winston was also there on Sunday, 12 April, the day on which his appointment to the Board of Trade was announced, and this time he seems to have charmed her.

Next day she left England with her mother on a six-week visit to the Continent, and for the following four weeks Winston was immersed in his by-election campaigns. But their friendship, so strangely achieved, was now established, if a trifle precariously, and they corresponded throughout the separation. In August Clementine was invited by the Duke of Marlborough to stay at Blenheim. She went there, 'down to my last white blouse', and on Tuesday 11 August 1908 Winston in a purposeful manner led her to the room over the boathouse, which lay on the verge of Capability Brown's great lake. He had clearly some major purpose in mind, but seemed in no hurry to approach it. His preliminary remarks were wide of the point, and a prey to acute anxiety, she wondered if he was ever going to reach it. During this agonizing period of suspense she watched a spider crawling across the floor, and thought that if Winston did not propose before the spider reached the end of the carpet she would shriek aloud. At last, in his own curious way, he reached his proposal, and was accepted, but in spite of this happy conclusion, there was still an element of uncertainty in Clementine's mind. She said that she 'was more dazzled by Winston than in love with him', and in fact tried to break off the engagement because he did not pay her sufficient attention.

They were to be married from Lady St Helier's house, and Clementine was sent to stay there the night before. But so uncertain was she of the immediate future that she was overtaken by a feeling of homesickness and desolation, and a yearning to return to her mother's house. The only garment available was her wedding dress, which was laid out ready for the morning. She borrowed a dress from the maid and returned to Abingdon Villas, where Minnie, Lady Blanche's servant, exclaimed in high excitement, 'Oh Lor'! Miss Clementine's come back again.' This unpromising situation was restored, and the wedding took place on 12 September 1908 at St Margaret's, Westminster. Lord Hugh Cecil was best man, and Dr Welldon gave the address. They spent the first two days of their honeymoom at Blenheim before going to Italy.

It was to be a curious marriage, although a long-enduring and most happy one. Winston's love for this girl was obviously compelling, but it was strangely intermittent, and the main preoccupation of his life was always liable to intrude on even these intimate regions. Lloyd George afterwards recorded that even during the signing of the register, Winston drew him aside and began talking urgently about the political situation. Whatever Winston may have thought, he had allied himself not only with a woman of exquisite beauty, but with a character as determined and committed as his own and an addiction to Liberalism far stronger. The atmosphere in which they moved after marriage was poisonous. Great ladies like Lady Londonderry cut them stone dead. Lady Crewe, although also a Liberal, told Clementine that Winston's association with Lloyd George was embarrassing her and should be stopped. Asquith's wife, Margot, was also one of those who were cold and hostile.

In order to give some indication of this hostility, Clementine recalled that on one occasion when returning home in a cab there was a slight accident which resulted in a cut on her face causing some blood to flow on the pavement; in the hall of her house this immediately caused rumours that Winston was in the habit of beating his wife. And later, when Lord Percy[6] had been found dead in Paris in a cheap hotel near the Gare du Nord a whispering campaign was started by political enemies that Lord Percy had been Clementine's lover and had been killed by Winston's brother Jack, who had been sent to Paris by Winston because he was too cowardly to do the deed himself.

Winston and Clementine were equally indifferent to this unpopularity, he because he had long become accustomed to it, she because she was a passionate Liberal and regarded it as a compliment. In any case, she insisted that owing to her poverty she had few acquaintances in London, and suffered less from the ostracism than would otherwise have been the case. The young couple were at first extremely short of money, although Clementine had an annuity from her father, and in 1921, Winston received a substantial legacy from Lady Londonderry. But for the moment they were dependent on Winston's earnings, and this financial situation was a source of constant anxiety to Clementine, who complained that she was never able to buy any smart clothes and often could not pay the servants.

It need hardly be said that Winston's lack of means did not prevent him from living in his usual comfort, employing five servants and ordering the most expensive food and wine. In these early days he told Clementine that he wanted duck for dinner and not unmindful that they cost 5s. each, she tried to dissuade him by pretending that they were out of season. But Winston had read in the papers that alligators at the Zoo were being fed with duck, and argued with some petulance that if the alligators could have them, it was intolerable that he could not.[7]

Their married life was deeply and consistently affectionate, but Clementine found it hard to share many of his friendships. Often the characteristics that attracted Winston seemed to repel her. She disliked F. E. Smith and disapproved of his influence on Winston (such as encouraging him to gamble). Later, after he was made Lord

6. Eldest son of the Duke of Northumberland and a former colleague of Churchill in the 'Hughligans'.

7. All the facts in this account of Churchill's courtship and early marriage are based on an interview with Lady Spencer-Churchill.

Birkenhead, she would refer to him, Bracken and Beaverbrook, with collective disapproval, as 'The Three B's', though she later became devoted to Brendan Bracken. She could not abide Winston's uncle Lord Wimborne or his two sons Ivor and Freddie Guest.

She did not always conceal her hostility. Although normally reserved she was capable of violent eruptions, often embarrassing to Winston at the time but recounted by him afterwards with pride. 'Clemmie gave poor — a most fearful mauling,' he would say, or, 'She dropped on him like a jaguar out of a tree!'[8] Their relationship with Sunny Marlborough was marred by one of these scenes in the autumn of 1913.

Clementine was staying at Blenheim without Winston at a time when party feeling was still intense. Sunny Marlborough made some provocative remarks at the dinner-table about Asquith being drunk the whole time. In the middle of the meal a telegram from Lloyd George was delivered to Clementine and she got up saying she must answer it at once. Marlborough then said, 'Please, Clemmie, would you mind not writing to that horrible little man on Blenheim writing-paper?' Clementine left the room, told her maid to pack, brushed aside Marlborough's apologies and took the train to London. Winston took her side in the row with reluctance, thus upsetting Clementine who felt she had earned his full support by her defence of his colleague, and should not appease Sunny Marlborough. Her hot temper was combined with an acute sensitivity. She was deeply upset by this incident, and burst into tears when discussing it with Margaret Smith soon afterwards. Later she wished she had accepted Sunny Marlborough's apology.

As it was, the Churchills did not meet him again until war washed away all petty squabbles. Then Sunny's son remembered going with his father to the Admiralty and hearing Winston trying in vain to get Cabinet consent to sink the German battle-cruiser *Goeben* trapped in the Straits of Messina[9] before the final expiry of the British ultimatum to Germany.

Winston's energy and versatility were such that it was the vocation of a lifetime being married to him. Clementine managed to subordinate the rest of her life to her marriage without losing her independence of character or her own opinions. She remained a Liberal of rather radical views to the end of her days, and she never voted Conservative till 1945. Apart from the normal duties of a politician's wife which she performed

8. Soames, p.231.
9. The two primary sources are the tenth Duke of Marlborough and Margaret Smith, later Lady Birkenhead. Lady Soames has described the scene in *Clementine Churchill*, p.96, using also her mother's account. The scene at the Admiralty was described to me by the tenth Duke, who had been summoned there by his father when his OTC camp closed down at the outbreak of war.

with grace and style, she was also able to bolster one of Winston's main weaknesses, for her perception of character was far deeper than his and she was not subject to the same dangerous bouts of hero-worship.

* * *

In 1908 England, like other Continental countries, was passing through a severe trade depression caused by the financial collapse in America the previous year. Unemployment was soaring, wages falling, and the state of the 'left-out millions' pitiable. Winston's interest in social welfare had been steadily increasing over the past years. He had met Sidney and Beatrice Webb, and had absorbed many of their Fabian principles. It is worth reminding ourselves that Beatrice Webb felt considerable reservations about Churchill, although realizing his great value as an ally. She noted that he was 'restless, egotistical, bumptious, shallow-minded and reactionary, but with a certain personal magnetism, great pluck and some originality – not of intellect but of character'. She had remarked in 1903 that he was 'bound to be unpopular – too unpleasant a flavour with his restless, self-regarding personality and lack of moral or intellectual refinement'. But even this arrogant and opinionated woman realized his quality sufficiently to concede: 'But his pluck, courage, resourcefulness, and great tradition may carry him far unless he knocks himself to pieces like his father.'[10]

On 8 January 1908, returning from his African journey, he had written to Arthur Wilson Fox, Comptroller-General of the Commercial, Labour and Statistical Department of the Board of Trade, asking for his opinion of a scheme for national insurance of workmen, which would combine the advantages of the German State-controlled system with the more flexible, voluntary machinery of the English system. His mind was already focused on this task:

> I am to speak at Birmingham on the 23rd, & these ideas of minimum standards of life & wages, of security against going to the Devil through accident, sickness, or weakness of character, & of competition upwards but not downwards, will be my general theme.[11]

When Churchill entered the Cabinet many ideas for social reform were already teeming in his mind, stimulated by the Webbs. During his twenty months as President of the Board of Trade his mind was mainly concentrated on Labour Exchanges, unemployment insurance, and sweated labour – unskilled labour and those who belonged to no trade union. The Board of Trade proved an admirable vehicle for his

10. Beatrice Webb, *Our Partnership*, pp.269-70.
11. Chartwell papers.

mood of the moment – social reform – on which, in the usual way, his mind was for the moment exclusively concentrated. But it should be remembered that the ground was by no means unprepared, and that he was well served by able and experienced lieutenants at the Board – Sir Hubert Llewellyn Smith, Permanent Secretary, Arthur Wilson Fox, and G.R. Askwith[12] who succeeded Fox in 1909.

Shortly before his appointment Winston was introduced by the Webbs to an alert young Oxford don called William Beveridge. He remembered that:

> At the end of 1907 I went to Germany with two objects in view: to supplement the argument for labour exchanges ... and to see for myself the German system of contributory insurance against sickness, infirmity and old age, and industrial accidents ...[13] ... By March 1908 the Webbs decided that the time had come to pass from propaganda for labour exchanges to action at the source of power ... The Webbs invited Mr Churchill to dinner and invited me also. The account of the party by Beatrice Webb can now be compared with what I wrote to my mother on the morning after: ... 'My dinner last night was of course very interesting and mainly about Labour Exchanges. Mrs Webb had sent their scheme (which is founded on me) to Winston Churchill and he has been converted and is now at work converting Asquith. I don't think he is at all points clear as to what Labour Exchanges mean – as Mrs Webb said afterwards you never quite know what he is going to hand back to you afterwards as his version of your idea – but still so long as he talks about the name it doesn't matter. I don't think I was as much impressed by his cleverness as I expected to be; he was or appeared to be rather tired and inconsecutive – but he was very amusing to listen to ...[14]

Beveridge went on to record how at some time during this period the Webbs advised Churchill: 'If you are going to interest yourself in unemployment, you must have the boy Beveridge', and on 3 July Beveridge wrote to his mother:

> I have just been offered and have accepted a permanent appointment in the Board of Trade – £600 a year – to begin at once or at any rate within a fortnight ... It all came about thus – On Wednesday I went by invitation to a conference on the unemployed – the President (Churchill), Sidney Webb, Llewellyn Smith, Wilson Fox and me. The upshot of this was that the President expressed his intention of taking up Labour exchanges seriously and wanted a memorandum to back his views

12. Afterwards Lord Askwith.
13. Beveridge, *Power and Influence*, page 56.
14. Beveridge, op.cit., p.66.

– which I undertook to prepare (voluntarily). However on Thursday I was called up again by telephone to see Wilson Fox – who is I think second in command – and he gave me to understand that the President was passing sleepless nights till he should obtain my personal paid services.[15]

With the bit between his teeth Winston was throwing himself into social reform with enormous energy and zeal. Objections and difficulties which conflicted with his desires were ignored, as were obstacles which might stand in his path. Llewellyn Smith thought it his duty to issue a warning that the way was not as clear as Winston imagined: 'Labour Exchanges do not seem simpler the more they are studied in detail. On the contrary the problem bristled with all kinds of difficulties.'[16]

As Robert Rhodes James truly wrote:

Churchill could never do' his abilities justice unless he was excited about a matter, and he quickly invested his work at the Board of Trade with a dramatic and romantic quality. It was indeed this very vitality and air of drama that alarmed even those who liked and admired him, and which aroused a certain scepticism about his motives among men who had been long concerned with the social problems that Churchill now so fervently espoused. As Gardiner commented – part in admiration, part in alarm – in 1908:

'More than any man of his time, he approaches an issue without mental reserve and obscure motives and restraints. You see all the processes of his mind. He does not "hum and ha". He is not paralysed by the fear of consequences, nor afraid to contemplate great changes. He is out for adventure. He follows politics as he would follow the hounds.'[17]

On 8 December Churchill presented a Memorandum on Labour Exchanges and Unemployment Insurance to the Cabinet. He wrote: 'The administration of the twin measures must become increasingly interwoven, as the draft Bill provides. Together they organise in due proportion the mobility and stability of labour.'[18]

In spite of the strong reasons for embracing Labour Exchanges and Unemployed Insurance in one Bill, it became evident to Churchill that it was necessary to present the Insurance policy as a whole, and he decided to introduce the Labour Exchanges Bill alone in 1909, explaining to Asquith:

I don't think I could press my Unemployment Insurance plan until Lloyd George has found a way of dealing with infirmity or (wh is possible) has

15. Ibid, p.68.
16. Chartwell papers, 11 August 1908.
17. Rhodes James, op.cit., p.34.
18. Chartwell papers.

found that there is no way. The insurance policy must I feel be presented as a whole, for it would never do to extract contributions from masters and men in successive years. One shot must suffice . . .[19]

Churchill set forth the Government scheme for Labour Exchanges and Unemployment Insurance in the House of Commons on 19 May 1909, and next day introduced the Labour Exchanges Bill, which reached the Statute Book by the end of the year. The Unemployment Insurance Scheme, providing for two and a quarter million persons, formed Part Two of Lloyd George's comprehensive National Insurance Act of 1911. Thus Lloyd George received the credit for this measure, although as Randolph Churchill pointed out, he also received the criticism and abuse.[20]

* * *

For twenty years unavailing efforts had been made to solve the sweated labour problem, an evil survival from the past which had its most devastating consequences among unskilled and unorganized labour, such as dockers, and those working in private workshops at tailoring, dressmaking and other trades. In the often Dickensian surroundings where these occupations were pursued unemployment and poverty were rife, and the struggle for existence brutally competitive. The machinery of the Factory and Workshops Act of 1891 had failed to solve this squalid anomaly, but in any case the Act did not cover domestic workshops. In every Parliamentary session since 1900, Sir Charles Dilke had introduced a Wages Board Bill to establish a minimum wage on the Australian model, but although the principle of such Bills was widely accepted, they had invariably been deferred.

In March 1909 Winston introduced his Trade Boards Bill, the central object of which was the necessity of establishing a minimum wage. The Board of Trade was to decide whether the minimum wage which had been prescribed by the Trade Board commanded enough respect in the trade to make its enforcement by inspection and prosecution likely to be effective. District trade boards would recommend local rates of wages; the Central Board would confirm them after hearing objections, and they would then become obligatory on all Government and municipal contractors.

The Bill would apply to factory and home workers, but different rates might be fixed for each. The scheduled trades were tailoring, cardboard box-making, machine-made lace and net finishing: other trades might be included by a provisional order subject to challenge by the House.

19. Chartwell papers, 26 December 1908.
20. Randolph Churchill, op.cit., Vo.l.II, p.306.

Only those employers who agreed to pay the prescribed rates would be eligible for Government contracts. After six months of the prescribed minimum rate the Trade Board, on application to the Board of Trade, might make it legally obligatory. The district boards would enforce the rates by a staff of inspectors.

The Second Reading of the Bill was moved on 28 April 1909, Winston writing to Clementine from the front bench: 'The Trade Board Bill has been beautifully received & will be passed without a division. A. Balfour and A. Lyttelton were most friendly to it, & all opposition has faded away. But the House was tired and jaded and speaking to them was hard work.'[21] This bloodless conquest of sweated labour was the removal of the greater part of a most ugly and discreditable survival from the past, and can be regarded as a bright feather in Winston's cap.

*   *   *

He filled his new office with incessant activity. He saw the Port of London Bill through Parliament in 1908, and in the same year supported the Licensing Bill, making impassioned and extremely incongruous speeches in the cause of temperance. He was now passing through the most radical period of his career. He was not above advocating a degree of State control, particularly in relation to the railways. Profoundly impressed by Germany's system of social and industrial organization, and despondent at the lack of it and the condition of the poor in England, he wrote to Asquith on 29 December 1908:

> . . .I feel compelled to state to you the conviction that has for a long time past been forming in my mind. There is a tremendous policy for Social Organisation. The need is urgent & the moment is ripe. Germany with a harder climate and far less accumulated wealth has managed to establish tolerable basic conditions for her people. She is organised not only for war, but for peace. We are organised for nothing except party politics. The Minister who will apply to this country the successful experiences of Germany in social organisation may or may not be supported at the polls, but he will at least have left a memorial which time will not deface of his administration . . .[22]

1908 was a year of constant industrial disturbance. There were strikes in the shipbuilding and engineering trades and a lock-out by the master cotton-spinners. Here again, Winston's Department was directly involved. By the Conciliation Act of 1896 the Board of Trade was empowered to appoint a conciliator in trade disputes, and

21. CSC papers.
22. Chartwell papers.

Conciliation Boards were set up in 1907. Churchill was a strong advocate of conciliation, and he established a Standing Court of Arbitration composed of two representatives of labour, two for the employers and a Chairman appointed by the Board of Trade, a scheme which came into operation in 1909. By this means State intervention became more systematic, and the Board of Trade was able to exert its influence at an earlier and sometimes less bitter stage of disputes.[23]

Churchill's achievements in social reform were therefore already impressive, and he was to carry them even further at the Home Office – as William Beveridge wrote, 'a striking illustration of how much the personality of the Minister in a few critical months may change the course of social legislation'.[24] Asquith's accession as Prime Minister had stimulated the Liberal Government's programme of social reform, and Winston and Lloyd George were his two most ardent paladins in this field. It is true that when Winston reached the Board of Trade the stage was already set for him, the climate of opinion propitious, and ambitious schemes already in preparation, but it was his own incomparable single-minded resolve that brought these plans to fruition.

*   *   *

With the whole of his mind thus concentrated on social reform, Winston was passing during this period through a phase of extraordinary and almost inexplicable blindness in international affairs. Blinkered and isolationist, he was indifferent to the growing arrogance and chauvinism in a Germany dangerously inclined to a war course and to her massive and increasing armaments. In April 1908 Germany introduced a new and ominous Navy Law, which increased her annual programme to four capital ships a year. This meant that unless the British rate of shipbuilding increased, Germany would be superior in capital ships by 1914.

On 12 April Reginald McKenna succeeded Lord Tweedmouth as First Lord of the Admiralty, and immediately agreed with the Sea Lords that it was imperative to lay down four new Dreadnoughts and if necessary six in 1909. In December he urged six upon the Cabinet, a demand which was of course bitterly opposed by Lloyd George. This occasioned no surprise, for Lloyd George was not as yet interested in defence or foreign affairs, had always been a Little Englander, and as Chancellor of the Exchequer needed every penny he could lay his hands on to finance the new social services and the unemployment insurance scheme then in preparation.

23. Randolph Churchill, op.cit., Vol.II, pp.285-8.
24. Beveridge, op.cit., p.87.

What appeared incredible, even to some who admired him, was that Winston should be standing at Lloyd George's side, urging similar courses, ridiculing the idea of Germany's aggressive intentions. The argument was between those who were convinced that national security demanded such a strengthening of the Navy and those who insisted that the extra expenditure entailed should be used on schemes of social reform. In ranging himself on this side Winston seemed not only to be trifling with great issues but also to be false to his own past when he had gloried in being a member of the 'Trust the Navy School'. What happened to his strategic judgment? Had he learned nothing from the Bosnia-Herzegovina crisis, a dress rehearsal for 1914? What had happened to his normal pugnacity in the face of danger? In making this choice for the social services rather than national security he seemed to be ignoring the cardinal principle that every thought for a country's embellishment must be paid for by ten thoughts for its actual preservation. His position seemed to many contemptible – a Little Navyite – and he lost the confidence of men who had before trusted him. Among these was no less a man than Asquith himself, who regarded the behaviour of this long-pampered subordinate as a personal affront: 'I am afraid that Winston is proving himself to be thoroughly untrustworthy,' he said to his daughter Violet with great sadness.[25]

Inside the Cabinet the battle continued until 1909, while outside a music hall song incited the public with the slogan: 'We want eight, we won't wait.' Grey, Runciman and Haldane supported McKenna, while Lloyd George and Churchill were upheld by Morley, Loreburn, Burns and Harcourt. Asquith, who was in favour of six Dreadnoughts, at last broke the deadlock by proposing that four should be laid down immediately and four more within the next financial year beginning 1 April 1909, or earlier if need be. Thus the matter was settled: the economists objected to six, insisted that four were sufficient and eventually compromised on eight.

Churchill was never afterwards able to offer any but the most feeble justification for his conduct in this affair, which did indeed tend to endorse Lloyd George's comparison of him on a later occasion to 'a chauffeur who apparently is perfectly sane and drives with great skill for months, then suddenly takes you over a precipice.'[26] Winston's explanation,[27] in *The World Crisis* is unrepentant and strangely unconvincing. He insisted that he and Lloyd George were right in holding that four ships would meet our needs, but added:

25. Bonham Carter, op.cit., p.169.
26. Thomas Jones, *Diary*, 8 June 1922.
27. Winston S. Churchill, *The World Crisis, 1911-1914*, pp.36-8.

But although the Chancellor of the Exchequer and I were right in the narrow sense, we were absolutely wrong in relation to the deep tides of destiny. The greatest credit is due to the First Lord of the Admiralty, Mr McKenna, for the resolute and courageous manner in which he fought his case and withstood his party on this occasion. Little did I think as this dispute proceeded, that when the next Cabinet crisis about the Navy arose our roles would be reversed; and little did he think that the ships for which he contended so stoutly . . . would be welcomed with open arms by me.

This explanation is a good example of the fact that Winston found it almost impossible to admit that he was wrong.

*   *   *

Shortly before the General Election of 1910, when Cabinet changes were in the air, a letter to Lord Morley from Churchill, written on 23 December 1909, throws further light on his strong views on naval expenditure and on his appointment to office both in 1908 and 1910:

I have no intention of going to the LGB [Local Government Board], and I do not want it to be offered to me. The PM pressed it upon me nearly 2 years ago. I then accepted it. At that time there were Pensions, Labour Exchanges, Unemployment Insurance, all within its scope. Now the Poor Law only remains, and I have not been studying the Poor Law. Secondly when I went at the last minute when the government was reformed to the Board of Trade, it was assigned to me as an office equal in all respects to a Secretaryship of State. It has not been possible for me to benefit from this promise in any way – had I done so, I could not have been of any use at this crisis. I make no complaint but I see no reason why I should a second time be placed in an embarrassing position. No statutory authority accords the new President of the LGB the higher status. It would be a simple act of the Executive – of wh I am a member. The same arguments which led me to refuse the advantages offered me at the B of Trade would apply in this case again. I should not in any circumstances expose myself to the taunts which would be directed upon me. It would be said that a mere shuffle of offices had been arranged to get round the definite decision of the House of Commons last session & for my personal benefit! I will not participate in that transaction.

If I am to be moved from the Board of Trade, there is no doubt in my mind where I should go. Two years ago when the P. Minister was forming his Government he spoke to me about the Admiralty as an office which 'would suit me very well'. I felt a great difficulty then in pressing for it. Tweedmouth was a relation and a dear friend. His fate hung in the balance. Further I did not then realise what a tremendous part these warlike issues played in the inner life of a Liberal Cabinet. I let the moment pass without a clear expression of choice. I have deeply regretted this ever since. The only troubles that have come to us come from this quarter. The only menace to our continued unity lies there. How serious it is you well know.

I believe we are about to gain a substantial victory at the polls. But the House of Commons which will meet will be one in which the Radicals, Labour & Irish will hold the balance. What such a Parliament will say to Navy Estimates of over 40 millions coupled with an exposed and derided scare, is a queer question to answer . . .

A resolute effort *must* be made to curb naval expenditure. This means hard fighting inside & outside at the same time. Still I think I could do it – without a smash in any direction – Westminster – Downing Street – Whitehall – the North Sea! . . .

McKenna and I were great friends before this miserable difference arose. I stood out of his way when he wanted the Financial Secretaryship to the Treasury and took a lower post. He offered when the Government was reformed to ask the Prime Minister to let me go to the Admiralty instead of him. Therefore I feel I can discuss the question upon a level altogether above personal claims & personal feelings. It will be much better for him to go to the Home Office which is a promotion & to leave the Admiralty at this juncture. It will be better for us all . . .[28]

* * *

On 1 February 1910, in the course of a letter congratulating Winston on his speeches during the election campaign, Asquith spoke of Cabinet reconstruction and offered him the Irish Office. With his eyes now fixed on the Admiralty, this was of course the last thing he wanted, but he replied with caution:

There are many circumstances connected with it that repel me . . .

Three or four years ago I would have gone; but now I am sure it would be more in the interests of the Government that Birrell should stand to his post. The Nationalists respect and trust him. He has all the threads in his hand. He has been through the unpleasant process of being disillusioned.

I do not know what other reconstruction you contemplate, but for myself I should like to go either to the Admiralty or to the Home Office. It is fitting, if you will allow me to say so – that Ministers should occupy positions in the Government which correspond to some extent with their influence in the country. No Minister holding an office of the second class can play a large part without producing awkward and doubtful relations with some of his colleagues in more important positions; & this in spite of much natural good will. It is convenient and it is fair that a true balance should be established. At a time so critical & with struggles so grave impending, there should be a generous appreciation of the real forces which contribute to the strength of the party & of your Government.

28. Chartwell papers.

One word more. Two years have passed since you offered me the Board of Trade as a Secretaryship of State. It has not been possible – for reasons which I have loyally recognised – to make that offer good; but the fact will I am sure weigh with you at the present time – sufficiently at any rate to justify me in writing to you openly.

Let me finally thank you for the kindness of your letter. It gives me the greatest pleasure to know that you are satisfied with my work.[29]

This letter, which Winston had laboriously drafted and redrafted in his own hand, was intended as a subtle bid for the Admiralty. But Winston's lifelong and abysmal ignorance of what was passing in the minds of others made him a clumsy intriguer, and the letter is neither adroit nor persuasive. It is probably too that the same radical fault made him unaware of Asquith's displeasure with his antics over the Dreadnoughts, or that if he realized it he had characteristically failed to gauge its strength. His bid misfired. McKenna remained First Lord and Churchill became Home Secretary. It is a fact of historical significance that he was not appointed to the Admiralty at this moment, and may even be regarded as a classic example of providential mercy, since his obstinate policy of drastic economy in naval construction would almost certainly have caused his removal from that office after the Agadir incident in 1911 with incalculable results, even though he had by then completely, and without a qualm, reversed his views on naval economy.

But his previous insistence upon it remains a baffling and not very creditable episode in his life, and it is strange indeed that he, of all men, should have been insensible to the 'deep tides of destiny'. The outcome of this struggle was that the Government was left with the need of paying for the Dreadnoughts without abandoning their programme of social reform. 'The People's Budget' was the fruit of this necessity.

---

29. Randolph S. Churchill, op.cit., pp.364-5.

Chapter 8

The Home Office

The Home Office which Churchill took over in February 1910 offered further scope for social reform. As at the Board of Trade, he began by investing the new office with excitement, romance and glamour. He saw the police force as a powerful army of which he would have sole and undisputed command. But his thoughts were above all focused upon the fate of this army's quarry, the criminals, and he relished in advance the prospect of exercising the luxury of mercy. He had never forgotten his own brief captivity and the horrors of confinement, and this tenacious memory, at such a moment, gave him a singular advantage in his office and ensured that he would be a good and humane Home Secretary.

Although his time at the Home Office was too short for him to place much legislation on the Statute Book, he devoted all his inexhaustible energy to thrusting forward plans that were already shaping, and carried through many administrative reforms that did not require legislation. Prison reform – the alleviation of the prisoner's soul-destroying tedium – this was the object closest to his heart, on which he laboured long and earnestly and with passionate conviction. As before, able men of like mind stood at his elbow, and of these Sir Evelyn Ruggles Brise, appointed by Asquith to be Chairman of the Police Commissioners in 1895, was perhaps the most knowledgeable and sympathetic. In Ruggles Brise Winston detected profound erudition, and a reforming ardour that matched his own, and drank deeply from this copious spring.

He did not confine himself to the help of officials, but also encouraged and absorbed the views of private citizens. One of these was Wilfrid Scawen Blunt, that eccentric landowner, poet and impulsive champion of oppressed people, who had served a two-months sentence in Galway and Kilmainham gaols under the Crimes Act in Ireland for calling a meeting in a proclaimed district. Winston had no intention of allowing any fish, however odd, to slip through the meshes of his net. He also consulted W.T. Stead, who, after his exposure of criminal vice in England, was imprisoned for three months for the manner in which he had obtained his evidence, and John Galsworthy, the dramatist and author of *The Forsyte Saga*. With these men he exchanged letters on prison reform and patiently elicited their opinions.

Blunt had known and admired Winston for some time, and, summarizing his impressions in the past, had written:

> In mind and manner he is a strange replica of his father, with all his father's suddenness and awareness, and I should say more than his father's ability. There is just the same *gaminerie* and contempt of the conventional and the same engaging plainspokenness and readiness to understand.[1]

Of these men, Winston particularly valued Galsworthy, and was always eager to rifle the treasury of his brain. He was also prepared to take the dramatist into his confidence, and acknowledging a letter from him in February 1910 on prison reform, concluded: 'My time may be short, so that if action is practically possible, it is essential that it should be prompt.'[2]

* * *

He therefore wasted no time before gutting the problem and propounding his solutions. Feeling as passionately as he did, he was determined that these should not be destined for the limbo of discarded experiments, and began to mitigate the lot of prisoners by a series of imaginative innovations. Always a man who could not bear to allow time to trickle through his fingers like sand, he felt in this case a particular urgency. He was ready by March to announce in the House his intention to differentiate between prison rules for criminals and so-called political prisoners:

> I feel, as did my predecessor, that prison rules which are suitable for criminals jailed for dishonesty or cruelty or other crimes implying moral turpitude, should not be applied inflexibly to those whose general character is good and whose offences, however reprehensible, do not involve personal dishonesty.[3]

This category, of course, embraced the suffragettes, who had spat poison at him on many a platform, and who had successfully organized

1. W.S. Blunt, *My Diaries*, Vol.II, pp.488-9.
2. John Galsworthy archives 999, 24.2.10.
3. Randolph S. Churchill, op.cit., Vol.II, p.387.

sympathy over the conditions in which they passed their prison sentences. Winston intended to treat political prisoners separately. They should not have to wear prison clothing, be searched or forced to take the regulation prison bath. They should be allowed food from outside, permitted to take regular exercise and to talk during those periods.

The whole of the prison services now came under the Home Secretary's review, and on 20 July, on the Prison Vote, he was ready to announce far-reaching reforms. As at the Board of Trade, he was conscious of an almost god-like power to soften the lot of unhappy people, and glowed with satisfaction in doing so. The following day he outlined some of the reforms in a letter to the King:

> ... A new effort is to be made to prevent people being sent to gaol for petty offences & thus familiarised with the degrading surroundings of Prison. The Probation of Offenders Act is to be strictly enjoined on magistrates all over the country. A bill is to be introduced to secure by law a period of grace for the payment of fines – (90,000 people go to prison each year in default of payment, a third of whom could probably have found money if a few days grace were allowed). Over 5000 lads between 16 & 21 are sent to prison each year for such offences as swearing, stone throwing, gaming, football in the streets. This is pure waste. Mr Churchill thinks that a system of defaulters' drills might be instituted – not military (wh would reflect on the possessing of arms) but physical exercise, vy healthy, vy disagreeable; that this might be done at the Police Station; that the boy might do his ordinary work besides, & not be sent to prison unless incorrigible or really dishonest.
>
> No lad between 16 & 21 ought to be sent to prison for mere punishment. Every sentence should be conceived with the object of pulling him together & bracing him for the world: it should be in fact disciplinary & educative rather than penal. The House was vy sympathetic to all this.
>
> In the prisons themselves Mr Churchill proposes to reduce solitary confinements to 1 months (instead of 9) for all except 'old lags' or as they are more decorously called 'recidivists'. Power is taken to pamper the suffragettes & the passive resisters. Further every quarter there will be either a concert or a lecture in each convict prison. These wretched people must have something to think about, & to break the long monotony ... The more strictly discipline is maintained, the more indulgence may follow on good behaviour. There are to be special provisions & regulations for aged convicts & for the weak-minded convicts. Lastly the whole system of Ticket of Leave is to be overhauled and reorganised ...[4]

Although some of these decisions required legislation and could not immediately be put into practice, many administrative measures could

---

4. Royal Archives, 21 July 1910.

be taken, and Prison Rules could be made by laying them in draft before Parliament for thirty days. These innovations were welcomed by both Parliament and public. Galsworthy, whose play *Justice*, which portrayed the mental and physical horror of solitary confinement, had been staged in London earlier in the year, wrote a letter to *The Times* praising the changes for their imagination and common sense. He also wrote to Winston, who had been moved by this work, and who replied on 30 July 1910:

> I am very much obliged to you for your kind letter, and for the excellent and valuable support you have given me in the public Press. There can be no question that your admirable play bore a most important part in creating that atmosphere of sympathy & interest which is so noticeable upon this subject at the present time. So far from feeling the slightest irritation at newspaper comments assigning to you the credit for prison reform, I have always felt uncomfortable at receiving the easily-won applauses which come to the heads of great departments whenever they have ploughed with borrowed oxen and reaped where they have not sown. In this case I can only claim a personal interest which has led me to seek the knowledge of others . . .
>
> I am now looking further afield and am bringing the whole subject of imprisonment for debt under review. I shall welcome from you any suggestions you may care to make on any branch of prison and criminal reform. 'Pit Ponies' are being examined by the Royal Commission.[5]

* * *

To eliminate short sentences of under a month, Churchill proposed a system of suspensory sentences for petty offences. He explained to Asquith that his intention was that when a person was sentenced to prison for certain offences (which did not involve violence, cruelty or wilful destruction of property) for any period of less than one month, the Court should declare the sentence to be suspensory in character. If the offender was convicted later of a similar offence, he would be compelled to serve his previous suspensory sentence, provided that this together with the new sentence amounted to more than one month: 'The rule-of-thumb principle which I wish to establish is prolonged admonition, no imprisonment under a month, and that month a very severe correction . . .'

In this long letter to Asquith, he set out Home Office business for the coming year, commenting upon it:

'A scientific and benevolent measure, dealing with prisons and the punishment of offenders, would be well suited to the Coronation year.' By his proposals he hoped to achieve simultaneously a marked reduction of committals on short sentences; a reduction in the prison population and easement in accommodation; and a relief in the work of prison staffs. He also proposed to make a complete administrative reorganization. 'Classification,' he remarked somewhat pontifically, 'is the essence of penology.'

It seemed to him that much ignorance on this subject prevailed in the Courts, and particular on the Benches of Magistrates. He now proposed to take authority by Parliamentary rule to set up a Board of Classification which:

> would consider the cases of all offenders after being sentenced, and distribute them to receive their appropriate treatment throughout the different penal and curative institutions of the prisons system: due regard of course being paid to the decision of the Court and provided always that any such modification or variation of treatment shall not be in excess or aggravation of the original sentences of the Court.[6]

The industrious apprentice was now restored to his master's favour, for Asquith warmly embraced Winston's proposals and was delighted when the *enfant terrible* had discovered such an ardent interest in penal reform. He was in entire agreement with his ideas, but feared that the attempt to abolish imprisonment for debt, although he was prepared to support it, would prove to be a measure bristling with controversy.[7] Churchill incorporated the substance of his long letter to Asquith explaining these matters in a confidential Cabinet Paper, 'Abatement of Imprisonment', dated 25 October 1910.

It seems that in the matter of Classification Winston was indulging that old fault of rushing his fences, for the question was not as simple as the Home Secretary imagined. On 23 August Edward Marsh had written to Winston, who was holidaying in Greece:

> Ruggles'[8] breath was rather taken away by your prisons minute and he burst into Homeric laughter when he read that it would be *easy* for the P Commrs to classify into 20 groups: but on the whole he was enthusiastic, and said your grasp of the subject was marvellous, and that *if* you or a Home Secretary like you were to be here for the next five years, it could be done – but that it is a five year job.[9]

*   *   *

6. Chartwell papers.
7. Ibid.
8. Sir Evelyn Ruggles Brise.
9. Chartwell papers.

The most odious and dreaded responsibility borne by Home Secretaries before the abolition of capital punishment – that of advising the Crown on the prerogative of mercy in murder cases – tormented him as much as it had any of his predecessors. He did not believe, like Bacon, that justice should contain an element of revenge, and in later years was to view with scant enthusiasm – and indeed an element of disgust – the punishment by death even of the Nazi war criminals. He told W.S. Blunt that 'it had become a nightmare to him to have to exercise the power of life and death in the case of condemned criminals, on an average of one case a fortnight', and he found that the duty merely became more excruciating as time passed. He who had once said with passion, 'Never abandon life. There is a way out of everything – except death' was awed and diminished by the thought that it was in his hands to deprive another of that unique gift, and he flinched from the duty whenever it recurred.

There were forty-three such cases during Churchill's two years at the Home Office, and he recommended twenty-three for mercy. Always on his desk were kept the name and date of execution of men under sentence of death. He examined every case personally, and with the utmost care. The whole miserable ground would be retrodden, and if at the end he was in the slightest doubt he would commit the pros and cons to paper and seek the opinion of expert advisers in the Home Office. Fulfilling this grim responsibility occupied many agonizing hours, but although so strongly inspired by the spirit of mercy, and so fearful of snuffing out the life of another, Churchill never rebelled against the principle of capital punishment, and to the end of his days was in favour of retaining the ultimate penalty for murder.

In Winston's absence during the summer recess of 1910 Sir Edward Grey undertook responsibility for the Home Office. There were at the time two capital sentences due for execution in August, on one of which Churchill had spent many hours of torturing reflection. He had finally decided that the law must take its course, but had forwarded the papers to Grey for his opinion, since he would be in charge at the time of execution. Grey, a sensitive man, devoted to birds and the countryside, relished these grim duties no more than his absent colleague, but saw no reason to intervene. Reporting to Churchill on 21 August, he expressed the anguish he felt in the responsibility for life or death:

> I think this part of the job is beastly & on the night before the two men were hung I kept meditating on the sort of night they were having until I felt that I ought not to let them hang unless I went to be hung too.[10]

10. Chartwell papers.

Winston, who so clearly understood Grey's unhappiness, replied from Greece:

> ... I know you must have felt keenly the painful duties wh I put upon you. There was however no doubt as to the course to pursue. The only capital decision with wh I have been dissatisfied was about a man I reprieved just before I started on the grounds wh I do not feel wholly convinced were adequate. He has since committed suicide! To most men – including all the best – a life sentence is worse than a death sentence.[11]

* * *

Although Winston accomplished so much useful and humane work at the Home Office, his general legislation was not always successful. On 4 July 1910 he introduced the long-anticipated Shops Bill to regulate the shop-opening hours and the hours and conditions of work for shop assistants. The proposals, although enjoying the general backing of public opinion, found scant favour with the shopkeepers. The Jews complained that the Sunday laws would mean that their total opening hours were less than those of the Gentiles, while the latter claimed that Sunday opening was unfair competition. After second reading the Bill was crowded out. The Home Secretary presented an amended version in March 1911, but his efforts to reconcile conflicting interests again failed, and the Bill was so mangled in Committee that it emerged a pallid and bloodless measure.[12]

Nor was he successful with the Aliens (Prevention of Crime) Bill. We have seen how in 1904 Winston, engaged in trying to ingratiate himself with the Jewish electors of North West Manchester, had strongly opposed the Aliens Bill introduced by the Tory Government. In 1906 the Liberals had been forced to enact a similar though modified measure. But it was the so-called 'siege of Sidney Street' that convinced Churchill that the regulations governing aliens must be strengthened.

This bizarre episode has been described so often that it is only necessary to make a brief reference to it here. The curious will find the most vivid account of the event, which revealed Winston in his most baroque and flamboyant mood and fanned the hatred of Conservatives, in his book *Thoughts and Adventures*.[13] The police had been searching for a gang of foreign criminals, and in the small hours of 3 January 1911 surrounded No. 100 Sidney Street off the Mile End Road, where they believed two of the wanted men were lodging. The criminals were armed

11. Ibid.
12. Annual Register 1911, p.69 and p.271.
13. Winston S. Churchill, *Thoughts and Adventures*.

with Mauser automatic pistols, and the police were unable to dislodge them. Scots Guards with long-range rifles were summoned from the Tower of London, and Horse Artillery from St John's Wood in case it was necessary to batter the house down. When it was seen to be on fire the Fire Brigade was brought to the scene, but was not allowed to operate for fear of being shot by the criminals. When the house was burned to the ground the bodies of two men were recovered, one dead from a gunshot wound, the other from suffocation.

The episode is remembered mainly because the Home Secretary could not resist driving down to the scene and, wearing a top hat and a cloak, recklessly exposing himself to gunfire. Those who liked him and knew him well regarded his behaviour as an endearing and wholly characteristic act of folly, Asquith saying with many a chuckle that 'it was Winston through and through', but his Conservative enemies, who saw in his conduct evidence of mental instability and deplorable lack of judgment, jeered. Wrote Mr Harold Macmillan: 'What we regard as his *joie de vivre* and fun – such as joining in the Sidney Street battle and wearing eccentric hats, to Conservatives appeared merely vulgar and exhibitionist.'[14]

Winston was, however, well able to exonerate himself from the charges of interfering with the police and 'directing operations'. He was called to give evidence at the Inquest on the two criminals on 18 January 1911.

> The Inquest resulted in a verdict of justifiable homicide, coupled with an expression of the desire for more stringency in the laws governing the admission of criminal aliens.[15]

Apart from Radicals, there was now general support for more effective measures, and Churchill introduced his Bill under the Ten-Minute Rule on 18 April 1911, but it was crowded out by pressure of Parliamentary business and made no progress. He therefore persuaded the House to give a second reading to Mr Goulding's Private Member's Bill, not because he agreed with its clauses but 'because I see a prospect of using it as a vehicle to carry the provisions of the Government Bill on the same subject into law.[16] However, the aliens regulations were not in the event altered till 1915.

He was more fortunate with the Coal Mines Bill for stricter safety

---

14. The Right Hon. Harold Macmillan to author.
15. Annual Register 1911, pp.3-4.
16. Chartwell papers, WSC to H.J.Wilson, 2 May 1911.

regulations in the pits. Second reading took place on Friday, 18 March 1911,

> and after a debate of only two hours, & despite the fact that it was in the power of any individual member to talk it out, it passed its second reading with unanimous consent. Considering that it was only published yesterday morning it is a great vote of faith & good will on the part of all parties to have allowed it to go so swiftly on its way.[17]

* * *

There was another aspect of Churchill's work at the Home Office which he tackled with a resolution as great as that for penal and other reform. This area of his responsibilities was industrial disturbance, and although his conduct and restraint were generally impeccable, he found himself in the end an object of loathing by organized labour.

In 1910 and 1911, there were strikes on an unprecedented scale in the docks, coalmines and railways, some of which ended in alarming violence. They were the backwash of the trade depressions from which the country was painfully recuperating. The first serious strike was at Newport docks in May 1910. It was caused by a loading argument between the Empire Trading Company and Houlder Brothers, Shippers, and the dockers' union. This dispute has a curiously contemporary ring about it. The dockers objected to the employers using labourers supplied by the Shipping Federation and prevented them from working. The docks were brought to a standstill, and looting and disturbances broke out.

The local authorities were frightened by the violent atmosphere, and the Mayor of Newport demanded reinforcements of 250 Metropolitan foot and 50 mounted policemen. The Newport Magistrates also asked the War Office to hold troops in readiness. This, as Winston was well aware, was the delicate element in such crises and, forearmed, he sought in advance to calm the militants. He was extremely anxious to avoid the use of soldiers but, if they had to be sent, asked for mounted troops:

> ... Mr Churchill, before he left, had considered the possibility of their applying for troops. He is most anxious to avoid their being used, and is doing all he can by offering to supply Metropolitan Police and otherwise to avoid the necessity; but of course if the Mayor or Magistrates requisition them, they must be ready to go. Mr Churchill asked me specially to impress on the War Office that *mounted troops* should be sent. They are

17. Royal Archives, 17 March 1911.

far more effective than infantry in dealing with a riot, and the risk of their employment leading to loss of life is much less.[18]

On the following day, 22 May, a settlement was reached between the Mayor of Newport, the Board of Trade and representatives of Masters and Men. The despatch of the Metropolitan Police was cancelled, as was the alert to the Officer Commanding troops at Chester.

So far Winston's touch had been confident and faultless, and it continued into a far more serious strike in the coal-mining district of the Rhondda Valley in the autumn of the same year, caused by a dispute concerning differentials in the working of hard and soft seams. Owing to the Coal Mines Act of 1908, the output of the South Wales mines had tended to diminish, with a resentment by the miners at a corresponding diminution of wages. By early November 1910, 30,000 men were idle, mainly at the collieries of the Cambrian Coal Trust in the Rhondda Valley, and at Aberdare.

On 7 November the miners at the Aberdare collieries suddenly turned out and prevented enginemen and surfacemen from going to work. Later they halted the ventilating machinery, imperilling the lives of hundreds of pit ponies. Police were summoned from Swansea, Bristol and elsewhere, and the Chief Constable of Glamorganshire demanded troops. The rioting, violent and dangerous, continued, and even the men whose duty it was to feed the pit ponies were not allowed to go down the mines. The worst rioting occurred in the town of Tonypandy, and from this moment Winston was branded with the smear of the word 'Tonypandy' which was flung at him by Labour opponents, who did not have the least knowledge of the facts, for the remainder of his political life.

If we are to adhere prosaically to the facts, it should be recalled that it was entirely due to Churchill's influence that the troops had been held back. He reported to the King that order had been maintained round the threatened collieries:

> No need for the employment of troops is likely to occur. They will be kept as far as possible out of touch with the population, while sufficiently near to the scene to be available if necessary ... The 400 Cavalry and Infantry which were sent for by the Chief Constable on Monday night were not started by the Secretary of State for War or by the Home Secretary, but were sent, pending superior instructions, by the General Officer Commanding of the Southern Command. Up to

18. Chartwell papers. Sir E. Troup, Home Office to Sir Edward Ward, Permanent U-S for War, 21.5.10.

10 o'clock on Tuesday morning the Home Office had no knowledge of this movement or of the necessity for it. At 11 o'clock Mr Churchill, after consulting with Mr Haldane and communicating with the Chief Constable of Glamorgan at Tonypandy, definitely decided to employ police instead of military to deal with the disorder, and, while moving troops near to the scene of disturbance, to keep them in the background until it was certain that police methods had proved insufficient. From this policy there has been no change whatever. 300 Metropolitan Police, of whom 100 were mounted, were ordered to start for Pontypridd as fast as trains could be got to convey them.

This force of picked constables experienced in the handling of crowds was for every purpose better suited to the needs of the situation than an equivalent body of infantry. Infantry soldiers can if attacked or stoned only reply by fire from long-range rifles which often kills foolish sightseers unconnected with the riot, or innocent people at distance from it. The Chief Constable of Glamorgan concurred in the substitution of the Metropolitan Police for the Infantry, who were halted at Swindon, and the Cavalry were told to proceed no further than Cardiff and to await further instructions there. General Macready was specially selected to take charge of any military forces which might be required to support the police . . . The train conveying the Metropolitan Police was delayed for about an hour in reaching its destination. All the attacks of the rioters upon the Glamorgan Colliery were, however, successfully repulsed by the Chief Constable with the County Police at his disposal, and when the Metropolitan Police arrived the rioters had already been beaten from the collieries without the aid of any reinforcement either of London police or military.

The insensate act of the rioters in wrecking shops in the town of Tonypandy, against which they had not the slightest cause for animosity, when they had been foiled in their attacks upon the colliery, was not foreseen by anyone on the spot, and would not have been prevented by the presence of soldiers at the colliery itself . . .[19]

It is clear from this document that, as during the Newport strike earlier in the year, Churchill's behaviour had been impeccably correct. He had been in constant liaison with the local authorities; he had been consistently against the use of troops to quell civil disorder, except in the last resort; and in each case he had used his influence with the War Office and the Chief Constable concerned to keep the military away from the scene of disturbance. The case is fully attested by General Macready, who wrote:

It was entirely due to Mr Churchill's foresight in sending a strong force of Metropolitan Police directly he was made aware of the state of

19. Chartwell papers, 10 November 1910. Draft.

affairs in the valleys that bloodshed was avoided, for had the police not been in sufficient strength to cope with the rioters there would have been no alternative but to bring the military into action.[20]

* * *

No agreement with the employers had yet been reached, and Winston was alarmed to an unusual extent by the situation, as can be seen in the appeal he made to Lloyd George on 13 November 1910:

> I am deeply concerned at the situation in South Wales. The tension has not at all diminished, and only the great force of police and military has prevented an outbreak. Unless the situation is relieved there will be a battle royal between the police and the rioters at no distant date. I believe the police will be found strong enough to beat all rioters without recourse being had to the military. But you will see that I cannot keep this great force of Metropolitan Police indefinitely occupied there, and the time will come in the course of the next week or ten days when I shall have to leave the soldiers in much more naked contact with the population than is now necessary. If the strikers delay rioting until the police force has been reduced they may come right up against the rifles with consequences of the utmost gravity . . .[21]

He therefore begged Lloyd George 'to tender your services to the Cabinet', and by using his influence in Wales, his knowledge of the Welsh language and his negotiating genius to seek to restore peace. The 'battle royal' which he forecast took place, again in Tonypandy, on the night of 21 November. Winston reported to the King:

> There was a hard and furious fight last night in Tonypandy. The police were quite strong enough to scatter the rioters & beat them out of the town. The military were at hand but did not have to fire. All is quiet now . . .[22]

Most of the miners returned to work towards the end of December. But the Labour Members in the House of Commons, led by Keir Hardie, violently attacked the Home Secretary for the impropriety of sending troops at all and for the harsh methods of the police at Tonypandy. He was engaged in creating a left-wing martyrology – Tonypandy – worthy to rank with the Tolpuddle Martyrs as an example of how enduring a *canard* based on mendacity, emotionalism and misrepresentation can prove. Yet there is not the slightest question that Churchill had handled

20. General Macready, *Annals of an Active Life*, Vol.I, p.155.
21. Chartwell papers.
22. Royal Archives, 22 November 1910.

industrial disturbance, at Newport and in the Rhondda Valley, with judgment and restraint, as the more honest members of the other side have since acknowledged. George Isaacs, a Socialist Minister of Labour, wrote in 1953: 'Looking back now, it is difficult to see what else a resolute Home Secretary could have done, given the situation in which such bitter industrial relations were allowed to develop.'[23] The industrial squalls of 1910-11 were of the utmost violence, which no Government worth its salt could tolerate, and Churchill's responsibility, as Home Secretary, was for the preservation of law and order.

* * *

In 1911, this first year of a new reign, there were far more protracted and widespread strikes, beginning with a seamen's strike in June which continued over the Coronation, and culminating in a serious railway strike in August. The Conciliation Boards set up in 1907 crawled at too slow a pace to keep abreast of the workers' grievances, and in late July Churchill was moved to express his fears in an undated memorandum:

> There is great unrest in the country. Port after port is called out. The police and the military are asked for at place after place. Fresh outbreaks continuously occur and will go on. The railways are not sound. Transport workers everywhere are getting to know their strength, while the 'hooligan' element are causing riots: and those conversant of labour matters in *practice* anticipate grave upheaval. Serious crises have been in recent years, and very often lately, surmounted only by a narrow margin of safety, and now specially a new force has arisen in trade unionism, whereby the power of the old leaders has proved quite ineffective, and the sympathetic strike on a wide scale is prominent. The general strike 'policy' is a factor that must be dealt with.[24]

Despite these forebodings, his actions remained careful and unprovocative, and during the London Dock Strike of 1911, the dockers' leader, Ben Tillett, described his influence as 'a moderate and responsible one'.[25] This reputation was sadly impaired by the railway strike of 1911. The Liverpool railwaymen were the first to come out, partly in sympathy with the dockers and partly because they had grievances of their own. On 13 August 1911 there was rioting and disturbance, started by hooligans and agitators and taken up by the strikers. A battalion of Scots Greys had already been sent to Liverpool, and these were followed by reinforcements. The example of Liverpool proved contagious, and partial strikes took place at many other centres. The

23. George Isaacs, *Churchill and his Contemporaries*, p.369.
24. Chartwell papers.
25. Ben Tillett, *History of the London Transport Workers' Strike, 1911.*

railway companies refused to negotiate, and the four railway unions called out their men on 16 August. There was no hesitation this time in the employment of troops. They were used to patrol the railway lines and to guard the signal boxes and those railwaymen who continued to work, so that the movement of essential supplies of food and fuel and the maintenance of services vital to the community, although disrupted, managed to continue. The strike ended on 20 August, but not before two men had been killed when troops opened fire during a riot at Llanelly for which the railwaymen themselves were not responsible.

Winston this time had taken the dangerous step of mobilizing thousands of troops, *without waiting for requests from the local authorities*, and sending them to all strategic positions. It was the first time that he had so stretched his powers, but before condemning him too hastily it is important to remember the circumstances in which the decision was taken.

In the words of J.A. Spender:

> Never in the memory of men living had a Ministry been beset with so many and great dangers as Asquith's Government during July and August 1911. The long, bitter struggle between Lords and Commons was entering its last stages. The Kaiser had set the furnace door ajar and given Europe a terrifying glimpse of the glare of war by sending the gun-boat *Panther* to Agadir, and at this moment the great railway strike broke out. The whole railways system of the country was suddenly threatened with paralysis, and the country itself with a failure of food, and a complete dislocation of industry. In the absence of a motor transport service, the railway was the vital artery of the nation, and it was essential that it should not be cut.[26]

It was in fact a major crisis, and as such Winston saw it, and did not hesitate to use troops to guard stations and protect the line. He was also aware, as the general public were not, that the danger of war was by no means over, and that Sir Edward Grey had warned the Admiralty that 'the Fleet might be attacked at any moment'.

On 19 August, thanks largely to Lloyd George's skilful negotiations with the Unions, the railways strike ended, the troops were withdrawn and the Enrolment of Special Constables was halted. In a telegram to King George V, Churchill generously said 'The Chancellor of the Exchequer is principally responsible for this happy result.'

* * *

These events offered a priceless opportunity to hostile elements, and the Home Office came under heavy, if erratic, fire. Mr Ramsay

26. Spender, op.cit., Vol.I, p.350.

MacDonald claimed that: 'The Department which has played the most diabolical part in all this unrest was the Home Office', and protested against 'this reversion to mediaeval ideas of the maintenance of law and order.' Winston now stood clearly revealed as the villain of the piece, and was duly hissed off the stage. Keir Hardie said that the two men shot at Llanelly had been murdered in the capitalist interest, and even Winston's Liberal friend Charles Masterman referred to his partiality for the 'whiff of grapeshot' technique.

He was completely unmoved by all the chatter and abuse. He saw himself as the Minister responsible for the protection of the transport system and the maintenance of law and order at a critical moment of danger. No Government, he said, could regard the crisis as a mere trade dispute and look on with tolerant impartiality. They had become 'active partisans of the food supply'. He would have regarded the failure to send troops as a gross dereliction of duty.

He never recovered his position with the Labour movement after this incident, and the martyr-makers ensured that it was never forgotten. Their propaganda was based on lies and *suppressio veri*, but it had the quality of persistence. They clutched the deaths at Llanelly as a weapon with which they belaboured Churchill over the years. In time, either unintentionally or with malice aforethought, it became confused in their minds with the earlier riots in the Rhondda Valley, and decades later Labour mythology was spewing at him the epithet 'Tonypandy' as a term of supreme abuse, although, as we have already noticed, he handled the disturbance there with a minimum of force and without calling on the Army.

It is a fact that although he was determined to do his duty, Churchill's sympathy, on the merits of the case, was largely with the men. The benefit of the social reforms which the Government were striving to pass into law had not yet accrued to the people, and the condition of the lower-class workers in industry was a disgrace to a civilized country. Winston was well aware of the facts: 'The strikers are vy poor,' he wrote to the King, 'miserably paid & now nearly starving.'[27]

In the summer of that momentous year of 1911, with all its alarms and excursions, passed into autumn, Winston's days at the Home Office were approaching their end. He was soon to fulfil his heart's desire and be transferred to the Admiralty. And when at last he reached this glittering and historic stronghold, it was in a very different and more worthy frame of mind than that in which he had twice before aspired to the office of First Lord.

27. Royal Archives, 18 August 1911.

Chapter 9

The Constitutional Struggle

Ever since riding to power on the avalanche of 1906 – or as F. E. Smith preferred to describe their arrival, 'floating into Parliament like corks on the top of a dirty wave' – the Liberal Government had been infuriatingly thwarted by the Tory majority in the House of Lords. Here the Conservative Peers had overwhelming numerical superiority, and used it recklessly to frustrate the Government's legislative programme either by rejecting Bills which the Lower House had passed by a large majority, or by amending them so brutally that they were entirely transformed or emasculated.

In 1906 they had so mutilated the Education Bill that the Prime Minister moved to discharge the order, and the Bill perished. In the same session the Plural Voting Bill was rejected by the Lords on Second Reading. Only a desire to conciliate organized labour saved the Trades Disputes Bill from a similar fate. To Liberals it not unnaturally seemed an intolerable state of affairs that a second chamber, composed on the hereditary principle, should use its powers in a wholesale massacre of progressive social measures put forward by a Government with the greatest majority in modern times.

Sir Henry Campbell-Bannerman clearly expressed his party's indignation when he announced the abandonment of the Education Bill:

> It is plainly intolerable that a Second Chamber should, while one party in the State is in power, be its willing servant, and when that party has received unmistakable and emphatic condemnation by the country, be able to neutralise and thwart and distort the policy which the electors show they approve . . . The resources of the House of Commons are not exhausted, and I say with conviction that a way must be found, and a way will be found, by which the will of the people, expressed through their elected representatives in this House, will be made to prevail.[1]

1. J.A. Spender, *Herbert Henry Asquith*, Vol.1, pp.185-6.

These ominous words gave clear warning that a struggle *à l'outrance* was impending between the two Houses of Parliament. 'A way must and will be found.' But there was much anxious discussion about how or where this was to be discovered. Many Conservatives too were interested in 'reform' of the House of Lords, while remaining affronted by the thought of curtailment of its powers. Campbell-Bannerman, however, knew that 'reform' would entail endless argument and delay, and was determined not to allow himself to be edged into this morass. He was resolved upon the 'clean cut' – the curtailment of the powers of the House of Lords, while leaving the question of its composition to a later Government. He wanted, in fact, to draw its teeth by an immediate surgical operation, and to leave the post-operational case in other hands, and eventually his will prevailed in Cabinet.

In June 1907 he introduced a resolution in the House of Commons declaring

> That, in order to give effect to the will of the people, as expressed by their elected representatives, the power of the other House to alter or reject Bills passed by this House must be restricted by law, so as to secure that, within the limits of a single Parliament, the final decision of the Commons should prevail.

The resolution, which was carried by 365 votes, became known as 'The Campbell-Bannerman resolution', and was the foundation stone of the Parliament Bill which was eventually passed in 1911.

* * *

When Winston entered the Asquith Cabinet as President of the Board of Trade he was not disposed to restrict himself pedantically to the narrow confines of his own department, and immediately took advantage of his new position to bombard his colleagues with memoranda on every conceivable subject, sometimes brilliant, frequently infuriating. These naturally included the House of Lords, and he was to become more and more closely involved in the constitutional struggle.

He soon found that his Cabinet colleagues formed an orchestra of gifted individual instrumentalists, frequently out of harmony, each with his own ideas as to how the baton should be wielded. Lloyd George, Edward Grey, Haldane, Morley, Crewe, Herbert Samuel, Augustine Birrell, John Burns – they were a talented but disparate assembly of men, and it is a tribute to Asquith's leadership that he was able to hold such a team together.

Various friendships and alignments grew up among this group, and the most remarkable was that now forged between Lloyd George and Winston Churchill, while Asquith relied increasingly on the advice of Lord Crewe. We have seen how Winston's wife recalled to the author, perhaps with a twinge of resentment even when so many years had passed, that Winston at this time was entranced by Lloyd George, 'that he was completely under Lloyd George's thumb'.[2] And in 1908 Winston's great friend, Violet Asquith, had already arrived at the same conclusion:

> To me the most curious and surprising feature of their partnership was that while it exercised no influence whatever on Lloyd George, politically or otherwise, it directed, shaped and coloured Winston Churchill's mental attitude and his political course during the next few years. Lloyd George was throughout the dominant partner. His was the only personal leadership I have ever known Winston to accept unquestioningly in his whole political career. He was fascinated by a mind more swift and agile than his own, by its fertility and resource . . . From Lloyd George he was to learn the language of Radicalism. It was Lloyd George's native tongue, but it was not his own, and despite his efforts he spoke it 'with a difference' . . . Lloyd George was saturated with class-consciousness. Winston accepted class distinction without a thought.[3]

It was indeed a strange relationship. One had been born in Blenheim Palace and was free of its magnificent rooms and lovely gardens. The other had been raised by his cobbler uncle in a mean Welsh village, and imbued with an abiding and rancorous hatred of wealth and privilege. Winston had once thrilled, and was to do so again, to Imperial glory and the broad sweep of history; Lloyd George was a Little Englander who had been shocked to the marrow by the Boer War in which Winston had so often risked his life. One was governed by reason, and reached his conclusions through mental processes, the other by flashes of dragonfly instinct. Winston was staunchly, fiercely loyal to Lloyd George; Lloyd George took pleasure in listening to spiteful anecdotes about his infatuated friend. And even though Winston must have been at least vaguely aware of Lloyd George's complete indifference to either scruples or principles, he was too deeply spellbound to be shocked.

*   *   *

On 27 November 1908 the House of Lords slaughtered one of the Government's sacred cows, the Licensing Bill, on Second Reading, giving clear warning of their defiant mood, and providing Winston

---

2. Lady Spencer-Churchill to author.
3. Violet Bonham Carter, *Winston Churchill As I Knew Him*, p. 161.

with the opportunity to display an incongruous ardour in the cause of temperance. They also in this session rejected the Scottish Small Landholders Bill, condescending, however, to pass the Old Age Pensions Bill [Asquith] and the Mines Eight Hours Bill [Churchill], in a desire to conciliate organized labour.

By the end of the year it was obvious that the Liberal Government would be unable to enact the major measures of policy which their great majority clearly empowered them to place on the Statute Book – Home Rule, temperance reform, land reform and Welsh Disestablishment – on which they had been elected in 1906, and that a fight to the death with the House of Lords was now inevitable. But although the Government had a more than plausible case to argue, some intelligent Conservatives were convinced that by 1909 this Liberal Government was no longer the trampling phalanx of 1906 welded together by triumph at the polls. In L. S. Amery's view:

> The great Liberal tide which had swept the country in 1906, had by 1909 completely spent itself . . . Liberalism had lost all momentum, and was in danger of early disintegration. It was essential at all cost to find some new issue, more particularly in the economic field, in order to regain the initiative and to recreate enthusiasm.

The Prime Minister was fully alive to the displeasing prospects ahead, and at the end of 1908, on 11 December, he made his views plain at a dinner at the National Liberal Club:

> To put the thing plainly, the present system enables the leader of the party which has been defeated and repudiated by the people at the polls to determine through the House of Lords what shall and what shall not be the legislation of the country. The question which I want to put to you and to my fellow Liberals outside is this: 'Is this state of things to continue?' We say that it must be brought to an end, and I invite the Liberal Party tonight to treat the veto of the House of Lords as the dominating issue in politics . . .[4]

The crisis between the Houses was precipitated by Lloyd George's Budget. New sources of revenue had to be found to finance naval construction and (far more precious to the Liberal mind) schemes for social embellishment – sickness and unemployment insurance – already in an advanced state of preparation. This Budget, regarded by Conservatives as a monstrous encroachment upon the rights of the landowning classes, now seems to our numbed senses stunned by modern exactions, a humble early violet. Its principal taxation proposals included a small

4. Spender, op.cit., Vol.1, pp.240-1.

increase in income tax, a more massive one on death duties; super-tax to be imposed on incomes of more than £3,000 per annum, and a higher taxation of the liquor trade. Four new land taxes of progressive financial value seemed to the Conservatives to be the knell of doom, and became charged with odium. Of these the two most important and controversial were the tax on the site value of undeveloped land, and the increment duty on the enhancement of site values.

*   *   *

The Opposition might well have accepted the Budget but for the land taxes. But these, which now seem so modest as to be almost derisory, were at the time regarded as dangerous and revolutionary, and passion was inflamed by the speeches made by politicians of both parties. Winston entered the struggle, as might be expected, by a series of attacks on the House of Lords. On 7 October 1909 he said at Abernethy, referring to the possible rejection of the Budget by the Upper House:

> The House of Lords has no scrap of right to interfere in finance. If they do, they violate the Constitution, they shatter the finances, and they create an administrative breakdown the outcome of which no man can foresee. If such a situation should occur a Liberal Government can only look to the people. We count on you and we shall come to you. If you sustain us, we shall take effective steps to prevent such a deadlock ever occurring again. That is the whole policy of His Majesty's Government – blunt, sober, obvious, and unflinching.[5]

But he could not believe that the rejection would take place, and two days later he was saying at the National Liberal Club:

> I have never been able to rank myself among those who believe that the Budget will be rejected by the House of Lords.[6]

The rejection by the Lords of a Finance Bill had long been in abeyance. They had a technical right to do so, but such a right had not been exercised in modern times, financial control being accepted by long custom as the prerogative of the elected representatives of the people. On 16 November 1909 Lord Lansdowne gave notice that he would move an amendment in the Lords on Second Reading of the Finance Bill: 'This that House is not justified in giving its consent to this Bill until it has been submitted to the judgment of the country.' And on 30 November the extraordinary event occurred. The House

5. W.S. Churchill, *Liberalism and the Social Problem*, p.240-1.
6. Ibid, p.405.

of Lord rejected the Finance Bill by 350 votes to 75, and a punishing battle clearly lay ahead.

* * *

The Prime Minister immediately advised the King to dissolve Parliament, and stated in the House of Commons: 'That the action of the House of Lords in refusing to pass into law the financial provision made by this House for the service of the year is a breach of the Constitution and a usurpation of the rights of the Commons.' Opening the election campaign on 10 December at the Albert Hall, Asquith made an important declaration which was widely misinterpreted, saying, 'We shall not assume office, and we shall not hold office, unless we can secure the safeguards which experience shows us to be necessary for the legislative utility and honour of the party of progress.'

This remark was taken by many to mean that the Prime Minister had obtained a guarantee from King Edward VII that, should the Liberals win the election and the Lords continue intransigent, he would create a sufficient number of peers to overcome their opposition. This was not in fact the case:

'The King had come to the conclusion that he would not be justified in creating new peers (say 300) until after a second election.'[7]

During the election campaign Winston attacked the Lords without restraint, reverting in the later stages to the Free Trade v. Protection issue. He retained his seat comfortably at Dundee, heading the poll with 10,747 votes, his fellow-Member, the Labour candidate, closely approaching him with 10,365. Winston's majority over the Conservative candidate was increased by 3,786 on the 1908 by-election. Polling continued for two weeks, and the final result was a Liberal majority of only 2 over the Tories. With Labour and the Irish Nationalists as their friends, vital but demanding, in support, they could achieve a majority of 124. The huge Liberal majority of 1906 had melted away like snow, and the Liberal subjection to the unrelenting pressure of the Irish Members had begun. Irish Home Rule had not been seriously discussed at the election, and even by stretching the facts and the use of a certain casuistry, it was difficult for the Government to claim that they had authorization, still less a mandate, for such a departure. But the Irish leader, Redmond, was not interested in their embarrassment. He did not like Lloyd George's Budget, and was not concerned with the Liberal Party's progressive social legislation. His prime interest was that the way should be cleared within the lifetime of the new Parliament for a Home Rule act which

7. Spender, op.cit., Vol. 1, pp.261-2.

would lead to a free Ireland, with its own parliamentary institutions, but still a Dominion of the Crown.

The Irish Nationalist Members were a stimulating element in the Westminster scene. Many of them were parliamentarians of supreme accomplishment, masters of lightning tactical moves, and although inclined to be dirty in-fighters, speaking with warm Celtic passion and all the fluency of their race. Indeed, it may be that power of speech, skill in debate, and biting wit were more widespread in the Irish Nationalist Party than in any other that has ever sat in the House of Commons. A cubit higher than all the others was Tim Healy, the man who broke Parnell; in private life charming and cultured, in politics dangerous as a panther. One of the finest speakers in an age rich in oratory, with a soft resonant voice and an unmatched natural eloquence, there was also in him that streak of silken brutality which had laid Parnell in the dust, and there were flashes of cruelty in his speeches, which were usually steeped in bitterness and gall. Dillon and Devlin were other Nationalist Members almost as formidable, but far less attractive, and therefore less readily forgiven. Several of the Irish, including Redmond's brother William, were to die bravely in the 1914 War.

There was a fascinating and extraordinary difference between Lloyd George's conduct of the Budget in the House of Commons and his contortions on the public platform. In the House, both in introducing the measure and at subsequent stages, his behaviour was restrained and impeccable. He was suave, humorous and good-tempered, showing an unnatural patience towards the Opposition, his murderous tongue under rigid control. On the platform, as though to compensate himself for this restraint, he indulged in a positive orgy of abuse of Tory landlords, particularly the Dukes, and his speeches at Limehouse and elsewhere remain gems of inspired scurrility. It was as though he was expelling by the cathartic of speech the rancid hatred which had accumulated since his poverty-stricken childhood, and the abuse was pierced by shafts of synthetic and maudlin pity, as when speaking of pensions:

> It's a shame for a rich country like ours that it should allow those who have toiled all their days to end in starvation. It's rather hard that an old workman should have to find his way to the tomb, bleeding and footsore through the brambles and thorns of poverty. We cut a new path through them, an easier one, a pleasanter one through fields of waving corn.

Such a *cri de coeur* was remote indeed from the merits of the land taxes, but it was none the less immensely effective at a mass meeting.

Family and Friends

Churchill arrives by taxi at Caxton Hall, London, to obtain his marriage licence. 1908. (*Press Association*)

Churchill's marriage to Clementine Hozier took place at St Margaret's, Westminster, on 12 September 1908. The couple spent the first two days of their honeymoon at Blenheim before going to Italy. Here, the bride is seen in her going-away outfit. (*Popperfoto*)

Mrs Churchill and the Mayor of Westminster (Lord Cheylesmore) at a bazaar at the Horticultural Hall, Westminster, in aid of the Browning Settlement. Circa 1910. (*Press Association*)

The Churchill children at a society wedding in 1915. *Left to right*: Diana Churchill, Randolph Churchill and their cousin John George Spencer Churchill. (*Press Association*)

With Mrs Churchill at a Chelmsford fête in September 1916. (*Popperfoto*)

On the beach at Sandwich, shortly before the outbreak of the First World War. (*Popperfoto*)

Churchill's mother Jenny in 1912. After the death of Lord Randolph Churchill she married George Cornwallis West, a man twenty years her junior. They were later divorced. (*Press Association*)

Churchill pictured with his daughter Diana, leaving his London residence to address a Liberal Meeting, in 1923, just before he left the Party. (*Popperfoto*)

F. E. Smith, first Earl of Birkenhead, and one of Churchill's closest friends. Two pictures showing him speaking at Bullyclare, Ireland, on the Ulster question in 1913. Churchill wrote: '. . . our friendship was perfect. It was never disturbed by the fiercest party fight. It was never marred by the slightest personal difference or misunderstanding. It grew stronger as nearly a quarter of a century slipped by, and it lasted until his untimely death.' (*Press Association*)

Asquith speaking at Ladybank in 1913. Miss Violet Asquith (later Lady Bonham Carter) is seated next to the Prime Minister. At one time Winston Churchill considered marrying Violet Asquith. (*Press Association*)

Stanley Baldwin (*right*) and Austen Chamberlain at Chequers in 1923.(*Press Association*)

One further masterpiece of this supreme vituperator deserves quotation:

> What is the chief charge against this Budget? That it is an attack against industry, and an attack on property. I am going to demonstrate to you that it is neither . . . only one stock has gone badly; there has been a great slump in Dukes. They used to stand rather high in the market, especially in the Tory market, but the Tory Peers have discovered that they are of no value. They have been making speeches recently. One especially expensive Duke made a speech, and all the Tory Press said: 'Well now, is this the sort of thing we are spending £250,000 a year on?' – because a fully equipped Duke costs as much to keep as two Dreadnoughts, and Dukes are just as great a terror, and they last longer . . .

Well might Winston's friend F. E. Smith remark that on the platform Lloyd George raised the naked issue of class hatred. His description of the eldest sons of peers as the first of the litter further beguiled his hypnotized listeners, and filled his Tory opponents with implacable hatred.

These outrages provoked some angry and cumbrous ripostes from the Dukes, which were of little service to their cause. The Duke of Rutland described the whole Liberal Party as 'a crew of piratical tatterdemalions', a far from accurate description of such elegant figures as Crewe and Grey. The Duke of Beaufort said that he would like to see Winston Churchill and Lloyd George 'in the middle of twenty couple of dog-hounds.' The Duke of Somerset saluted his impending financial doom by sacking his estate hands and curtailing his charitable gifts. The Duke of Buccleuch withdrew his subscription of one guinea to the Dumfriesshire Football Club in view of the pecuniary extremity in which the Budget was likely to place him.[8]

No one defended the Budget or attacked the House of Lords more vigorously than Winston, but he did so mainly without entering the contaminated waters in which Lloyd George so joyfully wallowed. But such was the influence of this man upon him that Winston himself could not always refrain from the sport of Duke-baiting; saying in a speech in Leicester that the dearth of Tory speakers was such that they had been forced to fall back on the Dukes:

> These unfortunate individuals who ought to lead quiet, delicate, sheltered lives, far from the madding crowd's ignoble strife, have been dragged into the football scrimmage, and they have got rather roughly mauled in the process . . . Do not let us be too hard on them. It is a poor sport – almost like teasing goldfish. These ornamental creatures blunder on every hook

8. Bonham Carter, op.cit., p.182.

they see, and there is no sport whatever in trying to catch them. It would be barbarous to leave them gasping upon the bank of public ridicule upon which they have landed themselves. Let us put them back gently, tenderly in their fountains; and if a few bright scales have been rubbed off in what the Prime Minister calls the variegated handling they have received, they will soon get over it. They have got plenty more.

The Opposition felt that this sort of language was to be expected from Lloyd George, an embittered little Radical smarting under a humble origin. He was in any case the villain of the piece with the green limelight on him – to be duly hissed off the stage. He was a common little man, and a cad, and little better could be expected from him. But when Winston lapsed into similar sneers, it was an entirely different matter. He was the grandson of one Duke of Marlborough, and now the first cousin and intimate friend of another. What was to be expected from the Welsh cobbler's nephew, consumed by bitterness and the yearning for a new order of society, was repulsive coming from one who had been born in a ducal palace and had been a guest in all the great houses of London. If Lloyd George was the principal object of Conservative detestation, all the old loathing of Churchill had revived with increased force, as a traitor to his own class and people.

* * *

But Winston, apart from such occasional aberrations, was thinking deeply about the Constitutional dilemma. During the next eighteen months he was, as we shall see, to modify his views considerably, but at this time, in 1910, he did not think that the Campbell-Bannerman resolution went far enough, and wanted a more far-reaching measure. He was in favour of the abolition of the hereditary principle, and of single-chamber government, but was prepared to accept a second chamber on an electoral system. These thoughts he set out and developed in two Cabinet Memoranda in January and February 1910.

> Since we are agreed in opposing the principle of a hereditary legislative Assembly, the only fundamental question open is – one Chamber or two? I would not myself be frightened of having only one . . . But I recognise the convenience and utility of a properly constituted and duly subordinated Second Chamber, to revise legislation, to revise it so far as possible from a non-party point of view, and to interpose the potent safeguard of delay. I recognise also its soothing effect upon large classes, who fear that their special interests may be ill-treated by the modern House of Commons. Moreover, we could not now agree upon a single-Chamber system, and at this juncture unity is vital.[9]

9. Chartwell papers.

He believed, however, that no policy would succeed which only acknowledged the necessity for a second Chamber, without also daring to decide on its exact construction:

> It would be highly dangerous to leave the void unfilled. The C.B. [Campbell-Bannerman] plan by itself will not command intellectual assent nor excite enthusiasm. But even if by a dead-lift effort we succeed in carrying it – which I greatly doubt – the work would remain unfinished. On the first return of the Conservative party to power the Lords would be reformed in the Conservative interest and their veto restored to them. To make any victory permanent in this field the captured ground must be strongly occupied by a new institution erected upon the ruins of the old.[10]

He proceeded to set out in profuse detail his own plans and suggestions for the constitution of a Second Chamber.[11]

The Cabinet was still divided on the form the Parliament Bill should take. Some senior members, notably Sir Edward Grey, believed like Winston that the Campbell-Bannerman plan did not go far enough, and that reform of the Second Chamber should be undertaken at the same time as the abolition of the veto. This was precisely the morass which Campbell-Bannerman had been determined to avoid. The compromise eventually reached was to dispose of the question of reform in the preamble to the Bill. During the long, wearisome passage of the Bill through the Commons, Winston came to recognize 'the deep sagacity of Sir Henry Campbell-Bannerman'. The fear that when the Conservatives were next returned to power they would immediately restore the Veto was not realized. Since the 1911 Act, after three-quarters of a century of argument on the subject of reform, the only accomplished legislation in regard to the House of Lords has been the Parliament Act 1949, which reduced its delaying powers from three sessions to two, and the Life Peerages Act 1958, intended to redress the unbalanced party representation in the House.

* * *

On 21 February 1910 the King opened Parliament, and in the Speech from the Throne announced that measures would be introduced to 'define the relations between the Houses of Parliament, so as to secure the undivided authority of the House of Commons over finance and its predominance in legislation.'

10. Ibid.
11. The details can be found in Randolph S. Churchill, *Winston S. Churchill*, Companion Volume II, Part 2, pp.965-71.

In his speech in the Debate on the Address later that day the Prime Minister was careful to expunge the impression caused by his Albert Hall speech on 10 December 1909, that the Government had already secured some kind of guarantee for the contingent exercise of the Royal Prerogative:

> I tell the House quite frankly that I have received no such guarantee, and that I have asked for no such guarantee ... to ask in advance for a blank authority for an indefinite exercise of the Royal Prerogative in regard to a measure which has never been submitted to, or approved by, the House of Commons, is a request which, in my judgment, no constitutional statesman can properly make and it is a concession which the Sovereign cannot be expected to grant.[12]

This pronouncement, crowning the known differences of opinion on the form the Parliament Bill should take, caused something like consternation among many Government supporters. C. P. Scott[13] referred, in a letter to Winston, to

> the confusion & almost despair which has spread through the party as a result of the announcements so far made. Men go about proclaiming loudly that they have been betrayed and that seats have been won on false pretences ... Then the suggestion of a complete change of policy on the Lords' Veto – the abandonment of the simple policy of the CB resolutions dealing with the power of the H of L and the substitution or addition of an elaborate scheme for constituting a new Second Chamber. People simply won't listen to it – for three years they have had the other policy placed authoritatively before them, they have just fought & won an election on it and to be asked when the very moment for action has arrived to sit still & wait till a quite different policy has been contrived & presented is more than they can stand.[14]

* * *

After the election of January 1910 Asquith entrusted Winston with the task of writing the nightly letter to the King about the day's proceedings in the House of Commons, a duty which he fulfilled for the monarchs until the end of the summer session of 1911. He took infinite pains with their composition, usually concentrating on one or two speakers and incidents, and bringing the whole scene vividly to life. He was careful to present a reasoned and careful analysis of the political position, and to avoid any

---

12. H.H. Asquith, *Fifty Years of Parliament*, Vol.2, pp.82-3. See also Harold Nicolson, *King George V*, p.128.
13. Editor of *The Manchester Guardian*.
14. Chartwell papers.

topic that could possibly offend the King. The Prime Minister also is treated throughout with fulsome respect.

These letters are of particular interest in that most accounts of the Parliaments of 1910 and 1911 suggest that they were continuously charged with drama and excitement, whereas according to Winston's daily eyewitness descriptions they were far more often marked by deadly boredom and apathy. From his letter of 25 February it is clear that Winston had by then recognized the necessity of shelving the reform of the constitution of the House of Lords, at least for the time being:

> . . . Reviewing the events of the week Mr Churchill feels that the position of the Government has become one of the utmost weakness. There can be no doubt that their supporters in the House and still more in the country are thoroughly disheartened and deeply angered by two grave disillusionments: first that Your Majesty's Ministers are remaining in office without any real prospect of carrying their Legislation upon the Lords' Veto; and secondly that the simple question (to them) of the limitation of the Veto according to Sir Henry Campbell-Bannerman's plan should have been clouded by the intention to deal with the constitution of the Second House . . . Unless the Prime Minister is able to make a statement which will reassure his supporters as to the simple issue of a limitation of the Veto being adhered to, and as to the resolution of the Government upon that point, the general situation must deteriorate rapidly.[15]

By 28 February he was able to inform the King that the situation in the House of Commons had been effectively relieved by a statement of the Prime Minister that afternoon:

> The statement makes it clear that the collision between the two Houses will not be reached before the 15th April . . . The gravity of the situation is not diminished, but its decision is postponed.[16]

The approaching crisis between the two Houses dwarfed all other issues, even the most important. On 14 March Winston told the King:

> The First Lord of the Admiralty is now reading his annual statement. A year ago this was the subject that electrified Parliament. Today the naval issues are no less important and the expense far greater. Yet so fickle is the House of Commons, so ready always to discard the old love for the new, that the Chamber is but half filled, and the members (including Your Majesty's servant) are off to the House of Lords to hear Lord Rosebery move the first of his Resolutions.[17] [for reform of the Second Chamber].

15. Chartwell papers.
16. Ibid.
17. Royal Archives.

And three days later, on 17 March, he informed the King:

> The debates upon the Naval Estimates have followed the course which
> Mr Churchill indicated in his letters last week as probable. The discussions
> have been lifeless, and enormous sums of money and vast programmes of
> reconstruction have been agreed to with an almost cataleptic apathy.[18]

At last, on 29 March 1910, the Prime Minister introduced the House
of Lords Resolutions. These were (i) that the veto of the House of
Lords upon Bills certified by the Speaker to be 'Money Bills' should
be abolished; (ii) other Bills, if passed by the House of Commons
in three successive sessions, should become law, whether the Upper
House agreed or not; and (iii) that the duration of Parliament should
be reduced from seven to five years.

Winston reported next day to the King:

> ... The Prime Minister made a magnificent speech yesterday in
> introducing the motion to go into committee upon the Veto Resolutions.
> Not in all this Parliament nor in the last has Mr Asquith been heard to
> such advantage ... Important as was the occasion, the House was still
> oppressed by the coma and even stupor which has been the extraordinary
> feature of this session. Nothing seems capable of arousing it. Your
> Majesty's new Parliament has been born in a trance. Two prevailing
> impressions are in everyone's mind – that its days are numbered, and
> that in the pass to which we are come, speeches are but empty words
> ... Mr Churchill is drawn increasingly to the conclusion that nothing but
> Your Majesty's intervention in some exceptional form or manner which
> cannot as yet be defined will relieve a constitutional deadlock which if
> prolonged indefinitely must prove injurious to the public welfare and to
> the structure of British institutions.[19]

*   *   *

When the Resolution abolishing the financial Veto of the Lords was
carried in April 1910 Winston wrote an amusing letter to the King
referring to a 'really delicious speech' by the Opposition Leader, Mr
Balfour, whose powers, he had thought before, were beginning to flag:

> Two years ago the Leader of the Opposition speaking at Dumfries
> said: 'It is the House of Commons, not the House of Lords which settles
> *uncontrolled* our financial system.' This and other similar utterances were
> expected to place Mr Balfour in a position of some difficulty in the
> present circumstances. His answer was conclusive. One must assume
> some knowledge in one's audience. The fact that the House of Lords

18. Ibid.
19. Chartwell papers.

has full powers to reject Budgets was so obvious that it did not need
to be stated. The suggestion that his words conflicted with this power
of rejection was too absurd even to be discussed. If he had said 'the
plain is perfectly flat,' it would have been understood all the time that
the statement was without prejudice to the fact that the world was round.
He would never have expected to be reproached for not having mentioned
specifically *the normal curvature of the earth's surface*. So when he said
the Lords could not touch Money Bills, he never meant that they could
not reject all the Money Bills of the year singly or at a stroke!

Mr Churchill thinks that this doctrine of 'curvature' may be found
very convenient by others besides Mr Balfour, who have from time to
time to explain away past speeches . . .[20]

There were further debates, in which Winston took part, on the
Resolution to restrict to two years the Lords' Veto on ordinary
legislation, and at their end the Prime Minister made the long-expected
declaration of intent:

I think it is not only convenient but necessary to give notice to the
House and to the country . . . of our future intentions. If the Lords
fail to accept our policy, or decline to consider it when it is formally
presented to the House, we shall feel it our duty immediately to tender
advice to the Crown as to the steps which will have to be taken if that
policy is to receive statutory effect in this Parliament. What the precise
terms of that advice will be, it will, of course, not be right for me to say
now, but if we do not find ourselves in a position to ensure that statutory
effect will be given to this policy in this Parliament, we shall then either
resign our offices or recommend a dissolution of Parliament. And let me
add this: that in no case would we recommend Dissolution except under
such conditions as will ensure that in the new Parliament the judgement
of the people as expressed in the election will be carried into law.[21]

At last there were signs of excitement and animation in the House,
and Winston told the King:

It is very rarely that such moments occur. This is the first time this
Parliament has really breathed and lived; and certainly it sprang at an
instant into an ebullition of energy and conflict which revealed the depths
of the quarrels of our time.[22]

The whole Liberal Party stood erect or even on the benches and
waved their hats, and an insulting shout from the Tories almost

20. Ibid.
21. Spender, op.cit., pp.278-9.
22. Chartwell papers.

caused a physical collision with the Irish Nationalist Members. In making his cautious statement – which caused some confusion in the public mind – Asquith's consistent purpose was to keep the name of the King out of party polemics.

> Interpreted in the light of that honourable and dominant intention his statements were not so contradictory as they seem.[23]

Winston's belief that the Irish would now drop their threat of opposing and seeking amendments to the Budget proved to be well founded, and during the latter part of April it passed 'swiftly and smoothly through the House of Commons', and on 28 April the House of Lords passed the Finance Bill without a division.

* * *

After the prolonged strain and argument of the constitutional wrangle, one thought was uppermost in the minds of all Members of Parliament – to escape from the atmosphere of Westminster. But they had hardly dispersed for their longed-for holiday when suddenly and unexpectedly King Edward VII died on 6 May. The King's death caused general grief and regret. His vulgarities and follies were forgotten, and his more endearing qualities recalled. His successor, King George V, was to win far greater respect and veneration in the hearts of his people, but he had not been trained for kingship. A sailor, he was now called upon in this crisis to pick his way through shoal water more baffling than any he can have known as a naval officer. It was evident from Asquith's statement in the House of Commons on 14 April that the Government had accepted the fact that in all probability a second General Election would be necessary before the Parliament Bill could be forced through. But, as a result of King Edward's death, the Prime Minister was reluctant to saddle the new and bemused King with an election upon such a grave constitutional issue. He therefore told King George V that he would try to come to an understanding with the Opposition. He did so, and Balfour at once agreed to a conference. This gesture was not received with general enthusiasm: 'The unselfish initiative on the part of the Prime Minister was much resented by the Irish Nationalists and by some of his more ardent supporters. But at least it gave the new Sovereign a six months' reprieve.' [24]

The Conference convened on 17 June in the Prime Minister's room in the House of Commons, the Government being represented by Asquith, Crewe, Lloyd George and Birrell, the Opposition by

23. Harold Nicolson, *King George V*, pp.128-9.
24. Ibid., p. 131.

Balfour, Lansdowne, Austen Chamberlain and Lord Cawdor. There was an arcane atmosphere about the proceedings, of which no reports were issued to either party, causing the suspicion that principles of vital importance were being discussed behind closed doors. Both sides wished to reach agreement, and Asquith was at first optimistic, but:

> Twelve meetings were held before Parliament rose for the summer recess at the end of July. As the weeks passed, the shock caused by King Edward's death, the common desire not to embarrass a new and untried Sovereign, lost something of their early and unifying impetus; party faiths, party loyalties, above all the party machines, intervened to hamper, and finally to disrupt, the unison of these eight men.[25]

The Conservatives had divided legislation under three headings: Financial, Ordinary, and Constitutional or 'Organic'. Under the first two headings some progress was made, but the Conference foundered on Constitutional or 'Organic' legislation. The Government insisted that after the first rejection of an Irish Home Rule Bill by the House of Lords a General Election should follow, and that if a majority in favour of Home Rule were returned to power, then the resultant Bills would be treated as 'Ordinary' and not as 'Organic' legislation. The Opposition maintained with equal obstinacy that after a second rejection of a Home Rule Bill by the House of Lords the Bill should be referred directly to the electorate as a special issue for a referendum. But

> Mr Asquith was ill disposed to plebiscites; in fact the very word 'referendum' would cause his usually tolerant features to writhe into an expression of contemptuous disgust. It was thus mainly on the question of Home Rule that the Conference broke down.[26]

The last session was held on 11 November.

Throughout the Conference Lloyd George had been the Liberal delegate most prepared to bend with the wind, and to go to the furthest lengths in compromise and concession. He was in fact meditating a plan which went far beyond the concrete issues to be resolved at the Conference. This aim, known to few, was nothing less than the formation of a Coalition Government, a proposal to which Winston gave ardent support. But although Balfour briefly coquetted with the plan, it was destined to fail. This was partly because the Conservative Chief Whip, Akers-Douglas, intimated that the Party would not tolerate so cynical a traffic with men they had been led to regard as revolutionaries and traitors. It was also because

25. Ibid.
26. Ibid, p.133.

Asquith, who although not completely *au courant* with the scheme, had
not the faintest belief that such a coalition could agree on either the
problem of the House of Lords or that of Home Rule, and was amazed
by the thought that either he or the Party should be willing to agree to
compulsory Military Service or Tariff Reform. He therefore watched this
attempted entry into Cloud-cuckoo-land with detached amusement, not
unmingled with contempt, and was in no way displeased or surprised
by the collapse of the scheme. Indeed, the only Liberals to mourn at its
graveside were Lloyd George and Winston Churchill.

But Asquith's daughter Violet was more interested in Winston's
evident enthusiasm for the abortive business, and puzzled to find
reasons for it:

> I could not guess at this time that except for 'the first fine careless
> rapture' of these early years in the Liberal Party he would only be really
> happy in coalition governments. Though a natural partisan he was never a
> party politician. In order to extend himself he needed a national, or better
> still, an international setting ... The Tory Party would have seemed to
> be his natural home. But despite his romantic feeling for the aristocracy
> his broad humanity transcended the boundaries of class. His intensely
> individual and adventurous mind, for ever on the move, could never be
> contained by the Conservatives, and its questing, restless brilliance often
> filled them with an unconcealed disquiet. The Liberals in their great days
> gave him more scope and a better run ... But he was never quite a
> Liberal. He never shared the reluctance which inhibits Liberals from
> invoking force to solve a problem ... He was by temperament an
> intellectual autocrat. He never liked having other people's way. He
> infinitely preferred his own.[27]

After the failure of the Conference, the situation reverted to what it
had been before the death of King Edward. The Prime Minister had
an audience of the King on Friday, 11 November at Sandringham, and
the King noted in his diary:

> At 6.30 the Prime Minister arrived. Had two long talks with him.
> He reported that the Conference had failed & he proposed to dissolve
> & have a general election & get it over before Xmas. He asked me for
> *no guarantees*. I suggested that the Veto resolutions should first be sent
> to the H of L & if they rejected them, then he could dissolve. This he
> agreed to do.[28]

On 16 November the Prime Minister and Lord Crewe went to
Buckingham Palace and received from the King an assurance that in the

27. Bonham Carter, op.cit., pp.196-7.
28. Nicolson, op.cit., p.133.

event of the Liberals being returned to power at the forthcoming election he would exercise his Royal Prerogative to create a sufficient number of Peers, if the Lords rejected the Parliament Bill. The King felt that he had been bullied and declared that he could never hold up his head again if he was obliged to create some 450 new peers. Asquith had said bluntly that if the King refused the next election would be fought on this theme of the King and the peers against the people. The Crown would thus be drawn into party politics.

On 21 November Lord Crewe moved the Second Reading of the Parliament Bill in the House of Lords, but no discussion of the proposals took place, for Lord Landsdowne moved to adjourn the debate, and brought forward a scheme of his own to reconstitute the Second Chamber which was to serve as Unionist policy at the election. Parliament was dissolved on 28 November, and the country went to the polls in December 1910 for the second time that year.

* * *

Winston continued with his Parliamentary letters to the new King. As in those to King Edward, he took infinite pains, and was careful to avoid any opinions that might cause the monarch offence, but there was a suggestion in August in an exchange of letters between the King's Private Secretary, Lord Knollys, and Lord Crewe, that the King did not look with undue warmth upon his Home Secretary. On 8 August Lord Knollys wrote: 'I am glad to say that the King has consented to ask Lloyd George to Balmoral. I suppose it does not signify his not inviting Winston Churchill as well. He would be *very* reluctant to do so . . .[29] The necessity for inviting even one of this abhorred pair must have been for George V a duty more distasteful than most.

During the election campaign Lloyd George reverted to his Limehouse form. The Conservatives, following a tour of John Remond and fellow Irish Nationalists in the United States, spread the accusation (in which Balfour joined) that the Irish were financing the election on American dollars. Balfour supported the press attacks on the 'dollar fund', remarking with somewhat impudent exaggeration that the Government were going 'to destroy the Constitution at the will of American subscribers'. Here Lloyd George intervened with a characteristically rapier thrust: 'But since when has the British aristocracy despised American dollars? They have underpinned many a tottering noble house.' This devastating comment not unnaturally enraged Winston's cousin the Duke of Marlborough, in whose own 'tottering' house, Blenheim, Lloyd George had been a guest, and who had married

29. Crewe papers.

Consuelo Vanderbilt, one of the greatest heiresses in America.

Asquith announced the coming dissolution on 18 November. Winston wrote to the King four days later reporting on the strange lethargy that still seemed to hold the House of Commons in its grasp: 'The Prime Minister's statement upon Friday last effectively extinguished the pallid flickering life of this House of Commons. It has never really lived, & now it is to die. No one cares about it any more.'[30]

Polling took place between 2 and 19 December, and the result showed scarcely any change. Liberal and Unionist representation was exactly equal, but with the support of the Irish Nationalists and Labour the Liberals could muster a majority of over 120. The election weakened Balfour's position with the Conservative Party. For any party leader to fail at three successive elections was to place a heavy albatross round his neck.

The Parliament Bill was reintroduced on 21 February and passed through all its stages in the House of Commons by 15 May 1911. On that day Lord Lansdowne's 'Reconstitution Bill', which he had introduced on 8 May, came up for Second Reading in the House of Lords. It was on the lines already put forward as the Conservative alternative to the Parliament Bill, and would have modified the hereditary principle. After four days' debate it was permanently shelved, and the Lords turned their attention to the Parliament Bill itself.

*   *   *

Winston took a large share in piloting the Parliament Bill through the House of Commons, and he was often left in charge of business, particularly after dinner. He described to the King the passage of the Bill and the atmosphere of the House. He related how Asquith introduced it with exemplary clarity,

> a speech so lucid that it defies summary. Mr Balfour was depressed & weary & his not unconciliatory remarks were received in a gloomy silence by the Unionist party. The House was vy orderly & there was a complete absence of excitement. When is the conflict going to begin? There is not any real danger ... No passion, no threats, no defiance – only a sort of sulky acquiescence ... peace broods sullenly over the Assembly and considerable events drift or flow steadily forward.[31]

In his letter of 28 February he reported that this strange apathy was continuing: 'There is a total absence of excitement or passion: &

30. Royal Archives.
31. Ibid.

no one would believe that business of fierce controversial importance was proceeding.'[32] He found that the Preamble to the Bill was the main difficulty, and that the Government supporters were opposed to it in the proportion of four or five to one. The Preamble contained the provision to reform the House of Lords after the Parliament Bill had passed into law. It was necessary to include this in order to compose the differences in the Cabinet on the subject, some important Ministers, particularly Grey, believing that the Campbell-Bannerman Resolution did not go nearly far enough, and that the 'reconstitution' of the Upper House should be undertaken at the same time as the Veto Bill.

It seemed to Winston curious that the Opposition should be anxious above all things to sweep away the House of Lords 'and put something or anything in its place'; that they reproached the Government for not declaring at once what form the reconstituted House should ultimately take. To the King he wrote: 'Mr Churchill . . . thinks the Opposition make a mistake in worrying too much about Reform. It would be better for them to wait for better times & make their own Reform. Some of them are beginning to see this.'[33] The Bill then dragged tediously through Committee like a scotched snake, until it was necessary to apply the 'Kangaroo' closure, by which the Chairman was empowered to select the amendments to be discussed down to a certain point in the clauses.

* * *

We have seen the deep respect with which Winston described Asquith in his Parliamentary letters. Partly on account of his daughter's strong admiration and affection for Churchill, Asquith had treated him generously, and had done much to advance his career. The younger man realized this, and was duly grateful. He could not however fail to be aware of the Prime Minister's increasing addiction to the bottle, a weakness to which others made frequent and malicious allusion. He referred to this, among other matters, in a letter on 22 April to his wife from Blenheim, couched in far less guarded terms than his communications to the King:

> You will see from the enclosed *Hansard* what a little pig Winterton made of himself . . . I have done with him. He showed real malignity – which I never forget . . .
>
> Lloyd George has practically taken Unemployment Insurance to his own bosom & I am, I think, effectively elbowed out of this large field in wh I consumed so much thought & effort. Never mind! There are many good fish in the sea.

32. Ibid.
33. Ibid.

On Thursday night the PM was vy bad: & I squirmed with
embarrassment. He could hardly speak: & many people noticed his
condition. He continues most friendly & benevolent, & entrusts me
with everything after dinner. Up till that time he is at his best – but
thereafter! It is an awful pity, & only the persistent free-masonry of the
House of Commons prevents a scandal. I like the old boy & admire both
his intellect & his character. But what risks to run. We only got him away
the other night just before Balfour began the negotiations wh I conducted
but wh otherwise wd have fallen to him – with disastrous consequences.
The next day he was serene, efficient, undisturbed . . .

We shall be up all night Monday – & I am going to put the screw on
the Parliament Bill as never before in the next few days. We must get on.
No peace till after the shock.[34]

By 26 April 1911 Winston was able to report to the King a
remarkable collapse in the opposition to the Parliament Bill in the
House of Commons, where the fight seemed to him politically over.
The extraordinary apathy still continued:

The dullness of the debates has led to very small attendances, though
the Government majorities have been well maintained. A complete
absence of anything like bitterness or passion has characterised the
whole proceedings.[35]

On 6 May he related how Lloyd George's 'Titanic proposals' for
National Insurance had introduced a new and healing factor into
the political situation, in a letter which gives a hint of his yearning
for coalition between the parties:

The two great parties hold each other in such effective equipoise on
most occasions, that when they appear ready to join forces a feeling of
enthusiasm & irresistible strength is created. Such an emotion pervades
political circles at the present time and cannot fail to mitigate the fierceness
of other disputations . . .[36]

*   *   *

The Parliament Bill passed its Third Reading in the House of Commons
by a majority of 121. Winding up for the Government, Winston
observed that he was 'almost aghast' at the Government's moderation.
'The powers retained by the House of Lords . . . will not merely be
effectual . . . they will be formidable and even menacing . . . We regard

34. Chartwell papers.
35. Royal Archives.
36. Ibid.

this measure as territory reconquered by the masses from the classes.'[37]

Lord Landsdowne had introduced his Reconstitution Bill a few days earlier. He and his supporters hoped to retain the powers of the Second Chamber while modifying and to some extent democratizing its membership, which was to be a fixed total of 320 of whom only 100 would be selected hereditary peers, 120 would be elected by the Commons and 100 appointed by the Crown in proportion to the strength of parties in the House of Commons.

Most Conservative Peers detested Lansdowne's proposal, and many thought the Parliament Bill to be the preferable choice in a grisly dispiriting selection. Nothing more was heard of it after Second Reading, Lord Morley having made plain the Government's decision that it could not possibly be a substitute or an alternative for the Parliament Bill. On 23 May, after a restrained debate, the House of Lords gave a Second Reading to the Parliament Bill, reserving the surgical cuts for the Committee stage.

* * *

The dreary wrangle was mercifully broken by the Coronation. The summer was one of abnormal heat. The remorseless thermometer, creeping upwards, was to reach its highest point – 100°F on the August day of the decisive debate in the House of Lords. So prolonged was the heat wave that the nerves, even of those inured to the tropics, became ragged. Nothing like it had ever been seen before – one sultry day followed another with the certainty of the hot weather in India. The water streamed down the windows of the florists' shops, and the water-carts laid the dust on Constitution Hill. The King was crowned on 22 June. In spite of the heat, there was a feverish social accompaniment, pursued with determined gaiety. Lord Winterton and F. E. Smith gave a fancy dress ball of such beauty that it resembled some bygone Venetian masque, and each night was occupied by similar distractions.

The Oxfordshire Yeomanry, in which both Winston and F. E. Smith were officers, was in camp in Blenheim Park that summer, and their wild frolics were of little pleasure to their wives. 'They behaved like Regency Rakes,' said F. E.'s wife Margaret. The Bucks, Yeomanry, in which their friend Fred Cripps (*bon viveur* brother of the austere Stafford) served, was brigaded with the Oxfordshire Regiment. There was an evening when F. E. took one of his horses without permission, and after a wild moonlight adventure rode it at full gallop into a chalk-pit. Heavy gambling with men far richer than themselves cost Winston and F. E. dearly, as their participation was usually disastrous. They made clumsy

37. *Hansard*, 15 May 1911.

and unsuccessful attempts to conceal enormous losses from their wives after nights such as that when Winston, F. E., Neil Primrose,[38] Cripps and the Duke of Marlborough sat on upturned barrels in F E's tent playing cards to the light of tallow candles until dawn; and the evening in the same tent when the Duke asked:

'What shall we play for, F. E.?'

'Your bloody palace if you like.'

There were balls in that palace which they attended in full-dress uniform trimmed with sable. Winston, as the veteran of five campaigns, no doubt took an interest in the rather perfunctory manoeuvres – hopefully described as 'Training' – but F. E. was an unorthodox officer with the habit of sending his men up a tree to see what was going on, and himself falling asleep beneath it.

On 28 June the House of Lords ripped the Parliament Bill to pieces in Committee. In Asquith's words:

> The Bill then went into Committee, where, in the course of six days, it was as completely transformed as though no General Election had been held. The principal Amendment moved by Lord Lansdowne, substituting the Referendum for the Suspensory Veto, and thereby deliberately overriding the express and emphatic decision of the constituencies only seven months before, was carried on July 5 by 253 to 46.[39]

The Cabinet immediately advised the King that the action of the Lords was destructive of the purpose of the Bill; that there was hardly a single Amendment that the Government could advise the House of Commons to accept, and that the Bill might just as well have been rejected on Second Reading. It followed that if, without any preliminary conference or arrangement, the Lords' Amendments were submitted to the House of Commons, they would be rejected *en bloc*, and that a complete deadlock between the Houses would be created. Parliament having been twice dissolved during the last eighteen months, and the future relations between the two Houses having been at both elections a predominant issue, a third dissolution was wholly out of the question.

Asquith then approached the heart of the matter:

> Hence ... it will be the duty of Ministers to advise the Crown to exercise its Prerogative so as to get rid of the deadlock and secure the passage of the Bill. In such circumstances Ministers cannot entertain

38. Lord Rosebery's younger son.
39. H.H. Asquith, *Fifty Years of Parliament*, Vol.2, pp.96-7.

any doubt that the Sovereign would feel it to be his Constitutional duty to accept their advice.[40]

The King accepted this advice, but thought that a creation of Peers should not take place until the Bill had been referred to the House of Lords after the rejection of their amendments by the House of Commons. He had been warned by influential Unionist Peers that many of their party believed that the Prime Minister was bluffing about invoking the Royal Prerogative. The Prime Minister therefore wrote to Balfour and Lansdowne stating emphatically that

> ... should the necessity arise, the Government will advise the King to exercise his Prerogative to secure the passing into law of the Bill in substantially the same form in which it left the House of Commons; and His Majesty has been pleased to signify that he will consider it his duty to accept, and act on, that advice.[41]

Lansdowne, whose nerveless leadership served him ill during this crisis, now felt that the Lords should give way rather than face the creation of up to 500 new Peers, which would make the House of Lords a laughing-stock and paralyse its action, without retarding the Parliament Bill. On this point Balfour was in agreement, but some Unionists, led by the aged Lord Halsbury (a former Lord Chancellor) declared that they would rather die in the last ditch. His motley and eccentric group, containing such bizarre champions as Lord Willoughby de Broke and the Duke of Bedford, became known as the 'Die-Hards' or 'Last-Ditchers', and against the advice of Balfour and Lansdowne canvassed in both Houses for support. The situation was approaching a climax.

On 24 July Asquith went down to the House to make his statement on the Lords' amendments and the Government's intentions, and ran into the full blast of the storm. The deep-seated animosity between the parties came at last to the surface on that sultry afternoon in the ugly scene that developed. Asquith's speech was overwhelmed, and in an orgy of resentment he was systematically howled down, and forced to send his unread statement to the press. His wife Margot, never one to be unduly deterred by opposition or hostility (which indeed she freely provoked) had driven with her husband to the House in an open motor-car, and they were cheered as it passed through the streets. The Galleries were packed to suffocation, and the House was densely crowded. Many of the ladies of both political persuasions were standing on their benches in excitement.

40. Ibid., p.97-8.
41. Ibid, and see also Harold Nicolson, op.cit., p.152.

Mrs Asquith listened with pride to the cheers which greeted her husband as he walked up the floor of the House, but her satisfaction was brief. For three-quarters of an hour the Prime Minister rose at short intervals and read a sentence or two from a manuscript, only for his words to be drowned by hootings and cries, of which 'Traitor!' was the most frequent, but with 'Redmond' (as the real ruler), and 'American dollars' often audible. Asquith, possibly the calmest man in the Chamber, repeatedly tried to make himself heard, brushing his hands down his thighs in a characteristic gesture, but the technique of interruption (afterwards brought to its repulsive perfection in other lands by the Communists) was anticipated by the leaders of this affray, who watched his lips narrowly, and drowned speech before it could issue from them. Asquith could only utter a few broken sentences, little of which could be heard.

'His mouth hardened, and he glared at his tormentors like a lion at bay, an impressive figure with straight-cut features flushed with anger, and heavy grey hairs.' There was a strident background chorus of 'Divide, divide!' The Speaker tried in vain to discipline the uproar. Mrs Asquith now appeared to her neighbours like a tigress defending her stricken mate. More accustomed to dealing out insolence than being on the receiving end of it, she must have felt that she was in the presence of some monstrous reversal of nature; scribbling futile notes to her friends below to protect the Prime Minister from 'the cats and the cads.'

The leaders in this lamentable scene, in which all restraint was abandoned, were Lord Hugh Cecil and F. E. Smith. Lord Hugh, that great gentleman, ardent Churchman and learned theologian, was as one wholly demented; his austere character seemed to make his behaviour particularly shocking, as he stood waving his arms in frenzy like some agonized Savonarola, and screaming: 'The King is in duress!' To one who sat watching: 'His transformation, and that of many other personal friends, was terrifying. They behaved, and looked, like mad baboons.'

Some believed that these excesses were a spontaneous outburst of rage at the Government's policy. Winston thought differently, and he was right. In a letter to the King on 26 July he wrote: 'The ugliest feature was the absence of any real passion or spontaneous feeling. It was a squalid frigid organised attempt to insult the Prime Minister & prevent debate.'[42] But it was also part of an attempt by Hugh Cecil, F. E. Smith and George Wyndham to revolt against Balfour's and Lansdowne's spineless leadership on the Veto Bill, and the Duke of Westminster had

---

42. Royal Archives.

turned Grosvenor House into an office where they held their meetings.

* * *

Then came a brief interlude in party strife thanks to the crisis caused by the arrival of a German gunboat at Agadir, Morocco. Winston was profoundly relieved at the way in which party bitterness was immediately dissolved and replaced by unity in the face of danger from without. He described the debate on the affair in a letter to the King on 27 July in 1911:

> ... A great moment in the House of Commons, showing at its very best the power and dignity of this country. The Prime Minister made his statement – careful & friendly in form & feeling, but strong & firm in substance. Then Mr Balfour – admirable – also vy short. No party dissensions even at their worst could affect national unity in great issues. Lastly Ramsay Macdonald [sic] – restrained, sombre but perfectly correct. The whole three speeches together occupying less than half an hour – in a dead hush with occasional deep murmurs of assent.[43]

But, with the foreign crisis passed, the political wrangle was resumed. On 2 August Winston summed up the confused situation and the Order of Battle in a letter to his wife:

> The Lords crisis is comical and complicated. The 'diehards' are about 100 (with the whole party at their back). Lansdowne has 324 abstainers: of which 50 to 60 will follow Cromer and St Aldwyns [sic] into the Government Lobby. We have 75 wh with stray bishops & Court Officials may be 85. *But* at least 20 perhaps more of Lansdowne's abstainers say that if any Unionists follow Cromer and vote with the Government, they will hold themselves freed from their pledge to Lansdowne and vote against the Government.
>
> Thus a creation [of Peers] wd be necessary or at least it is a damned near thing! And if one single peer is made Lansdowne & his gang will vote against the Govt. What a whirlpool! The split in the Tory Party is deep & bitter. We are going to take strong action; & it looks as if at least 300 will have to be made – if any are made ...[44]

The next move of the now desperate Opposition leaders was an attempts to unite their conflicting factions by putting down Votes of Censure on the Government in both Houses, or Votes of Censure 'on the pledges'.

43. Royal Archives.
44. CSC papers.

The tactical, and quite legitimate, object of this [wrote Spender] was
to enable the Unionist leaders, who had now decided to yield, to
put their protest on record in speeches which might have had the
opposite result of what they intended, if delivered when the Bill was
finally returned to the Lords.[45]

In the debate that followed Asquith made one of the finest speeches
of his life, and received a memorable ovation. He had asked Winston
to wind up for the Government, and this choice had been the cause
of considerable jealousy, but his speech was in no way provocative,
and provided the opportunity for some spuriously fierce banter at the
expense of his friend and opponent F. E. Smith. On the following day, 8
August, while the Censure debate was taking place in the Upper House,
the Commons considered the Lords' amendments. Asquith had lost his
voice, and Winston was in charge. As the King desired, they did not
dismiss the amendments *en bloc*, but dealt with them in detail, accepting
as a conciliatory gesture any that did not strike at the heart of the Bill.
'Mr Churchill,' Winston assured the King, 'took occasion yesterday to
make clear Your Majesty's complete detachment from political parties
& controversial party questions.'[46]

*   *   *

When the Bill returned to the Lords on Wednesday, 9 August, the
stage was set for the final battle. It was the hottest day in the whole
of that abnormal summer, and the temperature of 100° provided
a tropical background for the drama, making the atmosphere in
the House of Lords more tense and oppressive than ever. There
was still complete uncertainty which way the voting would go. In
spite of everything the Government had said and all the warnings
they had given, many Unionists still appeared to believe that they
were bluffing about the creation of Peers. The King was disturbed
by their false optimism, and instructed his advisers to write to Lord
Morley – who was in charge of the debate for the Government in
Crewe's absence through illness – saying that it was imperative to
dispel these illusions. A formula was therefore drafted by Morley, and
immediately accepted by the King.

Parliament had at last come fully and vibrantly alive. No one
present at this final scene would forget the excitement and tension in
the stifling heat of the packed Chamber that afternoon. The hour had
come, and the atmosphere was electric. In answer to an appeal from
Lord Rosebery, Morley dispelled the illusion that the Government was

45. Spender, *H.H. Asquith*, Vol.1, p.321.
46. Royal Archives.

bluffing by reading a short, devastating statement defining the terms of the Royal assent:

'If the Bill should be defeated tonight His Majesty will consent to the creation of peers sufficient in number to guard against any possible combination of the different parties in opposition by which the Parliament Bill might be exposed a second time to defeat.' There was a long moment of intense silence in the oppressive heat. Then, at the request of a peer, Lord Morley repeated his statement, adding: 'Every vote against my motion will be a vote for a large and prompt creation of peers.'

Although the Die-hard leaders assumed a bold front, and professed to be unaffected by the statement, many wavering and doubtful peers were at last convinced of the Government's resolution. The Archbishop of Canterbury strongly affected the issue by stating that he had been moved from his intention to abstain by 'the callousness – I had almost said levity – with which some noble Lords seemed to contemplate the creation of five hundred new peers', which he described as 'a course of action which would make this House, and indeed, our country, the laughing-stock of the British Dominions beyond the seas and of those foreign countries whose constitutional life and progresss have been largely modelled on our own.' This salutary reminder of the farcical aspects of the crisis made a definite appeal to common sense, but no one at this moment could forecast the outcome, until the motley levies entered the Lobbies, and the tellers declared the result of the division – a majority of seventeen for the Government. Thirty-seven Unionist and thirteen Bishops supported them, and there was wild uproar and cheering in the streets. It was in most respects a repetition of the drama attending the passing of the Great Reform Bill of 1832, when the threat of a creation of new peers, extorted from a reluctant King William IV, brought the recalcitrant House of Lords to heel.

This was the end of the great constitutional struggle. The belief that the Tories once in office would reverse the decision was not fulfilled, and the restriction of the veto of the House of Lords became an integral and accepted part of the Constitution. The Tories' defeat was not, however, marked by chivalrous acceptance. George Wyndham sneered bitterly that the Government was saved in the final division by 'the Bishops and the Rats', and that irreproachable High Churchman, Lord Robert Cecil, said that Bishops should be excluded from a reformed House of Lords. The Liberals were transported by joy, and the King, who had inherited so heavy a burden, and played his part so honourably, was conscious of an indescribable relief that he had been spared the odious necessity of a massive creation. In Winston's final report to him on the Parliament Bill, he wrote:

... The proceedings of the House of Commons yesterday were completely overshadowed by the memorable and dramatic events in the Lords ... When the keen feelings of the moment have passed away, the singular moderation of the change that has been effected will be apparent and will gradually be admitted with relief by the Conservatives & with regret by many of the supporters of the Government. It was a shocking thing that the tremendous issues of last night's division should have depended on the votes of a few score of persons quite unversed in public affairs, quite irresponsible & undistinguished who refused to accept guidance from all the most notable leaders of every political party in the State ... Mr Churchill feels certain that the course taken by Your Majesty in circumstances of such unusual gravity & difficulty was the only one wh could have averted vy evil consequences & that history will approve & justify all that has been done by those responsible. It is to be hoped that a period of co-operation between the two branches of the Legislature may now set in & that the settlement of several out of date quarrels may lead to a truer sense of national unity.[47]

47. Royal Archives.

Chapter 10

Home Rule

In his attitude to Ireland Winston Churchill had grown up a convinced Unionist, and remained one when he crossed the floor of the House in 1904. This intractable problem, which he was later to describe as 'The Irish Spectre', seemed in varying degrees of agony to be interwoven with his own life. When he was invited to contest North-West Manchester as a Liberal candidate he wrote to the local Liberal Association in April 1904 making his attitude plain: 'I remain of the opinion that the creation of a separate Parliament for Ireland would be dangerous and impracticable.'[1] And on 17 July 1904, when accepting the candidacy, he said:

> On the policy of administrative Home Rule – as my father said in 1890 – I do not look forward to the day when there shall be created a separate Parliament to be a rival of, and perhaps an enemy of the central Parliament here at home.[2]

Asquith had already given a qualified assurance in a speech in Sheffield in April that year: 'There is no question, say what you like, of a Home Rule Bill being introduced into the next session.'

After the Liberal triumph of 1906 the Government, with a majority of 130 over all other parties, was not dependent on their support of the Irish members who for another four years were not in a position to blackmail it into introducing a Home Rule Bill. In his election address Winston had said, 'I shall support no Irish legislation which I regard as likely to injure the effective integrity of the United Kingdom, or to lead, however indirectly, to separation.' But having said that, he

1. Chartwell papers.
2. Randolph S. Churchill, op. cit., Vol. II, p. 442.

235

seemed in his next words to be providing himself with a small trap-door of escape, for he added:

> I am persuaded that considerable administrative reforms are required in the Government of Ireland, and I would gladly see the people of Ireland accorded the power to manage their own expenditure, their own education and their own public works according to Irish ideas.

Although not committed to Home Rule, Sir Henry Campbell-Bannerman had always felt a vague and benevolent sympathy with Celtic yearnings, and it was during his two and a half years as Prime Minister that the Labourers (Ireland) Act and the Irish University Act were placed on the Statute Book. A few days before Campbell-Bannerman's resignation, the Irish leader Redmond introduced a Home Rule Resolution (30 March 1908), but Asquith, who was deputizing for the ailing Prime Minister, explained that he could not vote for it because it did not explicitly recognize the Imperial supremacy. Redmond therefore, no doubt thinking that Asquith was striking the first blow in a preliminary foray, accepted a Government amendment, which was carried by 156 votes, asserting the supremacy of the Imperial Parliament. Patience was of the essence in this issue, and although Asquith had made it clear that there could be no question of Home Rule legislation being introduced into the present Parliament, Redmond still felt that the result of the Division marked 'a distinct advance in the progress of the Home Rule cause'.

* * *

When Winston Churchill's elevation to Cabinet rank necessitated his re-election, there was a large Irish element in the electorate of North-West Manchester. At this by-election in May 1908 he was under strong pressure to state without ambiguity where he stood in regard to Home Rule. He was now on sufficiently friendly terms with Redmond to ask him to use his influence in winning the Irish vote in Manchester.

The local Irish leaders submitted three questions on his attitude which he forwarded with his proposed answers to Asquith, remarking that these 'have taken me a good deal of time to concoct'. The second question was:

> Is Mr Churchill of the opinion that Home Rule ought to form a leading issue in the programme to be put before the electors at the next General Election by the Liberal Party, and will he, as a member of the Cabinet,

use his best endeavours to have this done?

With the issue thus clearly set before him, Winston, after much thought, returned the following answer:

> At the last election I precluded myself as did others of my colleagues from attempting what is called 'the larger policy' in respect of Ireland during the present Parliament. By that I am bound so far as this Parliament is concerned. But I have for some time resolved not to be fettered in that way in any subsequent Parliament. I am encouraged by the striking success of a bold and generous policy in South Africa to approach Irish difficulties in a similar spirit – and when this Parliament has reached its close, I am strongly of the opinion that the Liberal Party should claim authority to deal with the problem of Irish self-government as indicated in Mr Redmond's resolve.

In a campaigning speech two days later, he offered an even more positive explanation of his complete reversal of policy:

> My opinion is that the Irish question has ripened during the last 2 years when I have lived in the inner or nearly in the inner councils of Liberalism. I have become convinced that a national settlement of the Irish difficulty on broad and generous lines is indispensable to any harmonious conception of Liberalism – the object lesson is South Africa ... At the next election I am strongly of the opinion that the Liberal Party should claim full authority and a free hand to deal with the problems of Irish self-government without being restricted to measures of administrative devolution of the character of the Irish Councils Bill.[3]

Despite this Redmond advised the Irish electors to abstain, and Winston's opponent Joynson-Hicks was elected by 449 votes.

* * *

It is clear that Winston had, and not for the first time, changed his mind. He was never ashamed to do so. He had travelled a long way indeed from his opinions of 1904, and even farther from his father's cause and his own youthful convictions of 1897. He had now firmly bound 'the millstone of Home Rule' round his own neck. There is no good reason to suppose that his *volte face* was prompted merely by electoral expediency. We have seen that he was unquestionably attached to the Union and, as in everything else, had adopted his father's views on the subject. But he had certainly studied the Irish question closely when

3. Chartwell papers.

writing Lord Randolph's *Life*, which was published in January 1906, a few weeks after he became Under-Secretary of State for the Colonies. All his warmest and most generous impulses had convinced him of the wisdom and justice of bestowing independence on the Transvaal and Orange River Colony after victory, and 'the striking success of a bold and generous policy in South Africa' coloured and influenced his attitude to Irish Nationalism.

One other aspect of his conversion was of importance, and was to serve him well in the struggle to come. He understood – far better than most Liberal leaders – the implacable resentment with which the Protestant majority in Ulster would regard the attempt to force them to live under an alien government and an alien religion. He was never, like other Liberals, to underrate this force. And he understood more clearly than others the lengths to which the people of Ulster would be prepared to go to avoid it, their stubborn and morose resistance, and the desperation with which they would regard the attempt to incorporate them as a Protestant minority in Catholic Ireland. For he had been reared on the Ulster case and knew it by heart.

Opening the Budget Election campaign in December 1909, Asquith had cautiously committed the Liberal Party to setting up in Ireland a system of full self-government in regard to purely Irish affairs. He made it clear that the new Liberal Government would safeguard the authority and supremacy of the Imperial Government.

'For reasons which I believe to have been adequate, the present Parliament was disabled in advance from proposing any such solution, but in the new House of Commons the hands of a Liberal Government will be entirely free.' He could perhaps scarcely have said less since Home Rule for Ireland had been a recognized Liberal policy since 1886. The question of separation from the Crown did not arise, nor had any responsible Irish leader put forward such a claim.

*   *   *

We have already seen the course of events from this moment – how the first election of that year, in January 1910, produced a Liberal majority of only 2 over the Conservatives, placing the Government at the mercy of the Irish Nationalists; and how in the second election, in December 1910, there had been little change in the position of the parties; and how the Parliament Bill was finally passed by the House of Lords in August 1911, opening the way to the passage of a Home Rule Bill. There was now no turning back for Asquith with that old Irish Man of the Sea clamped round his neck. Having forfeited his absolute majority in the House, his Government now lay at the mercy of Redmond and his 84 Nationalist followers, and he was forced to address himself urgently to the passage of a measure which he had safely ignored in the pride and power of 1906.

The Irish Nationalists were concerned with Home Rule, and with nothing else. They had little interest in 'soaking the landlords' and other darling projects of Liberal policy, and they had been kept waiting too long for that promised land to which Gladstone had tried to lead them, that 'debt owed by man to God'. Redmond, writing to Morley on the eve of the great battles, was soon to leave no doubt as to his position:

> Unless an official declaration on the question of Home Rule can be made, not only will it be impossible for us to support Liberal Candidates in England, but we will most unquestionably have to ask our friends to vote against them ... The opposition of Irish votes in Lancashire, Yorkshire, and other places, including Scotland, would most certainly mean the loss of many seats.

Nothing could be plainer than that.

Before giving an account of the turbulent events ahead, it should be noted that there were at least two Liberals with the foresight to realize the perils lurking in an attempt to coerce Ulster, and these two the most brilliant and by repute the most headstrong, in the party. Lloyd George and Winston Churchill had shared 'one prudent doubt' which was swept aside by a majority decision. They were both in favour of excluding Ulster at the outset from the operation of Home Rule.

> From the earliest discussions on the Home Rule Bill in 1909 [said Churchill] the Chancellor of the Exchequer and I had always advocated the exclusion of Ulster on the basis of county option or some similar process. We had been met by the baffling argument that such a concession might well be made as the final means of securing a settlement, but would be fruitless till then.

Winston was on friendly terms with many of the Irish Nationalists, whose quick minds and agile wits were much to his taste, and there can be no doubt that Redmond perceived an ally in him. He inquired of Redmond what books he ought to read on Ireland, and the historian Stephen Gwynn was asked to make a selection. After a speech by Churchill in the House, which he had missed, Redmond wrote on 15 February 1911, 'I have heard what you said and I feel most grateful. All of us count on *you* to put Home Rule through.'[4]

4. Chartwell papers.

* * *

That Ulster had no intention of supinely accepting the threat of Home Rule was shown on 25 September 1911 when the Ulster Unionist Clubs and Orange Lodges held a convention at Belfast, and declared for a Provisional Government. And a sharp change was noticeable in the attitude and tactics of the Opposition at Westminster when Balfour resigned from the Party leadership, and was succeeded by Bonar Law. It was soon evident that unexpected depths lay beneath that prim exterior, and it was with surprise and relief that Unionists realized that they now had a leader who was not only strongly bound to the Ulster cause, but was utterly reckless of consequences. Bonar Law was formidable in debate, and Sir John Simon once remarked that an attack by him in the House of Commons was like being pelted in the face by handfuls of fine, stinging gravel. Those who failed to understand Bonar Law may have forgotten that the dull-seeming, bridge-playing Canadian businessman was the son of a Presbyterian minister of Ulster farming stock. Although so dry and cautious, he was to show himself astonishingly violent and intemperate when the battle was joined, but to a discerning eye there was something spurious and synthetic in his passion, lashing himself with effort into a rage. It was not without reason that Asquith called him 'a conscientious fire-eater'.

> Conviction and background conspired to throw him wholeheartedly into the Ulster crisis. He saw in it the means of bringing together the Conservative Party, of getting over the weakness of dissension, inherited from Balfour's regime, and in giving his followers something they would really believe in fighting for ... It seemed to him monstrous that a Protestant section of the British people should be required to loosen, to however qualified an extent, their links with Westminster.[5]

The inspiration he needed he derived from Edward Carson, the Ulster leader, an heroic figure indeed, and to those who faced him from the witness box a terrible one, Carson the victor over the Lords of the Admiralty, and the scourge of Oscar Wilde; a man who boasted that devotion to the Union had been the guiding star of his political life, and who responded to the challenge of Home Rule with grim relish, seeming, as some mistakenly thought, to have Italian blood with that saturnine, Dantesque profile.

* * *

The sound of a few ranging shots in the battle were drowned in the

5. A. P. Ryan, *Mutiny at The Curragh*, p. 20.

growl of rage which greeted Winston's announcement in the New Year of 1912 that he would speak in that Holy of Holies of Orangemen, the Ulster Town Hall, where Lord Randolph had sounded a famous trumpet call in the cause of Ulster thirty-four years before, when he warned Ulster Loyalists to 'organize and prepare', so that Home Rule, if it came, should not descend on them 'as a thief in the night', and find them unprepared. Winston's brave if insensitive project was modified, but not before Carson had publicly described him as 'the most provocative speaker in the whole party going under the most provocative circumstances to a place where the words of his father are still ringing in our ears'.[6]

The Nationalists, who were responsible for the arrangements of this meeting, wished Redmond and John Devlin to appear on the same platform, but Winston, with unwonted caution, felt that their presence might give the extreme Orange faction occasion to make a disturbance, and wrote to Redmond:

> The arrangements have been made without my being consulted, otherwise I would have expressed my view at an earlier date. What we want in Belfast is not demonstrations but discussions. It is no use my coming to Ulster to appeal to the Nationalists. They are already the partisans of the Home Rule cause. But there may be great use in a Minister endeavouring to reassure any genuine apprehensions of anxieties which the Protestants of Ulster feel. No doubt there is very little words can do; but it will be a great gain even to give the appearance that a fair and reasonable discussion of the subject has begun in Ulster. I think I could do better alone at this moment.[7]

There is nothing more striking at this time than the contrast between the aggressiveness of Winston's public utterances – in which there was little to choose between him and his political enemy and beloved friend F. E. Smith – and the prudent and even sombre conclusions he reached in private. He had already fired a salvo in Dundee in October 1911, in which he stated baldly: 'Next year we proposed to introduce the Home Rule Bill and we propose to carry it through with all our strength.' He had gone on to explain Asquith's view that the Government put forward Home Rule not only in justice to Ireland, but also as the first step towards setting up a Federal system in Great Britain, in which Scotland and Wales would receive self-government, which might afterwards be extended to Lancashire, Yorkshire, the Midlands and other places. This idea was received with general derision, and Winston was mocked by the

6. Montgomery Hyde, *Carson*, p. 300.
7. Chartwell papers.

Opposition press as one wishing to return to the Heptarchy.[8]

Now, the Ulster Unionists had booked the Ulster Hall for the night before Winston's meeting, and announced that they would hold the premises, and prevent his appearance 'by force if necessary'. The shape of future events was becoming apparent. There followed an acrimonious exchange between Lord Londonderry and Churchill, Londonderry reminding him of Lord Randolph's connection with the Ulster Hall, and the advice he had given to the people of Ulster in 1886: 'Ulster will fight, and Ulster will be right.' Winston's answer to this untimely and irritating reminder was sharp, and effectively closed the exchange:

> One word more. Your letter forces me to refer to a personal matter. Your Lordship has a claim, to which I bow, to remind me of the memory of Lord Randolph Churchill. You were his friend through evil as well as good days. The Unionist party, who within a few months of the very speech which is now on their lips pursued him with harsh ingratitude, have no such right.[9]

* * *

The Ulster Hall sternly barred, the meeting was held in a giant marquee pitched in a football ground in the Catholic working-class Falls area. Clemmie was strongly advised not to accompany Winston in view of the violence anticipated, but with characteristic fearlessness she said that her presence might help to prevent it. They had a surly and hostile reception at Stranraer, and a miserable crossing, being 'disturbed all night by suffragettes who ran like Maenads round the deck shrieking "Votes for Women" into their cabin windows'.[10] At Belfast they were told that the windows had been removed from their cars because the dockers were preparing to throw iron bolts at them. An attempt was made to overturn their car, but the crowd was beaten off by the police. They drove through the streets where four battalions of infantry were on duty. At the hotel enraged businessmen shook their fists at Winston as he passed to his room, and when he parted the thick lace curtains to survey the crowd beneath he was greeted by curses and howls of menace. It was certain that Winston would be exhilarated by such scenes, but it should be noted that Clemmie, in every way as fearless as he, responded to them with equal defiance and enjoyment, and was to do so for the rest of her life.

In the afternoon he addressed an audience of 5,000 in the vast

8. *Morning Post*, 13 September 1912.
9. Chartwell papers, WSC to Lord Londonderry, 27.1.12.
10. Bonham Carter, op. cit., p. 283.

tent. There were no chairs and, as in medieval churches, the great audience stood throughout the proceedings. Both sides in the argument were represented in the crowd with equal violence and bigotry, and the rain drummed down upon the marquee. Winston had for some time been dogged by Lord Randolph's famous slogan, and now in his peroration, he tried, with almost rash boldness, to twist it effectively in exactly the opposite sense in a manner that was little to the taste of the Ulster sympathizers in the audience:

> It is in a different sense that I adopt and repeat Lord Randolph's words 'Ulster will fight and Ulster will be right'. Let Ulster fight for the dignity and honour of Ireland; let her fight for the reconciliation of races and for the forgiveness of ancient wrongs; let her fight for the unity and consolidation of the British Empire; let her fight for the spreading of charity, tolerance and enlightenment among men. Then indeed Ulster will fight and Ulster will be right.[11]

* * *

Against a background growing ever more sombre the Home Rule Bill was introduced in the House of Commons on 11 April 1912. Asquith's Bill followed closely the Gladstonian precedent: purely Irish matters were transferred to the Irish Parliament, while the Imperial Parliament retained control of all questions relating to the Crown, foreign relations and Customs duties, and certain other services either temporarily or permanently. The Irish Parliament was debarred from establishing or endowing any religion or imposing religious disabilities of any kind. It might raise new taxes, but could not add more than 10 per cent to income tax, death duties or Customs duties, except on beer or spirits. The common Treasury remained, and the Bill contained an elaborate financial arrangement. Irish representation in the Imperial Parliament was reduced to 42 Members to be at liberty to speak or vote on all subjects.

It was not an extreme measure, and there is some justification for the Liberal view that it amounted to little more than the establishment of local government with the same limited authority which was given to Northern Ireland in 1920. But at the same time Ulster was without doubt the most formidable obstacle, and some of the more percipient Liberals were fully aware of the fact. A young member of the Party, Agar Robartes, gave expression to their growing uneasiness by moving an amendment in the House during Committee stage, to exclude from the Bill the four counties of Antrim, Armagh, Down and Londonderry.

11. 8 February 1912.

'Orange bitters and Irish whiskey will not mix,' he said. The amendment was rejected.

The Cabinet had debated whether the predominantly Orange counties should be given an opportunity to contract out in the Bill as introduced, or whether this should be reserved as a concession for a later stage. They decided that the Bill as introduced should apply to all Ireland, and to warn the Irish leaders that

> the Government held themselves free to make changes, if it became clear that special treatment must be provided for the Ulster Counties, and that in this case the Government will be ready to recognize the necessity either by amendment or by not pressing it [the Bill] on under the provision of the Parliament Act.[12]

The policy the Government preferred and recommended was a policy for all Ireland, and they should not start by admitting it to be impossible.[13]

If they wished to avoid trouble with Ulster, this seems indeed to have been an extraordinary decision, and it is not surprising that Winston was baffled by it. It appears to indicate a fatal misassessment of Ulster's mood and temper, and a weak desire to postpone tackling it until it was already too late. Churchill in private recognized the force of the Ulster case, and was thus in advance of many of his colleagues, and, *sub rosa*, all his actions were designed to secure a compromise. But in public he continued to be positive and aggressive.

In a brilliant speech in the Second Reading debate on 30 April he put the onus of success or failure squarely on the Ulstermen:

> At one sweep of the wand they could sweep the Irish question out of life and history and free the British realm of the canker which has poisoned its heart for generations. If they refuse, if they take to the boats, all we say is that we shall not obstruct the work of salvage and we shall go forward at any rate to the end.

With virtuous indignation, rather in the manner of Satan rebuking sin, he went on to reprove Bonar Law and Carson for the violence of their language, and for inciting the Orangemen to bloodshed. He particularly deplored the violence of Bonar Law's speech and wrote sadly to F. E. Smith, with a hint of that caressing charm which F.E. had already noticed:

'My dear, I grieve more than I can say at B.L.'s speech; and if that is the answer to all we have offered then there is nothing for it but a trial

12. Cabinet Letter to the King, 6 February 1912.
13. Spender, *H. H. Asquith, Lord Oxford*, Vol. II, pp. 14–15.

of strength on which, believe me, I shall enter with the deepest sorrow but without fear. Alas! Alas!'

* * *

He was to receive a dusty answer on 27 July when a mammoth Unionist rally was held in the courtyard outside Blenheim Palace, for which three thousand people were brought in special trains to the sleepy Oxfordshire station. When the delegates were seated the gates were thrown open and the local people came in, bringing the gathering to fifteen thousand. At this enormous meeting in the hot sunshine of that summer, which seemed charged with menace, Bonar Law transcended even Carson and F. E. Smith in the violence of the language with which he inflamed the audience. Smith had already proclaimed that he would not shrink from the consequences of his convictions 'though the whole fabric of the Commonwealth be convulsed'; now Bonar Law, who had screwed himself up to the great act of defiance, permitted himself to utter an even more unambiguous threat.

> While I had still in the party a position of less responsibility than that which I have now, I said that in my opinion, if an attempt were made without the clearly expressed will of the people of this country, and as part of a corrupt Parliament bargain, to deprive these men of their birthright, *they would be justified in resisting by all means in their power, including force.*

Stimulated by the roar of approbation which followed this remark, Bonar Law continued:

> *I can imagine no length of resistance to which Ulster will go in which I shall not be ready to support them, and in which they will not be supported by the overwhelming majority of the British people.*

These reckless and defiant words, which can never before have been used by the leader of one of the great parties of the State, and which gave *carte blanche* to the Orangemen's most desperate intentions, brought the great audience to its feet wildly cheering for several minutes.

Winston was appalled by the speeches at this demonstration, which he thought would paralyse any attempts to compromise. He wrote to J. L. Garvin on 10 August:

> Do they think they will never come back to power? Have they no policy for Ireland except to make it ungovernable? They are the more inexcusable because no one that I know of has ever contemplated

the application of force to Ulster. The principle and doctrine lately enunciated would dissolve the framework not only of the British Empire, but of civilized society.[14]

The Prime Minister still appeared to nourish hopes that there was no substance in the Ulster agitation, that it was a gigantic bluff, and he was encouraged in these dangerous beliefs by Redmond, whose optimism was based on his knowledge of the rhetorical extravagance of his countrymen. But Winston's own aggressive bearing on the platform during the crisis masked a growing foreboding, and the rustle of the olive branch behind the sabre-rattling was always to be heard in private. It appears in a letter to Redmond later in August, telling him that he and his friends should now be thinking of a detour round the Ulster swamp:

> The Unionist Party have now staked their whole power to fight Home Rule on this foundation. Remove it, and the path in my judgement is absolutely clear. I do not believe there is any real feeling against Home Rule in the Tory Party apart from the Ulster question, but they hate the Government, are bitterly desirous of turning us out, and see in the resistance of Ulster an extraparliamentary force, which they will not hesitate to use to the full. I have been pondering a good deal over this matter, and my general view is just what I told you earlier this year – namely that something should be done to afford the characteristic Protestant and Orange counties the option of a moratorium of several years before acceding to an Irish Parliament. I think the time approaches when such an offer should be made – and it would come much better from the Irish leaders than from the Government.[15]

We may well inquire at this point how such an impasse had been reached. It must have been obvious that no moratorium with a time limit, as suggested by Winston, would have been acceptable to Ulster. If it was true that no Liberal Government could have contemplated the coercion of Ulster, why was it not excluded at the beginning, by the 'clean cut' which Carson demanded? Why not give both parts of Ireland what they wanted – allow Southern Ireland to have Home Rule, and Ulster to remain within the Union? It was the contention of the Liberals that this was not in fact what either of them wanted; that the partition of Ireland was repulsive to all parties in both islands in 1912, and that the object of

14. Chartwell papers. WSC to J. L. Garvin, 10 August 1912.
15. Chartwell papers.

Carson and many of his followers was not to rescue Ireland but to defeat Home Rule.

But it is easier to believe that Redmond and his Nationalists felt that they could not afford to accept Home Rule for a mere three-quarters of their island, even if they had wished to do so. They were uneasily conscious that there was a younger, tougher generation pressing on behind them, to whom the present Home Rule Bill was a mere stepping-stone to a demand for independence. They had little doubt what their own fate would be if they agreed to partition. Another objection to the 'clean cut' was that it was almost beyond human ingenuity to make it clean. Ulster was not a homogeneous unit, but a province where Nationalists, Unionists, Catholics and Protestants were closely intermingled. Another objection was that many Conservatives believed that to exclude Ulster would be to betray the Unionist minority in the South.

* * *

On 28 September 1912 Ulster acted. Ulster Unionists signed a solemn League and Covenant which pledged the signatories to 'use all means which may be found necessary to defeat the present conspiracy to set up a Home Rule Parliament in Ireland.' The way to this fervent scene of consecration had been paved by a series of dramatic preparatory meetings which those who attended never forgot, particularly those at Coleraine and Belfast. It was as impossible to witness these scenes without becoming convinced of the flaming purpose of Ulster as it was later to attend a Nuremberg rally under Hitler without becoming aware of the military fever in Germany.

At the meetings in Ulster the crowds were roused by the technique of psychological preparation of which Carson was a past master. Everywhere there were flags cracking in the wind like gunshots, orange collars and blue collars and hard-faced men pacing the streets. Visitors were struck everywhere by the ominous quiet of the preparations; during a meeting at the Ulster Town Hall in Belfast thirty thousands people waited outside tightly packed together, again in that deathly and ominous silence. The Covenant was signed next day after a service in the Ulster Hall. It lay on a round table covered by the Union Jack. Carson, the acknowledged leader of the Ulster movement, was the first to sign, and was followed by the Bishop, the Mayor and Corporation in full robes, and all the heads of Belfast business houses. And then the rank and file entered and began to sign at each side of the table, thousand of people, rich and poor, thronging into the hall together. And when Carson's ship left they decorated his cabin with roses. As it moved from the quay the crowd sang O *God our help in ages past*, and as the distance increased, the plaintive notes of *Come back to Erin* floated across the water, moving some of those on the ship to tears. The men in charge of lightships burned flares as they passed, and wireless messages came into the ship: 'We won't have Home Rule. God Save the King!'

The Home Rule Bill had a storm-tossed passage through the House of Commons, and the passions engendered led to scenes of constant uproar. One of the worst of these took place on 13 November 1912 when the Prime Minister moved the withdrawal of an Opposition amendment to the Financial Resolution of the Bill. The Prime Minister announced the Government's intention to rescind the vote, as it did not represent the considered view of the House. Pandemonium followed this somewhat dubious decision. Mr Harcourt was denied a hearing; Sir William Bull called Asquith a traitor, and was ordered to leave the Chamber by the Speaker; the Attorney General was howled down, and amid such a sustained tumult as had not been heard since the Parliament Bill, the House was adjourned for an hour in the hope that passions might cool. But on resumption it was worse even than before, the Opposition chanting continuously, 'Adjourn! Adjourn!' and determined to prevent debate, so that the Speaker was forced to adjourn the House for the night. Winston and Colonel Jack Seely left the House together to yells of 'Rats', and the former, accustomed to this form of address and thriving on such scenes, beamed with irritating benevolence and waved his handkerchief to the Opposition. An enraged Ulster Member took the Speaker's bound copy of the Orders of the House from his Chair and hurled it at Winston, cutting him on the forehead, and a stand-up fight seemed likely. As the House was technically adjourned the Speaker could take no action, but someone struck up 'Should Auld Acquaintance be forgot', and the fury dissolved in a gale of asinine laughter. Ronald McNeill,[16] the guilty Ulster Member, made a sheepish apology next day.

Such scenes marked the whole passage of the Home Rule Bill through the Commons. Lord Winterton, who was present throughout, refers to the 'roaring furnace' of controversy which the Bill caused, when 'Government and Opposition in the Commons roared and snarled at each other across the floor about Ireland like angry lions and tigers'.[17]

* * *

16. Subsequently Lord Craigavon, first Prime Minister of Northern Ireland.
17. Winterton, op. cit., p. 73.

The Home Rule Bill, having passed through the House of Commons, was next sent to the Lords, where on Second Reading it was rejected by 257 votes on 30 January 1913. The Ulster leaders then formally constituted the Ulster Volunteer force, for which Lord Roberts (who had played a well-meaning if somewhat naive part) secured Lieut. General Richardson as Commander. On 23 September Carson accepted the chairmanship of a Provisional Government, and two days later F. E. Smith acted as his 'galloper' at a review of the Belfast Volunteers, thus earning a sobriquet which was to pursue him in various degrees of obloquy for the rest of his life.

The Ulster Volunteers armed and drilled to resist Home Rule. Southern Ireland, bent on showing that two could play at that game, retaliated by forming a Provisional Committee in which Sinn Fein[18] joined with the Irish Republican Brotherhood[19] and the Gaelic Associations[20] to raise and arm their version of 'National Volunteers', in order to obtain far more than the moderate measure of Home Rule now before the Imperial Parliament.[21]

It was now becoming obvious to the Government that special arrangements would have to be made for Ulster if Home Rule (to which they were committed) was ever to become a reality. F. E. Smith had been making his own attempt at an agreed solution. Carson had been informed and had promised to tell his friends. At the end of September 1913 Asquith authorized Churchill, who was staying at Balmoral, to speak to Bonar Law; the outcome of these consultations can be seen in Robert Blake's biography of Bonar Law. From this it is clear that Bonar Law impressed his party's determination on Churchill with the utmost force, while inclining to the view which he and F. E. Smith had always shared with Carson – that it might be possible to 'leave Ulster as she is and have some form of Home Rule for the rest of Ireland'. He also made it plain that the Unionist Party under his leadership would positively encourage and recommend any refusal of the Army to obey orders.[22]

A cold wind blew from Lansdowne, bringing with it the chill of his Perthshire house where he was awaiting news from Balmoral. He felt that to exclude Ulster and establish Home Rule in the South would be to betray the whole past tradition of the Unionist Party. The miserable dilemma is clearly perceptible in Blake's words:

18. Literally 'Ourselves alone'. Founded by Arthur Griffith in 1905 to achieve the emancipation of Ireland by abstention from Westminster.
19. Or Fenians. A secret society founded in 1858, pledged to establish an Irish republic by force.
20. The Gaelic League was founded in 1893 to promote Irish cultural revival.
21. Spender, op. cit., Vol. II p. 21.
22. Robert Blake, *The Unknown Prime Minister*, pp. 156–7.

'Many other Unionists took the same view although, unlike Lansdowne, they possessed no acre in Ireland. The Right wing of the
party had always objected to Home Rule, not merely because it
was unfair to Ireland but because they denied the whole concept
of a separate Irish nation . . .'

While Winston was at Balmoral we find him deep in secret conclave
with his fellow platform firebrand, F. E. Smith. We see Winston writing
to his fanatical opponent, Bonar Law, discussing a conference, and
telling him that Balfour was hopeful about the 'limited solution of
leaving out Ulster'. He referred to 'my pleasant conversation with you':
'It was a vy pleasant conversation & I shall do my best to make it lead to
a good result.'[23] And we shall see F. E. Smith writing affectionately to the
Radical Lloyd George, describing his talks with the King and Winston on
the subject of the conference:

> The basis W and I discussed was:
> (1) Exclusion of Ulster with facilities for later adherence.
>
> (2) Acceptance of an agreed Bill by the Unionists for the rest of Ireland.
>
> (3) A genuine acceptance on our part to make the thing work in the south.
>
> (4) A conference to be summoned to discuss matters.[24]

These private conversations are another indication of Winston's sincere
desire, in private, for a settlement whatever his public indiscretions may
have suggested.

*   *   *

We have seen the turmoil which discussion of the Bill had caused
in the House of Commons and when Parliament reassembled in the
autumn Asquith introduced the closure and the guillotine. Bonar Law at
once tabled an amendment attacking the resolution with spirited vigour.
He warned the House that Ulster might explode at any moment: if
Home Rule was forced upon it, Heaven help Great Britain. If there
were bloodshed, the guilt would be on the Ministry. Winston replied
with what even for him was remarkable felicity that 'those who talk of
revolution ought to be prepared for the guillotine.'[25]

While his mind was concentrated mainly on the life-and-death
business of naval preparedness, and his chief work was at the

---

23. Bonar Law papers.
24. Lloyd George papers.
25. Randolph S. Churchill, op. cit., Vol. II, p. 471–2.

Admiralty, Ireland alone among other topics claimed a large part of his attention. He took a leading part in the Home Rule controversy, working at high pressure to keep abreast of it with so much else in his mind, and advocating the cause up and down the country with pleas for moderation and non-violence. At this time he was at full stretch at the Admiralty. The Chancellor of the Exchequer and the Liberal Radical press loudly demanded economy, and many Government supporters in the House of Commons were opposed to Admiralty policy. Winston frankly admitted that his absorption in the Irish problem was partly due to a desire to strengthen his position in the party. As he saw it:

> Eager partisans of the Home Rule cause were by no means anxious to see the Government weakened by the resignation of the entire Board of Admiralty. We were already so hard pressed in the party struggle that the defection of a single Minister might have produced a serious effect. No one expected me to pass away in sweet silence. The prospect of a formidable naval agitation added to the Irish tension was recognized as uninviting. In order to strengthen myself with my party, I mingled actively in the Irish controversy.[26]

* * *

26. Winston S. Churchill, *The World Crisis*, p. 102.

Chapter 11

The Ulster Crisis

Before the 1914 session opened Asquith told Redmond that he expected trouble in the Cabinet over the huge Navy Estimates, to which Lloyd George had referred pointedly in a New Year message on disarmament, and over opposition in the House to the Army Annual Bill, the Unionists urging that the troops should not be used against Ulster. It seemed, therefore, to Asquith that the Government should make an offer to Ulster, so depriving her resistance of moral force, and he suggested that Ulster MPs in the Dublin parliament might have the right to appeal to the Imperial Government against the Bills affecting Ulster.

By this time all parties realized with bleak certainty that some compromise was inevitable, and by 1914 opposition to any form of Home Rule on the basis of excluding part of Ulster either temporarily or permanently. Three courses were now discussed – the first being 'Home Rule within Home Rule'. This course commended itself to the Prime Minister, but to none of the parties concerned. The second was that the whole of Ireland should be included in the Bill, but that after a lapse of years an option should be given to the Ulster counties to remove themselves from the Irish Legislature and Executive. This too proved unacceptable. The third suggestion was exclusion, 'not as a solution, but as an expedient which might pave the way to a final settlement.'[1] It was on a compromise of this nature that the Government decided to advance.

But by the end of 1913 the situation had disintegrated, and the position between the parties was in its most extreme state of animosity. On 9 March 1914, when the Home Rule Bill came up for second reading on the third and last occasion under the Parliament Act, Asquith declared his proposal of an amendment enabling the Ulster

1. Lord Oxford and Asquith, *Fifty Years of Parliament*, Vol. II, p. 145.

counties to vote themselves out for a period of six years. Redmond then declared that in his view the Prime Minister had gone to 'the very extremest limits of concession. If these proposals be accepted as the basis of agreement and peace, then we, on our side, are prepared to accept them in the same spirit.'

It was soon evident what Carson's opinion was of this proposal. His answer was bleak and devastating. With an expression of impatience and contempt, and speaking in his rich brogue, he killed it at a blow. 'We do not want,' he said, 'sentence of death with a stay of execution for six years.'

On 13 March the Prime Minister wrote to the King, conscious that the Irish situation was now rapidly crumbling. He described a Cabinet meeting the day before:

> Some considerable time was given to a discussion of the military situation in Ulster, suggested by the latest series of police reports, which indicate the possibility of attempts on the part of the 'Volunteers' to seize by *coups de main* police and military barracks, and depots of arms and ammunition. A small Committee of the Cabinet, consisting of Lord Crewe, Mr Birrell, Mr Churchill, Colonel Seely and Sir John Simon, was appointed to look into the matter in all its aspects and report to the Cabinet . . .[2]

This Committee reported on 17 March that the guards on the depots were to be strengthened, and Churchill announced that the Third Battle Squadron of eight battleships would carry out exercises at Lamlash on the Isle of Arran. The Cabinet had approved this naval movement on 11 March.

On 14 March Churchill made a speech at Bradford which seemed calculated to inflame an already critical situation – partisan, violent and aggressive. He accused Bonar Law, with gross injustice, of using the Ulster crisis entirely for party advantage. 'Behind every strident sentence which he rasps out you can always hear the whisper . . . Ulster is our best card: it is our only card.' And having declared that 'there are things worse than bloodshed, even on an extended scale', he came to a challenging and truculent peroration:

> This is the issue – whether civil and Parliamentary Government in these realms is to be beaten down by the menace of armed force . . . If the civil and Parliamentary systems under which we have dwelt so long, and our fathers before us, are to be brought to the crude challenge of force, if the Government and Parliament of this great country and greater Empire are to be exposed to menace and brutality; if all the

2. CAB 41/35, 13 March 1914.

loose, wanton and reckless chatter we have been forced to listen to, these many months, is in the end to disclose a sinister and revolutionary purpose, then I can only say to you: 'Let us go forward together and put these grave matters to the proof!'

* * *

This speech and inept handling of the situation by the Secretary of State for War, Colonel Jack Seely, brought the whole issue to great tension. The Opposition accused Churchill and Seely of preparing to coerce Ulster, and of trailing their coats with the object of launching an 'Ulster Pogrom'. The suggestion of a pogrom and a plot were no doubt wildly exaggerated, but the Government were certainly preparing for the worst.

On 19 March Bonar Law moved a vote of censure on the Government. There were violent attacks on Winston. On 30 March F. E. Smith accused him of 'finessing for the firing of the first shot'. Winston replied: 'How easy it must be for a distinguished lawyer to procure the conviction of an innocent man.' Later, speaking on a vote of censure, he declared that the attacks on him were like a 'vote of censure by the criminal classes upon the police', a remark unlikely to lower the temperature. Bonar Law, in referring to the impending coercion of Ulster, said that the attitude of the Army was for the Army to decide. 'The debate was still proceeding when Sir Edward Carson strode starkly out of the House with a look of destiny upon his haggard Covenanter face. A whisper flew round the benches that he was taking the night mail to Belfast: there were few who doubted that next morning the Provisional Government of Ulster would be proclaimed.'[3]

Hints that the Army had been seduced from their allegiance and could not be relied upon in case of civil war had been strongly repudiated by Unionists, Carson calling it a 'foul lie'. Even so, disturbing reports continued to reach the War Office. It seems for some inexplicable reason to have been unknown to the Government that one of the highest officials in that Office, Sir Henry Wilson, Director of Military Operations, was actively fomenting unrest within the Army. This officer, one of the most incorrigible intriguers ever to have risen to the highest military positions, and a man with extraordinary conceptions of loyalty, was a passionate devotee of the Ulster cause, and revealed in his diary that he was in league with Ulster and with Ulster Unionist leaders in London, and in his own hand proved himself to be a traitor to the Government he served.

* * *

3. H. Nicolson, op. cit., p. 237.

It is not necessary here to describe in detail the so-called Curragh Mutiny which followed. It struck a deadly blow to the prospects of Home Rule, profoundly humiliated the Government and screwed the Conservative detestation of Churchill to the highest peg. It has been described by one of the principal actors, General Sir Hubert Gough,[4] and more recently by two modern historians.[5] We are concerned here only with the broad outline of events, and one cannot avoid the conclusion that nothing approaching a 'mutiny' took place on the Curragh. Rather was a comedy of errors played out in which the most culpable figures were a blundering Secretary of State, a buffoon as Commander-in-Chief in Ireland, and Sir John French at his unspeakable worst. Seely, the Secretary of State, was soon to be hissed off the stage.

The question of the British Army in Ireland had become acute. The doubt in the mind of the Government was whether the British troops would refuse to fight if ordered to invade Ulster, and Sir Arthur Paget, the Commander-in-Chief in Dublin, was ordered by Seely to take soundings among his senior officers. Paget told these officers, including Gough, that military operations were about to begin against Ulster, but that he did not expect bloodshed, owing to the strength of the British Army. But he added that in view of the qualms Irish Protestant officers might feel at fighting against fellow-Protestants in Ireland, he had obtained a concession that those officers 'domiciled in Ulster' might 'disappear', and would be reinstated later. This dispensation did not apply to all other Irish officers, nor was it explained how the 'disappearance' was to be stage-managed. These other officers were given the alternative of marching or being dismissed the Service. Gough had no hesitation in choosing dismissal.

On 21 March 1914 Paget again summoned the officers of the 3rd Cavalry Brigade, and begged them to withdraw their resignations. He was a stupid man, and wholly lacking in subtlety. 'He did not,' said Gough, 'mention that our resignations had been forced upon us by his words the day before . . . He never appealed to our honour, but harped much on the ruin of our careers.' He did not hesitate to assure them that the King had approved all these decisions. He made weak and futile suggestions as to their part in the coming operations. 'He would not ask us to fight. We could look on, and he would say nothing . . .' At one moment he said that his military moves were only to 'protect stores', and the next he said he would deploy 20,000 troops along the Boyne. Sadly floundering, and contradicting himself, Paget passed from clumsy seduction to warnings that all dissidents would be tried by court martial.

4. Gough, *Soldiering On*.
5. A. P. Ryan, *Mutiny on the Curragh*; Sir James Ferguson, *The Curragh Incident*.

This sorry farce was next transferred to London, whither General Gough and other officers were summoned to the War Office. Paget's folly had now been appreciated, and the War Office wished Gough and his officers to return to Ireland and resume their commands as though nothing had happened. But the news of events at the Curragh had already spread through the British Army.

> The first idea [wrote L. S. Amery] undoubtedly was to make a drastic example of General Gough ... But before many hours had passed, the Army Council and Ministers realized that if that course was persisted in there would be no War Office and very little British Army next day.[6]

The Government therefore was forced to climb down under the bitter compulsion of the hour. Gough had made up his mind that he would not return unless he was given a guarantee in writing that neither he nor his officers would be given orders to impose the Home Rule Bill by force on Ulster, and to this position he adhered with the utmost tenacity. His persistence was in the end rewarded after a difficult interview with Seely by a note from the Army Council which afterwards became known as the 'guarantee'. He wrote on a piece of War Office paper his own definition of it which was: 'that we should not be asked to impose Home Rule on Ulster by force'. The paper was incautiously initialled by Seely and by the C.I.G.S., Sir John French, who endorsed it: 'I should read it so.'

This document, which was intended to convince Gough's officers that the 3rd Cavalry Brigade would not be ordered north, got into the hands of the press, and this was the end of Seely. He had given an amended State document to General Gough twenty-four hours in advance of its publication, thus turning a public statement of Government policy on the Army into what appeared to be a clandestine deal between the Minister and a clique of officers, enabling Asquith to repudiate Seely's pledge on the grounds that it was made without Cabinet authority. Sir John French and the Adjutant General, who had both endorsed the 'guarantee', resigned. Seely was forced to do so: 'that it might not ever appear that a Minister of the Crown had made a bargain with servants of the Crown as to the terms of their service'.[7] The Prime Minister himself took over the War Office.

This episode marked one of Winston's lowest points. He was now the object of a Conservative venom greater even than that which had been spewed over him when he changed his party. To Conservatives his naval dispositions, as a so-called 'precautionary measure', had been

6. L. S. Amery, *My Political Life*, Vol. I, p.
7. H. H. Asquith, *Fifty Years of Parliament*, Vol. II, p. 151.

dangerous and provocative to the highest degree, while the humiliating failure of the Government to intimidate Ulster produced a complete loss of confidence in Southern Ireland in the Government's power to control the situation, and a realization that it had fatally underrated the strength of Ulster's resolve:

> The events of March 1914 made Churchill an object of peculiar hatred to the Conservatives. Throughout the summer their attacks on him, both inside and outside Parliament, were violent and persistent, and Bonar Law in particular did not forget or forgive what he regarded as Churchill's gross and unforgiveable irresponsibility.[8]

Even his ardent admirer Violet Asquith thought that his naval dispositions were 'open to the charge of being unnecessarily melodramatic and provocative'. But she acquitted him of any sinister intent: 'From childhood onwards he had always had a strong taste for moving soldiers. Now he could move ships. These congenial occupations at times went to his head and often got him into trouble . . .'[9]

* * *

In the meantime the King was in high dudgeon because he had never been informed of the War Office instructions to Sir A. Paget or of the proposed movement of military detachments to Ulster. The first he heard of the Curragh incident was from his newspaper on the morning of 21 March. He wrote to Asquith on 21 March complaining of this omission, and continued in a somewhat frosty manner:

> I . . . must further ask that I am kept fully informed of any proposed employment of the Navy in connection with Ulster, especially as I see in the press that some excitement has been caused already in Ireland by the movements of some ships & I have heard nothing from the First Lord of the Admiralty.[10]

As Asquith had reported to the King on 18 March, Churchill had informed the Cabinet the day before that the forthcoming practice of the 3rd Battle Squadron would take place at Lamlash, in the south-west of Scotland. It was, indeed, a precautionary measure, but one that aroused furious indignation.

8. R. Rhodes James, op. cit., p. 49.
9. Bonham Carter, op. cit., p. 295.
10. Asquith papers.

The Prime Minister countermanded the orders to the 3rd Battle Squadron on the evening of 21 March, and it was on Winston that anger concentrated. It was said that he had engendered the plot and led Asquith by the nose; a plot to provoke the loyal Ulster Volunteers to violent action and then shoot them down – to attack them by land and sea, and crush them with superior force. Some called it the 'Ulster Pogrom', and the phrase stuck like a well-aimed dart. *The Times* accused the Government of a 'calculated scheme for the investment of Ulster by land and sea', and Winston's orders to the Fleet and his belligerent words at Bradford were quoted in support of this charge.

*   *   *

The worst that can be said of Winston's conduct in this incident (which now seems like a storm in a teacup) is that although his policy was justified by events, its execution was inept. It seemed to confirm his reputation for sudden lapses of judgment. However, the Cabinet had apparently not contested the First Lord's intentions, which followed the Government's decision to protect certain depots in Ulster with reinforcements.

A Battle Squadron at Lamlash would be within easy distance of Belfast if trouble arose, and Churchill had promised Paget if required to carry troops by sea to Dundalk and Carrickfergus should the Northern Railway (as seemed likely) refuse to do so. In all probability Churchill had in mind more serious possibilities than the mere transport of troops for depot-protection. If H. A. Gwynne is to be believed, he told Sir John French on 20 March 'that if Belfast showed fight his fleet would have the town in ruins in twenty-four hours'.[11] This was doubtless simply an example of the Churchill taste for dramatizing a situation; but it does lend at least some justification to the theory that he was going further than the Cabinet realized, and was forcing the pace towards bringing direct pressure on Ulster.

The 'Plot' or 'Pogrom' storm raged for weeks with undiminished fury.[12] Churchill's explanation of the Lamlash affair in reply to Lord Charles Beresford in the Commons on 25 March was angrily rejected, amid scenes of frenzy rare even in those savage years. *The Times* of 23 March put the blame squarely on Churchill, Seely and French: 'These three men are responsible for an episode without parallel in the history of the Army.'

11. Robert Blake, *The Unknown Prime Minister*, p. 2.
12. See Randolph S. Churchill, op. cit., Vol. II, p. 499–504.

On 23 April Churchill wrote to his wife:

> The 'Ulster Pogrom' is in full swing as you will read in the papers. We have now published everything and I am confident that these wild charges will become gradually discredited. Bonar Law has exceeded himself in rudeness to the Prime Minister and feelings are on all sides bitter to a degree unknown hitherto.
>
> Seely goes about like a disembodied spirit, trying to return from the wastes of the infinite to the cosy world of men. He is terribly hard hit and losing poise. The world is pitiless to grief and failure . . .

And on 27 April:

> . . . Tomorrow I am to reply to Austen Chamberlain's vote of censure on the 'Pogrom'. The situation has from a parliamentary point of view been altered much in our favour by the gun-running escapade of the Ulstermen. They have put themselves entirely in the wrong, and justified to the full the modest precautions that were taken. My line will be a very stiff one.[13]

In the House Churchill offered an unexpected olive branch to Carson, asking him whether, if he were given the amendments to the Home Rule Bill which he sought to uphold the dignity and interests of Protestant Ulster, he would use all his influence to make Ireland an integral unit in a federal system.

On 29 April he wrote of this development to Clementine:

> I have just come back from the Pogrom debate. You must read all about it. We smashed the 'plot' altogether, but as you will see I yesterday at the end of my speech greatly daring & on my own account threw a sentence across the House to Carson wh has revolutionized the situation, & we are all back again in full conciliation. This is the biggest risk I have taken.
>
> So far all is well – but the Irish are vy restive & there is danger everywhere. I took my political life in my hands. The P.M. comes along with the main body. Carson made a gt & cheering advance, & Balfour also shd be read . . .[14]

Asquith, who now seemed to have become increasingly passive, stated in the House that although Winston had made the suggestion on his own responsibility, he was himself entirely in sympathy with it, an indication that the Prime Minister was wilting under the energetic force of a rising sun.

---

13. On the night of April 24/25 the Ulster Volunteers landed 30,000 rifles and three million rounds of ammunition at Larne.
14. CSC papers.

Winston was delighted by the result of his unauthorized initiative, and wrote to Clemmie on 30 April: 'You will see by the papers that the daring and perilous stroke I made has transformed the political situation. It was an inspiration . . . !'

* * *

The 'Pogrom' storm gradually died away, but the deplorable Curragh incident, besides embittering politics in England, had dangerous and far-reaching repercussions abroad, particularly in Germany where the impression was created that England would be so corroded and weakened by internal strife and a mutinous army that she was likely to be a negligible factor in European affairs.

Mr Asquith's Amending Bill, enabling any Ulster county to vote itself out of Home Rule for six years, was transformed by the House of Lords to exclude the whole of Ulster without a time limit. Returned to the Commons on 14 July, it was in this form totally unacceptable to the Irish Nationalists and the majority of the House of Commons. To add to the Government's tribulations, they were now realizing the danger from Germany. The European situation was so menacing that it was more than ever imperative to find a cure for this running ulcer at home. The Prime Minister therefore advised the King that the time was ripe for the conference of leaders suggested by His Majesty some months before.

The Government, the Opposition, the Irish Nationalists and the Ulster Unionists were represented at the Buckingham Palace Conference, but the presence of Lloyd George among them and the omission of Churchill is at first sight surprising. It was probably due to his intense unpopularity at that moment and the malevolence with which he had been pursued over the Ulster Pogrom. The discussions – which lasted four days, and were conducted in a friendly and courteous manner – turned entirely upon the demarcation lines of the area of Ulster to be excluded temporarily or permanently from the Home Rule Bill. The most difficult territory was in the counties of Fermanagh and Tyrone where the Roman Catholics were in a majority. All parties clearly wanted agreement, but the conference broke down on the time limit and boundary issues on 24 July, the day when the terms of the Austrian ultimatum to Serbia became known.

'What the Government now proposed, as Asquith told the King, was to proceed with County option but with the omission of automatic inclusion after a term of years and the substitution of fresh powers . of option as suggested by Sir Edward Carson at the conference.'[15]

15. Spender, op. cit., Vol. II, p. 55.

The Amending Bill was due to be debated on 31 July, but with the imminence of war it was (with the consent of Bonar Law, Redmond and Carson) indefinitely postponed.

* * *

The end of this melancholy conflict had not yet been reached. To the Government it was obvious that the Home Rule Bill must reach the Statute Book if the loyalty of Ireland was to be preserved during a European war. After Sir Edward Grey's historic speech on 3 August, Redmond had deeply moved the House when he assured the Government that they could safely withdraw all the troops from Ireland and that Nationalist Catholics in the South would join with armed Protestant Ulstermen in the North to protect the coasts of Ireland.

But in spite of these confident words, Redmond was a prey to deep anxiety. He felt that he was now approaching the heart of the matter, and that a false step would imperil the issue to a fatal degree. On the day following his speech he wrote to Churchill:

> I want ... to make an urgent appeal to you. In making my speech yesterday I was quite aware that I was taking very great risks. My people are sincerely anxious to make friends with this country but naturally enough they are full of suspicion & if the Home Rule Bill be postponed they will consider themselves sold & I will be simply unable to hold them. In that event deplorable things will be said and done in Ireland & the Home Rule cause may be lost for our time.[16]

Redmond went on to suggest that the Royal Assent should be given to the Bill, and that a pledge should be given that an Amending Bill would be introduced in the winter; and that pending the disposal of the Amending Bill, no step would be taken to put the original Bill into operation. He begged Winston to forward these views.

Redmond was confident that he could agree with Carson on the terms of the Amending Bill if this was done. But, on the following day, after an interview with that inflexible man, he was forced to report another dusty answer. In a revealing and confidential letter to Asquith, of which a copy was sent to Winston, he set forth his views on the *dégringolade* that would soon follow:

> I had an interview this afternoon with Sir Edward Carson in the Speaker's Library. The Speaker was also present. I found Sir Edward in an absolutely irreconcilable mood about everything. So much so indeed that it was impossible really to discuss matters calmly with him. The gist

16. Chartwell papers.

of our conversation was this – although, of course, I do not give you his words – that if the Government dared to put the Home Rule Bill on the Statute Book, that he and the Tory party would obstruct the Appropriation Bill and revive all the bitterness of the controversy. He would not listen to any suggested way out of the difficulty at all, and is evidently in the worst possible temper ... If the Government allow themselves to be bullied in this way by Sir Edward Carson, a position of the most serious difficulty will arise with us. It will be quite impossible for me to abstain from raising a discussion on the Second Reading of the Appropriation Bill, which would have most unfortunate and disastrous results in Ireland, and really would put us and our country in an absolutely cruel position. It would make it quite impossible for me to go to Ireland, as I desire to do, and to translate into action the spirit of my speech the other day.[17] It would revive all the suspicion and bitterness and controversy, all through the South and West of Ireland, and would exhibit us to the world as torn into a hundred fragments ...

After these sombre words, Redmond continued:

For my part I am not moved in the smallest degree by Sir Edward Carson's threats. In the present state of public opinion in England, and in the present state of the Tory Party in the House of Commons, I believe neither he nor the Unionist leaders dare take the extreme course which he threatened; and if they did so they would ruin themselves in the eyes of the public.

This to Redmond was the crucial moment, and the thought that at this late hour all his efforts might be frustrated was agonizing in the extreme. He concluded his letter:

This undoubtedly is the greatest opportunity that ever occurred in the history of Ireland to win the Irish people to loyalty to the Empire, and I do beg of you not to allow threats of the kind used to prevent you from taking the course which will enable me to preach the doctrine of peace, goodwill and loyalty in Ireland.[18]

*   *   *

Winston therefore devoted all his immense powers of persuasion to an effort to convince his Unionist friends that in the national interest they should accept the Government's proposal. He was particularly concerned, with a world war only beginning, to avoid

17. Redmond's speech assuring the Government that they could safely withdraw all troops from Ireland.
18. Chartwell papers.

a hostile Ireland, and equally to avoid alienating thousands of Irish Americans. His views at this moment can be seen in a letter to Lord Robert Cecil on 8 September 1914:

> ... I do beg of you to consider, as a military measure, the importance of giving the Irish their Bill, & so bringing them round in England and America to our side. The denial of this will certainly be disloyalty & rancour, & an element of weakness and discord introduced into our affairs. It is well worth while giving them their trophy, subject to proper conditions as to postponement of operation, and amendment.[19]

Winston also exercised his blandishments on Austen Chamberlain by correspondence between 11 and 14 September, but here he met with a reception as wounding as that accorded by Carson to Redmond. Chamberlain, the very mirror of uprightness and the soul of chivalry, was a zealot in this cause, and not prepared to make the most grudging concession even to an intimate friend. He ended the exchange of letters on 14 September in words of singular bitterness in a man so accustomed to polite intercourse – words that might have deeply wounded a man less self-sufficient than Churchill:

> The fact is, as you said to me on Friday, you 'do not care a damn about Home Rule' and you are utterly incapable of appreciating the feelings of those to whom opposition to Home Rule is a deep-rooted and sincere conviction. You have destroyed our belief in the honour of public men and have shattered the hopes that some of us entertained that union in the present crisis might produce a better feeling & greater agreement than would have seemed possible a few months ago. I see no gleam of light in the course that you have chosen. I would have staked my honour that you would not have done this thing and I am heart-broken to find that I am mistaken.[20]

Churchill replied:

> Compared to winning the war I do not care about Home Rule but that does not mean that apart from the comparison I do not care about it or think it a wise and helpful policy.
>
> With deep regret I must realize that we cannot understand each other's point of view and it remains for us to confront you with successful results at home as well as abroad.

* * *

19. Robert Cecil papers, British Museum.
20. Austen Chamberlain papers. AC/32.

The Home Rule Bill received the Royal Assent on 18 September 1914. It was accompanied by a Suspensory Act which postponed its operation until the end of the war. The lesser tragedy was thus submerged for four years in the greater; and when war came the ranks were temporarily closed.

We have seen that Winston Churchill, in spite of devouring anxieties at the Admiralty, played a leading and dominant part in the Irish struggle. His actions were sometimes marked by ineptitude but always by benevolent intention. His influence behind the scenes was a moderating one, and he perceived the intractable problem of Ulster far more clearly than many of his colleagues. His desire for a settlement was obvious, but much of the advantage gained by moderation was dissipated by public truculence. He devoted so much of his time and thought to the subject partly, at least, because the disputes in the Cabinet over the Naval Estimates made him feel that he was losing ground in his own party and that his position required strengthening. He believed that he had tried to introduce sanity into a situation which the Unionist leaders had whipped up into hysteria, and brought to the brink of civil war. Austen Chamberlain went too far in saying that he did 'not care a damn for Home Rule', as later events proved. His own position certainly ranked high in his mind, which was otherwise focused stonily on the German menace and naval dispositions. He would claim that he had continued his efforts to find a settlement until the early months of 1914, when he suddenly determined to force the issue.

Chapter 12

Prelude at the Admiralty

The Agadir incident finally caused Churchill to abandon any thought of an isolationist attitude, of which he had shown some sign at the Board of Trade and the Home Office . This crisis, which had burst upon the world, and particularly on rich and torpid England in July 1911, brought a sudden sense of impending doom. The Germans had sent the gunboat *Panther* to the port of Agadir on the Moroccan coast, in Asquith's sardonic phrase, 'in ostensible defence of some non-existent German interests against imaginary perils.'[1] This action, in the midst of German negotiations with France on Morocco and the French Congo, brought Europe to the verge of war.

By the terms of the Anglo-French Agreement of 1904, Great Britain could not remain indifferent if, as seemed possible, the Germans intended to establish a naval base on the Atlantic coast. To emphasize the fact, Sir Edward Grey told the German Ambassador, Count Metternich, that the British Government could not disinterest themselves in Morocco and awaited a disclosure of German intentions. A fortnight having passed without a reply, Lloyd George suddenly decided to take a decisive step. This incalculable man, who had always abhorred militarism and war, and who as a pro-Boer had run for his life from furious patriotic crowds, seized the opportunity of the Lord Mayor's Banquet to the bankers of the City of London (at which the Chancellor of the Exchequer is traditionally the principal guest) to utter a solemn warning.

He had already hinted to Winston that he intended to 'make it clear that if Germany meant war she would find Great Britain against her'. There was certainly no trace of the pacifist or Little Englander in Lloyd George's speech that night. Although he used no aggressive language, it was impossible to misunderstand his purpose:

1. H. H. Asquith, *Genesis of the War*, p. 91.

If a situation was to be forced upon us in which peace could only be preserved by the surrender of the great and beneficent position Britain has won by centuries of heroism and achievement, by allowing Britain to be treated as if she were of no account in the Cabinet of nations, then I say emphatically that peace at that price would be a humiliation intolerable for a great nation like ours to endure.[2]

The German government was staggered by this response to their clumsy diplomacy. Misled, as so often on great issues, by their lack of psychological understanding of the character of others, they had assumed that any firmness by Britain would be subdued by the champions of 'peace at any price', led by Lloyd George. The well-meaning but deluded Metternich was the next object of German resentment and made desperate efforts to retrieve the situation, demanding at one point of the Foreign Secretary that Lloyd George should be expelled from the Government. He was told by Grey that if that was his request the conversation must end.[3] The wretched man was recalled at the earliest opportunity.

Germany had received fair warning which caused her to hesitate on the brink, but it was for some time uncertain whether she really had recoiled. At least, she took heed of the *démarche*, and after much blustering resumed the conversations with France which had been so rudely interrupted.

On 6 August Winston felt justified in assuring Clementine, 'There is no doubt the Germans are going to settle with the French on a friendly basis. They sent their *Panther* to Agadir, & we sent our little Panther [Lloyd George] to the Mansion House: with the best results.[4]

But there was no certainty that Germany's negotiations with France would succeed, and they often seemed to be at breaking point. No precautions, therefore, were relaxed in Great Britain. The Fleet remained in a state of war readiness. The tunnels and bridges of the South Eastern Railway were patrolled round the clock; and in profound secrecy military conversations between the British and French General Staffs, which had been initiated five years previously, were accelerated and preparations began for landing an expeditionary force on the Continent. It should be remembered that while the earth trembled under the shock of Agadir and its aftermath, the Parliament Bill was engendering undiminished rancour, and the incredible heat-wave

2. Mansion House, 21 July 1911. Grey, *Twenty-Five Years*, Vol. II, pp. 224–5.
3. Stephen Roskill, *Hankey, Man of Secrets*, Vol. 1, p. 101.
4. Chartwell papers.

continued, bringing one burning day after another, and adding an enervating tropical heat to the general strain and tension.

* * *

As Home Secretary, defence and foreign policy were no part of Winston's business, but he now became obsessed by these themes. With a feeling of awe, not unmixed with pleasurable excitement, he sensed the approach of war. In August 1911 he went to stay with his friend Lady Horner at Mells in Somerset. She was one of the most remarkable women in England, the friend of Ruskin and Burne-Jones and other Pre-Raphaelites, and she was held in high regard by Asquith. The country round Mells was of exquisite beauty, lapped in stillness and peace. But this tranquillity found no echo in his heart. He could think of nothing but war:

'Sitting on a hilltop in the smiling country which stretches round Mells, the lines I have copied ... kept running through my mind. Whenever I recall them they bring back to me the anxiety of those Agadir days.'[5] In those peaceful scenes at Mells the lines from *The Shropshire Lad* were indeed charged with menace:

> On the idle hill of summer,
> Sleepy with the flow of streams,
> Far I hear the steady drummer
> Drumming like a noise in dreams.

> Far and near and low and louder,
> On the roads of earth go by,
> Dear to friends and food for powder,
> Soldiers marching, all to die.

An incident which had occurred in July emphasizes this new instinct of military vigilance. From a chance conversation with the Commissioner of Police at a garden party at 10 Downing Street Churchill learned that the Home Office was responsible for guarding the magazines at Chattenden and Lodge Hill, in which all the reserves of naval cordite were stored, and that they had been for many years protected only by a few unarmed constables. Shocked by this disclosure, he asked the Commissioner what would happen if a party of determined Germans arrived there well armed and at night. The Commissioner replied that they could do as they wished, and Winston abruptly left the garden party.

In a few minutes he was telephoning to the Admiralty demanding

5. *World Crisis.* See Abridged and Revised Edition, p. 57, and after Title Page - slightly different.

Marines to guard the arsenals. The First Lord and the First Sea Lord were away, and the Admiral in charge refused the request. Churchill then telephoned to the War Office, where he found the Secretary of State, Haldane, telling him that he was reinforcing and arming the police that night. Prompt and efficient as always, Haldane at once provided a company of infantry for each magazine.

This small incident, and the evidence it offered of a state of slackness and insecurity during a crisis which could result in war with Germany, so inflamed Winston's imagination that from that moment he could spare time for little else but internal security (for which he was in part responsible) and the military situation in Europe:

> It was only in a very small part of the field of preparation that the Home Secretary had any official duty of interference, but once I got drawn in, it dominated all other interests in my mind. For seven years I was to think of little else. Liberal politics, the People's Budget, Free Trade, Peace, Retrenchment and Reform – all the war cries of our election struggles began to seem unreal in the presence of this new preoccupation. Only Ireland held her place among the grim realities which came one after another into view.[6]

* * *

Winston Churchill had been a member of the Committee of Imperial Defence since his appointment as Home Secretary in February 1910, and he now seized upon every scrap of information that anybody could supply. Haldane requested his office to answer any questions Churchill might wish to put to them. With the gathering storm 'fiercely illuminated' in his mind, he plunged into foreign and military problems, studying every available document and extracting what information he could from the Foreign Secretary, Grey, and the Director of Military Operations, General Henry Wilson.

We have already met this bird of sinister passage in the Irish crisis. Insincere and dangerous, he was to pursue a career during the war of intrigue, disloyalty and opportunism, which was to be rewarded by his eventual promotion to Chief of the Imperial General Staff. At this moment he was in restrained mood, and offered sound advice. These meetings took place in August when Parliament had risen, and the weather was still tropical. Grey and Churchill often met in the afternoon, and afterwards strolled across the Park to the Royal Automobile Club for the refreshment of its swimming-pool.[7]

6. WSC, *World Crisis*, p.49.
7. Virginia Cowles, *Winston Churchill. His Life and Times*, p. 154.

Churchill did not share the optimism of the General Staff with regard to the strength and efficiency of the French army, and prepared a memorandum, *Military Aspects of the Continental Problem*, dated 13 August, for the Committee of Imperial Defence, in which he attempted, with almost clairvoyant accuracy, to foreshadow the course of military operations in a European war in which Great Britain, France and Russia were attacked by Germany and Austria.

> It was of course only an attempt to pierce the veil of the future; . . . to balance the incalculable; to weigh the imponderable. It will be seen that I named the *twentieth* day of mobilization as the date by which 'the French armies will have been driven from the line of the Meuse and will be falling back on Paris and the South', and the *fortieth* day as that by which 'Germany should be extended at full strain both internally and on her war fronts . . .' I am quite free to admit that these were not intended to be precise dates, but as guides to show what would probably happen. In fact, however, both these forecasts were almost literally verified three years later by the event.[8]

Asquith, whose legal mind was frequently exasperated by Winston's baroque exuberance, had always admired his clarity and vigour on paper, and, although the prophetic nature of this document escaped him, its argument impressed him profoundly. Certainly this paper was fresh in his mind when the Committee of Imperial Defence met at his summons on 23 August 1911.

The Services were represented by General Henry Wilson, for the General Staff, and Sir Arthur Wilson, First Sea Lord, for the Admiralty, who each expounded his views on the military and naval policy which should be pursued in the event of Great Britain being involved in war. There was an astonishing divergence in their opinions, and the performance of the War Office was so infinitely superior to that of the Admiralty that Haldane told Asquith that 'he could not continue to be responsible for military affairs unless he made a sweeping change at the Admiralty'.[9]

General Wilson had maintained at the meeting that the early despatch of an expeditionary force was a vital part of the plan agreed with the French General Staff. He had no doubt that the Germans would attack through Belgium, and that the six British divisions had an essential role in supporting the French left and in stiffening French morale. He asked the Admiralty for an assurance that these troops could be transported if

8. WSC, op. cit., pp. 55–7.
9. Haldane: *Autobiography*, p. 228.

the need arose. The Admiralty would give no such assurance, arguing that the German fleet must first be defeated. The British naval effort should be concentrated on blockading enemy ports, and then in landing detachments of the expeditionary force on the Baltic coast and the northern shores of Prussia. McKenna, the First Lord, supported the admirals, while Haldane with equal firmness backed his General Staff and urged that the Admiralty should establish a General Staff corresponding to that of the War Office, a suggestion that was immediately rejected. Haldane in fact had fixed his eyes on the Admiralty, where he saw much scope for his reforming zeal. Winston's eyes also dwelt longingly upon the same goal. Of this celebrated meeting he wrote:

> It was soon apparent that a profound difference existed between the War Office and the Admiralty view ... The serious disagreement between the War Office and the Admiralty Staffs in such critical times upon such fundamental issues was the immediate cause of my going to the Admiralty. After the Council had separated, Mr Haldane intimated to the Prime Minister that he would not continue to be responsible for the War Office unless a Board of Admiralty was called into being which would work in full harmony with the War Office plans, and would begin the organization of a proper Naval War Staff. Of course I knew nothing of this, but it was destined soon to affect my fortunes in a definite manner.[10]

*   *   *

At a moment so dangerous when 'we were in constant expectation of hostilities',[11] Asquith realized the havoc to be expected from divided counsels between War Office and Admiralty. He knew that Haldane believed himself to be the right man to perform the same miracles of organization at the Admiralty that he had already achieved at the War Office. The military office no longer offered any target for his reforming zeal, and his task there was accomplished. He believed himself to be the only person available and competent to create a new Naval Staff.

Yet although Haldane was his oldest friend, the Prime Minister hesitated before the prospect of introducing him as a new broom to sweep out the somewhat cobwebbed Admiralty stables, a move which would create apprehension and unrest. He was also reluctant to replace McKenna, for whom he had the highest regard, and it was not until the beginning of October that Winston received a summons to visit Asquith at Archerfield, a house lent to the Prime Minister on the East Lothian coast. Here, in autumn sunshine, he played golf inexpertly while the

10. WSC, op. cit., pp. 51–8.
11. Harold Nicolson, *Lord Carnock*, p. 346.

gulls wheeled above him, and the Prime Minister and his daughter Violet proved themselves equally incompetent on the links. There were some anxious moments for Winston. His rival Haldane drove over on two successive days, and was by no means pleased to find Winston so close to the fount of power, while Winston regarded Haldane's arrival with equal suspicion. Asquith's intentions were still not clear, and on one occasion he shut the two men up in a room together.[12] The course of events is best told in Violet's dramatic words:

> Winston left us for a night, I think to go to Dundee, and on the day after his return he and my father played golf together in the afternoon. I was just finishing tea when they came in. Looking up, I saw in Winston's a radiance like the sun. 'Will you come out for a walk with me – at once?' he asked. 'You don't want tea?' 'No, I don't want tea.' We were hardly out of the house when he said to me with grave but shining eyes: 'I don't want tea – I don't want anything – anything in the world. Your father has just offered me the Admiralty.'

Winston had for some time been uneasy even under Asquith's caressing hand, and he was for the moment as one transfigured by rapture, and already moving in a new and elevated atmosphere:

> I shall always remember, [she wrote] our walk through darkening woods down to the sea, where Fidra's lighthouse was already flashing out its signals and in his words "the fading light of evening disclosed in the far distance the silhouettes of two battleships steaming slowly out of the Firth of Forth. They seemed invested with a new significance to me."
>
> His whole life was invested with a new significance. He was tasting fulfilment. Never, before or since, have I seen him more completely and profoundly happy. The tide of happiness and realization was too deep even for exuberance . . .[13]

Winston never forgot this moment of exaltation, and the cleansing emotions of that memorable evening. Later he was to write of it:

> That night when I went to bed, I saw a large Bible lying on a table in my bedroom. My mind was dominated by the news I had received of the complete change in my station and of the task entrusted to me. I thought of the peril of Britain, peace-loving, unthinking, little prepared, of her power and virtue, and of her mission of good sense and fair

12. Haldane, op. cit. p. 236.
13. Bonham Carter, op. cit., pp. 236–7.

play. I thought of mighty Germany, towering up in the splendour of
her Imperial State and delving down in her profound, cold, patient,
ruthless calculations . . . I opened the Book at random, and in the 9th
chapter of Deuteronomy I read:

'Hear, O Israel: Thou art to pass over Jordan this day, to go in
to possess nations greater and mightier than thyself, cities great and
fenced up to heaven.

2. A people great and tall, the children of the Anakims, whom
thou knowest, and of whom thou hast heard say, who can stand
before the children of Anak!

3. Understand therefore this day, that the Lord thy God is he which
goeth over before thee; as a consuming fire he shall destroy them, and he
shall bring them down before thy face; so shalt thou drive them out, and
destroy them quickly, as the Lord hath said unto thee . . .'

It seemed a message full of reassurance.[14]

* * *

The step once taken, Winston was impatient to assume his new office.
The Naval Estimates would be brought before the Cabinet in November,
and the new Minister must have some hand in shaping them. Much
inconvenience would result from keeping the two departments hanging
in the air, and delay would be equally unpleasant for both Ministers.

On 20 October 1911 Sir Almeric Fitzroy wrote in his diary:

I saw Arthur Nicolson[15] at Brook's, who threw some light on Winston's
transfer to the Admiralty . . . He had told Arthur Nicolson that he
was thoroughly repentant of the part he had played in opposing naval
expenditure three years ago, and recognized the change of circumstances.
So much did he impress his hearer with the soundness and force of his
conclusions in the sphere of foreign policy that Nicolson assured me, in
the event of Edward Grey leaving the Foreign Office, there was no one he
would rather see there than Winston Churchill . . .[16]

On 24 October the change-over was finally announced:

Mr McKenna and I changed guard with strict punctilio. In the morning he
came over to the Home Office and I introduced him to the officials there.
In the afternoon I went over to the Admiralty; he presented his Board and
principal officers and departmental heads to me, and then took his leave. I
knew he felt greatly the change of office, but no one would have divined it
from his manner. As soon as he had gone, I convened a formal meeting of

14. WSC, op. cit., p. 63.
15. Afterwards Lord Carnock, a leading diplomatist and father of Harold Nicolson.
16. Almeric Fitzroy, *Memoirs*, Vol. II, pp. 456–7.

the Board, at which the Secretary read the new Letters Patent constituting
me its head, and I thereupon in the words of the Order-in-Council became
'responsible to the Crown and Parliament for all the business of the
Admiralty.' I was to endeavour to discharge this responsibility for the
four most memorable years of my life.[17]

They were certainly the most memorable years up to that point in
his career, and, before the shadows fell upon them, unquestionably the
happiest. For he was now at last conscious of 'walking with Destiny'. He
had authority over the greatest naval force in the world. No twinge of
morbid self-mistrust clouded his sense of triumph. He was determined
to master the new problems with an effort of concentration which even
he had never put forth before. There was a picture in his mind, clear as
a map, of the steps he intended to take. And he felt to the marrow of his
bones the traditional glories of his new office, the romance of sea-power,
and the part it had played in preserving England in the past, as it would
under his guidance in the future. This sense of history was strong upon
him: he saw it in the rooms in the Admiralty which had witnessed
transactions vital to England in the past; in the two stone dolphins
that guarded its entrance; in the furniture in Admiralty House with
its dolphin adornments, lovely relics of the days of Nelson.

But he was perhaps most exhilarated by the power to take decisive
action for which had long yearned. 'It was a joy,' said Violet Asquith,
'to see him buoyantly engaged in his new context, tasting complete
fulfilment. I remember telling him that even his brooding had assumed
a different quality. He travailed almost with serenity. 'That is because I
can now lay eggs instead of scratching round in the dust and clucking. It
is a far more satisfactory occupation. I am at present in process of laying
a great number of eggs – "good eggs", every one of them. And there will
be many more clutches to follow.'[18]

Even more was his imagination stirred by the mighty ships now
entrusted to him, the 'war castles foaming to their stations', and
by the part they would play in the destiny of mankind and the
preservation of Britain. He was to describe in a richly garnished
passage his first voyage in the Admiralty yacht *Enchantress* from
Portsmouth to the Fleet at Portland:

As I saw the Fleet for the first time drawing out of the haze, a friend
reminded me of 'that far-off line of storm-beaten ships on which the eyes
of the Grand Army had never looked', but which had in their day 'stood

17. WSC, op. cit., p. 63.
18. Bonham Carter, op. cit., p. 239.

between Napoleon and the dominion of the world'. In Portland Harbour the yacht lay surrounded by the great ships; the harbour was alive with the goings and comings of launches and small craft of every kind, and as night fell ten thousand lights from the sea and shore sprang into being and every mast-head twinkled as the ships and squadrons conversed with one another. Who could fail to work for such a service? . . .

For consider these ships, so vast in themselves, yet so small, so easily lost to sight on the surface of the waters . . . They were all we had. On them, as we conceived, floated the might, majesty, dominion and power of the British Empire. All our long history built up century after century, all our great affairs in every part of the globe, all the means of livelihood and safety of our faithful, industrious, active population depended on them. Open the sea-cocks and let them sink beneath the surface . . . and in a few minutes – half an hour at the most – the whole outlook of the world would be changed. The British Empire would dissolve like a dream; each isolated community struggling forward by itself; the central power of union broken; mighty provinces, whole Empires in themselves, drifting hopelessly out of control, and falling a prey to strangers; and Europe after one sudden convulsion passing into the iron grip and rule of the Teuton and of all that the Teutonic system meant.[19]

His mind occupied by such immense day-dreams, the problems of domestic politics, which had once so deeply engrossed him, receded and grew dim.

* * *

The most important of Winston's 'clutches of eggs', and the most difficult, was the creation of a Naval War Staff. As First Lord of the Admiralty, McKenna had declined to overrule the obstinate objections of the First Sea Lord, Sir Arthur Wilson, and the Board of Admiralty to this innovation, and this was the main cause of his removal. Churchill was totally unable to convince Sir Arthur of the necessity of such a staff, and it was clear to him that Wilson would have to go, and that a new Board of Admiralty must be constituted.

Sir Arthur was due for retirement in March, in the middle of the passage of the Estimates, a moment unpropitious for such an upheaval. Churchill therefore took time by the forelock and constituted a new Board with Sir Francis Bridgeman as First Sea Lord and Prince Louis of Battenberg as Second Sea Lord. He chose the youthful Beatty as his Naval Secretary. Perhaps he remembered the day when a young naval officer tossed a bottle of champagne from a gunboat on the Nile to a thirsty young lieutenant on the eve fo Omdurman. He had

19. WSC, op. cit., pp. 85–6.

never met Beatty since that day. On the advice of Admiral Fisher he also appointed Sir John Jellicoe, bypassing several senior officers, to be second-in-command of the Home Fleet, with certain reversion to supreme command in the future. These changes were announced in the House of Commons on 28 November.

Since their first meeting in 1907, Admiral Fisher, who was First Sea Lord for six years until 1910, and whose reforms had modernized the Navy, had exerted an extraordinary fascination on Churchill. He who was normally so insensitive to others was dazzled by this ageing naval genius – 'the greatest sailor since Nelson' – as by some spell or incantation. As soon as his own appointment as First Lord was assured, he sent for Fisher, then living in retirement on the tranquil shore of Lake Lucerne, and found him 'a veritable volcano of knowledge and inspiration'. Well knowing the turbulent history of this dangerous old man, and recalling, no doubt, Fisher's fury with him during his 'little navy' period, he had no intention at this time of recalling the stormy petrel to office. But after a few conversations the old Admiral impressed him so powerfully that he seriously considered placing him again at the head of the Naval Service; but apprehension of the renewal of old feuds and Fisher's advanced age caused him for the moment to restrain this impulse.

Fisher, none the less, remained his trusted counsellor, his oracle, and above all his friend. All was sunshine in the early phases of this disastrous partnership. The old Admiral treated the young First Lord with a breezy and indeed patronizing affection, and bombarded him with letters *de haut en bas* as from master to student, rich with heavy paternalism in which naval conceptions and doctrines are mingled with 'felicitous and sometimes recondite quotations, with flashing phrases and images, with mordant jokes and corrosive personalities'.

> I was regaled with eight or ten closely-written double pages, fastened together with a little pearl pin or a scrap of silken ribbon, and containing every kind of news or counsel, varying from blistering reproach to the highest form of inspiration and encouragement ... 'My beloved Winston', ending usually with a variation of 'Yours to a cinder', 'Yours till Hell freezes', or 'till charcoal sprouts' ... Alas there was a day when Hell froze and charcoal sprouted and friendship was reduced to cinders; when 'My beloved Winston' gave place to 'First Lord: I can no longer be your colleague.'[20]

But although Churchill was captivated by Fisher's bizarre extravagances,

20. WSC, op. cit., pp. 68–9.

he was sufficiently percipient to realize that there was something foreign to the Navy about him:

> He was never judged to be one of that 'band of brothers' which the Nelson tradition had prescribed. Harsh, capricious, vindictive, gnawed by hatreds arising often from spite, working secretly or violently as occasion might suggest by methods which the typical English gentleman are taught to dislike and avoid, Fisher was always regarded as the 'dark angel' of the Naval service ...

'Ruthless, relentless and remorseless' were the epithets he sought always to associate with himself. 'If any subordinate opposes me,' he used to say, 'I will make his wife a widow, his children fatherless and his home a dunghill.'

He lived up to these ferocious declarations. 'Favouritism,' he wrote brazenly in the log of the *Vernon*, 'is the secret of efficiency.' To be a 'Fisherite' – or, as the Navy called it, to be in 'the Fishpond' was during his first tenure of power an indispensable requisite for preferment.'[21] And in those strange, heavy Mongolian features was there perhaps a suggestion of a wild lack of balance, an arrogance almost verging on paranoia, which a more observant man than Churchill might have discerned? But Winston had no doubt of his own power to bridle the old man's dangerous caprices, and with Fisher's unofficial support studied his subject and grappled with his task. In the years that remained before the outbreak of war he spent nearly eight months afloat in the Admiralty yacht *Enchantress*. He visited every important ship until he knew 'what everything looked like and where everything was, and how one thing fitted into another. I could put my hand on anything that was wanted and knew the current state of our naval affairs.' 'He not only worked for the Navy, he lived for it.'[22]

Churchill's overall commission was to put the Fleet into 'a state of instant and constant readiness for war in case we were attacked by Germany', and the impact of his personality vibrated through the Admiralty.

> Our first labour was the creation of the War Staff. All the details of this were worked out by Prince Louis and approved by the First Sea Lord. I also resorted to Sir Douglas Haig, at that time in command at Aldershot. The General furnished me with a masterly paper setting forth the military doctrine of Staff organization and constituting in many respects a formidable commentary on existing naval methods.

21. WSC, *Great Contemporaries*, p. 261.
22. Cowles, op. cit., p. 159.

From all these sources Winston distilled a memorandum on the subject which bears the hallmark of his capacious intellect, and which he submitted to Haldane in January 1912. Haldane, that acknowledged master of organization, was deeply impressed by this document, and expressed his admiration to Winston in terms of ungrudging praise on 3 January:

> After reading it with close interest I can truthfully say that there is not a word I should have wished to change had I wanted to. In spirit and in substance it is an admirable document, and will mark a new and great departure in the history of the Navy ... This reform ought to have the greatest recognition. I am very happy about the Navy now. I could not have accomplished myself what you have done in so short a time, and the energy you have thrown into the general work is beyond praise. I am going to write to Asquith tonight to tell him so.[23]

Haldane may have been 'happy about the Navy', but a considerable part of the Navy was far from happy about the new reform. To many suspicious professional officers it appeared as a politician's device to undermine the authority of the First Sea Lord. Already they saw what they thought was the disease that would poison the fruit – the fact that that officer would necessarily be in frequent conflict with his subordinate, the Chief of the Naval Staff. Fisher wisely suggested that the two offices should be combined in the person of the First Sea Lord, and this proved to be the ultimate solution, but it was not one that Churchill was prepared to accept at the time.

The Germans had been strengthening their fleet ever since 1897 when a new Navy Law had been passed. This Law was superseded in 1900. In 1908 the Law was amended in a manner which made it clear that unless Britain increased her shipbuilding, Germany would attain superiority in capital ships by 1914. Britain therefore laid down eight Dreadnoughts in 1909, and we have already noticed the bitterness with which Winston, during his period of blindness, resisted this essential proposal.

In January 1912 Sir Ernest Cassel made an unofficial visit to Berlin in an attempt to obtain some mitigation of naval rivalry. Herr Ballin, a German shipping magnate and the Kaiser's adviser on maritime subjects, was his intermediary. Cassel returned with a statement of the new German Navy Law and an invitation from the Kaiser to the British Government to send one of their members

23. Chartwell papers.

to have discussions in Berlin. Churchill declined the invitation, which had originally been directed to him through Cassel. Sir Edward Grey felt that such an excursion would be premature for the Foreign Secretary, and it was finally arranged that Haldane should undertake the mission in February.[24]

Winston had planned to reinforce Haldane's mission by a statement of Great Britain's intentions in a speech at Glasgow. While waiting at the station for his train he bought a late edition of the evening papers which contained a report of the Kaiser's speech at the opening of the Reichstag conveying an ominous message of increases in the German Army and Navy. Winston seemed to detect a marked truculence, indeed a positive threat in the Emperor's words: 'It is my constant duty and care to maintain and strengthen on land and water the power of defence of the German people *which has no lack of young men fit to bear arms.*' [Author's italics.]

This arrogant flourish seemed to Winston unnecessary, provocative and demanding an answer. He would provide one in his speech at Glasgow. And here, on 9 February, he uttered words which caused deep indignation in Germany:

> The purposes of British naval power are essentially defensive. We have no thoughts of aggression, and we attribute no such thoughts to other great Powers. There is, however, this difference between British naval power and the naval power of a great and friendly Empire – Germany. The British Navy is to us a necessity, and, from some points of view, the German Navy is to them more in the nature of a luxury. Our naval power involves British existence. It is existence to us; it is expansion to them . . .[25]

This speech roused fury in Germany and irritation among Churchill's colleagues, although it merely conveyed the same warning as Edward Grey's speech in March 1909 which maintained that:

> Our navy is to us what the German army is to Germany. To have a strong navy would increase their prestige, their diplomatic influence, their power of protecting their commerce; but it is not the matter of life and death to them that it is to us.[26]

Now the Kaiser proclaimed Winston's speech a piece of arrogance requiring an apology. The term 'Luxus Flotte' (Luxury Fleet) became

24. H. H. Asquith, *Genesis of the War*, pp. 97–102.
25. Randolph S. Churchill, op. cit., Vol. II, p. 559 et seq.
26. H. H. Asquith, op. cit., p. 75.

an expression passed angrily from lip to lip, the word 'luxus' having implications in German absent in its English equivalent. Although, according to Churchill, Haldane found the speech useful on his mission because he had used identical arguments to the German Chancellor Bethmann-Hollweg, it was generally agreed by Liberals and Tories alike that 'Winston had dropped another brick'. Even the less offensive press commentaries included an element of derision, *The Times* observing:

> In short his text was 'We've got the ships, we've got the men, we've got the money too.' A more faithful expansion of the old saying could not be imagined and it will be difficult in future for Liberals to use the word Jingo any longer as a term of contempt.[27]

Conservatives were again delighted by what they saw as fresh proof of Winston's arrogance and tactlessness.

* * *

Haldane's mission was fruitless. All he was able to bring back with him was the text of the new German Navy Law, still unpublished, which provided for massive and continuous increases in naval strength. To the Admiralty the disclosure of this Law conveyed a disturbing message. For until they had studied the text they had imagined that new construction would be its most serious feature.

> But on examining the text they found that while the new construction was limited to three, or it may be two, capital ships in six years, the increase of personnel and the increases in vessels of all classes maintained in full commission constituted a development of the very highest importance. It practically amounted to putting about four-fifths of the German Navy permanently on a war footing. It would enable the German Government to have available at all seasons of the year twenty-five, or perhaps twenty-nine fully commissioned battleships; whereas at the present time the British Government have in full commission in Home Waters only twenty-two, even counting the Atlantic Fleet. Compared to this predominant fact, any alteration in the *tempo* of the proposed additional new construction appeared comparatively a small thing . . .[28]

It was, in fact, equivalent to a mobilization order.

Frustrating talks continued in London between Grey and Count

27. *The Times*, 10 February 1912.
28. Chartwell papers. WSC, Cabinet Memorandum, 9 March 1912.

Metternich, who was fettered by the closeness of his instructions and his imminent removal. Germany would not accept the Foreign Secretary's formula for a declaration of non-aggression towards her without the addition of the clause 'England will therefore observe at least a benevolent neutrality should war be forced upon Germany' or 'England will therefore, as a matter of course, remain neutral if a war is forced upon Germany.'

This brazen Teutonic request was completely unacceptable. Its acceptance would have disrupted the Entente by making it impossible for France or Russia to depend on British support, or for Great Britain to go to the aid of France should Germany, in a war 'forced upon her', attack France and seek to gain possession of the Channel ports. The conversations therefore ended in failure, with Germany refusing to make the slightest modification in her naval programme.

When introducing his first Naval Estimates in March Churchill clearly announced British policy – 'Sixty per cent in Dreadnoughts over Germany as long as she adhered to her present declared programme, and two keels to one for every additional ship laid down by her.' Presumably thinking that public opinion was still unprepared for increased Estimates, he confined himself to £44 million, which was not above the figure McKenna had had in mind for 1912. In July, however, it was necessary to introduce Supplementary Naval Estimates of £5 million, which caused Lloyd George – with how much jocularity one can only conjecture – to pass Winston a note in Cabinet: 'Bankruptcy stares me in the face.'[29]

In spite of the deadlock caused by German intransigence over the naval-construction race, the British Government continued its well-meaning efforts to placate that implacable power. The carrots of colonial advancement were dangled before the Germans in an attempt to appease their hunger – negotiations which they allowed to assume the appearance of success until *they* were at last ready to make war. With a similar intention Churchill proposed to Germany in April 1912 that there should be a 'naval holiday' from shipbuilding in 1913, an overture that was duly rejected.

To those who understood the character and mood of this formidable nation her unyielding attitude meant that she was bent on war. Such was the opinion of Arthur Balfour, who in a letter thanking Winston for showing him such documents commented on 22 March 1912:

29. Randolph S. Churchill, op. cit., Vol. II, p. 599.

I have read them with the deepest misgiving. A war entered upon for no other object than to restore the Germanic Empire of Charlemagne in a modern form appears to me at once so wicked and so stupid as to be almost incredible! And yet it is almost impossible to make sense of modern German policy without crediting it with this intention. I am told that many good observers in France regard a war in May as inevitable. Personally I am more disposed to think that, if war comes, it will come when the disparity between our naval forces is less than it is at present. But imagine it being possible to talk about war being inevitable when there is no quarrel, and nothing to fight over! We live in strange times![30]

* * *

With the First and Second Sea Lords and Rear-Admiral Troubridge, the first Chief of the new War Staff, Churchill reorganized the Fleets. The Home Fleet was divided into the First, Second and Third Fleets consisting of eight battle squadrons of eight battleships, each with their attendant cruiser squadrons, flotillas and auxiliaries.

One important result of the German naval challenge was the redisposition of the Mediterranean Fleet, and this subject was a bone of contention during the summer of 1912. Churchill believed that in the interests of security it was essential to concentrate the Fleet in home waters. In the past, and in a different age, the French had been the enemy in the Mediterranean: now it would appear in a new guise – Austria and Italy, who although they had as yet no Dreadnoughts would by January 1915 be jointly able to muster ten, a force which could overwhelm completely the British battle squadron of old battleships based on Malta. He thought that their crews would be more profitably employed in manning the new Third Battle Squadron so that it could be kept in full commission in home waters: 'The Malta Squadron,' he said, 'can do great good at home and no good where it is.'[31]

The Cabinet decided to withdraw the battleships, but held that Great Britain must still retain a force in the Mediterranean, and that a Dreadnought battle squadron should also be developed for service in that area by 1916. But even so, the withdrawal seemed to Churchill to carry a particular significance:

But the withdrawal – if only for a few years – of the battleships from the Mediterranean was a noteworthy event. It made us appear

30. Chartwell papers.
31. Ibid.

dependent on the French Fleet in those waters. The French also at the same time redisposed their forces. Under the growing pressure of German armaments Britain transferred her whole Battle Fleet to the North Sea, and France moved all her heavy ships to the Mediterranean. And the sense of mutual reliance grew swiftly between both navies.[32]

Admiral von Tirpitz, architect of the German Navy, had thus by his policy strengthened the Entente, causing England and France to draw closer together. It was in a sense characteristic of him that he should have calculated the consequences of these new dispositions, imagining that by forcing England to concentrate her Fleet in North Sea he had practically brought to an end her control of the Mediterranean.

Yet there was still a certain uneasiness in the relations of Britain and France, for there was no treaty of alliance between them. Nevertheless, the French were already enquiring, with obvious anxiety, about naval cooperation in the event of war, and in August 1912 the Cabinet sanctioned Anglo-French naval discussions. Churchill, while desiring closer Anglo-French relations, felt that the Government should not forfeit its freedom of choice in any future decision between war and peace. He thought it important to avoid a possible charge by the French that they had denuded their Atlantic seaboard and concentrated in the Mediterranean on the strength of naval arrangements made with Great Britain.

> . . . how tremendous would be the weapon which France would possess to compel our intervention if she could say: 'On the advice and by arrangement with your naval authorities we have left our Northern coasts defenceless. We cannot possibly come back in time.' Indeed it would probably be decisive whatever is written down now. Everybody must feel who knows the facts that we have the obligations of an alliance without its advantages, and above all without its precise definitions.[33]

The naval discussions were, for exactly this reason, far from easy, but the British negotiators remained firm, and the French were brought to realize that they could not be persuaded.

> We, however, declined to allow the naval arrangements to bind us in any political sense. It was eventually agreed that if there was a menace of war, the two Governments should consult together and concert before what common action, if any, should be taken. The French were obliged to accept this position and to affirm definitely that the naval conversations did not involve any obligation of common action. This was the best we

32. WSC, *World Crisis*, p. 81.
33. Chartwell papers. WSC, Secret Minute of 23 August 1912 to Sir E. Grey and H. H. Asquith.

could do for ourselves and for them.[34]

The Anglo-French agreement was signed on 10 February 1913. This bleak conclusion provided cold comfort for the French, and Winston's personal attitude appears to have been inconsistent, since it was he who, in the face of strong opposition, wished to withdraw the British battleships from the Mediterranean and yet did not want a definite treaty of alliance with France.

* * *

Towards the end of 1912 Churchill decided to replace the First Sea Lord, Bridgeman, by Prince Louis of Battenberg. Bridgeman had been in poor health. Churchill used this as a pretext for displacing him, but the First Sea Lord had no intention of going without a struggle. He produced doctors' opinions favourable to his cause, and an acrimonious correspondence developed between the two men. The dispute was given further publicity in Parliament on the Christmas adjournment on 20 December, when Bonar Law said that Bridgeman had been brutally 'ill-used' by Churchill, who at last closed an unpleasant episode by agreeing to a full publication of the correspondence between them in these words: 'If you desire that a further publication shall be made I shall not resist your wish. But I warn you most earnestly that it would be deeply injurious to your reputation. That is the last service which I can render to you.'[35] Winston's will prevailed, and Bridgeman went, but the First Lord undoubtedly lost some feathers in this unseemly encounter.

Meanwhile Winston's thrust and audacity allied to Fisher's genius was initiating a sequence of revolutionary reforms. They were united in the fervent belief that the supremacy of the Navy depended upon two factors – fire-power and speed. In 1909, when McKenna was First Lord and Fisher First Sea Lord, they had achieved an increase of 1½ inches in the calibre of guns – from 12 inches to 13.5 inches – and in 1912 twelve ships were building with this armament. It was entirely in keeping with his character that Winston should wish to enlarge these monsters still further, and when consulted on this point Fisher 'hurled himself into its advocacy with tremendous passion. "Nothing less than a 15-inch gun . . . what was it that enabled Jack Johnson to knock out his opponents? It was the big punch. " '

But no 15-inch gun had ever been made, and a certain doubt and even danger surrounded the project, its stresses still uncertain.

---

34. WSC, op. cit., p. 83.
35. For full correspondence between WSC and Bridgeman see Randolph S. Churchill, op. cit., Vol. II, pp. 628–39.

The safe procedure would have been to build a pilot gun and subject it to thorough tests before its installation in the new battleships. But this would mean the loss of a year, and in Winston's words, 'five great vessels would go into the line of battle carrying an inferior weapon to that which we had it in our power to give them'.[36] Many good authorities were for playing safe and forfeiting a year, and Winston was tormented by doubt. He consulted Fisher, who was 'steadfast and even violent and advised "Plunge".

'So I hardened my heart and took the plunge. The whole outfit of guns was ordered forthwith.' But he still felt a profound dread of the consequences of failure.

> Fancy if they had failed. What a disaster. What an exposure. No excuse would be accepted. It would all be brought home to me – 'rash, inexperienced,' 'before he had been there a month,' 'altering all the plans of his predecessors' and producing 'this ghastly fiasco,' 'the mutilation of all the ships of the year.'

It was indeed a fearful prospect, but it did not materialize. 'It proved a brilliant success . . . when I saw the gun fired for the first time a year later and knew that all was well, I felt as if I had been delivered from a great peril.'[37] This decision was an early example of Winston's radiant moral courage, of his willingness to risk extreme hazards when the stake was high enough. Even if it was, as some alleged at the time, a mere gambler's throw, it was an inspired one.

* * *

During the three years leading up to the Great War the strength of the Royal Navy increased to a greater extent than ever before. The main addition of strength was the creation of the Fast Division, five battleships costing £3 million each, of 75,000 horse-power, which could steam at a speed of 25 knots, mounting the new 15-inch guns and protected by thirteen inches of armour. The power to drive these ships at the four or five knots of extra speed required the use of oil, a more economical fuel than coal. The use of oil also reduced the time needed for refuelling and the labour and extreme fatigue of stoking, and enabled a ship of equal size to carry heavier gun-power.

When Winston went to the Admiralty in 1911 ships had already been built, or were building, solely dependent on the use of oil. A complete change-over from British coal to foreign oil was a decision of supreme gravity, and an expenditure of some £10 million was necessary

---

36. WSC, op. cit., pp. 87–8. The vessels referred to were the QE and her four sister ships.
37. Ibid.

to create the required reserves of oil with their installations. A Royal Commission on Oil Supply was set up, over which Fisher, who was called by his enemies 'the oil maniac', presided. At the same time, the Admiralty continued its search for oil, and Churchill sent a Committee of experts under Admiral Slade to examine the oilfields in the Persian Gulf. Negotiations led to the signing in 1913 of the Anglo-Persian Oil agreement and contract, which secured for the Navy a substantial proportion of its oil-supply and acquired for the Government a controlling share of oil properties and interests.

Winston estimated the return on this sum as £40 million, but with the enhanced value of the shares another £20 million could be added to this figure. This memorable transaction was described as 'the only measure of defence (with the exception of the Suez Canal shares) ever entered upon by the British Government which, instead of costing tax-payers money, has given them an enormous profit'. The credit of carrying through these contracts was due to Churchill alone, and to the forceful manner in which he dealt with the consequent Money Bill in the face of violent and ignorant opposition.[38]

These immense achievements – the conversion of the Fleet to oil, the Anglo-Persian Oil agreement which produced such a vast accumulation of wealth for Britain, the initiation and proving of the 15-inch gun and the creation of the incomparable Fast Division – alone in the years before the outbreak of war made Churchill's period at the Admiralty memorable, and it is certain that no other Minister in the Liberal Government could have matched his achievement. He had also laboured to improve the conditions and pay of naval ratings and to reform naval discipline and justice. He introduced a successful training scheme for young Warrant and Petty Officers so that those with talent could be promoted from the lower deck to commissioned rank.

There was a debit side to the balance sheet inseparable from this man's nature. Winston envisaged his task at the Admiralty as the responsibility for putting the Fleet into readiness for war. Nothing else concerned him beyond this absorbing task. He was autocratic and insensitive, and expected his orders to be obeyed immediately and without question. He was simply not aware of minor issues or the susceptibilities of others, and had such doubts occurred to him he would merely have brushed them away like intrusive flies.

But here he was dealing with the leaders of a great Service and the inheritors of an ancient tradition, who had commanded battleships, and having risen to the top in their careers, were disinclined to be harassed. The result was that some of his colleagues

38. Admiral Bacon, *Lord Fisher of Kilverstone*, Vol II.

came to nourish deep, if misguided grievances against him, of which the First Lord remained in complete and blissful ignorance. But others were not left in this condition. Sir Francis Hopwood, who had been appointed Additional Civil Lord at the Admiralty by Churchill, was far from loyal to his chief, and, an assiduous gossip, found malicious pleasure in relaying the Admirals' grievances to the King. Balfour's secretary, J. S. Sandars, was also similarly free with his pen in letters to Balfour.

The grounds for complaint by Winston's colleagues reveal nothing more sinister than normal tactlessness and brusquerie on the part of the First Lord. He had sent peremptory letters to the Sea Lords couched in arrogant terms; he had shown great irritability and bad temper. And later he had travelled round the coast holding reviews and inspections without reference to naval opinion or regulation, and was said to have sent for junior officers and discussed with them the proceedings of their superiors.[39] If there was substance in these charges – paltry on the face of them – one can only comment that they would not have arisen under a more sensitive man. It is easy to imagine a Melbourne or even a Balfour smoothing ruffled plumage, and gently indicating the triviality of the offence. And if there was a strong undercurrent of hostility among certain officials at the Admiralty, it must be attributed to the First Lord's indifference to the feelings of others – to the fact that he was the man he was, and that nothing would ever change him.

* * *

The Naval Estimates for 1913–14 provoked opposition from Treasury and Cabinet. Increased costs of shipbuilding materials, the addition of three battleships and one cruiser to what was already building, the rise in pay of naval ratings, the decision (to which Churchill had been opposed) to strengthen the Mediterranean Fleet at the cost of £8 million over the next four years were among the reasons which prompted the First Lord to ask for Estimates of £50 million. In fact he obtained £49 million. Even the prospect of war on a scale hitherto unknown could not blunt the innate pacifism of many members of the Liberal Government, who showed strong resentment at voting huge sums of money for weapons of war.

Churchill told the Chancellor of the Exchequer that in his opinion 'the proper and courageous action is for you to take Parliament fully into your confidence and to meet the expense either by new taxation or

---

39. Balfour papers. J. S. Sandars to Arthur Balfour, 10 October 1912. Royal Archives, Sir F. Hopwood to Lord Stamfordham, 9 November 1913.

by a substantial diminution during these years of strain of the Sinking Fund'.[40]

Long deliberations also took place with the Dominions on the co-ordination of Imperial Naval Defence, and plans for the exchange of manpower for training and contributions in shipbuilding were discussed and put in train.

In 1914 the First Lord estimated for a total expenditure of £50,694,800, and set the new programme out in detail in a memorandum dated 5 December 1913.[41] In 1913 the Estimates had had a rough passage, but in 1914 they produced a crisis and nearly brought about the First Lord's resignation. His main antagonist was Lloyd George, with whom his relations now approached breaking-point. Back with redoubled force came the Radical detestation of squandering money on the Navy in time of peace at the expense of the social services. If his colleagues in the Cabinet were deeply disturbed, there was also much uneasiness in the rank and file of the party, in which all the old doubts and suspicions were again being roused. They felt that Churchill was now obsessed with the mania of building up gigantic armaments, and that all interest in social reform had been wiped from his mind. To Lloyd George he now seemed so obsessed by his Navy he had lost all interest in home politics, and would do nothing but declaim about 'his blasted ships', or hold forth for hours about boilers.

Winston stood his ground with firmness. He was absolutely committed to four battleships. The three Dreadnoughts promised by the Canadian Prime Minister, Mr Borden, were designed for the Mediterranean, and the First Lord knew that he could not reduce his programme while expecting Borden to persuade a reluctant Canadian Parliament of the need for three battleships:

> How cd I argue in the H of C that the 'emergency' was so far removed that our forecasted programme cd be halved, at the very time that the unfortunate Borden was arguing in Canada that it was so real and serious that 3 ships must be built at once additional to the declared British programme? It wd destroy him. If on a general *revirement* of naval policy the Cabinet decide to reduce the quota, *it would be indispensable that a new exponent should be chosen* [author's italics]. I have no doubt at all about my duty . . .[42]

40. Chartwell papers.
41. Ibid.
42. Chartwell papers. WSC to H. H. Asquith, 18 December 1913.

Borden in fact failed to get his proposals through Parliament in time to
start building the three ships, thus making it necessary for Churchill to
add another £2 million to his Estimates. In the end, loyally supported by
Asquith and Grey, he prevailed over Lloyd George, and introduced his
Naval Estimates of over £54 million in a speech of two and a half hours.

* * *

Always receptive to new ideas and inventions, Winston from the first
had thrown himself with the avidity of a schoolboy into the fascinating
study of the art of flight. Always a doer rather than a watcher, he learned
to fly an aeroplane, although he never obtained a flying certificate. It was
not a happy experiment. Winston was too old to make a good or even a
safe pilot, and the marvellous aptitudes of youth were far behind him.
He was also, in the pilot's words, 'ham-handed' with the controls, and
his flying career was to end in tragedy, although not for himself.

He was sharply reproved by his friends and relations for this
dangerous self-indulgence. Sunny Marlborough sent him a severe letter
begging him to stop, and F. E. Smith wrote: 'Why do you do such a
foolish thing as to fly repeatedly? Surely it is unfair to your family,
your career & your friends.'

His incorrigible romanticism made him indifferent to these pleas, and
in May 1914 he spent two days at the Central Flying School, but in June,
in deference to his wife's wishes, he agreed, at least for the moment, to
renounce his new passion. 'This is a wrench,' he wrote to Clementine,

> because I am on the verge of taking my pilot's certificate. It only needed
> a couple of calm mornings; & I am confident of my ability to achieve it
> very respectably. I should greatly have liked to reach this point which wd
> have made a suitable moment for breaking off . . . Though I had no need
> & perhaps no right to do it – it was an important part of my life during
> the last 7 months, & I am sure my nerves, my spirits & my virtue were all
> improved by it. But at your expense my poor pussy cat! I am so sorry.[43]

This interest dovetailed well with his official work, and while at
the Admiralty Churchill founded the Royal Naval Air Service for
the aerial protection of harbours and other vulnerable points. By the
outbreak of war he had raised fifty naval machines, about one-third
of the number disposed of by the Royal Flying Corps. The War Office
did not look upon the First Lord's enterprise with favour, but, through
financial stringency, and as all the Army machines were assigned to the
Expeditionary Force, they were unable to provide for coastal defence
and were therefore obliged to put as good a face on it as they could.

43. Randolph S. Churchill, op. cit., Vol. II, pp. 704–5.

* * *

As a part of the economies sought by the First Lord when preparing his 1914 Estimates he decided that there should be no summer manoeuvres that year, and that a test mobilization of the Third Fleet should be substituted. The orders for this were issued on 10 July, and the test mobilization began five days later. A grand review of the Navy was held at Spithead:

> It constituted incomparably the greatest assemblage of naval power ever witnessed in the history of the world ... On the morning of the 19th the whole Fleet put to sea for exercises of various kinds. It took more than six hours for the armada, every ship decked with flags and crowded with bluejackets and marines, to pass, with bands playing and at 15 knots, before the Royal Yacht, while overhead the naval seaplanes and aeroplanes circled continuously.[44]

These tremendous armaments were his charge and his sole responsibility, and we can imagine the exultation with which he saw them foaming past the King – they were the true defence of the country.

The last sinister note in the overture was struck on 28 June, when the Archduke Franz Ferdinand, heir to the Austrian throne, was murdered by a Bosnian terrorist at Sarajevo; but, familiar with ghastly events in the Balkans, the British public had not been unduly disturbed. However, the storm signals were out, and they should have been clear enough to disturb the dullest mind. While the Government was harassed by the Irish crisis, and while the Cabinet 'toiled around the muddy byways of Fermanagh and Tyrone', the text of the Austrian note to Serbia was brought to the Foreign Office.

This note was clearly an ultimatum; but it was an ultimatum such as never been penned in modern times.[45] The Prime Minister's entry in his diary for 24 July gives a brief and succinct account of the Cabinet meeting:

> At 3.15 we had a Cabinet, where there was a lot of talk about Ulster, but the real interest was Grey's statement of the European situation, which is about as bad as it can possibly be. Austria has sent a bullying and humiliating note to Serbia, who cannot possibly comply with it, and demands an answer in 48 hours – failing which she will march. This means almost inevitably that Russia will come on the scene in defence of Serbia,

44. WSC, op. cit., p. 109.
45. Ibid.

and if so it is difficult both for Germany and France to refrain from lending a hand. So that we are within measurable distance of Armageddon.[46]

On 25 July Serbia replied to the Austrian ultimatum accepting her demands on all essential points, but Austria was 'resolved upon a complete and final humiliation', and broke off diplomatic relations with Belgrade that day. 'The Austrians,' said Asquith, 'are quite the stupidest people in Europe. There is a brutality about their procedure which will make most people think that this is a case of a big power wantonly bullying a little one. Anyhow, it is the most dangerous situation of the last forty years.'[47]

At such a moment Churchill was at his most inspired. On 26 July, Prince Louis of Battenberg, after speaking to Churchill by telephone, ordered the fleet, assembled at Portland, not to disperse. This decisive act ensured Britain's control of the naval situation a week before war was declared.

The Cabinet was divided, but Churchill had no doubts.

> His position was clear from the outset, and his principal contribution was to put pressure on Lloyd George, who was at first opposed to intervention, became hesitant, and finally cast his vote emphatically for war. Morley detected in this conversion the arguments of 'the splendid *condottiere* at the Admiralty' and Lloyd George's calculations of personal advantage.[48]

The crisis developed with ominous fatality. The Tsar promised to stand by Serbia, and a day later Austria declared war on that small kingdom. The dispute had now ceased to be a local one between Austro-Hungary and Serbia. If Austria were attacked by Russia, Germany must support her ally, and France, as an ally of Russia, would be embroiled. In Downing Street the Foreign Secretary continued to urge mediation by any method acceptable to Germany.

*   *   *

On 28 July Churchill, with the approval of the Prime Minister – but without the knowledge of the Cabinet – decided to send the Fleet secretly to its war station at Scapa Flow.

In the early morning of 29 July, the Grand Fleet sailed from Portland for the Orkneys, thus controlling the North Sea, and at the Cabinet on 1 August Winston asked for, and was refused, permission to begin full

46. H. H. Asquith, *Memories and Reflections*, Vol. II, p. 5.
47. Ibid.
48. Rhodes James, op. cit., p. 51.

naval mobilization. He explained in *The World Crisis* that his colleagues 'took the view after a sharp discussion that the step was not necessary to our safety'. Winston was obviously appalled by the blindness of many Liberal Ministers, and gave the meeting the rough side of his tongue, causing Asquith to report:

> Grey declares that if an out-and-out and uncompromising policy of non-intervention at all costs is adopted he will go. Winston very bellicose and demanding immediate mobilization. The main controversy pivots upon Belgium and its neutrality. I am still not quite hopeless about peace, though far from hopeful, but if it comes to war I feel sure that we shall have a split. Of course if Grey went I should go and the whole thing would split up . . .[49]

On that Saturday night Winston dined alone at the Admiralty, and sat reading the foreign telegrams which came at short intervals in red Foreign Office boxes. At last one arrived with the news that Germany had declared war on Russia. He knew that this was the writing on the wall, and sent a letter to Clementine, who was with the children at Cromer,

> Cat dear,
> It is all up. Germany has quenched the last hopes of peace by declaring war on Russia, and the declaration against France is momentarily expected. I profoundly understand your views. But the world has gone mad – & we must look after ourselves – & our friends. It would be good of you to come for a day or two next week. I miss you much – & your influence when guiding & not contrary is of the utmost use to me. Sweet Kat – my tender love – Kiss the Kittens.

Then he took another brave decision. Walking across the Horse Guards to 10 Downing Street, he found the Prime Minister with Grey, Haldane and Crewe. He told Asquith that he intended to mobilize the Navy instantly in the teeth of the Cabinet refusal, and that he would take full responsibility for his action at the meeting on Sunday morning. Asquith, still feeling bound by the Cabinet decision, 'looked at me with a hard stare and gave a sort of grunt', which Winston interpreted as agreement. He had no legal authority for calling up the Naval Reserves, but felt sure that the Fleet men would unquestioningly answer the summons. The vital decision was temporarily concealed from the Cabinet.

By 2 August Asquith believed that 'Things are pretty black. Germany is now in active war with both Russia and France and the Germans

49. H. H. Asquith, op. cit., pp. 7–8, 1 August 1914.

have violated the neutrality of Luxembourg.' Lichnowsky, the German ambassador, called upon him and, dissolving into tears, besought the Prime Minister not to side with France.

> Then we had a long Cabinet from 11 till nearly 2, which very soon revealed that we were on the brink of a split. We agreed at last with some difficulty that Grey should be authorized to tell Cambon [French Ambassador] that our fleet would not allow the German fleet to make the Channel a base of hostile operations. John Burns at once resigned . . . There is a strong party against any kind of intervention in any event. Grey, of course, will never consent to this and I shall not separate myself from him. Crewe, McKenna and Samuel are a moderating intermediate body. Bonar Law writes that the Opposition will back us up in any measure we may take for the support of France and Russia. I suppose a good number of our own party in the House of Commons are for absolute non-interference. It will be a shocking thing if at such a moment we break up.

In fact only Morley and Burns resigned from the Government. Beauchamp and Simon were persuaded to remain, although they could hardly have been described as a source of strength or courage. On 4 August, Asquith, describing the Cabinet meeting at which he received the news that the Germans had entered Belgium, and at which it was decided to send them an ultimatum expiring at midnight, remarked, 'Winston, who has got on all his war-paint, is longing for a sea-fight in the early hours of the morning to result in the sinking of the *Goeben*. The whole thing fills me with sadness.'[50]

Churchill was mainly concerned with bringing the Fleet to a state of full preparations, and in this he was successful. On the day before he sent the First Fleet on that secret journey to its northern station he was able to report to the King:

> The Second Fleet will assemble at Portland as soon as its men return in the ordinary course from leave on Friday. The Patrol flotillas have been raised to full strength and are moving in succession to their war stations. The two Irish blockades have been abandoned and all vessels engaged in them will conform to the general dispositions. The aircraft are collected at and around the estuary of the Thames to guard against airship attack . . . The reserves of oil & coal arrangements are satisfactory. The reserves of ammunition show large surpluses. The torpedo reserve is complete. There will be no deficiency of officers on a complete mobilization & we shall have at least 20,000 Reservists for whom no room can be found in any ship to send to sea.[51]

50. H. H. Asquith, op. cit., Vol. II, p. 21.
51. Royal Archives, WSC to the King, 28 July 1914.

And to his wife he wrote on the same day a letter which clearly reveals the quicksilver excitement of his mind and his ambivalence in the face of war:

> Everything tends towards catastrophe & collapse. I am interested, geared up & happy. Is it not horrible to be built like that? The preparations have a hideous fascination for me. I pray to God to forgive me for such fearful moods of levity. Yet I would do my best for peace, & nothing wd induce me wrongfully to strike the blow. I cannot feel that we in this island are in any serious degree responsible for the wave of madness wh has swept the mind of Christendom. No one can measure the consequences. I wondered whether those stupid Kings & Emperors cd not assemble together & revivify kingship by saving the nations from hell, but we all drift on in a kind of cataleptic trance. As if it was somebody else's operation! . . .

And then his excitement irrupts into the letter:

> We are putting the whole Navy into fighting trim (bar the reserve). And all seems quite sound & thorough. The sailors are thrilled and confident. Every supply is up to the prescribed standard. Everything is ready as it has never been before. And we are awake to the tips of our fingers. But war is the Unknown & the Unexpected! God guard us and our long accumulated inheritance. You know how willingly & proudly I wd risk – or give – if need be – my period of existence to keep this country great & famous & prosperous & free . . . I feel sure however that if war comes we shall give them a good drubbing . . .[52]

* * *

Asquith can have felt no surprise that Winston, during this supreme crisis, was 'bellicose', or that he had donned all his war-paint. His whole character was in startling contrast to most of his vacillating colleagues. To the majority of the Liberal Ministers war was the ultimate evil, and the military art an arcane and odious necessity indulged at the expense of social reform. They neither understood it nor wished to understand it. But Churchill, although he had witnessed at first hand the horrors of war, and understood from personal experience its reckless profligacy, was still fascinated by the military process and the grand strategy of mass encounters. He was, as Fisher called him, 'a war man', and it is impossible to doubt the truth of Hankey's[53] words:

52. CSC papers, WSC to CSC, 28 July 1914.
53. Sir Maurice (later Lord) Hankey.

Winston Churchill was a man of a totally different type from all his
colleagues. He had a real zest for war. If war there must be, he at least
could enjoy it. Churchill's courage was an invaluable asset to the Cabinet,
to Parliament, and to the nation in these early days. When all looked black
and spirits were inclined to droop, he could not only see, but could compel
others to see, the brighter side of the picture . . . He brought an element
of youth, energy, vitality, and confidence that was a tower of strength to
Asquith's Cabinet in those difficult days.[54]

And to the gentle, bird-watching Grey, who, although he faced
the approach of war with composure, regarded it with horror:
'His high-mettled spirit was exhilarated by the air of crisis and
high events.' The difference between him and the others, as Hankey
discerned, was that although he would go to great lengths to prevent
war, his temperament could not permit him to regard its arrival as an
unmitigated disaster, but rather as a new field of interest offering much
scope to his own particular gifts.

Winston's buoyant spirits were indeed in striking contrast to many
Liberals in the Administration, at least twelve of whom were at one
time in favour of neutrality. It is difficult at this distance of time to
follow the reasoning of these men, some of whom believed that they
could avoid the approaching agony by weak evasions and a base
seclusion; who imagined that Germany was being dragged unwillingly
into disaster by the brutality of Austria, and that all were victims of the
blind forces of history. Those who urged neutrality or caution revealed
a total ignorance of the predatory character of the German General Staff,
and of the fact that the approaching war was no sudden madness but
a consummation long and coldly planned – that *Der Tag* had been for
years toasted in every German officers' mess – the glorious day when,
Russia and France defeated, that detested country England would be
rolled in the dust and ground to pieces by the *furor teutonicus*.

Winston later wrote:

The differences which had prevailed about entering the war were
aggravated by a strong cross-current of opinion . . . that if we par-
ticipated it should be by naval action alone. Men of great power and
influence, who throughout the struggle laboured tirelessly and rendered
undoubted services, were found at this time resolutely opposed to the
landing of a single soldier on the Continent. And, if everything had
not been prepared, if the plan had not been perfected, if it had
not been the only plan, and if all military opinion had not been

54. Hankey, *The Supreme Command*, Vol. 1, pp. 185–6.

industriously marshalled round it – who shall say what fatal hesitancy might not have intervened?[55]

As a result of his own unorthodox decisions, Churchill was carrying a particularly heavy burden of responsibility. If peace had been preserved it would have been necessary to justify those measures to a Liberal and largely pacifist House of Commons whose furious reaction could be all too readily foreseen. It was not possible to discuss all technical details in that unwarlike Cabinet, and although the decision to move the Fleet to Scapa Flow had the approval of the Prime Minister, it had never been discussed there. Churchill's decision to mobilize the Navy had been taken in the face of a positive Cabinet refusal. But he was spared at least this unpleasantness by the fact that peace was not preserved. On 4 August as the chimes of Big Ben struck 11 p.m., the British ultimatum to Germany expired. The war telegram was despatched to HM ships and Naval Establishments all over the world:

COMMENCE HOSTILITIES AGAINST GERMANY.

55. WSC, op. cit., p. 137.

Part 3

The First
World War

Chapter 13

At War

At the outbreak of hostilities the post of Secretary of State for War was virtually unfilled. After Seely's resignation the position had been temporarily occupied by Asquith, but it was obvious that the Prime Minister could not continue to hold both offices, and a change was urgently required. Lord Kitchener was at that moment in England, and the Prime Minister summoned him to take the vacant post. No appointment could have made a stronger moral appeal to the whole nation, which had come to feel that it was impossible for him to fail. His name and fame placed him on a pinnacle above all other soldiers, so that he was in the public estimation an institution, a legend incarnate in his own time. His mind was powerful but inscrutable, and 'he had been so accustomed to deal with Eastern races that his approach to questions which called for decisions was slow, and sometimes tortuous. The sharp legal and political minds of his compeers were repelled by methods so foreign to theirs.'[1]

It was a fascinating speculation what the relations would be between this Titan at the War Office and the young Winston Churchill at the Admiralty. Past transactions between them augured ill for the future, and Kitchener's memory was known to be long and vindictive. We have seen how, as Commander-in-Chief, he had done everything in his power to prevent Churchill from fighting in the River War, but with all his might had not frustrated the young man's desperate ambition; and how when the war was over he had sought to exclude him from the victory march by placing him in charge of a convoy of sick camels as they slouched on their dusty journey along the Nile to Cairo from Khartoum; and how Winston had again foiled him by abandoning his charge. Lastly we have seen how the Commander-in-Chief was

1. Lord Esher, *The Tragedy of Lord Kitchener*, p.33.

forced to endure two volumes by the subaltern on the River War
in which his own conduct was subjected to blistering criticism. The
two men were the only members of this War Cabinet with experience
of war, and they met there on equal terms – Kitchener now sixty-four,
Winston still only thirty-nine.

At the first Cabinet after the declaration of war, Kitchener, according
to Winston 'in soldierly sentences proclaimed a series of inspiring and
prophetic truths'. Of these the most startling to his civilian colleagues
(who vaguely imagined that the war would be brief) was his confidence
that it would last many years, and that it would be necessary to raise
armies of millions and place them in the field.

Although Kitchener saw clearly that the struggle would be long and
bitter, and that Germany would never embark on war on such a scale
unless she was prepared to pursue it *à l'outrance*, he was thought by
many unwise and obstinate in refusing to use the Territorial Army as
the framework of his new force.

There was in existence nominally fourteen Territorial Divisions,
but Kitchener, who knew little about them, despised them as amateurs.
There was also, in that slow-moving mind, some intuitive instinct which

> led him to the conclusion that in order to obtain the vast numbers he
> had in view, as a voluntary offering from the youth of the nation, it was
> necessary to make a new and striking appeal upon fresh lines; that the
> essential point lay in the novelty of the summons he was about to issue.
> It was thus that 'Kitchener's Army' was born . . .[2]

When asked why he preferred raw recruits to those with years of
voluntary part-time training, he replied obstinately that he 'preferred
men who knew nothing to those who had been taught a smattering of
the wrong thing.' In this way he greatly increased his enormous task, and
when recruits poured in in their hundreds of thousands they found no
machinery to handle their training and equipment. In spite of Haldane's
pleas, he refused to use the County Territorial Associations which
existed for this purpose, and the birth of Kitchener's armies required
prodigies of improvisation.

*   *   *

Meanwhile Winston at the Admiralty had been agonizing over the
fate of the *Goeben*, the only ship in the Mediterranean faster and
more powerful than any vessels in the French Fleet, which he felt
would attack French troopships carrying their African army to France.
The Commander-in-Chief Mediterranean, Sir Berkeley Milne, had been

2. Bonham Carter, op.cit.

told on 30 July that his first task in the event of war would be to aid the French in the transportation of their African army to France. If possible, too, he had been instructed to bring into action individual fast German ships – particularly *Goeben*, which might interfere with French transports. News came from the Mediterranean on 4 August that the battle-cruisers *Indomitable* and *Indefatigable*, which could alone compete with *Goeben*, were shadowing her and her attendant battle-cruiser *Breslau*.

Winston's mouth at this moment watered for *Goeben*, and he believed that during the hours before the expiry of the ultimatum he held her in his grasp. From Asquith and the First Sea Lord he procured agreement that if *Goeben* attacked French transports British battleships should engage her. The Prime Minister, however, qualified his agreement by insisting that the Cabinet (which was about to meet) should first be informed. Before going into Cabinet, 'wearing all his war paint', Churchill sent his telegram to the Commander-in-Chief, but the Cabinet vetoed the decision until England and Germany should be in a state of war. The Cabinet felt in honour bound to observe the strict rules and formalities and held 'that the moral integrity of the British Empire must not be compromised at this solemn moment for the sake of sinking a single ship'.[3]

Churchill was therefore forced to cancel his authorization to engage *Goeben* if she should attack French transports. But the pursuit continued, although the Italian declaration of neutrality hampered the pursuing ships which were ordered not to infringe the six-mile limit off the Italian coasts. At 5 o'clock on 4 August the First Sea Lord remarked that there was still time to sink *Goeben* before darkness, but Winston, shackled by the Cabinet decision, could not issue the necessary order. It was hoped to sink her next day.

Excitement was mingled with Winston's terrible anxiety during that fruitless chase:

> Throughout the long summer afternoon three great ships, hunted and hunters, were cleaving the clear waters of the Mediterranean in tense and oppressive calm. At any moment the *Goeben* could have been smitten at under ten thousand yards range by 16 twelve-inch guns firing nearly treble her own weight of metal. At the Admiralty we suffered the tortures of Tantalus.

But the *Goeben*, as it happened, did not attack the French transports. Under cover of darkness she slipped away, outdistancing the pursuing battle-cruisers, and the German commander, Admiral Souchon, brought

3. WSC, op.cit., pp.132-3.

Goeben and *Breslau* to Messina on the morning of the 5th, where they lay coaling for thirty-six hours. While there Souchon received news that a treaty had been concluded between Germany and Turkey and was ordered to proceed immediately to Constantinople.

Sir Berkeley Milne sent two battle-cruisers to guard the northern exit from the Straits of Messina. He despatched *Indomitable* to coal at Bizerta instead of Malta, intending to watch to northward with his two remaining battle-cruisers and leaving the southern escape route open. It was then free to *Goeben* to escape south-eastward, or, as seemed more probably, to run up the Adriatic into Admiral Troubridge's squadron which was poised to prevent the Austrians leaving, or the Germans entering, the Adriatic. Troubridge at first decided to intercept *Goeben* on his own authority, and after reporting his intention to the Commander-in-Chief began to steam south, but having received no reply or orders from Berkeley Milne, and realizing the disparity between his own and the German ships, he abandoned the pursuit.

Winston was in a state of impatient suspense while the German ships were in the Straits and the issue still in doubt, for he was painfully alive to the havoc this German vessel would cause if she escaped his grasp, 'carrying with her for the peoples of the East and Middle East more slaughter, more misery and more ruin than has ever before been borne within the compass of a ship'. Admiral Souchon chose the easterly course to the Greek islands, steaming irresolutely about, and delaying for thirty-six hours to confirm that the Turks would admit him to the Dardanelles.

And finally, on the evening of 10 August, he entered those waters unmolested and lay at Constantinople for the duration of the war.

Churchill has placed on record in vivid prose and minute detail the reasoning and actions of the admirals and the misunderstandings which led to the escape of these ships, and on Prince Louis's analysis of Admiral Troubridge's report on this episode made the laconic comment: 'The explanation is satisfactory; the result unsatisfactory.'[4]

* * *

Meanwhile at home the Navy was instrumental in transporting the British Expeditionary Force, product of Haldane's executive genius, to France. This task, considered by many a hazardous operation, was safely accomplished between 9 and 22 August, while on 12 August the Grand Fleet under Admiral Jellicoe, the new Commander-in-Chief, sailed from its Northern Station.

4. Chartwell papers.

In deadly secrecy and without the loss of a single man or ship, the whole of the British Regular Army – six Infantry Divisions and one Cavalry Division – was safely transported across the Channel and disembarked in France. It was a triumph for British sea power, and for Churchill, who had the responsibility – a triumph that must have done something to cleanse his mouth of the bitter taste left by the escape of *Goeben*. Three days later the BEF was fighting at Mons. As well as this forbidding task, the Navy was required to convoy troops needed in France from all parts of the Empire.

On 18 August, when the news of the passage of the Army was given to the public, Asquith wrote:

> The curtain is lifted today and people begin to realize what an extraordinary thing has been done ... The poor old War Office, which has always been a by-word of inefficiency, has proved itself more than up to date, for which the credit is mainly due to Haldane and the Committee of Imperial defence. The Navy too has been admirable; not a single torpedo has slipped through either end of the Channel.

* * *

On 23 August British and German troops were fiercely engaged. Late that evening Kitchener described the situation to Winston, who found him still 'darkly hopeful'. The Secretary of State explained that it was still possible for the French, using Namur as their base, to thrust through the German lines, cutting off the German armies from their supply bases in Germany, and attacking them from behind.[5]

There were several aspects of the news in the next few days which seemed to Winston ominous in the extreme – the German capture of Namur, the clear threat to the 'naked Channel Ports'; and Sir John French had advised the fortification of Havre. There was also the unpalatable fact that the Allied armies were in full retreat, and Winston was shaken by the sombre words: 'It will prove a difficult operation if the enemy remains in contact.'

Then followed the dark days of the retreat from Mons in which the British Army often seemed doomed, and, while it was in retreat Winston wrote to his brother Jack with sombre hope. 'Our men seem to have stood up to them well & no doubt exacted a heavy forfeit. No one can tell how far this great adventure may carry us all. Unless we win, I do not wish to live any more. But win we will.'[6]

---

5. Martin Gilbert, *Winston S. Churchill*, Vol.III, p.54.
6. John Churchill papers, WSC to JSC, 24 August 1914..

* * *

A shaft of sunlight penetrated the gloom and anxiety on 28 August in the form of an aggressive and brilliant naval action, this time blessed by fortune and success. Winston had ardently wished to attack the Germans in the Heligoland Bight, and invited Commodores Tyrwhitt and Roger Keyes, in command of the Harwich Striking Force and the Submarine Service respectively, to produce a plan.

British submarines, prowling in the Bight since early August, had discovered the habits of the enemy, and knew that a flotilla of destroyers patrolled to the north of Heligoland during the night hours, and was relieved after daylight by another flotilla which carried out a less extended patrol. The plan was to take two flotillas and two destroyers from Harwich and six submarines, supported by two battle-cruisers from the Humber, and, reaching a point inside the northern coast of the Heligoland Bight shortly before dawn, to attack the relieving flotilla as it emerged. They would then turn westward for home in a long line abreast, hoping to meet and destroy the incoming flotilla patrol. On hearing of this enterprise, Jellicoe offered to send three battle-cruisers and six light cruisers in further support under the command of Admiral Beatty.

This action on 28 August, although marred by mist and faulty Admiralty staff-work in not apprising Tyrwhitt and Keyes of Beatty's presence, was an overwhelming and much-needed success. Flotillas and light cruisers were engaged in a series of encounters until 4 o'clock in the afternoon, and Admiral Beatty led his squadron far into the Bight. One German destroyer and one cruiser were sunk; two destroyers smashed to pieces and several others damaged. More than a thousand Germans perished, and 224 wounded were picked up and brought to England as prisoners. British casualties amounted to 35 killed and about 40 wounded, and no British ship was sunk or seriously damaged.

The chief importance of this action, apart from its invigorating contrast with the disturbing news from Belgium, was its effect upon German morale: 'They felt as we should have felt had German destroyers broken into the Solent and their battle-cruisers penetrated as far as the Nab.'[7] Naval losses of this kind were distasteful in the extreme to the German Emperor, who 'muzzled' the Battle Fleet. Von Tirpitz (one of whose sons had been taken prisoner during the action) protested against 'muzzling' policy, only to forfeit the Emperor's capricious favour. The Imperial resentment gradually increased until the architect of the German Navy requested his own dismissal in March 1916 after a further wrangle with his master over the U-boat war.

7. WSC, op. cit., p.183.

* * *

But the news from the armies indicated that Sir John French believed that his position had now become critical. By no means *en rapport* with Kitchener – with whom he had already begun to quarrel – French sent an alarmist telegram on 31 August which filled Asquith, Kitchener and the Cabinet with consternation. In it the Commander-in-Chief stated that he was no longer willing to co-operate with the French Army, and that he intended to withdraw his force from the fighting line and to fall back behind Paris.

This defeatist message reached London shortly before midnight on 31 August, and Asquith at once summoned an emergency conference with Kitchener, Winston, Lloyd George and McKenna. It was decided to send Lord Kitchener immediately to France in an effort to retrieve the situation. Winston provided him with a destroyer, and he was in Paris next morning and closeted with Sir John French in the afternoon.

The meeting was strained, and its harmony was in no way increased by the fact that Kitchener was dressed in a Field Marshal's uniform. Sir John French, whose fiery temper was belied by a somewhat bovine exterior, was bitterly wounded by this inadvertent slight. To him the appearance of Kitchener in Paris at such a dark and critical moment, as a Field Marshal senior to himself, was humiliating and injurious, and could only suggest to the French that as a senior officer had been sent, his own authority was in hazard. In spite of this unfortunate chance, Kitchener was able to report to Asquith later that evening:

'French's troops are now in the fighting-line, where he will remain, conforming to the movements of the French Army, although at the same time acting with caution to avoid being in any way unsupported by his flanks.'

Although the situation had been readjusted, Sir John was still simmering with resentment against Kitchener, and Asquith asked Winston to keep the peace between them. The employment of Churchill – so tactless, brusque and insensitive – in the role of conciliator was at first sight a strange one, but he and Sir John French were old friends. Winston performed his mission with unexpected delicacy, explaining with such skill the reason which had prompted the Government to make their *démarche* that French wrote to him: 'As usual you have poured balm into my wounds.' This was perhaps the first tribute of the kind that Churchill had received in public life.

Sir John's resentment of Kitchener was not easily quenched, and on 3 September he wrote to Churchill:

    ... K's visit was really most unfortunate – He took me away from the front to visit Paris on a very critical day when I should have been

directing the operations most carefully ... I do beg of you, my dear
Friend, to add one more to all the many and great kindnesses you have
done me & *stop this interference* with field operations. Kitchener *knows
nothing* about European warfare. Of course he's a fine organiser but he
never was & never will be a commander in the field.[8]

*   *   *

In order to make the greatest possible use of the surplus reservists
of different classes, the First Lord had in August 1914 constituted the
Royal Naval Division. This consisted of three Brigades, two composed
of men drawn from the Royal Navy, Royal Fleet Reserve, RNR and
RNVR, and the third consisting of men of the Royal Marines, including
Reserves of that Corps. The Division was under Naval discipline and
wore khaki naval uniform. Service was to be for '3 years or war'.
Two Naval Brigades went into camp on 19 August 1914, and the
three Brigades were fully constituted by 24 August. They were to be
available for service afloat should any unexpected need arise, but if
at any time the naval situation permitted they could be released by
the Admiralty and handed over to the Army for military service.[9]
The Royal Naval Division was in fact used as a land force in the
diversion at Antwerp, and was later handed over to the Army during
the Dardanelles operation.

The men of this force were regarded by Winston and his friends
as glowing with loyalty and enthusiasm and consumed by an ardent
desire to engage the enemy. Those who mistrusted the First Lord, on
the other hand, viewed with considerable suspicion the raising of this
new force. To them it seemed that Churchill's wild ambition, having
slaked itself at the Admiralty, was now urging him towards another
element, and one already engrossed by the Secretary of State for War
– that he was in fact about to encroach on Kitchener's territory. Nor
were the men in the Division as happy about the switch from sea to
land as Winston fondly supposed.

*   *   *

The rot in France had been stopped by the gallantry of the troops and
by Kitchener's visit to Paris; but there was still acute anxiety in England
over the thousands of missing men and the rumour that the French
were about to evacuate Paris. It was at this moment that the miracle
happened. The Russian armies had invaded East Prussia, and, although
they had been mangled in the marshes of Tannenberg, the Germans had

8. Chartwell papers.
9. PRO. ADM. 116. 1322.

thought it prudent to withdraw two army corps from Belgium. This withdrawal caused the German flank in France to become exposed, and on 6 September, in Winston's words, the French and British armies 'turned on their pursuers and sprang at their throats'. The great saving tide of the Marne had begun to flow, its 'miracle' to unfold and for the moment the German strategy in the West had failed.

The Admiralty was now stretched tight and working at a pace set by the tireless First Lord, whose day began at nine and frequently extended until two in the morning. He accomplished these exertions by that judicious use of the siesta he had learned in the dripping woods of Cuba. His task was to seize, and hold, supremacy on the seas throughout the world, and he was at all times conscious of that fact.

In August the Cabinet – looking, as Asquith said, 'more like a gang of Elizabethan buccaneers than a meek collection of black-coated Liberal Ministers',[10] – had drawn up a plan to seize German colonies in all parts of the world. 'A month before,' reflected Winston, 'with what horror and disgust would most of those present have averted their minds from such ideas!' But now it could not ignore the fact that 'our sea communications depended largely on the denial of these bases or refuges to German cruisers.' The Admiralty also carried the heavy burden of convoying troops from all parts of the Empire needed for France, and sometimes replacing them with Territorials from home. All this, he said, 'lay heavy upon us'.

From the middle of September the Admiralty came under its greatest strain. 'The great map of the world which covered one whole wall of the War Room now presented a remarkable appearance. As many as twenty separate enterprises and undertakings dependent entirely upon sea-power were proceeding simultaneously in different parts of the globe.'[11]

Churchill's responsibility was enormous, but still inadequate for his fantastic energies, and by the end of August he had become active in three elements – land, air and water. We have seen his fascination with the art of flight, and it was to be expected that his imagination would grasp, before most men, its future dominance and efficacy in war. At this time the number of machines was small, and they were divided into two separate independent air forces under the War Office and the Admiralty.

Kitchener, whose aircraft were engaged in support of the armies of France, invited Winston on 3 September to take over from the War Office full responsibility for the aerial defence of Britain. He

10. Asquith, *Memories and Reflections*, Vol.II, p.25.
11. WSC, op.cit., p.185.

accepted eagerly, and from that moment was in charge of the machines of the Royal Flying Corps earmarked for home defence, as well as the Royal Naval Air Service. There was full scope here for his energies, for air attacks on London were certain, and it was necessary to provide anti-aircraft guns and searchlights. He tackled the many problems of defence with his usual energy and confidence. But as in naval matters, so now, every instinct in him revolted against a purely defensive role, and he lost no time in deciding that his aircraft would defend by attacking, that they would locate the Zeppelins, smoke them out of their own holes and then destroy them.

On 27 August Churchill sent a squadron of Royal Naval Air Service machines to Dunkirk under C. R. Samson[12] with orders to establish an air base from which Zeppelins were to be attacked before they left on the last stage of their flight to England. Air bases were set up by Samson at Dunkirk and Calais, from which, according to Sir Sefton Brancker: 'with a handful of men, a few nondescript aeroplanes, and some commandeered cars with improvised armour, he was here, there and everywhere, terrorizing marauding Uhlans and inspiring French Territorials.[13]

One of Winston's objects in this enterprise was to put the Royal Naval Air Service to immediate military use and condition its pilots to battle. The RNAS carried out successful raids on Zeppelin sheds at Cologne, Düsseldorf, Friedrichshafen and other places, and within a year claimed the destruction of six Zeppelins on the ground and in the air. But there remained the problem of defending the air bases, and this need led directly to the development of armoured cars. All available Rolls Royce cars were bought by the Admiralty, fitted with improvised armour and used for the protection of Samson's air operations and his advanced air bases. The German cavalry quickly retaliated by digging trenches across roads, and by October these had reached the sea. Winston refused to accept defeat, and ordered that a method must be found of bridging these trenches, and it was at his direction that a car was designed carrying a bridge in front which could be dropped to cross an obstacle and then drawn up again behind it.

*   *   *

Another unorthodox sortie, first suggested by Hankey, and ardently supported by Winston, was the dispatch of a diversionary force of Marines to Ostend. As this enterprise was followed by much chatter and abuse at Winston's expense, it is well to remember that it had

12. A pioneer flyer of exceptional skill and boldness, and a Commander in the RNAS.
13. Norman Macmillan, *Sir Sefton Brancker*, p.77.

Political Life

Aged 24, Churchill stood for Parliament as Tory candidate for Oldham in 1899 and lost. *(Press Association)*

A portrait taken in 1904, at the time Churchill joined the Liberal Party, while MP for Oldham, a move that enraged the Conservatives. *(Topham Picture Library)*

(*Opposite*) David Lloyd George (Chancellor of the Exchequer) with Winston Churchill (then Home Secretary) in 1910. At one time Mrs Churchill formed the impression that Winston was 'completely under Lloyd George's thumb – wholly absorbed and fascinated by him'. *(Press Association)*

Churchill wearing a warm overcoat in 1912.
Throughout his life he was subject to fits of
depression, as his expression indicates here.
(Mary Evans Picture Library)

Leaving the War
Office. 1919.
Churchill was
Secretary of State for
War and Air from
January 1919 –
February 1921.
*(Topham Picture
Library)*

Churchill speaking at the Enfield Lock Munition Works in 1915. Mrs Churchill is seated at the table. *(Press Association)*

Sir Frederick Guest with Churchill who had just returned from a tour of Egypt (he was then Secretary of State for Air and the Colonies). Leaving the Colonial Office, April 1921. Guest was then Chief Whip of the Coalition Party. *(Press Association)*

Churchill speaking on behalf of the Liberal Party in Manchester in 1923. Front row figure with beard is C. P. Scott, editor of the *Manchester Guardian*. *(Mary Evans Picture Library)*

Electioneering: Churchill addressing brewery workers at Victoria in March 1924. At the time he was Independent Anti-Socialist candidate for the Abbey Division of Westminster. *(Topham Picture Library)*

Churchill and his wife listen intently to a question put to them on the same occasion. *(Popperfoto)*

Churchill speaking during the Epping Election in 1924. *(Topham Picture Library)*

Churchill, MP for Epping, Essex, was returned with an increased majority on 30 October 1924. Mr and Mrs Churchill being hauled in triumph through the streets after the declaration. He represented Epping from 1924–1945. *(Press Association)*

the highest official backing. The Prime Minister made an entry in his diary on 26 August:

> When I came back from the House I had a visit from Winston & Kitchener and we summoned Edward Grey into our councils. They were bitten by an idea of Hankey's to dispatch a brigade of Marines, about 3,000, conveyed and escorted by battleships to Ostend, to land there and take possession of the town and scout about in the neighbourhood. This would please the Belgians and annoy and harrass the Germans who would certainly take it to be the pioneer of a large force, and it would further be quite a safe operation as the Marines could at any moment re-embark. Grey and I consented ... Winston I need not say was full of ardour about his Marines.[14]

It should be added that the expedition also enjoyed Kitchener's full approval. The crossing of the Marines was not opposed by hostile submarines, and no men were lost while the Brigade was in Belgium. On 27 August Asquith noted:

> Winston has been scoring some small but not unimportant points. His 3,000 Marines have taken Ostend and are scouting about the country in the region and the *Kaiser Wilhelm*, a huge and armed German liner, has been sunk by the *Highflyer*.

In order to invest this little wasp's sting with the menace of a major operation, Winston announced in the House of Commons that a British force was in the process of landing at Ostend, and the consternation in the German command more than justified the whole operation:

> The German commanders were constantly looking backwards apprehensively over their right shoulders, fearful of an Allied stroke against their ever-lengthening communications in Belgium and northern France ... The earlier idea of landing the British expeditionary force on the Belgian coast had been overruled in favour of the policy of dispatching it, and attaching it, to the French left wing. But the Belgian field army, though under German guard at Antwerp, had at least caused a serious detachment of German strength to this guard, and was a chronic irritation to German nerves.[15]

The result of this impudent piece of bluff at Ostend was to induce a condition satisfactorily verging on panic in the German high command. On 5 September, the day when the French troops from Paris were advancing to attack von Kluck's First Army – the

---

14. Asquith's Diary [*Memories & Reflections*, Vol.II, pp.28-9].
15. Liddell Hart, op. cit., pp.184-5.

flank army of the German encircling movement into France – Colonel
Hentsch, the representative of the German Supreme Command, came to
that threatened army with the ominous warning:

> 'The news is bad. The VII and VI armies are blocked. The IV and V
> are meeting with strong resistance ... The English are disembarking
> fresh troops continually on the Belgian coast. There are reports of
> a Russian expeditionary force in the same parts. A withdrawal is
> becoming inevitable.' The 3000 Marines had now become, in the fevered
> imagination of the German High command, a force of 40,000 men, and
> the non-existent Russians a host of 80,000.[16]

The German flank army was thus left to face the ordeal of the
counter-offensive in the belief that its rear was seriously threatened,
and that its supreme command was contemplating a withdrawal, a
belief which insidiously weakened its purpose at a moment of strain. The
supreme command became convinced of the need of a retirement, and,
when Hentsch came again on 9 September with full powers to organize
it, he found that it had already begun:

The German retreat gathered momentum. With it the immediate
danger passed. We should not overlook the effect of Hankey's
inspiration and Churchill's implementation of it, helped by that strange
Russian myth, which may have originated from a proposal by Churchill
to request the despatch of a Russian expeditionary force to the Belgian
coast. The suggestion seems to have leaked.

*   *   *

Winston was soon involved in another colourful excursion far removed
from his official duties, which provided his enemies with ample field
for comment. In September 1915 Joffre asked Kitchener to send British
reinforcements to the Dunkirk garrison, to defend the city in the event
of a German attack and to alarm the enemy on his flank. The request
was submitted by Kitchener to Winston, who agreed to contribute the
Marine Brigade on condition that the War Office would add a force of
Yeomanry. It was perhaps unfortunate that Kitchener decided to send
a whole Regiment, and that the one chosen was that in which Winston
and Jack had for long served, and of which his cousin Marlborough was
Colonel-in-Chief; unfortunate, too, that this force, under the First Lord
of the Admiralty, should have required such an enormous quantity of
motor transport which had to be provided by the War Office.

There was therefore from the start a whiff of patronage about
the affair, and the fifty motor-buses from the London streets which

16. Ibid.

accompanied the expedition lent it something of the air of a harlequinade distasteful to many in the context of a bloody war. The 'Dunkirk Circus', as this venture was soon contemptuously called, appeared where it was least expected, showing itself unexpectedly in Ypres, Lille, Tournai and Douai, accompanied by a large reconnoitring force of aeroplanes. Winston found the greatest stimulation in this private army, and frequently crossed the Channel to superintend its operations. No casualties were sustained by the Circus in its *opéra bouffe* war, but the Prime Minister's benevolent approval became strained, and the circus was wound up.

Winston himself, this time with more reason, became the object of criticism and derision. What was he, the First Lord of the Admiralty, doing, it was asked, playing at Red Indians with this ridiculous force in the fields of France? Why could he not concentrate on his own office? Was it not his fantastic egotism and theatricality that caused him to neglect his proper work and become absorbed in such humiliating masquerades? His enemies, in full cry, neglected any useful reconnaissance work accomplished by the force and the absence of casualties; neglected also the fact that the enterprise sprang from a request by the French Commander-in-Chief, endorsed by Kitchener.

There were now sections in his own party in which he was held in suspicion, while among Conservatives, in Beaverbrook's words: 'He was hated, he was mistrusted, he was feared.'[17] To all these gathering doubts and fears his involvement in the 'Dunkirk Circus' marks a positive contribution, and it may be regarded as a small but definite episode in his decline at the Admiralty.

17. Lord Beaverbrook, *Politicians and the War*, Vol.1, p.31.

Chapter 14

Antwerp

The 'Dunkirk Circus', although a factor in undermining Churchill's position at the Admiralty, was only a minor one compared with the attempt to relieve Antwerp in October 1914, and later to force the Dardanelles. No event, with the single exception of the Dardanelles, did him greater or more undeserved damage than the Antwerp episode. Although it was Churchill's initiative, it was as part of an agreed plan and basically sound that the enterprise was launched.

The battle of the Marne had been fought and won, and the Germans driven back to the Aisne. It had been followed by successive attempts on either side to envelop the other's western flank in a process sometimes called inaccurately 'the race to the sea'. But before these efforts could reach a conclusion a new factor intervened. Antwerp, with the Belgian field army, was still a thorn in the German side, and they determined to neutralize it.

The danger to Great Britain if the Channel ports fell into German hands was obvious, and was always present in Churchill's mind:

> The struggle of *armies* and *nations* having failed to reach a decision, *places* recovered their significance, and geography rather than psychology began to rule the lines of war. Paris now unattainable, the Channel Ports – Dunkirk, Calais and Boulogne – still naked, and lastly Antwerp, all reappeared in the field of values like submerged rocks when the tidal wave recedes.[1]

Antwerp guarded the whole line of these ports and threatened the rear of the German armies in France. It was therefore of strategic significance to both German and British high commands. It was a strange omission that

---

1. WSC, op. cit., p. 200.

the latter had hitherto neglected to guard against its capture, although Winston, as First Lord of the Admiralty, had urged the necessity even before the battle of the Marne.

On 9 September the Emperor ordered that Antwerp be taken, but nothing was known of this until 28 September when the Germans began shelling the outer forts of the city with 17-inch howitzers firing projectiles of over a ton. The outer fortifications were quickly demolished, and four days later the King of the Belgians sent out an urgent demand for help, saying that without reinforcements the Belgian army would be placed in jeopardy, and that plans for evacuating the city were already in hand.

Winston was in the train to Dover *en route* to one of his jaunts with the Dunkirk Circus when this chilling news arrived. His train was stopped by a message from Grey to intercept him, and he hurried back to London to attend a meeting in Kitchener's house. Here he found Grey, the First Sea Lord (Prince Louis of Battenberg), and Sir William Tyrrell of the Foreign Office, who showed him the telegram containing news of these alarming events. It appeared that the Belgian Government had decided to leave Antwerp for Ostend, and that the King and the army intended to withdraw towards Ghent. It was thought that Antwerp might hold out for five days, but the British minister there, Sir Francis Villiers, considered that resistance would be briefer once the King and the Government had departed.

There was general consternation at the news, as unexpected as it was frightening. The Belgians had so far stood well, and believed that they could soon expect massive reinforcements.[2] It was incomprehensible that they should suddenly panic and throw up the sponge. The small midnight conference of Ministers, so hastily summoned, decided that Antwerp could not be abandoned without a struggle, although there are different versions of how the decision was reached. Grey recalled the scene with particular clarity, and if we accept his memory as accurate there can be little doubt that Winston responded with ardour to the challenge, and indeed usurped the function of leadership.

> Churchill's mind was already made up. Immediately he entered the room he said that the abandonment of Antwerp *must* be stopped, and announced that he was going there to stop it.
>
> I said something cautious, deprecating the enterprise, not because it seemed foolhardy or undesirable in itself. On the contrary, anything

2. The French had offered to contribute a division, and the use of the British 7th Division was contemplated.

that would avert the fall of Antwerp was worth much risk; and if, as seemed possible, the proposed abandonment of such a place was due to panic, the energy, resource and courage of Churchill might save the situation. But the risk of having the First Lord of the Admiralty shut up in Antwerp was startling. Kitchener reserved his opinion, while Churchill developed his plan. Shortly stated it was this. The Germans were not attacking Antwerp in force. One big gun was the sole trouble. This was knocking out, one after the other, forts that had been deemed ... impregnable. The German Field Force supporting this gun was not strong; the assumption was that the Germans could not easily or quickly strengthen it; if two allied divisions could be spared, the German force could be driven off and Antwerp saved. What was essential, therefore, was to delay the abandonment of Antwerp. This Churchill felt sure he could do by his presence there . . .[3]

Kitchener agreed to the British 7th Division, which was not yet in the battle-line, being diverted to Antwerp, and was ready to ask the French to spare a second division for the enterprise. At 12.45 a.m. on 3 October the assembled Ministers sent a telegram to Sir Francis Villiers emphasizing the vital importance of Antwerp's defence and promising to send a brigade of Marines that day, to be followed in all probability by heavy reinforcements from the main army. Winston's offer to stiffen the defence in person had been accepted, and the telegram informed the Minister that: 'First Lord of the Admiralty will be at Antwerp between 9 and 10 tomorrow.'[4] His mission was first to examine the position at Antwerp and report on it, and it should be noted that Lord Kitchener expressed 'a decided wish that he should go,' although other Ministers may have felt instinctive reservations. Asquith, who was not at the meeting, wrote:

I fancy with Grey's rather reluctant consent, the intrepid Winston set off at midnight and ought to have reached Antwerp at about nine this morning. Sir John French is making preparations to send assistance by way of Lille. I have had a talk with Kitchener this morning and we are both rather anxiously awaiting Churchill's report. I do not know how fluent he is in French, but if he was able to do himself justice in a foreign tongue, the Belges will have listened to a discourse the like of which they have never heard before. I cannot but think he will stiffen them up.[5]

3. Grey, *Twenty-Five Years*, Vol. 2, p. 79.
4. Chartwell papers.
5. Asquith, *Memories and Reflections*, Vol. II, p. 41.

Whatever the deficiencies of his French, Winston did indeed exercise a galvanizing influence on the wilting Belgians. As a result of his exhortations, at once hectoring and persuasive, they abandoned their intention of retreating to Ostend and prepared to defend Antwerp as long as possible, in the assurance of outside reinforcement. The two Naval Brigades of the Royal Navy Division embarked on 3 October for Antwerp: the Marine Brigade was moved to Antwerp that afternoon.[6] Kitchener was able to arrange for the 7th Division and the Cavalry Division to join the force as soon as possible, and received from the French the promise of the Fusiliers Marins and a Territorial Division. The British force was to be commanded by General Rawlinson and described as the British IV Corps.

We are safe in assuming that Winston enjoyed himself even more at Antwerp than at Dunkirk. He was in high authority and at the heart of a battle of great strategic consequence. One can picture the Napoleonic cogitations, the gathering together of threads, the frenzied activity, the melting appeals in atrocious French. It was as though he was reliving the dangerous but invigorating battles of his youth, and he was exhilarated by the experience. His old friend, Jack Seely, arriving in Antwerp from Sir John French's headquarters, found him at the centre of his web:

> From the moment I arrived it was apparent that the whole business was in Winston's hands. He dominated the whole place – the King, Ministers, soldiers, sailors. So great was his influence that I am convinced that with 20,000 British troops he could have held Antwerp against any onslaught.[7]

He achieved this predominance over others because he was, in his own eyes, the central figure in a 'tremendous and highly local situation' – the Man of Destiny. A. G. Gardiner had of old noticed his mien, sombre but resolved, his troops fighting in the last ditch, and looking to him for guidance and inspiration. His powerful but one-track mind was completely engrossed by the current crisis. His Marines were already fighting in the Antwerp trenches, and the rest of the Naval Division were soon to follow. The 7th Division and French forces were on their way. If Antwerp could stand firm until they arrived the ugly situation could be retrieved, but every passing day brought growing danger to the Belgian army.

Asquith was right in his conviction that Winston would inspire the Belgians with a measure of his own courage. He had appeared at their headquarters wearing the uniform of an Elder Brother of

6. Chartwell papers.
7. Major General J. E. B. Seely, *Adventure*, p. 189.

Trinity House and breathing fire. He lost no time in beginning the process of rehabilitation:

> 'Before the car had fairly come to a stop,' said a press correspondent, 'the door of the *tonneau* was thrown violently open and out jumped a smooth-faced, sandy-haired, stoop-shouldered, youthful-looking man in undress Trinity House uniform.
>
> As he darted into the crowded lobby ... he flung his arms out in a nervous characteristic gesture, as though pushing his way through a crowd. It was a most spectacular gesture, and reminded me for all the world of a scene in a melodrama where the hero dashes up on a foam-flecked horse, and saves the heroine, or the homestead, or the family fortune as the case may be ...
>
> The Burgomaster stopped him, introduced himself, and expressed his anxiety regarding the fate of the city. Before he had finished Churchill was part way up the stairs. 'I think everything will be all right now, Mr Burgomaster,' he called in a voice which could be distinctly heard throughout the lobby. 'You needn't worry. We're going to save the city.'[8]

And, although the defences of Antwerp had been reduced to rubble by heavy artillery, and guns, ammunition and other equipment were by now in short supply, he managed to infuse some of his own blazing confidence into the weary Belgian staff, and to convince them that with so much help on the way they could still continue fighting.

* * *

Winston was soon in such a state of exaltation that he convinced himself that if he personally was placed in command of all operations in the field, the city could be saved. On 5 October he performed an action so puerile and baffling that one is reminded of Lloyd George likening him to a chauffeur who, after months of impeccable conduct, suddenly drives over a precipice. His telegram to Asquith, wholly adolescent in character, places a devastating question-mark against his judgment and the sudden impulses of his mind.

In it he offered to resign his office at the Admiralty and assume command of all forces assigned to Antwerp, provided that he was given the appropriate rank and authority and the full powers of a commander of a detached force in the field: 'I feel it my duty to offer my services. I am sure that this arrangement will offer the best prospect of a victorious result to an enterprise in which I am deeply involved ... I wait your reply. Runciman would do Admiralty well.'[9]

8. E. A. Powell, *Fighting in Flanders*.
9. Beaverbrook papers.

This offer, which suggests an excitable boy who had been reading too many adventure stories, was read out in Cabinet where it provoked roars of incredulous laughter – described by Asquith as a 'Homeric laugh'.[10] So weird an aberration is a measure of Winston's utter absorption in the matter in hand, his delight in exchanging an office desk for a battlefield, and the romanticism which made him long to command great armies in war. It showed too his blindness to facts when his emotions were deeply engaged.

For he, ex-Lieutenant of Hussars, would if his folly had been indulged have been in command of two eminent Major-Generals, several Brigadiers and countless Colonels. There was little harmony in this war between politicians and soldiers, and one shudders to contemplate the shambles that would have followed. But stranger far than this was that he was prepared to leave his great office, on which he had lavished so much thought and effort, whose historic grandeur he so deeply venerated and in which he was one of the three men directly conducting the war; and, by a sudden instinctive option, chose to become a mere Major-General in the field, one among many others. It was simply not adult behaviour and revealed a startling absence of the power of self-scrutiny, as well as a deplorable black-out of judgment.

> He would be abdicating his part in the grand strategy of the war which he had always seen in world-wide terms, in order to play a personal part in a small patch of it. On the great issues of war aims and peace terms he would have no say. He would be exiled from the inner councils of the nation at the greatest crisis of its history. Had he imagined life without his telegrams and boxes, his access to the heart of things?[11]

He had not so imagined, being inured to this form of reflection, but his decision was no sudden brainstorm reached in the heat of battle and soon to be forgotten, for he renewed his suggestion to the Prime Minister when four days after leaving London he returned to the Admiralty on 7 October.

> Winston ... became suddenly very confidential and implored me not to take a 'conventional' view of his future. Having, as he says, 'tasted blood' these last few days, he is beginning, like a tiger, to raven for more, and begs that sooner or later – the sooner the better – he may be relieved of present office & put in some kind of military command ... His mouth waters at the sight and thought of Kitchener's new

10. Montagu papers.
11. Bonham Carter, op. cit., pp. 335–6.

armies. Are these 'glittering commands' to be entrusted to 'dug-out trash' bred on the obsolete tactics of 25 years ago, 'mediocrities who have led a sheltered life mouldering in military routine' &c &c. For about three-quarters of an hour he poured forth a ceaseless cataract of invective and appeal, & I much regretted that there was no shorthand writer within hearing . . . He was, however, quite three parts serious.[12]

Asquith, after receiving his first message, at once saved him from the consequences of his own rashness, declining the offer firmly and telling Winston that he could not be spared at the Admiralty. He returned to Antwerp.

* * *

Meanwhile Asquith, who was usually mildly diverted by Winston's private operations, found himself becoming distinctly irritated, an irritation which was to turn into black anger when the operation was concluded. The Naval Brigades sent at Churchill's urgent request, and largely composed of untrained naval reservists, had already arrived, and the main force of 20,000 troops was on its way. Among the reservists were the Prime Minister's third son, Arthur [Oc] Asquith, the poet Rupert Brooke, the musician Dennis Browne, and two ill-starred Oxford scholars, Patrick Shaw-Stewart and Charles Lister.

When Winston went to meet the reservists, he was able to indulge one of his most peculiar pleasures for he came immediately under heavy shell-fire. As he discussed the dispositions with the General in charge, 'the whole house thudded and shook from minute to minute with the near explosions of shells whose flashes lit the window-panes'. An Italian journalist reporting the siege of Antwerp was astonished by his calmness:

> He was still young and was enveloped in a cloak, and on his head wore a yachting cap. He was tranquilly smoking a large cigar and looking at the progress of the battle under a rain of shrapnel, which I can only call fearful. It was Mr Churchill, who had come to view the situation for himself. It must be confessed that it is not easy to find in all Europe a Minister who would be capable of smoking peacefully under that shell-fire. He smiled, and looked quite satisfied.[13]

12. Montagu papers, H. H. Asquith to Venetia Stanley, 7 October 1914.
13. *Giornale d'Italia*, 7 October 1914.

The Naval Brigades summoned by Winston consisted of some six thousand men, untried in battle, ill-equipped, only partially trained, and with scant military experience. Some of the harshest abuse afterwards levelled against Churchill was for his decision to send these 'raw astonished ranks to slay or to be slain'. Yet this motley band, a cross-section of all classes in the community – stokers, sailors, poets and classical scholars – fought with superb courage and played an essential part in prolonging the resistance, although before the battle ended many were killed, nine hundred were taken prisoner and more than fifteen hundred, losing their way, blundered into Holland and internment.

* * *

At Dover they had been embarked for Dunkirk, where Rupert Brooke imagined that they would spend at least a month in much-needed training. But they were told instead that they were to proceed directly to Antwerp. The officers had no revolver ammunition, and many men had never fired a rifle or dug a trench. On the way to Antwerp they were led through an armorial gateway into the grounds of a deserted *château*. It was night, and, as Rupert Brooke so clearly remembered:

> Little pools glimmered through the trees, and deserted fountains: and round corners one saw, faintly, occasional Cupids and Venuses – a scattered company of rather bad statues – gleaming quietly. The sailors dug their latrines in the various rose-gardens and lay down to sleep – but it was bitter cold - under the shrubs . . . But by 2 the shells had got unpleasantly near . . . and some message came. So up we got – frozen and sleepy – and toiled off through the night.[14]

These men were among the last to leave the stricken city, for Antwerp was now about to fall. In spite of strong appeals from General Rawlinson and Churchill to continue the fight, the Belgians decided that their communications were imperilled to such an extent that they must move their army across the Scheldt. Rawlinson, in view of the obvious exhaustion and imminent demoralization of the Belgian army, ordered a general retirement to the inner lines of forts which were to be defended to the utmost by the Naval Division.

Winston's little army held on to the last and then withdrew at night, marching for thirty miles through the shattered burning town, across a pontoon bridge over the Scheldt, earth and sky suffused with red from the flames, the river blazing with burning petrol. 'That was like Hell,' wrote Rupert Brooke, 'a Dantesque Hell, terrible . . . Antwerp that night

14. Christopher Hassall, *Rupert Brooke*, pp. 464–5.

was like several different kinds of Hell – the broken houses and dead horses lit by an infernal glare.'[15]

* * *

When Antwerp fell a savage inquest was opened, with Winston chosen and garnished for sacrifice. Venomous attacks were made on him in the Conservative press, and public opinion, ignorant of the strategic implications of the operation, was poisoned against him. This indeed was easily accomplished, for to the ordinary man the position was simple: Winston had descended, *deus ex machina*, to save Antwerp, and the city had fallen. There seemed no need to inquire further.

He was inured to hatred and abuse, and remained calm in the face of a failure so closely associated with himself:

> We have been so absorbed in events, that I for one have not given a thought to opinion. After all, in war results are the only things that matter. Success carries all before it, & no explanation of non-success is worth making . . .
>
> The loss of Antwerp was a bitter pang to me. But you must not suppose that sentiment dictated our movements. The sudden and total collapse of the Belgian resistance, & the diversion of the promised French aid, were factors that destroyed a good & reasonable chance of saving the place – even at the last moment. I take the fullest responsibility for my share . . .[16]

More serious for Churchill was the fact that the event had shaken the Prime Minister's confidence in his judgment. No longer the father-figure glowing with pride at his *enfant terrible* and tolerant of his lapses, he now wrote harshly to Venetia Montagu about the employment of the untrained naval reservists, and the brutal abuse by Winston of these raw levies with whom his own son Oc had served:

> Oc came to London yesterday & I had a long talk with him after midnight, in the course of which he gave me a full & vivid account of the expedition to Antwerp & the retirement. Strictly between ourselves, I can't tell you what I feel of the *wicked* folly of it all. The Marines of course are splendid troops & can go anywhere & do anything: but nothing can excuse Winston (who knew all the facts) from sending in the two other Naval Brigades. I was assured that all the recruits were being left behind, and that the main body at any rate consisted of seasoned Naval Reserve

---

15. Ibid.
16. Chartwell papers. WSC to Colonel Repington, 15 October 1914. General Joffre did not fulful his promise to send a sufficient force in time to co-operate with the British in the relief of Antwerp.

men. As a matter of fact only about a quarter were Reservists, and the rest were a callow crowd of the rawest tiros, most of whom had never fired off a rifle, while none of them had even handled an entrenching tool . . . It was like sending sheep to the shambles . . .[17]

Winston's defence of his actions, advanced later in *The World Crisis*, was that the naval detachments prolonged the defence of Antwerp for several days, but here he did himself an injustice, for they prolonged it for a week. The Belgians were on the point of surrender on 3 October, and the week's respite was crucial, as it almost certainly enabled Calais and Dunkirk to be made secure. Today Churchill's actions at Antwerp are seen to be largely to his credit, and the verdict of one of the leading modern military historians endorses this fact:

> . . . Viewed in the perspective of history, this first and last effort in the West to make use of Britain's amphibious power, inspired by Churchill, applied a brake to the German advance down the coast that just stopped their second attempt to gain a decision in the West. It gained time for the arrival of the main British force, transferred from the Aisne to the new left of the Allied line. While the heroic defence at Ypres, aided by the French and Belgians along the Yser to the sea, was the human barrier to the Germans, it succeeded by so narrow a margin that the Antwerp expedition must be adjudged the saving factor.[18]

Such considerations were obscured from contemporary vision, and Churchill was the obvious, the uncomplaining, scapegoat. At the Admiralty the Antwerp failure drove another nail into his coffin which was to be screwed down finally at the Dardanelles. Perhaps some obscure understanding of the public mood came to him later when, indirectly acknowledging the force of his critics, he wrote:

> Those who are charged with the direction of supreme affairs must sit on the mountain-tops of control; they must never descend into the valleys of direct physical and personal action.

17. Montagu papers. 13 October 1914.
18. Liddell Hart, op. cit., pp. 186–7.

Chapter 15

The Naval Scene

The Prime Minister had certainly acted wisely in rejecting Winston's quixotic attempt to lay down his office and years later Churchill came to realize the fact, writing of the Cabinet decision: 'I certainly have no reason to regret that they did so.' But he was at this time yearning for action and the stink of cordite, particularly the physical direction of battle. As early as 26 August he wrote to his brother Jack, who was about to leave for France: 'As soon as the decisive battle has been fought at sea – I shall try to come out too, if there is any use for me. P.S. The result of the big battle governs the future. We must wait.'[1]

That decisive battle in blue waters was not to be. The German High Seas Fleet, after its stinging reverse in the Heligoland Bight, lay low by the Kaiser's orders, licking its wounds in harbour, to the disgust of Winston Churchill and von Tirpitz. Winston, although passionately eager to bring it to battle, had no doubt as to the wisdom of the German policy. Writing to Sir John Jellicoe on 9 October 1914, he said:

> I am in full agreement with your letter. No change is required in the naval policy to which we have steadily adhered since 1911. The main point is to secure the safety of the British Fleet during the long and indefinite period of waiting for a general action ... The enemy, in my judgment, pursues a wise policy in declining battle. By remaining in harbour he secures for Germany the command of the Baltic, with all that implies, both in threatening the Russian flank and protecting the German coast, and in drawing supplies from Sweden and Norway. This is an immense advantage to the Germans, and this is the best use to which, in present circumstances, they can turn their Fleet. It is to secure the eventual command of the Baltic that British naval operations must tend. I have already pointed out, in papers which I showed you, the three

1. John Churchill papers.

alternative conditions under which this would be possible, and I hope that
. . . you will make a study of the actual method by which the entrance to
the Baltic could be effected when the time arrived.[2]

On 21 September Winston had indulged his frustration at the German
strategy by making a bombastic speech at Liverpool. Addressing an
expectant audience of fifteen thousand, he declared with ill-timed
annoyance: 'Although we hope the Navy will have a chance of settling
the question of the German Fleet, yet if they do not come out and fight
in time of war they will be dug out like rats in a hole.'

It was an unworthy gibe, for (as he had himself admitted) the German
Fleet was sequestered for strategic purposes. His audience rose to him as
a man, but public opinion thus encouraged was staggered by the news
next day that three British cruisers, *Aboukir*, *Hogue* and *Cressy*, had
been sunk off the Dogger Bank. Winston's stock, already depreciated,
again sagged, and in the irrational and resentful thinking of thousands
it appeared that the arrogance and *hubris* of his Liverpool speech had
been a direct invitation to disaster.

Churchill's relations with George V had never been happy in spite of
prolonged efforts at ingratiation by Winston, and at this moment Lord
Stamfordham wrote, 'Seeing . . . today the rats came out of their own
accord and to our cost, the threat was unfortunate and the King feels it
was hardly dignified for a Cabinet Minister.'[3]

But in this matter he had been the sport of cruel mischance. When
visiting the Grand Fleet he had heard Commodore Roger Keyes referring
to these three old cruisers as 'the live-bait squadron', remarking that
they were of the *Bacchantes* class, patrolling off the Dogger Bank,
and particularly vulnerable to German attack. Appalled that these old
ships had been exposed to such risk, Churchill ordered their instant
withdrawal. But there was a fatal delay in executing this order, and
1,400 men were drowned. An even worse blow followed on 27 October
when the Dreadnought *Audacious*, one of the most powerful ships in
the Navy, was sunk by a German mine off the north coast of Ireland.
This was a major blow to the Admiralty, and to Jellicoe, who begged
Churchill to suppress publication of the news. As the liner *Olympic* had
witnessed the episode, this was clearly a difficult request, but Churchill
persuaded the Cabinet to demand at least a temporary secrecy, although
the newspapers complied with ill grace.

* * *

2. Chartwell papers: 13/27.
3. Gilbert op. cit., Vol. III, p. 87 (Asquith papers.)

Churchill's reputation was now tarnished. He was smeared with the failure of Antwerp, and the internment in Holland of the men of the Naval Brigades was attributed entirely to his folly. A disgusting slander that the sailors in the three cruisers had perished because Churchill had refused to recall them from the patrol until it was too late was widely believed. The loss of *Audacious* completed this cycle of misfortune.

At this inopportune moment it was found necessary to unship the First Sea Lord, Prince Louis of Battenberg. The atmosphere of censure and reproach against those responsible for the conduct of the war, and particularly Winston's part in it, found another target in this blameless and dedicated man on account of his German birth. It is sad but not surprising in a country pervaded by an anti-German hysteria so intense as to cause dachshunds to be put down, German-sounding shops to be attacked, and trusty Fräuleins to be sent packing that Prince Louis should become the victim of a sickening witch-hunt on account of his German parentage. Although he spoke English with a thick German accent, the First Sea Lord was completely anglicized, and had devoted his whole life to England and the Royal Navy, being equally responsible with Churchill for the Fleet's readiness for war. No voice had been raised against him at the time, but now a poisonous chorus in clubs and newspapers was directed against him, while anonymous letter-writers added their pathological voices to the tumult.

Although Winston was as disgusted as anyone by this campaign, he had doubted for some time whether Battenberg was a man with the force and dynamism his office demanded, and regarded him as one exhausted by his labours.

'He [Churchill] has quite made up his mind,' Asquith wrote to Venetia Stanley on 27 October, 'that the time has come for a drastic change in his Board; our poor blue-eyed German will have to go . . . We both enlarged on the want of initiative & constructive thought of the present naval advisers . . .'[4] An additional pathos was lent to this shabby transaction by Prince Louis's last private letter to Churchill. His health had been seriously impaired by the merciless campaign against him, and he felt himself a broken man, but it is obvious that he bore no grudge against the First Lord and still regarded him with affection. Although there had been a painful interview between the two men, Prince Louis had carried himself with dignity and restraint:

My dear friend,
I am deeply touched by your letter, which shall be treasured by my sons. I beg of you to release me. I am on the verge of breaking down & I cannot

4. Montagu papers.

use my brain for anything. . .

Do me the favour to assemble the Board for five minutes this afternoon. If you would merely read my letter to you & say that you have accepted it, not another word need, or indeed should be spoken & I can leave the room after a silent handshake with my colleagues.[5]

* * *

This was an unsavoury episode with no credit to anyone concerned, and it was now necessary to find Lord Louis' successor. Winston at last decided (despite strong objections by the King) to recall the ageing Fisher from retirement, although he was conscious of the risk he was taking.

After their reunion had broken later in inconceivable disaster for Winston, he was fond of saying that he had taken his political life in his hands in making this appointment, and so it appeared to many. But apart from the spell Fisher always cast upon him, there was another compelling reason for his choice. Recent events had diminished his own stature at the Admiralty, and he was anxious to restore it. Conflicting with his doubts about Fisher, and overriding them, was his own conviction that this vindictive Puck, with his inventive energy and brilliant unorthodoxy, was the only man in the country who as First Sea Lord could perform this task. He deliberately ignored the fact that Fisher was now seventy-four; he disregarded his record of truculence and discord, and remembered only his genius. There was also a magnetic mutual attraction between these two men which drew them together to their own discomfiture.

'It was in some respects an inspired choice, for it brought back from retirement one of the most dynamic and determined men in British naval history; in others, it was an invitation to disaster, for Fisher came on his own terms and with his own ideas . . . Churchill was heedless of the many signs that Fisher was intent upon supremacy.'[6] Here once again we see Winston being deluded by his own lack of psychological perception. Had he noticed this tendency of Fisher's, he would either have tried to crush it or more probably have sought to disarm the old man by some form of cumbrous blandishment. As it was, 'Churchill co-opted Fisher to relieve the pressure against himself, but he had no intention of letting anyone else rule the roost. Here, then, were two strong men of incompatible tempers both bent on autocracy.'[7]

5. Chartwell papers: 13/27.
6. Rhodes James, op. cit., p. 59.
7. Beaverbrook, *Politicians and the War*, p. 98.

Winston overbore all nagging doubts – 'For good or ill I had my way.' Unfortunately for him, it was for ill, and the warm embraces between the First Sea Lord and his young master, those buoyant hulloos that had once flown between them, became sour and ended in the kiss of death. But at first there was no signal of disaster. The two blood-brothers swore that neither would take an important decision without the knowledge of the other. The working hours at the Admiralty were staggered to suit Lord Fisher's age and habits. Fisher would retire to bed at eight o'clock and rise, charged with energy, between four and five a.m.

Winston, who had carefully gauged Fisher's physical resources before appointing him, recorded that: 'as the afternoon approached the formidable energy of the morning gradually declined, and with the shades of night the old Admiral's giant strength was often visibly exhausted.' Winston adjusted his own working hours to suit Fisher's physical condition. He was called at eight instead of seven, took an hour's siesta after lunch, and was able to work into the small hours of next morning without the slightest fatigue. 'Between them this "unsleeping watch" was kept throughout the day and night. Winston's minutes were written in red and Fisher's in green.' In Winston's words: 'As long as the port and starboard lights shone together all went well.'

* * *

Certain other changes were made at the Admiralty as a result of Fisher's appointment, Admiral Oliver becoming Chief of the Naval Staff. On 4 November came the dispiriting news of the battle of Coronel off the coast of Chile. Admiral Cradock, commanding the South American station, had for weeks been anxiously scanning the horizon for the German Commander-in-Chief, Admiral von Spee, who had been roaming the Pacific unlocated, with a powerful squadron which comprised *Scharnhorst*, *Gneisenau*, *Leipzig*, *Nürnberg* and *Dresden*.

At the beginning of November the German squadron was at last located off the west coast of South America. Without the support of his most heavily armoured ship *Canopus*, which was too far distant to reach the scene in time, and without *Defence*, which had been ordered from the east coast of South America to support him, Cradock attacked the German squadron at 7 p.m. on 1 November with his flagship *Good Hope*, *Monmouth*, *Glasgow* and *Otranto*. In a battle lasting under an hour, and in a rough sea, Cradock's ships were illuminated against the sunset, while the Germans were shrouded against the dark background of the coast of Chile. The battle was quickly lost, and *Good Hope* and *Monmouth* were sunk with no survivors. This disaster was a heavy blow to the Admiralty, where the greatest anxiety was felt about the threat presented by von Spee to merchant shipping and to the New Zealand and Australian convoys; and there was criticism of the failure to reinforce Cradock with a faster and more powerful ship than *Canopus*.[8]

The action was also seen as a humiliating blow to British naval prestige, and as such it was represented by Asquith to the King:

> This mishap is the more regrettable as it would seem that the Admiral was acting in disobedience to his instructions which were express to the effect that he must concentrate his whole squadron, including *Canopus* and *Defence*, and run no risk of being caught in a position of inferiority . . . The Cabinet are of the opinion that this incident, like the escape of *Goeben*, the loss of the *Cressy* and her two sister cruisers, and that of *Hermes* last week, is not creditable to the officers of the Navy.[9]

After his victory Von Spee disappeared into the immensity of the Pacific, leaving alarming uncertainty as to where he would strike next. At this critical moment the genius of Fisher immediately asserted itself. He detached two battle-cruisers, *Invincible* and her sister ship *Inflexible*, from the Grand Fleet, ordered them to coal at Devonport and to sail within three days, on 11 November, for the Falkland Islands. Protests by the Dockyard that the *Invincible*'s boilers could not be repaired before midnight on 13 November were brusquely dismissed, and they were told that bricklayers and material were to sail in *Invincible* if the work was not finished by the date laid down. The battle-cruisers sailed with workmen on board, and they sailed in time.

Admiral Sturdee, recently Chief of the Naval Staff, was given command of the South American station with the main object of hunting down von Spee. He hoisted his flag in *Invincible*. Joined by Admiral Stoddart's squadron in the South Atlantic, they arrived at the Falkland Islands on 7 December, where they found *Canopus*, which had been ordered to defend the British colony should von Spee descend upon the Islands. This was apparently his intention. On 6 December he steamed east from the Straits of Magellan, and his leading ship, *Gneisenau*, was in sight of the Falklands at 8 o'clock on the morning of the 8th. Believing that von Spee was at Valparaiso, Sturdee coaled his fleet at the Falklands on the 7th, intending to sail round the Horn the following day.

When *Gneisenau* saw the fatal tripod masts of the battle-cruisers, those harbingers of death, she turned and rejoined her main body.

8. For Churchill's explanation of Admiralty action see WSC, *The World Crisis*, pp. 235–47.
9. Royal Archives. HHA to the King, 4 November 1914.

Sturdee pursued the enemy, now some fifteen miles distant, still visible, hull down on the horizon. He had no difficulty in overhauling them, as the German ships had been so long at sea that their speed was much restricted. Von Spee ordered his light cruisers to escape to the South American coast, and with *Scharnhorst* and *Gneisenau* bravely turned to fight it out with his pursuers. Admiral Sturdee stood off far enough to make the German fire ineffective and with the 12-inch guns of *Invincible* and *Inflexible* pounded the enemy ships to pieces.

Scharnhorst sank with all hands at 4.17 a.m., and von Spee and his two sons perished in her. *Gneisenau* fought on with desperate courage until 6 o'clock when, a completely disabled hulk, she opened the sea-cocks and, with her flags still flying, disappeared into the ocean. The battle had lasted six hours, and the British battle-cruisers had almost exhausted their ammunition. The other cruisers had given chase to the three escaping German ships, and they were remorselessly hunted. Not one of them save *Dresden* escaped (to be brought to book three months later), and in this manner was Coronel avenged. After four months of war the outer seas were swept clear of the enemy, and commerce could proceed unmolested in these waters. As a result of this action, many British warships were ordered to return to home waters, and the Admiralty found themselves with an enormous surplus of older ships, manpower and supplies with which to plan new naval operations. But above all, Winston could reflect 'No German ships of war remained on any of the oceans of the world.'

It was a glorious and sorely needed victory, and was widely acclaimed as Fisher's work, a thrilling augury for the naval future under his inspired direction. Nor was Winston disturbed by the First Sea Lord's sudden effulgence, and there was generosity in his warm letter of congratulation:

> My dear—
> This was your show & your luck. I should only have sent one Greyhound & Defence. This wd have done the trick. But it was a sizzling coup. Your flair was quite true. Let us have some more victories together & confound all our foes abroad – & (don't forget) – at home . . .[10]

In spite of this warmth, there were already little rifts between them, too small perhaps for Winston's insensitive antennae to register, but precursors none the less of the tempests that were to follow. But the ice had not really begun to crack, and his admiration of the old sailor was still intense: 'He was far more often right than wrong and his drive and life-force made the Admiralty quiver like one of his great

10. Bacon, op. cit., Vol. II, p. 178 [And Fisher papers, Comp. Vol. III, Part 1, p. 302.].

ships at its highest speed.'

One further naval action must be recorded before we contemplate the tragedy of the Dardanelles. The German naval code had been broken when the body of a German officer was picked up from the wreck of the *Magdeburg* in the Baltic, his dead hand still clutching the cipher and signal books of the German Navy. This invaluable discovery was handed to the Admiralty by the Russians on the grounds that Britain was the greatest naval power in the Alliance, and could put it to the best use. The 'sea-stained priceless documents', as Winston described them, when decoded, revealed enemy plans and dispositions in the Heligoland Bight.

On 14 December a movement of battle-cruisers was reported apparently aimed against the coasts of Britain. Orders were immediately issued for a strong force of battle-cruisers, light cruisers and destroyers to intercept them. For thirty-six hours there was no further news until on the morning of the 16th, when Winston was lying in his bath, a signal was brought to him from the War Room, which he 'grasped with a dripping hand':

> 'German battle-cruisers bombarding Hartlepool.' I jumped out of the bath with exclamations. Sympathy with Hartlepool was mingled with what Mr George Wyndham once called 'the anodyne of contemplated retaliation'. The war-map showed the German battle-cruisers within gunshot of the Yorkshire coast, while between them and Germany, cutting off their retreat, 'steamed in the exact positions intended, four battle-cruisers and six of the most powerful battleships in the world . . .[11]

Only one boon could have enabled the German ships to avoid annihilation – fog – and that was vouchsafed to them.

> And while the great shells crashed into the little houses of Hartlepool and Scarborough, carrying their cruel message of pain and destruction to unsuspecting English homes, only one anxiety dominated the thoughts of the Admiralty War Room.

The word 'Visibility' assumed a sinister significance.[12]

While angry questions were flying as to how the Navy had permitted the bombardment, and what it was doing, and what it was intending to do, the veil of mist over the North Sea became a curtain under cover of which the invisible enemy eluded their hunters and escaped their doom. Winston's carefully set trap could not close its jaws, and he was to

11. WSC, op. cit., p. 259.
12. Ibid.

write ruefully: 'Thus ended this heart-shaking game of Blind Man's Buff.' We can sympathize with his agony when, through a mere turn in the weather, 'this tremendous prize – the German battle-cruiser squadron whose loss would fatally mutilate the whole German Navy and could never be repaired – ' eluded his grasp. Five hundred civilians had been killed and wounded in the bombarded towns, and the public indignation at the Admiralty failure to avenge them was loud and shrill. The Admiralty could not defend itself without compromising its secret information which must at all costs be kept inviolate, and could only hope that the future would disclose a similar opportunity – without the interference of fog.

* * *

Such an opportunity seemed to be at hand on 23 January 1915 when Sir Arthur Wilson and Admiral Oliver broke into Churchill's room without ceremony and with thrilling news:

'First Lord, these fellows are coming out again!'

'When?'

'Tonight.'

An intercepted message revealed that the German High Seas Fleet would leave harbour that night, and the three men took the signal to Fisher, who was in bed with a chill in his room at Archway House, next door to the Admiralty. He shared their excitement at the prospect of a decisive battle, and a strict silence was preserved.

'We shared our secret with none,' wrote Churchill afterwards. 'That night I attended a dinner which the French Ambassador was giving to Monsieur Millerand, the Minister of War and in London on a mission of consequence.'

A more cheerful event followed in the New Year. On Sunday morning, a succession of telegrams poured into the Admiralty proclaiming that the battle of the Dogger Bank had begun, and excitement was screwed to the topmost peg. By early afternoon the battle was over – less decisive indeed than Churchill had hoped, but a victory none the less, which would have been even greater had not Beatty's flagship *Lion* been seriously disabled and forced to drop out of the line. The German battle-cruiser *Blücher* was sunk with 1,200 men on board, and the other German ships fled for harbour.

The public, so capricious in its endearments, acclaimed the victory, and the neutral world drew its own conclusions. Confidence in the Admiralty was restored, and the German Navy did not emerge again for fifteen months. Only Winston was disappointed, for this was not the decisive victory on blue water for which he had yearned.

'Today a chance offered,' he wrote to Sir John French, 'but only one forfeit cd be exacted. I had hoped for more. We hit them vy hard. But their strong armour protected their motive power: & they fled so fast, we cd not obtain a decision.'[13]

13. Gilbert, op. cit., Vol. III, p. 262 [And Churchill papers: 26/2, 24 January 1915. Comp. Vol. III, Part 1, p. 448.]

Chapter 16

Prelude to The Dardanelles

The German influence in Turkey was a matter of growing concern, and various efforts were made to wean the Turks from it. In 1912 Churchill had appointed Rear Admiral Limpus as Naval Adviser to the Turkish Government, and this officer, as Head of the British Naval Mission, trained and modernized the Turkish Navy. Churchill was sympathetic towards the Young Turks who had deposed Sultan Abdul Hamid in 1908, but their Minister of War, Enver Pasha, was awed and impressed by German power and preferred to seek military advice from that quarter. A strong German Military Mission was established in Constantinople.

In 1911 the Turkish Admiralty ordered a dreadnought to be built at Barrow-in-Furness, and the *Reshadieh* was launched in 1913. There was no dock suitable for such a ship in Turkey, and so Admiral Limpus persuaded Armstrong-Vickers to negotiate with the Turkish Government to provide the necessary installations. On 3 December 1913 he reported to the First Lord on the progress of the negotiations. We have seen how Churchill's manner frequently irritated officers older and more experienced than himself, and his reply to Limpus (who was eleven years his senior, and had encountered him in the Boer War) is a good example of this failing. After acknowledging his letter, Churchill admonished the Admiral like a pedantic schoolmaster to an errant pupil:

> ... I find it necessary to criticise the general style and presentment of your letters. A flag officer writing to a member of the Board of Admiralty on service matters ought to observe a proper seriousness and formality. The letters should be well written or typed on good paper; the sentences should be complete and follow the regular British form. Mere jottings of passing impressions hurriedly put together without

sequence, and very often with marked confusion, are calculated to give an impression the reverse of that which is desirable. You do not do yourself justice in these matters. No one can be so busy as not to be able to cast a letter to a superior in a proper form. You should make up your mind beforehand exactly what you mean to say, and study to say it in the clearest and shortest way, if necessary re-drafting your letter. In your latest communication three letters appear to be mixed up without beginning or end. Knowing the good work which you did in South Africa and your zeal in your Turkish mission, I am able to dispel from my mind the impression which the chaotic character of your correspondence would otherwise convey.[1]

* * *

The Turks now ordered a still larger battleship, the *Sultan Osman I*, from Armstrong-Vickers. Both ships were to be ready for action in 1914, and at the end of July, when war seemed certain, Churchill decided that they must not be allowed to sail:

> The builders shd by every means prevent & delay the departure of these ships while the situation is strained: & in no case shd they be allowed to leave without express permission. If necessary, authority will be given to restrain them.[2]

The Turkish crews, which had arrived in England a short time before to sail the ships to Turkey, were not allowed to board, and the Turkish flag was never hoisted. On the outbreak of war the two ships were commandeered and served throughout the war with the Royal Navy, the *Sultan Osman* as HMS *Agincourt*, the *Reshadieh* as HMS *Erin*.

This action was endorsed by the Foreign Office, and justified as a necessary means of maintaining British naval supremacy in time of war, but to the Turks it seemed an act of pure brigandage and produced an ugly reaction which the Germans were quick to exploit. Leading Young Turks who advocated a neutral or even pro-British attitude were disillusioned, and the arrival of *Goeben* and *Breslau* in Turkish waters a week later was a visible reminder of German might.

The seizure of the Turkish ships ensured that Enver Pasha's pro-German policies would prevail, and on 2 August he concluded a treaty with the German Ambassador so secret that its terms were unknown to those members of the Turkish Cabinet who had favoured a neutral or pro-British policy. The treaty, while not committing Turkey to enter the war on the German side, gave the Germans

1. Chartwell papers, 10 December 1914.
2. Gilbert, op. cit., p. 192. WSC to First and Third Sea Lords, 29 July 1914., p. 283.

paramount influence at Constantinople. Germany agreed to become Turkey's ally in the event of war between Turkey and Russia, and on 11 August Admiral Souchon, now in the Sea of Marmara with *Goeben* and *Breslau*, received secret instructions from Berlin: 'It is of the greatest importance to go to Constantinople as quickly as possible in order thereby to compel Turkey to side with us on the basis of the treaty that has been concluded.'[3]

The Germans next tried the elephantine deception of announcing that they had sold *Goeben* and *Breslau* to the Turkish Government, and Admiral Souchon solemnly hoisted the Turkish flag. In London, the Cabinet decided to insist that the German crews must return to Germany and be replaced by Turks. With the approval of Grey, Churchill sent a personal message to Enver pointing out that alliance with Germany would be a supreme disaster for Turkey, and this was followed by a second and more persuasive communication on 19 August, to be delivered to Enver by Admiral Limpus. The gist of this was that both Turkish battleships would be returned to Turkey after the war, having been thoroughly repaired in British dockyards. If either was sunk, Britain would pay the full value to Turkey on the declaration of peace.

As compensation for delay in delivery, he proposed to pay Turkey £1,000 a day in weekly instalments for every day the ships were detained:

> This arrangement will come into force on the day when the last German officer and man belonging to the *Goeben* and *Breslau* shall have left Turkish territory definitely and finally, and will continue binding as long as Turkey maintains a loyal and impartial neutrality in this war and favours neither one side nor the other. Do you agree?[4]

*   *   *

But Enver had already made up his mind. Surrounded by emblems of German power, he saw Germany as invincible, and was determined that Turkey should share her triumph. He refused to receive Churchill's message. On 22 August the Turkish officers and men who were to have manned *Reshadieh* and *Sultan Osman* reached Constantinople from Tyneside, and Enver used the occasion to strengthen his position by stimulating and nourishing Turkish opinion hostile to Britain. On the following day twenty-eight German military officers reached

3. Ibid, p. 193.
4. Foreign Office Archives: 371/2137.

Turkey. On 26th came the news that ninety German sailors had passed through Sofia on their way to Constantinople, and Churchill minuted:

'The evident intention of the Turkish Government to put their Fleet as well as their army into German hands and to let the Germans use Turkish ships as well as German ships (wh ought to have been interned) as an effective part of the German naval forces can only have one significance.'

Confirming this sombre conclusion, Admiral Limpus reported to Churchill:

> In fact I consider that Constantinople is almost entirely in German hands. It appears to me that Enver and the Army wish and intend this. That Djavid [Minister of Finance] knows that anything but neutrality means ruin; that Talaat [Minister of the Interior] *probably* understands this; that the Grand Vizier certainly does; and that Djemal [Minister of Marine] is a little uncertain – but has French leanings.
>
> The lesser Ministers and the bulk of the people are on the whole averse to the Germanophile policy of the few: but as long as the Army remains German they cannot do much . . . I continue to use what influence I can wield to keep Turkey from finally committing suicide.
>
> In giving my reasons to the authorities here why Turkey should not join the German group I have studiously omitted all talk of action that England might take, such as keeping the requisitioned ships without payment, and fomenting Arabian and Persian Gulf troubles against Turkey: or might encourage Greece to take, such as a landing between Smyrna and the Dardanelles, taking the forts on the south side of the Straits, admitting Torpedo craft to the Marmara, cutting off and starving first the Gallipoli Peninsula, and soon after cutting off all communications between Constantinople and the South. But they are each and all things which, methodically undertaken and persistently carried out, would succeed, and would annihilate the remaining power of Turkey.[5]

On 27 August the Ambassador forwarded to the Foreign Office a report from the Military Attaché that *Goeben* and *Breslau* would be ready for sea on 2 September. He believed that there was little likelihood of the German personnel being removed. The Turkish Fleet was thought to be completely under the control of German officers, and German merchant vessels in the Bosporus were being converted into armed cruisers:

> It may be advisable to consider the question of our fleet entering the Straits. In respect of this, if mines can be negotiated, there

5. Chartwell papers: 13/45.

should be little apprehension of difficulty in running past the shore defences, and once off Stamboul, position would be a commanding one, completely paralysing all military movements between European and Asiatic shore.

The Military Attaché added even more significant sentences to his despatch:

On the other hand reconstructed Turkish fleet would have also to be dealt with, and a mere fleet entry is not calculated to have any permanent effect nor might fleet be able to remain without simultaneous action on the part of the Russian fleet at Bosporus and Russian military occupation of adjoining country. Personally, except for giving Russia immediate assistance and possibly casting a balance in Balkans on our side, I should be against a fleet enterprise only. Probability is that it might succeed, but to command situation properly at Dardanelles, requires also use of military force and point arises whether substantial enterprise should be attempted in quite subsidiary theatre of war.[6]

Thus two British officers on the spot, with intimate knowledge of Turkey, had already given serious thought to an attack on the Gallipoli Peninsula.

* * *

On 19 August M. Venizelos, Prime Minister of Greece, had offered, with the approval of the Greek King Constantine, to place all the naval and military resources of Greece at the disposal of the Entente when they should be required. 'He added that this offer was made in a special sense to Great Britain with whose interests those of Greece were indissolubly bound.'[7]

Sir Edward Grey, after much thought, advised the Cabinet to decline this proposal, fearing that alliance with Greece meant immediate war with Turkey, and possibly with Bulgaria, and being particularly anxious not to foster a Greek enterprise against Constantinople in such a way as to cause offence to Russia. Grey still nourished a hope – sanguine, perhaps – that the Ambassador in Constantinople, close to the Grand Vizier and the leaders of the Turkish neutrality party, would even now be able to keep the peace. The wisest course seemed to Grey to be maintenance of the offer to guarantee the integrity of the Turkish Empire in return for her neutrality. It was not one about which

6. Admiralty papers: 116/1336.
7. WSC, op. cit., p.280, p. 192. WSC to First and Third Sea Lords, 29 July 1914, p. 283.

Churchill could feel happy. 'I naturally conformed to the Cabinet decision, but with increasing misgivings. I still continued to work and hope for a Balkan confederation.'[8]

It is obvious in what direction his mind was turning when after discussing the Turkish situation in detail with Kitchener he wrote, on 1 September, to the Chief of the Imperial General Staff:

> I arranged with Lord Kitchener yesterday that two officers from the Admiralty should meet two officers from ... the War Office today to examine and work out a plan for the seizure by means of a Greek Army of adequate strength of the Gallipoli Peninsula with a view to admitting a British fleet to the Sea of Marmara ... the matter is urgent, and Turkey may declare war on us at any moment ... I will explain verbally to the Committee the points on which His Majesty's Government desire information.[9]

The Director of Military Operations submitted a report to Kitchener on 3 September in which he stated that any attack on Gallipoli was 'likely to prove an extremely difficult operation of war', but he thought with a force of 60,000 men such an attack would be justifiable. He and Churchill assumed that for such an attack, naval and military forces would be combined, and that the main burden would fall upon the army, which, at that time, all presumed would be Greek.

By 9 September, Churchill, believing that with German influence dominating Constantinople, war with Turkey could no longer be avoided, recalled Limpus and his mission. Bearing in mind this officer's intimate knowledge of the Turkish Navy and territory, his immediate wish was to place Limpus in command of the Dardanelles Squadron, but the British Ambassador argued that such an appointment would push the Turks into war on the German side, whereas if Limpus was sent to Malta they would be convinced that Britain still desired peace.

This diplomatic frustration infuriated Churchill, and he rejected the reasoning. He had intended his telegram of recall to be shown by Limpus to Djemal, the Turkish Minister of Marine:

> I do not myself believe, he told Grey, that the withdrawal of the [Naval] mission, the delivery of my message, & the appearance of the Admiral in command of the Mediterranean Sqn, would have had any other effect than to cow and embarrass the Turks ... Nothing appeals to the Turkish Govt except force; & they will continue to kick those who they think are unable or unwilling to use it against them ... If he is to

8. Ibid, p. 281.
9. Churchill papers, 26/1.

be vetoed, another Admiral must go from home at once. In case you take Mallet's[10] view, the mission had better remain until the Germans decide to make it prisoner of war.[11]

Grey did accept Mallet's advice, and Admiral Carden was sent to the Mediterranean, Limpus replacing him as Admiral-Superintendent, Malta Dockyard. Thus, in Winston's opinion, 'we lost the advantages of having on the spot the Admiral who of all the others knew the Turks, and knew the Dardanelles with all its possibilities'.[12]

Still convinced that the Turks were about to enter the war on the German side, Churchill became more incensed with their duplicity. In strong disagreement with Grey, he wrote to the Foreign Secretary on 16 September:

> I must repeat that grave injury has been done to our naval position by the flagrant violations of neutrality committed by the Turks. The British naval mission was ordered off the ships entrusted to them, and has now after many humiliations resigned.
>
> The appointment of a German C in C of the Turkish Fleet as well as of the Turkish Army may not lead directly to war, but the whole attitude of Turkey has been & still is to look for a chance of striking at us if she dare. We ought to have absolute freedom to deal with her at the peace as the general convenience & interests of the allies require. I earnestly trust that this freedom will not be compromised.[13]

* * *

Deprived of Limpus, Churchill lost no time in galvanizing his successor, telegraphing to Carden on 21 September:

> Assume command of the squadron off the Dardanelles. Your sole duty to sink *Goeben* and *Breslau*, no matter what flag they fly. We are not at war with Turkey but German Admiral Souchon is now C in C Turkish Navy and Germans are controlling and largely manning it. Turks have been told that any Turkish ships which come out with *Goeben* and *Breslau* will equally be attacked by us. You are authorized to act accordingly without further declaration or parley . . . remembering that we do not want to pick a quarrel with Turkey unless her hostile intention is clear.[14]

10. Sir Louis Mallet, British Ambassador in Constantinople.
11. Grey papers, 11 September 1914.
12. WSC, op. cit., p. 283.
13. Grey papers.
14. Admiralty papers: 137/96.

By 23 September the British Cabinet policy had hardened to the point of instructing Mallet to inform the Porte that:

> we are grievously dissatisfied with the recent attitude of the Turkish Government, which has resulted in placing Constantinople under German, and no longer Turkish control. Unless the 'peace party' soon succeeds in getting the upper hand we shall be compelled to adopt an attitude of hostility & to take measures accordingly.[15]

On 27 September Carden stopped and examined a Turkish torpedo boat which wished to enter the Aegean. The presence of German sailors on board was another glaring breach of neutrality, and the ship was ordered to turn back. The German General in charge of the fortifications at the Dardanelles next ordered the waterway to be sealed, and contrary to all Treaty obligations to keep the Straits open to shipping of all nations not at war, the Dardanelles were closed. The minefields across the Straits were completed on 29 September.

On 23 October intelligence reports suggested that a Turkish attack on Egypt was imminent, and even the most optimistic or timid members of the British Cabinet could no longer entertain extravagant hopes of Turkey's benevolence. Grey, who had already given her a great deal of rope, telegraphed to Mallet on 28 October:

> It is reported that four Turkish gunboats are intending to proceed from Alexandretta. You should warn Turkish Government that as long as German officers remain on *Goeben* and *Breslau* and Turkish Fleet is practically under German control, we must regard movement of Turkish ships as having a hostile intention, and should Turkish gunboats proceed to sea we must in self defence stop them.[16]

But neither threat nor warning could deflect the Turkish Government from its course. On 30 October *Goeben* and *Breslau*, flying the Turkish flag but commanded by Admiral Souchon, bombarded the Russian Black Sea ports of Odessa, Nikolaev and Sevastopol. The next day Grey sent Mallet an ultimatum to the Turks, demanding the dismissal of the German military and naval missions and the removal from *Goeben* and *Breslau* of all German personnel within twelve hours. If this was refused, Mallet was to ask for his passports and leave Constantinople with the Embassy staff. In London the Cabinet still did not propose a formal declaration of war on Turkey, preferring, according to Asquith's letter to the King, 'to wait for the development of the next two days before

15. Royal Archives.
16. Draft Foreign Office papers: 371/2144.

taking ourselves, or suggesting to other powers, a new departure'.[17]

While these patient diplomatic efforts were pursuing their futile course, Winston's combative mind was already addressing itself to the prospect of action. He asked the First Sea Lord to obtain Admiral Slade's opinion on the possibility and advisability of the bombardment of the sea face forts of the Dardanelles. The Admiral sent Churchill a plan of bombardment on 30 October, and his comments on the feasibility of this operation should be carefully noted:

> A bombardment of the sea face of the Dardanelles Forts offers very little prospect of obtaining any effect commensurate with the risk to the ships. The Forts are difficult to locate from the sea at anything like the range at which they will have to be engaged ... It would not be advisable to risk serious damage to any of the battle cruisers as long as the *Goeben* is effective.

But Slade added in italics: '*A little target practice from 15 to 12 thousand yards might be useful*'[18] and Churchill underlined this sentence in red ink.

The British ultimatum to Turkey expired at noon. At 5 p.m., and while England had still not declared war on Turkey, Churchill telegraphed Carden, ordering him to begin hostilities, and on 2 November he instructed the Admiral:

> Without risking the ships demonstration is to be made by bombardment on the earliest suitable day by your armoured ships and the two French battleships against the forts at the entrance to the Dardanelles at a range of 14,000 to 12,000 yards. Ships should be kept under way approaching as soon after daylight as possible retirements should be made before fire from the forts becomes effective. Ships guns should outrange older guns mounted in the forts.

On 3 November, according to these instructions, the bombardment was carried out over a period of ten minutes, one shot destroying almost all the heavy guns of the fort at Sedd-el-Bahr. And although hostilities had begun, Britain had still not issued a formal declaration of war against Turkey. But at last, on 4 November, Grey gave the Turkish Ambassador in London, Tewfik Pasha, his passports, telling him that the conflict between the two countries could still be ended by dismissal of the German naval and military missions, and regretting the curtailment

17. Gilbert, op. cit., p. 215.
18. Admiralty papers 137/96.

of the friendly relations between the Ambassador and himself.[19]

In the meantime the course for the Dardanelles campaign had been set. After the bombardment of 3 November, Churchill discussed with Fisher, Oliver and Jackson the best method of forcing the Dardanelles:

> The effects of the bombardment of November 3 were studied by Sir Henry Jackson early in the New Year, and used by him to form the basis of a major naval assault.[20]

19. Foreign Office Archives.
20. Admiralty papers 137/96.

Chapter 17

Disaster at The Dardanelles

The failure of the attack on the Dardanelles was the most shattering episode in Churchill's life, and at no other moment, before or after, did he reach a state of equal despair. The memory of his agonizing fall from grace, and the humiliation – infinitely galling to him – which clung to it until his last years, made him the object of a reproach and a distrust from which he could never shake himself completely free. And the tragedy was enhanced by the fact that the Dardanelles attack was a brilliant strategic conception squandered. Had all gone well, it might have been the shortest road to victory.

A contributory cause of the disaster was the haphazard manner in which important issues of state were decided at the beginning of the war. Britain had not been involved in a general war since the days of Napoleon, and had no adequate executive machinery for its efficient conduct. We are told by Lloyd George, the Chancellor of the Exchequer in that administration, that:

> During the first two months . . . there was no established War Council. There were sporadic and irregular consultations from time to time between the Secretary of State for War and the First Lord, between each of them individually and the Prime Minister and, now and again, between the War Lords and the Prime Minister sitting together. The Foreign Secretary was occasionally brought it. I was not summoned to these conferences except when there were matters to be decided that directly affected finance.[1]

Even more prejudicial to the effective waging of the war was the fact that there was no machinery of liaison between the naval and military

1. Lloyd George, *War Memoirs*.

staffs and no joint staff planning committee. The two Services operated as though sealed in their own compartments. It was difficult with such an arrangement to achieve unanimity of opinion, and at the end of 1914 the leading Ministers were trying to forward different and uncorrelated schemes for the offensive.

Even when a War Council was set up, it was dominated by Kitchener, as he brooded heavily over its proceedings – the 'K of K', massive and inarticulate, armoured in his prodigious reputation, the 'legend incarnate' in their midst. We have seen the Liberal leaders as men almost entirely ignorant of war, some pacifist in conviction and all finding this brutal arbitrament repugnant to their finer senses. What could such men do except nod and acquiesce when Kitchener delivered judgment? Even one so fiery and independent as Lloyd George was to admit to the Dardanelles Commission:

> On military matters he [Lord Kitchener] laid down the law and we never confronted him. Some of us did in a feeble sort of way venture to express doubt, but the moment he said 'That is not so', we had neither knowledge nor experience of the position to be able to challenge what he said. His position was very paramount.

But there was one other man in that group with an affinity with war, who could meet Kitchener on his own ground – Winston Churchill – and the old antagonism between them was gradually replaced by a certain friendship. In this manner the position – a dangerous one, perhaps – arose, when the two men on the Council who understood war and had known it at first hand came to bear the joint responsibility for conducting it. In Lloyd George's words:

> . . . At that time you must remember that the conduct of the war was entirely in the hands of Lord Kitchener on land and Mr Churchill at sea, subject to the Prime Minister's supreme authority. You had not constant meetings in the War Council such as you have now to consider every big military and naval operation.[3]

Over this combination Asquith presided with remarkable dexterity, although his mind occasionally wandered from the point at issue, when he glanced surreptitiously at a letter from Venetia Stanley, to whom his devotion was now complete. The Prime Minister's letters to this young woman still in her twenties – letters which, in Winston's

2. PRO ADM. 1437 B and 1437 C.
3. Ibid.

words, were addressed to one 'with brighter eyes than those which peer through political spectacles' – prove that another essential ingredient of war – security – was still in its infancy, for they reveal an astounding indiscretion, often disclosing to her the most secret information about military operations, sometimes even before they were known to his colleagues in the Cabinet.

* * *

The proposal to attack the Dardanelles sprang largely from the trench deadlock on the Western Front. British solutions to this petrified trench system stretching from Switzerland to the North Sea were twofold – an attempt to unlock the trench barrier by an engine, the tank, impervious to machine-gun fire 'which would restore the tactical balance upset by the new preponderance of defensive over offensive power', and a strategic solution, which was to outflank it. The advocates of this second course (who became known as the 'Eastern' as opposed to the 'Western' school), believed that the bloody attrition on the Western Front could be curtailed by a blow in some other theatre, an attack on the enemy's flank. The reason why the Dardanelles operations was not given sufficient support to ensure victory lay in the opposition of the French General Staff, supported by Sir John French. Joffre was obstinately confident of his power to achieve a swift and decisive victory in France. The British Commander-in-Chief, also obsessed with the dream of an early break-through, argued strongly against an alternative strategy and in favour of a concentration of military effort on the Western Front. To some, particularly Churchill, Kitchener and Lloyd George, the trench barrier in France appeared impregnable to frontal attack, and they felt the strongest repugnance at the prospect of the new armies grinding themselves to pieces in assaulting it. They were also apprehensive that the Russian army might at any moment collapse.

* * *

When Churchill was still Home Secretary he had written a Cabinet Paper[4] dated 15 March, in which, *inter alia*, he remarked, 'It should however be remembered that it is no longer possible to force the Dardanelles, and nobody would expose a modern fleet to such peril.' He was to explain this apparent inconsistency to the Dardanelles Commission in 1916 by saying that he had in the meantime been deeply impressed by the devastating effect of artillery attacks on forts in Flanders. 'This war had brought many surprises. We had seen fortresses

---

4. *The Mediterranean Fleet.*

reputed throughout Europe to be impregnable collapsing after a few days attack by field armies without a regular siege.'

The idea of forcing the Dardanelles was raised by Churchill at the end of August 1914. On 1 September he asked the General Staff to prepare a general plan for the seizure of the Gallipoli Peninsula by the Green army with a view of admitting a British fleet to the Sea of Marmara, and it was, as we have seen, on his orders that a British naval squadron shelled the outer forts on 3 November. After this bombardment Churchill began to discuss the question of forcing the Dardanelles with Fisher, Jackson and Oliver, using obsolete battleships whose loss would not weaken Jellicoe's Grand Fleet but which could still effectively fire heavy shells into a strategic target.

The General Staff reply to his question about the Gallipoli idea was not optimistic, but Winston pursued the idea doggedly. He was convinced that this was the right place to attack Turkey – the Achilles heel – and as Lloyd George observed, when Churchill 'has a scheme agitating in his powerful mind ... he is indefatigable in pressing it upon the acceptance of everyone who matters in the decision'.[5]

On 25 November he was therefore ready, when serious pressure was being exerted on Egypt by Turkey, to argue that the ideal way of defending Egypt was by an attack on the Gallipoli Peninsula, since this if successful would give the allies control of the Dardanelles, and enable them to dictate terms to Constantinople. It was, however, he conceded, a difficult operation requiring a large force.[6] The idea was not at that time accepted.

The military situation in Europe steadily declined in November. Enormous losses were accepted as the price for stabilizing the line at Ypres. The defeat of the Russians at Tannenberg was a triumph for German arms: the Austrians began an offensive against Serbia, the only Balkan state in the alliance, and frantic efforts were made to bring Bulgaria and Rumania to the Allied side. Reports reached the Government from Petrograd of the chaotic state of the Russian armies, the lack of food and equipment, the dwindling of ammunition, and the complete breakdown of logistics.

Winston cast about for some means of sustaining the ailing Russian giant, and on 29 December referred to Asquith an old plan of Fisher's – to seize the island of Borkum and invade Schleswig-Holstein. It was hoped that British domination of the Baltic would enable Russia to

5. Lloyd George, op. cit., Vol. I, p. 395.
6. PRO. CAB/37/105.

land troops near Berlin. For 'why,' asked Winston, 'should the new armies be sent to chew barbed wire in Flanders?' Hankey submitted a memorandum at the same time, also seeking a detour round the hideous swamp of trench warfare – an attack on Turkey. This was a lucid, calm and persuasive document which increased Hankey's influence and reputation. Winston was still faithful to his Baltic plan, but he did not think that the position of himself and Hankey was incompatible. 'We are substantially in agreement . . .' he told Asquith. 'I wanted Gallipoli attacked on the Turkish declaration of war. But Kitchener does not look far afield or far ahead, *vide* Antwerp.'[7]

But before he could offer a final opinion to Asquith, outside events beyond his control imposed their own pattern on the situation. On 2 January 1915 a telegram was received from the British Ambassador in Petrograd with a disturbing message. The Grand Duke Nicholas reported that the Turks were threatening the Russian forces in the Caucasus, and made an urgent request to Lord Kitchener to

> arrange for a demonstration against the Turks elsewhere, either naval or military, and to spread reports which would cause the Turks . . . to withdraw some of their forces now acting against the Russians in the Caucasus.

In the known plight of the Russian armies, this was an appeal that Kitchener could not ignore.

* * *

He at once asked Churchill if he thought any naval action could prevent the Turks sending more men to the Caucasus. Later in the day the two men had a long discussion. Kitchener was anxious to help the Grand Duke, but insisted that he had no troops to spare. That evening he wrote to Churchill:

> We have no troops to land anywhere . . . The only place that a demonstration might have some effect in stopping reinforcements going to the East would be the Dardanelles . . . We shall not be ready for anything big for some months.[8]

On 3 January 1915 Kitchener sent the following telegram to the British Ambassador in Petrograd:

7. Asquith papers, 31 December 1914.
8. Chartwell papers: 26/4.

Please assure Grand Duke that steps will be taken to make a demonstration against the Turks. It is however feared that any action we can devise and carry out will be unlikely to seriously affect numbers of enemy in the Caucasus, or cause their withdrawal.

Britain was thus pledged to act and Hankey's plan had been accepted by Kitchener. Fisher, who had been impressed by Hankey's memorandum, had read all the Cabinet papers and was aware of Winston's conversation with Kitchener, wrote to Churchill:

I CONSIDER TURKEY HOLDS THE FIELD – BUT ONLY IF IT'S IMMEDIATE.[9]

Churchill telegraphed to Vice-Admiral Carden: 'Do you consider the forcing of the Dardanelles by ships alone a practicable proposition? . . . Let me know your views.'

Churchill was afterwards to claim: 'All this was purely exploratory. I did not commit myself at this stage even to the general principles of an attack upon Turkey.[10]

It should be remembered when considering these exchanges that the Russian appeal for help dwarfed all other anxieties in the minds of the English leaders. If the Russians collapsed the Germans would at once transfer their enormous armies from the Eastern front to the West, with results terrible to contemplate in a theatre where the Allies were already barely holding their own. Besides jeopardizing their armies on the Western Front, a Russian collapse would ensure the destruction of Serbia, and enable the Turks to concentrate their forces on Egypt. It would be a climacteric in the war.

On 5 January Winston read out Carden's reply to an expectant War Council: 'With reference to your telegram of 3rd instant, I do not consider Dardanelles can be rushed. They might be forced by extended operations with large numbers of ships.'

Fisher remained an enthusiastic supporter of Hankey's plan, and wrote to Balfour on 4 January urging him to support it. Kitchener's insistence that the War Office could not spare any troops had thrown the responsibility squarely upon the Admiralty, and Winston was under heavy pressure.

He was not yet committed to the Dardanelles venture, which Kitchener (although refusing to supply it with any teeth) was now

9. Chartwell papers: 13/56.
10. WSC, op. cit., p. 324.

definitely advocating. Kitchener estimated that 150,000 men would be sufficient to capture the Peninsula, but as usual no one in the Council questioned the demigod's assertion that there were no soldiers to do so, or called for reports or estimates as to what troops were available then or in the near future.[11]

* * *

Winston returned to the Admiralty in the afternoon of 5 January. He had now concluded that the Dardanelles offered a strategy with good prospects of success and immense potential rewards, although it was not yet paramount in his mind. In his office at the Admiralty he found that two men, Admiral Oliver, the Chief of Staff, and Admiral Jackson favoured, *en principe*, the 'extended operations' mentioned by Carden. With this limited endorsement, he sent a telegram to Carden: 'Your view is agreed with by high authorities here. Please telegraph in detail what you think could be done by extended operations, what force would be needed, and how you consider it should be used.'

Carden might have been expected to assume from this signal that the 'high authorities' were the Board of Admiralty speaking with the agreement of the War Council, instead of two Admirals, Oliver and Jackson. Nor was the assent of these two as full and binding as the message suggests. Oliver had been cautious, suggesting merely that 'we should push on slowly until we overcome the enemy's defence, or till the enemy's defence brought us to a standstill'. Jackson was even more noncommittal. Carden afterwards thought that his telegram had been far too buoyantly interpreted, explaining in his evidence to the Dardanelles Commissioners that the operative word was 'might'. We are entitled to suspect that Winston in this transaction was guilty of investing the words of others with far more significance than they were intended to convey.

The War Council met again on 8 January. After its members had been reduced to a state of gloom by Kitchener's forecast of a new German offensive, Lloyd George argued strongly for the opening of an alternative theatre of war, suggesting that a British Expeditionary Force could be landed in Southern Austria, a move which might bring Rumania and Italy into the war to ensure their share of the spoils. But Kitchener returned at once to the Dardanelles project, saying:

The Dardanelles appeared to be the most suitable objective, as an attack here could be made in co-operation with the Fleet. If successful, it would re-establish communication with Russian; settle the Near Eastern

11. PRO. CAB/19/1.

question; draw in Greece and, perhaps, Bulgaria and Rumania; and release wheat and shipping now locked up in the Black Sea.[12]

Churchill, while agreeing that the suggested Mediterranean operation should be studied, was anxious that the chance of action in Northern Europe, which might bring Holland into the war on the Allies' side, should not be overlooked. Several possible strategies had already formed in his fertile mind – a threat to Berlin by the Russians as the result of winning dominance of the Baltic, a landing in Schleswig-Holstein directed against the Kiel Canal which might bring Denmark into the war, and a landing at Emden which would strike at Wilhelmshaven and the German heartland.

'. . . the greatest hope in the N[orth],' he wrote to Sir John French on 11 January,

> is . . . bringing Holland in. If in the summer we are in a position to offer Holland the protection of an army of 700,000 or 800,000 men, it is by no means impossible that she might join the Allies. Her fate is bound up in our victory . . . It is not until all the Northern possibilities are exhausted that I wd look to the S of Europe as a field for the profitable employment of our expanding milty forces.[13]

Such was Churchill's opinion on January 11. Germany was the principal foe; her northern flank the primary and most vulnerable objective. Fisher remained an Eastern enthusiast. That day he discussed the possibility of an attack on Turkey with Grey's Private Secretary, William Tyrrell. The Foreign Office wanted to know, Tyrrell explained, what chance there was of British capturing Constantinople, as the diplomatic advantages of such a victory would be considerable . . . On the following day Fisher wrote to Tyrrell that 'if the Greeks land 100,000 men on the Gallipoli Peninsula in concert with a British naval attack on the Dardanelles I think we could count on a quick and easy arrival at Constantinople . . .'[14]

* * *

On 12 January Carden's detailed plan was received for forcing a passage into the Sea of Marmara. It was proposed that the bombardment should be undertaken by old battleships, shortly destined for the scrapheap, supported by two battle-cruisers, and many ancillaries. It was hoped that the French would contribute a squadron under a

12. Chartwell papers.
13. Copy, Chartwell papers: 26/2.
14. Gilbert, op. cit., p. 247.

French Rear-Admiral. The plan was greeted with enthusiasm by the war group at the Admiralty. By naval power alone, and without troops, these men saw the pressure on Russia relieved, the southern flank of the enemy turned and, without depriving the Western Front of men, Greece, Bulgaria and Rumania drawn into the Allied net. And all of this would be accomplished by obsolete battleships, the loss of which would not weaken Jellicoe's force in the North Sea.

The naval experts had not begun with the slightest optimism about a purely naval attack, none of them believing that ships alone could prevail, and Admiral Sir Henry Jackson had written a strong memorandum against it. Churchill, with his devastating power of exposition, had swung them round by arguing that to help Russia was a vital strategic necessity, that only obsolete battleships would be used, and that if the operation did not prove successful the Navy could in any case withdraw.

Until he received Carden's plan Churchill had been far from happy about the prospects of forcing the Dardanelles by ships alone without the co-operation of troops. But he now swung round strongly. He had always believed that Turkish defeat would quickly follow the appearance of overwhelming naval power in the Sea of Marmara. He thought that Enver Pasha might be induced by it to turn from the German to the Allied cause. In justifying this attitude in after years Churchill has been accused of exaggerating the enthusiasm of his advisers at the Admiralty. It is suggested that their attitude was one of surprise rather than eager agreement, and that Fisher's silence at the War Council masked strong apprehension.

The War Council met on 13 January. Much preliminary business was transacted before the question of the Dardanelles was reached in the evening, and it was after sunset when Churchill began his exposition. Most of those present agreed that the way he outlined the plan was cogent, skilful and persuasive, and Hankey afterwards recalled:

> The idea caught on at once. The whole atmosphere changed. Fatigue was forgotten. The War Council turned eagerly from the dreary vista of a 'slogging match' on the Western Front to brighter prospects, as they seemed, in the Mediterranean . . . Churchill unfolded his plans with the skill that might be expected of him, lucidly but quietly and without exaggerated optimism.[15]

The prospects so seductively offered were indeed alluring. The forts, Winston said, would be systematically reduced 'within a few weeks.

15. Hankey, op. cit., Vol. I, p. 265.

Once the forts were reduced, the minefields could be cleared and the Fleet would proceed up to Constantinople and destroy the *Goeben*. They would have nothing to fear from field guns or rifles which would be merely an inconvenience.[16]

Lloyd George 'liked the plan'; Kitchener thought it 'worth trying'. He added that the bombardment could be broken off if it did not prove effective, indicating that if it failed, the attack could be abandoned and the operation regarded as a feint. Thus primed, the Council decided that 'the Admiralty should prepare for a naval expedition in February to bombard and take the Gallipoli Peninsula with Constantinople as its objective'.

A strange confusion followed this resolution. Fisher left the Council without being aware that a decision had been taken. Another point of grave misunderstanding was that one section of the Council left under the impression that the Navy had been ordered only to *prepare* for an attack, and another (which included Churchill) took it to be a definite decision.

Three facts should be emphasized here – that although Churchill had moved from doubt to enthusiasm for the naval attack, and from that moment threw all his dynamic energy into sustaining it – Kitchener's responsibility for its initiation was equal, if not greater. Fisher was to say as much to the Dardanelles Commissioners when questioned as to whether the idea had come from Kitchener.

'Without any doubt whatever. That is to say, he came to Mr Churchill and said: "Look here, we must do something for the Grand Duke; you do something at the Dardanelles; I have no army; I have no troops." Of course it did.'[17]

Secondly, it is strange that Kitchener and Churchill, to say nothing of other War Council members, should have seriously believed that Constantinople could be conquered and held by ships alone, and not have realized that by taking this naval decision they were in fact committing themselves to military action on a large scale.

Certainly it seemed incredible to the Dardanelles Commissioners:

> It is almost inconceivable that anyone, whether military, naval or civilian, could have imagined for one moment that Constantinople would be captured without military help. It is clear that by the decision of Jan 13th, the War Council, although only pledged for the moment to the naval action, were committed to military action on a large scale in the event of

16. Minutes of the War Council, 13 January 1915.
17. PRO. ADM. 1437B and 1437C.

the attempt to force the Dardanelles by the Fleet along proving unsuccessful ...[18]

Lord Fisher and Sir Arthur Wilson, the two naval advisers present
at the War Council, were not asked to express any opinion, and
remained silent, although neither was more than lukewarm about
the scheme, and both would have preferred a joint naval and military
attack. They considered the naval operation purely experimental and
such as could be discontinued if first results were unfavourable. One
of the many criticisms which can be levelled against this weird conclave
was that no one, from the Prime Minister or First Lord downward, made
any attempt to elicit their views – a failure that was to draw a stern
comment from the Commission which later explored the Dardanelles
disaster. They declared:

> We think that there was an obligation first on the First Lord, secondly on
> the Prime Minister and thirdly on the other members of the War Council
> to see that the views of the Naval Advisers were clearly put before the
> Council, we also think that the Naval Advisers should have expressed
> their views to the Council whether asked or not, if they considered that
> the project which the Council was about to adopt was impracticable from
> a naval point of view ... We do not consider that the urgency was such as
> to preclude a short adjournment to enable the Naval and Military Advisers
> of the Government to make a thorough examination of the question. We
> hold that the possibility of making a surprise amphibious attack on the
> Gallipoli Peninsula offered such great military and political advantages
> that it was mistaken and ill-advised to sacrifice this possibility by hastily
> deciding to undertake a purely naval attack which from its nature could
> not attain completely the object set out in the terms of the decision.[19]

*   *   *

However valid this criticism, Winston was full of excitement and
expectation, and could talk of little else but the plan. The difficulties in
his path were brushed aside. Completely happy and fulfilled, he forecast
the glorious consequences of the attack to Violet Asquith: 'It's possibilities,' she said, 'seemed limitless and he unrolled them before my dazzled
eyes.'

> Once the Fleet had forced the Straits and entered the Sea of Marmara,
> Greece and Bulgaria would probably join us in attacking Turkey. Italy
> would probably abandon her neutrality: Rumania would hasten to join
> the victors, and the Balkan States with their powerful armies might well
> form a solid block to sweep the Turks from Europe. But he thought most

18. PRO. CAB. 19/1.
19. Bonham Carter, op. cit., p. 353.

of all of helping Russia. When Constantinople fell the shipping bottled up in the Black Sea would be released: she could export her grain, and in turn receive arms and ammunition from us. The situation would be retrieved. 'He painted with a master-brush upon his glowing canvas a vision of the Fleet appearing at the Golden Horn.[20]

It was this power of auto-intoxication through words which was to lead to Lord Esher to write of Winston: 'He handles great subjects in rhythmical language, and becomes quickly enslaved by his own phrases. He deceives himself into the belief that he takes broad views, when his mind is fixed upon one comparatively small aspect of the question.'

Within a fortnight a storm had erupted in the person of Fisher. Only the final approval of the War Council was now needed to put the Dardanelles plan into operation, and a meeting had been arranged for 28 January. But on the morning of that day Fisher sent a note to the Prime Minister protesting against an attack on the Dardanelles without troops, and saying that he did not intend to be present at the Council Meeting. He sent another letter – one of resignation – to Churchill. On receiving this Churchill hurried across to 10 Downing Street, where he found the Prime Minister infuriated by Fisher's threat to leave London permanently. It was arranged that Winston should at once communicate with Fisher, ordering him in the Prime Minister's name to attend the Council, and before it to come to Downing Street for a meeting with Asquith and Churchill.

The Prime Minister described this meeting in one of his confidential letters to Venetia Stanley. It cannot have been an easy occasion:

> ...Another personal matter which rather worries me is the growing friction between Winston and Fisher. They came to see me this morning before the War Council, and gave tongue to their mutual grievances. I tried to compose their grievances with a compromise, under which Winston was to give up for the present his bombardment of Zeebrugge, Fisher withdrawing his opposition to the operation against the Dardanelles.[21]

Fisher was obviously not mollified, and, although he was forced to attend the Council meeting, entered it as a most reluctant and surly consultant and continued his eccentric behaviour in the Cabinet Room. When Winston had given his report on the preparation for the Dardanelles operation Fisher said that he had understood that the question would not be raised at this meeting and that the Prime Minister was aware of his views on the subject. Asquith replied that the question

20. Montagu papers.
21. PRO. ADM. 1437B.

could not be left in abeyance, and Fisher rose and left the Council table, making as if to leave the room. Kitchener followed him and asked him what he intended to do. The furious old man replied that he would not return to the meeting, and would resign his office as First Sea Lord. With some difficulty Kitchener persuaded him to return to the table, where he sat listening to the discussion on the Dardanelles in what Asquith described as 'an obstinate and ominous silence'.

Yet so mercurial was Fisher's temper that when Winston summoned him to his room that afternoon because he did not know what had happened between the Admiral and Kitchener, and wished to discover Fisher's present mood, he found that it had changed again. It required more than an hour's discussion, sometimes passionate, to bring Fisher round, but as he had once admitted of Churchill, 'He always out-argues me.' After this hour Fisher definitely consented to undertake the Dardanelles attack, and he was later to tell the Dardanelles Commissioners: 'When I finally decided to go in, I went in the whole hog, *totus porcus*.' No more reluctant hog had ever allowed himself to be driven to the stockyards.

*   *   *

It was perhaps characteristic that when this severed bond had been for the moment spliced, Winston should have felt entirely free from anxiety. He accepted the old man's foibles, although he misunderstood their meaning. He was confident that he could manage him, and knew that Fisher was as prone to resignation as a dog to fleas. It was natural that he did not seek to probe further. But there were others, more perceptive, who wished Churchill well and saw in Fisher unlimited possibilities of danger, who recognized his appalling vindictiveness and irresponsibility, and did not believe that his naval genius compensated for a temperament so mobile as to verge on madness.

Who but a madman, they argued, could have seriously proposed, as he had done earlier in that month, that all German prisoners of war should be shot in reprisal for air raids? He was a man who worked by a series of instinctive flashes of conviction which he was unable to justify by any logical process. By yielding weakly under the pressure of superior argument he had become doubly dangerous, for he was committing himself to an enterprise in which he did not believe, and to which he was certain to be disloyal.

His explanation of why he had remained silent at the War Council was feeble in the extreme:

> Mr Churchill knew my opinion ... I did not think it would tend towards good relation between the First Lord and myself nor to

the smooth working of the Board of Admiralty to raise objections in the War Council's discussions. My opinion being known to Mr Churchill in what I regarded as the proper constitutional way, I preferred to remain silent.[22]

Although he seemed for the moment to have given the Dardanelles plan his approval, Fisher had been the prey of festering doubts about it. He had come to believe that the operation would absorb too much time and too many ships, to the detriment of Britain's naval strength in the North Sea, and he was encouraged in these beliefs by Jellicoe who had been alarmed to hear that the *Queen Elizabeth* and other powerful ships had been assigned to the Mediterranean. He had been edging his way towards a purely defensive position – a negation of action, and on 25 January, in a memorandum presented to Churchill, and aimed at members of the War Council, he had written: 'Being already in possession of all that a powerful fleet can give a country, we should continue quietly to enjoy the advantage without dissipating our strength in operations that cannot improve the position.'[23]

Behind that aggressive exterior and craggy Mongolian face had begun to appear unmistakable signs of the erosion of time and age, revealing themselves in a desire for caution, for playing safe, and it is probable that his nerve was weakening. Richmond, the Assistant Director of Operations at the Admiralty, although a censorious critic, was perhaps justified in writing in his diary on 19 February 1915: 'He is old & worn out & nervous. It is ill to have the destinies of an empire in the hands of a failing old man, anxious for popularity, afraid of any local mishap which might be put down to his dispositions.'[24]

After the War Council of 28 January detailed plans were worked out by the Admiralty for the naval attack on the Dardanelles. Churchill had arranged for a French force to take part under British command. While preparations were in progress he was asked by the War Council to visit France and persuade Sir John French to release some of his troops for service in the Balkans, for constant telegrams from that area warned of the danger to Serbia from Austria and Bulgaria. Grey was anxious that the attack on the Dardanelles should succeed, to counteract the effect produced by the appearance of German troops on the Balkan frontiers. His opinion was that the present enemy intention was to intimidate Rumania and Greece, and to impress Bulgaria by an offensive against Serbia.

One of the convictions which bedevilled the Dardanelles operations

22. Chartwell papers: 13/56.
23. Quoted Gilbert, op. cit., p. 260.
24. Chartwell papers: 26/3. Grey to Churchill, 2 February 1915.

was the belief that the Turks were bad soldiers incompetently led, and the failure on 3 February of a Turkish force which crossed the Sinai Desert and was driven off from the Suez Canal seemed to lend credibility to this belief. In the meantime bad news continued to be received from the Balkans, and it appeared likely that Bulgaria would abandon her neutrality and attack Serbia.

These anxieties were reflected in the War Council held on 9 February, when Churchill described his preparations for the Dardanelles attack. He was negotiating with the Greek Prime Minister, Venizelos, for the use of the island of Lemnos which, with its fine harbour at Mudros, would provide perfect shelter for the Fleet. But Serbia still held the main place in their councils. The Ministers decided that the best way to help her was to send a division of 20,000 troops to Salonika from where they could march north to the Serbian frontier. It was decided after some argument that the first-class 29th Division should be offered to Greece.

Although a naval attack on the Dardanelles had been agreed on, the possibility of using troops as well in a combined operation was still a major topic in February. Fisher and Jackson were particularly insistent that troops were essential, and Kitchener sent Lieutenant General Birdwood, the commander of the Australian and New Zealand Army Corps then training in Egypt, to the Dardanelles to report to him on the prospects.

In the meantime further doubts had been expressed about a purely naval attack. On 13 February Hankey told the Prime Minister 'very strongly' that it should be supported by a strong military force, and Asquith noted that he had himself for some time been coming to the same conclusion. And on 14 February Richmond issued a memorandum warmly endorsed by Fisher, in which he wrote: 'The bombardment of the Dardanelles, even if all the forts are destroyed, can be nothing but a local success, which without an army to carry it on can have no further effect.' Jackson followed suit with a paper in which he insisted that 'the naval bombardment is not recommended as a sound military operation unless a strong military force is ready to . . . follow it up immediately the forts are silenced.'[25]

'The First Lord,' Hankey told Balfour, 'still professes to believe that they can do it with ships, but I have warned the Prime Minister that we cannot trust to this . . .'[26]

* * *

25. Gilbert, op. cit., p. 287.
26. Balfour papers.

Churchill was by no means blind to these warnings, and had begun to wonder whether Carden's plan was too sanguine. He had started by insisting on the need for a powerful military force in any attempt to take Constantinople. He had next allowed himself – too hastily, perhaps – to be so attracted by Carden's scheme as to believe that ships alone might win the day. At least the plan offered the prospect of action, which always lured him strongly, and since Kitchener had so far refused troops it was the only strategy which did so. For on the day Winston received Jackson's memorandum the Greek Government, through the pro-German inclination of the Greek King, refused to accept the British expedition to Salonika, thus leaving the Dardanelles as the only remaining field of operations immediately available in the East. It was hoped that the 29th Division, which had been destined for Salonika, could now be sent instead to the Gallipoli Peninsula.

Fisher added his own warning to those given by his naval colleagues. 'Not a grain of wheat,' he told Winston, 'will come from the Black Sea unless there is a military occupation of the Dardanelles, and it will be the wonder of the ages that no troops were sent to co-operate with the Fleet with half a million soldiers in England.'[27]

An emergency meeting of the War Council was called on 16 February. At this meeting Kitchener, influenced against his will by his brilliant Intelligence officer, Wyndham Deedes, agreed with palpable reluctance that the 29th Division should be sent to Lemnos at the earliest possible moment to support the attack on the Dardanelles, and that the Australian and New Zealand troops should join it there. Winston was profoundly relieved by this decision, writing to Kitchener on 18 February, and showing that his confidence in the 'naval attack' was now at least doubtful:

> . . . And I think that at least 50,000 shd be within reach or 3 days notice, either to seize the Gallipoli Peninsula when it has been evacuated, or to occupy C'nople if a revolution takes place. We shd never forgive ourselves if the naval operations succeeded & the fruits were lost through the army being absent.[28]

The decision to mass troops in the neighbourhood of the Dardanelles marked a critical stage of the inception of the operation and a withdrawal from it could no longer have taken place without a dangerous loss of face. Such at least was the opinion of the Dardanelles Commissioners:

27. Gilbert, op. cit., p. 287.
28. Chartwell papers (Copy: Churchill papers: 13/47).

It ought to have been clear at the time that, when this was once
done, although the troops might not have been actually landed, it would
become apparent to all the world that a really serious attack was intended,
and that withdrawal could no longer be effected without running serious
risk of loss of prestige . . .[29]

Churchill and Kitchener were agreed that the Fleet should pass the
Narrows before troops needed to be used, Winston being particularly
anxious that ample reinforcements should be at hand. Their relations
were not always easy, being clouded by an irritating argument over an
offer to Sir John French by Winston of a Brigade of the Naval Division,
and two squadrons of his famous armoured cars which were now
being hawked round from pillar to post. The offer was made without
Kitchener's knowledge or consent, and made him extremely angry. It
was an example of Winston's insensitiveness in personal matters, and
he refused to budge an inch, although Asquith took Kitchener's side.

* * *

It was unfortunate that this foolish and unnecessary quarrel should come
to a head by the day of the War Council Meeting on 19 February. At this
meeting Kitchener went back on his promise to sent the 29th Division to
the Dardanelles, and Churchill was staggered by the *volte-face*; for only
three days before Kitchener had agreed to release it. In strong language
he begged the War Council to confirm the earlier decision and despatch
the 29th Division. Although Kitchener had agreed that troops from
Egypt might be sent in its place, Churchill insisted that they would be
no substitute for the highly trained 29th. Kitchener was adamant. This
obstinacy led to a quarrel, and on the following day, the orders which
had been given on the 16th for the collection and fitting of the transports
for the 29th Division were cancelled without Churchill's knowledge.[30]

On 24 February Kitchener said that 'if the Fleet could not get
through the Straits unaided, the Army ought to see the business
through. The effect of a major defeat on the Orient would be very
serious. There could be no going back.' But in spite of Churchill's
strenuous arguments, he still refused to send the 29th Division. The
attack on the Dardanelles, he argued, had been planned as a naval
operation. Did Mr Churchill contemplate a land attack as well? The
First Lord replied that he did not, but that it was conceivable that the

29. PRO. CAB/19/1.
30. Chartwell papers.

naval attack might be temporarily held up by mines, and some local military operation required.

A considerable change had come over Kitchener's attitude towards the Dardanelles enterprise. The idea of breaking off the attack in case of naval failure now disappeared, and military operations on a massive scale were contemplated. Kitchener nevertheless clung to the idea that success could be won by naval action alone.

On the morning of 19 February Carden had begun his bombardment of the outer forts of the Dardanelles. It was thought that to reduce all the forts up to Gallipoli might require a fortnight. Reports on the preliminary bombardment were not particularly encouraging: none of the guns in the forts had been hit directly, although magazines in two had exploded, and for the next two days sudden bad weather delayed operations.

The naval bombardment was resumed on 25 February, and the outer forts silenced. Carden then began to plan for the second stage of the operations – minesweeping and clearing of the inner forts – which he hoped to begin in March. At a Council Meeting on 26 February Churchill made another passionate appeal for the 29th Division. In three weeks' time, he argued, 'Constantinople might be at our mercy. We should avoid the risk of finding ourselves with a force inadequate to our requirements and face to face with disaster.' But he denied any intention of using troops to force the Dardanelles, emphasizing that they 'were required to occupy Constantinople and to compel a surrender of all Turkish forces remaining in Europe after the fleet had obtained command of the Sea of Marmara . . . The actual and definite object of the army would be to reap the fruits of the naval success.'[31]

Kitchener's continued obstinacy over the 29th Division caused Winston to lose his temper at this meeting, and, in the opinion of the Prime Minister, to cut no very dignified figure. He said angrily that he wished it placed on record that he dissented altogether from the retention of the 29th Division in this country, and that he must disclaim responsibility if a disaster occurred in Turkey owing to insufficiency of troops. So disgusted was Asquith that he had called Winston into his study after the meeting like an errant schoolboy. He told Venetia Stanley: 'Winston was rather trying today & I felt constrained to talk to him afterwards a little for his soul's good: a task wh as you know I do not relish, & in which I fear do not excel.'[32] Earlier on the same day he had written to her: 'The War Council lasted nearly 2 ½ hours. Winston

31. Chartwell papers?
32. Montagu papers.

was in some ways at his worst – having quite a presentable case. He was noisy, rhetorical, tactless, & temperless.'[33]

At this point Churchill's robust optimism began to fade. Having impressed the War Council with his earlier belief in an entirely naval attack, he had now lost that confidence. But since he was still convinced of the importance of a victory in this theatre, he was prepared to go ahead with his plans for just such an attack, and thus, in Martin Gilbert's words, 'made himself responsible for the very disaster that he forecast'.[34] Round him he saw everywhere vacillation and doubt. 'The capacity to run risks is at famine prices. All play for safety.'[35]

In this mood of caution and in his demands for the 29th Division he was later supported by the Dardanelles Commissioners, whose opinion was that after the decision of 16 February there were only two defensible courses open to the Government —

> one to recognize that by reason of our commitments elsewhere, an adequate force could not be found for expeditionary action in the Eastern Mediterranean, and to have abandoned the naval attack on the Dardanelles once it had become apparent that military operations on a large scale would be necessary. The other was to accept the risk boldly, and make a determined attempt to force the passage of the Dardanelles by a combined operation in great strength.
>
> The Government adopted neither of these courses. Time, as Mr Asquith very truly said to us, was all-important. Yet for at least three weeks the Government vacillated and came to no definite decision in one sense or the other. The natural result ensued. The favourable moment for action was allowed to lapse. Time was given to the Turks, with the help of German officers, to strengthen their position, so that eventually the opposition to be encountered became of a far more formidable character than was originally to be anticipated. Moreover, even when the decision was taken, it was by no means thorough . . . The hope of dispensing altogether with military assistance, save in respect to what were called 'minor operations', was not abandoned. We think that Mr Churchill was quite justified in attaching the utmost importance to the delays which occurred in despatching the 29th Division and the Territorial Division.[36]

*　　＊　　＊*

On 29 February there began a noticeable stirring among the uneasy

---

33. Ibid.
34. Gilbert, op. cit., p. 311.
35. J. C. Paysers WSC to Jack Churchill 26 Feb 1915.
36. PRO. CAB/19/1.

and calculating Balkan states in the face of a possible British triumph. On the evening of 1 March Violet Asquith was sitting with Clementine Churchill in Admiralty House when Winston entered the room 'in a state of wild excitement and joy. He showed us, under many pledges of secrecy, a telegram from Venizelos promising help from the Greeks, both naval and military – an Army Corps of three Divisions for Gallipoli! Our joy knew no bounds.' Violet asked him if the Greek King, who had a German wife, was 'sound', and he replied that the King was in favour of war. Churchill then began to hypnotize himself with his own words:

> Winston totted up our combined forces: we now had the Anzac Army Corps on the spot, the Royal Naval Division on the way, the French division, the promise of the Greek divisions and the British Army Corps at Batoum. The 29th was still in the balance. In the background Bulgaria, Rumania and Italy were still waiting – ready to pounce – all determined to play a part in the fall of Constantinople. All these tremendous consequences had flowed from our united naval enterprise. And why? Not because of its scale or power but because of its true timing and direction – because it was aimed at the heart of Eastern Europe when we could wrest it from the Central Powers and commit it to our cause.

In this manner did Winston reveal a glorious vista of certainty which left his listeners entranced:

> I went back across the Horse Guards treading on air. Turkey, encircled by a host of enemies, was doomed, the German flank was turned, the Balkans for once united on our side, the war shortened perhaps by years, and Winston's vision and persistence vindicated.[37]

But alas, it was all the stuff of dreams, and with their passing there came a bleak awakening. Within a day a disastrous message was received that the Tsar would not at any price accept the co-operation of Greece in the Constantinople expedition. This was shattering news for Winston, perhaps the worst he had so far received. He reflected bitterly upon the fact that Russia, reeling before the German onslaught, her soldiers betrayed by gross logistical incompetence, should yet retain the power and the will to inflict this wanton injury upon the Allied fortunes.

The bombardment of the forts continued during the second week of March, but with difficulties caused by bad weather and increased Turkish activity. Carden's reports on his progress were so negative as to be disturbing. The War Council next met on 10 March. Kitchener

37. Bonham Carter, op. cit., pp. 368–9.

had hitherto justified his refusal of the 29th Division by the fact that it was essential to have a first-class unit as reinforcement in case of a serious reverse on the Western Front. Now, to the general surprise, he announced that the general situation was sufficiently stabilized to warrant its release. He had received an adverse report from Birdwood on the chances of the Navy getting through, and had changed his mind. But the delay had been such that the 29th Division could not reach the scene of action in under a month. It may be noted that both in *The World Crisis* and in his evidence to the Dardanelles Commissioners Churchill laid great stress on the importance of this delay, even stating in one account that he should have broken off the naval attack when Kitchener went back on his undertaking. But a significant passage in his evidence suggests that Churchill's grievance against Kitchener was ill-founded:

> At this time I must make it clear that I was pressing for the collection of an army in the Eastern Mediterranean for contingencies, among which helping the fleet through was one, reaping the fruits if they got through was another, and general action in support of our diplomacy to bring in Greece was a third. I had no right to complain at this stage if Lord Kitchener said: 'I am not going to land on the Peninsula.' I could not have said, 'Oh! you have broken faith with the Admiralty.' On the contrary, we had said we would try it without committing him to that, and he would have had a right to complain if we had turned round and immediately demanded that he should undertake this very serious military operation.[38]

*   *   *

But no one suggested breaking off the operation. Winston told his colleagues that the Admiralty were still confident that they could pass the Straits by naval means alone. He still believed that if the naval action failed, the ships could be withdrawn and the enterprise abandoned. He welcomed the appointment of his old friend, Sir Ian Hamilton, to command the Mediterranean Expeditionary Force, and told him he was confident that the Navy alone could force the Straits, though he would value a simultaneous attack by troops.

In the meantime Carden, after his initial setbacks, had seemed hesitant about renewing the attack. He was strongly harried by Winston, disturbed by what he saw as the defeatist nature of his telegrams. Carden explained that minesweeping had been hampered by heavy fire, but that he had suffered no casualties, and Churchill told him sharply:

38. PRO. ADM 1437B. Q. 1251.

I do not understand why minesweeping should be interfered with by fire which causes no casualties. Two or three hundred casualties would be a moderate price to pay for sweeping up as far as the Narrows ... This work has to be done whatever the loss of life and small craft and the sooner it is done the better.[39]

When Hamilton arrived at the Dardanelles on 17 March he found that Carden had suffered a complete breakdown, an ominous misfortune on the eve of the full-scale naval attack which had been planned for 18 March. Carden recommended to the First Lord that Vice-Admiral de Robeck should succeed him in the command, and to this officer Churchill entrusted the Mediterranean Detached Fleet with Admiral Wemyss as his second-in-command. The First Lord asked de Robeck if he was in full agreement with the instructions to Admiral Carden. He replied that he was.[40]

39. Chartwell papers [Copy, Chartwell papers, 13/54, 13 March 1915.]
40. For exchange of telegrams see WSC, *The World Crisis*, pages 387 and 389. [or Chartwell papers, 13/65]

Chapter 18

The Naval Attack

The decisive moment had now come, but not in propitious form. Kitchener was careful to emphasize to Ian Hamilton that 'we soldiers were to understand that we were string number two'. The Navy had said that they could force the Dardanelles on their own, and 'we were not to chip in unless the Admiral definitely chucked up the sponge'. At no time did it seem to occur to Kitchener to suggest a combined naval and military operation of the sort Churchill had demanded in January and February. It was the Navy's task.

All immediately concerned were uneasily conscious of the immense rewards which victory in this assault would bring, and Lloyd George had clearly pointed to the glittering prizes awaiting the victor:

> Its influence may be decisive as far as the Balkan States are concerned. This means that if we have a large force ready, not merely to occupy Gallipoli, but to take any other military action which may be necessary in order to establish our supremacy in that quarter, Roumania, Greece, and I think, very probably, Bulgaria, will declare for us . . . To bring Bulgaria, Roumania and Greece in with Serbia means throwing an aggregate army of 1,500,000 on the Austrian flank. This will not only relieve the pressure on Russia, but indirectly on France . . . and thus give us time to re-equip the Russian army.[1]

With such immense issues at stake the assault opened on the morning of 18 March, when in brilliant sunshine the whole Allied Fleet of fourteen British and four French battleships advanced to the attack on the Narrows. Most naval actions had been fought over vast

---

1. Copy, Chartwell papers: 13/56. Memorandum by D. Lloyd George, 22 February 1915.

areas of blue water and could not be wholly observed by an onlooker, but this famous assault took place within the confines of the Dardanelles and was clearly visible in all its phases to those on the hills overlooking the Straits. Another notable feature of the attack was that it was between warships on one side and artillery and mines on the other, and that no enemy ships were deployed from beginning to end of the battle.

This action has often been described, and we need not concern ourselves here with details. De Robeck's first line of attack consisted of four powerful British ships – *Queen Elizabeth*, *Agamemnon*, *Lord Nelson* and *Inflexible* – accompanied by two further battleships, *Prince George* and *Triumph*. Behind them was the French Squadron – *Gaulois*, *Charlemagne*, *Bouvet* and *Suffren* – under Admiral Guépratte.

The ships entered the Straits at 10.30 a.m. on 18 March and opened the assault at 11.30, the *Queen Elizabeth* shelling the fortresses on both sides of Chanak with her 15-inch guns while her consorts attacked the forts at Kilid Bahr on the opposite bank. The range of the Turkish batteries made it impossible for them to reach their attackers, and they were forced to hold their fire and endure in silence the murderous battering from the British guns.

At noon de Robeck decided that it was time for his allies to engage the enemy and sent in the French Squadron, whose Admiral had requested this role, to bombard the forts at close range.

The most vivid chronicler of these events wrote in these terms:

> One can perhaps envisage occasional flame spurting out of the debris, the ships slowly moving through a sea pitted with innumerable fountains of water, and sometimes disappearing altogether in the fumes and the spray, the stabs of light from the howitzers firing from the hills, and the vast earthquake rumbling of the guns.[2]

Then the casualties began. *Gaulois* and *Inflexible* were badly damaged, and *Agamemnon* also seriously disabled. But the enemy at the Narrows was also in a critical condition. Guns were jammed and communications severed between the gunners and those directing the fire. The smooth functioning of gun-drill broke down; fire became intermittent and feeble, and although the forts had not yet been destroyed, the morale of the artillerymen appeared to have collapsed. De Robeck decided to withdraw the French Squadron and bring up the six British battleships waiting at the rear. But at 2 p.m. *Bouvet* was seen to be shattered by a gigantic explosion, and sank with nearly all hands in two

2. Alan Moorhead, *Gallipoli*, p.64.

minutes. In the meantime *Swiftsure*, *Majestic*, *Ocean*, *Irresistible*, *Albion* and *Vengeance* closed the range and pressed the attack, and by 4 p.m. the guns at the Narrows, which had been firing erratically, had almost fallen silent.

It was now the turn of the minesweepers to clear the way, but when the trawlers sent to clear the Turkish minefields came under fire, they turned tail and fled out of the Straits. After this lamentable fiasco the next blow fell. *Inflexible*, which although damaged had remained in the line, struck a mine and listed heavily to starboard. *Irresistible* was also struck and sank, and an hour later a general retirement was ordered. Later in the day the battleship *Ocean* was mined and sank, following *Irresistible* to the bottom.

A fearful hush had now come over the battlefield:

> All was silent on either shore, and except for the Turkish searchlights which kept sweeping back and forth across the water there was no sign of life anywhere . . . There was nothing to be seen or heard: nothing but this extraordinary silence, the utter lassitude of the battlefield after the day's fighting is done.[3]

De Robeck, staggered and mystified by these losses, ruefully contemplated the sinking or disablement of six of the nine battleships involved in the attack, and called a halt to the day's operations.

If De Robeck was shaken by this disaster Winston regarded it only as a reverse on the first of several days' fighting, and although the losses in ships were heavy, those in men were remarkably light. 'It never occurred to me for a moment that we should not go on.' He was, after all, as Fisher called him, a 'War Man', and he knew that war could not be waged without casualties. He was not in the least deterred by the loss of a few obsolete battleships, and was astonished that others should be, particularly when he compared those losses with the frightful carnage on the Western Front, where endless casualty lists of dead and missing were accepted with resignation. Nor had the idea of withdrawal occurred to Commodore Roger Keyes, De Robeck's Chief of Staff, who asked permission to take a destroyer and try to salvage two damaged battleships. He described later the macabre silence.

> I had a most indelible impression that we were in the presence of a beaten foe. I thought he was beaten at 4 p.m. and at midnight I knew with still greater certainty that he was absolutely beaten; and it only remained for us to organize a proper sweeping force and devise some means of dealing with drifting mines to reap the fruits of our efforts.

3. Ibid, p. 69.

So convinced was Keyes of a supreme opportunity going begging
that he added:

> I wish to place on record that I had no doubt then, and have none
> now – and nothing will ever shake my opinion – that from the 4th
> April, 1915, onwards, the Fleet could have forced the Straits, and
> with losses trifling in comparison with those the Army suffered,
> could have entered the Marmara with sufficient force to destroy
> the Turco-German Fleet.[4]

And Winston himself, equally convinced, later recorded:

> If the Navy had tried again they would have found that the door was
> open. Their improved sweeping forces could have concentrated upon
> clearing the few remaining mines out of the Eren Keui Bay. The battle of
> March 18 could have been resumed a month later in overwhelmingly
> favourable condition; and had it been resumed it would, in a few hours,
> have become apparent that it could have only one ending.[5]

It is not possible to prove or disprove the truth of these confident
assertions, but the secret Admiralty Inquiry in 1919 did not uphold
them. Those who reject the claims of Churchill and Keyes maintain
that the key to the door which Winston said was open was the
clearing of the minefields, not the amount of ammunition available
in the Dardanelles forts. But even such critics are forced to admit that
the improved minesweeping force of converted destroyers, proposed by
Keyes, offered a new and promising chance of success.

*   *   *

Churchill, then, took it for granted that the attack would be resumed,
and Lord Fisher and Sir Arthur Wilson were of the same mind. 'Both
met me that morning with expressions of firm determination to fight it
out. The First Sea Lord immediately ordered two battleships to replace
casualties.' A War Council on 19 March, after listening to Churchill's
account of the battle and hearing that he had evidence from a secret
source that the Turks were short of ammunition, authorized him to
inform De Robeck 'that he could continue the operations against
the Dardanelles if he saw fit'. There was no wish expressed at the

4. Admiral Sir Roger Keyes, *Naval Memoirs*, p. 186.
5. WSC, op. cit., pp. 405–6.

meeting to break off the attack, and there as an air of surprising vagueness in its proceedings. Kitchener was unable to produce a War Council plan for the disembarkation of troops, and said that Hamilton would have to improvise one. No one raised the nature or timing of any contemplated military operation, and no one asked whether a second naval attack should be postponed until the Army had made its preparations to land.[6]

We know now that De Robeck had been far more heavily stricken by the failure of the attack than appeared at the time. 'It had,' he said, 'been a disastrous day', but his morale had been restored by a reassuring telegram from Winston on 20 March, praising his 'resolute attack' and promising four more battleships to replace his losses.[7] Destroyers were being equipped with a sweeping apparatus to deal with the mines, and a squadron of aircraft under Commander Samson were to be sent out and identify enemy guns. Refreshed like a watered flower, De Robeck said that he hoped to resume operations in a few days, writing to General Hamilton, 'We are all getting ready for another go and not in the least beaten or down-hearted.'

It was therefore with astonishment and 'consternation' that Winston received a telegram from De Robeck which seemed to indicate a disastrous weakening of purpose. De Robeck now felt unable to move again without military support, and, as the Army would not be ready until the middle of April, he proposed to delay the attack for another three weeks. Winston at once drafted a reply in which he stressed the perils of delay, particularly through the danger of submarines, and ordered De Robeck to prepare to renew the action at the first favourable opportunity. In this sense of urgency he had the agreement of Asquith who told Venetia Stanley, 'The news from the Dardanelles is not very good . . . and the Admiral seems to be rather in a funk. I agree with Winston and K that the Navy ought to make another big push, so soon as the weather clears. All this was rather kept back from the Cabinet . . .[8]

Having drafted his reply to De Robeck, Winston next summoned a meeting of Lord Fisher and the War Staff at the Admiralty, and placed the telegram before them. And at this extremely inopportune moment he encountered the full force of his colleagues' long-suppressed opposition – what he described as 'insuperable resistance'. Fisher, Wilson and Jackson flatly refused to renew the naval attack. They had been willing to underwrite the operation when it was recommended by the Admiral on the spot, but as De Robeck and Hamilton were now

6. Cabinet Office papers, 22/1.
7. Copy, Churchill papers, 13/65.
8. Montagu papers.

agreed that a combined operation was necessary, they were opposed to overruling their judgment.

The dynamic First Lord, who had so dominated the Admiralty, found himself outnumbered and outgunned by his own naval advisers. Only the Chief of Staff, Commodore de Bartolomé, supported him, and he was the most junior of those present. Churchill saw with sickening lucidity the vista of terrible consequences disclosed by this infirm relaxation of purpose. 'For the first time since the war began, high words were used round the octagonal table.'

The thwarted Churchill brought the question before the Cabinet on 23 March. The Prime Minister instinctively believed that Churchill was right, and he was accompanied in this view by Kitchener. But Asquith either felt himself too deficient in technical knowledge or was too weak to override the opinion of Fisher and his senior colleagues, based on the wishes of the Admiral in command, so Churchill was compelled 'under extreme duress' to abandon the attack. There was an explanation of De Robeck's *volte-face* apart from a failure of nerve. On 22 March he had attended a conference at Lemnos in the *Queen Elizabeth* with Generals Hamilton, Birdwood and Braithwaite, of which Hamilton recorded:

> The moment we sat down De Robeck told us *he was now quite clear he could not get through without the help of all my troops.* Before ever we went aboard Braithwaite, Birdwood and I had agreed that, whatever we landsmen might think, we must leave the seamen to settle their own job, saying nothing for or against land operations or amphibious operations until the sailors themselves turned to us and said that they had abandoned the idea of forcing the passage by naval operations alone. They have done so . . . So there was no discussion. At once we turned our faces to the land scheme.[9]

Was it right to abandon the naval attack or should it have been pressed forward at all costs, and its losses accepted as a normal hazard of war? It will ever remain a matter of opinion and argument, but we should note the passage devoted to this question in the Report of the Dardanelles Commission:

> It is interesting, but perhaps not very profitable, to speculate on what might have occurred if subsequent to the bombardment of March 18th, the naval attack had been at once pressed on, aided by such troops as were then on the spot. We have already stated that Mr Churchill was strongly in favour of adopting this course, and that he received some support both from Mr Asquith and Mr Balfour. The idea, however, had

9. Hamilton, *Gallipoli Diary*, Vol. 1, pp. 41–42.

to be abandoned because the weight of both naval and military authority was much opposed to it. But there were exceptions. Commodore de Bartolomé agreed with Mr Churchill. Sir Ian Hamilton also stated that General Birdwood wished to 'land at once', and he added: 'I think there was a good deal to be said for it.' Sir Ian, however, held that 'Lord Kitchener's original orders not to land if he could avoid it', held good. Enver Pasha, at a much later date, is reported to have said: 'If the English had only the courage to rush more ships through the Dardanelles they could have got to Constantinople, but their delay enabled us thoroughly to fortify the Peninsula, and in six weeks time we had taken down there over 200 Austrian Skoda guns.'[10]

However this may be, Churchill's great enterprise was over. He could reflect bitterly that he had been forced to abandon the most glittering opportunity of his life in spite of the fact that no crippling losses such as were common on the Western Front had been sustained, and no compelling argument advanced that the naval victory could not be won. It was a moment for Winston of profound unhappiness and dejection, for he had suddenly lost the power to organize and direct.

He continued to advocate the need to defeat Turkey; he pressed for military action on the Gallipoli Peninsula at the earliest opportunity and with the maximum force. But from the moment that military preparations began, the power to act passed from Churchill's hands. As Secretary of State for War, Kitchener controlled all military initiatives at the Dardanelles.[11]

Since Winston was no longer at the centre of planning we need not trace in any detail the military assault on the Peninsula. It ended in a military failure, hideously expensive in human life, and a splendid opportunity was squandered. He was bitterly conscious that power had slipped from his hands, and was kept in humiliating ignorance by Kitchener of the plans for landing in Gallipoli. His fears were aggravated by the elapse of five vital weeks between the breaking off of naval operations and the military attack.

During those five weeks the Turks were feverishly strengthening their defences under the expert supervision of German officers. The element of surprise had been lost, and when at last, on 25 April, the troops landed on the Gallipoli beaches, they were unable to reach their objectives. The Army found itself fighting on the beaches with heavy casualties from a withering fire poured down upon the troops from the cliffs and heights

10. PRO. CAB/19/1.
11. Gilbert, op. cit., p. 380.

that towered above them, and succeeded in gaining only a precarious foothold on the southern tip of the Peninsula.

Winston was gravely disturbed by the slow progress, and by the enormous losses that accompanied it. With Fisher, he went to the War Office to entreat Kitchener to send reinforcements from Egypt. After some argument the Secretary of State yielded, and ordered a Territorial Division and an Indian Brigade to be sent from Egypt to the Dardanelles. Even in this hour of depression his dramatic instincts were alert, and he wrote in an unsent letter of 26 April to Kitchener's Military Secretary, FitzGerald:

> I hope K will not cut Hamilton too fine. I have a feeling that there ought to be another 20,000 men in it. They could get there in a week from Egypt. A valiant and successful attack like this may go well for a time: but there must be *stuffing* behind and inside it. So far all is well, but watch carefully that these two or three precious days that decide things are not lost.
>
> I think there ought to be more men: at any rate more *near* the spot.
>
> *Remember every minute of this is history*: [author's italics] and every attack requires backing.[12]

It was all in vain.

* * *

Winston visited Paris on 5 May with Sir Henry Jackson to conduct the final naval negotiations for Italy's switch from her alliance with Germany and Austria to the Franco-British side. It was an indication of Asquith's continued confidence in him. He returned to London on 10 May when he received a letter from de Robeck offering to renew the naval attack upon the Straits, for like other sailors, he had witnessed the cruel sufferings and bitter sacrifices of the Army and been mortified that the Navy was unable to make a more positive contribution. He now suggested that the Fleet should engage the forts at the Narrows and test their alleged shortage of ammunition.

But Churchill realized that circumstances had changed since the first naval attack. Now the presence of a great army on the Gallipoli Peninsula, which depended for its survival on British dominance of the Aegean, and the suspected arrival of German submarines, made a total commitment of the Navy an unacceptable risk. Churchill therefore decided that the most he could safely do was to encourage de Robeck to clear the minefield and advance as far as the Narrows, destroying the Turkish forts en route.

12. Copy, Chartwell papers: 13/45.

Fisher was, however, strongly opposed to any independent action by the Fleet until the Army had effectively occupied the shores of the Narrows, and on 11 May there was a sharp and acrimonious exchange between him and Churchill at the Admiralty, in which 'I used every argument which the situation presented, and made every appeal that our long and intimate association rendered possible. I encountered an absolute refusal, accompanied by signs of the most extreme distress.'

Although Winston did not realize it, the Admiral's nerve was beginning to crumple. He was beset 'with the deep empirical misgivings of old age.' During the First Lord's absence in France, Fisher had become automatically responsible for the conduct of the Admiralty, and had found the responsibility a deeply oppressive one. Under the strain his never stable character had begun to show signs of disintegration. Clementine Churchill had observed this, and in an effort to placate him invited the old man to luncheon at Admiralty House. They had a pleasant meal and the Admiral left in cheerful mood. But when she later left the house she was astonished to find him still lurking in the passage outside her room:

'You are a foolish woman,' he said; 'all the time you think Winston's with Sir John French he is in Paris with his mistress.' 'Be quiet, you silly old man,' she said, 'and get out.'

This ridiculous observation was clearly not the remark of a man in full possession of his reason, but although angered by it, she divined its cause. 'The Admiral,' she said later, 'was as nervous as a kitten,'[13] and it seemed clear to her that his mind was unbalanced. In fact Fisher, in his then condition, was convinced that Winston was again courting disaster by trying to 'rush the Dardanelles'. He believed that if the limited attack on the forts and the minefield was successful Winston would be tempted to advance further into the Sea of Marmara. He sent Churchill a memorandum on 11 May, drafted by Hankey, setting forth his objections to separate naval action, and stating that another attempt by the Fleet to force the Narrows was doomed to failure.

When Churchill read this document and the defiant letter that accompanied it he realized that the Admiral was for once *au grand sérieux*, and wielded his own pen with equal vigour:

My dear Fisher,
    You will never receive from me any proposition to 'rush' the Dardanelles; & I agree with the views you express so forcibly on this subject. It may be that the Admiral will have to engage the forts & sweep the Kephez minefield as an aid to the military operations; & we have always

13. Gilbert, op. cit., p. 419. Soames. 120.

agreed in the desirability of forcing them to fire off their scanty stock of ammunition . . . and it is my most earnest hope on public & still more on personal grounds that any real issue will find us as always hitherto – united. That shall be my endeavour.

We are now in a vy difficult position. Whether it is my fault for trying or my misfortune for not having the power to carry through is immaterial. We are now committed to one of the greatest amphibious enterprises of history. You are absolutely committed. Comradeship, resource, firmness, patience, all in the highest degree will be needed to carry the matter through to victory. A great army hanging on by its eyelids to a rocky beach, and confronted with the armed power of the Turkish Empire under German military guidance: the whole *surplus* fleet of Britain – every scrap that can be spared – bound to that army & its fortunes as long as the struggle may drag out: the apparition of the long-feared submarine – our many needs & obligations – the measureless advantages – probably decisive on the whole war – to be gained by success.

Surely here is a combination & a situation wh requires from us every conceivable exertion & contrivance wh we can think of. I beg of you to lend your whole aid & good will; & ultimately then success is certain.

Yours ever
W[14]

* * *

Fisher, who was by now confident that he could rely on Asquith's support, rejected this warm appeal. On 12 May the battleship *Goliath* was torpedoed and sunk in the Dardanelles, and there were reports that German submarines had appeared in the eastern Mediterranean. Churchill resolved on a gesture of appeasement towards the Admiral. Knowing that the old man's main cause of anxiety was the presence of the *Queen Elizabeth* at the Dardanelles and the risk of her destruction, he agreed that she should return to home waters and be replaced by two monitors with 14-inch guns.

Although this gesture may have placated Fisher, it caused deep resentment in another quarter. When Kitchener was told at a conference that evening that *Queen Elizabeth* was to be withdrawn he was alarmed and angry. In Winston's words, 'His habitual composure in trying ordeals left him. He protested vehemently against what he considered the desertion of the army at its most critical moment.'

It was impossible that Fisher would remain silent after such a remark. 'The *Queen Elizabeth* would come home,' he said angrily: 'she would come home at once; she would come home that night, or he would walk out of the Admiralty then and there.'

14. Copy: Churchill papers: 13/57.

The following day, 13 May, Churchill sent a telegram to de Robeck indicating that forcing the Dardanelles with ships was no longer a feasible operation:

> We think the moment for an independent Naval attempt to force the Narrows has passed and will not arise again under present conditions. The Army is now landed ... Your role is therefore to support the Army in its costly but sure advance and reserve your strength to deal with the situation which will arise later when the Army has succeeded with your aid in its task . . .[15]

Churchill had in fact yielded to Fisher's demands, hoping that by so doing the lamentable differences between them would be healed, but in this wishful thinking he underrated the Admiral's growing paranoia and excitement. So far his agitation resembled the premonitory rumblings of an ancient but far from extinct volcano. He had begun to ventilate his complaints in a letter to Asquith on 12 May;

> It will be within your recollection that you saw me and the First Lord of the Admiralty in your private room, prior to a meeting of the War Council (28 January 1915), to consider my protest against the Dardanelles undertaking when it was first mooted. With extreme reluctance, and largely due to the earnest words spoken to me by Kitchener, I by not resigning (*as I now see I should have done*) remained a most unwilling beholder (and indeed a participator) of the gradual draining of our Naval resources from the decisive theatre of the war. The absence, especially at this moment, of destroyers, submarines, and mine-sweepers (which are now at the Dardanelles) most materially lessens our power of dealing with the submarine menace in home waters – a menace daily becoming greater . . .[16]

After talking over his grievances with Churchill that evening Fisher seemed to become calmer, but the following day the antagonism and resentment that had always accompanied his love for Winston reasserted itself. Again the Admiral addressed himself to a Prime Minister long wearied of this fruitless wrangle, but this time with a sharply rising note of protest:

> Thank you for your letter of yesterday, in which you state that you had long been given to understand that an arrangement had been come to between the First Lord and myself and you kindly added that you were very glad. But I regret to say that within four hours of the pact

15. Copy: Churchill papers: 13/65.
16. Admiral Sir R. H. Bacon, *The Life of Lord Fisher*.

being concluded the First Lord said to Kitchener 'that in the event of the Army's failure, the Fleet would endeavour to force its way through,' or words to that effect ... I desire to convey to you that I honestly feel that I cannot remain where I am much longer, as there is an inevitable and never-ceasing drain *daily* (*almost hourly*) of our resources in the decisive theatre of the war. But that is not the worst – instead of the whole time of the whole of the Admiralty being concentrated on the daily increasing submarine menace in Home Waters, we are all diverted to the Dardanelles, and the increasing activities of the First Lord, both by day and night, are engaged in ceaseless *prodding* of everyone in every department afloat and ashore in the interest of the Dardanelles Fleet, with the result of a huge Armada now there, whose size is sufficiently indicated by their having as many battleships out there as in the German High Sea Fleet! Therefore this purely private and personal letter, intended for your eye alone and not to be quoted, as there is no use threatening without acting, is to mention to the one person who I feel OUGHT to know, *that I feel my time is short.*[17]

Fisher's mistrust of Churchill was now becoming an obsession. He was determined to ignore every olive branch, and he disseminated poison against the First Lord wherever it could produce the most corrosive effect. The issue between them was straightforward: Churchill was convinced that the Fleet must continue to take part in the Dardanelles operation; Fisher was determined that it should not. Neither was prepared to budge an inch. But the animosity was all on Fisher's side, and Churchill, even at this penultimate stage, still pathetically believed that he could 'manage' his turbulent friend.

At a War Council meeting on 14 May – at which the atmosphere was described by Winston as 'sulphurous' – Fisher repeated his familiar dirge that he had been opposed to the Dardanelles from the beginning, and in answer to that claim Winston wrote the same afternoon to the Prime Minister in a manner which betrays little rancour at Fisher's behaviour, and no comprehension of the fact that his frequently threatened resignation was really about to take place:

I must ask you to take note of Fisher's statement today that he was against the Dlles & had been all along, or words to that effect. The ISL [First Sea Lord] has agreed in writing to every executive telegram on which the operations have been conducted; & had they been immediately successful, the credit would have been his. But I make no complaint of that. I am attached to the old boy & it is a great pleasure to me to work with him. I think he reciprocates these feelings. My point is that a moment will probably arise in these operations when the Adl & Genl on the spot

17. Asquith papers.

will wish & require to run a risk with the Fleet for a great and decisive effort. If I agree with them, I shall sanction it & I cannot undertake to be paralyzed by the veto of a friend who whatever the result will certainly say 'I was always against the Dlles . . .

It is also uncomfortable not to know what Kitchener will or won't do in the matter of reinforcements. We are absolutely in his hands, & I never saw him in a queerer mood – or more unreasonable. K will punish the Admy by docking Hamilton of his division, because we have withdrawn the 'Q Elizabeth'; & Fisher will have the Q Elizth home if he is to stay. Through all this with patience & determination we can make our way to one of the gt events in the history of the world.

But I wish now to make it clear to you that a man who says 'I disclaim responsibility for failure' cannot be the final arbiter of the measure wh may be found to be vital to success.

This requires no answer, & I am quite contented with the course of affairs.[18]

*   *   *

Winston, unperceptive to the last of Fisher's state of mind, visited him in his room in the Admiralty in the late afternoon of 14 May. The Admiral, who had been so angry and unmanageable before, had undergone one of his lightning changes of mood, and was calm and reasonable, not a feather out of place. Winston, who still believed that the differences between him and Fisher could be resolved, was encouraged by the prevailing calm, and for several hours the two men discussed naval reinforcements for the Dardanelles not only without bitterness, but with much of their old friendship. Winston, with somewhat cumbrous tact, tried to limit his suggestions to requests to which he thought Fisher would agree and, when they had finished, remarked affectionately, 'Well, good night, Fisher. We have settled everything, and you must go home and have a good night's rest. Things will look brighter in the morning and we'll pull the thing through together.'

Fisher was also satisfied with the conversation, and told his naval secretary that his relations with the First Lord were again amicable. 'But,' he added lightly (though at the same time ominously), 'I suppose he'll soon be at me again.'[19]

Winston remained working out in detail in his room the arrangements just agreed with Fisher, and finished this task by eleven o'clock. Then he made a last-minute, almost casual, but quite fatal decision to add two more E class submarines to the ships earmarked for the Dardanelles. It should be noted that this addition in no way bound Fisher. It was a

18. Copy: Churchill papers, 13/52.
19. Gilbert, op. cit., p. 435–6.

proposal, not an order, and Winston, to emphasize this fact, told the Admiral in a personal covering note:

> My dear Fisher,
>   I send this to you before marking it to others in order that if any point arises we can discuss it. I hope you will agree.
>   Yours ever
>   W

The proposal about the submarines caused a sudden and synthetic eruption of fury in the Admiral, which suggests that his mind had already been closed, that his amiable conversation with Winston was meaningless, and that he was prepared to grasp any straw which provided him with an excuse for extricating himself from a position which he feared and loathed. When the Admiral, like a prima donna after many abortive farewell performances, at last decided on 15 May to resign he stage-managed his departure with a sort of lunatic panache. In Asquith's words: 'Fisher has levanted.' He deserted the Admiralty, his post and his work, pulled down the blinds in his house in the Admiralty Arch, and set a red-herring trail in the direction of Scotland. [Winston's private secretary, Masterton-Smith, in the belief that Fisher was making for France, was scouring the Continental railway stations; others were following different scents. Asquith had provided the beadle with a paper to serve on him:- 'Lord Fisher – in the name of the King I command you to return to your post.']

Winston first heard this dire news from Fisher's letter of resignation on the morning of 15 May:

> First Lord,
>   After further anxious reflection I have come to the regretted conclusion I am unable to remain any longer as your colleague . . . I find it increasingly difficult to adjust myself to the increasingly daily requirements of the Dardanelles to meet your views – as you truly said yesterday I am in the position of constantly veto-ing your proposals.
>   This is not fair to you besides being extremely distasteful to me.
>   I am off to Scotland so as to avoid all questionings.
>   Yrs truly
>   Fisher.[20]

It was characteristic of Churchill that he was still not unduly alarmed. He could look back on all the other petulant occasions when Fisher had sworn he was resigning, and therefore treated this last one with

20. Chartwell papers: 13/57.

a lightness it did not deserve. But he searched in vain at the Admiralty for the First Sea Lord whose movements were unknown, except that he had told his Naval Secretary that he was going to Scotland immediately. Winston crossed Horse Guards Parade to Downing Street where he showed the Prime Minister Fisher's letter.

The Admiral, after some time, was run to ground in London and brought to Number Ten. He was in a morose and truculent mood. While Fisher waited for Asquith (who had gone to a wedding) Lloyd George appeared, and spoke to the Admiral. He was immediately struck by what he saw as a 'dour change' in Fisher's mood:

> A combative grimness had taken the place of his usually genial greeting; the lower lip was thrust forward, and the droop at the corner was more marked than usual. His curiously oriental features were more than ever those of a graven image in an Eastern temple, with a sinister frown.
>
> 'I have resigned' was his greeting, and on my inquiring the reason he replied, 'I can stand it no longer.' He then informed me that he was on his way to see the Prime Minister, having made up his mind to take no further part in the Dardanelles 'foolishness', and was off to Scotland that night.[21]

Lloyd George began to reason with Fisher, reminding him that he had never opposed the Dardanelles expedition at the War Council, but his unanswerable arguments were ignored, Fisher insisting that he would leave for Scotland immediately, and it was at that moment that Asquith returned. But he was no more successful with the sullen Admiral than Lloyd George. Fisher refused to return to the Admiralty, and although Asquith thought that he had shaken his determination to resign, he was far from sure. By this time both Winston and the Prime Minister realized the gruesome political crisis that would descend upon them if they could not persuade Fisher to return, and it was clear to them that the Admiral must be appeased. Asquith considered that this pacification should take the form of a letter from Winston which would combine an emotional appeal with some positive assurance that naval reinforcements sent to the Dardanelles would be confined to the needs of the Army. The letter was sent on 15 May:

> ... It is true that the moment is anxious and our difficulties grave. But I am sure that with loyalty and courage we shall come through safely and successfully. You could not let it be said that you had thrown me over because things were for the time being going badly at the Dardanelles.
>
> In every way I have tried to work in the closest sympathy with you ...

21. Lloyd George, *War Memoirs*.

My own responsibilities are great and also I am the one who gets the blame for anything that goes wrong. But I have scrupulously adhered to our original agreement that we should do nothing important without consulting each other.

If you think this is not so, surely you should tell me in what respect. In order to bring you back to the Admiralty I took my political life in my hands with the King and the Prime Minister – as you well know. You then promised to stand by me and see me through. If you now go at this bad moment and thereby let loose upon me the spite and malice of those who are your enemies even more than they are mine it will be a melancholy ending to our six months of successful war administration. The discussions which will arise will strike a cruel blow at the fortunes of the Army now struggling on the Gallipoli Peninsula and cannot fail to invest with an air of disaster a mighty enterprise which with patience can and will certainly be carried to success . . .

I hope you will come to see me tomorrow afternoon. I have a proposition to make to you with the assent of the Prime Minister which may resolve some of the anxieties and difficulties which you feel about the measures necessary to support the army at the Dardanelles.

Though I shall stand to my post until relieved, it will be a very great grief to me to part from you; and any rupture will be profoundly injurious to every public interest.[22]

* * *

But the bell had already begun to toll for Winston Churchill, and its first note was struck harshly by his friend Lloyd George, who said to his secretary, Frances Stevenson, that if Fisher could not be lured back into the fold Churchill would have to leave the Government:

It is the Nemesis of the man who has fought for this war for years. When the war came he saw in it the chance of glory for himself, & has accordingly entered on a risky campaign without caring a straw for the misery and hardship it would bring to thousands, in the hope that he would prove to be the outstanding man in this war.[23]

Brutally unjustified as this opinion was, and probably expressed at a moment of irritation and fatigue, it represented exactly the views of Winston's numerous and implacable enemies.

Fisher lurked in seclusion for the whole of 15 May, and Churchill's letter only reached him that night. The Admiral replied next morning in a manner which proved that he was destitute of any adequate excuse

22. Fisher papers.
23. Frances Stevenson, *Diaries*, p. 440.

for his conduct, and he was thrown back on the explanation that it was due to Churchill's addition of two submarines to the Dardanelles reinforcements. He said not a word about the fact that this addition was a suggestion, not an order, and one which Churchill was perfectly willing to discuss with him, and his long-pent-up resentment seemed to explode into angry phrases as he wrote, refusing any further meeting with the First Lord:

> YOU ARE BENT ON FORCING THE DARDANELLES AND NOTH-ING WILL TURN YOU FROM IT – NOTHING – I know you so well!
> I could give you no better proof of my desire to stand by you than my having remained by you in this Dardanelles business up to this last moment against the strongest conviction of my life as stated in the Dardanelles Committee Memorandum . . .
> *You will remain* and I SHALL GO – it is better so . . .[24]

In this manner and on an insolently frivolous pretext did Fisher inflict upon his Chief and friend the most murderous blow in his political career. He had assiduously fostered the impression that he had always been against the Dardanelles, and that he had fought it tooth and claw and been overborne. In fact, although at no time enthusiastic, he had never raised his voice against it in the War Council, and had signed every executive order for it in his own hand. Had it succeeded, he would have claimed a large share of the credit, and the operation would have been said to have borne 'the Fisher touch'. He had engaged in indecorous intrigue against Churchill behind his back with leaders of the Opposition, his unruly tongue wagging in the ears of anyone who would listen, and he was strongly suspected of inspiring a poisonous campaign against him in the press. By resigning at this moment he deserted Churchill at his hour of greatest need, and precipitated a political crisis which seemed to put a full stop to Churchill's career. It was not a record of which he had any cause to be proud. Where was his 'Totus Porcus' now?

We should observe the characteristic fact that up to the last moment Winston had not fathomed the brain-storm that had seized the Admiral – 'We have always got on well – differed on no principle – I had always supposed him to be perfectly loyal.' Once again we realize that the working of the human mind was a force he could not comprehend: 'Poor darling W,' wrote Violet Asquith

> there is a naive and utterly disarming trustfulness about him. He is quite impervious to the climatic conditions of other people. He makes his own

24. Chartwell papers: 13/57.

climate and lives in it and those who love him share it. In an odd way there was something like love between him and Fisher – a kind of magnetic attraction which often went into reverse. Theirs was a curiously emotional relationship – but as in many such they could neither live with, nor without, each other.[25]

*　*　*

Churchill made a final attempt at blandishment in a letter to Fisher on 16 May, but received a dusty answer in which the Admiral again refused to meet him: 'Please don't wish to see me. I could say nothing as I am determined not to. *I know I am doing right*.'[26]

The old man had another arrow in his quiver, and it was discharged in a devious manner. On 15 May he had sent to the Leader of the Opposition, Bonar Law, a press cutting which recorded that Lord Fisher had been received in audience of the King and had remained with him for half an hour. It was his tortuous method of informing the Conservative Leader of his resignation.

When the fact that Fisher meant business at last penetrated Winston's mind he began to mend his fences. He learned on 16 May from Sir Arthur Wilson that the other Sea Lords were prepared to remain at their posts. He then asked Wilson whether he was willing to accept the position of First Sea Lord, and he consented. Winston told Asquith of this transaction and offered to go if the Prime Minister wished to make a change. Asquith replied that he did not desire to do so.

For a moment Churchill felt that the crisis was over and that he would be able, on 17 May, to satisfy Parliament. But during his visit to Asquith he learned that the combination of Fisher's resignation and Colonel Repington's disclosure of the shell shortage on the Western Front was so dangerous that the Prime Minister might be forced to consult the Conservative Opposition. Churchill realized from this that the crisis would not be confined to the Admiralty, but he was still reasonably confident that if he announced the new Board of Admiralty without delay and explained Fisher's resignation to the House the threatening explosion might still be prevented. He was not therefore in a despondent mood as he sat preparing his speech for 17 May, still hoping that the issue could be restricted to Admiralty policy which he was confident of defending, and that a general crisis could be circumvented. His optimism was not justified by events.

25. Bonham Carter, op. cit., p. 392.
26. Chartwell papers: 13/57.

Chapter 19

The Bitter Cup

Alerted by Fisher's melodramatic warning in the press cutting, Bonar Law responded on 15 May with suspicious alacrity. He went to see Lloyd George and asked him if he could confirm the fact of Fisher's resignation. On being told that it was true, Bonar Law stressed the gravity of the political situation, aggravated by the failure of the Dardanelles expedition and the scandal over the shell-shortage. He told Lloyd George that if Fisher resigned it would be impossible for Churchill to remain at the Admiralty. We should remember that Fisher was a pampered darling of the Tory Party, Churchill its *bête noire*. On this question the Opposition was adamant, and would certainly force a major Parliamentary challenge.

Lloyd George, aware of what this involved, said that he must consult the Prime Minister. Using the internal access from No.11 Downing Street to No.10, he placed the circumstances before Asquith, arguing with all his persuasive power that an immediate Coalition provided the only hope of neutralizing the Conservative attack. Although this advice implied throwing Winston (so often protected and forgiven before) to the wolves, Asquith acquiesced in it with a strange lassitude, and said that he would invite the Conservatives to join his Administration.

Winston was not to be the only sacrifice to appease Conservative hatred. Haldane, the creator of the General Staff and Territorial Army, and the greatest Secretary of State for War in modern times, was also discharged like an errant footman after a disgraceful press campaign against him, his main crime in Tory eyes being that he had been educated in Germany and had once said that she was his spiritual home.

In fact, at that moment and unknown to his colleagues, the Prime Minister had been temporarily deprived of fighting spirit and initiative by an agonizing personal dereliction. Venetia Stanley, the young woman he adored, the Egeria who had solaced him in moments of depression and weakness, the person whose advice he sought on questions of high strategy; with whom he shared all the secrets of the State; the engrossing influence which alone made his burden tolerable – had told him three days before that she was to marry Edwin Montagu. This man, referred to by Asquith in their correspondence as 'the Assyrian,' and afterwards Secretary of State for India and co-author of the Montagu–Chelmsford Reforms, had supplanted him.

Asquith was utterly shattered by these tidings, and consumed by jealousy and despair. Venetia had severed herself from him, and he made desperate efforts to re-establish contact. Anyone, he told her, who wished to get rid of him could do so

> effectively, & without a moment's delay, when any veil is dropped between me and you – soul of my life . . . You alone of all the world – to whom I have always gone in every moment of trial & trouble, & from whom I have always come back solaced and healed & inspired – were the one person who could do nothing wrong, & from whom I could ask nothing. To my dying day that will be the most bitter memory of my life.[1]

Asquith's devouring grief at this moment dumbed his will. He could not now face Bonar Law's threats, with all they implied, and he listlessly gave way. He was aware that Churchill had successfully reconstituted his Board, and that with Sir Arthur Wilson as First Sea Lord the Admiralty would continue to work efficiently, and he had every reason to believe that Churchill could defend the naval position in Parliament; but, a prey to torturing emotions, he was past caring and declined the challenge.

Ignorant of the Prime Minister's debilitation, Churchill went down to the House of Commons, anxious but confident, on 17 May to deliver his speech of explanation and announce his new Board of Admiralty. On reaching the House he was told by Lloyd George that a Coalition was inevitable and must be brought into being without delay. Winston made no objection to this, but wished first to complete the new Board of Admiralty, only to be told that the Coalition must be formed immediately.

He then went to Asquith's room to ask permission to make his speech. It was a moment of tragedy, reminding us of another searing occasion when Lord Curzon, in the absolute conviction that he was to become Prime Minister, and with a list of his Cabinet in his pocket, was informed at the last moment that the post was to go to Mr Baldwin.

Now Asquith made it clear to Winston that he no longer wanted a debate. When Churchill tried to show him the list of his new Board, the Prime Minister said curtly, 'No, this will not do. I have decided to form a

1. Montagu Papers. Quoted Gilbert, op.cit., p.447.

National Government by a coalition with the Unionists, and a very much larger reconstruction will be required . . . What are we to do for you?'[2]

In this laconic fashion was Churchill informed that his tenure of the Admiralty was at an end.

* * *

This episode came as a profound shock to him. His long unbroken success was abruptly shattered, and he saw with dismay that his career was in jeopardy. But he remained defiant and a trifle high-handed. When Lloyd George, who had joined them, suggested that Winston should be sent to the Colonial Office, he replied haughtily that he would only accept a Service department. But he was in no position to pick and choose. The Conservatives did not wish him to play any part in a Coalition Government, or if he did, only in a minor office.

In the middle of this discussion a message was brought to Winston summoning him back to the Admiralty on business of immediate importance. He left at once to be told that the German High Seas Fleet was about to enter the North Sea. It seemed that the great sea battle for which he had long yearned was about to begin at a moment when he knew that his days at the Admiralty were numbered. With Oliver and Wilson, he gave orders for the Grand Fleet and all other available ships to be sent to the scene of action. He remained at the Admiralty for five hours, personally superintending every detail of the approaching battle which he believed would take place next day. His malaise about his own political future was wiped from his mind by the zest of action, but by morning it was clear that the Germans did not intend to make a major challenge and had returned to their bases.

'The episode was over,' wrote Churchill in *The World Crisis*: 'All our fleets, squadrons and flotillas turned morosely away to resume their long-drawn, unrelenting watch, and I awoke again to the political crisis. But my hour had passed . . .' Indeed, had there been a full-scale battle between the two Fleets resulting in a British victory Churchill's position would have been transformed, for it would have been manifestly impossible to degrade the hero of the hour, the victor over the High Seas Fleet.

On the next morning Winston had time to regret his haughty rejection of the Colonial Office suggestion, and in his naive way even now nourished a pathetic hope of remaining at the Admiralty.

'Above all things,' he wrote to Asquith on 18 May, 'I shd like to stay here — and complete my work, the most difficult part of wh is

2. WSC, op.cit., p.454.

ended . . . If Balfour were to go to the War Office the two departments wd work with perfect smoothness.'[3]

Sir Max Aitken was astonished at this ill-founded optimism. Having called on Winston that night with F. E. Smith, Aitken noted:

> What a creature of strange moods he is – always at the top of the wheel of confidence or at the bottom of an intense depression . . . That Tuesday night he was clinging to the desire of retaining the Admiralty as though the salvation of England depended on it. I believe he would even have made it up with Lord Fisher if that had been the price of remaining there. None the less, so little did he realise the inwardness of the whole situation that he still hoped.[4]

By that time it was evident that in reality nothing could retrieve Winston's position although, dimly conscious of approaching changes, he made desperate efforts to do so. He became aware of the sour taste of disfavour when he was excluded from all discussions on the formation of the Coalition – the first time for five years that he had been denied entry into the highest counsels. It was a moment full of bitterness.

The Prime Minister had not yet formally accepted Fisher's resignation, and there were some Liberals, as well as Conservatives, unaware of Fisher's behaviour in the crisis, who thought that, with Churchill finally ousted, Fisher might take his place as First Lord. But the Admiral quickly invalidated this suggestion and placed himself beyond the pale by an action of such staggering stupidity that those aware of it, from the King downwards, concluded that his brilliant but disordered mind had given way. Seeing himself on the verge of becoming the supreme naval authority, he submitted a paper to Asquith containing the six conditions on which he was prepared to 'guarantee the successful termination of the war.' There is megalomania in every line of this preposterous document, and Fisher could have devised no more effective method of digging his own grave:

1. That Mr Winston Churchill is not in the Cabinet to be always circumventing me, nor will I serve under Mr Balfour.
2. That Sir A.K. Wilson leaves the Admiralty and the Committee of Imperial Defence and the War Council, as my time otherwise will be occupied in resisting the bombardment of Heligoland and other such wild projects, also his policy is totally opposed to mine and he has accepted position of First Sea Lord in succession to me, and thereby adopting a policy totally opposed to my views.

3. Copy: Chartwell Papers; 13/52.
4. Beaverbrook, *Politicians and the War.*

3. That there shall be an entire new Board of Admiralty, as regards the Sea Lords and the Financial Secretary (who is utterly useless). *New Measures* demand new men!

4. That I shall have complete professional charge of the war at sea, together with the absolute sole disposition of the Fleet and the appointments of all officers of all ranks whatsoever, and absolutely untrammelled sole command of all the sea forces whatsoever.

5. That the First Lord of the Admiralty should be absolutely restricted to policy and parliamentary procedure . . .

6. That I should have the sole absolute authority for all new construction and all dockyard work of whatever sort whatsoever, and complete control of the whole of the Civil establishments of the Navy.

Fisher added to all this: 'These six conditions must be published so that the Fleet may know my position.'[5]

Asquith did not show this document to Winston, and he remained unaware of the full extent of Fisher's treachery, for it was not until 1927 that Asquith sent him a copy while writing his memoirs.

*   *   *

Max Aitken, in many ways a shrewder observer of personalities than Churchill, had assured him that he had not the slightest chance of making an accommodation with the Conservatives, and that their dislike of him was unqualified and absolute. Himself a man without vindictiveness, Churchill had no comprehension of an emotion so poisonous and so enduring. In any case, by 19 May he was becoming desperate and felt no qualms in presenting himself in the unnatural role of suppliant to Bonar Law, a man whose character he found unsympathetic and whose intellect he despised.

Churchill had always underestimated Bonar Law because he did not understand him – had underrated his mathematician's mind, his Covenanter's ruthlessness, his power to debate which was like having 'showers of gravel thrown in one's face'. He saw only the dullness of the man, the grey neutral character, the lack of intellectual resources and the joyless routine of his daily life. During the Home Rule crisis their differences had been acute, and Bonar Law had frequently winced under the lash of Churchill's tongue. For Winston had seemed to find a particular relish in spraying this dull creature with those wonderful *roulades* of contemptuous phrases chosen unerringly by his perfect ear, which were not intended to wound, although they invariably did so,

5. Copy, Chartwell Papers: 2/153.

and which their author regarded as he might a boisterous game of polo – rough but unmalicious.

But when Winston wrote to Bonar Law on 19 May these insults had not been forgotten:

> My dear Bonar Law,
>   Now that there is I rejoice to think a good prospect of our becoming colleagues, I feel entitled to send you the enclosed papers.
>   I have borne in silence all these anxious months the charge that I am to blame by my interferences with the naval experts for the loss of 3 cruisers & the faulty dispositions wh led to the action of Coronel.
>   I also send you the telegram wh as it happened – tho this was good luck – had such a decisive effect on the operations culminating in the action at the Falklands.
>   You must not suppose that in sending you these I want to claim all the credit or avoid the blame, only hitherto the principle has been that the blame only came to me.[6]

Bonar Law naturally felt no interest in this raking over the past, but Winston would not abandon his efforts. No Government changes had been made public, and he continued to work at the Admiralty on routine matters and in an unreal atmosphere, while sticking like a limpet to his plans for remaining in that office.

Incredibly, after all that happened, his thoughts turned again to Fisher. It occurred to him that by offering the Admiral some preferential position enhancing his powers, Fisher could be persuaded that, like Kitchener, he was *inter pares* with the politicians whose superior position had proved so irksome to him in the past. With an exuberance worthy of Fisher himself, he offered the Admiral any terms he liked, an extraordinary *carte blanche* which he was certainly not empowered to present. He had fallen into a trap baited by a forgotten loyalty. This strange gesture merely inflamed Fisher's paranoia, because it caused him to believe that his presence at the Admiralty was considered essential to victory. With despicable disloyalty Fisher immediately conveyed this offer to Bonar Law, adding virtuously, 'I rejected the 30 pieces of silver to betray my country.'[7]

At the Admiralty the senior officials were in favour of Balfour as First Lord with Sir Arthur Wilson or Sir Henry Jackson as First Sea Lord. They were now also agreed that both Churchill and Fisher

6. Bonar Law papers.
7. Gilbert, op.cit., p.456.

should go, a view which was passed on to Asquith by the Director of Naval Intelligence.[8]

The strain was now affecting even Winston's iron nerves, making him moody and excitable. When Lord Riddell called on him at the Admiralty on 20 May

> He looked very worn and harassed. He greeted me warmly and said, 'I am the victim of a political intrigue. I am finished!' I said, 'Not finished at forty, with your remarkable powers!' 'Yes,' he said. 'Finished in respect of all I care for – the waging of war; the defeat of the Germans . . .'[9]

On the same day he made another futile attempt to enlist Tory support. That night he had a long discussion with Bonar Law, doomed in advance to failure, in which he sought to justify his record at the Admiralty and his actions over the Dardanelles. It was to no avail. But like a boxer who although in desperate straits refuses to surrender because the prize is so great, Winston grimly persevered. He addressed himself again to the same frigid court of appeal next day in a long letter, now carrying the marks of despair, and again misjudging Bonar Law's attitude to him:

> The rule to follow is what is most likely to please the newspapers. The question of the Dardanelles operations and my differences with Fisher ought to be settled by people who know the facts and not by those who cannot know them. Now you and your friends, except Mr Balfour, do not know the facts. On our side only the Prime Minister knows them. The policy and conduct of the Dardanelles operations should be reviewed by the new Cabinet. Every fact should be laid before them. They should decide and on their decision the composition of the Board of Admiralty should depend.
>
> It is not in justice to myself that I am asking for this; but primarily because of the great operation which is in progress, and for which I bear a tremendous responsibility. With Sir Arthur Wilson's professional aid I am sure I can discharge that responsibility fully. In view of his statement to the Prime Minister and to the naval Lords that he will serve as First Sea Lord under me, and under no one else, I feel entitled to say that no other personal combination will give so good a chance.
>
> If this view of mine should prove to be true, it affects the safety of an Army now battling its way under many difficulties, and the success of an operation of the utmost consequence for which more than 30,000 have already shed their blood: and I suggest to you that it is your duty to refuse to judge so grave an issue until you know the facts.

8. Captain, later Sir Reginald, Hall, M.P.
9. Lord Riddell, *War Diary*.

My lips are sealed in public, but in a few days all the facts can be placed before you and your friends under official secrecy. I am sure those with whom I work as colleagues and comrades in this great struggle will not allow a newspaper campaign – necessarily conducted in ignorance and not untinged with prejudice – to be the deciding factor in matters of such terrible import.

Churchill then proceeded to justify at length his conduct of the Admiralty from 1911 until the present time, and concluded:

Many Sea Lords have come and gone, but during all these 4 years (nearly) I have been according to my patent 'solely responsible to Crown and Parliament' and have borne the blame for any failure: and now I present to you an absolutely secure naval position; a Fleet constantly and rapidly growing in strength, and abundantly supplied with munitions of every kind; an organisation working with perfect smoothness and efficiency, and the seas upon which no enemy's flag is flown.

Therefore I ask to be judged fairly, deliberately and with knowledge. I do not ask for anything else.[10]

He followed this appeal by writing to the Prime Minister with harrowing persistence and growing desperation on 21 May. It was a *cri de coeur* in which he described the torturing reflections which now disturbed every waking moment, and which could be so easily dispelled by a word of confidence and reassurance from on high:

. . . My responsibility is terrible. But I know I cd sustain it, & without the slightest impairment of our margin here, cd bring this vast Dardanelles business safely through in spite of the submarines. Arthur Wilson & I together can do it. We alone know the whole position . . .

It is no clinging to office or to this particular office or my own interest and advancement wh moves me: I am clinging to my *task* & to my *duty*. I am straining to make good the formidable undertaking in wh we are engaged; & wh I know – with Arthur Wilson – I can alone discharge.

I do not believe it possible to endure such anxiety.

None of the ordinary strains of war – wh I have borne all these months – have been comparable to this feeling. It grows upon me each of these long drawn days . . .

You alone know the whole situation and that it is my duty to carry the burden safely: and that I can do it.

I can only look to you. Let me stand or fall by the Dardanelles – but do not take it from my hands.[11]

10. Copy, Churchill papers: 13/52.
11. Asquith papers.

The same day, 21 May, he wrote again to Asquith:

> I am very sorry for your troubles, and sorry to have been the cause of a situation wh has enabled others to bring them upon you – I will accept any office – the lowest if you like – that you care to offer me, & will continue to serve in it in this time of war until the affairs in which I am deeply concerned are settled satisfactorily, as I think they will be.[12]

Gladstone had once said that a Prime Minster should be a good butcher: now, apathetic in his secret misery, and wearied by Winston's importunity, Asquith decided to close the score. He did so without apparent remorse, although his daughter assured us that he was repelled by the odious duty, and the agonized flounderings of the stricken creature were cut short by a passionless blow of the pole-axe:

> My dear Winston,
> I have your letters. You must take it as settled that you are not to remain at the Admiralty. I am sure that you will try to take a large view of an unexampled situation. Everyone has to make sacrifices; no one more than I, who have to part company with valued and faithful colleagues, who have served me loyally & well. I hope to retain your services as a member of the new Cabinet, being, as I am, sincerely grateful for the splendid work you have done both before and since the war.
> I cannot, of course, make any definite offer of any particular place, until I am able to realise & appraise the competing claims of others.[13]

After this frigid dismissal Winston at last realized that his glorious adventure at the Admiralty was over, and if he still nourished any hope of Tory support, it was extinguished by a brief note from Bonar Law the same day: 'I thank you for your letter which I shall show to my friends beginning with Austen Chamberlain but believe me what I said to you last night is inevitable.'

* * *

Winston accepted the fact that Asquith's letter was final:

> My dear Prime Minister,
> All right, I accept your decision. I shall not look back.
> I have tried my hand but without success to persuade Sir Arthur Wilson to hold himself at Mr Balfour's disposition. In the circumstances I wd advise Sir Henry Jackson. But a complete understanding exists between me & Mr Balfour, & I daresay he will let me talk to him about it.
> I must wait for the march of events at the Dlles.

12. Copy, Churchill papers: 13/52.
13. Ibid.

I am grateful to you for your kindness to me & belief in my vision of things.

Count on me absolutely – if I am of any use. If not, some employment in the field.

Yours vy sincerely
WSC[14]

Having reached this solution, the Prime Minister felt able to assume a friendly, even breezy tone:

21 May. I was delighted to receive your letter of today this afternoon, and I recognise with gratitude, but without surprise, the spirit in which it is written.

We have all for the moment to put up with unwelcome new facts, and nothing is more unwelcome than the disappearance of old comrades, and the process of transplantation from one place to another, especially from one of greater to one of lesser interest.

I know you will ply a stout & labouring oar, whatever seat in the boat may be assigned to you.[15]

On 22 May he saw Asquith briefly, but no specific offer of employment was made. Winston was calm and well behaved. He had determined that if he had to go he would at least do so like a gentleman. And on the same day he made his farewells to the Admiralty officials – a poignant ordeal – looked (as he assumed) for the last time on the octagonal table, the dolphins and the places where so much history had been made. During the weekend Asquith offered him a post – a low post indeed, almost a sinecure – the Chancellorship of the Duchy of Lancaster, a minor office in the Cabinet, 'a bone,' as his cousin Sunny wrote, 'on which there is little meat.' He accepted this paltry award mainly because it provided him with a seat on the War Council from which he could continue to influence events in the Dardanelles, but also perhaps through an atavistic fear of resignation, an extreme reluctance to isolate himself from the fountain of power. On 27 May he was given the seal of the Duchy of Lancaster by the King.

* * *

After this disaster Winston fell into a profound dejection, an *accidie* so deep that it seems that he would never emerge from it.

'The worst part of our life together,' Clementine Churchill told the author, 'was the failure of the Dardanelles Expedition. Winston was filled with such a black depression that I felt he would never recover

14. Asquith papers. Copy, Churchill papers.
15. Churchill papers: 13/52.

from it, and even feared at one time that he might commit suicide. His despair was only alleviated when he was given useful work which really contributed to the winning of the War at the Ministry of Munitions [by Lloyd George in July 1917].'

Although Winston was to forgive Fisher, the real architect of his ruin, and even try to recall him, Asquith remained the object of a sustained antagonism wholly alien to Churchill's character. His instinctive sense of language could not be blunted even by despair, and a year later he wrote to his brother Jack, stringing together as in a necklace three abusive adjectives unerringly chosen:

'Meanwhile Asquith reigns, supine, sodden and supreme.' He was amazed by the Prime Minister's ruthlessness at the moment of decision:

> When Lord Fisher resigned in May and the Opposition threatened controversial debate, Asquith did not hesitate to break his Cabinet up, demand the resignation of all Ministers, end the political lives of half his colleagues, throw Haldane to the wolves, leave me to bear the burden of the Dardanelles, and sail on victoriously at the head of a Coalition Government. Not 'all done by kindness'! Not all by rosewater! These were the convulsive struggles of a man of action and of ambition at death-grips with events . . . He defended his authority by every resource in his powerful arsenal.[16]

He had forgotten all Asquith had done for him, how swiftly he had advanced his career, until at the age of forty he was one of the two men directing the war. Indeed, Asquith would even now have kept Churchill in a Liberal Administration, but he knew that in a coalition government there could be no place for him.

Encased in his own strange armour of insensitivity and heedless of the sounds outside, Winston had failed to read the signs and was bewildered by the speed of his own destruction. When Asquith's support was withdrawn he was as exposed as a snail without its shell, detested by Conservatives, and with hardly any support in the Cabinet or the Liberal Party. He felt with every reason that he had been made the scapegoat for the Dardanelles. All the odium of failure descended upon his head. The equal responsibility of Asquith and Kitchener for the project – from which they had never wavered – was unknown to the public, and they were uncontaminated by the association.

Winston saw no reason why Fisher's resignation should lead to the fall of the Government or to him leaving the Admiralty, and he

16. WSC, *Great Contemporaries*, pp.108-9.

believed that Asquith could in any case have postponed the Coalition. He failed to realize the force of the pressures driving the Prime Minister in this direction, and was unaware of the defection of Venetia Stanley which had so enfeebled his purpose. Nor was he aware that the Prime Minister's attitude towards him had changed, that his old confidence in him had faded, and that of late Winston's rhetoric and excitable exhortations had begun to fill him with boredom and exasperation.

* * *

It was the first serious reverse of Churchill's career, and it was a terrible one. The whole apparatus of power had suddenly dropped from him, and he was stunned by the brutality of the fall. 'Like a sea-beast fished up from the depths, or a diver too suddenly hoisted, my veins threatened to burst from the fall in pressure . . . At a moment when every fibre of my being was inflamed to action, I was forced to remain a spectator of the tragedy, placed cruelly in a front seat.'

> He had fallen virtually unmourned. In the hour of disaster his considerable achievements at the Admiralty in the three years before the war were forgotten, his deficiencies magnified out of true proportion. The public could not know, nor was it to know for many years, the extent of his contribution to the expansion of the Navy in 1911-1914, nor of his actions in the first vital weeks of the war, nor above all of his initiation of the tank in the teeth of official scepticism . . . Beatty wrote that 'the Navy breathes freer now it is rid of the succubus Churchill.' Jellicoe described him as 'a public danger to the Empire'. The King curtly commented that Churchill was 'impossible'. Many Liberals, chagrined by their downfall, saw him as the author of all their woes. Mrs Asquith wrote with bitterness that the Cabinet had been 'smashed', 'by the man I always said *would* smash it – Winston'.[17]

And Churchill, as he sadly surveyed the wreckage of his political career, could have reflected again as he had before on another occasion: 'Thus the beaver builds his dam, and thus when his fishing is about to begin comes the flood and sweeps away his work and luck and fish away together. So he has to begin, again.'[18]

* * *

Churchill was thus left the sole scapegoat of the Dardanelles fiasco, which ended with the final evacuation of the Peninsula on 8 January 1916. The stigma of this ill-starred venture clung to him for the greater

17. Rhodes James, op.cit., p.80.
18. WSC, *My Early Life*, p.159.

part of his life, and when hostile audiences wished to anger him they would shout, 'What about the Dardanelles?'

He was regarded by an ignorant public as the author of all our disasters, and his mighty achievements at the Admiralty were drowned in the general growl of hatred. But in fact Churchill's responsibility ended with the pressure he brought to bear on the War Council to land an army on Gallipoli, and with the failure of the naval attack on 18 March. For the active operations of the Navy as an independent force ended with that repulse, and from that moment the control of the expedition passed to Kitchener and Hamilton. Churchill's role thenceforward was merely to use his influence to extract reinforcements and munitions from a sometimes wavering and sceptical Government.

The idea of seizing Constantinople by forcing the Dardanelles or occupying the Gallipoli Peninsula may not have first germinated in Churchill's mind, but it was he who translated theory into action by a strategy which would surely have been endorsed by his great ancestor – opening the southern line of communication with Russia. There can be no doubt it was a brilliant strategic conception, stultified by events and by military procrastination. If successful the attack, as Churchill conceived it, might well have shorted the war by two years: the Revolution in Russia might well have been prevented, or at least postponed, with all which this would have meant to the civilization of Europe and the security of the world. And had Churchill only been supreme with the uncontrolled power of appropriating from the Western Front the little that was needed to make the Dardanelles campaign a sure success, he would have been acclaimed as the statesman whose intuitive genius won the war.

For we should remember again the dazzling opportunities disclosed by this conception. By occupying the fortifications on both sides of the Straits, communication would have been severed between European and Asiatic Turkey. The Turkish armies in Armenia, Syria, Palestine and the Sinai Desert, cut off from their supplies and arsenals, would have been paralysed. Serbia would have been spared the horrors of invasion; Rumania would almost certainly have declared herself; Bulgaria would never have thrown in her lot with the Central Powers and might well have joined the Allies.

The capture of a city of such historic renown as Constantinople would have stirred the whole world, and settled the doubts of millions of waverers. It is difficult to imagine a more decisive blow to enemy prestige than the capture of Constantinople – Byzantium – in 1915, or one that would have created more electric shock-waves throughout the Muslim world. Its fall would have led to immediate peace with demoralized Turkey and doubtless to the downfall of the pro-German junta which had seized power in the land. Success in the Dardanelles operation would also have enabled Britain to supply the Russian armies with the weapons and equipment they so desperately needed, and in return import wheat, oil and wood.

* * *

In the part of the campaign in which he was directly concerned, certain fair and valid criticisms can be made against Churchill. We have already noticed a tendency in that ardent imagination to assume that successful accomplishment would be the logical corollary to an exciting project that had taken possession of his mind. It was then that he displayed his well-known failing of 'rushing his fences'. He realized how far-reaching the results of the fall of Constantinople would be, but there is little to suggest that he carefully evaluated what forces were required to ensure victory. 'Once the Cabinet had decided on the general principle of an attempt to force the Dardanelles, Mr Churchill's sole determination was to set about the task as soon as possible. He saw the huge prize, and tried to seize it with inadequate means. This precipitancy paved the way to our subsequent disasters.'[19]

It is unlikely that any other first-class Power would have charged so blindly at the Dardanelles without months of reflection and preparation by the General Staff, the results of which would have been found in plans pigeon-holed before war even began. In 1915 there were none, and Sir Ian Hamilton was faced by a task of forbidding improvisation.

When we consider Churchill's part in this affair we are always driven back by his agreement to the naval attack, and the question arises whether it was a legitimate hazard of war; whether it would have succeeded if it had been immediately renewed after the first reverse; and whether if the Fleet had caused Constantinople to surrender, it could have maintained its position without military support.

At the time of the attack on the Dardanelles Turkish morale, particularly in Constantinople, was at its lowest ebb. Basra, in the Persian Gulf, had fallen to the British: the expedition into Egypt had been a pitiable and humiliating failure, and in Enver's offensive against Russia his army had been decimated at Sarikamish. So despairing had the mood of the Turks become that their German masters feared they might make a separate peace. There was a general conviction that the Fleet's attack against the Dardanelles would succeed and that Constantinople would fall in a few days.

The Turkish State archives and gold reserves had been moved from the city, art treasures buried and plans prepared by many for

19. E. Ashmead Bartlett, *The Uncensored Dardanelles*, p.14.

a flight into the interior. Such was the despondency of the leaders that some, like Talaat, had taken similar precautions. Other Young Turks, more hawk-like and caring nothing for the Christian treasures of Byzantium, had already made plans to destroy the city rather than allow it to fall into the hands of the Allies. Even apart from their danger from the approaching enemy Fleet, they realized that their own power was beginning to crumble: 'With every day that went by it became more evident that a great part of the population – and not only the Greeks and the Armenians – looked upon the arrival of the Allied warships, not as a defeat but as a liberation.'[20] In this state of defeatism the city was peculiarly vulnerable, and after the first naval assault most Turks were convinced not only that the attack would be renewed next day, but also that it was certain to succeed. Would it in fact have succeeded if it had been immediately renewed, and could it have achieved its purpose?

*   *   *

Churchill and Keyes were certainly seized by a common instinctive conviction that they had reached the crisis of the battle and that the enemy was on the point of collapse; but this view was not shared by others, and in the Cabinet and the Admiralty old misgivings were reviving. The conception of a naval attack had enjoyed at best the tepid support of most high officials at the Admiralty, and had been strongly opposed by some. They could not know at this critical moment that ammunition was nearly exhausted, nor that the Turkish Government was prepared to abandon Constantinople. They became convinced that an entirely naval operation could not succeed and that an army must be provided.

Winston Churchill has described in *The World Crisis* his conviction of complete impending victory at the end of the first day's action, and his words are confirmed by the view of the official historian:

> The Turkish Commander in the Dardanelles was weighed down by a premonition of defeat. More than half the ammunition was expended, and it could not be replaced. The antiquated means of fire control had been seriously interrupted. The Turkish gun crews were demoralized and even the German officers present had, apparently, little hope of successful resistance if the Fleet attacked the next day ... A German journalist describes the great astonishment of the defenders of the coastal forts when the attacks suddenly ceased. He records that the German naval gunners who were manning the batteries at Chanak told him later that they had made up their minds that the Fleet would win, and that they themselves could not have held out much longer.[21]

20. Moorehead, op.cit., p.74.
21. Brigadier-General C.F. Aspinall-Oglander, *Military Operations. Gallipoli.*

There was therefore reasonable cause for Churchill's belief that a renewed attack with fresh battleships ruthlessly employed, without regard to losses, and supported by a new fleet of destroyer-minesweepers manned by resolute crews, would have forced the Straits. If we pursue another hypothetical question, we may ask whether, if the Fleet had done so, it could have compelled the capitulation of the city and maintained its own position there.

The German commander at the Dardanelles, General Liman von Sanders, a leading authority, did not believe that the forcing of the Straits would have achieved this end:

> In my opinion even if the Allied Fleet had been successful in breaking through the Dardanelles and victorious in a sea-fight in the Sea of Marmara, its position would have been scarcely tenable unless the entire shore of the Straits of the Dardanelles were strongly occupied by enemy forces. Should the Turkish troops be successful in holding their positions along the shores of the Straits, or should they be successful in recapturing these, then the necessary flow of supplies through ships and colliers would be rendered impossible. Measures of defence taken rendered a landing by troops near Constantinople, who might have lived on the country, almost without prospect of success.
>
> A decisive success could only be gained by the enemy if a landing by troops upon a great scale occurred either simultaneously with the break-through by the Fleet or if it preceded this. A landing by troops following the break-through would have been obliged to renounce artillery support by the Fleet which would have had to occupy itself with other tasks.[22]

We may conclude that Churchill's most far-reaching error was his acquiescence in the naval attack, and his acceptance of the fact that Kitchener would not supply the troops essential to its success. Shortly before the battle Kitchener had changed his mind and said that troops would be forthcoming. If Churchill had stayed the naval attack, and waited for military support (as urged by Fisher and Jackson), a joint operation might have been successfully launched if no time had been wasted and no warning given to the enemy. As it was, the Dardanelles expedition ended in utter ruin, and for Winston in a fall and a humiliation excruciating in their pain. Sadly, he wrote of it thirty years afterwards: 'I was ruined for the time being over the Dardanelles, and a supreme enterprise was cast away, through my trying to carry out a major and cardinal operation of war from a subordinate position. Men are ill-advised to try such ventures.'

22. General Liman von Sanders, *Five Years in Turkey*.

It was left to Asquith, who had supported the enterprise throughout and unlike Winston politically survived it, to claim that the Dardanelles expedition had not been in vain. Scratching together a few alleged and meagre advantages derived from it, he appeared before the Dardanelles Commission and told them why he thought it had been justified:

> I will give you two reasons. There are a great many I might give, but I will give two. In the first place it undoubtedly staved off and postponed for months the adhesion of Bulgaria to the Central Powers. There is no doubt whatever about that. In the second place – and this was the point Lord Kitchener always insisted upon to the end – he said to me a hundred times it contained and immobilised 300,000 Turkish soldiers for the best part of nine months, who otherwise would have been a most formidable accretion to the enemy forces. Even though it failed, I consider it had very effective and powerful results.[23]

But these were paltry gleanings from a field which had promised so golden a harvest.

---

23. PRO ADM. 1437B and 1437C.

Chapter 20

An Unhappy Pause

I t was obvious from the beginning that Churchill would not long
remain in his sinecure office. His only reason for accepting it – that
he could influence the Dardanelles Campaign in the War Council
– had been an illusion, for he was reduced to the role of an impotent
spectator. He who had sent great armadas to sea now found himself
concerned with the appointment of county magistrates. He remained
plunged in depression, but even at this time of despair could still muster
a rueful humour, a sour panache. Writing to his friend Jack Seely in June
1915, he reported: 'The Duchy of Lancaster has been mobilized. A strong
flotilla of magistrates for the 1915 programme will shortly be laid down.
"Already I feel the machine beginning to move." '[1]

The War Council now became known as the Dardanelles Committee,
and Churchill attended all its meetings. He pelted it with memoranda,
but soon realized that he had little if any influence upon its counsels.
When the memos, so eloquently written, so powerfully reasoned, were
received by the Committee they produced an impression of *déja vu*,
of arguments all too familiar and no longer tolerable. His colleagues
were surfeited with the baroque exuberance of his style but Austen
Chamberlain wrote to his wife that 'Winston takes his fall with much
dignity. He is always at his best in adversity.'

His new office contained no facilities for a Minister seeking to
influence high policy, and was even lacking a messenger. Perhaps
such squalid deprivations, in contrast with his mighty resources at the
Admiralty, made him realize more clearly than anything else the full
extent of his fall. He was forced to ask Edwin Montagu at the Treasury
for three rooms and a messenger, and in these he installed himself with
the faithful Edward Marsh and a shorthand writer.

1. Chartwell papers. [Copy, Churchill papers: 2/67.]

399

Nor were these his only troubles. His salary had fallen from £4,500 to £2,000 a year on leaving the Admiralty, and although Asquith was prepared to allow him to remain at Admiralty House, Clementine Churchill refused to consider what she regarded as an act of charity. He moved instead temporarily into his cousin Lord Wimborne's house in Arlington Street, with the intention of transferring his family later to Jack Churchill's house in Cromwell Road opposite the National History Museum, where Jack's wife, Lady Gwendeline Churchill, was living with her two sons. 'It seems to me,' Winston wrote to Jack, 'that in the uncertain situation during the war we must not have two establishments and that the families must live together. Clemmie and Goonie are so fond of each other that this is vy attractive & easy.'[2]

The reduction in Winston's salary was averted by a decision of the Coalition Government to pool all ministerial salaries for the duration of the war, and under this new scheme he received £4,360 a year. But it is improbable in the extreme, even if he had been confined to £2,000 a year, that there would have been any noticeable difference in his mode of living. For he had never allowed these sordid considerations, which torment so many, to have the slightest bearing on his own comfort. 'He is just prepared to accept the best of everything,' said his friend, F. E. Smith, and this was the truth.

After his departure from the Admiralty he leased a farmhouse in Surrey near Godalming. This little building, Hoe Farm, which lay in a quiet green valley, had been converted by Sir Edwin Lutyens into a country house. Although so near London, it was quiet and peaceful, and a refuge from the tension which now held him day and night. He was to be seen in there stalking up and down, up and down, between the grass path at the top of the garden, from a copse of young trees at one end to a wooden summer-house at the other, sunk in sombre reflections. But this time it was like Napoleon after Waterloo.

As he had to suffer, he would at least do it in comfort. Tortured by an obsessional concern for the Dardanelles and unable to tear his mind from it, he could yet write to Jack about Hoe Farm:

> How I wish you could be there. It really is a delightful valley and the garden gleams with summer jewelry. We live vy simply – but with all the essentials of life well understood & well provided for – hot baths, cold champagne, new peas, & old brandy.
>
> The war is terrible: the carnage grows apace, & the certainty that no result will be reached this year fills my mind with melancholy thoughts. The youth of Europe – almost a whole generation – will be shorn away. I find it vy painful to be deprived of direct means of action, but I bear the

2. John Churchill papers. 'Goonie' was Lady Gwendeline's nickname.

pangs because I see and feel the value of my influence on general policy. I do not think the present arrangements will last for ever, and I hope to regain a fuller measure of control before the end of the year.[3]

* * *

At this moment there was most opportunely revealed to him an occupation which was to rest and solace his mind until the last days of his life, and provide a sure refuge in moments of anxiety and depression. He was encouraged, by the sight of Lady Gwendeline sketching, to attempt to paint. He became quickly enthralled, and it was a potent therapy which even made him forget at moments his miserable political situation. Using water-colours, he painted the pond in front of the house, the winding tree-lined drive, and the house with its Tudor sprawl of chimneys and sharply pointed roofs. Thus began to germinate what Graham Sutherland was to describe as 'an extraordinary talent as a painter, particularly when he was not under the influence of some artist or other.'[4]

And so, in his misery: 'the Muse of Painting came to my rescue – out of charity and out of chivalry because after all she had nothing to do with me – and said, "Are these toys any good to you? They amuse some people." '

But although so naturally gifted, he was abashed by his first attempt to paint in oils. His description of this venture is well known, but it should be quoted as an example of the effective (if rather ponderous) humour with which he could invest a personal matter which had left an indelible impression upon his mind:

> The palette gleamed with beads of colour; fair and white rose the canvas; the empty brush hung poised, heavy with destiny, irresolute in the air. My hand seemed arrested by a silent veto. But after all the sky on this occasion was unquestionably blue, and a pale blue at that. There could be no doubt that blue paint mixed with white should be put on the top part of the canvas. One really does not need to have an artist's training to see that. It is a starting-point open to all. So very gingerly I mixed a little blue paint on the palette with a very small brush, and then with infinite precaution made a mark as big as a bean upon the affronted snow-white shield. It was a challenge, a deliberate challenge; but so subdued, so halting, indeed so cataleptic, that it deserved no response.
>
> At that moment the loud approaching sound of a motor-car was heard in the drive. From this chariot there stepped swiftly and lightly the gifted wife[5] of Sir John Lavery. 'Painting! But what are you hesitating about?

3. Ibid.
4. Graham Sutherland, O.M. to author.
5. Lady Hazel Lavery, wife of the well-known painter Sir John Lavery.

Let me have a brush – the big one.' Splash into the turpentine, wallop into the blue and white, frantic flourish on the palette – clean no longer – and then several large, fierce strokes and slashes of blue on the absolutely cowering canvas. Anyone could see that it could not hit back. No evil fate avenged the jaunty violence. The canvas grinned in helplessness before me. The spell was broken. The sickly inhibitions rolled away. I seized the largest brush and fell upon my victim with berserk fury. I have never felt any awe of a canvas since.[6]

*   *   *

He continued to advise and exhort about Gallipoli, but he was becoming weary of fruitless admonitions, and as always at such moments his thoughts turned to the field of action, though for the moment he could see no obvious outlet. In early July he was incensed by Lord Fisher's appointment as Chairman of the Admiralty Board of Inventions and Research. He saw himself as mouldering on the beach while Fisher, the cause of his ruin, was restored to power and place, and protested angrily but vainly to Asquith. Jack Churchill had suggested that he might visit Gallipoli as an observer and reporter, and the idea had attracted him. He was therefore pleased when Kitchener, with the approval of Asquith and Balfour, suggested that he should pay an official visit to the Dardanelles.

He was excited by this prospect, which he invested with considerable importance, and even with an aura of destiny. It offered a relief from dreary stagnation, a sense of involvement and the solace of movement. He wrote to his wife almost with the air of one going to certain death with a passionate desire to convince posterity. [This letter was to be handed to Clemmie *only if he was killed*]:

> I am anxious that you should get hold of all my papers, especially those wh refer to my Admiralty administration . . . There is no hurry; but some day I shd like the truth to be know. Randolph will carry on the lamp. Do not grieve for me too much. I am a spirit confident of my rights. Death is only an incident, & not the most important wh happens to us in this state of being. On the whole, especially since I met you my darling one I have been happy & you have taught me how noble a woman's heart can be. If there is anywhere else I shall be on the look out for you. Meanwhile look forward, feel free, rejoice in life, cherish the children, guard my memory. God bless you.[7]

6. WSC, *Thoughts and Adventures*, pp.307-8.
7. Spencer-Churchill papers.

But all this emotion was premature. The new Conservative Ministers, particularly Bonar Law, whom Churchill had once patronized, later wooed and always underestimated, imposed a sudden veto on his journey. He was upset and wounded by this rebuff, and his anger communicated itself to the Dardanelles Committee, where he strongly but vainly questioned the Government's policy at Gallipoli. But by now even he had begun to realize that his bolt was shot. Meanwhile he had formed an absolute contempt for Asquith's and Kitchener's direction of the war, but, powerless in his isolation to affect the issue, he could do nothing to underwrite his own conviction that it would be disastrous to abandon the Dardanelles campaign.

The Prime Minister met the growing criticism of the Government, Kitchener and himself, by the decision to wind up the Dardanelles Committee, and to substitute for it a small body of himself, Kitchener and Balfour.[8] This was the tolling of the bell for Churchill, for it meant that he was now excluded from all power to influence war policy. It was time to go, and this time he knew that his destination was the trenches. On 29 October he sent a letter of resignation to Asquith, at last severing their long relationship, which had lasted from the days of Asquith's greatest power and Winston's precocious genius:

> I had hoped to see you yesterday to tell you that our ten years work in office must now end.
>
> I agree with the principle of a war executive composed of the Prime Minister & the heads of the two military departments. But the change necessarily deprives me of rendering useful service.
>
> After leaving the Admiralty five months ago I have only remained in the Government at your request in order to take part in the work of the War Council. It would not be right for me at this time to remain in a sinecure. The views I have expressed on war policy are on record, and I have seen with deep regret the course which has been followed. Nor could I conscientiously accept responsibility without power. The long delays in coming to decisions have not been the only cause of our misfortunes. The faulty & lethargic execution and lack of scheme and combination over all military affairs & of any concert with our Allies are evils wh will not be cured merely by the changes indicated in yr memorandum – good though these are in themselves.
>
> I therefore take leave of you not without many regrets on personal grounds but without any doubts. There is one point however on which it would perhaps be well for us to have a talk. It is now necessary for the truth to be made public about the initiation of the Dardanelles expedition.[9]

8. In its final form it consisted of Asquith, Lloyd George, Balfour, Bonar Law and McKenna.
9. Draft, Churchill papers: 2/67.

[This letter was *unsent* because Asquith persuaded him to withhold his resignation until after 2 November when he (the P.M.) was to make a policy statement to Parliament.]

The last meeting of the Dardanelles Committee was on 6 November, and the question of Gallipoli was left in the air when the Committee was wound up. Churchill knew that he would be excluded from the new Cabinet War Committee, and he wrote again to Asquith on 11 November, somewhat unnecessarily, as he had already resigned, asking the Prime Minister to submit his resignation to the King:

> I am an officer, and I place myself unreservedly at the disposal of the military authorities, observing that my regiment is in France.
>
> I have a clear conscience which enables me to bear my responsibility for past events with composure . . .[10]

The escape route before him was to go to France as a Major in the Queen's Own Oxfordshire Hussars, and he had decided upon this course. It only remained for him to make his farewell speech to the House of Commons, and this he did on 15 November. Knowing that a traditional courtesy and restraint was shown to speakers on these occasions, Winston embarked on a long and major attempt at self-justification. In a speech which filled twenty-two columns of Hansard he offered a powerful defence of his record over the past fourteen months, with the Dardanelles always foremost in his thoughts. He repeated the familiar and not altogether valid argument 'that the attack on the Dardanelles was a Naval plan, made by Naval authorities on the spot, approved by Naval experts in the Admiralty, assented to by the First Sea Lord, and executed on the spot by Admirals who at every stage believed in the operation . . . I will not have it said that this was a civilian plan, foisted by a political amateur upon reluctant officers and experts.' He spoke coldly about Fisher, and at one point referred to the Dardanelles as 'a legitimate gamble', which shocked some of his listeners. But the speech was well received, partly because the words of a resigning Minister demanded sympathy, and partly because it was the utterance of a man who was exposing to public scrutiny the most crucial transaction of his life, and passionately desired to convince.

But this he could do only briefly, if at all. His reception was warm but deceptive: a cool mood of re-examination quickly replaced the enthusiasm in the House, and a letter in *The Times* by Ellis Ashmead Bartlett, the brilliant correspondent who had followed the Dardanelles operation so closely – 'Mr Churchill's Defence – a Criticism' – summoned back all the doubts that had been focused on Winston's conduct of affairs.

10. Copy, Spencer-Churchill papers.

Cartoons and Illustrations

Attacking Chamberlain's protectionist policy, 1905, after crossing the floor. First published in *Graphic*. (*Mary Evans Picture Library*)

Drawing by S. Begg published in the *Illustrated London News* in 1907. (*Mary Evans Picture Library*)

UNDER HIS MASTER'S EYE.

Scene—*Mediterranean, on board the Admiralty yacht "Enchantress."*

Mr. Winston Churchill. "ANY HOME NEWS?"
Mr. Asquith. "HOW CAN THERE BE WITH YOU HERE?"

Cartoon by Cravenhill published in *Punch*, May 1913. *(Mary Evans Picture Library)*

BONAR AND HIS BOGIES

(The absurd attempt of the Tories to humbug the public by concocting a ridiculous charge against the Government of deliberately plotting a wholesale massacre of Ulsterites, has been completely exposed by the evidence laid before Parliament during the past week.)

JOHNNY BULL : *" Take them away, Bonar. You can't curdle my blood with those silly things ! They've had all the stuffing knocked out of them ! "*

A cartoon published in *Reynolds' Newspaper,* 26 April 1914. *(John Topham Picture Library)*

The Victory Chorus: a cartoon published in the *Evening News,* 30 November 1914. *(John Topham Picture Library)*

First Sea Lord, 1914.
Cartoon by David Wilson in
*Graphic. (Mary Evans
Picture Library)*

Another cartoon on the
vexed subject of the Navy
Estimates. Published in
Punch, 14 January 1914.
(Mary Evans Picture Library)

CHURCHILL S'EN VA-T-EN GUERRE

WINSTON (through force of nautical habit) to SIR JOHN FRENCH : " *Come aboard, sir !* "

Churchill joining Sir John French as a Major after the fall of the Dardanelles, one of the blackest moments of Churchill's life. Drawing by F. H. Townsend published in *Punch*, 24 November 1915. (*John Topham Picture Library*)

THE CRISIS IN ESSENCE

ERIC: *"Russia is nothing to this, Churchill, my boy! Now we'll finish this nonsense of an 'England Fit for Heroes' once and for all"*

Daily Herald cartoon with Sir Eric Geddes. Published in 1919. *(Mary Evans Picture Library)*

Chapter 21

Return to Arms

On 16 November 1915 Winston Churchill made his farewells. There was a small gathering of intimate friends and relations at Jack Churchill's house in the Cromwell Road. Violet Asquith and her stepmother Margot, Goonie, Clementine's sister Nellie Hozier, and Edward Marsh were assembled to speed him on his way. There was an atmosphere of suppressed grief among them, with Marsh blinking back his tears, although Clementine was calm and brave, and Winston carefree, gay and brilliant.

'For most of us,' said Violet, 'it was a kind of wake. My heart ached for Clemmie, and Eddie was very pathetic. Winston was not unmindful of his plight and had asked my father to take him on as an extra Private Secretary as he could not bear to think of poor Eddie being plunged back into the bowels of the Colonial Office, sans personal function, sans friends, sans anything.'[1]

Max Aitken called next evening at 41 Cromwell Road, where the finishing touches were being put to Winston's equipment. He found the place in a state of chaos: 'The whole household was upside down while the soldier-statesman was buckling on his sword,' he wrote. Downstairs the derelict Eddie was still in tears, while above, 'Lady Randolph was in a state of despair at the thought of her brilliant son being relegated to the trenches. Mrs Churchill seemed to be the only person who remained calm, collected and efficient.'[2]

On 18 November, the evening of Winston's departure for France, his former private Secretary, Masterton Smith, wrote to Clementine:

> It is half after ten of the clock and the shutters of the old familiar Private Office are just going up, but I cannot let the day pass without telling you

---

1. Bonham Carter, op.cit.
2. Beaverbrook, op.cit.

that you no less than Winston have been much in the thoughts of many of us. Not even the high gods (whether their home be Fleet Street or Mount Olympus) make things that have been as if they had never been, and to those of us who know and understand, Winston is the greatest First Lord this old Admiralty has ever had – or is ever likely to have.

With those of us who shared his life he has left an inspiring memory of high courage and tireless industry, and he carries with him to Flanders all that we have to give him – our sincere good wishes.[3]

* * *

On that day, three days after his resignation speech, Winston Churchill had crossed to France to join his Yeomanry Regiment, the Queen's Own Oxfordshire Hussars. Once again he was going to the wars, but to a conflict that bore no resemblance to the fields of battle he had once known – the harsh outcrops of the North West Frontier, or the baking plains of the Sudan. For this was a war of position, static on a front petrified between Switzerland and the North Sea, a war of snipers, mud and rats, of trench feet and lice, of shattering barrages, of tedious routine and waiting between bloody frontal assaults. But although it was so different from anything he had known before, Winston fell into the military life without the slightest difficulty, and transferred his mind from international to local problems with no sense of incongruity or waste.

On the day of his arrival he was invited to dinner at GHQ at St Omer by his old friend, Sir John French, the Commander-in-Chief, and afterwards wrote to his wife:

> French as ever an affectionate friend. He wished me to take a Brigade as soon as it could be arranged. I said . . . that beforehand I must feel myself effectively master of the conditions of trench warfare from the point of view of the regimental officer; and I suggested the Guards as the best school. This is therefore to be arranged & I expect to go into the line on Saturday for a week or two. You must not let this fret you in the least. No action is in prospect & only a vy general & ordinary risk need be contemplated. But I shall always be vy glad to have served with this famous corps. It is indeed much safer than going into the line with the QOOH. [Oxfordshire Yeomanry].

Sir John French invited Lord Cavan, in command of the Guards Division, to St Omer, '. . . to whom after some talk I said "I shd regard it as a vy gt honour to go into the line with the Guards" to wh he replied – I thought sincerely "we should be *proud* to have

---

3. Churchill papers: 28/152.

you." ' Lord Cavan sent Winston to the 2nd Battalion of the Grenadier Guards, commanded by Lt. Colonel 'Ma' Jeffreys, which was going into the line next day. 'If you come to lunch with me at 1 o'clock,' said Cavan, 'you will be in plenty of time.'

> Accordingly the next day, having packed what I thought was a very modest kit, I repaired to the headquarters of the Guards Division ... As soon as the frugal lunch was over, the General took me himself in his car to the Grenadier battalion which I was to join as Major under instruction previous to higher appointment. The Companies had already begun their march to the trenches, and the Colonel, the Adjutant and the Battalion staff were on the point of setting out. There were salutes and smiles and clicking of heels between the Divisional General and the Battalion officers; and then His Lordship got into his car and drove off, leaving me very like a new boy at school in charge of the Headmaster, the monitors and the senior scholars.[4]

Lt. Colonel Jeffreys[5] was an officer at once courageous, honourable and austere. His mind was narrow, and he had that withering contempt for politicians common to senior officers in this war, though he later became one himself. So widespread and general was his mistrust that the soldiers seldom mentioned 'politicians' without the prefix 'bloody', and it required another World War to convince both groups that their aims were in fact identical, and that the need for victory enjoined harmony.

Now, after riding for half an hour in silence, the Colonel suddenly remarked: 'I think I ought to tell you that we were not at all consulted in the matter of your coming to join us.' Winston was in no way put out by this churlish greeting, and remained polite and attentive. He was fully aware of hostility, and determined not to be discountenanced by it:

> It took about forty-eight hours to wear through their natural prejudice against 'politicians' of all kinds, but particularly of the non-Conservative brand. Knowing the professional Army as I did and having led a variegated life, I was infinitely amused at the elaborate pains they took to put me in my place and to make me realise that nothing counted at the front except military rank and behaviour. The weather remains atrociously cold, but the Colonel gradually and appreciably thawed. He took immense pains to explain to me the economy and discipline of his battalion. I asked if I might accompany him on his rounds which he made to the trenches once each day and once each night. He accepted the suggestion, and thereafter we slid or splashed or plodded together through the snow or mud – for the weather alternated cruelly – across the bullet-swept fields and in and amid the labyrinth of trenches.

4. WSC, *Thoughts and Adventures*, pp.100-1.
5. Lt. Colonel Jeffreys, afterwards Major General, became Conservative MP for Petersfield.

* * *

The trenches taken over by the 2nd Battalion of the Grenadiers were near Neuve Chapelle, and Battalion forward headquarters were established in a ruin called Ebenezer Farm. The Guards spent forty-eight hours in the line and forty-eight hours in reserve billets in support, three times repeated, and followed by six days rest. Having spent a miserable first night in the stifling signallers' compartment at Ebenezer Farm, Winston found a friend, Edward Grigg, commanding No.1 Company, and slept in his dug-out on the Sunday night, and when the Colonel's thawing-out process had reached a sufficient point of warmth, Winston suggested (not without guile) that he would learn more quickly if he lived with a company in the trenches rather than at Battalion headquarters. Henceforward, when in the forward line he took up his abode with No.1 Company. A desire for military experience no doubt prompted him in this decision, but another reason why he found it more agreeable was that under 'Ma' Jeffreys' Cromwellian dispensation hard liquor was prohibited at Battalion headquarters when the Guards were in the line, and only sweet tea provided – a beverage by no means to Winston's taste.

By 23 November he had already achieved a sort of grey peace, and reported to Clementine:

> I have lost all interest in the outer world and no longer worry about it and its stupid newspapers ... I spent Sunday night in the trenches – with Grigg's company: & when we go in again tomorrow night I am going to stay with them for the whole period. This gives me the opportunity of seeing and learning thoroughly ... It is a wild scene. The line of trenches – or rather breast-works we are now holding is built along the ruins of other older lines taken from the Germans or built later by the Indians ... The neglect & idleness of the former tenants is apparent at every step. Filth & rubbish everywhere, graves built into the defences & scattered about promiscuously, feet & clothing breaking through the soil, water & muck on all sides; and about this scene in the dazzling moonlight troops of enormous bats creep and glide, to the unceasing accompaniment of rifle & machine guns & the venomous whining & whirring of bullets wh pass overhead. Amid these surroundings, aided by wet & cold, & every minor discomfort, I have found happiness & content such as I have not know for many months ... [6]

6. Spencer-Churchill papers.

* * *

Back in the trenches on another forty-eight-hour spell of duty, he was again, as so often before, grazed by Death, and described his escape to Clementine on 26 November:

> Yesterday a curious thing happened. We were eating some food in the dugout (not this one) when a telegram arrived that the Corps Commander [General Haking] wished to see me & that a motor car wd meet me at 4.30 on the main road. I thought it rather a tall order to bring me out of the trenches by daylight – a 3 miles walk across sopping fields on wh stray bullets are always falling, along tracks periodically shelled. But I assumed it was something important and anyhow I had no choice . . . I started off just as the enemy began to shell the roads in revenge for the shelling he had been receiving from our provocative and well fed artillery.
>
> I just missed a whole bunch of shells wh fell on the track a hundred yards behind me; and arrived after an hours walking, muddy, wet & sweating at the rendezvous where I was to meet the motor. No motor! Presently a Staff Colonel turned up – saying he had lost the motor wh had been driven off by shells. He added that the General had wanted to have a talk with me and that it was only about things in general & that another day wd do equally well. I said that I was obeying an order, that I regretted leaving the trenches at a moment when they were under bombardment, that if I was not wanted for any official duty I wd return at once. And this I did – another hour across the sopping fields now plunged in darkness. As I walked I cd see our trenches in the distance with great red brilliant shells flaring over them in fours & fives & cd hear the shriek of the projectiles rising like the sound of a storm. It looked fierce & formidable but by the time I got near silence had descended . . .
>
> I reached the trenches without mishap & then learned that a quarter of an hour after I had left, the dugout in wh I had been living had been struck by a shell wh burst a few yards from where I wd have been sitting; smashing the structure & killing the mess orderly who was inside . . . & all our effects buried in mud & debris . . . Now see from this how vain it is to worry about things. It is all chance and our wayward footsteps are best planted without too much calculation . . .[7]

He was also able to assure Clementine that his old robust indifference to shellfire was unimpaired:

> This morning we were shelled & I expect there will be more tonight. It has not caused me any sense of anxiety or apprehension, nor does the approach of a shell quicken my pulse, or try my nerves or make me about to bob as do so many. It is satisfactory to find that so many years of luxury have in no way impaired the tone of my system.

7. Spencer-Churchill papers.

In these early days Winston nearly always stressed his happiness in his present surroundings, and his remoteness from the past: 'I do not feel the least revolt at the turn of events. L.G. & McK [McKenna] & the old block [Asquith] are far away & look like Mandarins of some remote province of China.'

But he left no doubt of his continuing interest in this vanished world nor of his intention to return to it:

'If I survive the war, I shall have no difficulty in taking my place in the House of Commons & it must ever be a good one.' As he had once, as a boy in India, badgered his mother to use her influence with the great on his behalf, so now he indicated to his wife the names of those whose favour would sweeten his return:

> Garvin, Scott, Rothermere & others shd be cultivated. Keep in touch with the Government. Show complete confidence in our fortunes. Hold your head vy high. You always do. Above all don't be worried about me. If my destiny has not already been accomplished I shall be guarded surely. If it has been there is nothing that Randolph need be ashamed of in what I have done for the country.[8]

* * *

Winston had been only dimly aware of the prejudice against him in France. He had struggled hard to neutralize it with a success undeniable, but perhaps less complete than he imagined. His daring, and his unquestioning acceptance of the squalid conditions, could not fail to help him gain the respect of men who regarded physical courage as the sole element in front-line life. Lord Cavan remained kind and friendly; he told Winston it was unnecessary for him to go back to the trenches, and offered him employment at his own headquarters.

'But I said I wouldn't miss a day of it. Nor did I. I also scorned the modest comforts of Battalion H.Q. & lived in the wet & the mud with the men in the firing line. My physique is such that I support these conditions without the slightest ill effect.' His mind – always concentrated on the affair of the moment – had been immersed in this strange new world of mud and star-shells, harsh and entirely masculine. But occasionally thoughts of Clementine and home pierced him with a bitter-sweet reminder of another life:

> I reciprocate intensely the feelings of love & devotion you show to me. My greatest good fortune in a life of brilliant experience has been to find you, & to lead my life with you. I don't feel far away from you out here at all. I feel vy near in my heart; & also I feel that the nearer I get to

honour, the nearer I am to you . . . But I feel quite safe and at home with the Army, and am sure that I have taken the steps to win their respect. Presently they will realise they have a skilful servant at their disposal, for whom Asquith & Co have no further use.[9]

While the Grenadiers were having a week's rest period, Winston was invited to stay at GHQ. He arrived on 1 December to find that on the previous day Sir John French had gone to London and, it was widely believed, to his dismissal. He found the atmosphere at GHQ thick with tension and intrigue. He also found two birds of ill omen, Lord Esher and Sir Henry Wilson, bringing to the antiseptic theatre of war a disturbing atmosphere of rumour and political gossip. Esher, fresh from the centre of affairs, wrote of Winston: 'He has forgotten politics and thinks of nothing but his section . . . Jeffries [sic] is his Colonel, and gave him a more than cold welcome. But apparently he has won over those who were hostile to him by his quite modest behaviour.'[10]

He had reached the point almost of forgetting politics, but the arrival of the inconstant friend Esher, and the *faux bonhomme* political soldier, Wilson, with his hearty manner and loud, insincere laugh, brought back their atmosphere in an instant. He amused Esher by describing himself as 'the escaped scapegoat', and was taken riding by Wilson. There had been serious differences between them in the past, but these were now composed. Wilson was impressed by his strategic vision, and at his suggestion Winston embodies his ideas in a paper, 'Variants of the Offensive', which contained, among other suggestions, the outline of an attack by caterpillars [tanks] in force. 'None should be used until all can be used at once.'

* * *

Winston was appalled by Esher's report on politics at home which revealed

> a continuance of the same utter inability to take a decision on the part of the Government. What they settle one day is upset the next. Months have now passed in this condition: & now the great twin disasters of Gallipoli & Salonika are drawing near . . . the guilt of criminality attaches to those responsible . . . Kitchener returns are 25 days futile banging about the Near East and making silly proposals. It seems likely that in order to get rid of him a large number of troops will be diverted to Egypt & locked up there . . .
>
> Well I am jolly glad to be out of it. It has indeed distressed & unsettled me to come again into the area of secret information. The able soldiers are

9. Spencer-Churchill papers.
10. Esher papers, Lord Esher to his son, 2 December 1915.

miserable at the Government's drifting. Some urge me to return and try
to break them up. I reply no – I will not go back unless I am wounded;
or unless I have effective control.[11]

This was self-deception.

When French returned, with his fate still undecided, Winston
suggested to him that he was now ready to take a battalion. French
rejected this idea, saying that he must take a brigade at once and that
'he would settle it quickly in case any accident shd happen to him.'

> Meanwhile I live here [at GHQ] in gt comfort. I have just got back from
> a vy long walk with French – talking about all things in heaven & earth.
> I am so sorry for him. No man can sustain two different kinds of separate
> worries – a tremendous army in the face of the enemy: a gnawing intrigue
> at the back. He seems to have told a good many people of my refusal of a
> Brigade and insistence on going into the trenches. He said the P.M. spoke
> with emotion about me. But Asquith's sentiments are always governed by
> his interests. They are vy hearty & warm within limits wh cost nothing.[12]

His short stay at GHQ was a pleasant interlude for Winston. For the
moment he was able to live in comfort, to ride every day, and visit different parts of the front. He was able to renew old friendships, and form
new ones, particularly that of Edward Louis Spiers[13] who, bilingual in
French and English, was serving as Liaison Officer with the French 10th
Army. Under his guidance Winston visited its grisly battlefields, where
100,000 men had died. On returning late one night to GHQ he found
correspondence from London, including a letter of 30 November from
Curzon, which greatly agitated him. It disclosed the intended evacuation
of Gallipoli and predicated a battle *à l'outrance* in the Cabinet.[14]

'I am still in uncertainty,' he told Clementine next day, 'as to my
immediate employment. Whether a battalion or a brigade – nothing is
settled. French is away in Paris & general instability is in command . . .
I shall therefore return tomorrow to the Grenadiers for another cycle
in the trenches. I shall be quite happy with them.' He sent Curzon's
disturbing letter to his wife:

> Keep in touch with Curzon & the others. Don't fail to keep the
> threads in yr fingers. Let me know who you see. Curzon's letter &
> enclosures . . . have of course revived distressing thoughts. My scorn for
> Kitchener is intense. If they evacuate in disaster – all the facts shall come

---

11. Spencer-Churchill papers.
12. Ibid.
13. He later changed the spelling to Spears.
14. Churchill papers.

out. They will be incredible to the world. The reckoning will be heavy &
I shall make sure it is exacted.

Curzon's letter was by now eight days old. On 8 December, the same
day that Churchill was writing this letter, the Cabinet formally took the
decisions to evacuate Suvla and Anzac. Ignorant of this fact, he replied
to Curzon, rejoicing in his own peace of mind:

Except for the distressing thoughts wh yr papers & letters revive I have
been entirely happy & free from care. I do not know when I have passed
a more joyous three weeks; & to let that tremendous melancholy situation
of our affairs all over the world slide from one's mind having fixed it so
long in mental gaze, has felt exactly like laying down a physical load . . .[15]

* * *

On 9 November he returned to the trenches near Neuve Chapelle where
the Grenadiers were now holding a far stronger line than before. He had
been given a blue steel helmet by the French, which he invariably wore
and which lent a bizarre distinction to his appearance in the trenches. He
was much flattered when the haughty 'Ma' Jeffreys sufficiently unbent to
make him acting second-in-command of the Battalion, 'wh considering
all things is a gt compliment.'

But French had promised him a brigade, and on his return to
St Omer on 10 December Winston learned that he was to be
given command of the 56th Brigade in the 19th Division under
General Bridges. He would remain with the Grenadier Guards until
he assumed his command, and meanwhile stayed for a few days at
GHQ with French. He asked Clementine to order him a Brigadier
General's tunic and to be careful that secrecy was observed by the
shop.

French was recalled to London on 14 December, and there were few
who doubted that he was there to receive his dismissal. The next day he
telephoned Churchill from London to say that the Prime Minister had
written to him that Churchill was not to have a brigade, adding: 'Perhaps
you might give him a battalion.' Winston at once instructed his wife to
cancel the order for the tunic.

Winston was furious with Asquith over this egregious piece of
disloyalty, and, in a state of black depression, wrote two letters
to Clementine on 17 December so despairful that he afterwards
asked her to destroy them.

15. Curzon papers. WSC to Curzon, 8 December 1915.

French returned that evening, having duly received his dismissal as Commander-in-Chief, and on the following day Winston described to his wife what had happened:

> French has returned. The position is as follows. He saw Asquith, told him that he had given me a Brigade & Asquith said he was delighted. A few hours later, being I suppose frightened by the question in the House, Asquith wrote a note to French (wh French showed me *vy privately*) saying that 'with regard to our conversation about our friend – the appointment might cause some criticism' – & should not therefore be made – adding 'Perhaps you might give him a battalion.' The almost contemptuous indifference of this note was a revelation to me. French was astonished; but in his weak position he cd do nothing, & now he is no longer C in C. Meanwhile he had told everyone he had given me a Brigade & is of course deeply distressed at the turn of events.

Winston continued to rage against what he considered to be the latest manifestation of the Prime Minister's treachery:

> Altogether I am inclined to consider that his conduct reaches the limit of meanness and ungenerousness. Sentiments of friendship expressed in extravagant terms; coupled with a resolve not to incur the slightest criticism or encounter the smallest opposition – even from the most unworthy quarter. Personally I feel that every link is severed: & while I do not wish to decide in a hurry – my feeling is that all relations shd cease.[16]

* * *

In the meantime French explained the difficulty to his successor, Sir Douglas Haig. Winston was called in to their interview and treated with the utmost consideration by Haig. In the circumstances Winston consented to take a battalion, and asked that Spiers and his friend Archibald Sinclair should be allotted to him. He had earlier remarked: 'Taking a battalion means living with utter strangers of a common class, but I hope if it is settled thus Archie will come as Adjutant or something – as I must have a pal.' No battalion was immediately available, and Churchill left for England on 22 December for a few days' leave, to spend Christmas with his family.

When Winston returned to France Clementine wrote on 30 December offering political advice, and urging him to beware of Lloyd George:

> I think my Darling you will have to be very patient. Do not burn any boats. The P.M. has not treated you worse than LlG has done, in fact not so badly

16. Spencer-Churchill papers.

for he is not so much in your debt . . . It's true that when association ceases with the P.M. he cools & congeals visibly, but all the time you were at the Admiralty he was loyal & steadfast while the other would barter you away at any time in any place. I assure you he is the direct descendant of Judas Iscariot. At this moment although I hate the P.M., if he held out his hand I could take it, (though I would give it a nasty twist) but before taking LlG's I would have to safeguard myself with charms, touchwords, exorcisms & by crossing myself. I always can get on with him, & yesterday I had a good talk, but you can't hold his eyes, they shift away.[17]

Winston was not unaffected by this letter, but we can see by his letter that Clementine had only partly succeeded in making him change his mind:

. . . You are a vy sapient cat to write as you did in yr last letter. But I feel that my work with Asquith has come to an end. I have found him a weak and disloyal chief. I hope I shall not ever have to serve under him again. After the 'Perhaps you might give him a battalion' letter I cannot feel the slightest regard for him any more. L.G. is no doubt all you say: but his interests are not divorced from mine. After all he always disagreed about D'lles. He was not like H.H.A. [Asquith], a co-adventurer – approving & agreeing at every stage. And he had the power to put things right as regards my policy & myself. But his slothfulness & procrastination ruined the policy, & his political nippiness squandered his agent. However there is no reason why ordinary relations should not be preserved.[18]

* * *

On 1 January 1916 Churchill learned that he was to command the 6th (Service) Battalion of the Royal Scots Fusiliers in the 19th Division under General Furse. 'Now that I shall be commanding a Scottish battalion,' he told Clementine,

I shd like you to send me a copy in one volume of Burns. I will soothe & cheer their spirits by quotations from it. I shall have to be careful not to drop into mimicry of their accent! You know I am a vy gt admirer of that race. A wife, a constituency, & now a regiment attest the sincerity of my choice!

He was able to give her news of the progresss of the tank:

I was sent for this afternoon to the Operation division. They have at last been ordered to get a move on about the caterpillars in consequence of my letter wh I wrote for Haig. They wanted to know who to apply to in England about them etc. This is after 9 months ofactual manufacture and

17. Churchill papers: 1/118. Quoted Gilbert, op.cit., p.623.
18. Spencer-Churchill papers.

committees unending. God, for a month of power & a good shorthand writer![19]

At last, on 5 January, Churchill assumed command of his battalion at Moolenacker near Meteren. He was able to take his friend Archie Sinclair with him, whom he promptly appointed his second-in-command, but Spiers was not released. The Battalion had been savagely mangled in the battle of Loos, and then after a brief rest had spent months in the mud and filth of the Ypres Salient. They were now in reserve billets for rest and training. Morale was low, and officers and men viewed the arrival of their new commander with deep misgiving.

'When the news spread,' said one of the officers, Captain Gibb, 'a mutinous spirit grew. Everyone liked the old C.O. and nobody could see why any prominent outsider should come in and usurp his place so easily.'[20] It is improbable that Winston was aware of the resentment caused by his arrival, no doubt feeling that such emotions could more properly be indulged by himself for being forced to accept a battalion rather than a brigade, and it will become evident that this malaise was soon completely dispelled by his personality and charm.

Winston learned that the men were largely Lowland Scots, with a sprinkling of Englishmen, and that the battalion had been built up by reinforcements after its crippling losses at the battle of Loos. The Scots Fusiliers were the Ayrshire and Galloway regiment, and he was to discover that some of its finest soldiers were the miners from the Ayrshire coalfields. Winston wasted no time in getting down to work:

> First of all the Company Commanders were called into the orderly-room and were introduced formally by the retiring Colonel. Then the rest of the officers came in and were presented. After each officer had come up and saluted and shaken hands Winston relapsed into his chair and scrutinised him, silently and intently, from head to foot. It was not easy to know how to parry this unconventional attack on one's composure. It was necessary to stand at attention, of course, so that no relief could be sought in the diversion of a mere social and friendly observation. I found myself forced to stare hard back at him and trust to time to bring this, like all other trials, to an end.[21]

* * *

After his experience with the Grenadier Guards Winston was aware how much smartness and discipline contributed to combative ability,

19. Spencer-Churchill papers.
20. A.D. Gibb, *With Winston Churchill at the Front*, p.10.
21. Ibid, p.20.

and was determined to apply similar methods to his new battalion and turn it into an efficient fighting force before its next spell in the trenches. One of his innovations, much resented by his officers, was that all orders should be acknowledged by the single word 'Sir', as in the Guards. His initial parades were rendered farcical by Winston giving cavalry commands which were naturally incomprehensible and caused much merriment and confusion.

One of the first orders he issued was: 'Gentlemen, war is declared on the lice,' and a committee of company commanders was created to concert measures for the utter extermination of all the lice in the battalion. After three or four days of unsavoury toil this miracle was accomplished, and Gibb wrote: 'We were certainly a liceless battalion.' He was insistent that his men should take care of their feet, and that they should sing on the march, writing to his friend, Edward Grigg, of No.1 Company, 'I wish you would write me a brief description of your "trench feet routine" & also send me a short list of the principal songs (of a respectable character) wh are popular with No.1.'[22]

Like the sudden melting of snow, the reservations about the new Commanding Officer disappeared.

> ... It is only just to say that he improved us greatly. Meantime he improved *on* us. All the company commanders were invited to dine in the H.Q. mess and there learnt a little of the charm and courtesy of the man as distinct from the Colonel. No doubt he sought to win us, but for that he is only to be admired, and his capacity for coaxing the best even out of the most boorish is a gift which I have never ceased to wonder at. He materially altered the feelings of the officers towards him by his kindliness and by the first insight we thus gained into the wonderful genius of the man. And so began a conquest which when he left us was complete – a complete conquest achieved in one or two short months and over men of a race not easily moved or won over.[23]

Such was the opinion of the Battalion officers of their Colonel. He gave his own estimate of them in a letter to his wife on 6 January:

> This regiment is pathetic. The young officers are all small middle class Scotsmen – vy brave & willing & intelligent; but of course all quite new to soldiering. All the seniors & all the professionals have fallen. I have spent the morning watching each company in turn drill & handle their arms. They are vy good ... The regiment is full of life & strength, & I believe I shall be a help to them.[24]

22. Altrincham papers.
23. Gibb, op.cit., pp.24-5.
24. Spencer-Churchill papers.

Sometimes there came to him, even in his new surroundings, a painful twinge at his isolation from the world of power:

> ... I watch in the Times ... the movement of political things & I must confess it excites & disturbs my mind. I try however not to look back too much, having not only put my hand but fettered it to the plough. I must rely on you to keep constant touch with the friends and pseudo friends I have. I do not like feeling forgotten and déconsidéré out here – especially when I am not in the trenches but only waiting in reserve billets – i.e. squalid little French farms rising from a sea of sopping fields & muddy lanes.[25]

Although he was now constantly occupied with his new problems, his mind was also filled all the time with thoughts of Clementine:

> You cannot write to me too often or too long. The beauty & strength of your character & the sagacity of yr judgments are more realised by me every day. I ought to have followed yr counsels in the days of my prosperity. Only sometimes they were too negative. I shd have made nothing if I had not made mistakes. Ungrateful country.[26]

The novelty of the present had begun to give way to bitter reflections about the past. No longer does he speak of the happiness of his release from the political treadmill, and memories of recent and irretrievable disasters lingered with more persistence:

> Whenever my mind is not occupied by work, I feel deeply the injustice with wh my work at the Admiralty has been treated. I cannot help it – tho I try. Then the damnable mismanagement wh has ruined the Dardanelles enterprise & squandered vainly so much life & the opportunity cries aloud for retribution: & if I survive the day will come when I will claim it publicly.

Churchill made every effort to keep his men cheerful by arranging more recreation – football, sports and concerts – 'Poor fellows they do not get much to lighten their lives – short though they may be.' But he was unable to agree with his officers on the subject of discipline. In their view Winston, ever inclined to compassion, interpreted the rules governing punishment far too leniently. Perhaps memories of his clemency as a reforming Home Secretary floated back to him now as he contemplated such serious acts of indiscipline as disobeying orders. Winston thought that if the man was a first offender, he should be severely reprimanded and given a second chance.

25. Ibid.
26. Ibid.

'We permanently differed on this matter,' wrote Captain Gibb, 'and I am afraid the men began to realize that they might at least once indulge themselves in the luxury of telling their sergeants to go to hell!'[27]

* * *

The Battalion did not leave rest billets for the trenches until 24 January 1916. They were to relieve the 8th Border Regiment in a line of trenches, about 1,000 yards, in the neighbourhood of Plooegsteert, or, as the soldiers immortalized it, 'Plugstreet'. They spent two nights in a village and then moved forward to their support billets. Battalion support headquarters were at the Ouvrier of the Sisters of Charity, known as the Hospice, on the western side of the road from Ploegsteert to Armentières. Before first light on the morning of 27 January the 6th Battalion of the Royal Scots Fusiliers took over their sector of the trenches and, according to the Colonel, 'the relief was accomplished with the utmost precision in under two hours. I don't think the Grenadiers ever did better.'

Advance headquarters were in the ruined Laurence Farm, close to No-man's-land. Their first spell in the trenches was for only forty-eight hours, but from 1 February they spent six days in the trenches, six in support, then another six in the trenches followed by six days' rest.

Winston was able to note with satisfaction that on their first spell in the trenches they had no losses, although there was shelling and sniping, and the parapet was blown in at one point. He spent three hours in the trenches making a thorough inspection and deciding what improvements he would make. Going round the trenches was, he found, an arduous business: 'It takes nearly two hours to traverse this labyrinth of mud.'

When in the trenches Churchill was at all times conscious of his responsibility as Battalion Commander:

> You know a Colonel's day in the line is almost the greatest personal demand on a man's qualities – vy like being Captain of a vy big ship in submarine infested waters.
>
> I have telephones to each of my companies, to the brigadier, & to the artillery. In 30 seconds I can turn on a horrid blast of shells – if an attack is made . . . We are vy careful about gas. That is an odious peril.[28]

On the evening of 29 January Winston was back in his support headquarters at the Hospice. He was well lodged there with a good bedroom looking out across the fields to the German lines 3,000 yards away. Two nuns remained in the building to tend the

27. Gibb, op.cit., p.77.
28. Spencer-Churchill papers, WSC to Clementine Churchill, 27 January 1916.

small chapel, armoured in their faith and indifferent to their exposed position. They welcomed the British troops as the saviours of this part of Belgium, and made them appetising soup. The sound of gunfire was always about the place, but Winston, realizing that the German gunners were not aiming at the Hospice but at a battery beyond it, was not disconcerted. On his first day there he described the scene to Clementine: 'On the right & left the guns are booming; & behind us a British field piece barks like a spaniel at frequent intervals. But the women & children still inhabit the little town & laugh at the shells wh occasionally buff into the old church.'

He was further endeared to the Hospice by the discovery of a piano, 'a splendid bath (portable) and a tolerably hot water supply.' After the filth of the trenches this was bliss indeed, and he wrote, 'I am now just going to sample it, after 3 days deprivation of that first of comforts.'[29]

* * *

Churchill was visited at the Hospice by his friend F. E. Smith, then Attorney General in the Coalition Government, who arrived in time for dinner in the mess. Winston was delighted to see him, and welcomed his brilliant conversation as a tonic after the limited resources of his own officers. After a pleasant evening they retired to bed, Winston looking forward to a long political talk with his friend next morning. But in the small hours, at 4 a.m., a Provost Marshal appeared at the Hospice and arrested the Attorney General. Although the Attorney General had applied for a pass to visit the forward zone he had not yet received it. Protesting furiously, he was driven to the Hôtel du Commerce at St Omer, where he spent the rest of the night. When he woke in the morning, he found two Military Policemen guarding his bedroom door.

On being told that he was under close arrest, and that he would be shot if he tried to leave, F. E. stalked out of the hotel and invaded the office of the Adjutant General, Major General Macready. This officer – showing a marked lack of sympathy with the fuming Minister, and perhaps gratified by having one of the most deadly cross-examiners at the Bar at his disposal – inquired coldly, 'If you are a civilian, why are you here in uniform? If you are a soldier, why don't you obey the regulation?'

Even F. E. Smith could think of no obvious reply to these carefully premeditated questions, for he was wearing the uniform of an officer of the Oxfordshire Hussars. He then took refuge in Sir Max Aitken's house, the Canadian Office in St Omer.

The reason for this outrageous affront to a Law Officer of the Crown charged with the ultimate appeal in all court-martial cases was that the

29. Spencer-Churchill papers.

telegram from GHQ to the Headquarters of 2nd Army, requesting that Sir Frederick Smith should be supplied with a pass to the forward zone to visit Colonel Churchill, had been altered in transit by a malicious hand. This was yet another shot fired in the despicable subsidiary war between soldiers and politicians which continued in petty futility throughout the great struggle. On the excuse of a technicality, a Minister of the Crown had been arrested and treated with every circumstance of ignominy as a common prisoner. It was a heaven-sent opportunity for insulting a civilian who had the added stigmata of being a politician and a lawyer, and the story of his humiliation was gleefully passed, with many a titter, from mess to mess – a classic discomfiture of a 'bloody politician'.

Winston at first found the episode humorous, but soon realized its serious implications and his friend's humiliation, and extorted complete satisfaction from the Adjutant General's Branch:

> I am sure they had it in their minds that F E was trying to break their rules & they wished to obstruct his movements & make him come to heel . . . Once the impetus was given it gathered momentum as it passed from GHQ to Army & from Army to Corps & at some point someone with real malice or utter stupidity gave the necessary nasty twist. However the contrary impulse from on high has now been so unmistakeable that I fancy such a piece of cheek & folly will go long without a repetition.[30]

This lamentable episode was closed at a luncheon with Haig at GHQ, attended by a still sullen F. E., Bonar Law and Lloyd George. It was agreed that the matter should be allowed to rest, and the Commander-in-Chief indulged his usual practice of observing the amount of brandy consumed by his guests and entering the total in his diary.

* * *

The Battalion returned to the trenches on the following day. At first Winston concentrated on strengthening the defences, but later organized various provocations of the enemy which caused retaliation. The Battalion was altogether 100 days in the trenches while under his command, during which time 15 men were killed and 123 wounded. On 29 January the Hospice was shelled. Winston 'had just had a splendid hot bath – the best for a month & was feeling quite deliciously clean, when suddenly a tremendous bang overhead, & I am covered with soot blown down the chimney by the concussion of a shell these careless Boches have fired too short.'[31]

He had another and far narrower brush with death on 3 February

30. Spencer-Churchill papers.
31. Leslie papers. WSC to Lady Randolph Churchill.

when in his advance headquarters at Laurence Farm. As on all his campaigns, Winston had provided himself lavishly with the basic comforts of life:

> We had just finished an excellent lunch and were all seated round the table at coffee & port wine, when a shell burst at no gt distance making the window jump. Archie said that at the next one we shd all go into our dugout in the barn just opposite & we were discussing this when there was a tremendous crash, dust & splinters came flying through the room, plates were smashed, chairs broken. Everyone was covered with debris and the Adjutant [Jock McDavid] (he is only 18) hit on the finger. A shell had struck the roof and burst in the next room – mine & Archie's. We did not take long in reaching our shelter – wh is a good one! My bedroom presented a woebegone appearance . . . The wonderful good luck is that the shell (a 4.2) did not – & cd not have – burst properly. Otherwise we should have had the wall thrown in on us – & some wd surely have been hurt . . . I have made them put up another still stronger dugout – quite close, on wh they are now hard at work . . .[32]

From this time the Hospice was regularly shelled, and on one of these occasions Churchill had lost a Most Secret document which he should not have kept in the front line. Vistas of appalling disgrace seemed to confront him, but after a few days he found the paper he had been feverishly seeking in an inner breast-pocket: 'Seeing it once again safely in my hand, I gave a gasp of delight and relief, and the precarious battered abodes of "Plugstreet" under rainy skies and bitter winds seemed as safe and comfortable as home.[33]

*   *   *

The Hospice became too vulnerable a target for 'rest' Battalion headquarters, and he decided to move them to Soyer Farm, about eight hundred yards farther from the front line, where one of his companies was billeted. But he found it overcrowded and cramped, and soon began to return to dine and sleep at the Hospice – to the nuns, the piano and the tin portable bath.

Although still pierced by envious shafts of regret about the political scene from which he was a self-banished exile, he had now become completely immersed in his military duties. He no longer noticed the ravished landscape round Plugstreet, the blackened tree-stumps, the smell of corruption. Early and late, at dawn and in darkness, he was in the line. In

---

32. Spencer-Churchill papers.
33. WSC, *Thoughts and Adventures*, pp. 113-20.

wet weather he would appear in a complete outfit of waterproof stuff, including trousers, or in overalls, and with his French light-blue helmet presented a figure impossible to confuse with any other.

In the Mess he had reconciled himself to the company of brave but dull young men, and found that he had become fond of them. In the recollection of Gibb:

> There was absolutely no reticence about Churchill during ordinary social intercourse with his officers in the Mess. If he was asked a question about even the most delicate-seeming subjects he always gave a frank and honest reply. He would sit and discourse of Antwerp and the Dardanelles with perfect freedom . . . He amused us much by his stories of Lord Fisher, for whom he seemed to have the greatest admiration. He regarded Fisher as the type of man that was needed to win the war . . . Fisher was to him an unscrupulously wholehearted fighter for his country's good – a 'ferocious brute', he called him *à propos* of his conduct of the war. There was never any trace of hostility or animosity towards him – nothing save the most profound admiration. Regarding Lord Kitchener, on the other hand, he was less enthusiastic. He did not regard him as the awe-inspiring, relentless, terrifying being which the country thought him. He told us that on first going to meet him in conference he, Churchill, was rather nervous and subdued, thinking that Kitchener would be as awe-inspiring as he was painted, but he assured us that he got on well with him and found him to be 'a very nice old cup of tea.'[34]

It is agreeable to note that Winston, intolerant and socially spoilt, accustomed for years to choosing his own company (and that in the highest political and intellectual circles) should have been able to accommodate himself to that of lesser men. It is obvious that he not only tolerated the company of these Scottish boys with whom he had been forced into propinquity, but even experienced a strong affection based upon shared danger. But his unexpected success with the officers was equalled, if not excelled, in his relations with the men:

> It always struck me that Colonel Churchill achieved in a remarkable measure of success in dealing with the rank and file of the battalion. His attitude towards them was ideally sympathetic and was not marred by that condescending *hauteur* which goes so far to frustrate the efforts of a number of our regular officers.

He found the sentries less enthusiastic in their duties than he desired, and made a particular point of explaining their duties to them, walking along the front line and selecting positions for the men which gave a maximum shelter and enabled them to keep a perfect look-out:

34. Gibb, op.cit., pp.95-7.

To the young boys among them, especially, it seemed an unpleasant thing to stand up for an hour and expose oneself to the all too frequent bullets that came over to us from the German sentries. Winston used to get up on the firestep and encourage them, demonstrating to them what a small chance, after all, there was of their being hit and pointing out too how vital were the duties they were performing. In all this there was such a complete absence of the 'superior person' that the men welcomed his presence and his advice, and responded most loyally to his orders.[35]

He held strong views on the subject of sentries sleeping at their post, for which the penalty was often death, and took endless pains to obviate such disasters. It was also observed that he showed constant and humane concern for the wounded. Churchill had long been familiar with the horrors, the appalling debris of war, and felt no aversion to them; but 'he was always first on the scene of misfortune and did all in his power to help and comfort and cheer. It did not matter where he was or what he was doing, if he heard that a man was wounded he set off at once to see him.'[36]

*   *   *

Although this static war was dull and brutish, Winston managed by his own imagination to invest it with a certain panache. Desmond Morton, then a young Artillery major who did not know Churchill but afterwards became a close associate, was ordered to visit the Colonel commanding a neighbouring formation which had applied for artillery for a trench raid. Morton was directed to the Colonel's headquarters, which he found in an advanced and exposed position. He was then told that the Colonel was Winston Churchill:

> I went over dead ground to his H.Q., and found Churchill with a sketching block in his hand, making a drawing of the enemy lines. He was 'doing a Marlborough', calling up fire, demanding help on the flank, and turning the whole thing into a major campaign, rather than a trench raid of which the object was to collar a few Germans.[37]

And so, for a moment, in the midst of the squalor of modern war, he saw himself on the battlefields of Blenheim and Malplaquet, disposing of vast resources.

He took leave on 2 March, after the battalion had come out of the line for a rest period, and on arriving in London learned that Balfour was to introduce the Naval Estimates on 7 March. Here was

35. Ibid, pp.72-4.
36. Ibid.
37. Sir Desmond Morton to author.

his opportunity to attack the Government for its lethargy and defend his own record in naval and air administration, and he immediately began to draft his speech. This contained no word about Fisher, but after a dinner party attended by F. E. Smith, as well as by C. P. Scott[38] and Garvin[39], who were united in their desire to bring back Fisher, the 'old Malay' was, to Clementine's dismay, invited to luncheon at 41 Cromwell Road. F. E. Smith's recollection of this unhappy meal was of Clementine, like a tigress defending her stricken mate, saying furiously to Fisher, whom she abhorred since he had destroyed Winston and told her quite untruthfully that he was in Paris with his mistress – 'Keep your hands off my husband. You have all but ruined him once. Leave him alone now.'

On the evening of 5 March Winston read his speech to Fisher and told him that he intended to end it with a plea for Fisher's recall to the Admiralty. Fisher's enthusiasm for this insane act of generosity knew no bounds, and in the brief interval before the debate he bombarded Churchill, as of old, with extravagant letters. C. P. Scott, to Clementine's annoyance, was constantly in the house, like some unwanted sacristan, stiffening Winston's resolve and trying to persuade him not to return to the front. On 6 March Asquith dined with the Churchills, and Winston openly told him that he intended to demand Fisher's recall in the debate next day.

* * *

Churchill had written to his wife as recently as 3 February: 'I am rather anxious about old Fisher. I cannot trust the P.M. not to put him back. He & his press are vy active now. The general apathy at the Admiralty excites dissatisfaction. Fisher without me to manage him wd be disastrous.' Yet it seems inconceivable that Churchill can have hoped that there was the slightest prospect of his own reinstatement as First Lord, even in the improbable event of his bid for Fisher's recall succeeding.

Winston's speech, which was a well-reasoned criticism of the Admiralty's lack of driving force, ended in disaster and humiliation.

> Churchill's appeal for Fisher's return destroyed in a few minutes the whole impact of his speech, turning what had been to that moment one of the most serious and skilful speeches he had ever made into an object of derision. Churchill's hammer-blows of criticism were forgotten. The Government, Parliament and, on the morrow, the British public, gaped in amazement.[40]

38. Editor of the *Manchester Guardian*.
39. Editor of *The Observer*.
40. Gilbert, op.cit., p.722.

Only Lord Fisher was enthusiastic, and Winston's humiliation was complete. On the following day he was forced to endure a douche of Balfour's elegant ridicule, to which he was only able to make a most feeble response. Yet he remained convinced that the Army and Navy were in dire straits, and wished to remain in London for the Army Estimates debate. He was persuaded by Clementine to return to France, and she accompanied him to Dover on his way back.

From Dover he wrote to Asquith asking to be relieved of his command, and he gave Clementine a statement to the press. At that moment he felt that his place was on the front opposition bench, but when once again under the familiar weeping skies of Flanders, he felt wasted and drained dry after the week's emotional turmoil. An impression came to him that he had acted hastily, and he asked Asquith to delay action on his request. And he wrote to his wife:

> My dearest soul, you have seen me very weak & mentally infirm this week. Dual obligations, both weighty, have rent me. But I am sure my true war station is the H of C. There I can help the movement of events. I cannot tell you how much I love & honour you and how sweet & steadfast you have been through all my hesitations & perplexity.[41]

And again, a few days later:

> I reproached myself for having got so involved in politics when I was home that all the comfort & joy of our meeting was spoiled ... But the next time I come home it will be with a set purpose & a clear course, & with no wild & anxious hurry of fleeting moments & uncertain plans. I am going to live calmly.[42]

Clementine was a woman of high mettle, with a strong temper, and although she loved and admired Winston, and gave him unwavering loyalty, her letter of 23 March [the same date as Winston's letter to her, above] might almost be construed as a warning, revealing as it did her exhaustion by Winston's internal struggle:

'When next I see you I hope there will be a little time for us both alone. We are still young, but Time flies, stealing love away and leaving only friendship which is very peaceful but not very stimulating or warming.'

Winston was clearly wounded by these reflections, replying emotionally:

> Oh my darling do not write of 'friendship' to me – I love you more each month that passes and feel the need of you & all your beauty ...

41. Ibid. WSC to CSC, 19 March 1916.
42. Ibid. WSC to CSC, 23 March 1916.

Sometimes also I think I wd not mind stopping living vy much – I am so devoured by egotism that I wd like to have another soul in another world & meet you in another setting & pay you all the love & honour of the gt romances ... But I am not going to give in or tire at all. I am going on fighting to the vy end in any station open to me from wh I can most effectively drive on this way to victory. If I was somehow persuaded that I was not fit for a wider scope I shd be quite content here – whatever happened. If I am equally persuaded that my worth lies elsewhere I will not be turned from it by any blast of malice or criticism.[43]

* * *

During April the demand for universal military conscription suggested to the impulsive Churchill that the Government was about to break up, and that his own opportunity might be at hand. On 8 April he wrote a letter marked SECRET to F. E. Smith, begging him to bear his interests in mind:

I must await the *coup* out here. This letter is the only course open to me now. I must rely on you. Generally speaking L.G. [Lloyd George] is the key to my position at the moment. However a new system might be formed; it seems to me that L.G. and I shd be together. If he came in to what might be in substance a Tory Administration, he would need above all Liberal associates ... I have a feeling that B.L. [Bonar Law] and L.G. have a supreme chance now, if they have the resolution to act. It does not seem to me material whether B.L. is first & L.G. or *vice versa*. Either place would afford the basis of an effective war organisation – compared to wh nothing matters. Munitions will seem to me the easiest opening for me, tho of course you know my wishes, if they are obtainable.

The party of the future might be formed. I am sorry the crisis comes now – if it does: but in that case it is to you I must look and do look with entire confidence that you will set my affairs first in yr thoughts. Burn this wh is for your secret eye alone.[44]

Clementine did not agree with Winston's buoyant fantasies. Nor did she believe in the imminence of a crisis, and still thought his return would be premature. In this her shrewd common sense was superior to his instinct:

What I do think is that remaining there you are in an honourable *comprehensible* position until such time as at least a portion of the country demand your services for the state. If you come back before the call you may blunt yourself. People will always try to deny you power if they think you are looking at it. To gain a share of war direction you are contemplating a terrible risk, the risk of lifelong disappointment and bitterness ...

43. Ibid. WSC to CSC, 26 March 1916.
44. Birkenhead papers.

I could not bear you to lose your military halo. I have had cause during the 8 years we have lived together to be proud and glad of you so often, but it is this I cherish most of all. And it is this phase which when all is known will strike the imagination of the people: The man who prepared and mobilised the Fleet, who really won the war for England – in the trenches as a simple Colonel. It would be a great romance . . .[45]

Sage counsel – but of the kind which Winston found most difficult to follow. On 18 April he learned that there was to be a Secret Session, and his monomania swept all Clementine's shrewd, prudential advice from his mind. He at once applied for leave to attend the Session, and obtained it on condition that he returned to the front after the debate. He therefore spoke in the Secret Session on 25 April. There was, of course, no report of the proceedings. He had also applied for an extension of leave in order to stay in England for the open session on 27 April, but his Divisional Commander and his Brigadier insisted on his return while his Battalion was in the trenches. During his leave Winston – now with Clementine's probably grudging agreement – decided to leave the Army.

The complete reorganization of his Battalion and its amalgamation with another simplified matters and gave him a plausible excuse for departure. He consulted Haig, the Commander-in-Chief, who agreed that he could do more for the war effort by returning to Parliament and using his energy and skill to get conscription through the House. After this interview Winston added with sublime and no doubt unconscious hypocrisy that 'he had seen the force of Haig's arguments and had reluctantly agreed to return to England.'[46]

*   *   *

We can follow Winston's last days at the front in a series of episodes – a farewell luncheon party and farewell parades, and a general feeling of sadness at his departure. There was a Battalion photograph taken by 'an unwashed and Semitic artist from Armentières', with Winston 'playing the man' and wearing his Glengarry bonnet. There was his last evening with the Battalion, and his last farewells next day in the orderly room in an atmosphere charged with emotion, when the nervous Adjutant made a halting speech, touching in its affection and gratitude, to which Winston replied with mellow felicity.

He was accustomed to the society of men of his own choice and from his own world. Yet he had bridged any gulf, and triumphantly bestowed his charm and innate benevolence upon the young men. At this moment

45. Gilbert, op.cit., pp.753-4. [or Churchill papers: 1/118]
46. Gilbert, op.cit., p.759.

of departure every one of them felt his going as a sharp personal loss. No more convincing tribute could have been paid than that of the Adjutant:

> I am firmly convinced that no more popular officer ever commanded troops. As a soldier he was hard-working, persevering and thorough. The expected fireworks never came off. He was out to work hard at tiresome and indispensable details and to make his unit efficient in the very highest possible degree. I say nothing of his tactical and strategical ability – these were not tested in our time, but I cannot conceive that exceptionally creative and fertile brain failing in any sphere of human activity to which it was applied. And, moreover, he loved soldiering: it lay very near to his heart and I think he could have been a very great soldier. How often have we heard him say by way of encouragement in difficult circumstances, 'War is a game to be played with a smiling face.' And never has precept more consistently practised than this.
>
> I speak with all possible warmth and affection of him as the friend of his officers. This was most strikingly demonstrated in the last days of his command when he was anxious to find employment, congenial employment, for those who were to be thrown out into the cold when the battalions amalgamated. He took endless trouble: he borrowed motor cars and *scoured* France, interviewing Generals and Staff-officers great and small, in the effort to do something to help those who had served under him . . . The early months of 1916 are by far my most treasured war-memory. It was my happiest time and my most interesting time. For work in intimate association with Winston Churchill was the last experience in the world any of us expected – our course did not lie in that way. At first the prospect frightened us, but those feelings did not survive the first week. We came to realize, to realize at first hand, his transcendent ability. He came to be looked upon by us as really a possession of our own, and one of which we were intensely proud. And much more, he became our friend. He is a man who is apparently always to have enemies. He made none in his old regiment, but left behind these men who will always be his loyal partisans and admirers, and who are proud of having served in the Great War under the leadership of one who is beyond question a great man.[47]

Winston Churchill returned to England on 7 May 1916, having served in France and Flanders for five and a half months.

47. Gibb, op. cit.

Chapter 22

Out in the Cold

The break-up of his Battalion gave Churchill a plausible reason for returning to Parliamentary life, but the moment of political opportunity had not yet come. He did not expect to return to office under Asquith, whose enervating leadership he had long deplored, and whose removal he considered essential to the successful prosecution of the war.

He lost no time in making his voice heard in the House, speaking against the clause in the Military Service Bill which allowed Ireland to retain the voluntary system of recruitment, attacking the conduct of the war, criticizing the functions and powers of the Air Board of which Lord Curzon was to be President, and taking the opportunity to defend his own record in air defence. He sought an Air Ministry with full departmental powers, but this was not to be created until November 1917. When the Air Board was constituted Curzon invited Churchill to appear before it 'to advise us what are the points to which in your judgment we could best turn our immediate attention with a view to strengthening the air arm.'[1] Balfour, his successor as First Lord, also threw him an acceptable crumb when, after the indecisive battle of Jutland on 1 June, he asked Winston to draft a second communiqué to restore public confidence. This was issued on 3 June. These were small steps indeed on the road back, but they were as welcome as water to a parched man.

But however hard he sought to address himself to present realities, Winston could not refrain from worrying the carcase of his old grievance, for whenever he attacked the Government on its conduct of the war he was invariably taunted with the cry (inexpressibly galling to him): 'What about the Dardanelles?'

1. Chartwell papers, Curzon to WSC, 25 May 1916.

He was now convinced that his political reputation would never be restored until Parliament and public were made aware of the truth about this operation. He persuaded Asquith to agree to publication of the main documents in so far as military security would allow, and on 1 June Bonar Law informed the House of Commons that this would be done. Asquith was opposed to publication of the War Council Minutes, and Winston agreed that this presented difficulties. As he wrote to Asquith on 2 June:

> The main point I want to establish from them is my demand on behalf of the Admiralty on 27th Feb for the immediate despatch of the 29th Division & two Territorial Divisions in addition to the other troops. I also think that the decision of each War Council meeting about the Dardanelles shd be shortly stated, with the names of those who were present. This last I think vy important. Nearly everyone of consequence was present when the original decision to begin the purely naval attack was taken . . .[2]

Ian Hamilton's papers contained evidence that Kitchener had ignored his protests at the troops being held up in Cairo and had not even shown them to the War Council. This evidence of Kitchener's vacillation and neglect seemed unanswerable. On 6 June Hamilton was with Winston at 41 Cromwell Road. At midday, and while the two men were immersed in their documents, they heard Kitchener's name shouted in the street. Startled, Winston threw open a window, and heard the cry of a newsvendor: 'Kitchener drowned! No survivors!'

On the evening of 5 June Kitchener had sailed in HMS *Hampshire* on a secret mission to Russia, a journey welcomed by the Prime Minister to keep the discredited Minister away from London. A few hours after leaving Scapa Flow, the *Hampshire* struck a mine laid by the Germans before the battle of Jutland. Kitchener perished, and there were but a dozen survivors. He had become a legend in his lifetime, and now that he was no longer at hand to defend himself evidence about the Dardanelles could not be allowed to rest upon adverse criticism of the vanished hero.

Nevertheless, Winston continued to press the Prime Minister on the subject of the War Council Minutes, writing to him on 8 June:

> On reading through the Minutes of the War Council meetings wh dealt with the Dardanelles, I was convinced that they ought to be published & that they cd without any public disadvantage or personal unfairness be published . . . You will readily understand my wish that

2. Chartwell papers.

the truth shd be known. Not a day passed without my being the object of unjust reproach & now that poor Kitchener is gone I cannot see that the fortunes of the Ministry will be in any way prejudiced. The genesis of the operation is the vital point & your interest in showing that it was soberly and carefully entered upon is the same as mine. Meanwhile your acceptance of general responsibility in the House though most full & frank helps me not at all. Only the facts can tell the tale: and the public ought now to have them.[3]

Unfortunately for Winston, Asquith was already beginning to change his mind about publication of the documents. The War Council Minutes were by no means the only obstacle he saw looming in his path, and General Calwell, who had been asked by the War Office to examine the Dardanelles papers and to advise on what could be published, wrote to Sir Ian Hamilton on 4 July:

It seems quite impossible to publish correspondence and telegrams dealing with the operations subsequent to your successful landings, because they must give away Lord K if the story is fairly told. The tragedy of the 'Hampshire' simply precludes publication at present . . .[4]

The Prime Minister eventually decided to repudiate the pledge given to Parliament, and told Churchill that the documents could not, after all, be laid before it. On 20 July Asquith announced the setting-up of a Select Committee under the chairmanship of Lord Cromer 'to inquire into the conduct of the Dardanelles operations.'

Winston was disappointed and aggrieved beyond measure by this abject surrender. The dead hand of Kitchener seemed to have imposed a paralysing if not final veto. The evidence before the Commission was to be taken in secret, and there was no prospect of its early release. At this bitter moment Winston wrote to his brother Jack:

The Govt have decided to repudiate their pledge to publish the Dlles papers. My dossier was more than they could face. There will be a row, but there are many good arguments in the public interest against publishing: and many more good arguments in the Government interest![5]

Winston duly appeared before the Commission: his evidence was a *tour de force*, and the Report fairly exonerated him from the wild charges that had been levelled against him.

---

3. Chartwell papers.
4. Copy, Churchill papers; 2/74.
5. John Churchill papers. WSC to JSC, 15 July 1916.

* * *

He was tormented by uncertainty about his own future, and on 21 June he had written to Jack:

> The situation here is vy uncertain: & I do not know whether I shall be offered munitions or not. The Press is amazingly vicious & I count only on the Dlles papers to turn their mood. These will much embarrass the Government. I am sorry that the end of poor old K should have come at this moment. For his own sake it was a good exit – the glory had departed, the clouds were gathering & night drew near.[6]

When Lloyd George's appointment to the War Office was announced it was Edwin Montagu and not Winston who replaced him at the Ministry of Munitions. It was another moment of bitterness and humiliation for Churchill but Lloyd George showed himself friendly, though he was in no doubt of the difficulties confronting anyone who sought to repair the Churchill fortunes. Conservative hatred had in no way abated, and the fact that Winston had resigned his commission in the field caused it to break out again like an explosion of marsh gas. For the passage of time had done nothing to refresh the hate-withered garden of the Tory mind. Many of Winston's friends were baffled by the persistence of such implacable mistrust, and concluded lamely that the hatred was blind. But Lloyd George, with his subtle perception, interpreted it with greater insight, and even invested it with a convincing logic:

> They admitted that he was a man of dazzling talents, that he possessed a forceful and a fascinating personality. They recognised his courage and that he was an indefatigable worker. But they asked why, in spite of that, although he had more admirers, he had fewer followers than any prominent public man in Britain? They pointed to the fact that at the lowest ebb of their fortunes, Joseph Chamberlain in Birmingham and Campbell-Bannerman in Scotland could count on a territorial loyalty which was unshaken in its devotion. Churchill had never attracted, he had certainly never retained, the affection of any section, province or town. His changes of Party were not entirely responsible for this. Some of the greatest figures in British political life had ended in a different Party from that in which they had commenced their political career ... They asked: What then was the reason?
>
> Here was the explanation. His mind was a powerful machine, but there lay hidden in its material or its make-up some obscure defect which prevented it from always running true. They could not tell what it was. When the mechanism went wrong, its very power made the action disastrous, not only to himself but to the cause in which he was engaged

6. John Churchill papers.

and the men with whom he was co-operating. That was why the latter were nervous in his partnership. He had in their opinion revealed some tragic flaw in the metal. This was urged by critics as a reason for not utilizing his great abilities at this juncture. They thought of him not as a contribution to the common stock of activities and ideas in the hours of danger, but as a further danger to be guarded against.

I took a different view of his possibilities. I felt his resourceful mind and tireless energy would be invaluable under supervision ... It was interesting to observe in a concentrated form every phase of the distrust and trepidation with which mediocrity views genius at close quarters ...[7]

Some idea of the strength of this prejudice can be gained from a letter of the Under-Secretary of State for War, Lord Derby, described by Clementine as 'a fat sneak', to Lloyd George in August:

... I know your feelings about him and I appreciate very much that feeling which makes you not want to hit a man when he is down, but Winston is never down or rather will never allow that he is down and I assure you that his coming to the War Office as he does is – not to put it too strongly – most distasteful to everybody in that office. If as I hope there will be a new Party formed at the end of the war which would break down all old Party ties, Winston could not possibly be in it. Our Party will not work with him and as far as I am concerned personally nothing would induce me to support any Government of which he was a member ... He is absolutely untrustworthy as was his father before him, and he has got to learn that just as his father had to disappear from politics so must he, or at all events from official life.[8]

*   *   *

Winston had been in a state of constant depression since his return to London. His own uncertain future was by no means the only cause of this, for 1916 was also the year which witnessed the ghastly slaughter of the Somme, when the flower of the British Army was thrown in bloody frontal assaults against machine-guns and strong defensive positions, to maintain the insatiable demands of the 'war of attrition'. Although Winston admired and had been befriended by Haig, he regarded the carnage in France with feelings akin to nausea. He was by no means squeamish and knew better than most men that war cannot be waged without casualties, and he had been prepared, at the Dardanelles, to accept heavy losses to achieve a crucial victory. But he was revolted by the cold-blooded and ill-rewarded butchery on the Western Front.

---

7. David Lloyd George, *War Memoirs*.
8. Lloyd George papers, E.1.1.1., 19 August, 1916.

He recognized Haig's fearful responsibilities and the conflicting interests by which he was torn, but he was none the less appalled by his strategy. It was not in his character to abuse those who had treated him well, but his later estimate of the Commander-in-Chief, although attempting objectivity, was as devastating as any frontal assault launched by Haig:

> He presents to me in those red years the same mental picture as a great surgeon before the days of anaesthetics, versed in every detail of such science as was known to him: sure of himself, steady of poise, knife in hand, intent upon the operation; entirely removed in his professional capacity from the agony of the patient, the anguish of relations, or the doctrines of rival schools, the devices of quacks, or the first-fruits of new learning. He would operate without excitement, or he would depart without being affronted, and if the patient died, he would not reproach himself.[9]

* * *

Asquith's downfall – in which Churchill played no part, and which has been described by one of its leading participants, Max Aitken, in *Politicians and the War* and in Lord Crewe's Memorandum on the break-up of the First Coalition[10] – did not take place until early December. The new Prime Minister, Lloyd George, had of course to form his own Government; he desired to indulge his long-starved friend, had in mind to offer Churchill the control of Air, but the unslumbering Conservative hatred thwarted this intention, Bonar Law saying he would rather have Churchill against him than with him, and Austen Chamberlain, Walter Long, Lord Robert Cecil and Curzon making his exclusion a condition of their joining the Cabinet. The antagonism expressed by Derby was shared by nearly all the Conservative Party, and reflected by a majority of the most powerful organs of the press.

Lloyd George, therefore, however well intentioned, was unable to prevail on the strong Conservative group which he was obliged to include in his Coalition Government, and Churchill remained for a further seven months in a state of miserable ostracism. By the summer of 1917 the Prime Minister was prepared to make a bolder move. General Smuts, who had carried admiring recollections of Winston from the aftermath of the South African War, saw him on 5 June and advised him that Air offered a greater scope than Munitions.

> The result is [Smuts reported to the Prime Minister next day] that although he prefers Munitions, he will accept an offer of Air on the

9. WSC, *Great Contemporaries*, p.165.
10. Asquith, *Memories and Reflections*, Vol.II, pp. 128-39. See also Gilbert, op. cit. pp.820-3.

assumption that real scope is given him & that he must control the higher patronage in the Air Service.

In spite of the strong party opposition to his appointment I think you will do the country a real service by appointing a man of his calibre to this department, the vital importance of which will more and more appear.[11]

But it was not until 16 July 1917 that Lloyd George felt strong enough to invite Churchill to join the Government, offering either the Ministry of Munitions or Air. Winston chose the former. Lloyd George acted with his usual swift secrecy, and without allowing time for any resentment of his choice to gather force. The changes were announced next day – Churchill becoming Minister of Munitions, and Sir Eric Geddes First Lord of the Admiralty in place of Carson. Edwin Montagu became Secretary of State for India, from which position he was (to the consternation of many) to initiate reforms which accelerated the progress of Indian self-government.

Once again, one is astonished by the persistence of the Conservative hatred of Churchill. As Lloyd George said:

I knew something of the feeling against him among his old Conservative friends, and that I would run great risks in promoting Churchill to any position in the Ministry; but the insensate fury they displayed when later on the rumour of my intention reached their ears surpassed all my apprehensions ... Some of them were more excited about his appointment than about the war ...[12]

Winston himself later recalled:

There was an outcry among those who at that time had accustomed themselves to regard me with hostility. An immediate protest was made by the Committee of the National Union of Conservative Associations, and an influential deputation of Unionist Members presented themselves to the leader of the Party in strong complaint. Mr Lloyd George had, however, prepared the ground with his accustomed patience. Lord Northcliffe was on a mission to the United States, and appeased. Sir Edward Carson and General Smuts were warm advocates. The group of Ministers who had prevented my entering the Government on its formation was no longer intact. Some had been previously placated: the remnant acquiesced.[13]

One of those who limply acquiesced but whom Lloyd George had disdained to neutralize in advance was Lord Derby, now Secretary of State for War. This infirm politician, his mind swept by every passing

11. Lloyd George papers, F.45.95, 6 June 1917.
12. David Lloyd George, op.cit.
13. WSC, *World Crisis*, p.706.

Sports and Pastimes

Churchill enjoyed golf, fishing, riding, hunting, shooting, painting, bricklaying and flying, among other pursuits.

Churchill out shooting, 1900. *(Popperfoto)*

Enjoying a game of golf in 1913. Churchill was then First Lord of the Admiralty. *(Popperfoto)*

Churchill learning to fly. A picture taken in 1914. *(Popperfoto)*

And as a passenger. Mr Churchill, piloted by Lieutenant A. M. Longmore, RN, made a long flight in a seaplane at Portsmouth, starting from Portsmouth Harbour and proceeding over Spithead, where a flotilla of submarines was followed, Churchill is pictured leaving the seaplane after his flight. 1914. *(Mary Evans Picture Library)*

Winston Churchill on his polo pony, ready for the match, in Madrid, 1914. *(Press Association)*

Homes

Two views of Blenheim Palace, Oxfordshire, seat of the Duke of Marlborough.
Churchill was born two months prematurely and his mother was hurried to a
dingy room on the ground floor, a dark refugee known as the Dean Jones' room.

Aerial view of Blenheim. *(Popperfoto)*

West Front of Blenheim. *(By kind permission of His Grace the Duke of Marlborough, JP, DL)*

Chartwell, Westerham, Kent, Churchill's last home. It is now a shrine to his memory.

Chartwell: 'a tall house in mellow red brick built on the side of a steep slope, with rooms at dramatically different levels.' (*Popperfoto*)

Sir Winston's study at Chartwell – close-up of his desk. (*Popperfoto*)

gust, wrote on 21 July with weak indignation to Sir Philip Sassoon, who occupied the ornamental but bloodless position of 'Extra ADC' to Haig, mercifully secluded from the scenes of carnage:

> . . . Strictly between ourselves Lloyd George has made a *coup-de-main* when he appointed Geddes, Winston Churchill and Montagu. I never knew a word about it until I saw it in the paper and was furious at being kept in ignorance, but you can judge of my surprise when I found that the War Cabinet had never been told . . . Winston is the great danger because I cannot believe in his being content to simply run his own show and I am sure that he will try to have a finger in the Admiralty and War Office pies. We have an assurance that he will not do so, and I do not think that Geddes or I would stand for it for a moment, but I feel convinced that he will try it on . . . There is no doubt that the appointment of Winston and Montagu is a very clever move on Lloyd George's part. He has removed from Asquith his two most powerful lieutenants and he has provided for himself two first-class platform speakers . . .[14]

14. Derby papers.

Chapter 23

Ministry of Munitions
17 July 1917-10 January 1919

C hurchill returned to office, after twenty months' exclusion, and with such an immeasurable relief at being again at the centre of affairs that Clementine Churchill, who had been infected by his deep, brooding depression, felt a burden lifted from her own mind. She was convinced that his recovery began at that moment.[1] Now there was a task to perform, intractable problems with which to grapple and above all a sense of full participation.

Lloyd George, the first Minister of Munitions when the Ministry was created in 1915, had assembled a large number of the ablest industrialists and business-men in the country, but the task of supplying the Forces was enormous and ever more exacting, so that the Ministry, expanding to meet it, was now a vast organization. Churchill moved swiftly:

> I found a staff of 12,000 officials organized in no less than fifty principal departments each claiming direct access to the Chief, and requiring a swift flow of decisions upon most intricate and interrelated problems. I set to work at once to divide and distribute this dangerous concentration of power.
>
> Under a new system the fifty departments of the Ministry were grouped into ten large units each in charge of a head who was directly responsible to the Minister. These ten heads of groups of departments were themselves formed into a Council like a Cabinet . . . The big business men who now formed the Council were assisted by a strong cadre of Civil Servants, and I obtained for this purpose from the Admiralty my old friends Sir William Graham Greene and Mr Masterton Smith. Thus we had at once the initiative, drive, force and practical experience of the open competitive world coupled with those high standards of experience, of official routine, and of method, which are the qualifications of the Civil Service.[2]

1. Lady Spencer-Churchill to author.
2. WSC, *World Crisis*, p.708.

This reorganization freed the Minister from a morass of paper-work for which he had little inclination, and from many of the day-to-day decisions which could now be competently discharged by the ten Members of the Council, while he confined himself 'to the assignment and regulation of work, to determining the emphasis and priority of particular supplies, to the comprehensive view of the war programmes, and to the initiation of special enterprises.[3]

The reorganization was in every way successful, and Churchill was later to write: 'Instead of struggling through the jungle on foot I rode comfortably on an elephant, whose trunk could pick up a pin or uproot a tree with equal ease, and from whose back a wide scene lay open.'

* * *

The war was now in what Churchill called its 'Slogging Phase':

> This lasted from the beginning of the Battle of the Somme, the 1st July 1916, to the end of the Passchendaele attacks in November 1917. During the whole of this period the British armies, sometimes alone and sometimes assisted by the French, were hurled almost continuously, or with the briefest intervals for recovery, in assaults upon the fortified German lines.[4]

These terrible offensives placed a strain on the Ministry of Munitions. Supply was mainly dependent on shipping steel, skilled labour and dollars. The U-boat campaign had rendered the shipping situation acute. Steel-output from British sources alone had almost doubled, but the greater part of the necessary iron ore had to be shipped through dangerous waters from the north of Spain. Finished steel was bought from America to the limit of its availability. Skilled men were continuously pillaged from the factories to make good the staggering losses on the Western Front. The entry of the United States into the war in April 1917 relieved the dollar shortage, but a year must pass before their armies could take their place on the battlefield. By the autumn of 1917 Churchill was gravely disturbed about the supply position for the following year and found it necessary to issue a warning:

> The situation is very serious. Our labour, skilled and unskilled, is being drafted away at a time when we need a largely increased supply. It is not possible unduly to press the workmen at the present time. Our dollar credits in Canada have been severely curtailed. Our

3. Ibid, p.709.
4. Chartwell papers. Cabinet Memorandum by WSC, 22 June 1918.

importations of iron ore are scarcely two-thirds of our requirements from overseas. At the same time the Commander-in-Chief in France and the War Office demand an artillery programme nearly half as much again as that provided for this year. The Admiralty demand double as much shipbuilding materials as last year. Their claims upon every kind of material, including especially the rarest, are rapidly increasing; and at the present time they already absorb between 35 and 40 per cent of the entire labour supply of the country available for munitions of war. The Air Board have laid down a programme which requires our supply of aeroplanes to be at least tripled, in addition, of course, to the Admiralty airships. Meanwhile the maintenance of the railways in this country and other civil services essential to its war-making capacity has fallen heavily and dangerously into arrears; and the demands of the Allies become more insistent every week . . .[5]

This catalogue of needs gives some indication of the problems facing the Ministry of Munitions. Churchill also made a particularly intense effort to accelerate the tank programme. He had believed in the potential of this machine from the beginning, and at every stage encouraged its development, seeing in it the only means by which the petrified trench system could be decisively breached. The military mind had been slow to embrace the conception, protesting that tanks became bogged down in mud, and they had been used only in driblets, thus disclosing their existence without compensating results. On 10 October 1917 Winston wrote to Lord Robert Cecil, who had reported complaints from Tank headquarters in France:

... I have been giving a good deal of attention to tanks lately, and have held two conferences with the representatives of the War Office and of the Tank Corps, as a result of which I hope things will be put on a sounder basis. Broadly speaking, I consider a year has been lost in Tank development, and the most strenuous efforts will now be made to repair this melancholy state of things. A very complete agreement was reached at our conference last Monday between all concerned.

Apart from the defects in supply, and the lack of concord between the users and the makers, there has been a failure to use the Tanks under conditions which are favourable to their action, or for which they were originally conceived. It is hoped that under the new arrangements we may secure (a) a better supply of Tanks, and (b) a better use of the supply.[6]

5. Chartwell papers. Cabinet Memorandum by WSC, 1 November 1917.
6. Chartwell papers.

The occasion was supplied by the battle of Cambrai on 20 November, when the conception of the tank was triumphantly vindicated by its skilful and proper use. No artillery barrage preceded the battle, and nearly 500 tanks were engaged. This, under General Sir Julian Byng, was the employment of the Tank Corps as it was designed to be used, and the results were a revelation of its powers:

> As the tanks moved forward, with the infantry following close behind [wrote the historian of the Tank Corps] the enemy completely lost his balance, and those who did not fly panic-stricken from the field surrendered with little or no resistance . . . and by 4 p.m. on 20 November one of the most astonishing battles in all history had been won and, as far as the Tank Corps was concerned, tactically finished, for no reserves existing it was not possible to do more.[7]

This attack achieved complete success, and the rolling downland near Cambrai had been chosen as lending itself to tank movement. A penetration of six miles was achieved, far deeper and less expensive than any past British offensive; 10,000 prisoners and 200 guns were captured at the price of 1,500 British casualties. Above all, the battle revealed that surprise and the tank were the combination by which the trench barrier could be unlocked and completely vindicated the confidence Winston had always reposed in this weapon. The War Cabinet, which had hitherto been lukewarm in its attitude to the tank, began to show a belated interest in what Churchill called 'moving power', and there is perhaps some justification in his claim that had he been able to convince them of the significance of this new weapon in 1915, the war would have ended that year.

*　　*　　*

As the winter of 1917 drew on the picture grew ever more sombre as one disaster followed another – the U-boat campaign, the failure of General Nivelle's offensive against the Chemin des Dames ridge followed by mutinies in the French armies, the fearful carnage of Passchendaele where many British soldiers drowned in the mud, and the Italian rout of Caporetto – all these events formed a picture stark and terrifying. The Russian armies, crippled by the incompetence of their staff, and now rotted by subversion, collapsed and were soon removed from the war by revolution. The American armies were still far from the field of battle.

At a dark moment, on 10 December, Winston made a speech of defiance and exhortation at Bedford on Allied War Aims. He

7. Clough Williams Ellis, *The Tank Corps*.

acknowledged that the country was now in its greatest danger since the battle of the Marne saved Paris. He urged his audience to be steadfast and patient, not to be misled by sophistries and dangerous counsels, and to reject all thought of pacifism or treating with the enemy:

> We have never fought, and we are not fighting, for booty or revenge . . . We shall be satisfied when the Prussian militarism is unmistakably beaten and the German people are saved from its evil spell . . . We must raise the strength of our army to its highest point. Every service – the most scientific, the most complex – must be thoroughly provided; we must make sure that in the months to come a large proportion of our Army is resting, refreshing, and training behind the front line ready to spring like leopards upon the German hordes. Masses of guns, mountains of shells, clouds of aeroplanes – all must be ready, all must be there; we have only to act together and we have only to act at once.[8]

None the less, he was disturbed about the strength of the Army in France. Shaken by the major reverses of 1917, Lloyd George was in favour of remaining on the defensive until the arrival of the American troops in the main theatre. Winston's instinct was sure. While agreeing with this policy, he was convinced of an impending heavy German offensive, and did not think that the armies were being brought up to strength with sufficient speed. He saw this need as a matter of the greatest urgency, writing to Lloyd George on 19 January 1918:

> . . . I don't think we are doing enough for our army. Really I must raise that point with you. We are not raising its strength as we ought. We ought to fill it up at once to full strength. It is vy wrong to give men to the Navy in priority to the Army. To me it is incomprehensible. The imminent danger is on the Western Front; & the crisis will come before June. A defeat there will be *fatal*. Please don't let vexation against past military blunders (which I share with you to the full) lead you to underrate the gravity of the impending campaign, or to keep the army short of what is needed . . . I do not like the situation now developing and do not think all that is possible is being done to meet it . . . The Germans are a terrible foe, & their generals are better than ours . . .[9]

* * *

Since becoming Minister of Munitions Winston had resumed his visits to France in order to discuss the needs of the Army, visit Allied munitions and aeroplane factories, and confer with the French Minister of Armaments, Loucheur. He invariably flew on these excursions, and

8. Chartwell papers.
9. Lloyd George papers. F.8.2.19.

as all the best aeroplanes were required at the Front, his machines were often far from safe.

He had several narrow escapes from death, once when a valve burst over the Channel, nearly forcing the pilot down into the water. He managed to turn and limp back to an aerodrome near Cap Gris Nez. Here Winston was provided with another indifferent machine which broke down as soon as they were over England: '. . . another snap in the engine led to a repetition on the part of my pilot of those gestures which indicated that we had no choice but to descend. He side-slipped artistically between two tall elms, just avoiding the branches on either side, and made a beautiful landing in a small field.'[10] He felt excitement rather than fear after such escapes, and regarded his journeys to France with the exhilaration of one escaping from an office desk. He visited the Front whenever possible, and was a frequent visitor at GHQ.

His visits, whether strictly necessary or not, were so frequent that in May he asked Haig 'if I cd have a permanent lodging assigned to me in France somewhere in the zone of the armies. I do not like trespassing on your unfailing hospitality each time I come over . . .'[11]

The Commander-in-Chief, friendly as always to Winston, was agreeable to this request, and he was provided with the Château Verchoq, which he used for the rest of the war. His instinct for comfort cushioned his every movement: he was ferried backwards and forwards in what he called 'my private aeroplane'. The Duke of Westminster placed a car at his disposal in France, while in London he had the use of his friend Sir Abe Bailey's car and chauffeur in addition to a Ministry car. We may conjecture that these visits to France were chiefly memorable for the opportunities they provided for observing the war at close quarters. He found that he could work at the Ministry in the morning, fly to Verchoq at lunch-time, and spend the afternoon at the Front, so that he was able to boast with naive satisfaction: 'I managed to be present at nearly every important battle during the rest of the war.'

* * *

He was at the Front on 21 March 1918 when the Germans launched their last terrific assault on the British army along a fifty-mile sector of their line. This was Ludendorff's 'All or Nothing', his last desperate attempt to win the war, and so stupendous was the attack, and so prolonged, that defeat seemed to stare the Allies in the face. After the collapse of Russia a million extra men and three thousand extra guns had

10. WSC, *Thoughts and Adventures*, p.188.
11. Chartwell papers.

been added to the strength of the German armies on the Western Front, giving the Germans for the first time a preponderance in numbers. The sector between Arras and St Quentin was chosen as the point of attack, on the western face of the great salient formed by the German front in France. The strategic object was the separation of the British and French armies, and driving the British back against the Channel coast.

The German General Staff were now dominating the political as well as the military scene. Ludendorff and three of the ablest senior staff officers dictated the policy. All others, however exalted – commanders of armies and groups of armies – were disregarded. The Kaiser had become a mere impotent figurehead. This terrible offensive was planned on a scale and intensity never before conceived, and was designed to smash the British in a final knock-out blow before the American armies could appear in force upon the field. It was indeed All or Nothing, and its underlying purpose was, in Ludendorff's words: '*Wir müssen die Engländer schlagen*' – 'We must beat the British.'

This offensive decided the issue of the war. It lasted forty days and cost the British Army 300,000 casualties, and before it was over men were asking themselves for the first time whether Germany might after all win the war. The opening phase of this terrific onslaught, in Winston's words, 'the greatest onslaught in the history of the world', launched with new methods of infiltration and a plentiful use of gas, is well recorded – the devastating assault on the 5th Army, the fear that the French would break contact with their allies, and the dangerous rumours that they regarded the defeat of the British armies as inevitable.

By contrast Lloyd George was disturbed at the apparent inactivity of the French, who had moved only lethargically into action, and early on the morning of 28 March he sent for Winston and asked him if he could get away for a few days to undertake a mission to France: 'I can't make out what the French are doing. Are they going to make a great effort to stop the German inrush? Unless they do, the Germans will break through between us to the sea. Our Headquarters don't seem to know what they are going to do. The reports show a few French divisions arriving here, but what is going on behind? Are hundreds of thousands of men coming up? That is what I want to know. Can't you go over and find out? Go and see everybody. Use my authority. See Foch. See Clemenceau. Find out for yourself whether they are making a really big move or not.'[12]

Lloyd George, disturbed by the magnitude and power of the offensive, could see no reason why, having been driven from their fortified position, the British should not be able to stand farther in the rear. Winston explained that all offensives eventually lose their

12. WSC, *Thoughts and Adventures*, pp.165-6.

momentum. It was like a bucket of water thrown on the floor. The water lost its force as it advanced. He told Lloyd George that what was required from the French army was 'a strong upward punch' into the southern flanks of the ever-extending German bulge.

* * *

He set forth with the Duke of Westminster as his only companion, and crossed the Channel in a destroyer. He remained in France for five or six days. On 29 March he was able to reassure Lloyd George as to the role of the French:

> I had a most satisfactory talk with Clemenceau and every personal facility will be accorded to me. Spiers has been very helpful. I also saw Loucheur who has been continually with the Armies. These men know the real intentions of the French Government and I am completely reassured as to their policy. It is quite right. What I cannot judge is whether they will be able to carry it out. But at any rate there is a clear, bold policy being pushed to the utmost limit with all available resources and with the agreement of all concerned. Put briefly it is the upward punch of which I spoke to you . . .[13]

Clemenceau was a statesman after Winston's own heart. He recognized the old 'Tiger' as indomitable in courage and dangerous in enmity. On 30 March he and Clemenceau, accompanied by the Chef de Cabinet and M Loucheur, spent the day with the British and French commanders, receiving reports from each. On their journey Winston discovered that Clemenceau was even more reckless than himself in courting shell-fire. He, the embodiment of French resistance, insisted on crossing the river Luce to the actual battle area, where he was exposed to such instant danger that even Winston became nervous for his safety, and persuaded him to return. '*C'est mon grand plaisir,*' he protested, as in the midst of shrapnel and bursting shells he was respectfully directed to a safer place. Winston wrote to Clementine describing the scene:

> Yesterday was vy interesting, for I saw with Clemenceau *all* the commanders: – Haig, Foch, Petain, Weygand, Rawlinson etc; & heard from each the position explained. The old man is vy gracious to me & talks in the most confidential way. He is younger even than I am! and insisted on being taken into the outskirts of the action wh was proceeding N of Moreuil. Seely's Brigade had just stormed the wood above the village & were being attacked by the Huns there. Stragglers, wounded horses, blood and explosives gave a grim picture of war. I finally persuaded the old tiger to come away from what he called 'un moment délicieux.'

13. Chartwell papers. Telegram from WSC to Lloyd George, 29 March 1918.

We dined with Pétain in his sumptuous train and I was much entertained by Clemenceau. He is an extraordinary character: every word he says – particularly general observations on life & morals – is worth listening to. His spirit & energy indomitable. 15 hours yesterday over rough roads at high speed in motor cars. I was tired out – & he is 76!

He makes rather the same impression on me as Fisher: but much more efficient, & just as ready to turn round and bite! I shall be vy wary . . .

I think we ought to hold them for the time being, but a most formidable prolonged tremendous struggle is before us – if we are to save our souls alive.[14]

*   *   *

This was eventually accomplished after the extremity of suffering and at a terrible price. But the attack of 21 March precipitated two important developments. The first was that Foch was appointed Commander-in-Chief of all the Allied Armies in France. This decision was the result of the weakness and tardiness of Pétain's assistance, and his intention – communicated to Haig on 24 March, at the height of the battle – to withdraw French troops to cover Paris should the Germans continue to press on to Amiens. Had he been allowed to carry out this intention, contact between the British and French armies would have been severed. It was a change of which Winston strongly approved:

> Thus there was established for the first time on the Western Front that unity of command towards which Mr Lloyd George had long directed his cautious, devious but persevering steps, and to which, whatever may be said to the contrary (and it is not little), history will ascribe an inestimable advantage to the cause of the Allies.[15]

The second result was that Lloyd George and Clemenceau, through their countries' ambassadors at Washington, sent a most urgent request to the President of the United States 'to give immediate instructions so that 120,000 American infantry may be embarked monthly for Europe, from now onwards till the end of July.'[16]

The attack of 21 March was the prelude to a series of desperate German offensives, among the most bloody and protracted battles of the war, which continued throughout the summer of 1918. Ludendorff was well aware that this was his last chance of victory before the Americans arrived in full strength upon the battlefield, and it was not until the end

14. CSC papers. WSC to CSC, 31 March 1918.
15. WSC *The World Crisis*, p.763.
16. Chartwell papers. Telegram from WSC to Lloyd George on message sent by Clemenceau to America, 31 March 1918.

of July, after this prolonged agony, that the tide began to turn.

Churchill had given a formidable undertaking that all losses in material would be immediately replaced, and it is by his performance at this moment that his capacity as Minister of Munitions should be judged. Faced by the tremendous wastage of these battles, he was forced to lash his willing slaves at the Ministry to ever more urgent labours, to a peak of effort greater than ever before:

> and for this the Munitions Council, its seventy departments and its two and a half million workers, men and women, toiled with a cold passion that knew no rest. Everywhere the long-strained factories rejected the Easter breathing space which health required. One thought dominated the whole gigantic organization – to make everything good within a month. Guns, shells, rifles, ammunition, Maxim guns, Lewis guns, tanks, aeroplanes and a thousand ancillaries were all gathered from our jealously hoarded reserves. Risks are relative, and I decided, without subsequent misadventure, to secure an earlier month's supply of guns by omitting the usual firing tests . . .

He was able to write to Asquith on 6 April:

> I have been able to replace everything in the munitions sphere without difficulty. Guns, Tanks, aeroplanes will all be ahead of personnel. We have succeeded in pulling the gun position round so completely since last summer that we can deliver 2000 as far as they can be shipped.
>
> It has been touch and go on the front. We stood for some days within an ace of destruction.[17]

* * *

Since his return from France in 1916 Churchill had become closer and more intimate with Lloyd George, although he strongly disapproved of his method of government with only a small War Cabinet (of which he was not a member, although he belonged to the War Committee which settled the day-to-day programme of military and administrative business). He therefore felt unable to accept any responsibility for policy, explaining to the Prime Minister in April after one of their many political conversations:

> Certainly I will never accept political responsibility without recognised and regular power. As you know, I do not think that the new system . . . of governing without a regular Cabinet is sound or likely to be successful. But I am content in this war crisis to serve you and the Govt. to the best of my ability in an administrative capacity, without

17. Chartwell papers.

troubling myself about the political or party combinations, and to offer you personally in your intense labours for the material safety every aid & encouragement that a sincere friend can give.

It was a vy warm-hearted & courageous act of yours to include me in yr Government in the face of so much Conservative hostility, and I have ever had yr interests at heart.[18]

A Cabinet reconstruction was in the air, and on 15 May Winston wrote to the Prime Minister, offering to efface himself and remain outside a reconstructed Coalition Cabinet in order to strengthen Lloyd George's hand:

My only desire is to take part in the war, and I shall always be very grateful to you for giving me such interesting work. It would be a great relief to me to be freed from coming to decisions in political & party matters which would be at once premature & final. That is why I have so often disappointed you when our conversation has turned on party organisation & election preparations. I shd therefore be very glad to facilitate the creation of a political Cabinet by remaining exactly where I am.

When in France, and particularly at the scene of action, he felt a sense of freedom and exhilaration, and a complete release from the irksome political considerations in the change of scene and the stimulation of battle.

Coming out here [he told Clementine] makes me thoroughly contented with my office. I do not chafe at adverse political combinations, or at not being able to direct general policy. I am content to be associated with the splendid machines of the British army, & to feel how many ways there are open to me to serve them.[19]

After the battle of Amiens in August 1918, at which Rawlinson achieved a brilliant success with the tanks, Winston, who sent Haig a telegram of congratulation, received a reply which filled him with gratification and made clear the debt owed him by the armed forces for his feverish efforts: 'Many thanks for your welcome congratulations. I shall always remember with gratitude the energy and foresight which you have displayed as Minister of Munitions, and so rendered our success possible.'[20]

* * *

18. Lloyd George papers. F.8.2.19. WSC to Lloyd George, 4 May 1918.
19. CSC papers. WSC to CSC, 15 September 1918.
20. Ibid.

It is a matter of history that the cruelly battered British did not break, that they closed by a miracle the gap which had been torn in their line at St Quentin, and that contact was not lost between them and their French allies. By the late summer of 1918 the Americans were pouring in enormous numbers into France, and all prospect of a German victory had disappeared. When the collapse came, it was swift. Ludendorff's tremendous, coldly calculated gamble had failed, and in October the end was at last in sight. Winston realized better than most what a desperately close-run affair it had been, saying afterwards: 'We only just got through. The more one knows about the struggle the more one realises on what small narrow perilous margins our success turned . . . It was neck and neck to the very end.'

On 7 November Churchill wrote to Lloyd George saying that it was not possible for him 'to take the very serious & far-reaching political decision you have suggested to me without knowing definitely the character & main composition of the new Govt. you propose to form for the period of reconstruction.' He said that he was anxious not to be an embarrassment to the Prime Minister, and did not wish to be pressed on the reluctant Conservatives. He would make no complaint whatever on quitting the Government then or at the end of the war.[21]

Lloyd George took strong exception to this letter, and for once replied in writing rather than by means of conversation. His answer was tart and showed every sign of exasperation:

> After the conversation we had on Wednesday night, when we arrived at an understanding on questions of policy, your letter came upon me as an unpleasant surprise . . . It suggests that you contemplate the possibility of leaving the Government, and you give no reason for it except an apparent dissatisfaction with your personal prospects. I am sure I must in this misunderstand your real meaning, for no Minister could possibly adopt such an attitude in this critical moment in the history of our country. I am confronted with a problem as great as that of the war – fuller of difficulties and as vital to the people of the country. If you decide to desert me just as I am entering upon this great national task . . . the responsibility must be yours . .
>
> You say that before you come to the 'very serious and far-reaching political decision' which I invited you to take you must know how the Government is going to be constituted. Surely that is an unprecedented demand! The choice of the Members of the Government must be left to the Prime Minister, and anyone who does not trust his leadership has but one course, and that is to seek leaders whom he can trust.[22]

21. Chartwell papers.
22. Ibid.

Winston send an undated but soothing answer to this tirade, denying that he was contemplating desertion, and the Prime Minister's anger must have abated, for he was not moved to write another letter.

The Armistice was signed on 11 November, and in his office Winston heard Big Ben strike the hour of eleven, which told him that the bloodiest war in human experience had at last ended. He could look back on it with little personal satisfaction in spite of his brilliant beginning at the Admiralty. Foremost in his mind was the sour memory of an unfruitful experiment, for which he had been coldly selected as scapegoat, while his wife for her part recalled all too well his long, disastrous intercourse with Fisher. Nor would he forget that for nearly half of the long struggle, for which he recognized his own outstanding aptitude, he had been kept in humiliating seclusion. However, his re-employment and success at the Ministry of Munitions had done much to cleanse his mind of despairing thoughts, and his presence at battles helped to raise his drooping spirits. When Big Ben had struck he drove to Downing Street to see the Prime Minister and to speak of the future.

Part 4

The End of
The Coalition

Chapter 24

A Service Department

On December 1918 Lloyd George's wartime Coalition appealed to the country in what became known as the 'Coupon Election'. Candidates supporting the Coalition were provided with coupons testifying to their loyalty. They were opposed by Liberal followers of Asquith and by Labour candidates. The election revived the Prime Minister's temporarily suppressed demagogic instincts, and he felt safe in indulging the electorate's revengeful mood by wild promises about trying the Kaiser and demanding from Germany the whole cost of the war, which were afterwards to be a source of embarrassment but at the time served his purpose. One Minister raved about 'squeezing the lemon until the pips squeaked', and such myopic folly matched the public mood. Lloyd George swept the board, and the Labour Party with 59 seats found themselves the official Opposition. A mere handful of Asquithian Liberals survived the debacle, and that without their leaders. Lloyd George's coalition won 526 seats, giving him a majority of 337 over all other parties.

He reconstructed his Government with what Churchill regarded as 'masterful despatch'. Churchill was allowed to decide between the War Office and the Admiralty, and was told: 'You can take the Air with you in either case; I am not going to keep it as a separate department.'[1] It proved to be an unfortunate decision.

Churchill met the Prime Minister's obvious preference by accepting the War Office, although privately yearning to be a *revenant* to the Admiralty. He was again at the head of a Service department, but now with a significant difference. For he was not there to command loyal soldiers in war but to disband a sullen army and to create a new one. The soldiers considered that, being subject to discipline, they

1. WSC, *The World Crisis: The Aftermath*, p.52.

were being handled with indifference in the post-war adjustments. The demobilization scheme, influenced mainly by civilian opinion and intent upon the revival of industry, had insensitively ignored the rights of the Army. Drawn up in 1917, it decreed that the 'key men' for industry should be the first released. But those who were to be the first to come home had often been the last to go out as their part in industry had preserved them as civilians until the needs of the Army became desperate. This order of release was already proceeding, to the rage of less pampered and longer-serving soldiers and in spite of forceful criticism by Sir Douglas Haig.

The result of this crass and unjust policy was demoralization, and it was the deplorable situation with which the new Secretary of State was faced. It was one he was well qualified to understand:

> The ordinary soldier without these advantages saw his lately joined comrade hurrying home to take his job ...while he, after years of perils and privations on a soldier's pay, wounded and sent back to the carnage ... was to be left until all the plums at home had been picked up and every vacancy filled. The fighting man has a grim sense of justice which it is dangerous to affront.[2]

Mutinies had already taken place on both sides of the Channel, and in every unit of the Army discipline was rotted and undermined. It was an odious situation.

Although the problem of reviving a dispirited army was less familiar to him than directing a confident one, he perceived the cause and devised the remedy:

'My only difficulty was to secure the assent of others; my only apprehension, whether we were not too late.' He had already insisted that his will should prevail against all civilian departments in matters affecting the discipline of troops. His policy was:

> First: Soldiers should as a general rule only be released from the front in accordance with their length of service. Those who had served longest at the front were to be the first to be demobilised, and any man with three wound stripes or more was to be discharged forthwith ...
> Secondly: the pay of the Army was to be immediately increased to more than double the war rate, in order to lessen the gap between the rewards of military and civilian employment.
> Thirdly: In order, whilst still maintaining the necessary forces in the field, to release the men who had fought in as large numbers and as quickly as possible, the 80,000 young lads who had been trained but

2. WSC, op.cit., p.54.

had not quitted our shores, must be retained compulsorily for a period of two years and sent abroad.[3]

But it was not easy to get endorsement for this obvious programme. The Prime Minister was in Paris: the Cabinet was uneasy at the thought of presenting a new Conscription Bill to Parliament so quickly after the war.

* * *

The Government viewed this scheme with misgiving, and Bonar Law conveyed it to Lloyd George, who was furious:

> I have just heard that you propose bringing before the Cabinet on Tuesday the question of continuing military service for an army of 1,700,000. I am surprised that you should think it right to submit such a scheme to my colleagues before talking it over or at least submitting it in the first instance to me. It is hardly treating the head of the government fairly . . . and I ought to have been consulted in the first instance. A memo ought to have been sent to me by aeroplane which would have reached me in a few hours . . .[4]

This was a characteristic tiff between two men who understood one another so well. Yet Winston was anxious to propitiate Lloyd George. He assured him that the scheme was entirely provisional, and that he had already arranged to send it by aeroplane . . .

> Briefly the scheme consists in releasing two men out of three and paying the third man double to finish the job. I am extremely anxious about the present state of the army and am serving you to the very best of my ability in preparing a comprehensive scheme for your approval.[5]

Lord Esher would not have been surprised by the Prime Minister's petulant outburst. He wrote to Winston on 23 January:

> You have made a splendid start from all I hear nothing but eulogy comes my way.
> Everybody who matters is delighted.
> What will that funny jealous little devil LG say at having a S of S who *acts* instead of talking. *Nous verrons.*[6]

3. Ibid.
4. Chartwell papers, LlG to WSC, 18 January, 1919.
5. Ibid, WSC to LlG, 20 January 1919.
6. Ibid.

Taking the Adjutant-General with him, Churchill crossed to France to seek the Prime Minister's approval. This was obtained the next day, and the new Army Orders were issues, which announced the Government's intention to increase the remuneration of those retained in uniform and to create Armies of Occupation.

Lloyd George's sudden exasperation seemed to be appeased, and Winston wrote to Clementine on 24 January:

> ... I was taken by the PM to the Conference this morning & placed in a seat of honour among the great ones of the earth ... I breakfast lunch & dine with the PM who is splendidly installed close by this hotel. It is a good thing to get in touch again. We were diverging a good deal. I think I influence him in a considerable degree, & there is no one with whom he talks so easily ... PS I hope to launch my big scheme Thursday.[7]

On returning to London he wrote to Lloyd George about the proposed new Military Conscription Bill:

> It is not true to say that the signature of peace affects the military problems of the British Army. That problem exists in the fact that we have got to find garrisons on the reduced scale proposed during the whole of this year, for both France and other theatres, and it is physically impossible to organise a voluntary army in that period.
>
> Therefore, it seems to me that the manly course – and the honest course – is to take Parliament fully into our confidence and rely on the good sense of the nation, which having won so great a victory, would never forgive us if we cast the fruits away ...
>
> You realise, I suppose, that all the men of the present army are serving on one or other of the following bases:–
> *either (a) 'the duration of the war', which means the signature of the Peace Treaty; or (b) 'six months after the cessation of hostilities', and this is universally interpreted by the men as six months from November 11th, i.e. May 11th.*
> We therefore automatically lose all authority over the whole of our armies in every theatre and in India if the Peace Treaty is signed at any moment after May 11th; or on May 11th if it is signed at any moment before ...[8]

These arguments proved unanswerable, and Parliament passed the Bill by a large majority.

*   *   *

In the meantime widespread insubordination and indiscipline were bedevilling the Services, more than thirty cases being reported in

7. Chartwell papers, CSC papers, 24 January 1919.
8. Chartwell papers.

one week. The most disturbing incident was a mutiny at Calais, launched by the big Army Ordnance detachments and the Mechanical Transport, at the end of January 1919. It was noteworthy that these men, the least disciplined in the Army, had also seen least of the fighting, and paid their principal loyalty to political trade unionism rather than to their own officers. They now refused to obey orders. They met the leave-boats and persuaded so many of the returning soldiers to join their ranks that they were soon at the head of three or four thousand men.

There was no fighting force to hand to deal with this menace, and so the Commander-in-Chief recalled two divisions from their march to Germany, placing them under the command of General Byng, who with great tact and restraint brought the situation under control without bloodshed. The ringleaders were arrested and all the other men returned to duty. The austere Haig at once advocated the most extreme form of punishment, and demanded the death penalty for the rebel leaders, writing to Churchill, 'If any lenience is shown to them the discipline of the whole Army will suffer, both immediately & for many years to come.'[9]

Fortunately for his reputation, although he had not yet received a detailed account of the disorders, Churchill disagreed with this harsh request. Ever since his days as Home Secretary he had hated the supreme penalty and shrank from applying it. He now wrote to Haig:

> Unless there was serious violence attended by bloodshed or actual loss of life, I do not consider the infliction of the death penalty would be justifiable. The death penalty should be used only under what may be called life and death conditions, and public opinion will only support it when other men's lives are endangered by criminal or cowardly conduct ... I will, of course, await your full report before forming a final opinion.[10]

In the sequel the court martial condemned the three ringleaders to five years' penal servitude, one year's hard labour, and ninety days' field punishment respectively.

When the new system came into operation, and its working was grasped by all ranks, discipline swiftly returned and demobilization proceeded smoothly:

> For a period of nearly six months we maintained an average rate of 10,000 men a day discharged to civil life. This immense body, equal to a whole peace-time Division, was collected daily from all the theatres of

9. Chartwell papers.
10. Ibid. WSC to Sir Douglas Haig, 31 January 1919.

war, disembarked, de-trained, disarmed, de-kitted, demobilized, paid off and discharged between sunrise and sunset.[11]

* * *

Simultaneously with demobilization Churchill was confronted by the equally urgent problem of the reconstruction of the Regular Army on a voluntary basis. He sought to solve it on the following lines, as he explained to Austen Chamberlain in February: 'There will be two after-war armies: one long service for our foreign garrisons, and the other short service with a long reserve period for home defence. The former will be as small as we can manage, and the latter as large as we can afford.'[12]

It was necessary to undertake this tremendous task in circumstances of uncertainty, for it was impossible to predict how long the armies of occupation would be required, or what Great Britain's ultimate foreign commitments would be. Churchill was also aware that all planning was subject to the available financial resources. One profitless commitment which particularly irritated him was the retention of the 250,000 German prisoners of war in British hands. The cost of maintaining them was heavy, and the 50,000 British soldiers involved in guarding them were due for demobilization. There were no available men to replace them.

The intransigence of the French was mainly responsible for this impasse, and it is not difficult to understand. When they thought of their ravaged country, and the irreparable blow to their manpower, their hearts hardened. 'When they thought of all the slaughter represented by their capture, and of the depleted manhood of France, they could not bring themselves to let these hundreds of thousands of unlucky men go home. It was like surrendering captured cannon.'[13] With dogged patience Winston continued to urge repatriation, until at last, at the end of August 1919, he took matters into his own hands and himself issued the necessary instructions.

* * *

It was inauspicious for Churchill's political reputation that Lloyd George decided that the element of Air should not be administered as a separate department after the war. With the Army as his main preoccupation, he gave less attention to the newly named Royal Air

11. WSC, op.cit., p.65.
12. Chartwell papers. WSC to Chamberlain, 4 February 1919.
13. WSC, op.cit., pp.67-8.

Force than was appropriate. In Sir Basil Liddell Hart's words:

> Churchill himself was War Minister and Air Minister combined from 1918 [sic] to 1921, the crucial period for the reconstruction of the forces. The Air Force had evolved a plan under which the post-war R.A.F. was to consist of 154 squadrons of which forty were for home defence. Under Mr Churchill's aegis this was whittled down to a mere twenty-four squadrons, with only two for home defence, and the plan for state-aided airways covering the Empire was discarded. When he moved to a fresh office in 1921, *The Times* had this comment on his regime at the Air Ministry: 'He leaves the body of British flying well nigh at the last gasp when a military funeral would be all that would be left for it.'
>
> In the War Office, too, he sadly disappointed all the progressive young soldiers who had built their hopes on his vigour and activity as foster-parent of the tank early in the war. To their dismay, he allowed the older school to refashion on 'back to 1914' lines, thus missing the best opportunity of reconstructing it on a modern basis . . .[14]

* * *

This dispiriting survey of a period of retrenchment and *laissez-faire* seems completely out of harmony with the Churchill we know, the 'War man' who had directed the Navy in those early golden years at the Admiralty, and honed it to a fine cutting edge when the great incentive came. But Churchill is entitled to be judged in the context of the moment. Stringent economy was the demand made of all spending departments; and we know that it was one which for filial reasons struck a ready echo in Winston's heart. Had he not once tried to emasculate the Navy he was later to transform? And was he not always prone to accept whatever demands a new office disclosed with exclusive and almost obsessive concentration?

And at this moment – even if he had ardently wished to carry them out – Utopian plans for the reconstruction of the Army and the development of the Royal Air Force were literally impossible to achieve within the prescribed financial limits. The Chancellor of the Exchequer, Austen Chamberlain, no enemy of Winston, was compelled always to sing to him the same enervating descant of economy and prudence. It was irksome to Churchill's nature to be fretted by financial considerations, but now, with enormous military responsibilities abroad and inadequate resources, he found himself in that frustrating position:

> The public will no doubt be disappointed whatever happens. They have hoped for the most drastic terms against Germany coupled with almost immediate dispersal of our army. They expect to maintain a great

14. Liddell Hart, op.cit., p.200.

and increasing Empire and at the same time largely to diminish their military establishment. They look forward sanguinely to large reductions of expenditure while at the same time they insist on the highest possible wages, salaries, gratuities and remuneration of all forms being paid to everybody who has at any time been connected in any way with the public services during the war.[15]

In August 1919, he again commented morosely, 'Everyone is delighted to rail at expenditure, but the moment the axe is laid to the root of any particular tree a perfect scream of protest goes up.'[16]

In spite of the demands for economy, it was necessary to meet the emergencies that arose. These presented themselves in urgent guise and repeatedly in Egypt, India and Ireland, on the Rhine and in Great Britain. He must provide for the obligation to remain in military occupation of Constantinople, Mesopotamia and Palestine, often in circumstances of great uneasiness and unrest. He was also vexed by the fact that demobilization was postponed by the delay in making peace with Germany, and then in ratifying it, which long hampered the release of prisoners.

* * *

As to Liddell Hart's charges that Winston had limply acquiesced in the desire of *passé* senior officers to allow the Army to relapse into an obsolete instrument – that he had sought to refashion it on 'back to 1914' lines – it should be emphasized that he was, on the contrary, an ardent protagonist of its mechanization. He had seen at first hand, and with horror, the fearful price paid for incessant frontal assaults on heavily defended positions, on machine-guns and barbed wire, and was anxious to regain the superiority of free operations. Writing to Austen Chamberlain on 22 June 1919, he said:

> In all the clearing up that remains to be done after the war, the armoured car will play a vital part. Instead of large forces of infantry, cavalry and heavy artillery maintained as garrisons, we require in many places smaller forces with machine guns in armoured cars which are very mobile and can move into streets and villages and push out across deserts in suitable country and support civil and police administration. There is no other way of holding and administering the very large regions we have in our charge except by an undue expenditure of troops organised on the old lines. Everyone is crying out for armoured cars – India, Egypt, Mesopotamia, Denikin, Ireland, the Army of the Rhine – and I am sure that in the next few years great reliance will be placed upon this means of maintaining order which can so often operate without loss of life.

15. Chartwell papers. WSC to Austen Chamberlain, 5 July 1919.
16. Ibid. WSC to Austen Chamberlain, 26 August 1919.

On the other hand the Treasury is resisting even the armouring of 100 lorries which are most urgently required, and their opposition has already resulted in a delay of some weeks.[17]

On 30 October 1919 Churchill again wrote to the Chancellor of the Exchequer in a manner which suggests that he was trying to sweeten his own conviction that the nature of the Army must be changed by a coating of economic prudence:

From your point of view, namely the reduction of military expenditure, it seems to me that you are most unwise to resist the substitution of machinery for manpower. The only result of doing so is to force the military authorities to solve all their problems in terms of numbers ... Now that the cost of the individual soldier cannot be less than £250 a year, enormous expense is bound to result from trying to defend our increased possessions on old-fashioned lines. On the other hand ... the preponderance of military opinion is quite content to carry on along those lines, dealing in factors which they understand and have been familiar with all their lives ... namely, infantry, cavalry and artillery in as large numbers as possible in each particular theatre.

I cannot hope to carry military opinion with me ... unless I am able to show these new weapons not as a mere experimental pattern but as definite features in the military organisation. There is no comparison between the best tank used in the war and the new model ... Unless these new tanks can be made and the military authorities impressed with their practical utility, it is hopeless to look for a speedy transition to a mechanical army ... My plan is to do away with at least half of the cavalry and substitute for them a much smaller number of these very fast tank units (which alone possess the swiftness of cavalry). But I shall never get military opinion to accept this, except under violent duress, unless and until it is possible to show the definite tactical results which can be achieved by the use of this new arm manoeuvring with the others. Before these proofs can be offered, it is necessary not only to have the weapon but to train men to use it, and for this purpose every month counts. Nine had already been consumed in fruitless discussion and correspondence.[18]

These letters render absurd Liddell Hart's allegations that Churchill acquiesced in a return to now obsolete weapons and methods of war, and he seems totally unaware of Churchill's views on the mechanization of the Army. On the contrary, Churchill intended above all else to restore mobility to the battlefield, and he made a strong fight for it while Secretary of State for War. It was not his fault that he did not remain at his post long enough to prevail over the Devil's Advocate at

17. Chartwell papers.
18. Ibid.

the Treasury or the reactionary elements in the War Office. If Liddell Hart and *The Times* newspaper believed that Churchill had left the Royal Air Force in so moribund a condition that it was only fit for the final offices of the undertaker and the strains of defunctive music, it is only fair to comment that this view was not shared by the Chief of the Air Staff, Sir Hugh Trenchard (now generally regarded as the 'father' of the RAF), who was to write to Bonar Law in February 1921 giving his reasons for wishing to revert to a separate Air Ministry:

> These reasons are quite apart from the point that it was possible to run a joint Secretary of State for War and Air in the case of Mr Churchill with his enormous capacity for work & quick comprehension by once reading through the vast number of long & complicated questions that continually arise. I am perfectly certain that no other man I have yet met could have done this work without seriously handicapping the development of the Air Service & also militating against economy, except Mr Churchill, & owing to his capability in doing this he has enormously assisted in the formation of the Air Service on a very economical basis.[19]

The fact that Churchill had combined in his person the functions of the War Office and the Air Ministry invited the creation of a Ministry of Defence embracing the three Service Departments, of which, according to Roskill, Winston 'saw himself as the first incumbent.'[20] The idea found little favour in the Air Ministry, which sensed a reversion to the old pre-war state of affairs when it was divided between the Navy and the Army, and neither Trenchard nor Hankey lent a kindly ear to the suggestion. But the reform was urged repeatedly over the years, only to be resolutely scotched by its opponents. Churchill had, of course, worked out the details in a minute which suggests a personal interest, and conveyed them to the Prime Minister.[21]

But it was forty-five years before a Ministry of Defence of the sort over which Winston sought to preside came into being, in 1964.

*   *   *

As Secretary of State for War one theme seemed to become dominant in Churchill's mind, and his immersion in it, at once chivalrous and logical, became a source of irritation to his colleagues. It was the need to support the anti-Bolshevik forces in Russia.

To some, and particularly to Lloyd George, it appeared that his mind

19. Bonar Law papers, 100.2.12.
20. Roskill, *Hankey*, Vol.2, p.32.
21. Chartwell papers, WSC to Lloyd George, 14 July 1919.

had set in a familiar and exasperating mould – that he was in the grip of an *idée fixe*, devouring and threatening to exclude all else. Perhaps the Prime Minister was reminded of the metaphor he himself had used, of the chauffeur who, after months of impeccable driving, suddenly drove his car over a cliff. To judge from his letters he now feared that Churchill was on the verge of such an aberration.

Certainly Churchill's chivalrous instincts were roused by the plight of Russia. Perhaps there was substance in Lloyd George's jibe that 'his ducal blood revolted against the wholesale liquidation of Grand Dukes'. Certainly his profound respect for the mystique of kingship had been outraged by the butchery of the Imperial family at Ekaterinburg. In one of the most striking of his literary images he had described the despatch of Lenin to Russia in a sealed train 'like a plague bacillus', and more deadly than any bomb. He saw the collapse of Russia as the moment when 'with victory in her grasp, Despair and Treachery assumed command, she fell upon the earth, devoured alive, like Herod of old, by worms'. He detested what he described as 'the foul baboonery' of Bolshevism, and described Lenin as 'the monster crawling down from the pyramid of skulls'.[22] The vast stricken country was in a state of disintegration, like some huge animal horribly wounded but refusing to die. The Tsar had been overthrown in March 1917, the Bolsheviks had seized power in the following October and, in March 1918 they signed a treaty of armistice with the Germans at Brest-Litovsk. This released a million German soldiers from the Eastern Front to face the hard-pressed Allies in France.

In November 1918 there were detachments of Allied troops on Russian soil, most of whom had been despatched from the treaty. There were 8,000 troops, mainly British, at Murmansk and Archangel in the far north, and a further 1,000 at Omsk on the Siberian railway. The object of these forces was to prevent oil-supplies and other sinews of war from falling into German hands.

In the meantime the Bolshevik advance had not been uncontested. White Russian counter-revolutionary forces, separated by vast distances, were continuing to fight the war. Admiral Kolchak, formerly Commander of the Black Sea Fleet, and since November head of the Provisional Government at Omsk, was fighting the Bolsheviks in the east, and General Denikin, a soldier who welcomed with a certain relish the political and diplomatic commitments of his new role, in the south. Both were fighting in the face of great difficulties, and in tones of growing desperation both begged Great Britain for help.

22. Rhodes James, op. cit., p.106.

* * *

It was an appeal which Churchill was temperamentally incapable of resisting. Chivalry and prudence alike prompted his conclusions. Loathing cruelty to man and beast, he had grasped with unusual subtlety the real character of the emerging phenomenon. He was repelled by the cold erasure of all humanity from this new secular religion. When starry-eyed simpletons were already rhapsodizing over the 'great social experiment' he saw only leaders committed beyond recall to a régime whose victims were left rotting and freezing through the Arctic night, under which mercy was annulled and God blasphemed, and which rejected with contempt the small, the local, the kindly. In a flash of incandescent understanding, he realized that the Christian tolerance which alone lent glory to life was not only to be abolished but to be rendered heinous.

It is to Churchill's eternal credit that he grasped the unforgiving nature of this philosophy in the dawn of its baneful power, and recognized the presence of authentic evil. It can be seen in his writings on Lenin and Trotsky, whose genius he accepted, but whose influence he found pernicious. This first conviction and the instinctive repulsion were never to leave him, and years afterwards he was to write:

> For all its horrors a glittering light plays over the scene and actors of the French Revolution. The careers and personalities of Robespierre, of Danton, even of Marat, gleam luridly across a century. But the dull squalid figures of the Bolsheviks are not redeemed in interest even by the magnitude of their crimes. All form and emphasis is lost in the vast process of Asiatic liquidation. Even the slaughter of millions and the misery of scores of millions will not attract future generations to their uncouth habiliments and outlandish names.[23]

Apart from instinct, it seemed to him crass folly to allow a system to prevail in Russia whose leaders were admitted terrorists, who believed in the doctrine that the end justified the means, and whose openly proclaimed objective was world revolution.

For three months the Allies delayed, infirm of purpose, but at last, in June 1919, the five leaders in Paris decided to support Kolchak. Winston was aware that this decision was hedged round by reservations and doubts:

> The reader might well suppose that the decision of the Big Five to support Koltchak ... marked the end of doubt and vacillation. They had no

23. WSC, *Great Contemporaries.*

troops; they could not spend much money. But they could give a steady aid in surplus munitions, in moral countenance and in concerted diplomacy . . . But their decision to support Koltchak, and later to support Denikin, represented only half a mind. The other half had always been, and was throughout the summer of 1919. uncertain of itself, sceptical about the prospects of the anti-Bolsheviks, ill-informed about the true nature of the Third International, and anxious to see whether the extremists in Moscow would not respond to the exercise of reason and patience.[24]

It was Churchill's responsibility to withdraw the troops who had been sent to Murmansk and Archangel while the German war was still in progress. It was a task of extreme delicacy. Confined to those ice-locked shores through the interminable Russian winter, they were exposed to serious danger from the Bolsehevik forces. In order to secure the safe withdrawal of these men, reinforcements would have to be sent, and again the responsibility was Churchill's. In March the War Cabinet authorized him to make the necessary dispositions, and he raised 8,000 volunteers from the demobilizing armies who were despatched as soon as the ice-bound ports were opened.

His direction of even this limited force to the war zone caused a flurry of unease in England. Churchill was again despatching large numbers of men to a theatre of war, and the British public, searching misty and uncertain memories of Antwerp and the Dardanelles, found little comfort in their reflections. He was sending them, furthermore, to interfere in the affairs of a country which should be allowed to settled its own problems, in however beastly a way, free from foreign interferences.

When this new, well-equipped, battle-hardened force disembarked and relieved the garrisons, the hitherto friendly Russian troops – who realized that the withdrawal of British troops was their own death-sentence – mutinied, and from that moment had to be regarded as an uncertain if not hostile force. It had been hoped that Admiral Kolchak, who knew that all Allied troops would be withdrawn from North Russia before the following winter, would join forces with the local troops and stabilize the position before the Allied evacuation. This did not happen, and so grave was the situation considered that Lord Rawlinson was sent to conduct the operation.

* * *

He embarked on 4 August with a further naval and military force at his disposal. When the North Russian Government realized that

24. WSC, *The Aftermath*, pp.235-6.

the Allies were definitely leaving they courageously decided to continue their resistance to the Bolsheviks. Their operation began with a swift and carefully planned offensive against them. While the enemy was temporarily paralysed the withdrawal was made. Archangel, in September, and Murmansk, in October, were evacuated by all British and Allied troops, with more than six thousand Russians seeking refuge in the liberated Baltic States.

This difficult operation was bitterly resented by the Socialist and Liberal Opposition, and public opinion found it difficult to tolerate the despatch of thousands of soldiers to Russia when the war was over. There was an ignorant misunderstanding of the fact that to extricate the Allied troops further supplies of men and arms must be made available, and once again the Secretary of State for War was saddled with the blame. Meanwhile the armies of Denikin in the south, which had all but reached the former Grand Duchy of Moscow, were too little concentrated, were slowly pierced by Bolshevik forces, and began to disintegrate. By February 1920 the Great Powers had no alternative but to withdraw such aid as they had provided.

Winston's ardent and idealistic support of the anti-revolutionary forces had disturbed not only the British public but also his colleagues. The Prime Minister was particularly sensitive. Although Lloyd George could not be accused of pro-Bolshevik sympathies, he was a man of humble origin who had devoted much of his life to espousing the cause of the under-dog, and was in any case anxious to make massive cuts in military expenditure. Churchill was an aristocrat profoundly convinced of the virtue of preserving the continuity of the old order. Even in the flush of his radical conversion this had been an obstacle between them.

Some idea of the resentment of Churchill's colleagues at his absorption by the subject is provided by a letter of unusual sharpness from Lloyd George in September 1919, which clearly indicates the perils of their love-hate relationship, and in which exasperation breathes through every line:

> I have found your mind so obsessed by Russia that I felt I had good ground for the apprehension that your great abilities, energy & courage were not devolved to the reduction of expenditure. I regret that all my appeals have been in vain. At each interview you promised me to give your mind to this very important subject. Nevertheless the first communication I have always received from you after these interviews related to Russia. I invited you to Paris to help me to reduce your commitments in the East. You there produced a lengthy and carefully prepared memorandum on Russia. I entreated you on Friday to let Russia be for at least 48 hours &

to devote your weekend to preparing for the Finance Cttee this afternoon. You promised faithfully to do so. Your reply is to send me a four page letter on Russia, and a closely printed memorandum of several pages – all on Russia. I am frankly in despair . . .

You confidently predict in your memorandum that Denikin is on the eve of some great and striking success. I looked up some of . . . your statements made earlier in the year about Koltchak, & I find that you use exactly the same language in reference to Koltchak's success.

Lloyd George proceeded to relate instances of British action taken on Churchill's advice in Russia which had failed:

Not a member of the Cabinet is prepared to go further . . . I wonder if it is any use my making one last effort to induce you to throw off this obsession which, if you will forgive me for saying so, is upsetting your balance. I again ask you to let Russia be, at any rate for a few days, & to concentrate your mind on the quite unjustifiable expenditure in France, at home, & in the East, incurred by both the War Office & the Air Dpt. Some of the items could not possibly have been tolerated by you if you had given one fifth of the thought to these matters which you have directed to Russia . . . You won't find another responsible person in the whole land who will take your view. Why waste your energy and your usefulness on this vain fretting which completely paralyses your other work . . .[25]

This was a daunting and, some might have thought, ominous letter from a Prime Minister to a subordinate. But Churchill had had ample time and experience to develop that hard politician's carapace which protected him from such shocks, and he was not unduly disturbed. Still less were his convictions on Russia, which had set hard like cement, softened by the Prime Minister's reproaches.

*   *   *

It is not difficult to sympathize with Lloyd George's extreme irritation, for Winston, in the grip of an *idée fixe*, was frequently impervious to reason. But the Prime Minister was not justified in accusing Churchill of a failure to apply his mind to departmental economy. The letters already quoted to the Chancellor of the Exchequer in no way support this charge.

Churchill in *The Aftermath* describes the Russian civil war in language which leaves no doubt of his passionate involvement. With a sense of revulsion and disgust he writes of the murder of Kolchak and his Prime Minister in their cells in the prison of Irkutsk, and the final horror and desolation of the collapse in the Crimea in July 1920,

25. Lloyd George papers: F.9.1.20.

after which shiploads of infected and destitute human beings – often dead or moribund – arrived continuously in the already overcrowded, impoverished and straitened Turkish capital. These are scenes on which men are reluctant to reflect, and, like thoughts on death itself, are inclined to put aside, and, in Winston's words: 'A veil has been drawn over the horror of the final scenes.'

Churchill's belief in the indefinite menace presented by Bolshevism to future generations did not blind him to the problem presented by the presence in Europe of the greatest Continental Power in a condition of impotence and defeat. We have already noticed that in the first vindictive flush of victory many who should have known better had expressed a short-sighted desire that Germany should pay in unlimited measure for the miseries she had inflicted on the world. Winston's thinking on this cardinal subject, to his great credit, avoided these extremes of emotion. His instinct about Germany, which seldom betrayed him, warned him urgently against ruthless peace terms and the illusory reparations demanded by the French, which he knew the Germans could never pay. And his words to Lloyd George of Janaury 1919 have, in retrospect, great prescience:

> If the Germans handle their situation well now and we handle ours badly I see no reason why they should not be relatively more powerful than ever in a few years time. The removal of the Russian menace ... goes far to compensate them for their losses of territory and population in the West. If the Austro-Germans affiliate with them, they will be stronger than ever. When the British and American Armies have disappeared, the French will be left face to face with an enemy twice as numerous as they are. The great crops of children which are coming forward in Germany every year are three times as great as those on which France will have to depend ...[26]

And again in May 1919:

> On every ground ... I strongly urge settling up with the Germans now. Now is the time, and it may be the only time, to reap the fruits of victory. 'Agree with thine adversary whilst thou art in the way with him.' Everything shows that the present German Government is sincerely desirous of making a beaten peace and preserving an orderly community which will carry out its agreement ... Let us beware lest in following too far Latin ambitions and hatreds we do not create a new situation in which our advantages will largely have disappeared. Settle now while we have the power, or lose perhaps for ever the power of settlement on the basis of a military victory.[27]

26. Chartwell papers, 29 January 1919.
27. Lloyd George papers, 20 May 1919.

* * *

The end of the Russian civil war was followed by a sort of grey relief, and the Bolshevik threat – always more apparent to Churchill than to others – lost some of its Hallowe'en terror. But the year which followed, 1921, was scarred by personal tragedy. In its first days Blanche, Lady Airlie, Clementine's grandmother who had meant much to her in her childhood, died at the age of ninety. Later in January Winston's cousin Lord Herbert Vane-Tempest was killed in a railway accident, leaving him as residuary legatee of Frances, Lady Londonderry, an estate in Ireland worth £4,000 a year. It was the first financial security he had known. This stroke of good fortune was marred in April when Bill Hozier, Clementine's brother, shot himself in a hotel bedroom in Paris for reasons that remain mysterious. When Hozier had found himself in difficulties because of his wild gambling Winston had helped him out and made him promise never to gamble again. There was no sign that he had broken this promise; indeed, he had just paid a considerable sum into his bank.[28] Then at the end of June Winston's mother died. In 1918 she had married Montagu Porch, her third husband and a man more than twenty years younger than herself, but to everyone's surprise they were happy together. In the summer when he was abroad she fell downstairs; gangrene set in, and a leg had to be amputated. At first she seemed to be recovering; then she suffered a violent haemorrhage and died before Winston could reach her bedside. He had always adored her, and now was deeply moved. He wrote to Lord Curzon: 'The wine of life was in her veins. Sorrow and storms were conquered by her nature and on the whole it was a life of sunshine.'[29]

But the worst blow was still to come. Marigold, 'The Duckadilly', their youngest daughter, was a sweet child loved by all. She had learnt to sing the song 'I'm for-ever blowing bubbles' in a true little voice, and had made it her signature tune. In August the children were sent to Broadstairs with a governess for a seaside holiday while Clemmie stayed with the Westminsters and Winston remained in London. The plan was for the family to join up in Scotland. But on August 14 Marigold fell seriously ill; a sore throat that had been troubling her for some time developed into septicaemia and the doctors could do nothing for her. Winston and Clemmie hurried down to Broadstairs and summoned a specialist, but without antibiotics he was as helpless as the local GP. Lady Soames's account continued:

28. Soames, p. 199.
29. Ibid., p. 200.

On the evening of 22nd August, Clementine was sitting by Marigold's bedside; the child was smiling; suddenly she said to her mother: 'Sing me "Bubbles".' Clementine, summoning all the control she knew, began the haunting, wistful little song that Marigold loved so much; she had not struggled very far, when the child put out her hand and whispered, 'Not tonight ... finish it tomorrow.' The next day Marigold died; she was two years and nine months old; both her parents were with her. Clementine in her agony gave a succession of wild shrieks, like an animal in mortal pain.[30]

All this happened just after Lloyd George had transferred Winston from the War Office to the Colonial Office, scene of his first political achievements, and his attention was diverted to the unending entanglements of the Middle East.

30. Soames, pp. 201-2.

Chapter 25

Colonial Office

13 February 1921-19 October 1922

Winston Churchill in the role of conciliator, a pourer of oil on troubled waters, a soother of inflamed passions – it is difficult to reconcile such a tranquilizing figure with the man we have been studying. Yet although he held this office for less than two years, he helped to bring about two lasting peace settlements of the utmost delicacy, presenting a formidable challenge. For this he received only ephemeral credit at the time, and too little afterwards.

The first was in Palestine and its neighbouring territories, an area which was in a state of seething discontent caused (at least in part) by the British failure to redeem wartime promises of independence for the Arabs. To the intense resentment of the Arab world, the mandate in Syria had been assigned by the Peace Conference to the French. When the Arabs resisted this award by force the French troops ejected the Emir Feisal from Damascus, and settled down in the occupation of the province with a large army, repressing subsequent revolts with the utmost severity.

The result was that other parts of the Arab world were in a state of rebellion and fury, and a bloody uprising was suppressed in Iraq in 1920. In Palestine the strife between Jew and Arab seemed likely to erupt into violence, and when Winston surveyed the Middle East scene he saw that 'The Arab chieftains, driven out of Syria with many of their followers – all of them our late allies – lurked furious in the desert beyond the Jordan. Egypt was in ferment. Thus the whole of the Middle East presented a most melancholy and alarming picture.' Churchill formed a new department of the Colonial Office, the Middle East Department, to deal with this menacing situation.

It had been found necessary to keep a large army in the area to maintain order at a cost of thirty million pounds a year. Winston was urged by his superiors to settle the trouble, and cut expenses –

instructions easier to issue than to fulfil. One of his first actions was to enlist that wayward genius T. E. Lawrence, the 'Lawrence of Arabia' of a legend at least partly inspired by his own incomparable persuasiveness as a self-advertiser. It was to be expected that Winston would add such a figure as Lawrence to his simple pantheon of heroes, where he joined the other often-wounded demigods, the men with many orifices, who dwelt there. It was to be expected too that it was the authentic courage of Lawrence, the glamour that invested him, and his power over words that won Churchill's heart, and that other and stranger aspects of his character completely eluded him. The melancholy which possessed Lawrence after the war he dimly understood, attributing it to his remorse at British failure to redeem his promises to his Arab friends, but of the masochism, the suppressed sexual inversion, the habit of sometimes shameless invention – all traits utterly alien to him – he had not an inkling. He realized, however, that Lawrence's form of self-effacement caused the limelight to beat upon him all the more fiercely.

He had first met Lawrence in the spring of 1919 in unfavourable circumstances, when it transpired that the legendary figure had, with a characteristic and irritating gesture, refused to accept the Companionship of the Bath and the Distinguished Service Order from the King at a private audience. Winston was incensed by what he considered an insolent and discourteous gesture, and gave Lawrence the rough side of his tongue. Lawrence accepted the rebuke with charming good humour, and made no attempt at explanation or defence.

But once the ice was broken he seemed exactly the stamp of man to exercise the strongest appeal to Churchill's romanticism, and as the legend of Lawrence in the field was unfolded to him and his fierce loyalty to the Arabs with whom he had fought became apparent, Winston came under the spell. Their relationship was fruitful, and remembered with gratitude by both. But when Churchill first spoke to the men in his new Middle East Department of adding Lawrence to their number:

> They were frankly aghast – 'What! Wilt thou bridle the wild ass of the desert?' Such was the attitude, dictated by no small jealousy or undervaluing of Lawrence's qualities, but by a sincere and entirely justified conviction that in his mood and with his temperament he could never work at the routine of a public office.[1]

It was a source of immense satisfaction to Winston that it was he who had domesticated this wild creature, and kept it for a time docile by his side, until it suddenly took fright and fled. It was a pleasure like cajoling some shy and exotic bird into eating out of his hand.

1. WSC, *Great Contemporaries*, p.117.

* * *

Churchill felt it necessary to handle the situation on the spot, and shortly after becoming Colonial Secretary he summoned a conference at Cairo, to which he was accompanied by Lawrence, Trenchard from the Air Ministry, and others, and which was attended by the principal officers concerned in the administration of Middle East affairs. He first addressed himself to repairing the injury done to the Arabs in general, and to the Sherifian family in particular. The Sherifians or Hashemites were guardians of the holy places at Mecca and as such were venerated throughout the Islamic world; accordingly the Emir Feisal was placed on the throne of Iraq as King, and the Emir Abdullah was entrusted with the government of Transjordania. It was also decided to remove nearly all the British troops from Iraq, and to rely upon the Royal Air Force for its defence. This last arrangement (in which the hand of Lawrence can be discerned) besides being effective, provided the economies which Churchill had been entreated to make. In 1921 the British Garrison in Iraq cost more than £2 million: by 1928 this sum had been gradually reduced to £1,648,038.

The settlement arrived at satisfied even Lawrence, who felt that a great burden had been removed from his conscience. Winston was one of the first of those invited to subscribe for a copy of *The Seven Pillars of Wisdom*, and was much gratified by the words Lawrence wrote in the flyleaf of the volume which eventually reached him:

> Winston Churchill
> who made a happy
> ending to this show.
> 1.12.26. T.E.S.
> W.S.C.
>
> and eleven years after we set our hands to making an honest settlement, all our work still stands: the countries have gone forward, our interests have been saved, and no body has been killed, either on our side or the other. To have planned for eleven years is statesmanship. I ought to have given you TWO copies of this work!
> T.E.S.[2]

It should be noted that Winston at this point conceived an immense – indeed, excessive – veneration for Lawrence as a man of letters; and to him *The Seven Pillars* was his masterpiece. Putting his own literary pride in his pocket, he referred to his own style deprecatingly, calling it the work of a mere journalist in comparison with that of

2. Lawrence had changed his name to Shaw on entering the Royal Tank Corps in March 1923.

this master of prose. He refers to *The Seven Pillars* as 'this treasure of English literature':

> It ranks with the greatest books in the English language. If Lawrence had never done anything except write this book as a mere work of the imagination his fame would last – to quote Macaulay's hackneyed phrase – 'as long as the English language is spoken in any quarter of the globe'. *The Pilgrim's Progress, Robinson Crusoe, Gulliver's Travels* are dear to British homes. Here is a tale originally their equal in interest and charm. But it is fact, not fiction. The author was also the commander . . . In Lawrence's story nothing that has ever happened in the sphere of war and empire is lacking. When most of the vast literature of the Great War has been sifted . . ., when the complicated and costly operations of its ponderous armies are the concern only of the military student, when our struggles are viewed in a fading perspective and a truer proportion, Lawrence's tale of the revolt in the desert will gleam with immortal fire.[3]

Later he adds: 'Through all, one mind, one soul, one will-power, a tale of torment, and in the heart of it – a Man.' This seems, in retrospect, to have been one of Churchill's least prescient predictions.

* * *

There had been indignant protests against the Iraq settlement and the withdrawal of the troops. The French Government deeply resented the promotion of Feisal, whom they regarded as a defeated rebel, and the British War Office was horrified by the departure of the troops, predicting carnage and ruin. But the proposals were accepted, although it required a year of delicate and anxious administration to give effect to them. In this task, seeing the hope of redeeming most of the promises he had made to the Arab chiefs, Lawrence loyally co-operated. There can be no doubt that when it was all over, with Feisal acclaimed King, Abdullah settled in Transjordania, the Army out of Iraq and the Air Force 'installed in a loop of the Euphrates', he felt that Churchill had honoured his work. In a draft preface to an abridged and unpublished edition of *The Seven Pillars* he wrote in 1922:

> This book dates itself to 1919, when powerful elements in the British Government were seeking to evade their war-time obligations to the Arabs. That state ended in March 1921 when Mr Winston Churchill took charge in the Middle East. He set honour before expediency in order to fulfil our promises in the letter and in the spirit. He executed the whole MacMahon undertaking . . . for Palestine, for TransJordania and for Arabia. In Mesopotamia he went far beyond its provisions,

3. WSC, op.cit., p.120.

giving to the Arabs more, and reserving for us much less than Sir Henry MacMahon had thought fit. In the affairs of Syria he was not able to intervene . . . I must put on record my conviction that England is out of the Arab affair with clean hands.[4]

And he was to add later: 'It is my deliberate opinion that the Winston Churchill settlement of 1921–1922 (in which I shared) honourably fulfils the whole of the promises we made to the Arabs, in so far as the so-called British spheres are concerned.'[5]

* * *

While Winston was negotiating a settlement in the Middle East he was also a member of the Cabinet Committee grappling with the still nagging question of Ireland. We left this harrowing theme after the suspension of the Home Rule Bill at the end of 1914. Since that time the 'Irish spectre' had never altogether ceased to haunt Churchill, and was now beginning to reassert itself in sinister form.

At that time of suspension it seemed as though the true spirit of Ireland, ardent, passionate, prepared to close ranks in the face of foreign menace, had been reflected in Redmond's patriotic speech of 3 August 1914. But this fugitive goodwill had swiftly eroded, and Anglo-Irish relations entered on a new and deteriorating phase. The Irish Nationalists, at once the bulwark and the bane of pre-war Liberal Governments, had been obliterated at the Coupon Election of 1918, and their place taken by the extremist group Sinn Féin (Ourselves Alone), whose intention was complete severance of the English connection, whose objective was a Republic and whose method was stealthy terror. Utterly ruthless in the name of patriotism, steeled by long memories of Ireland's subjection, they were ready to turn their hands to any method, however dirty, to achieve their purpose. This took the form of burning houses and murdering English officials.

The Sinn Féin group had at once – like the IRA fifty years later – renounced representation in the English House of Commons. On 21 January 1921 its parliamentary assembly, Dáil Éireann, consisting of the Irish Members elected to the British Parliament at the General Election, met and issued a Declaration of Independence. The same body, a few days later, elected a Cabinet and gradually built up an administration in rivalry with that of the British Government. But that Government, intent on its great task of post-war reconstruction, hardly noticed this significant event. It required the summer of 1919, with

4. David Garnett, *The Letters of T.E. Lawrence*, pp.345-6.
5. Ibid, p.671.

its record of the murder of British police and soldiers, ambushes and sudden death, to remind legislators that the Irish problem still awaited a solution and was now lowering over the British Government, stark and unresolved. These murders, perpetrated by the Irish Republican Army and the Irish Republican Brotherhood, so cold-blooded, so clandestine, provoked reprisals on an equal scale from the security forces, the Army and the police.

* * *

In August 1919 the British Government proclaimed the suppression of Sinn Féin, and in September Dáil Éireann was declared a dangerous association and banned. The Government was driven to the conviction that Home Rule must be introduced, and on 22 December Lloyd George outlined the Cabinet's intentions in the House of Commons. The new Bill superseded the suspended Act of 1914. It provided for two Parliaments in Ireland, and authorized the establishment of a Council which might be the nucleus of an all-Ireland Parliament. After prolonged debate this Bill reached the Statute Book in December 1920. The overwhelming might of the Coalition Government ensured its passage, but it was accepted only under bitter protest by the North, which exercised its option to contract out of the Dublin Parliament and set up its own legislature in Belfast. Southern Ireland refused to recognize this Act, but characteristically took advantage of its electoral machinery to elect a new 'Dáil'. All the Sinn Féin candidates were returned unopposed.

In the meantime the frightful catalogue of murder and outrage continued, and so brutally was this terrorism accomplished that the British Government was stung into the unwise decision to repay the murderers in kind. The decision to raise a contingent of ex-Servicemen arose from the continuing resignations from the Royal Irish Constabulary, and from the difficulty of providing sufficient troops from dwindling resources. The Secretary of State for War at the time, Churchill, incurred much of the odium for these men's excesses committed in retaliation for the murder of their military or RIC comrades. A special police force was enlisted of unemployed officers from the wartime army, a para-military *gendarmerie* who, owing to their scratch uniforms, became known as the 'Black and Tans', and were soon the object of general fear and loathing in Ireland. Whether they liked to admit it or not, the British had been provoked into a policy of counter-terrorism.

The two sides in this repulsive strife approached the problem from diametrically opposite angles. To the English the snick of a rifle bolt at a moonlit ambush indicated merely a cowardly and clandestine form of murder. It was difficult for even the most cool-headed to avoid the conclusion that there was something horribly and characteristically degenerate in the Irish methods when cattle were mutilated for political reasons, and when on 'Bloody Sunday', 21 November 1920, fourteen men were killed including six British officers, some of whom were pulled out of bed and shot in front of their wives.

The Irish regarded the matter in quite a different light. They believed the English should plainly realize that Ireland, in spite of centuries of oppression, had never been a colony of England, that they were a different race who were bent on independence even if it meant dying for it, and that their moment was at hand. If the British objected to their soldiers being killed, they had a simple remedy for the problem by withdrawing their forces from Ireland. What the British regarded as stealthy terror, and murder in its most cowardly and disgusting form, they idealized as the calm, passionless shooting down of an alien army of occupation.

The worst aspect of such conflicts is the savage craving for revenge which invariably accompanies them, and no amount of historical sifting can gauge the emotions of a soldier who comes upon his friend whom he has last seen jesting and drinking lying mutilated in a ditch with his throat cut. We must realize, whether we like it or not, that in this imperfect world such experiences do cry aloud for revenge. The Black and Tans were sent to Ireland ostensibly to buttress the forces of law and order, but it was hardly to be expected that men chosen in the manner they were would long content themselves with police functions when they saw the outrages which were a common spectacle in Ireland in those bloody days.

* * *

The British Government did not yet fully grasp the tenacity and vindictiveness of their opponents, and there had not been even a muffled hint in Government statements in either House of Parliament that the Cabinet might soon come to the conclusion that it had become unrealistic to pursue the will o' the wisp of coercion into the bogs of Ireland. But by the spring it seemed clear that the unlovely choice lay between an all-out war to crush the rebellion – a war in which many innocent lives would be lost – or of some further concession to the South in order to reach a peaceful settlement. The situation was complex and apparently intractable. The Northern and Protestant counties of Ireland were loyal to Great Britain, and with a passion equal to that animating the South in the opposite sense, determined to remain a part of her. Southern and Catholic Ireland, containing a majority of the whole country's population, was demanding complete independence. Should the British Government decide to crush the rebellion by force of arms or partition the country, giving the South some form of Dominion Status which would provide the independence they sought, yet preserve the link with the Crown?

Churchill followed his usual formula for such occasions: '. . . to couple a tremendous onslaught with the fairest offer'. He told his colleagues on the Cabinet Committee that it was essential to avoid the belief that Britain was giving way through weakness or apprehension, but that after complete victory had placed British authority beyond question, he thought that fair words and a generous settlement should be offered to Southern Ireland.

He saw that the Prime Minister was impressed by the number of Conservatives who adhered to this course, and by the arguments of the Ministers who advocated it in the Cabinet discussions in April.

Lloyd George rightly judged that a campaign of repression à l'outrance would not meet with the degree of wholehearted support, even from Conservatives, necessary to carry through such a policy successfully. He had been driven by harsh experience to realize that the programme of compulsion had failed and could only lead to unlimited bloodshed and further reprisals. A chill autumnal blight had settled upon the Anglo-Irish struggle. Neither side had yet yielded an inch – the British clinging to their hegemony over Ireland and the Southern Irish insisting on freedom. Those, including the Prime Minister, who had spoken of 'taking murder by the throat', and, like Birkenhead, of using 'force in its most extreme and vigorous application', had been forced at last by the realities of office to swallow a sour gruel. It had dawned on Lloyd George that the Irish Resistance was a real force that would not yield to coercion, and adverse reports from senior officers on the condition of the Army drove him in the same direction.

He had already made several efforts to negotiate a settlement provided the rebels were ready to accept the Crown and the Imperial connection. These efforts were now renewed. An element of comedy softened these grim proceedings when Lord Derby, uneasily relying on dark glasses to sustain the alias of 'Mr Edwards', had a fruitless interview with de Valera in Dublin. Next Sir James Craig, the first Prime Minister of Northern Ireland, agreed to meet the Irish leader. This mission was not only abortive but acutely tedious for the unhappy Ulsterman, who was subjected to a long harangue on Irish history and grievances, which after four hours had advanced no further than Poynings' Law in the reign of Henry VII.

All the Sinn Féin members having been returned unopposed in the May elections in Southern Ireland, the British Government made preparations for the introduction of Crown Colony Government for which provision had been made in the Government of Ireland Act.

Sinn Féin was fighting not for Home Rule under the Crown but for a separate Revolutionary Republic. The issue of an all-out war to the finish or a final effort at reconciliation could no longer be evaded.

* * *

On 24 June 1921 an astonished world, expecting further instalments of tragedy in Ireland, learned that the Prime Minister had invited de Valera and Sir James Craig to meet him in conference in London with the object of ending the conflict. Three weeks later, they did; de Valera rejected offers of Dominion status for Ireland. The public were, of course, ignorant of the direction in which the Prime Minister's mind had been moving in recent weeks, and the constant talk of force, the ruthlessness of the Black and Tans and Lloyd George's grim promise to 'take murder by the throat' had occluded the possibility of negotiations in the public mind. The news therefore broke upon the people with a tremendous shock and an element of utter bewilderment. Of this apparently baffling change of direction Churchill was afterwards to write:

> No British Government in modern times has ever appeared to make so complete and sudden a reversal of policy . . . In May the whole power of the State and all the influence of the Coalition were used to 'hunt down the murder gang': in June the goal was 'a lasting reconciliation with the Irish people'.[6]

The transformation had been brought about by Lloyd George's instinctive desire to change course, and by a melting appeal for reconciliation drafted in the Prime Minister's office, and placed in the mouth of the King, who was opening the first session of the new Ulster Parliament. Many were afterwards, in the cold light of reason, to regard the Irish Settlement as a great remedial measure of enlightened statesmanship, but at the time so bitter were the feelings of many towards the Government for inviting to conference men whom they had themselves stigmatized as murderers, that it required high moral courage for them to pursue their chosen path. For Churchill the *détente* had come, and the conference started, before England had as he wished proved her irrestible superiority in arms.

* * *

The Truce was announced on 9 July 1921 and came into operation on the 11th. One of the factors which may have prompted the Irish to accept this breathing-space was that by June that year the insurgent forces in Ireland were in a precarious position. Clementine Churchill

6. WSC, *The Aftermath*, p.290.

took the success of the negotiations for granted, as well as Winston's exclusion from any group that might be conducting them:

> ... But I do wish my *Dear* one that you were in this Irish Settlement. Would you have been if you were not 'en froid' with LlG? I do feel that as long as he is P.M. it would be better to hunt with him than to lie in the bushes and watch him careering along with a jaundiced eye ...[7]

It was only under considerable pressure from Lloyd George that de Valera agreed to treat, and to enter a conference on 11 October 'free on both sides', and Churchill was not excluded. The British delegation was built round a hard core of Lloyd George, Chamberlain, Birkenhead and Churchill. So strong was this team that it was possible to relegate Churchill (then Secretary of State for the Colonies) to the fourth place in the counsels. He thus played only a part of second rank in the Treaty discussions, and his main contribution to the settlement was to come later, when he piloted the consequent legislation through the House of Commons.

The Prime Minister's most important colleagues were Austen Chamberlain, the leader of the Unionist Party, and Lord Birkenhead, the Lord Chancellor. Courage was needed by both of them, and particularly by the Lord Chancellor, who had taken a tremendous decision. With full awareness of what he was doing, he had jeopardized his position in the Unionist Party and exposed himself to the charge of treachery to a trust. He knew that many old friends would despise him as a renegade; for he, more than any other Minister in these negotiations, had identified himself with resistance to Irish Home Rule. In the turbulent days before the war he had grazed the very frontiers of treason when he shared and matched the risks run by Carson. He stood to gain by frustrating a settlement and to lose by advocating it. Yet once he had decided to embrace the negotiations, he remained throughout their most resolute advocate, no mere sorcerer's apprentice to Lloyd George, but the man who won the friendship of the Irish Republican leader, Michael Collins, and entered most deeply into his heart and mind. Commenting on the part played by Chamberlain and Birkenhead, Lord Longford wrote in his lucid account of the negotiations:

> Without the original consent, initiation even, of Chamberlain and Birkenhead, the path to settlement could never have been trodden. Without their firm adherence to his own person, without their prompt suppression of each incipient Conservative revolt, Lloyd George must

7. Churchill papers, 1/39. CSC to WSC, 11 July 1921.

have been driven from the path of settlement by one or other incident long before December was reached. When Irishmen think of England politicians as self-seeking, they should honourably except Sir Austen Chamberlain and Lord Birkenhead.[8]

The Irish delegation were naturally weaker, and having never been in conference with men of experience before, understandably nervous. De Valera elected to stay in Dublin, but the two leading members of the Delegation, Arthur Griffith and Michael Collins, were formidable. Griffith, quiet, deceptively nondescript, deeply versed in history, was 'that unusual figure – a silent Irishman'. He was the real power in Sinn Féin. Michael Collins was the man of action who had loomed before the British of late in official reports as a man of violence, a gunman and a murderer, but who displayed qualities of heart and mind which astonished these seasoned politicians. The state of recklessness and peril in which he lived appealed to the panache in Churchill and Birkenhead, who became convinced that Griffith and Collins were men of high calibre, who would honour their word once they had given it. Collins had inspired and directed the rebellion, of evil repute to many, and stood closer to the terrible incidents of the conflict than his leader; a Cork man, impetuous and excitable, but 'passing readily to grimness and back again to gaiety, full of fascination and charm – but also of dangerous fire. That was Michael Collins, one of the most courageous leaders ever produced by a valiant race'. The other Irish delegates were, in Churchill's opinion, dwarfed by the two leaders.

* * *

Since Churchill was in a relatively subordinate position, it is no part of this story to repeat the oft-told story of the negotiations, with their fluctuations and moments of despair, conducted against a background of excitement and rising tension on both sides of the water, and darkened by the internal stresses of the Conservative Party and the convulsions of the Irish Dáil. It was not to be expected that the way to a settlement would, after such long bitterness, be smooth. From Dublin de Valera, as self-proclaimed 'Head of an Independent State', clearly felt it necessary to harass the infant understanding as far as he safely could with a series of irritating pinpricks. One of General Smuts's many services to the Commonwealth was the mature wisdom with which at this moment he soothed the prickly prima donna.

The formidable English delegation included Sir Hamar Greenwood, the Irish Secretary. The presence of Greenwood, creator and inspirer of

8. Longford, *Peace by Ordeal*, p.257.

the Black and Tans, made necessary a number of those delicate adjustments of which Lloyd George was a master. It was thought improbable
that the Irishmen would have shaken hands with Greenwood, as they
believed that those hands were as drenched in blood as he considered
theirs. Like a sophisticated hostess anticipating an initial *bêtise* that
might wreck her party, the Prime Minister settled the English on one
side of the table, and led the Irishmen to the other. Summoning all his
winning charm, he introduced the delegates across it. Churchill was to
record the Conference in one of his finest books. He was struck by the
immense differences which insulated the two sides, and by the abiding
animosity that seemed to scar the Irish mind.

> We found ourselves confronted in the early days not only with the
> unpractical and visionary fanaticism of the extreme Irish secret societies,
> but also with those tides of distrust and hatred which had flowed between
> the two countries for so many centuries . . . Hatred plays the same part in
> Government as acids in chemistry. And here in Ireland were hatreds which
> in Mr Kipling's phrase would 'eat the live steel from the rifle butt', hatreds
> such as, thank God, in Great Britain had not existed for a hundred years.[9]

Churchill did his utmost to soothe relations between the two sides.
He particularly directed blandishments towards Collins, who seemed
to him a man of similar kidney to himself, but his efforts at ingratiation
were at first less successful than he imagined. He saw himself appealing
to a kindred spirit – fighter to fighter, soldier to soldier, adventurer to
adventurer.

> Our settlement with the Boers, with my own vivid experiences in it, was
> my greatest source of comfort and inspiration in this Irish business . . . I
> remember one night Mr Griffith and Mr Collins came to my house to meet
> the Prime Minister. It was at a crisis, and the negotiations seemed to hang
> only by a thread. Griffith went upstairs to parley with Mr Lloyd George
> alone. Lord Birkenhead and I were left with Michael Collins meanwhile.
> He was in his most difficult mood, full of reproaches and defiances, and
> it was very easy for everyone to lose his temper.
>   'You hunted me day and night!' he exclaimed. 'You put a price
> on my head.'
>   'Wait a minute,' I said. 'You are not the only one,' and I took from
> my wall the framed copy of the reward offered for my recapture by the
> Boers. 'At any rate it was a good price – £5,000. Look at me – £25 dead
> or alive. How would you like that?'

By such means Winston sought to strike an echo in this formidable
man. But Collins was morose and intensely suspicious, and although he

9. WSC, *The Aftermath*, p.304.

admired Birkenhead without reserve, he was at first hostile to Churchill and merely irritated by his man-to-man approach, noting: 'Don't quite know whether he would be a crafty enemy in friendship. Outlook: political gain, nothing else . . . Inclined to be bombastic. Full of ex-officer jingo or similar outlook. Don't actually trust him.'[10] But the two men had much in common, and these early suspicions were soon dissolved.

*   *   *

The Conference lasted from 11 October 1921 until 5 December, and after several moments of torturing difficulty the Treaty was at last signed at ten minutes past two on the morning of 6 December, but not before Lloyd George had confronted the Irish delegates with an ultimatum threatening the immediate use of naked force. The Treaty provided self-government in a 'Free State' for Southern Ireland, out of which Ulster was entitled to opt. The link with the Crown was preserved.

But when the Irish delegates returned to Dublin, exhausted by strain, they found the Sinn Féin party in deep division over the settlement, half of it supporting the Treaty, and the rest, led by de Valera, regarding it as a cowardly and treacherous surrender, and demanding nothing less than an independent republic. This split was ultimately the cause of the Irish civil war, but the Treaty was endorsed by Dáil Éireann on 7 January by the narrow majority of 64 votes to 57.

Members of the anti-Treaty faction worked with bloody fanaticism to prevent Griffith and Collins implementing the agreement signed in London. De Valera formed the Republican party to combat Griffith's Provisional Government, and Ireland was soon plunged into the agony of civil war. In April the Four Courts (the law buildings) in Dublin were seized by rebels. In June fighting began and the four Courts were burned. The war, shocking in its savagery even for Ireland, dragged on until May 1923, producing unlimited misery and a chilling death toll. When Birkenhead signed the Treaty he had remarked to Collins, 'I may be signing my political death-warrant', and the Irishman had grimly replied that he might be signing his own actual death-warrant.

In August 1922, when the civil war was waning, and just before Lloyd George's Coalition Government fell, this prophecy was fulfilled. Collins was ambushed and shot dead a few miles from his birthplace in County Cork. His last message was: 'Tell Winston we could never have done it without him.'[11] He was referring to Churchill's successful piloting of the Irish Free State Bill through Parliament and defence of the Government's Irish policy. A week earlier Arthur Griffith had died of heart failure.

10. Rex Taylor, *Michael Collins*, pp.153-4.
11. Rhodes James, op.cit., p.132.

Their places were taken by two new leaders of a stature worthy of their fearful responsibilities – William Cosgrave and Kevin O'Higgins.

* * *

By the time the Treaty was signed Churchill had carried out his undertakings in the Middle East, and was comparatively free apart from routine work. He was asked by the Prime Minister to assume responsibility for British–Irish affairs and became Chairman of the Cabinet Committee on Ireland. He led for the Government in the Treaty debates and on all Irish business in the House of Commons until the end of October 1922. It was in this role that he made his greatest contribution to the cause of the Irish settlement.

He proved successful in this thankless task, and we can follow his activities in the words of Austen Chamberlain, whose duty it was at this time to report to the King on the progress of Parliamentary debates. On 15 December 1921 he wrote:

> ... Mr Churchill rose and the House and Galleries were again crowded. He spoke with great force and power and with equal skill and tact. The case for the Government could not have been better put ... But it is impossible to summarise the speech. It had a profound effect upon the House ...[12]

After the Christmas Recess Parliament debated the Irish Free State Bill, and on Churchill's speech on the Second Reading Chamberlain told the King:

> ... He [Churchill] thought it useless to speculate on such ugly eventualities as the possible victory of de Valera, but in the worst event the moral and material position of this country was immensely strengthened by the steps we had taken. Ireland, not Britain, was now on her trial before the world. Her best fighters were on the side of peace. It was the 'talkative gentlemen' who were now opposing the Treaty – men whom we had never troubled to arrest or had released at once if by some mishap they had been arrested 'as you return an undersized fish to the water'. The House was full while he spoke and listened with attention ... to his fine speech.[13]

On the Third Reading Churchill wound up for the Government, and Chamberlain reported:

> For some reason he spoke with less than his usual ease and the House listened rather coldly; but in his handling of the Irish Questions and in his general handling of this Bill he has shown Parliamentary talent of the

12. Austen Chamberlain papers. AC to HM, 15 December 1921.
13. Ibid. AC to HM 17 February 1922.

highest order and greatly strengthened his parliamentary position.[14]

Chamberlain's admiration for Churchill's performances seemed to grow as the debates unfolded, and when the time came for him to comment on the 'election pact'[15] his admiration is sincere and convincing:

> It was a masterly performance – not merely a great personal and oratorical triumph, though it was both of these, but a great act of statesmanship. Mr Chamberlain ... commends to Your Majesty's particular attention a speech faultless in manner and wording, profoundly impressive in its delivery and of the first consequence as a statement of policy. It gripped the attention of the House from the opening sentence and held it, breathlessly intent, to the end.
>
> Mr Speaker described it as the best Parliamentary speech he had ever heard.[16]

Churchill had discharged his difficult talk with extraordinary skill and persuasiveness. His speeches, increasing on each occasion in authority and effect, were a blend of firmness and conciliation, lit by incomparable humour and winged with irony. The fact that every speech had to be laboriously composed, polished, memorized and rehearsed gives us an inkling of this man's prodigious labours.

*   *   *

It was not until 6 December 1922 that the Irish Free State Constitution came into force. The civil war which was ravaging the South removed the last vestige of hope, if any existed, that Northern Ireland would relax her opposition to political unity with the South. On 7 December the Northern Ireland Parliament, acting under Article 12 of the Treaty, voted an address to the Crown, praying to be excluded from the jurisdiction of the Irish Free State.

Like a bad dream, Ireland then drifted out of British politics for the next forty years and the hideous memories of the strife receded. But the Treaty was fatal to the Prime Minister and the Coalition Government, and within a year he had been driven from power, although we shall see in a later chapter that there were contributory causes which hastened his fall. The terms of the Treaty had produced

14. A.C. Papers. AC to HM, 9 March 1922.
15. On 20 May 1922 Collins and de Valera signed an agreement by which in 57 Constituencies Republican Candidates were not to be opposed. Thus the anti-Treaty party would have 57 seats against 64 for the Treaty's supporters. Further, as a result of this so-called election, there would be a Southern Irish Government containing 5 pro-Treaty and 4 anti-Treaty ministers, with the President of the Dail and the minister for the army added.
16. A.C. Papers. AC to HM, 1 June 1922.

consternation in the Unionist Party, and Birkenhead and Chamberlain became objects of particular criticism for surrendering to a campaign of murder. The fact that the Treaty had led not to peace but to civil war enraged those Conservatives who had voted for it, and who felt that they had been given promissory notes that were now rubbish on the market. The Treaty and its circumstances were not forgiven by the most tenacious elements in the Party. Yet even if this instrument was a prime cause of Lloyd George's downfall, he had little with which to reproach himself on his record in Ireland. He had shielded Ulster from falling under an alien regime and religion which she feared and detested, and when the dust of the civil war settled it was found that Lloyd George had in an act of remedial statesmanship, brought peace to a tormented country by granting a Home Rule which had long been her due but had been obstinately withheld. Winston Churchill, who was to describe these events with glowing eloquence, pronounced a verdict which was temporarily justified:

> Yet in so far as Mr Lloyd George can link his political misfortunes with this Irish story, he may be content. In falling through Irish difficulties he may fall with Essex and with Strafford, with Pitt and with Gladstone; and with a long line of statesmen great or small spread across the English history books of 700 years. But Lloyd George falls with the weighty difference, that whereas all the others, however great their efforts and sacrifices, left behind them only a problem, he has achieved – must we not hope it? – a solution.

It was, alas, wishful thinking, for most of what Lloyd George and his colleagues had fought to establish crumbled into dust.

Chapter 26

A Last Nail in the Coffin

ow much easier is it for a man to carry with him like a birthmark the stigma of a character inclined to violence as a means of policy, and warped by some inexplicable malaise of judgment, than to retain for more than a brief space the more negative repute of a conciliator! Winston's new-won laurels as a man of peace became in an instant sadly withered when the Chanak crisis in Turkey in September 1922 suddenly restored the image of a man of war, of dangerous decisions instinctively reached, wild in judgment and willing to risk plunging the nation into war for the mere excitement of doing so.

The origins of this crisis, the final solvent of the Coalition, can be traced to the fascination exercised by the Greek statesman Venizelos on Lloyd George. Hypnotized by this magnetic and persuasive man, and by his own anti-Turkish prejudices, the Prime Minister had incautiously underwritten the Greek campaign in Asia Minor and sanctioned a Greek advance into Anatolia, entirely Turkish in population apart from the Greek coastal settlement, notably in Smyrna. Churchill initially took the strongest exception to this policy, even enjoying a moment of fugitive agreement with the Foreign Secretary, Lord Curzon; and France and Italy joined in this mistrust.

It was a strange chance that twice associated Chanak, that drab little town at the Narrows, on the Asiatic shore of the Dardanelles, with a sharp decline in Churchill's reputation. He had consistently expressed his dislike of that preference of Lloyd George which had made him lend a friendly ear to Greek chauvinistic ambitions in Asia Minor. By the end of 1920 he had come to the conclusion that the moment was ripe for a *détente* with the Muslim world and the establishment of peace and friendship with Turkey. He had also decided that the restoration of Turkish suzerainty was 'an indispensable step towards the pacification of the Middle East.'[1] In June 1921 he warned Lloyd George that 'if the Greeks go off on another half-cock offensive, the last card will have been played and lost and we shall neither have a Turkish peace nor a Greek army.'[2] This warning was disregarded. To Churchill it seemed that although Turkish policy in the Great War had been cold-blooded and malignant, the attitude of the Peace Conference towards her was so harsh that right had now changed sides. 'Justice,' he wrote, 'that eternal fugitive from the councils of conquerors, had gone over to the opposite camp.'

* * *

By the summer of 1922 the Greek armies in Asiatic Turkey were *in extremis*, as Churchill had predicted, and Kemal had driven them towards the sea to Smyrna. At the end of August they collapsed before the Turkish nationalist forces, and in less than a fortnight the exultant victors entered the city with fire and sword, driven by a corrosive hatred of this ancient enemy – now an intruder on their soil – and by a lust for revenge. The same gruesome retribution of massacre and exile which befell the inhabitants of Smyrna awaited a further million Greeks in Constantinople and Eastern Thrace if the Turkish army were allowed to cross the Straits.

Kemal then turned his armies north and advanced to the boundaries of the neutral zone at the Dardanelles, which had been created by the Treaty of Sèvres of which the French and the Italians were also guarantors. It was still occupied by a small British force at Chanak. Churchill, who had so consistently opposed Lloyd George's encouragement of the Greeks, now became the convinced, indeed passionate, advocate of a policy of resistance to the Turks. He was not without supporters. Curzon, in a moment of understandable petulance, complained that in Cabinet 'Lloyd George, Churchill and Birkenhead excelled themselves in jingo extravagance and fury'. Winston was to describe the episode, as usually in his historical writing, dramatizing it, with himself as a central figure, and buoyantly assuming the firmness of all those who agreed with him:

> I found myself in this business with a small group of resolute men: the Prime Minister, Lord Balfour, Mr Austen Chamberlain, Lord Birkenhead, Sir Laming Worthington Evans ... We made common cause. The Government might break up and we might be relieved of our burden. The nation might not support us: they could find others to advise them. The Press might howl, the Allies might bolt. We intended to force the Turk to a negotiated peace before he should set foot in Europe.[3]

1. PRO.CAB.23/231. Quoted Rhodes James, op.cit.
2. WSC, *The Aftermath*, p. 396.
3. Ibid, pp.395-6.

Although the Cabinet was already committed to accepting a large part of Turkey's requests for a settlement, Lloyd George, Churchill and Birkenhead were foremost among those who resented being forced to do so under duress. They were united in the conviction that it was essential to deny the Turks possession of the Gallipoli Peninsula and in the determination to fight rather than allow this to happen. The obvious need for acting in agreement with their allies, the French and Italians, was ignored. The situation now appeared one of the greatest danger. Would Kemal attack, and if he did would this mean war? The Cabinet decided that he must be stopped, at least until terms of a peaceful transfer could be arranged and provision made for the security of the Straits.

At a long meeting on 15 September it was agreed to try to promote a peace conference, but meanwhile to take defensive measure against the Turks, if need be single-handed. Telegrams were sent to the Dominions and the European allies requesting support in resisting the danger to Constantinople and the Straits. The following day, the Foreign Secretary, Curzon – whose functions Lloyd George had so frequently and shamelessly usurped before – was conveniently absent at his country home, Hackwood. Churchill and Birkenhead were asked by the Prime Minister to draft a manifesto on the crisis for the public. Both men were determined not to negotiate with the Turks under threat of force: both were masters of the English language in its most aggressive form. This document, although a desire for peace could have been said to underlie it, was in essence bellicose and defiant.

* * *

By some gross bureaucratic error, Canadian and South African Ministers read of the appeal in the newspapers before its official arrival and returned a dusty answer, and only Australia and New Zealand sent helpful replies. The French and Italians, after sniffing the air and disliking the aroma, hastened to withdraw from a situation that had become intolerable to them, and the British Government seemed to have isolated itself completely from its own friends.

Winston, in a rare admission of possible error, wrote of the declaration concocted by him and Birkenhead that it 'has been censured for being alarmist', but this was a pallid reflection of British public opinion at the time. The nation had not long been delivered from the Great War. That had left agonizing and indelible memories of the slaughter of trench warfare and frontal attack which were to haunt the minds of leaders and people until the eve of the Second World War, inhibiting action and paralysing decision, because the recollections of the past summoned reflections so baleful that it was unthinkable to contemplate its renewal. Now men seemed to see the Coalition leaders wantonly courting another disaster. It was as though through a chink they suddenly caught the angry glow of a new furnace. It is easy to understand this grave public uneasiness, but not all modern historians interpret Churchill's actions in a sinister manner, and it is worth noting Harold Nicolson's comments in his acute study of Curzon's last phase:

> To Mr Lloyd George, and above all to Mr Churchill is due our gratitude for having at this juncture, defied, not the whole world merely, but the full hysterical force of British public opinion. The effect of Mr Churchill's communiqué had, as Curzon foresaw, produced in M. Poincaré an outburst of reckless indignation. He was determined not to become the Leonidas of Mr Lloyd George's Thermopylae. He at once telephoned orders that the French contingent which . . . had been sent to help us at Chanak should be recalled. The Italians, two days before, had already assured Kemal of their neutrality. Our slender forces, abandoned by their Allies in the moment of danger, faced Kemal alone . . . Yet Kemal had also read the Churchill communiqué. He sheered away from Chanak and marched on to the Ismid Peninsula. Great Britain was thereby granted a respite of ten incalculably valuable days.[4]

At this moment a revolution in Athens, in which King Constantine was for the second and last time driven into exile, caused Kemal to fear a revival of pro-Greek feeling in England, and to order his troops to advance on Chanak where they stationed themselves 'grinning through the barbed wire', not without amiability. On 29 September the Cabinet, overruling the unhappy Foreign Secretary, ordered General Harington, commanding the British forces from Constantinople, to deliver an ultimatum to Kemal, threatening war unless the Turks withdrew.

The military commander found himself in the most difficult position in which a soldier can be placed, and he handled the problem with courage and tact. He was forced to make a political decision, using such latitude as his instructions permitted. He ignored the Cabinet order, and did not deliver the ultimatum. By 1 October he was able to report that the crisis seemed to be over, and that he had arranged to meet Kemal, who eventually agreed to sign an armistice convention. So courageous and sensible had been the actions of the British General that few would dispute the verdict of *The Times* that 'An immediate conflict between the British and Kemalist troops has been avoided mainly by the

4. Harold Nicolson, *Curzon: The Last Phase*, pp.272-3.

tact and wisdom of Sir Charles Harington.'[5] The armistice convention in fact gave Kemal everything he had hoped for, including the restoration of Eastern Thrace to Turkey, and he no doubt recognized the folly of challenging the British power if he could gain his ends by easier means. But Winston's feeling was one of sombre regret. On 17 October Hankey wrote in his diary:

> I walked across the Park with Winston one evening towards the end of the crisis and he quite frankly regretted that the Turks had not attacked us at Chanak, as he felt that the surrender to them of Eastern Thrace was humiliating, and that the return of the Turks to Europe meant an infinity of trouble. I don't think the Prime Minister felt very differently . . .[6]

But the British people certainly 'felt differently', and the Chanak crisis, by seeming to bring them again to the verge of war, was neither forgiven nor forgotten, exposing the Government to charges of criminal recklessness and exercising a decisive political influence on events:

> The daring displayed by Mr Lloyd George and Mr Winston Churchill in thus saving Great Britain from humiliation at the hands of Mustapha Kemal was not, at the time, appreciated, by the British press or public. An attack was launched accusing the Coalition Government of having with reckless levity brought Great Britain to within an inch of war. The rank and file of the Conservative party, who had for months been chafing under the dictatorship of Lloyd George, could no longer be restrained . . .[7]

The Coalition, behind a still imposing façade, had been for some time disintegrating from within, and before long, portentous cracks were to appear in its structure. Its leaders, Lloyd George, Austen Chamberlain and Birkenhead, had become almost insolently aloof from their restless subordinates, and had little inclination to analyse the anatomy of their discontent. They were indifferent to what their underlings thought, provided that they continued to do what they were told.

The Coalition was six years old, ample time for alliances to be formed and grievances to mature, and such governments do not long cohere when the period of national danger which caused their formation has passed. It is also a fact, as one rebellious Under-Secretary at this time remarked, that

> there is an inherent tendency in all coalitions to coalesce more closely at the top than lower down in the scale of party organisation. Cabinet business gets despatched more expeditiously and more amicably if the

5. *The Times*, 2 October 1922.
6. Roskill, Hankey: *Man of Secrets*, Vol.2, p.295.
7. Nicolson, op. cit., p.267.

issues dividing the parties are kept out of the discussions. Tacitly side-stepped, they presently come to be regarded as of secondary importance, or even as a rather tiresome element to be postponed, or, if possible, eliminated by some compromise.[8]

To the party rank and file it appeared that by putting forward from the first anti-Socialism and the defence of the Constitution as a policy and continually harping on them, the Government had proved themselves bereft of any other aim and negative in their attitude towards unemployed, wage reductions and the other pressing economic problems still unsolved. The great shadow of Ireland was the blackest to darken the Government's last phase, and there had been consternation when the terms of the Treaty were revealed. Birkenhead and Chamberlain, for 'surrendering to the campaign of murder', became the objects of particular loathing.

Amery, F. E.'s friend since Oxford days, emphasized another alignment which had a strong bearing on the issue:

> Of the personal relationships which affected the situation the dominating one was the close association between Churchill and Birkenhead. They had been intimate friends personally even when most strongly divided in public affairs. Carson's Galloper Smith, and the minister who was prepared, if need be, to suppress Carson's Ulstermen by force were also mess-mates as officers of the Oxfordshire Hussars . . .Both were, in the better sense of the word, political adventurers, fundamentally patriotic and public spirited but not unwilling to throw themselves into any fray in which they might distinguish themselves and win promotion. Both had a rare gift of eloquence; in Birkenhead's case vividly fluent; in Churchill's diligently studied and continually maturing. Birkenhead had the more brilliant mind, but Churchill's was the stronger character.

* * *

The Irish issue was one of the main causes of the Government's downfall. The leaders had made the Treaty, confident in their statesmanship and wisdom, but few of their Conservative supporters welcomed the settlement, and most of them abhorred it. If the Irish Treaty provided much of the explosive which was to blow Lloyd George's government to pieces there were other corrosive agencies at work on the fabric, and many wondered that it had so long survived. The scandal over the sale of honours, bringing the stink of corruption into government, was a powerful contributory cause of its downfall. They had been traded cold-bloodedly across the counter as a grower

8. L.S. Amery, *My Political Life*, Vol.II, p.224.

dispenses figs, and this cynical commerce had repelled men of strict principle like Stanley Baldwin and Edward Wood.[9]

At last the offer of a barony to a South African millionaire of the most murky antecedents brought the matter to a head and produced an uproar. Churchill, then Secretary of State for the Colonies, was enraged by Lloyd George's failure to inform him of his intentions, and the King sent for the Lord Chancellor and expressed his disgust at the transaction. The repercussions startled even Lloyd George, who hastily instructed the Coalition Whip, Captain Guest, to tell the old gentleman that he must write a letter declining the honour. Guest, reinforced by a colleague, called upon the South African to acquaint him with this unpalatable news. The man was stone deaf, and throughout an agonizing encounter laboured under the impression that the Whip had come to congratulate him. Such was his elation that he uncorked a magnum of champagne, and much indecorous shouting and mime was necessary before the delegation could convey its real and bleak message.

Lloyd George and his intimate colleagues found much to recommend an early election when internal discontents would be met by the promise of distracting remedies, and for over a year discussions had been in progress in these inner councils about a propitious moment to seek a fresh mandate from the people. Such a moment seemed to have come at the beginning of 1922, when they believed that a General Election in defence of the Constitution and the existing economic system would rally both wings of the Coalition. All was planned when Sir George Younger, head of the Unionist organization, denounced the intention as a betrayal of his Party. Younger, who was later described by Birkenhead as 'the cabin boy who tried to steer the political ship', was far closer to the rank and file of the Party in the country than the leaders, and although Birkenhead's contemptuous sneer stuck like a burr, it only further diminished his influence. Had their leaders known it, the Conservatives, far from approving an election fought as a coalition, were fast approaching the conclusion that Lloyd George and his Liberal followers were no longer an asset but an albatross heavy round their necks which the moment was ripe to dislodge.

* * *

If the Irish Treaty had brought immediate peace to Ireland, Conservatives, however much they were repelled by it, might have brought themselves to swallow this sour gruel. But there was now a state of civil war in Ireland, and Bonar Law expressed the real Conservative view when he said that in spite of the endorsement of the Irish Treaty

9. Afterwards Lord Halifax.

by a general election in Southern Ireland, they would never have voted for it if they had had any inkling of its outcome. All through the spring and summer of 1922 resentment against the Cabinet, particularly Lloyd George, Birkenhead and Austen Chamberlain, grew even more bitter in the ranks of the Tory Party.

All these fears and resentments came in the end to be focused squarely upon Lloyd George. In his frequent absences from the country he had little time to spare for the House of Commons, leaving the conduct of business to Bonar Law and Chamberlain; and this self-effacement was to cost him dear. The junior Ministers now saw that, apart from the deluded inner circle at the summit, the whole Conservative Party was in a state of simmering revolt. They felt bereft of a policy of their own, and resented being dragged along in the wake of an unpredictable Prime Minister whom they profoundly mistrusted, and a group of Ministers who had lost not only their principles but their heads.

The Prime Minister's long absences abroad had a most injurious effect on the process of government. During the Peace Treaty negotiations he was continuously in Paris, and often after the signature of the Treaty in June 1919. Courting still greater unpopularity, he became ever more convinced of his dexterity in foreign affairs. On returning from his foreign excursions, Lloyd George would retire exhausted to the country for a few days' recuperation and summon a few chosen intimates to confer with him. In the spring of 1922, before the Genoa Conference on economic problems, he was on the verge of nervous collapse and was forced to rest at Criccieth for three weeks. His preoccupation with European problems distracted his mind from domestic issues, which in the post-war period were many and clamant – economic recession, industrial unrest, unemployment, the housing shortage, serious coal strikes – all were subordinated to the demands of the international scene. It was not, as many believed, that the problems were unrecognized, but it was impossible to get swift policy decision from the Prime Minister. In the sort of life he was leading there was simply no time to address his mind to these matters, and in his periods in England it was always occupied with planning the next conference. His exertions were prodigious, but the task he had set himself was beyond the compass of one man.

* * *

Thus withdrawn from the House of Commons and secluded from opinion in Parliament and the constituencies, the Prime Minister was forced to rely on his Conservative Cabinet Ministers to ensure the loyalty of the Tory Party in the House, where they formed two-thirds of his supporters. But here it was a case of the blind leading the blind, for Chamberlain and Birkenhead were as little *en rapport* with public opinion as the Prime Minister himself. The frustrations of Ministers attempting a co-ordinated policy is reflected in a letter from Churchill to Lloyd George on 8 October 1921:

> I had a feeling we made great progresss in cutting our way into the post-war monetary & financial mystery ... But it seemed to me that all this progress stopped short of reaching any conclusions of a definite character on which a policy or even a provisional policy cd be based; that we have not at the present time got a clear view on the fundamental questions to which I have drawn attention. *I* certainly do not pretend to have a clear view upon them, tho' I have a feeling that if we went on hammering away for a week or two we shd get to the bottom of it & frame a definite policy which wd carry us through the temporary & baffling fluctuations which are affecting us so violently at the present time. It is quite true that owing to your very great skill in navigation we have avoided many dangerous rocks & shoals & in the coal strikes have come through one of the greatest industrial hurricanes that have ever blown. But for all that we are drifting about in a fog without a compass.[10]

To sustain the isolated and god-like part in which he had cast himself, Lloyd George established a private secretariat at 10 Downing Street and with the help of gifted extraneous advisers frequently usurped the functions of the resentful Lord Curzon, who at such moments became almost a cipher in his gilded room at the Foreign Office.

> Lord Curzon, the Foreign Secretary, was obliged to accept these intrusions upon the responsibility of his office: but he did not do so light-heartedly, or without many a groan of warning, without many sighs of discontent. His friends in the Conservative Party were well aware that the Foreign Secretary viewed with grave misgiving some of the more imaginative of the Prime Minister's excursions. The blame for the checks, the disappointments and the calamities that followed was thus increasingly, but not always quite fairly, attributed to Mr Lloyd George alone.[11]

An episode in the summer of 1922 provides a vivid glimpse of the complete divorcement by that time of the Coalition leaders from the minds of their subordinates, and their sublime indifference to their opinions. The junior Ministers, almost entirely hostile to their leaders and far more closely in touch with the rank and file of the Party in Parliament and the constituencies, were in a quandary. As members of the Government they shared responsibility, while not in fact having the slightest part in framing policy. In August 1922 they asked to be

10. Lloyd George papers, F.10.10.
11. Nicolson, *King George V*, pp.317-17.

allowed to submit their anxieties to the whole body of Unionist Cabinet Ministers, and did so in a fair and temperate manner. Chamberlain then asked Birkenhead to reply:

> F E began by rating them for their impertinence in having asked for a meeting at all, when they had already been informed of the Cabinet Ministers' views, and then went on in the most astonishingly arrogant and offensive manner to lecture them for their silliness and want of loyalty. I could see them all bristling more and more with every sentence . . . Whatever chances F E may have had of the Unionist leadership of the future they are not likely to have survived this unfortunate performance . . . Austen wound up with a few pontifical sentences, and we dispersed, most of the juniors spluttering with indignation.[12]

But although Lloyd George might have overcome the unpopularity of the Irish Treaty among a large section of the Conservative Party, had it not been for the civil war, the failure of the portentous Genoa Conference was impossible to disguise. This conference, into which Birkenhead (recovering from an illness) sauntered from his yacht, and, clad in a blue blazer with brass buttons and yachting cap, held seven hundred journalists enthralled with an impromptu speech of astonishing brilliance, provided the opportunity for Lloyd George to make a decision about British relations with the Bolshevik régime; he was anxious to resume trade with Russia as part of a general arrangement for trade revival in Europe. This, as we have seen, was a policy which Churchill was not prepared to stomach, and his long and violent disagreement with Lloyd George on the matter was probably the main cause of the *froideur* between the two men to which Clementine had referred. His hatred of the Bolshevik regime had in no way abated. If anything it had increased. On 24 March 1920 we find him writing to Lloyd George:

> Since the Armistice my policy would have been 'Peace with the German people. War on the Bolshevik tyranny.' Willingly or unavoidably you have followed something very near the reverse . . . We are now face to face with the results. They are terrible. We may well be within measurable distance of universal collapse & anarchy throughout Europe and Asia. Russia has gone into ruin. What is left of her is in the power of these deadly snakes. But Germany may perhaps still be saved. I have felt with a great sense of relief that we may perhaps be able to think and act together in harmony about Germany: that you are inclined to make an effort to rescue Germany from her frightful fate – which if it overtakes her may well overtake others. If so time is short and action must be simple. You ought to tell France that

12. Amery, op.cit., pp.234-5.

we will make a defensive alliance with her if *& only* if she entirely alters her present treatment of Germany & loyally accepts a British policy of help & friendship towards Germany . . .[13]

The conference proposed by Lloyd George, which he saw, *couleur de rose*, as achieving the triumphant resettlement of Europe, was arranged to assemble in Genoa on 10 April 1922. The instructions to the British delegates envisaged the *de jure* recognition of Russia subject to a probationary period. Churchill was bitterly opposed to such recognition, and Curzon shared his opinion. These doubts were also expressed by Austen Chamberlain, who reminded the Prime Minister that Winston's hostility would have a devastating effect upon their own fortunes:

> The Lord Chancellor and I have done our best to restrain him, but he has said to both of us that he could not remain a member of the Government if *de jure* recognition were granted to the Soviet Government. Putting aside any feelings of our own, you will readily perceive that our position would be impossible if Winston retired because he was more Tory than the Tory ministers . . .

Chamberlain reminded Lloyd George that the United States had declined to grant recognition and to be represented at Genoa. He advised him that the right formula to adopt was to concert his action with France, and only give recognition in agreement with her:

> Isolated recognition by us would in any case raise great difficulties among our followers in the House of Commons, and if it led to a breach with Churchill it would be quite fatal to us. I think we are entitled to expect from Russia something more than paper recognition of the ordinary obligations of a civilised State before we grant recognition. Our experiences with regard to the assurances given at the time of the trade agreement do not encourage us to place much faith in her word.[14]

Thus beset on all sides Lloyd George reacted with fury. He refused to treat France as though he were a dictator: he even nourished a vague hope of a party in Russia 'prepared to surrender its Bolshevism and to make terms with the Western capitalists' and 'return to the community of civilised nations'. His old exasperation with Churchill's Russian obsession revived in a sudden flare of malice when he informed Chamberlain:

> If Winston, who is obsessed with the defeat inflicted upon his military projects by the Bolshevik armies, is determined that he will resign rather

13. Lloyd George papers, F.9.2.20.
14. Austen Chamberlain papers, 21 March 1922.

than assent to any recognition, however complete the surrender of the communists, and whatever the rest of Europe may decide, then the Cabinet must choose between Winston and me.[15]

And he complained to the Chancellor of the Exchequer, Sir Robert Horne, with equal petulance:

I told you I thought Winston would be a real wrecker ... To go to Genoa under the conditions that would satisfy Winston would be futile and humiliating in the extreme. Unless Genoa leads to a real European peace it is no use going there. It is an essential part of the Genoa programme that there should be a European pact of peace which will involve an undertaking by Russia not to attack her neighbours ... I cannot see how this is possible without recognising Russia .... I certainly could not go to Genoa on Winston's terms.[16]

But Horne's reply merely deepened his resentment:

I understand from Austen, he is to see Winston & put to him a proposition based on solemn & public declarations from Russia ... F E wd agree on that line if Winston will. We cannot, however, disguise from ourselves that if Winston & F E were to go out on this matter it wd break up the Coalition.[17]

* * *

The position was serious enough, even without this threatened disaster, for the Genoa Conference proved a fiasco; France had no intention of recognizing Russia, and Curzon, who had been against the conference from the beginning, succumbed to phlebitis and was unable to attend. To crown all else, on the sixth day of the meeting, the Russians confirmed all Winston's dark suspicions of treachery and bad faith by signing a secret bilateral treaty with the Germans at Rapallo in April, agreeing to the immediate establishment of full diplomatic relations and the renunciation of all reparations between the two countries. This was a blow from which the conference could not recover, and it quickly expired. Although Lloyd George performed its obsequies with his usual skill, there were many who would have been in agreement with Lord Curzon's sour comment to Austen Chamberlain: 'I hope that this will be the last of these fantastic gatherings which are really only designed as a stage on which he is to perform.'[18] And to the last the Foreign

15. Ibid, 22 March 1922.
16. Lloyd George papers, F.27.6.57.
17. Lloyd George papers, F.27.6.58.
18. Nicolson, *Curzon: The Last Phase*, p.245.

Secretary was fearful that Lloyd George, to save face, would conclude some agreement with the Soviet even more devious than the Treaty of Rapallo. 'To have dealings,' he wrote, 'with such people is bad at all times ... But to do it in the conditions described in order to scrape something out of Genoa would be the nadir of humiliation.'

* * *

These events merely confirmed Winston's detestation of the Soviets. The 'deadly snakes' had fulfilled his expectations by acting in their treacherous, snake-like way. As though his position was not already painfully familiar to the Prime Minister, he continued to emphasize it, nagging him in July when all appeared to be over:

> I must make it plain that I feel it quite impossible to recognise the Bolsheviks in view of all that has happened ... The issue does not arise now & may never arise; but if it does − I do not see the slightest chance of my ever being able to stay. I shd be very sorry indeed to leave you, but it will be for me a decisive act. There has been no improvement of any kind in their character & behaviour & I do not believe there ever will be ...[19]

The Genoa conference, so widely proclaimed, so extravagantly boosted, had raised hopes of settlement which were dashed by its complete and humiliating failure. To the Prime Minister's anxious followers this was merely the latest and the most futile of those 'imaginative excursions' into foreign affairs. He was never to recover the political ground he had lost there, and after the Chanak crisis − which we have seen interpreted as a reckless provocation of war − rebellion in the Conservative ranks could no longer be ignored. The Prime Minister confronted the situation with calm but with few illusions. Exhausted by his prodigious labours, he had been offered £80,000 (a huge sum at the time) to write his memoirs. He decided to appeal to the country as a coalition, regarding his own possible dismissal with a fair degree of equanimity.

On 13 October he warned the King that he might have to ask for a dissolution. He seemed already to be pervaded by a mellow afterglow. In Manchester, at his most irresistible, and revelling in his waspish tongue, he dazzled the Reform Club in a speech in which after a powerful vindication of his Near East policy he relished the sharp antidote of revenge. This was at the expense of Lord Gladstone, who had provoked him, referring to Gladstone as 'the best embodiment of the Liberal doctrine that quality is not hereditary'. Pleased with the success of this sally, he went on plaintively and amid loud laughter to speak of himself as an old actor for whom fashionable London had no

19. Lloyd George papers, F.10.3.22.

further use: 'but I can still go on on touring the provinces'. He savoured
with relish and in advance the malicious pleasure of watching his critics
tackling the problems which they upbraided him for failing to solve, and
he seemed to emphasize his own indifference to what might happen with
an irresponsible detachment. He would welcome freedom – he longed
to be free. He offered to resign in favour of others – Balfour, Bonar
Law or Chamberlain – with wild prodigality, and this speech with its
reckless denunciation of the Turks and its criticism of the French further
convinced Conservatives that the Prime Minister was a menace and the
Coalition a rickety building fit only for demolition.

It was this speech, too, which finally resolved Curzon's vacillation
between loyalty to the Coalition and rage at Lloyd George's intrusions
into foreign affairs. The decision to make an immediate appeal to
the country as a coalition had been confirmed at a dinner party in
Churchill's house on 11 October. Among those who solemnly agreed to
this step was Curzon, who was reported to have said firmly, 'I'm with
you.' But next day he thought better of this incautious gesture of loyalty
and changed his mind, an action which left a clinging taint of duplicity
on Curzon's memory and later drew Birkenhead's memorable sneer: 'He
was penultimately loyal to the Coalition, and if when it deliquesced he
found salvation a trifle quickly – well, so, to be sure, did Balaam.'

*   *   *

The annual conference of the National Union of Conservative Associations was to be held in November, when the profound discontent of
the Party would find certain expression. It was to anticipate this that a
decision was taken to convene a meeting of the Parliamentary Party at
the Carlton Club on the morning of 19 October. This famous gathering,
which destroyed the Coalition, has been too frequently described to
concern us in detail. All were agreed that there was an atmosphere of
the utmost tension and excitement in the Club, which according to one
member was 'humming like a bee-hive'. Chamberlain's opening speech,
at once dictatorial and banal, produced little enthusiasm, but Stanley
Baldwin spoke with extraordinary effect and dominated the meeting.

Conservatives were sated by long experience of the erratic wizardry
of Lloyd George and the rhetorical genius of Birkenhead. They were
now ready for a direct approach and for less sophisticated methods.
And Baldwin's plainsong appeal was sustained by a sense of moral
outrage, his unbending attitude to the Prime Minister far transcending
political mistrust and amounting to a belief that he was almost the Devil
incarnate, responsible through his evil example for all the distempers of
the realm. 'Baldwin laid the blame for a degenerate society squarely on

Lloyd George whom he regarded as a real corrupter of public life.'[20] Uxorious and impeccable in his own moral behaviour, he was shocked to the core by the stories that reached him of the Prime Minister's wildly disordered private life. Such deviations he found not only repellent but incomprehensible, and it was his habit among intimates to refer to Lloyd George as the 'Goat'.

Sustained by such indignation, his forthright words fell upon the meeting with extraordinary effect, free from guile and passionately emphatic. The Prime Minister might be a great dynamic force. That force had already broken up the Liberal Party. Baldwin did not want it to break up the Conservative Party. Behind his unadorned words, his argument that to avoid this fate the Party must fight on its own and above all free itself from its destructive leader, the emphasis throughout his speech was upon personal and moral issues and the essential need to return to an uncontaminated conduct of affairs.

The appeal was perfectly attuned to the mood of the moment. The finishing touches were put to the wrecking process by Bonar Law. Ailing and despondent, and recently contemplating resignation, with an effort and seeming to think his way on his feet he arrived at the conclusion that the Party should come out of the Coalition and go to the country on its own. This was decisive, and the cheers that greeted him left him in no doubt that he represented the wishes of the great majority. Few who listened to him understood what was passing through that enigmatic mind at the moment of decision. Fully aware of the discontent of the Conservative rank and file with Lloyd George, and of the fact that his own support was vital to the success of the anti-Coalition Conservatives (for he had no rival to the leadership and they could do nothing without a leader), he still felt he could not intervene without disloyalty to Chamberlain. He had already warned Lloyd George of his danger:

> It is difficult to say how far Lloyd George heeded these warnings. Probably he wrote them off as typical examples of Bonar Law's pessimism. After all, everyone else said that Lloyd George was indispensable . . . Why should he, Lloyd George, a statesman of world renown, the architect of Allied victory, give up the great game because a few die-hard back-benchers murmured at his rule?[21]

But Bonar Law had long delayed in his painful hour of doubt; he had been stiffened by Max Aitken, now ennobled as Beaverbrook, like some limp lay figure without volition of its own. Sick in body but

---

20. Middlemas and Barnes, *Baldwin*, p.98.
21. Robert Blake, *The Unknown Prime Minister*.

buttressed by *The Times*, he had been promised the support of Derby's Lancashire, and he was strong in the knowledge that the anti-Coalition Conservatives were behind him almost to a man. The motion to free the Party from Lloyd George was carried by 187 votes to 87, and a momentous and painful morning came to an end.

* * *

Lloyd George resigned that afternoon, and Chamberlain and Birkenhead, staunch in defeat, followed him into the shadows. When a man shouted 'Judas' at him at a public meeting Birkenhead replied with contempt and pride, 'Judas is abhorred for betraying his Master. Am I to be reproached for refusing to betray mine?' The Prime Minister had fallen after sixteen years of continuous office, still the most illustrious figure in Europe. He fell 'like Lucifer, never to rise again'. He had cut his own bonds with the Liberal Party and was now rejected by the Conservatives. With all his wonderful aptitude in negotiation, his melting eloquence and withering invective, he was deficient in the one quality which might have enabled him to retrieve his position – the ability to inspire confidence. The step had faltered, the image become tarnished; yet some believed that the Prime Minister was not the only cause of their discontents, and that Churchill's ascendancy over weaker-minded colleagues and his obstinate Free Trade convictions were the real menace to their future.

Winston was excluded from the last scene by a rare failure of health. Until the Second World War he regarded the session of 1922 as his period of most sustained achievement. He recalled the fruitful settlements in Iraq and Palestine, and his triumph in steering the Irish legislation through Parliament. Just as in the writing of history he often succumbed to *suppressio veri*, so now he excised from his mind the disasters of the Russian intervention, the unwise economies in the Air, scars of Chanak and the sour aftertaste of the Irish Treaty. It is an example at once of the strength and weakness of his mental endowment which was able to exclude unwelcome facts so that much of the pain was removed by the anodyne of Nature.

As a Liberal he could not have attended the Carlton Club meeting in any event, but a day or two before it he had been taken ill and rushed by an ambulance to hospital for an emergency operation for appendicitis. In his later years he became more circumspect in his approach to sickness, but now he tried to shoo it out of his room like an intrusive hen. On awaking from the anaesthetic he immediately cried, 'Who has got in for Newport? Give me a newspaper.' He was told sharply by the doctor that he could not have one and must lie still, but when the doctor returned he found Winston again unconscious with four or five newspapers lying on the bed.[22]

He was affected by events no less than his two closest colleagues. No longer a Minister, he was to lose his seat in the ensuing General Election, and he was to recall this in 1932, a a typical example of the vicissitudes of politics. Emphasizing his recent unbroken success, he wrote:

> Suddenly everything fell in pieces. I was hurried off in an ambulance to hospital, and had hardly regained consciousness before I learned that the Government was destroyed and that our Conservative friends and colleagues, with whom we had been working so loyally, had in a night turned from friends to foes. I was no longer a minister. And then in a few weeks the constituency which had sustained me so long repudiated me in the most decisive manner. And all this, mind you, at the close of a year when I had been by general consent more successful in Parliament and in administration than at any other time in my life. In the twinkling of an eye I found myself without an office, without a seat, without a party, and without an appendix.[23]

22. Roskill, op.cit., Vol.2, p.297.
23. WSC, *Thoughts and Adventures*, p.213.

Epilogue

Chapter 27

The Wilderness Years

The greater part of Churchill's long exile was spent at Chartwell, and all his literary work was composed there. Here the last volumes of *The World Crisis* were finished; here *Marlborough* and *A History of the English-Speaking Peoples* and *Thoughts and Adventures* were written; and here the flow of memoranda and the speeches were composed with which from 1932 onward he vainly sought to rouse a torpid nation to awareness of the German menace, and to impart some understanding of the urgency of events to its ruinous leaders.

We have noticed how unthinkable it was for him even in moments of dejection to become weary of the human condition. He could not bear the sterile inertia of idleness, or the thought of time trickling irrevocably away like sand through his fingers. When deprived of office and the bustle of power he generated his own activity, and in this peaceful and idyllic place he so dominated time that not a moment of the day was wasted, and little space was left for torturing reflections. If ever there was a man who could 'fill the unforgiving minute with sixty seconds worth of distance run', it was he, and Winston could write in retrospect with perfect truth of this period of his life: 'Thus I never had a dull or idle moment from morning to midnight, and with my happy family around me dwelt at peace in my habitation.'[1]

Partly for this reason, the house in its lovely setting, constantly embellished, stole ever more strongly into his affections, associated with the joy of creation in many forms, so engrossing that it abolished gloom, and with a life richly productive and intensely rewarding which never seemed to be disturbed with the restlessness which usually accompanied his exclusion from power. It was his home for forty years.

1. WSC, *The Gathering Storm*, p.62.

* * *

Although the Churchill family moved to Chartwell in 1924, he had
bought the property in 1922, captivated in an instant by its position,
surroundings and closeness to London.

> A few miles north of Penshurst a combe climbs to the timbered
> summit of the Kent hills. Its suave green slopes evoke a sense of
> pastoral peace and somewhere about the 600-foot contour, it is flanked
> by the sheltering woods. Fertile soil overlays the local ragstone, and the
> trees, mainly chestnut, beech and oak, grow to great size. Their shadows
> at dawn and sunset are thrown far across the combe. Southward the view
> stretches to the Weald. On one side of this little valley rises a clear spring,
> the Chart Well, from which its name derives. Wooded, watered, smoothly
> pastured, this place must have commended itself to the eye and spirit since
> the Kentish landscape was first tamed.[2]

It had commended itself at once to Winston and his family. His
daughter Sarah had lasting memories of the occasion when he drove
her with Randolph and his eldest daughter Diana to see the property.
With Winston precariously at the wheel of an ancient Wolseley, they
drove from London to Chartwell, and on the way he explained with a
certain deceit to the children that the object of the journey was to inspect
a house he might buy, and to ask their opinion on the purchase. The
house was then gaunt, weed-choked and long abandoned, but it seemed
to the children to possess all the romance of a deserted place, brooding
among its nettles and encroaching rhododendrons like some mysterious
dwelling in a poem by De la Mare or Poe. They begged him to buy it.
They were all so excited by the inspection that Winston was unable to
make the car start, but with his usual skill in enlisting the aid of others
he soon assembled a large crowd to push it to the top of the hill, where
it was pointed out to him that the ignition had been off and the brake
on. He did not tell the children until they reached Parliament Square on
the homeward journey that he had already bought the property.[3]

* * *

The Chartwell estate comprised more than eight hundred acres, but
he had bought the house with eighty acres including the park and the
topmost reach of the Chart combe with its embracing woods for £5,000.
It is unlikely that the proceeds of *The World Crisis* provided the cash
for this transaction, and more probable that the purchase money and

2. Fedden, op.cit., p.13.
3. Sarah Churchill, *A Thread of Tapestry*, pp.22-23.

the funds for the complete transformation of the house were derived from the legacy received from the will of his great-grandmother, Lady Londonderry, two heirs with priority having died childless.

The possibilities disclosed by this tangled demesne, the views it commanded on every side, and particularly over the Weald, added to the fact that it was only twenty-five miles from London, had caused him to make his decision. He was not interested in the house, and probably scarcely noticed it, but although Sarah had been so captivated by its mystery, there was much in it to give an adult pause for thought, for not even the most obstinate devotee of the Victorian scene could have found cause for admiration in this unsightly survivor, though some of the interior dated from the sixteenth century. The front was smothered with ivy, and unchecked rhododendrons muzzled walls adorned by graceless bays and oriels, while rampant laurel bushes and sombre firs darkened the house inside, where dry rot had for long been eroding the fabric. Over the derelict building brooded an air of desolation and sadness.

We are safe in assuming that a single glance was sufficient to bring the light of battle into Clementine Churchill's eyes and to convince her of the absolute necessity of a major architectural operation, but Winston's first impression as he stood by the entrance of this forlorn building had not been one of bricks and mortar but of the superb beech wood rising steeply beyond the lawn to the sky, and eastwards of the level of the land falling sharply to combe and water and seeming to invite embellishment. From the beginning Winston had concerned himself mainly with the landscaping of his own property, and to bringing an added grandeur to that which nature had already fashioned.

The defects of the house, though daunting enough, could at least be overcome, but Chartwell also contained a fault about which nothing could be done. On the bank overlooking the house there was a mass of rhododendrons which each spring burst into a sea of mauve and purple – two colours which Clementine could not abide. Neither these nor their over-storey of trees that shut out the light from the house could be touched by the owners of Chartwell, since they lay on common land.

Clementine's distaste delayed the purchase of Chartwell, which Winston eventually completed without informing her. It was the only time, Lady Soames tells me, in a marriage of fifty-seven years when he acted with less than candour towards her.

Winston was certain that she would come to share the enchantment that Chartwell had cast over him and the children, but while his mind was fixed on plans for lakes and landscaping, hers was appalled by the thought of the cost of it all. Nor did time soften her attitude; she accepted the situation and worked hard to improve the house and

garden without ever feeling the affection for the place that Winston
had so confidently forecast.

He started modestly enough by ordering a consignment of fruit
trees – quinces, damsons, plums, pears, apples and Kentish cobs[4],
but such tentative beginnings were soon to yield to far more significant
changes. Just as in painting he preferred a bold technique, so on his land
he showed an equal enterprise, making improvements and changes with
growing confidence and imagination. Thus in time the landscape came
to bear in an unmistakable manner the impression of his own character
– its impetuosity, its insistence on grandiose effects, and its demand for
water, and ever more water and lakes which seemed almost to proclaim
a *folie de grandeur*. While Winston's attention was thus concentrated
upon the adornment of his land, Clementine's practical mind busied
itself with immediate necessities, some of which caused him misgivings.
'He watched with apprehension,' said Sarah, 'my mother's determined
actions. Away went the mysterious but suffocating rhododendrons, ivy
and goodness knows what which had tried to eat and smother the house
in its twenty years of emptiness.'

He was disturbed by the ruthlessness of her preliminary destructions.
Large trees – even a fine, long-established cedar – were felled without
mercy to make way for building additions, causing him to object
plaintively but in vain:

'If you go on like this, Clemmie, we had better rename the house
One Tree Hill.'[5] She showed equal decision in transforming the old
Victorian building into a tall house in mellow red brick which, since
it was built on the side of a steep slope, had rooms at dramatically
different levels. Looking at the estate that emerged, one saw clearly the
division of their labours. His hand is apparent in the masterful additions
to the landscape and in the open lawn in front of the house flanked by
two gigantic limes, fragrant in flower and humming with bees, hers in
the many flower gardens, and in the planting, for simple effect, of such
flowers as fuchsias, potentillas and lavender, massed white geraniums,
tulips and cherry pie. But the house was almost entirely her work, and
her skill and the resourcefulness of the architect, Philip Tilden, were
at once evident, particularly in the striking room levels, and in the
drawing-room which overlooked the view he loved, the superb vista
of the Weald giving an impression of dim blue, assuming this colour
through the mere depth of distance, and in Winston's library, the real
engine-room of the house, where he wrote his books and composed his
speeches, and brooded over the darkening political scene. None of this

4. Fedden, op.cit., p.17.
5. Sarah Churchill, op.cit., p.24.

mollified Clementine's unalterable antipathy to Chartwell.

* * *

We should remember, when thinking of his life there, that for Winston Chartwell was a refuge in which his family could be happily raised and where he could work without disturbance. It was a place so pastoral wherever the eye turned that it might have been a hundred miles from London instead of little more than twenty. One had the sense there of always unbroken country tranquillity, of sharply descending slopes and woods astir in the breeze, of a house so cunningly devised as to appear almost part of the garden, and opening on to it at every possible point, and a garden which itself seemed to melt into the surrounding combe and become a part of it. And over the place in high summer was the sense of green leafy places, and of the water which Winston loved, trickling through ferns down its green channels – the perfect raw material for the creative ambitions that at once filled his mind.

The water flowing gently from the Chart Well was the foundation on which his plans were based. It had been dammed at one point by the farmer occupant and a large lake created which merely whetted his appetite. Another lake above the dam was excavated, but after inspecting the two sheets of water (and perhaps using as a pretext the fact that they were choked by weeds and dangerous for the children's bathing) he left them to the waterfowl and built another dam higher in the valley. The new lake was cemented for swimming, but it too developed irritating faults and was in turn abandoned. Baffled but obstinate, he built yet another pool, this time on the other side of the valley and nearer the house. The gentle flow from the spring was unable to fill it, but company water was added and an electric pump installed to send it through a filter from the large lake to the swimming pool and back. In all these projects Winston was not only the author but also invariably a labourer.

Desmond Morton had taken a cottage near Chartwell at Crockham Hill, and was a weekly visitor there until the War. When making his swimming pool he told Morton, 'I want something that will raise the temperature to boiling point on Christmas Day,' and when he invited Morton to bathe the following Christmas steam was rising from the bath. A large and cumbrous heating apparatus had been installed – unusual at the time – which Winston's friends thought had sufficient capacity to heat the Ritz Hotel.

For all technical advice he relied on Professor Lindemann, the Oxford physicist, and it was on his assurance (after mathematical calculation) that the spring would yield a sufficient flow to fill the second lake that the work was put in hand. It was his friend Birkenhead's daughter who had nicknamed the scientist 'Prof' in an idle moment, and the sobriquet stuck like a dart. This saturnine, reserved man, at once shy and forbidding, loved by friends and abhorred by his many enemies, was now a member of Churchill's inner circle of intimates, and was to remain there, admired, loved and teased, until that day when as an old and infirm man Churchill paid his last respects at Lindemann's funeral.

* * *

Winston had also become immersed in wild life, and found the company of birds and animals both stimulating and soothing. This characteristic in him had never been so marked before, perhaps because he had never had leisure to indulge it. He also seemed now to regard the countryside in a different manner. As he pointed out one of the additions he had made to the landscape, he did so with such transparent love that he might almost have been possessed by a pathetic fallacy and be investing the land itself with human emotions.

A similar awareness now marked his attitude to animals. The new lakes he had created provided the opportunity to stock them with wild fowl. Canada Geese and black swans were added to those already there. Although more successful in ingratiating himself with the Canada geese, he was fascinated by the swans, so strange and seductive, black as night, and their movement stately as a *pavane*. But it was soon painfully obvious that the cygnets offered particular temptations to the foxes which infested the many woods round the estate. Winston's attitude to all wild life was humane, indeed sentimental. He who had pushed aside a goose placed on the sideboard, refusing to carve it with the words: 'This goose was a friend of mine,' and would allow no animal to be slaughtered for food to which he had said 'Good morning,' now found himself on the horns of a dilemma. He refused to allow foxes to be shot below the house, yet took infinite pains in other ways to safeguard the swans, consulting the London Zoo and experiments with protective devices, but since he refused to sanction the one obvious remedy the cygnets continued to be taken before they were fledged.

Now that he had time to observe them he came to love animals and all wild things, and was happy to find that he had the gift of winning their confidence. A robin at Chartwell fed from his hand; one of the Canada geese would waddle from the lake on his approach and accompany him faithfully on his walk round the garden, and among the animals under his special care at different times were a fox cub, a badger, a sheep and a succession of cats, one of which was drawn by his artist friend William Nicholson.

It was generally felt that in the case of the ram his sentimentality degenerated into self-indulgence. It was an unrewarding and aggressive creature with an appalling smell and a tendency to butt all passers-by. Winston had reared this animal from a lamb and fed it from the bottle, and his affection for it was apparently unassailable. It was inappropriately known as Charmayne. It is believed to have been doctored to curb its ferocity, but with little result, and he resisted all attempts to dispose of it – did so, indeed, with mulish obstinacy until Charmayne rounded upon his protector, and, butting him in the back of the knees, knocked him flat. Even Winston's sentimentality was not proof against this assault on his person, and the ram, at last deprived of his protection, was banished from the farm. Since his immersion in nature had become so absorbing it was to be expected that it would include an affection for dogs. Rufus, his brown poodle, was held in besotted affection, and he was sad that the lives of dogs were so pathetically short.[6] There was also a pug which belonged to his youngest daughter Mary, and Sarah Churchill tells us that when this dog was so ill that it appeared to be dying, Winston was even stirred into verse to comfort the children:

> Oh, what is the matter with poor Puggy-Wug?
> Pat him and kiss him and give him a hug.
> Run and fetch him a suitable drug,
> Wrap him up tenderly all in a rug,
> That is the way to cure Puggy-Wug.

* * *

The objects of his interest were thus wide, but one had the impression that he valued each species for a different reason. There was something soothing and conducive to reflection in the golden orfe moving slowly in their pool below the rose garden; something of challenge and novelty in making friends with the geese and black swans, and a satisfaction of his passion for colour in butterflies.

For he was still as captivated by these as he had been as a boy in Bangalore, and had long treasured 'the flying beauties flaunting their splendid liveries' that he had collected in Uganda. Now, deploring the decline in their numbers caused by modern artificial fertilizers, he asked his wife to plant clumps of buddleia which, he had been told, would draw to them in summer as by a magnet, brimstones, tortoiseshells, red admirals and peacocks.

And he found yet another occupation in the garden which also involved the pleasure of creation in the area covered by an old kitchen garden. This was the main scene of his new activity as

6. WSC to author.

builder and bricklayer. Altogether he built with his own hands the greater part of two cottages and extensive garden walls as well as a summerhouse for his youngest daughter and a two-storied tree-house for the other children which was perched like an eyrie high in one of the great limes. The foundations of the wall and cottages were built by a professional bricklayer to knee-height, and Winston was also instructed by him in the use of the plumb-line and the art of cementing bricks. The rest was entirely his own work.

He was never one to stand by watching others. The act of building undoubtedly provided him with a sense of achievement, of something positively accomplished to show for his efforts, and he was an arresting sight when engaged in it, often wearing one of his eccentric hats and smoking a cigar, with a whisky and soda sometimes placed thoughtfully on the wall beside him. As one approached him from behind, that unmistakeable silhouette seemed to stamp itself upon his surroundings, proclaiming that this was he, and could be no other, silently dominating the scene. On the invitation of the General Secretary, Churchill took out a card as an adult apprentice in the Amalgamated Union of Building Trade Workers, but his unpopularity, added to the incongruity of his new position as a trade-union member, caused acute resentment in the industrial world and led to the passing of angry resolutions. His Union Card was withdrawn after the General Strike, but restored, with honeyed words, at the end of the Second World War.

* * *

In this paradisal garden, now preserved by the National Trust, there are many corners where it is pleasant to linger – water gardens, gardens heavy with the scent of roses, vine-covered loggias and a terrace overlooking the Weald – but of these perhaps the most evocative of the past is the Goldfish Pond, fringed by magnolia, bamboo and wisteria. It was here that he came every day to sit in reflection and to feed the golden orfe. Here more than anywhere else one feels the real force of remembrance. Nothing has been changed:

> His garden chair stands beside the pond and, though empty, his ample presence still seems to fill it, while his gleaming carp, those long-lived fish, still cruise the unruffled water. Such is the impress of habit that they glide expectantly towards the casual visitor as though a lesser hand might scatter the maggots, regularly despatched from Yorkshire, that they were long accustomed to receive from a prime minister . . . If the twentieth century can apprehend a numen, this place is hallowed ground. Here the aged statesman sat in contemplation, and here he must often have reflected on his long career and the mutability of human fortune, on the brevity of fame and the span of eternity.[7]

7. Fedden, op.cit., pp.20-21.

In other parts of the garden were further indications of the activities which occupied every day, the studio where he painted, and the Marlborough Pavilion whose walls were decorated with a frieze portraying Marlborough's campaigns by his artist-nephew John Churchill, son of his brother Jack.

John Churchill had been brought up with his uncle and regarded him almost as a father, and while painting the Pavilion he was sometimes with him for months. He did not find Winston receptive to outside thinking, and noticed that when William Nicholson tried to explain to him the greatness of Hindu mural painting he could not understand, and refused to accept his views. Direct and logical, he could not comprehend theories of art: he would paint always what he directly saw and could never have evolved it from his mind in a studio. His nephew formed the opinion that he had a strange jealousy of professional artists, but he was fond of cross-examining John about his painting, about how he worked and how he saw a picture in his imagination before embarking on it. He noticed too that Winston had inherited no gift for music. As in poetry his appreciation inclined to the more robust of Kipling's poems, so in music he seemed limited to the Harrow Songs which he knew by heart. John, also a Harrovian, knew them too and could accompany his uncle, and when Winston would bellow the songs in a lusty but unmelodious voice.[8]

Whatever lacunae there may have been in his aesthetic appreciation, there were not wanting experts who believed that he was blessed by a natural aptitude for painting. One, Sir John Rothenstein, saw his work as reflecting 'sheer joy in the simple beauties of nature; water, still, bubbling, or agitated by wind; snow immaculate and crisp; trees dark with the density of their foliage or dappled by sunlight; fresh flowers; distant mountains, and, above all, sunlight at its fiercest.'[9]

Graham Sutherland, who years later painted a controversial picture of Churchill which Clementine caused to be destroyed, considered that

> he had extraordinary talent as a painter, particularly when he was not under the influence of some artist or other. But Sickert had a good influence in that, under it, Winston's pictures became less competent and more profound. The painting became more probing, and less an unquestioning acceptance of everything Winston saw before him. His style bcame much more conceptual.[10]

Sutherland added that Picasso was believed to have said that Churchill

8. John Churchill to author.
9. Sir John Rothenstein, *Time's Thievish Progress*, p.143.
10. Graham Sutherland, O.M. to author.

would have been a great painter if he had not been a politician, and he was inclined to agree with that judgment. But he emphasized that 'to achieve greatness a man must devote his whole life and soul to art. It cannot be arrived at by using it as a hobby or for escapism.'[11]

Winston spoke a good deal to Sutherland about painting, but with extraordinary and excessive modesty almost amounting to self-abasement, similar to that he showed about his literary style when writing to Lawrence of Arabia, and betraying unease in relation to the masters of an art to which he also aspired but in which he probably felt retarded by his lack of artistic training.

The great majority of the paintings in Churchill's garden-studio were landscapes rather than portraits, for painting sharpened his close observation of the countryside, and there can also be little doubt of the truth of Rothenstein's words:

> It is surely not mere chance that men and events, with which nine-tenths of his life were passionately concerned, should be rigorously excluded from his work. It was to gain respite from their pressures, to establish contact with a world unrelated to elections, manoeuvres, and the preoccupations of the body politic, that Churchill repeatedly set up his easel. From this world, enriched and fortified, he returned to the combat.

He had in fact, almost by chance, discovered (perhaps unconsciously) a perfect instrument of emotional release, a time machine which transported him far from the cares of the day, and a diversion which left behind it a visible accomplishment in the form of the finished picture.

* * *

It is the scope and resourcefulness of Churchill's mind in exile and the extraordinary diversity of his interests that astonish us. It was a mind which focused itself with absorbed interest on each separate object or activity under scrutiny at the moment. There was no difference or overlapping, no confusion of interest or waste of time. One imagined, but did not see, a meticulous and powerful organization pre-empting every minute of the day. Everything to which he set his hand – writing major books, researching speeches, composing articles for the press which commanded enormous prices, directing a staff of

11. Graham Sutherland, O.M. to author.

European experts in a scouring of the foreign scene, building lakes and houses, painting landscapes, breeding tropical fish, studying butterflies and birds – all advanced with the certainty of a machine.

How it was done, how organized, remained his secret, but he confided in his nephew John his advice

> that in order to control the mind, it is essential to be able to switch the interest from one subject to another absolutely. Thus he would quite suddenly switch his activities from dictating and writing to building a wall or painting a picture. The concentration being such that the previous interest was completely dismissed from his mind.[12]

But the pattern of his days at Chartwell was regular. He was called at 8 o'clock with a hearty English breakfast, for his appetite was one of his greatest physical assets, and read all the papers before starting his morning's work, still in bed, with a room-temperature controlled at 74° Fahrenheit. Until luncheon he wrote memoranda or dictated to a secretary, often continuing his dictation while dressing.[13] After luncheon he would walk in the garden, feed the golden orfe or the waterfowl on the lake, or work on his building. As though conscious of the brevity of life, he abhorred a wasted minute. Any that fell free he filled by dictating stray thoughts that occurred to him about Marlborough. Nor could he bear to squander an idea. He kept what he called a 'box of rejects' into which he threw fragments cut from the drafts of previous speeches, turning to it to search for a thought or phrase that might help him with the work in hand. His siesta, that habit acquired so many years ago when the dark-skinned soldiers slung their hammocks in the steaming Cuban woods, followed, and provided him with the vitality for hours of further work, more dictation in study or bedroom until dinner. And at midnight, when others were retiring, a night shift stenographer appeared, with whom he continued his labours, once at least, in the author's personal experience, until 4 a.m.

In contrast, mealtimes were for Winston a period of relaxation, when he ate the delicious food provided by Clementine with that remarkable appetite, drank wine and brandy freely, and demanded conversation in which he played the principal part or no part at all as his mood prompted. Sometimes, when tired, he would sit hunched in what seemed to be surly meditation, disturbing to some, but to those who knew him well indicating only that

12. John Churchill to author.
13. Fedden, op.cit., p.41.

he was tired and recharging his batteries, and when at last he re-entered the conversation he did so in the form of a monologue often scintillating in its brilliance.

He was at his best in the company of those with weapons as sharp as his own, although they were few in number. But in his friend F. E. he found a controversialist with a mind sharpened upon the legal grindstone. Birkenhead's advantage over Churchill as a natural orator was neutralized in private exchanges so that they were perfectly matched, and their arguments so glittered with sustained wit and *tours de force* that it seemed to their fascinated listeners extraordinary that these should have emerged from casual discussion and been called forth on the spur of the moment. They might almost have been part of some carefully written play, catching fire from one another; and it was impossible to predict the victor. Again, and even more strongly, the conviction reached one at this period that although this man had been sustained since adolescence by a ravening ambition, he had remained innocent-minded, devoid of all subtlety, and incapable of dissimulation, and the dogged hatred of his enemies seemed even more difficult to understand.

Watching Winston at this time with his children, one noticed that his attitude to them was affectionate and indulgent. His nephew John remembers his playing Gorillas[14] with them when they were small and building a Meccano bridge so large that the central section had to be removed to let visitors into the house. At Chartwell the children were organized into work parties controlling the waters on the lakes. He was proud of their accomplishments and worried over their health; he loved having them about him – 'Come to luncheon,' he would say, 'You'll find us all bunged up with brats' – but he was often a distant if loving father. For Winston work always came first: equally for Clementine he always came first. She was distanced from her children partly by the daunting demands of being married to Winston and partly by her own nature. Her daughter writes:

> From the day she married him until his death fifty-seven years later, Winston dominated her whole life, and once this priority had been established, her children, personal pleasures, friends and outside interests competed for what was left . . .
>
> Clementine had no real understanding of the childish mind or outlook, and applied her own perfectionist standards not only to manners and morals but to picnics and garden clothes. But the circumstances of her life and her own nature combined to place her goddess-like on a pedestal. But on any big issue, once the courage was screwed up to broach the subject,

14. A game in which he chased them up trees and came climbing up after them.

the children could be sure of her attention, astonishingly quick action, and, if justified, the championing of their cause . . .[15]

Clementine's forebodings about the cost of Chartwell were to be more than realized. Not only did the house cost a small fortune to make habitable (dry rot having eaten deep into it) but the cost of running two establishments was ruinous. Some indication of the expenses involved may be seen in the fact that by November 1924 the cost of improving Chartwell had risen to £17,648.8s.3d., a figure already greater than the original valuation of £15,000.[16] In spite of this enormous expenditure a series of domestic misfortunes struck two years later, the most spectacular event being a fall of plaster from the ceiling which destroyed two rather expensive chandeliers. All Churchill's eloquence and persuasive powers failed to convince the builders responsible that they should pay for the repairs. The next year the ceiling fell down again.

His life was conducted on a grand scale. When he wrote a book, instead of sending out half a dozen copies to his closest friends he would cast his bread on the waters with a vengeance and give over a hundred copies away.[17] In 1925, a year of exceptionally high expenditure, he spent £259 on coal and fuel at Chartwell and £275 on cars there. The next year he spent £309 on wines and spirits and £163 on cigars.[18] In the early 1930s he would pay Clementine £300 for housekeeping expenses on the first day of every month. Multiply all these figures by 25 times to reach a rough modern equivalent and the scale of his expenditure becomes clear. When one considers that all this rested on the literary earnings and eventually on the health of one man it is not surprising that Clementine worried.

As Randolph grew up he became a source of concern to his parents. Precocious, impudent, wilful, arrogant and resentful of any form of authority, he made the lives of a series of nannies and nursery-maids miserable. As each incumbent left the house, he and Diana would bump their suitcases down the stairs crying 'Nanny's going, Nanny's going. Hurrah! Hurrah!'[19]

When he was five Randolph had an experience that might have blighted a more sensitive plant.

> . . . I said to a little boy at school (it makes me blush to recall the episode), 'Will you be my chum?' He said, 'No.' I said, 'Why not?' He said, 'Your father murdered my father.' I said: 'What do you mean?' He said, 'At the

15. Soames pp. 235-238.
16. Churchill Papers 1/173.
17. Gilbert p.311, 496.
18. Ibid. 1/192.
19. Randolph Churchill, *Twenty-One Years*, p.12.

Dardanelles.' So when I got home I told this to my mother who was naturally distressed at what had happened and explained to me about the Dardanelles. I am sorry to say it made me feel immensely proud for I realised my father was a boss man who could order other fathers about.[20]

Occasional trips abroad with Winston were the most exciting experiences for his children. He descended once in 1923 and took Diana and Randolph off to Le Touquet. The visit made such an impression on Randolph that forty years later he remembered the tune ('Yes, we have no bananas') played at the Thé Dansant in the outer rooms of the Casino.

Winston, deeply and surprisingly though he loved and revered his own father, was conscious of how distant a figure he had been. He over-compensated in his relationship with Randolph, making light of his bad reports, spoiling him and encouraging impertinence and independence which were already extraordinary in a child of his age. He treated Randolph as an adult when he was still quite young, and yet fussed over him like a small child long after such treatment was fitting. When he was twelve and the time came for Randolph to go to a public school, Winston allowed him to choose between Eton and Harrow. 'I went down and inspected both institutions. It seemed that there were fewer rules and much less discipline at Eton than at Harrow. Accordingly I opted for Eton.'[21] Randolph was encouraged from his early teens to stay up and join in the arguments after dinner with Winston's distinguished guests. At the same time Winston would write back from Italy where he and Randolph were on holiday.

'The Rabbit is a very good travelling companion. He curls up in the cabin most silently and tidily; we have played a great deal of chess in which I give him either a Queen or two castles, or even castle, bishop and knight – and still wallop him.'[22]

You might think that he was describing a ten-year-old boy, but Randolph was nearly sixteen at the time of this letter.

Perhaps with his own sufferings at St Georges in mind, Winston determined to spare Randolph as much corporal punishment as possible. He asked F.E., whose son was Captain of Colonel Sheepshanks's house at Eton when Randolph arrived there, to make sure that he was not caned. This prohibition put some strain on filial obedience when Randolph added to his natural impudence an extraordinary incompetence as a fag. Later Winston wrote to Sheepshanks saying that as Randolph was

20. Ibid., p. 17.
21. Randolph Churchill p. 28.
22. Gilbert v.224.

now nearly a man he hoped he would no longer be caned unless there were some special reason. '. . . I think it would be a mistake if he were to be caned in the House without any serious cause . . . As boys begin to grow up an incident of this kind, without just and good cause, might well have an embittering effect upon a mind rapidly forming and already in some respects startlingly mature.'[23]

Randolph's relations both with other boys and masters were uneven. His housemaster, Colonel Sheepshanks, once warned him off seeing a much younger boy in another house, quoting the text '. . . whoso shall offend one of these little ones . . .' Randolph, after threatening to sue him for slander if he repeated this accusation of unnatural vice, continued, 'though it's none of your business, sir, you may be interested to know that the reason I see so much of Mercer-Nairn is that I happen to be in love with his sister.' This for a sixteen-year-old Etonian was precocity run riot and afterwards, Randolph records, he had no more rot from Sheepshanks.[24] He did, however, get some bad reports from that source. In December 1928 Sheepshanks sent a long letter to Churchill:

> I think he might easily be rather a subversive influence in the House . . . one of his present complaints is that there is no one in the House of any intelligence, except, of course, Churchill. I do not mind him thinking this, though it is fearful conceit, but I do think it objectionable or, rather, bad taste when he airs this grievance in public. It seems to show that he has not much feeling of loyalty to the House. This is, I think, the root of the matter. At present he is too self-centred, and is not capable of having any real feeling for home or school or anything or anyone except himself . . .
>
> I have tried to talk to him about all this, but it is almost impossible. He gets so angry and talks so fast and interrupts so much that one cannot get anywhere . . . In a way perhaps it is a pity he is not leaving now.[25]

A more sympathetic assessment made by Mr Robert Birley, later Headmaster of Charterhouse and Eton, identified facility as Randolph's main problem. He found it so easy to work up an acceptable answer that he could get by without really thinking about the subject. Birley described his answers as good journalism. He had a first class mind and effortlessly churned out second class work. His handwriting (for which he was receiving special tuition) was dreadful, his style 'at the moment abominable, extremely rhetorical, windy and involved, full of clichés and pomposity.' These faults did not worry Birley who saw them as springing from Randolph's efforts to develop his own style. He was more concerned by his failure to get on with his contemporaries; as a

23. Churchill papers 1/199.
24. Randolph Churchill pp. 36-7.
25. Churchill papers 1/200.

result of this he made friends with boys either more stupid or younger
than himself, whether or not he was in love with their sisters. Birley's
report continued:

> He is quite one of the most interesting pupils I have had, and he is
> a very pleasant one. His mind is vigorous and his interests are wide.
> At the moment he is going through a mental crisis. I consider it almost
> inevitable that a boy with a mind as logical as his should experience very
> real religious difficulties. It is almost a sign of mental honesty. But while it
> is good that he should be honest in this, and that he should be ambitious,
> I hope he will not become too self-centred. There *is* a danger of this.[26]

An excellent example of Randolph's facility and his improved though
still florid style came when he left Eton while still seventeen and went
up to Oxford, where Professor Lindemann had secured him a place at
Christ Church. His preparations for the preliminary examination in
history were sketchy, and the dons, who looked in vain for any dates or
statements of facts in his papers, were regaled instead with this passage
on Louis XIV: 'This Monarch was disfigured by all the vices that might
have disgraced an Eastern potentate, swigging his wine and dandling his
concubines while France mouldered into ruin.'

Part of Randolph's impatience with the whole educational process
sprang from ambitions formed at the time he went to Eton. From the
age of thirteen or fourteen, he was convinced 'That the only career for
me was politics like my father and grandfather – if anyone had said to
me that I wouldn't get to be in the House of Commons by the time I
was twenty-one, or immediately afterwards, I would have thought them
absolutely too ridiculous for words.'[27]

When he was still nineteen an extraordinary chance of advancement
came Randolph's way. He was lying in bed at 10.30 a.m., he
remembered, when a friend, Boy Scheftel, disturbed him at this early
hour with a telegram suggesting a lecture tour of the United States. It
was an offer that could not have arrived at a more opportune moment;
Randolph had acquired a taste for America when he accompanied his
father there in 1929; the tour had possibilities for making a name in
the world beyond anything that Oxford could offer, and, best of all,
the generous fees would enable him to pay off his debts. Winston,
though proud and excited by the offer, was displeased that Randolph's
studies should be interrupted, and predicted that he would come back
with his tail between his legs.

Randolph was said to have chosen as the general title of his
lectures *Young England looks at America*, though this may have

26. Churchill papers 1/199–200.
27. Randolph Churchill 117.

been an invention of his friends. His average fee was between $250 and $300, well above the standard rate, and he was much in demand.[28] His letters home show a desire to plunge into British politics at Winston's side: 'Baldwin is becoming increasingly fatuous and Irwinian', he wrote to his father as the Indian issue gathered pace, 'I do not believe that we are going to continue forever to be governed by people who are almost incapable of thought and entirely devoid of the capacity for resolute action.'[29]

His American hosts, though generous and appreciative, did not win his unqualified approval. 'I cannot genuinely pretend to any ardent affection for the people of this country,' he wrote in the same letter. 'They are undoubtedly a friendly and hospitable race, but the men are all so incredibly boring, unattractive, and narrow minded that it is difficult to acquire any high intellectual stimulus in their company.' The women, however, were another matter. Winston must have been alarmed to read: 'As to all the rumours of engagements I shall say little as the position is still very complicated – But you may feel certain that I shall do nothing without the greatest consideration.'[30]

Clementine crossed the Atlantic in February 1931, accompanied Randolph on his tour and met and approved of the girl he was thinking of marrying (but never did). It was an idyllic trip, and possibly the last time when Randolph and his mother enjoyed and sustained a deep pleasure from each other's company. When she left he wrote to Winston: 'Americans of every age and both sexes have been amazed at my producing such a young and beautiful mother. Mummie has had a success unsurpassed by the most fascinating and eligible debutante.'[31] Clementine wrote, 'He [Randolph] is a darling. He had quite captivated me . . . It is quite like a honeymoon.'[32]

On his own return from America, still in debt, Randolph decided that his education was complete; a successful lecturer could hardly resume his fitful attendance at others' lectures. He arranged a job with ICI to obtain Winston's consent to his departure from Oxford, but it was a temporizing move. Politics remained the only career that Randolph contemplated. When finally he set out on his chosen path it was with a violence and impetuosity that were self-defeating. While Winston had always maintained personal friendships with political enemies, Randolph insulted anyone whose views deviated in the smallest degree

28. C.P. 1/222.
29. Ibid.
30. C.P. 1/222.
31. Ibid.
32. Soames p. 242.

from his own. He spurned advice even from his father; moderation and compromise were alien to his nature; and the debts piled up.

In 1932 the eldest daughter, Diana, married John Bailey, the son of Winston's friend Şir Abe Bailey. According to her sister Sarah, she was worried about still being a spinster at the advanced age of twenty-three.[33] The family were resigned rather than enthusiastic; the marriage was not a success, and within a year the couple were separated. But in 1935 when helping Randolph's candidate at the Norwood by-election she met his successful rival, Duncan Sandys, who won the seat for the Conservatives. They were married within a few months. With her husband in politics and rapidly become a disciple of her father, Diana saw much of her parents in those early years, though latterly she was much less close to them than her two sisters.

The more outgoing characters of Sarah and Mary learnt to come to terms with their mother's remote nature, but Diana was herself too shy and inward-looking to do the same. Clementine would be highly critical of her. Yet behind all misunderstandings there lay affection, concern and unwavering loyalty, even when in later years she became difficult and unbalanced.

In the Christmas holidays of 1937 Diana and Duncan Sandys joined Clementine and Mary for a skiing holiday:

'Duncan and Diana are having a renewed honeymoon [Clementine wrote to Winston] They are very sweet together and his devotion to her makes me like him better. I think when he is in London he is so taken up with his 'career' and the excitement of Parliament that he has no time to talk to her or play with her and she is a lovely fragile little flower which droops when neglected.'[34]

Both Diana and Sarah had ambitions to go on the stage. Diana soon realized that she lacked the gift and gave it up, but though Sarah too lacked the talent she craved she persisted and won occasional success, due more to her alluring personality than to the reality of her performance. She had also grown up to be startlingly attractive with Titian red hair of exceptional beauty. Her parents looked on the prospect of her joining the chorus with some concern. As Mary Soames writes: 'They both belonged to the generation of which several ladies of the chorus became duchesses but on the other hand, ladies simply did not become chorus girls.'[35] But since Sarah wanted to go on the stage a great deal more strongly than her parents wanted to prevent her, her wishes

33. S. Churchill, *Keep on Dancing*.
34. C.P. 1/322.
35. Soames p. 245.

prevailed. In the autumn of 1935 she went for an audition with C.B. Cochran, the famous impresario.

> When my turn came [Sarah remembered] Sarah Michaelovitz, the impressive Russian name coined for the occasion, was forgotten and I gave my right name. I waited for Mr Cochran to tell me to touch my toes or turn a few cartwheels but instead, much to my astonishment, he asked 'Does your father know you are here?' . . . I felt like a naughty child.[36]

Cochran had behaved in the most courteous manner, asking Churchill's permission before allowing her to perform. Afterwards in November 1935 he wrote a report on how the audition had gone.

> . . . Your daughter, Sarah, danced for me yesterday afternoon. I can say in all sincerity that had she been entirely unknown to me and my Ballet Mistress, she would have been engaged forthwith.
>
> From meeting her, I expected to find a certain amount of natural grace of movement, but I was very surprised to find that she had received good training and must have worked hard to fit herself for the profession she wishes to adopt . . .
>
> Were your daughter a poor girl, dependent upon the stage for a living, I feel pretty certain that within a year or so she would break away from the crowd and make headway towards achieving some position in the theatre.

When she started work with Cochran, Sarah naturally met the rest of the cast including the leading man, Vic Oliver, an Austrian comedian whose real name was Samek. Oliver was amusing and with a fundamentally nice character, seventeen years older than her and already married twice. They fell in love. Winston was horrified by this alliance with 'an itinerant vagabond'[37]; nor would he have been placated had he known the motives Sarah later attributed to herself. 'Maybe I was looking for a substitute father,' she wrote after the failure of her marriage. 'Indeed I have sometimes thought that I was trying to marry my father.'[38] Despairing of obtaining her parents' consent to the marriage, she ran off to New York to join Vic there. Randolph, grotesquely miscast as a diplomat, followed hot-foot in pursuit, forcing his way on to the *Olympic* by the use of his father's name.

Sarah on her liner, the *Bremen*, found to her embarrassment that Lady Astor was a fellow-passenger. The evening entertainment invariably consisted of a rendering of *Deutschland über Alles* by the crew. Meanwhile the race across the Atlantic – with at one

36. Sarah Churchill, *Keep on Dancing* p. 27.
37. Ibid, p.36.
38. Ibid. 56-7.

stage both liners delayed by a hurricane, excited the American Press – who responded with headlines like 'Brother chases Cupid.' Once in New York Randolph performed his mission with surprising tact and skill.

> I had a talk with Sarah today, he wrote on 2 November 1935. She seemed very touched by your letter which arrived today and which she showed me. I am afraid that she is very set on her purpose and doubt whether there is much chance of a change. However she sees the advantage of waiting for Samek to obtain U.S. citizenship and seems prepared to do this ... Undoubtedly Baruch, whom Sarah has asked to facilitate and hasten the signing of the papers could obtain a delay instead of an acceleration. But I do not see that we should gain anything by that. I am sure if they failed to get the citizenship they would go ahead with the marriage once the divorce was valid, more especially if they suspected, as I fear they would, that we were responsible for the hitch.[39]

With Baruch's help Churchill had engaged an American lawyer to look into Oliver's background, particularly the validity of his passport and last divorce. These inquiries imposed some delay but he agreed with Randolph that it would be wrong to put more obstacles in the couple's path. 'It will not be our policy to delay the naturalisation and once the divorces are definitely valid we shall acquiesce in the marriage. There is nothing more to be done.'[40] There was some bitterness on both sides. The Churchills felt that Sarah had broken her promise to wait for a year, while she was wounded by the somewhat cumbersome legal barriers put in her way. 'My father seemed to start acting like Mr Barrett of Wimpole St.'[41] Fortunately, they were too fond of each other and too sensible to bear lasting grievances. When she heard that he had withdrawn his opposition she wrote:

> Please believe me that I never resented the fact that you made inquiries about Vic, and I know you acted entirely out of love – I am sorry for the pain and shock I must have caused you and Mummie – and I do thank you from the bottom of my heart that you have withdrawn your opposition. All other difficulties look silly with the one and truly important obstacle gone.[42]

39. C.P. 1/288.
40. Ibid.1/288.
41. S. Churchill, *Keep on Dancing*, p. 46.
42. C.P. 1/288.

The wedding took place in New York on Christmas Eve 1936. A week later Churchill wrote to Baruch thanking him for his help:

> Sarah and her husband came to luncheon with us yesterday. You have indeed been a good friend through all this tiresome business, and Clemmie and I are most deeply grateful for all you have done.
>
> I gathered from Randolph that you formed the opinion that Mr Oliver's attachment was serious, and did not think ill of him. Certainly I feel that after what has virtually been an engagement of almost a year, it would be wrong for us to withhold our consent. We are bound to wish for nothing but their future happiness. Morever one has neither the right nor the power to do more than advise and make sure that everything is in order.[43]

Sarah was Churchill's favourite child, 'The Mule' as he called her, and he remained tolerantly affectionate throughout all the vicissitudes of her varied and finally tragic life.

After poor Marigold's death, Mary was born, isolated by a gulf of years from the other children. She was eight years younger than Sarah, and as a result was brought up almost as an only child. She spent most of her time at Chartwell under the care of a cousin, Miss Whyte, known to her as Nana. In her own words she 'had a lovely life', but it was one dominated by Nana. Her mother remained an aloof figure, her father affectionate but preoccupied with higher things. The other Churchill children had faced the same situation, but unlike them Mary lacked the company of children her own age. She made do with a series of pets, moved easily in the society of grown-ups and was happy; but when she was fourteen a change took place.

Clementine had always been athletic and active, a fine rider and tennis player. Now, at the age of fifty, she developed a liking for skiing, a sport that she had never tried before. This would not be considered remarkable nowadays, when skiers are wafted up the mountains in gondolas and chair lifts, when the snow is compacted for them by machines and when elaborate technology has reduced the effort of the sport (if not its expense) to a minimum. Even with such aids people today often give up skiing at about the age that Clementine, with none of them, adopted it. In her time many of the mountains had to be climbed on foot, on skis with skins attached to stop them sliding. The snow had to be negotiated in its natural state with equipment that was cumbersome, primitive and dangerous. Clementine's intrepid spirit rose above these disadvantages, and considering the age at which she started, she became a remarkably good skier. She was attracted as much by the beauty of the mountains as by the challenge of a new and demanding sport. She would use this

43. C.P. 1/298.

beauty to try and entice Winston out to the Alps. 'Lovely colours in the snow for painting,' she would write, or 'You would love this. I wish you would try. Only I'm afraid you would be too bold and come the most frightful purlers.'[44] But Winston knew his own tastes and stayed in the South of France.

The greatest of pleasures that skiing gave to Clementine was to bring her closer to Mary, who accompanied her mother to the Alps for three successive Christmases in 1935-7. On their first expedition to Zurs one of their party was Judy Montagu[45] who noticed with astonishment that 'Clemmie and Mary were just like two people falling in love. It was as though they had suddenly discovered one another and withdrawn from the others, behaving like Romeo and Juliet.'[46]

Winston and Clementine, as we have seen, often went on trips abroad without each other, and the correspondence that accompanied these separations always gave a vivid picture of their lives. This was never more true than in the first four months of 1935 when Clementine was Lord Moyne's guest on an extraordinary voyage on his yacht, *Rosaura*. She and Winston had sailed with him round the Eastern Mediterranean in the summer of 1934; afterwards he asked them both to join him on a more ambitious expedition to capture monitor lizards for the London Zoo at Komodo, one of the Lesser Sunda Islands in the Dutch East Indies. Winston faced a critical time in his political life with the India Bill remorselessly approaching its climax, with Nazi Germany becoming a clearer and more serious threat to peace in his eyes (but not in those of others) and with Randolph embarking on a series of madcap enterprises, which threatened at times to rebound on his father, and expecting his father to pay his large debts. Nor could he leave *Marlborough* for the four months that was the least that the cruise in the *Rosaura* would last; but with some reluctance he agreed to Clementine going.

She joined the yacht at Messina and sailed to Madras and Rangoon, where they were joined by their host, then on to Singapore, Borneo, Celebes, The Moluccas, New Guinea, Australia and New Zealand, before turning north again and continuing their circuitous route to the island of Komodo, which they reached on 18 March 1935. Throughout this time the Churchills exchanged streams of letters and telegrams, his a mixture of domestic affairs and politics, entitled the Chartwell Bulletins, hers accounts of coral beaches, uncharted waters, naked savages and strange monsters. The contrast could not be more striking, but both are overflowing with affection.

44. Soames, p. 247.
45. Later Mrs Grendel.
46. Mrs Grendel to author.

Winston described his trials with a digger he had hired to make a haha and island at Chartwell. At first he looked on this machine as a benign and versatile monster capable of extraordinary feats of landscaping; later, after it had been stuck in the lake for many costly days, simply as a monster. Randolph's electioneering exploits were related with alternating enthusiasm and exasperation. 'Sarah has already gone up to work for Randolph'; he wrote in Bulletin 3, 'and Diana follows tonight, so at any rate he has two supporters. Though unhappily neither has a vote in the Wavertree division.' Randolph's opponent, he continued,

> is a thoroughly unattractive nonentity, with no knowledge of politics, but a socially ambitious wife and a large fortune, which no doubt weigh with the caucus committee which chose him . . . Randolph of course is in the seventh heaven. This is exactly the kind of thing he revels in and for which his gifts are particularly suited . . . That he will emerge a new public figure of indisputable political force is certain.[47]

But after his performance at Wavertree, where he split the vote and let the Socialist candidate in Randolph 'became quite uncontrollable and now wants in defiance of everyone else's opinion to bring out another splitting candidate at Norwood – he does not seem to wish to consider any interests but his own and we had sharp words upon the subject.'[48]

An embarrassment to Winston was that Randolph's exploits at Wavertree had caused a reaction in the constituencies, encouraged and nurtured by Central Office, against the diehards who had supported him. Winston was coming under increasing pressure from his constituency party at Epping, so much so that it seemed for a time that Randolph might lose his father his seat without winning one of his own. When Randolph ignored his advice and introduced a candidate at Norwood Winston wrote:

> He knows he is a thoroughly bad thing, but means to brazen it out. I shall of course having nothing to do with it, except to bear a good deal of the blame . . . Baldwin said to me in the Lobby two days ago that Mrs B had said to him 'One's children are like a lot of live bombs. One never knows when they will go off or in what direction.'[49]

Later his annoyance changed to modified admiration as Randolph 'virtually had to fight alone making the speeches, answering the

47. CP 1/273. Chartwell Bulletin No.3.
48. Ibid Bulletin No.6.
49. Ibid No.9.

questions, writing the election address, interviewing the press etc.'[50] He thought the 2,700 votes Randolph's candidate won was quite creditable considering that he was without any support.

When the children were not electioneering they were ill. Sarah was exhausted; Mary had whooping cough 'and barks away with great regularity'; but Randolph's condition was more worrying. He had contracted a rare disease resembling jaundice with effects which for a time defied diagnosis. Eventually it was identified as Sewerman's Disease, a very rare and new form of infection derived from the bacilli in the urine of rats, and consequently contracted by sewermen. But Randolph could not recall having encountered any rats – except Buchan Hepburn![51] During this illness Randolph's appearance, already alarming enough, was not improved by the growth of 'a hideous scruffy beard which makes me positively sick to look at . . . He declares he looks like Christ. Certainly on the contrary he looks very like my poor father in the last phase of his illness.'[52]

Much of his correspondence is occupied with domestic matters: walls were being built, cottages repaired, orchards re-turfed. All important decisions and some apparently trivial ones were deferred until Clementine's return. Animals feature prominently in the Bulletins. Two goats died after eating weedkiller, but 'All the black swans are mating, not only the father and mother, but both brothers and both sisters have paired off. The Ptolemys always did this and Cleopatra was the result.' A heifer they had bought 'has committed an indiscretion before she came to us and is about to have a calf. I propose however to treat it as a daughter.'[53] The dogs had ruined another carpet and been banished to a less vulnerable part of the house: 'The pug is getting intolerable. He commits at least three indiscretions a day, and if his actions stain the carpets, his protests when chastised fill the air.'[54] The animal life at Chartwell was to be augmented. On 9 February Clementine telegraphed from Sydney 'Just spent delightful day with Streetie purchased pair black swans at zoo two wallabies and opossum tonight New Zealand love Clemmie.' 'Menagerie welcome Winston', he replied the same day.

Underlying all Winston's correspondence were the two great political issues of the time, the India Bill and German rearmament. Neither campaign was going as he would have wished. The India Bill was voted

50. Ibid No.11.
51. Ibid Nos 11 & 12. Patrick Buchan Hepburn was briefly Churchill's Secretary (when he fell foul of Randolph) then a Conservative MP, Chief Whip, Minister of Works, and finally Governor General of the West Indies.
52. Ibid No.3.
53. Ibid No.9.
54. Ibid No.9.

through clause by clause by a mass of well-disciplined lobby fodder, not even interested enough to attend the debates, but whenever Winston himself failed to attend clauses were voted through with alarming speed. Perhaps inspired by Randolph, who used to mock him for the elaborate preparation of his speeches, he took to making a series of short impromptu speeches and found them effective. 'At sixty,' he wrote,

> I am altering my method of speaking, largely under Randolph's tuition, and now talk to the House of Commons with garrulous unpremeditated flow. They seem delighted. But what a mystery that art of public speaking is! It all consists in my (mature) judgment of confining to three or four absolutely sound arguments and putting them in the most conversational manner possible. There is apparently nothing in the literary effect I have sought for forty years![55]

In Germany things were even worse. He reported Hitler's claim to have an air force equal to Britain's, and gloomily forecast that it would soon be ten times the size of ours. 'On the whole since you have been away,' he wrote in one of the later bulletins,

> The only great thing that has happened is that Germany is now the greatest armed power in Europe . . . Rothermere rings up every day. His anxiety is pitiful. He thinks the Germans are all powerful and that the French are corrupt and useless, and the English hopeless and doomed. He proposes to meet this situation by grovelling to Germany. 'Dear Germany, do destroy us last!' I endeavour to inculcate a more robust attitude.[56]

He was depressed by the response of the country's leaders.

> . . . Baldwin remains with all his cards in his hand, a power-miser I am going to call him. With the utmost skill and industry, and self-repression, he gathers together all the power counters without the slightest wish to use them or the slightest knowledge how! Ramsay continues to decompose in public.[57]

While Winston's letters ranged from the death of goats to the fate of empires, Clementine's were full of new experiences and unexpected adventures. Deep-sea fishing made her feel so sea-sick that the only fare she could stomach at lunch was an improbable combination of claret and strong peppermints. The size and depth of the ocean, the distance from home, the cruel coral reefs around the islands, the alien scenery seemed sometimes to be sinister as well as beautiful. On one

55. Ibid No.12.
56. Ibid No.12.
57. Ibid No.12.

expedition to a small uninhabited island this sense of menace came to the surface. They were looking for lizards called tuataras which Lord Moyne wished to add to his collection for the Zoo. Clementine set off with her usual enthusiasm, scrambling on hands and knees through the steep bush. She soon became completely lost and unable to retrace her footsteps. She was soaked by a rainstorm and became exhausted trying to escape. Eventually her shouts for help were answered by one of the yacht's officers. 'I almost kissed him . . . I was really lost for only 1 hour, but it felt like much more in that dense, enchanted wood – Of course there was no danger really I suppose, but I thought of lying there and dying of hunger as far away from you as I can be on this earth.'[58]

In the middle of March they arrived at their destination, the island of Komodo, home of the monitor lizard. It was, she wrote,

> The most beautiful thing I have ever seen and is perhaps one of the loveliest, wildest, strangest spots in the world. It is deeply indented with bays and lagoons. It has innumerable paradise beaches – some of the finest sand. (There is a pink one of powdered coral) some of wild rocks with coral gardens far lovelier than at Nassau, and accessible. That is if you are not afraid of being observed by a giant polyp or tickled by a sea snake 12 foot long.[59]

They stayed in this faintly sinister paradise for a week during which five small lizards were caught. Their photographer, however, managed to photograph a twelve foot monster escaping with half a pig in its jaws.

On this impossibly romantic journey, Clementine was thrown into the company of a handsome and charming younger man Terence Philip, a London art dealer. It is not surprising that they fell briefly in love, though it was an affair doomed to wither 'like a fragile tropical flower which cannot survive in greyer, colder climes.'[60] She would look back on this uncharacteristic lapse with amusement and a trace of nostalgia.

* * *

Randolph, meanwhile, thwarted of a seat in Parliament was making his name as a journalist, first on the *Daily Mail* then on the *Evening Standard*. His exuberant style, like his father's, became seasoned with a pithy wit, while his irreverence remained with him all his life. 'Dear Papa,' one of his letters began, 'I am just off to Aldershot to learn

58. Soames, 265.
59. Ibid. 266.
60. Ibid. 266-7.

the goosestep.'[61] It was an appropriate beginning to a military career which was to include a remark made by Randolph as a young captain to his Commander-in-Chief, General Alexander, and overheard by the author: 'Of course, I'm not accusing you personally of cowardice, my dear General.' It would be hard to improve on the opening sentence of his autiobiography: 'I was born in London on 28 May 1911 at 33 Eccleston Square of poor but honest parents.' Winston watched his activities with admiration, amusement, concern and often fury.

Randolph worshipped his father, but as time went on their relationship became more and more stormy. Randolph was blinkered in his outlook, unable to see any merit in those whose interests or opinions clashed with his father's. He would himself criticize Winston in violent and intemperate language, then when his attack was destroyed, indulge in a series of incriminations and self-justifications, anything to avoid the apology that was obviously due.[62] If Randolph had won a seat in Parliament and been able to fight at his father's side, many of these difficulties might have disappeared.

On the other hand, there was some substance to Randolph's complaint that when he was a child his father treated him almost as an adult but that once he had grown up he started treating him as a child. When Randolph was going to cover the Spanish Civil War, Winston wrote:

Feb 15 1937

My dear Randolph,

I am consenting to your going to Spain on the very strict understanding that you will under no circumstances expose yourself to any risk.

You will be under the tutelage of Cardozo who has similar instructions from me.

I suggest you stay in Spain for six weeks. You ought to collect quite a lot of material for a good book.

Regarding my bet with you, you have my full permission to drink the wine of the country and beer but no spirits or foreign wines. When you return you will of course go out to win your bet in regard to a strict teetotal regime.

Affectionately yours,

P.S. Never forget you are an only son.[63]

Danger to his children touched him on the raw even after they had grown up and left home. The year after this letter to Randolph

61. C.P. 1/325.
62. See CP 1/325 for a good example.
63. C.P. 1/301.

he heard that Duncan Sandys was planning to take Diana to Spain with him. He wrote:

31 March 1938

My dear Duncan,

You will do a very wrong act and one which the world would judge harshly if you take Diana with you to Barcelona. There is no excuse whatever for bringing her into this scene of misery, privation and danger. You may easily have great difficulty in getting out if the front breaks while you are there. I am bound to let you know how very strong my opinion is.

Yours ever.

In the winter of 1938-9 Clementine went to the West Indies on a final cruise in the *Rosaura*. From Haiti she suggested that Winston should write a book 'or a tragedy' about the black general Toussaint l'Ouverture. In Jamaica she was welcomed with prolonged cheers in a remote mountain village as the wife of the future Prime Minister of England. There were no Chartwell Bulletins for this cruise, Winston no doubt being too preoccupied with events in Europe, and Clementine was unhappy about it:

'My Darling,' she wrote on New Year's Day of 1939,

Do you know that I am starved for a letter from you. Mary, Horatia, Moppett and Sarah have written but Alas not you ... Do you think you could dictate a few words every day to a secretary and she could send it twice a week. Never mind about writing yourself. I used to mind about that, but I'm accustomed to type written letters now and would much rather have them than nothing ... *Please* don't telegraph. I hate telegrams just saying 'all well rainy weather love Winston'.[64]

There was a moment of sadness when Sidney Peel, an old admirer of hers, died and her mind was drawn back to the days before she met Winston.

He was good to me and made my difficult rather arid life interesting. But I couldn't care for him and I was not kind or even very grateful. And then my Darling you came and in that moment I knew the difference.

I am glad you wrote about it because at that moment I longed for you. I wanted to put my arms round you and cry and cry.

* * *

The main impression of Churchill at the beginning of the 1930s had been one of contentment. Deeply immersed in his labours on *Marlborough*,

64. C.P. 1/323.

in the wild life on his property and in his own creative zest, he had not yet begun to taste the bitter fruit of ostracism, and although he was not included in the National Government – predominantly Conservative – which succeeded the Labour Government in 1931, he showed no particular irritation or restlessness.

But after a visit to Munich in the summer of 1932, his mind haunted by Marlborough's struggle against a single aggressive power seeking to dominate Europe, he had been forced to listen to much ominous and vainglorious chatter about the Hitler movement. With long memories of the awe-inspiring German military might in the past, of the ugly chauvinism which he knew that national character could assume, and with his own experience of the havoc of which the *furor teutonicus* was capable, he formed settled and sombre conclusions about his new development. Henceforward he spent much of his time studying and warning against the gathering storm in an unheeded campaign which will be described later in this account.

In the meantime he began forming an intelligence service, called by some a 'Little Foreign Office', of his own at Chartwell of remarkable efficiency to advance his cause. He believed that in the next war the air might be the decisive factor. For advice on this he relied on Lindemann, who spoke German perfectly and had been an experimental pilot in the Great War when he had personally conducted dangerous tests of the spiral spin which had killed so many airmen. Now a physicist of repute and an expert on aerodynamics, the 'Prof', for long an intimate, was constantly on hand to advise on the needs of air defence, to estimate German progress in the air and to supply statistics. Desmond Morton, by then Director of the Industrial Intelligence Centre under the Cabinet Office, obtained permission from the Prime Minister, Ramsay MacDonald, to speak freely to Churchill and keep him well informed. He became a close adviser.

Morton was in fact instructed by MacDonald and Hankey in 'what to do with Winston if he talked rot'.[65] He was allowed to impart in general all information about foreign affairs, but was not authorized to show Churchill documents. Morton was impressed by the amount of money Winston was prepared to spend to increase the efficiency of his intelligence service, observing that he had a permanent telephone line to the GPO and the Central Telegraph Agency which, according to Morton, cost him £4,500 a year.[66]

But a close knowledge of foreign affairs and an awareness of every new development were what he principally needed, and they

65. Sir Desmond Morton to author.
66. Ibid.

were supplied by a brilliant recruit to his campaign, Ralph Wigram of the Foreign Office.

> I had also formed a friendship with Ralph Wigram, the rising star of the Foreign Office and in the centre of all its affairs. He had reached a level in that Department which entitled him to express responsible opinions upon policy, and to use a wide discretion in his contacts, official and unofficial ... He saw as clearly as I did, but with more certain information, the awful peril which was closing upon us ... All this helped me to form and fortify my opinions about the Hitler Movement. For my part, with the many connections I now had in France, in Germany and other countries, I had been able to send him a certain amount of information which we examined together.[67]

*   *   *

From this time the menace of a renascent German militarism, so agonizingly apparent to Churchill, but about which most others preferred to remain in placid suspense – as though reluctant to contemplate even the possibility of another general war in which they believed civilization would perish – dominated Winston's mind, but with no detriment to his spirits or the continuance of his own work. One noticed that his conversation was now sometimes spiced by a strong Rabelaisian emphasis which his personality somehow contrived to render innocuous, and the author recalls the end of a later monologue delivered shortly before the Second World War to two of his most fervent admirers who were also men of more than Victorian propriety and extreme squeamishness. He was deploring the locust years, and explaining how easy it would have been to eliminate Hitler if the necessary steps had been taken in time, concluding: 'And then we could have turned on him and said: "Arseholes to you." ' A *gamin* smile deprived the remark of offence, but one was left to watch repulsion and idolatory at war on his listeners' faces.

His growing preoccupation with Germany, with all the work and time demanded by it, did not exclude his other activities. It was merely added to them, and the way he discharged the double task is clear proof not only of his power of organization but also of his abnormal stamina. His working day at Chartwell was seldom less than eighteen, and sometimes even reached twenty, hours, and as much time was now spent on sedentary work, he took little if any violent exercise. Yet whatever strains he imposed on it, his physique appeared impregnable. Although during the exile at Chartwell his alcoholic intake was sometimes greater than at other periods of his life, his digestion was unimpaired and his

67. WSC, *The Second World War: The Gathering Storm*, p.63.

appetite enormous. He was an almost complete stranger to illnesss, and on the rare occasions when he suffered from some minor disorder would summon a succession of doctors until he found one who pronounced the diagnosis he required.[68]

He had been brought up to believe that drunkenness was contemptible and disgusting, a fault in which no gentleman indulged, and he was not in the slightest danger of infringing this principle. Alcohol, even in considerable quantities, produced no discernible effect on him, and the brilliance of his conversation was enhanced rather than diminished. His habit of drinking whisky and soda at unconventional hours caused some to think that he drank more than he did, but he had the rare gift of using alcohol freely but always remaining its master instead of its slave. Moreover, the amount of whisky in his glass was small and, in truth, it was for him more a heavy cigar-smoker's mouthwash than an alcoholic indulgence. This, with his rock-like head, was no doubt the reason why malicious and ill-informed rumour accused him of excess in this direction.

But it is true that Churchill relied much upon alcohol, and would have been miserable deprived of it. He liked to have a glass by him, and would nurse a whisky and soda for at least an hour. The habit of playing with weak drinks for a long time gradually increased, and in the later part of his like he drank far less. He was particularly fond of brandy, and of champagne, which was served both at lunch and dinner, a practice which, as he explained, saved him the trouble of specifying the wine when telling the butler to bring another bottle.

* * *

One of the Oxford historians who advised Churchill on Marlborough was a young Fellow of Wadham College and Tutor in Modern History, William Deakin, who had been recommended to him by Professor Feiling, and who spent more than half of his time with Winston at Chartwell between 1935 and 1939. Churchill became devoted to this young don, who was soon included in the circle of intimates who could do no wrong, and found himself the object of almost paternal affection. He was later to endear himself even further when he was parachuted into Yugoslavia in the war and awarded the DSO for his part in Marshal Tito's most critical and terrible battle.[69] Deakin, a man of exceptional charm and powers of observation, spent a great deal of time alone with Churchill, and we receive a clear picture of him at this time through his eyes. He was struck immediately by

68. Lady Spencer-Churchill to author.
69. The fifth German offensive in Montenegro.

his extraordinary power of mental and nervous concentration, by the manner in which he became completely absorbed by whatever he was doing at a given moment – painting, writing or building. 'He was either totally with you, or else you were not there at all.' He also noticed that Winston had a Napoleonic memory and was always convinced that he was right, and when it was conclusively proved that he was wrong, resembled a crestfallen schoolboy. He had an uncertain and rather peculiar feeling about the academic establishment, and when shown to be mistaken would exclaim, using the word in the pejorative sense: 'You are a God-damned don.'

He was strangely nervous of anyone professionally well-equipped in the academic sense, an uneasiness which was the legacy of his own sparsity of formal education. 'But, if a certain man was known to be bloody-minded and unpopular with his contemporaries, Winston automatically felt a *penchant* for him. This was no doubt due to his own long unpopularity.' He was wholly unaware of the impression he produced on others, and could never, for example, conceive that he might be intimidating to a young man. The historian saw him as 'a perfectly rounded personality':

> But he had made himself. Everything he had done and learned had been achieved the hard way. He was not a sort of genius from childhood. He had made it all, and to do so he had displayed not only great imagination but an inhuman application. He had the wonderful quality of making you feel better than you were.'

His close association with Churchill exposed him to all sides of Churchill's character and left him with a feeling of 'limitless affection'. He came to realize that he was at once generous by nature but fundamentally simple. He was at times confronted by Churchill's egotism and tendency to bully, but was amused rather than disturbed by these symptoms which he saw as essentially comical and immature.

'And they were so much more compensated for by what he gave out. He gave out so much that you felt better than you were. He transmitted a heightening of perception.' And here Deakin was echoing the words of Harold Macmillan, who believed that Churchill was extremely selfish, 'but made amends for it so magnificently that it was usually forgiven him.'[70] 'He could be bullying and unfair,' thought Deakin, 'but was at all times without rancour. He was ruthless in shutting others out of his life, but never held whatever they had done against them.' He thought that Churchill's interests and abilities had set in about 1910, and that his character had remained unchanged in essentials since then. He never said

70. The Right. Hon. Harold Macmillan to author.

in those days: 'If only I was in control now.' Sometimes there was an air of gloom about him, but no restlessness for office. It seemed to Deakin in retrospect that 1940 coincided with something that had long been expected and prepared for in Churchill's mind. He had an aristocratic aloofness in politics and was in no way oppressed by his isolation and the fact that he had only a handful of followers

> He had a heroic attitude to life. Easily hurt himself in private, he believed that public figures should be exposed to attack, and that this was as necessary concomitant of public life. His family relations by the time I arrived were firmly rooted. His private life was simple and strong, particularly in his relations with Clemmie who was a good deal sharper in her judgment of men than he.[71]

* * *

Those who now visit this lovingly tended shrine will find the most significant imprints of the man in his upstairs library, in the objects which seem to embrace all he wished to remember – Lord Randolph's mahogany writing-table; a drawing of his brother Jack, so much beloved, so lacking in his own qualities; a water-colour of a four-in-hand in Jerome Park with Leonard Jerome haughty on the box; two porcelain busts, one of Napoleon, whose baseness he could not see in the dazzle of his glory, and Nelson, representing an element he also had sought to control; a bronze cast of Lady Randolph's shapely hand; a piece of shrapnel that nearly killed him in the Great War; and, still conveying an undefinable arrogance, a painting of Lord Randolph with his wild eyes and fierce moustaches writing at his desk with a quill pen. Lastly, in a poignant effort to establish a *rapport* and continuity between their lives, the Chancellor's black despatch box which he had used to present his budget is placed under Lord Randolph's picture. So, framed and on one sheet of paper, is that budget.

71. F.W. Deakin to author.

Select Bibliography

Besides Sir Winston Churchill's own numerous writings, and the various biographies of him already existing, (most especially Martin Gilbert's monumental work) the following peripheral studies may be of interest:

Bacon, Admiral Sir R.: *The Life of Lord Fisher of Kilverstone* (Hodder & Stoughton, 1929).

Bennet, Daphne: *Margot: A Study of the Countess of Oxford and Asquith (Gollancz, 1984).*

Balfour, Lord: *Chapters of Autobiography* (Cassell, 1930).

Birkenhead, second Earl of: *The Life of F.E. Smith, the First Earl of Birkenhead* (Cape, 1984). (Eyre and Spottiswoode, 1960).

Bonham Carter,Lady Violet: *Winston Churchill As I Knew Him* (Eyre and Spottiswoode and Collins, 1965).

Bush, Captain Eric: *Gallipoli* (Allen and Unwin, 1975).

Cassar, George: *Kitchener* (Kimber, 1977).

Colville, Sir John: *The Churchillians* (Weidenfeld and Nicolson, 1981).

Dugdale, B.: *Arthur James Balfour* (Hutchinson, 1930).

Egremont, Max: *Balfour* (Collins, 1980).

Garvin, J.L.: *Life of Joseph Chamberlain* (Macmillan, 1935–69).

James, Robert Rhodes: *Churchill: A Study in Failure* (Weidenfeld and Nicolson, 1970).

James, Robert Rhodes: *Lord Randolph Churchill* (Weidenfeld and Nicolson, 1959).

Jenkins, Roy: *Asquith* (Collins, 1964).

Judd, Dennis: *Radical Joe: A Life of Joseph Chamberlain* (Hamish Hamilton, 1977).

Koss, Stephen: *Asquith* (Allen Lane, 1976).

Lloyd George Papers (House of Lords Record Office).

Mackay, Ruddock: *Balfour: Intellectual Statesman* (Oxford University Press, 1985).

Morgan, K.O.: *Lloyd George* (Weidenfeld and Nicolson, 1974).

O'Brien, Terence: *Milner* (Constable, 1976).

Robbins, Keith: *Sir Edward Grey: A Biography of Lord Grey of Fallodon* (Cassell, 1971).

Rosebery, Lord: *Lord Randolph Churchill* (1906).

Spender, J.A.: *Herbert Henry Asquith* (Hutchinson, 1932).

Spender, J.A.: *A Life of the Right Hon. Sir Henry Campbell-Bannerman* (Hodder and Stoughton, 1923).

Wilson, John: *CB: A Life of Sir Henry Campbell-Bannerman* (Constable, 1973).

Young, Kenneth: *Arthur James Balfour* (Collins, 1980).

Index